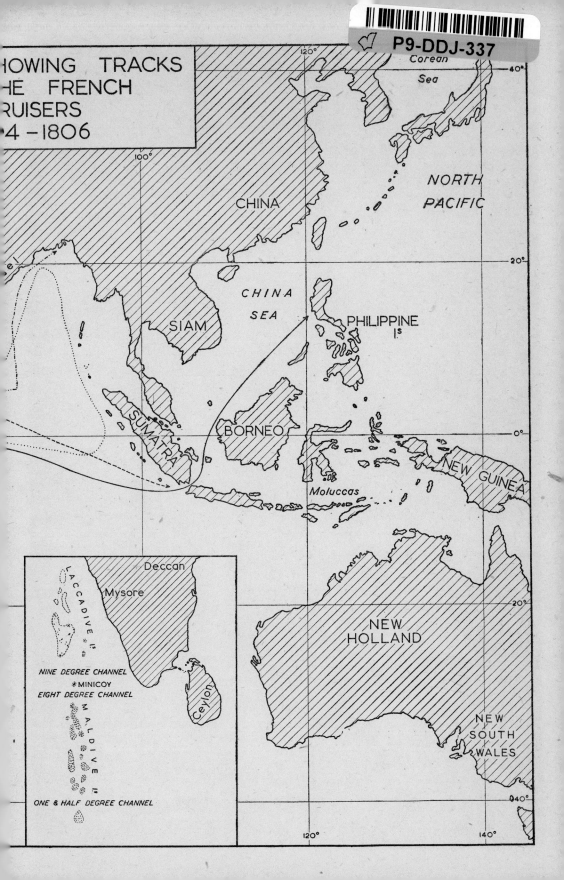

...HOWING TRACKS
...HE FRENCH
...RUISERS
...4 — 1806

War in the Eastern Seas

Edited by C. Northcote Parkinson

THE TRADE WINDS
A Study of British Overseas Trade during the French Wars
1793–1815

PLATE I. Admiral Peter Rainier (1741?–1808)
Commander-in-Chief on the East Indies Station

WAR IN THE EASTERN SEAS

1793-1815

C. Northcote Parkinson

Raffles Professor of History
University of Malaya

George Allen & Unwin Ltd
RUSKIN HOUSE · MUSEUM STREET · LONDON

FIRST PUBLISHED IN 1954

FOR

ANN

PRINTED IN GREAT BRITAIN
in 12 point Fournier type
BY UNWIN BROTHERS LIMITED
WOKING AND LONDON

PREFACE

THE naval wars of 1793–1815 have been called, and with some reason, the classic age of British Sea Power. But this classic age has not been recorded by historians with anything like the care which its importance would seem to merit. During that great conflict, or fairly soon after its conclusion, appeared the works of Steel, Ralfe, James, Brenton and Ekins, together with a spate of biographies. Of these contemporary or nearly contemporary works, that by William James, *The Naval History of Great Britain* (1826), is by far the most valuable. James himself, however, in defining his field of study, was careful to disclaim any intention of writing what we should now regard as history. 'It appeared to me,' he wrote in his preface, 'of little consequence whether an action, purely naval, was fought off the North Cape or the coast of Peru.' To the historian the place of conflict is of the greatest consequence. James emphasizes further that he had 'neither the talent nor the inclination to descant on the consequences' of any combat and that he deliberately 'left the field of politics open to those who know better how to traverse it. . . .' To the historian the consequences are seldom without interest, and James left it to the historian to discover what the consequences may have been.

Many years were to pass before any historian made the attempt. At last, in 1892, there appeared *The Influence of Sea Power upon the French Revolution and Empire*, by Captain A. T. Mahan of the United States Navy. Mahan had the advantage of having already written *The Influence of Sea Power upon History*, 1660–1783. Added to this he had naval experience in sail, a general knowledge of history and something like genius in comprehending the strategic problems of the past. It is true that his knowledge of the sailing ship is no longer wholly an advantage—for he naturally refrained from telling his contemporaries what he and they already knew—but it is also true that he brought the French Wars into some sort of perspective. Our current version of what happened is very largely his. And while there has been published since 1893 a wealth of detailed studies and a mass of documentary material, no revised naval history of the period has as yet appeared.

Sixty years would be a long period for a historical work to hold the field even if its original conception and execution had been faultless. In fact, however, Mahan's work was imperfect in two major respects. He did not use the original sources. He did not continue the story after 1805. His rate of compilation would have been inconsistent with actual research even had the naval archives been available to him as a serving officer. And then, Mahan was too impressed by the Nelson legend to pay much attention to events between 1805 and 1812. From 1812 he could fairly allow his interest, like his sympathy, to centre upon the United States Navy, so that the main naval war of 1805–15 was closed to him and has since remained virtually closed to everyone else. To such of Nelson's contemporaries as were still at sea in 1815 this historical treatment of the war would have seemed grotesque, but for these last ten years no history has been written, not even such an undocumented history as Mahan provided for the period 1793–1805.

To describe a history as undocumented is no criticism if the documents do not, in fact, exist. But the documentary evidence relating to the Royal Navy in this period is daunting in its mere bulk. We have copies of every operation order issued by the Board of Admiralty and

5

of every dispatch that Board received. We have the Minutes of the Board itself for a part of the period and the log of every ship in commission. We have so much material that we scarcely know where to begin—and almost as much again, perhaps, in Paris, Madrid and the Hague. Nor is this all. For work in the political, diplomatic and economic aspects of this period has given us a background knowledge of the wars which, illuminating the documentary sources, should long since have given us a new narrative of the war at sea.

Some day I may have the opportunity of attempting to write what is so evidently needed. In the meanwhile, this present work is at least some contribution towards that greater theme. My account is based on the correspondence of the successive commanders-in-chief, taken together with such French sources as were available to me. I have used as background my own previous work, *Trade in the Eastern Seas*, 1793–1813, without writing which I should scarcely have understood campaigns which, without their commercial context, might have been meaningless.

If I was qualified in any way to write this book, and if I may be thought qualified to attempt its greater sequel, it is the result of a long apprenticeship. Any feeling I may have for the realities of history I owe, in the first place, to Mr. E. Welbourne, the present Master of Emmanuel College, Cambridge. My first introduction to the French Wars was under the guidance of the late Sir John Clapham. To naval history I was led by the late Sir Geoffrey Callender, with whom I worked for three years at Greenwich. On my return to Cambridge I came under the influence of Sir Herbert Richmond, a former commander-in-chief on the East Indies Station. To all of these scholars I am indebted, as also to Professor Mark Thomson of Liverpool, for giving me the opportunity of teaching to others something of what I had tried to learn. The recent war, moreover, did more for me than merely interrupt my studies. Any understanding I have of the basic problems of time and distance and supply I owe to the senior officers under whom I worked when attached to the Royal Air Force and when serving, later, on the General Staff. Any knowledge I have of the Royal Navy I owe to those with whom I served at the Royal Naval College, Dartmouth; and not least to the cadets themselves.

In the actual preparation of this book for press, much of the burden has fallen on my secretary, Mrs. Y. J. G. Lawton, to whom I am deeply grateful for her assistance. I owe the material in Appendix E to Captain J. W. Rainier, R.N., who has been most helpful in every way. The maps were efficiently drawn by Mr. J. M. Taylor, and owe any defects they may have to me rather than to him. To M. Pierre J. Charliat, the distinguished French historian, I owe, among many other kindnesses, my introduction to the French naval archives. To my brother, Mr. R. C. Parkinson, late R.N.V.R., I owe several extracts from the logs of East Indiamen; logs to which distance prevented me referring in person. To my sister-in-law, who was Miss Pamela Willoughby, I hope to owe forgiveness for anything I may have written about the faults of Sir Nesbit Willoughby. To my publishers I am indebted for their patience with an author who lives so near to the scene of his story and so far from everywhere else. Above all am I beholden to the person to whom this book is dedicated, without whose encouragement it would never have been finished.

C. NORTHCOTE PARKINSON.

University of Malaya,
   Singapore.

CONTENTS

PREFACE   page 5

    Introduction   11

PART ONE

   I   Cornwallis Returns to England   55

  II   Rainier Sails for India   65

 III   Danger from the Dutch   78

 IV   Sercey at the Ile de France   91

  V   The End of Sercey's Squadron   112

 VI   The Threat from Egypt   132

VII   Java Reprieved   156

VIII   The Red Sea and Peace   173

PART TWO

  IX   Decaen and Linois   187

   X   New Outbreak of War   203

  XI   The Battle of Pulo-Aur   221

 XII   Cruise of the *Marengo*   236

XIII   Pellew and Linois   250

XIV   The Command Divided   276

 XV   Pellew and Decaen   300

XVI   Drury in China   320

PART THREE

 XVII   The Navy in India   337

XVIII   Health and Sickness   353

 XIX   The French Islands Blockaded   364

XX Lord Minto and Admiral Drury   page 375

XXI The Battle of Grand Port   383

XXII The Capture of Mauritius   397

XXIII The Conquest of Java   412

XXIV The End of the War   418

Appendices:

    A. Note on Duclos-Legris   425

    B. Ship's Company of the *Marengo*   426

    C. List of Prizes taken by Linois's Squadron   427

    D. Officers of the China Fleet   429

    E. Note on the Rainier Family   431

    F. General Orders of Sir Edward Pellew   437

    G. Note on an Inscription by Charles Baudin   441

    H. Remarks on Nagasaki Harbour   443

    K. The Blockade of Mauritius   447

    L. The Garrison of Mauritius in 1810   449

List of Documentary and Printed Sources   450

Index   460

ILLUSTRATIONS

Plate

I Admiral Peter Rainier (1741?–1808), Commander-in-Chief on
the East Indies Station   *frontispiece*
*From an oil painting by Devis in the National Maritime Museum,
reproduced by permission of the Trustees*

facing page

II The Rt. Hon. Henry Dundas, first Viscount Melville (1742–1811),
Secretary of State for War and President of the Board of Control   64
*From a portrait in oils by Sir Thomas Lawrence, reproduced by
permission of the Trustees of the National Portrait Gallery*

II The Rt. Hon. second Earl Spencer (1758–1834), First Lord of the
Admiralty   64
*From an oil painting in the National Portrait Gallery, repro-
duced by permission of the Trustees*

III Two-decked man-of-war shortening sail   128
*From a watercolour with etched base by W. I. Pocock after N. Pocock,
published in 1815, reproduced by permission of the Trustees of
the National Maritime Museum*

III The Honourable East India Company's Ship *Pitt*   128
*From an aquatint by J. Edy after D. Serres, published by I. Harris
in 1789, reproduced from the print in the National Maritime
Museum, by permission of the Trustees*

IV Action between H.M. frigate *La Sybille* and the French frigate *La
Forte* (28th February, 1799)   192
*From a coloured aquatint by T. Sutherland after T. Whitcombe,
reproduced by permission of the Trustees of the National Maritime
Museum*

V The French 74-gun ship *Marengo*, refitting at Brest in 1803   193
*From a drawing made by Duclos-Legris and included in his journal,
now in the National Maritime Museum and here reproduced by
permission of the Trustees*

VI Captain Sir Home Riggs Popham (1762–1820)   256
*From an oil painting by M. Brown in the National Portrait
Gallery, reproduced by permission of the Trustees*

Plate   *facing page*

VII   Rear-Admiral Sir Edward Pellew (1757–1833), Commander-in-
      Chief on the East Indies Station   257

      *Reproduced from an oil painting by James Northcote in the National
      Portrait Gallery, by permission of the Trustees*

VIII Rear-Admiral Sir Thomas Troubridge (1758?–1807), Commander-
      in-Chief on the East Indies Station   320

      *Reproduced by permission of the Trustees, from the oil painting by
      Sir William Beechey in the National Maritime Museum*

IX   Captain Peter Rainier (*d.* 1836)   321

      *Reproduced from the portrait in oils by John Hoppner, by kind
      permission of Captain J. W. Rainier*

X   Captain Fleetwood Pellew (1789–1861), in the raid on Batavia
      harbour in 1807, which he led at the age of seventeen   352

      *From a pencil drawing by George Chinnery in the National Mari-
      time Museum, reproduced by permission of the Trustees*

XI   Admiral Sir Nesbit Josiah Willoughby (1777–1849), called 'The
      Immortal'   416

      *From the oil painting by Thomas Barber at Birdsall House, Malton,
      reproduced by kind permission of Lord Middleton*

XII   Launch for landing troops, from a model in the Science Museum   417

      *Reproduced from a copyright photograph by permission of the
      Director*

MAPS AND DIAGRAMS

Pondicherry   14
The Dutch East Indies and Batavia   24
The Philippines   41
The Coast and Ceylon   79
Penang   102
The Red Sea and Bombay   144
First and Second Voyages of Admiral Linois   209
Third and Fourth Voyages of Admiral Linois   270
The Capture of the *Marengo*   273
Java, Sourabaya and the Straits of Bali   296
Canton and Macao   322
Fort St. George, Madras   344
Admiral's House, Madras   345
Madras Naval Hospital, 1808   356
The Battle of Grand Port   391
Port Louis   404
The Capture of Mauritius   409

Introduction

THE years between 1783 and 1793 represented the aftermath of a war in which England had been more or less defeated. North America had been lost, Canada and the West Indies saved with difficulty. Such naval successes as there had been were mainly defensive —the holding of Gibraltar, the rescue of Jamaica. In India the fighting had been indecisive at best, and the peace treaty might well have brought France some territorial gain. A continuance—or rather a revival—of the policy of Dupleix, implemented by the naval administration of a Choiseul and the tactical brilliance of a Suffren, might have been fatal to British India. But Louis XVI was in no mood for colonial expansion and had, moreover, no such galaxy of talent at his disposal. In point of fact, the French had been half-hearted in their Indian policy ever since 1754. Many influential Frenchmen had urged then, and many had believed since, that territorial possessions in India were a waste of money and an overhead charge on the profits of trade. This idea was reflected in the peace treaty of 1783, from which France gained little in the East beyond a restitution of territory and a concession (which proved valueless) of unlimited trade with India. The alliance with the Mahrattas was abandoned and no effort made to strengthen the restored possessions. It had become an admitted principle that, in India, the French were to appear only as merchants. In India, therefore, the British remained supreme.

British India centred on Fort William, or Calcutta, nearly a hundred miles up the Hooghly; too far up, in fact, for the larger Indiamen. Calcutta was a city of palaces—as seen, at any rate, from one angle—and was the gateway to the Ganges basin, the only part of India worth an invader's trouble. It was the seat of government for Bengal and indeed for the whole of British India. It was a fortress, a garrison town, a treasury and a high court; everything, in fact, but a naval base. Subsidiary to it were two other centres of government, Madras and Bombay. Madras, or Fort St. George, on the Coromandel Coast, existed partly by historical accident and partly in order to checkmate the French at Pondicherry. It was well placed for the latter purpose, blocking an approach to Bengal by land and useful for a squadron defending it by sea. But if its position was suitable

II

its harbour was not. To put it more exactly, there was no harbour at all; just an open roadstead, a dangerous lee-shore for half the year and an inconvenient landing place during the rest. Bombay, on the other side of India, was of less importance as a town but of greater use as a port. Here there was, and still is, a deep natural harbour, well sheltered and with sufficient tidal range for docking Indiamen and men-of-war. Here was stationed the East India Company's own Navy, the Bombay Marine, used for police-work on that side of India. Through Bombay was organized the Overland Mail, by which European news, via Constantinople, might arrive in as little as three months—half the normal time. Here again, the settlement was, in some sort, an outpost of Bengal, a defence of western India. And this was the base to which the Navy resorted during the north-east monsoon. The Coromandel coast had no comparable seaport except in Trincomalee, which belonged to the Dutch and lacked any hinterland from which a squadron might draw supplies.

One lesson of the recent war had been that Trincomalee, in French hands, could be a serious menace. Another lesson had been that Calcutta and the whole Bay of Bengal was vulnerable to a naval foe operating during the north-east monsoon from a base to the eastwards. Thus, Suffren, in the winter of 1782, had been not at Mauritius (where, in all reason, he should have been) but at Acheen in Sumatra. His presence had been so inconvenient that the question arose as to whether there should not be a British base in that area. This was one motive behind the foundation of Fort Cornwallis, on Prince of Wales Island, in 1786. There was, it is true, an almost simultaneous inquiry (in about 1788) into the possibilities of New Harbour, near Calcutta itself. But, by 1791, the strategic value of Fort Cornwallis, now called Penang, was recognized and even, soon afterwards, overestimated. Penang is an island in the Straits of Malacca, separated from the mainland of Malaya by the strait which forms its excellent anchorage. The island is mostly mountainous and the fort was built close to the shore on the eastern side. As a fort it came in for a good deal of criticism, especially from the future Duke of Wellington. It was easy to bombard from the sea, it was alleged, and houses masked what should have been its field of fire on land. As against this it might be urged that—unlike most rival fortifications—it is still there. And if insufficiently open to the public view, that is merely because it is still, up to a point, operational. At the time this story opens Penang was rapidly growing, with a population that was to total ten thousand by the turn of the century. The settlement owed its existence mainly to Francis Light, the first governor, who was still in office when war began but who died in 1794.

It owed something, incidentally, to Lieutenant Home Popham, who surveyed the South Channel in 1791–92 and showed it to be practicable. It was, as a settlement, rather isolated and vulnerable. But an attack by the Sultan of Kedah had been beaten off in 1791 and future danger was more likely to come from the Dutch or the French.

Still more isolated than Prince of Wales Island was the settlement at Bencoolen (or Benkulen), officially known as Fort Marlborough. Although near the Straits of Sunda it was badly placed from the point of view of local trade. It produced pepper but its importance lessened as that of Penang increased. Like Penang, it lay on the route to China. It was in China, at Canton, that the purely commercial interests of the East India Company centred. At Canton there was no settlement but merely a factory—one among several European factories—and that used only in the trading season. This establishment was governed by the Company's supercargoes, who bought the tea and saw it shipped each year and then withdrew—as compelled by Chinese regulation—to Macao. From a strategic point of view, Canton needed no protection. On the other hand, the China fleet of Indiamen, especially on the homeward voyage, was extremely important and fairly easy to waylay on a known and largely inevitable route. From the French point of view, several of the English trade routes were vulnerable. By contrast, any attack on Calcutta would have been almost impossible, and an attack on Madras or Bombay would have needed larger forces than could easily be embarked. Penang and Bencoolen were easily assailable but offered relatively little to the captors.

As against British India the French had only the most trifling footholds on the mainland. Besides Pondicherry, their capital, they had the isolated factory of Mahé on the Malabar Coast, Chandernagore and two or three villages in Bengal. Pondicherry, it is true, was fortified and even capable of standing a short siege; but it was scarcely tenable unless the French should be able to establish a naval superiority in the Bay of Bengal. The town was surrounded by a nearly circular line of ramparts, weaker only where the sea aided the defence. Unfortunately, however, for the garrison, the fortifications were too extensive, being designed to encircle the whole town instead of merely the white quarter. The thirteen bastions and twelve ravelins implied a larger garrison than the settlement could ever maintain. Grandpré, like his hypothetical ancestor mentioned by Shakespeare, 'a valiant and most expert gentleman,' did more than 'measure the ground.' He drew conclusions from what he saw. 'That unfortunate town,' he wrote, 'was destined to become a school of fortification; for the Dutch and English have never failed, when they got possession of it, to raze everything at all connected with military defence; so that, when ceded to France after a war, it was always to be rebuilt.' The Chevalier de Fresne, its last rebuilder, had perpetuated its too extensive system of fortification, so that Pondicherry could not be taken very seriously as a fortress. As a trading port it was even less likely to inspire respect, having little to boast of except a traffic with Bengal in salt and blue dye. The trade with France, such as it was, centred rather on the factory of Yanaon on the coast of Golconda. This place, however, like Mahé and Chandernagore, included

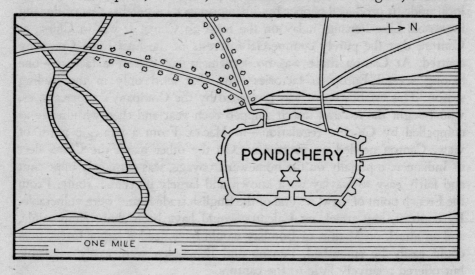

no stretch of territory. As for the factories in Bengal—Balasore, Patna, Dacca and Chatigam—these were trifling possessions, as impossible to defend as Karikal or the French part of Masulipatam. Taken together, these footholds gave the French a certain scope for trade or even for intrigue with the native powers; but as bases for any military operation, they amounted to little or nothing.

The French policy of self-effacement in India did not apply to all French possessions east of the Cape. Although Suffren had tried to carry on the war in the Bay of Bengal he had been based, ultimately, on the Isle of France, otherwise known as Mauritius. With that island the French also held the neighbouring island of Bourbon, two or three settlements in Madagascar and several outposts in the Seychelles. All these were subordinate to the Isle of France, which was the stronghold, the naval base, and the seat of government. Implicit in the theory that Pondicherry was not to be held in force was the corollary that the Isle of France was to be held to the last man and the last round. Held in force, this island might constitute an active menace to the English trade passing the Cape and a base also for raiding any part of the Indian Ocean. For these purposes the Isle of France was very well fitted indeed.

Mauritius was sometimes called 'the Gibraltar of the East'; not inappropriately, either as regards its position or its natural strength. Lying centrally between what used to be the two main trade routes by which the Indian Ocean was entered from the westward, Mauritius takes the form of a rocky island, 'an irregular oval somewhat more than eleven leagues in its greatest length, and rather more than eight in its greatest breadth.'

> The land gradually rises from the shore, towards the centre of the island, which is a woody plain, elevated about 200, or 250 fathoms above the level of the sea. In the middle of this plain is a very sharp conical mountain, which, from its situation, is termed the middle peak. The other mountains, which are separated from each other are, the Montagne de Faience, Grand Port, Savane, Rivière Noir, Rivière Rampart, Corps-du-Garde, and the Ponce. Of the last-mentioned chain, Piter Bort, says M. Bory de St. Vincent, is the most elevated point; and according to the Abbé de la Caille, it is 424 fathoms perpendicular height above the level of the sea. Its summit, generally covered with snow, is formed by an enormous and inaccessible rock, bearing a striking resemblance to a head and distinguishable at a great distance out at sea. . . . Another chain, in the course of which is a very large and remarkable roundish rock, termed Morne des Pretres, runs in a direction towards the north: it is the Montagne Longue, on the extremity of which are signal posts, elevated 2,400 feet above the level of the sea.
>
> The isle of France is watered by above sixty rivulets, some of which deserve the name of rivers, but others do not contain any water in the dry season. . . .
>
> *Naval Chronicle*, Vol. 25, p. 144.

The Mauritius had been first colonized by the Dutch, who, however, abandoned it in 1712 on account of a plague, it is said, of locusts and rats. Some Frenchmen had settled in Bourbon as early as 1664, so that it was not long before the neighbouring island also came into their hands. The first settlement was in 1734, when the French East India Company sent out M. Mahé de la Bourdonnais as the first governor. La Bourdonnais was an exceedingly able man, a good sailor and a skilled engineer. The development of the colony was almost entirely due to him, and it may be said that the island bears the impress of his character to this day.

> . . . the island is indebted to him, and to him alone, for its aqueducts, bridges, hospitals, and principal magazines. In short, every thing useful that still exists there is the work of that truly great man. La Bourdonnais had a

very extensive knowledge of those mechanic arts which are most common and most necessary for our wants. Often was he seen by the break of day, at the head of his labourers, driving a wheel barrow, or handling the trowel and the compass, merely with a view to excite and keep up a spirit of emulation. After the example which he himself gave, it was hardly possible for any one not to concur, as far as he was able, in promoting the public advantage. Whatever, therefore, he planned or undertook for the benefit of the colony, during the twelve years of his administration, was always attended with speedy and complete success.

(Alexis Rochon, *A Voyage to Madagascar and the East Indies.*)

The only serious mistake made by the early settlers was in destroying too great an extent of the forests, and thus lessening the rainfall. Despite this blunder, however, it was found possible to put about a third of the land under cultivation. The chief crops were wheat and maize, grown alternately, but efforts were also made in other directions. Coffee, sugar, indigo, cotton and spices were all grown with varying success, and the rearing of sheep and cattle was not wholly neglected. From the first, the French settlers depended on slave labour, and it was La Bourdonnais who introduced, from Brazil, a crop intended for the feeding of slaves. This was the manioc (sometimes spelt manihot or magnoc), a plant from the root of which a kind of bread is made, called cassada or cassavi. In its green state this root is poisonous, but it is made edible by being dried over a fire and grated into powder. The French sometimes called it Madagascar bread. This, with grain, coffee and sugar, formed the chief product of the island.

The population of the Isle of France was estimated in 1799 as consisting of 10,000 white men and mulattoes, and 55,000 slaves. At a later date, the average population over the period 1804–25 was stated as being over 82,000. The exact figures were as follows: 7,108 white men, 9,416 free people of colour, and 65,633 slaves. These slaves were nearly all negroes brought from Madagascar, Anjouan, Quiloa, Zanzibar and, above all, Mozambique. To keep up their numbers, a yearly supply was necessary. To maintain this supply a regular trade existed, mostly in the hands of the Portuguese, which the French referred to as 'La Traite.' The Portuguese and French traders used to pay from 30 to 80 piastres for each Mozambique or Madagascar slave; those from Quiloa and Zanzibar being somewhat cheaper. The market prices at Zanzibar were said to range from 50 dollars for a prime slave to 4 dollars for a child; young girls, on the other hand, sometimes fetching as much as 60 dollars. The export trade from Zanzibar alone was estimated at some 10,000 slaves a year. Only a proportion of these went to the Isle of France, for there was a similar demand for slave-labour at Muscat and in certain parts of India. It is clear, nevertheless, that the numbers imported annually by the French were very considerable. They were paid for, it seems, in cash rather than in goods; which brings us to the question as to how the Isle of France could maintain a balance of trade, a question which can be answered only after some attention has been given to her seaports.

When La Bourdonnais was choosing a position for his capital, he had two alternatives open to him. There was the harbour to the south-east where the Dutch had made their settlement, and the harbour to the north-west, facing the trade wind. Only at these two points could a seaport be founded, as the rest of the island is almost unapproachable, the coast being everywhere fringed with coral reefs. His temptation was to follow the example of the Dutch, the south-east side of the island being the pleasanter and the harbour affording easy ingress before the wind. In resisting this temptation he was guided by strategic considerations. The harbour on the leeward side of the island, being more difficult to enter, was so much the more easy to defend. For an enemy seeking to attack the port the wind was always blowing the wrong way except during the hurricane season when it was rash to be near the island at all. It was possible, of course, to work up the channel into the harbour by a process of warping and towing, provided only that the garrison did not object. But to have attempted such a slow approach under the fire of the batteries would have been virtual suicide. La Bourdonnais was too good a seaman not to realize how easily the north-west port could be rendered impregnable.

Port Louis was the name given to the town which grew up round the north-west harbour, but the inhabitants, at the time of which we are speaking, still called it 'The Camp.' Built at the head of a triangular bay, at the foot of the mountains, Port Louis depended on trade for its prosperity. It owed much to a resourceful officer who had enlarged the harbour. This was M. de Tromelin, a retired naval captain. He obtained the sanction of the Duc de Praslin and then proceeded forthwith to deflect the course of the silt-bearing streams which tended to fill up the harbour. That done, he dredged out the channel. The coral basin known as Trou Fanfarron was then a sort of lagoon, unconnected with the harbour. By dredging and by explosives, Tromelin managed to add this basin to the harbour, breaking down the reef which had lain between. Thus was formed a safe and capacious port, capable of sheltering upwards of fifty large vessels. The commercial future of the island, if not assured, became possible.

As to the town, or camp, it is composed of wooden houses, which have only a ground floor, on account of the winds and the heat. They are separated from each other, and surrounded with palisadoes. The streets are tolerably straight, and it were to be wished, that rows of trees were planted to render them cool. . . . The town has no regular fortification, but to the left of it in looking towards the sea, there is an intrenchment of dry stones, extending from the mountain to the harbour. On the same side is Fort Blanc, which defends the entrance; and opposite to it, on the other side, is a battery on the island of Tonneliers. . . .

(Charles Grant, Viscount de Vaux, *History of Mauritius*.)

Port Louis was an unattractive town and so uncomfortably hot in the warmer months that most of the white inhabitants sought refuge elsewhere. The business done there was of two kinds. First, there was the exchange of commodities with Europe and with other parts of the East. Sugar, coffee, cotton, indigo and cloves were exported to France and all the necessities of a civilized life were imported from thence. Slaves, as we have seen, were imported from Madagascar and East Africa. Cotton cloth was imported from India, and grain occasionally from the Cape of Good Hope. From Batavia came rice, arrack, cordage, oil and wood. Second, and distinct from the exchange of produce, was the business done with foreign ships calling at the island. These were sometimes supplied not only with provisions and water, but also with a market and even a cargo. American ships, for example, when first tentatively rounding the Cape, would often find all the Eastern goods they wanted at the Isle of France, and so would spare themselves the trouble of going further afield. By 1790, it is true, many American ships had found their way to China, but the habit of calling at Port Louis remained with them. Danish ships were apt to do the same, and there was more than a tendency for the Isle of France to become a regular market and exchange for the products of East and West. During the war circumstances greatly intensified this kind of business while discouraging any other type.

Most of the trade, of whatever description, centred on Port Louis. The harbour on the south-east side of the island, called Grand-Port because of its larger expanse of water, was regularly used only by smaller craft. Under stress of weather, however, ships often put in there for temporary shelter. A town grew up there, becoming second in importance to the capital.

Revenue of the Isle of France was derived from a customs levy of from 5 per cent to 10 per cent on imports—especially foreign imports. Some 200,000 piastres were raised annually in this way—the Spanish coinage was the most widely used in the East—and with this, the equivalent of between £40,000 and £50,000, the expenses of administration were met. This financial basis was sound so long as no considerable garrison was needed. As soon as it became necessary to support a body of regular troops, the island was run at a loss and became, theoretically, a drain on the mother country. The word 'theoretically' is used because the French Revolutionary Governments were apt to lose sight of the colony's existence for years at a time, which usually prevented the troops being paid at all.

To what extent the Isle of France was self-supporting in the matter of food, it is very difficult to determine. In normal times foodstuffs were imported, as we have seen, from Java, the Cape and elsewhere. Subsequent events, moreover, proved that a cutting off of these supplies produced a real shortage, though no actual famine. When the island was under a close blockade there were instances of its coffee and sugar being used as manure. The rendering valueless of its exports, however, caused only financial difficulties. It is far from clear that there was any real starvation. What the shortage amounted to was probably this, that the more prosperous inhabitants had to pay very high prices for their food, some of them being ruined meanwhile by the failure of their business, while the poorer white inhabitants had to submit at times to an unaccustomed diet of turtle and manioc. Before the war ended the Government must often have had reason to feel grateful to the great La Bourdonnais, not only for introducing the manioc plant but for compelling every planter to cultivate 5,000 square feet of it for each slave he kept.

In discussing this question of the degree in which the Isle of France was self-supporting, no account has so far been taken of the part played in its economy by the neighbouring island of Bourbon. This island lies about 130 miles south-west of Port Louis, a distance which would be thought considerable in many parts of the world, but which dwindles into insignificance when compared with the 3,000 miles separating the Isle of France from the East Indies or with the 2,000 miles between it and Ceylon. Bourbon is somewhat larger than the Isle of France and has been defined as 'a circular volcanic mountain intersected by fertile valleys.' It had, during the period with which we are dealing, a more agricultural character than the Isle of France; chiefly through the absence of an adequate harbour. The chief products of Bourbon were coffee and cotton, cloves also having been grown with success since 1770. The foodstuffs cultivated were wheat, maize, potatoes, manioc and yams—both the last being intended for the slaves. Fruit was plentiful but cattle scarce, owing to lack of pasture. Most of the island's supply of meat and rice came from Madagascar, being paid for in dollars and small-arms. Grain, on the other hand, was so plentiful that quantities were exported to the Isle of France. The relationship between the two colonies was, to some extent, that of town and country. Taken together, it would probably be true to say that they were essentially self-supporting. Considered separately, the Isle of France was not altogether so.

In 1799 the population of Bourbon was estimated at fifty-six thousand; of which number some eight thousand were white men or mulattoes and the remainder slaves. There were two towns on the island, St. Denis, the capital, and St. Paul, which had the better harbour. Neither could be said to be very important in a commercial sense. There was a trade with France, coffee and cotton being exchanged for slave-trade goods. There was the slave-trade; and, finally, there was the trade with the other French settlements, and more especially with the Isle of France. The public revenue of Bourbon was derived chiefly from import duties. The island had its own Government, which was subordinate, however, to the governor either of Pondicherry or the Isle of France. During the period with which we are concerned the government-general was vested almost continuously in the latter administration; necessarily, in that Pondicherry was only momentarily in French hands.

Of the settlements subordinate to Port Louis, perhaps the next to consider should be Roderigue or Rodriguez, known formerly as Diego Rais. This is a small island lying 375 miles to the eastward of the Isle of France.

> Roderigue is situated in lat. 19°41′S., long. 63°10′ E. by the best accounts, the variation 13′ W. in 1802. It was the practice, when navigators had no means to correct their longitude but the variation, for ships bound to Mauritius to get a sight of Roderigue, and then steer westward for their port; such circuitous tracks are no longer requisite, since marine chronometers and lunar observations are in general use . . . [at Roderigue] This road or harbour (called Matheuren Bay) is safe when you are in, but the channel is intricate. . . . There is a small level spot of land between two hills, with some houses, where a resident and some soldiers are stationed, with a few slaves, who collect land and sea turtle; these are carried to Mauritius in vessels employed constantly on this service. . . . The only inducement a ship can have to touch at this place is the want of fresh water, there being plenty of this necessary article in the harbour, and also wood for fuel. Fish may be caught in abundance, but some of them are of a poisonous quality. . . .
>
> (*Naval Chronicle*, Vol. 28, 1812.)

The inhabitants of Rodriguez seem to have numbered about twenty. A little market gardening was done, mainly for the benefit of such shipping as should put in there. The importance of the island lay in its position to windward of the Isle of France. When ships sighted Rodriguez before steering for Port Louis it was to avoid the risk of falling to leeward of the latter place. In time of war this island was found to have its uses.

In Madagascar the French had, it seems, only one settlement. This was Fort Dauphin, a harbour which the French had sought to develop in the seventeenth century. In 1805 the ruins of the old fort were still to be seen, the gate carved with the words 'Etablissement de La Compagnie des indes en 1661, sous La Regne de Louis 14. . . .'—the rest of the inscription having been obliterated by time. At that time the station consisted of about a dozen cottages under the rule of a certain M. Ykel, who had been there for sixteen years. He had under him a clerk, some coopers, carpenters and slaves. His duty was to supply French ships with water, rice, cattle, goats, turtle and fruit. As the former French settlers had been massacred by the natives, M. Ykel was fortunate in having secured their confidence. French vessels would sometimes call at other points on the coast of Madagascar, St. Augustin Bay, Foul Point or Tamatave. At this last-named place, also called Tamatava, the French had a fort, at any rate during the later years of the war; but this may have been but a temporary measure. There was no settlement at St. Augustin; this was merely a harbour where friendly natives would supply cattle, sheep, goats and poultry in exchange for bottles, hardware, old iron, bad powder and unreliable muskets. The more fierce of the Madagascar tribes lived, apparently, on the other side of the island, so that there was no serious difficulty in arranging this traffic.

The remaining French possessions east of the Cape were in the Seychelles. These islands, over 800 miles to the north of the Isle of France, were described as 'a cluster of nearly twenty islands and rocks, all dependencies of Mauritius, and absolutely necessary for some of her commercial purposes.' Most of these islands were uninhabited, but there was a tolerable anchorage between two of them, St. Anne and Mahé, and on the latter a settlement had been formed. In 1805 there were about two hundred white men living there, mostly deported convicts, and nearly twice as many slaves. Coffee and cotton were grown, turtle were caught and business was done with ships in the slave-trade. As a useful port of call, and undefended, Mahé was always changing hands. English cruisers took possession of it from time to time in the course of the war, and French cruisers repossessed themselves of it as regularly. It was merely a matter of hoisting flags, the same resident being willing to govern in the name of either country. A formal agreement of neutrality was once drawn up by the islanders, but it was cancelled by the governor of the Isle of France. Men-of-war used to approach the Seychelles cautiously, not knowing whether the enemy might be there. The southernmost of this group was called Frigate's Island. Midway between the Seychelles and the Isle of France are the Galega or Agalega Islands. They were described as 'two patches of earth, rocks, and a scanty vegetation. . . . The largest is about six miles in length. . . .' These islands were at this time wholly uninhabited, but cruisers sometimes called there for coco-nuts and fish. They were of some little use to navigators voyaging from one to another of the scattered French possessions.

No attempt has yet been made to describe the strength, the strategic value or the garrison of the French Islands. Such military considerations may well be postponed until a later page, leaving us free at this point to survey the eastern dependencies of Holland. The Dutch, if inferior to the French in sea-power, were commercially far more important. Their principal possessions were Java, the Spice Islands and the Cape of Good Hope. Java was the centre of the Dutch East Indies. It was there that the Dutch had established their capital and it was from there that the Dutch maintained a sphere of influence extending to Borneo, Celebes, Ternate, Ceram, Timor and Sumatra. Of the islands actually occupied by them the Dutch valued most the Spice Islands; that is to say, Amboyna and its dependencies together with the Banda Islands. To Amboyna they had confined the cultivation of cloves, and to Banda the cultivation of nutmegs. By thus limiting the supply and by garrisoning their outposts such as Fort Nassau and Fort Belgica, the Dutch East India Company contrived at least partially to retain a monopoly in spices. Their efforts were directed more towards excluding interlopers than towards developing the trade. Java itself produced, not spices, but pepper, rice, sugar, coffee, salt, cotton-yarn and indigo. A part of the exports from the Dutch East Indies were derived from the native rulers, some of whom were compelled to deliver produce at a fixed price; at a price, indeed, so low as to make the transaction a thinly disguised paying of tribute. Thus, the Kingdom of Bantam yielded six million pounds of pepper annually; but, although it was 'esteemed second in quality to that grown on the coast of Malabar,' the buying price was fixed at twopence-halfpenny a pound. Spices and tin were obtained elsewhere on similar terms. Besides the clusters of islands from which the Dutch drew their merchandise, Holland had another possession of importance in Malacca, which was held for strategic and political reasons. The ancient Malay capital, situated in the straits which take their name from it, Malacca had a special value in the eyes of the native. Like the other Dutch towns and forts, however, it had small commercial value when compared with Batavia, the capital of Java and of the whole Dutch East Indies.

Batavia, being at the western end of Java, had a strategic position close to the Straits of Sunda. This, together with an excellent harbour, gave the town its unquestioned predominance in the East Indies.

> The city of Batavia, which was the capital of the Dutch possessions in the East, as well as of the Island of Java, lies . . . on the northern shore of the empire of Jacatra, in the deepest part of a bay formed by the points of Ontong, Java, and Crawang; from the former of which it lies about four Dutch miles south-east, and from the latter about five miles south-west. Ten or twelve small islands, at the distance of from two to four leagues from the city, shelter the bay from north-west to north by east from the swell of the sea; the road is between a quarter and half a league from the city. The ground upon which the city is built, bears evident marks of having been left, or thrown up by the sea; as is the case with a great extent of the land on each side, the shore of which is chiefly soft mud, which increases every year. Above, or to the south of the city, towards Tanabang and Weltervreeden, the ground rises by degrees; and the soil becomes firmer and dryer on approaching the mountains, which lie twelve or more Dutch miles inland. . . .
>
> (*Naval Chronicle*, Vol. 27, 1812.)

In the low-lying situation of Batavia the Dutch had what they doubtless valued, a splendid opportunity to reproduce Holland. The proper approach, however, to Batavia is by sea, and it is as a seaport that it must first be considered.

The roadstead at Batavia was exceptionally sheltered, being surrounded by a number of islands, all of which served as breakwaters. On one of the islands, Onroost, the Dutch East India Company had its dockyard. Of Onroost Captain Cook said 'there is not a marine yard in the world where a ship can be laid down with more convenience, safety and despatch, nor repaired with more diligence and skill.' It may be added at this point that Java furnished all, and more than all the timber needed for shipbuilding and repairing. Into the basin formed by the islands, including Onroost, there flowed the River Jacatra. Unfortunately, this river tended to silt up the harbour, so that the anchorage, as time went on, became more distant from the town. When the first settlement was made a fort had been built at the point where the river entered the sea. By the end of the eighteenth century, however, the mud banks had grown to such an extent that the nearest place for a ship to drop anchor was far out of range of the guns. It had therefore ceased to be a place of safety for shipping in time of war. The difficulty of transporting goods between the ships and the wharves was met by prolonging the banks of the river by brick piers stretching

out seawards for three-quarters of a mile. Nevertheless, the river itself
having become shallower, only small vessels could lie alongside the piers

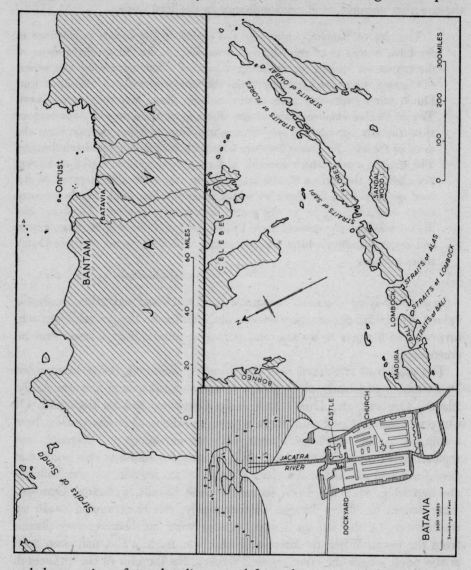

and the carrying of merchandise to and from the city was left to a type of
flat-bottomed craft designed for the purpose.

> Batavia . . . is considered one of the best harbours in India, having a
> number of small islands about two or three leagues from the city, which
> shelter the bay from N.W. to N.E., the principal of which are Onrust,

Edam, Cooper's Island, and Purmerend. Large ships generally ride at single anchor in the roads, at about $1\frac{1}{2}$ miles from the shore, in six fathoms, the dome of the principal church bearing about south; but smaller vessels approach within a mile of the shore.

Fronting the small river, or canal, which leads to the city, there is a bar, on which there are about three feet at low water. The channel for boats to enter, is to the eastward of the bar; and as there is at times a surf upon it at low water, when blowing strong in the N.W. monsoon, strangers ought not to send their boats to the river, as many have been overset upon the bar, and the crews devoured by alligators, which are of a large size, and very numerous. . . . The breadth of the river within the city is about 180 feet; it runs into the sea, past the Castle and the Admiralty Wharf. On both sides of the mouth are long piers of wood and brick-work, about 3,800 feet in length, taken from the moat of the city. The vessels belonging to the merchants are laid up and repaired between these piers, on the west side; but along the east side, the passage is kept open for the lighters, which go in and out of the city with the cargoes of the ships. At the outward point of the eastern pier there is a shed, which serves for a stable for the horses which draw the small vessels and boats up and down the river. Opposite this is a hornwork, called the Water Fort, built at a considerable expense. It is constructed of a kind of coral rock, and defended by heavy cannon; within it are barracks for the garrison, and there is no other approach to it than along the western pier. . . .

(Milburn, Oriental Commerce, Vol. II.)

The Water Fort and the older fort in the town itself, known as the castle or citadel, were sufficient to defend the Dutch capital and even to protect such of the shipping as could run between the piers. But they afforded no protection to large vessels in the roadstead, which were undefended except by some batteries on the islands.

The island of Onrust is about three leagues N.W. from Batavia, and is nearly round. It rises six or eight feet above the surface of the sea, and is of small extent. . . . In the centre of the island, and within the fort, consisting of four bastions and three curtains, stand the warehouse and other buildings. . . . On the north side of the island are two saw-mills; and on the south side there is a long pier-head, on which are three large wooden cranes, erected for the purpose of fixing or unstepping masts. Three ships can lie here behind each other, alongside the pier, in deep water, to be repaired, or to receive or discharge their cargoes. There is another pier, a little more to the westward, called the Japan pier, where one more ship can lie to load or unload. There are 20 or more feet of water against the piers, and it rises about 5 feet once in 24 hours. All ships that require it, are hove down at the wharfs along the piers, and receive every necessary reparation with convenience, safety, and dispatch. The government of this island is under the master carpenter, and his situation is reckoned a very profitable one.

Edam is about three leagues N.N.E. from Batavia; it is very woody, and has abundance of large and ancient trees. The Company have some warehouses on this island for salt; but the chief use they make of it, is as a place of exile for criminals, who are employed in making cordage, and over whom a ship's Captain is placed as commandant.

Cooper's Island is about 1,600 yards from Onrust, and about one-third less in size. The Company have several warehouses upon it, in which coffee is chiefly laid up. There are two pier-heads, where several vessels may load and discharge at its south side. There are two batteries mounting 12 guns on this island.

The Island of Purmerend is to the eastward of Onrust, and about half as large again. It is planted with shady trees, and in the centre is a large building, which serves for a hospital, or lazaretto. . . .

(Milburn, *Oriental Commerce*, Vol. II.)

Beyond the islands, with their wharves and workshops, and beyond the mud-flats which cumbered the river mouth, lay the city of Batavia itself. It was thought to be 'among the neatest and handsomest cities in the world,' rivalling even Calcutta in the amount of its trade though not in size. The population, to be exact, was estimated at 116,000 in 1793, at 160,000 in 1805. The former figure, taken from John Barrow's *Voyage to Cochin China*, may be an underestimate. Accounts agree, as to the latter figure, that the Europeans numbered between 1,200 and 1,500, that there were 100,000 Chinese, and that the remainder consisted of Javanese, Armenians, Parsees, Hindoos, Persians and Arabs. Barrow makes the white population number about 9,000, but he is probably including half-castes. These were said to be numerous, owing to the shortage of white women. The mass of the population lived in the suburbs which had grown up outside the fortifications. Most of the more prosperous Europeans, whether officials or merchants, had country houses to which they could retire when hours of business were over.

Batavia was roughly oblong in shape, the River Jacatra dividing it longitudinally into two tolerably equal parts. A moat, connected with the river, surrounded the whole. Coming into the city by boat from the sea, one saw, first of all, the castle or citadel, defended by its own moat, to the left; the dockyard, on the opposite bank, to the right. As if a slow-moving and tidal river, together with the moats of the city and castle, did not provide stagnant water enough, a series of canals had been dug, both inside and outside the ramparts, most of them being either parallel with or at right-angles to the course of the Jacatra. These canals had streets on either bank, the town having been regularly planned in a chess-board fashion.

The digging of the canals, which dated from the middle of the eighteenth century, had been part of a conscious effort to reproduce Holland. This effort, in other respects as well as in this, was remarkably successful. The houses were in the Dutch style, built for the most part of brick, stuccoed and white-painted on the outside, with sash windows and mahogany or green-coloured woodwork. Intersecting each other at right-angles, and made very broad, the streets (like the canals) were everywhere lined with rows of trees. To save walking in the heat, the white inhabitants were conveyed about the town in gondolas. The general effect seemed to most visitors very attractive.

> . . . The streets are broad and airy . . . and planted with trees along the canals as well as the foot-paths which adjoin the houses; between these rows lies the carriage-road; and, notwithstanding the stigma sometimes cast on Dutch taste for the intermixture of vegetation, I own I admire the arrangement. I will not, however, say so much for the style of Dutch architecture. The houses, indeed, are commonly large and roomy, substantially, though not perhaps very elegantly built; within, they possess all the conveniences adapted to the national taste in this climate; without, they sometimes look heavy, although in extent frequently trenching on the outline of palaces. . . .
>
> . . . There is, after all, something neat in the aspect of a Dutch town; it may sometimes want animation and variety . . . yet fine houses, with wood and water intermixed, ought, when tolerably arranged, to please even a fastidious eye. . . .
>
> (James Prior, *Voyage in the Indian Ocean*.)

English visitors to Batavia, whether or not possessed of a fastidious eye for architecture, usually boasted a fastidious nose for drainage. It was here that the Dutchman's copy of his native land broke down. Risks can be taken with stagnant water in the Netherlands which will only produce disaster in the tropics. Prior, as a surgeon, regarded the canals of Batavia as little better than cesspits; while even the trees were to him objects of great suspicion.

> They (the canals) are about thirty feet broad, and two or three deep; some have a languid stream, others scarcely any; but all crowded with the very germ and soul of putrefaction, to which the sun speedily gives life and action. In the Chinese suburb, one or two were completely stagnant, the surface covered by decomposed animal and vegetable matters, converted into the usual green scum of such filthy places. . . . Over these are several small bridges, not at all of a piece with the other buildings of the city, the

inhabitants being too fond of boats to care much about bridges. Some bad qualities are attributed to the trees that line the streets, such as preventing a free circulation of air, and forming a receptacle for the concentration of the noxious vapours arising from the filthy pools around them; to these I may add the doctrine of the vegetable physiologists, that they give off carbonic acid gas during the night. . . .

At the hottest time of year the water in the canals at Batavia dwindled until there was practically no current and but one or two feet in depth. In the absence of any system of sanitation, all the filth and refuse in the city were thrown into the canals. The situation was not much improved, from the point of view of health, when the latter overflowed in the rainy season, flooding the lower parts of the town and polluting afresh the houses of a none too cleanly population. The chief diseases which resulted were dysentery and malaria.

The diseases prevalent in Batavia are chiefly of a putrid nature. The disorder most common is a tertian ague, which, after two or three paroxisms, becomes a double tertian, and then a continued remittent, which frequently carries off the patient in a short time. In many instances, even the most hale and robust men are attacked, and taken off in a few hours, in consequence of the rapid progress of putridity in the viscera. The most efficient means of preserving health are, to avoid the night air, to eat and drink very moderately, and to take much exercise on horseback. [Prior].

Java as a whole was not particularly unhealthy and it was thought by many that Batavia would be greatly improved if the canals were filled in. It must, however, be remembered that the soil was wet and marshy in any case, and that the mud-flats round the river mouth collected most of the sewage of the town.

In the eyes of other nations, and especially the English, Batavia was a mere graveyard. This reputation was very largely based on a reading of Captain Cook's voyages. In his circumnavigation of 1768–70, Cook had called there to refit, losing a great many men from disease out of an otherwise healthy crew. This made a great impression, particularly because of Cook's reputation for a knowledge of hygiene. The impression was confirmed by the experiences of other ships. Batavia was thought to be exceptionally unhealthy and it was often asked why the Dutch did not remove their capital elsewhere. Even the Chinese and Malay troops employed to man the batteries were decimated by disease, it was said, needing perpetual recruitment to maintain their numbers. In short, 'Batavia has generally been regarded as one of the most unwholesome spots on the face of the globe.'

It would seem that the city's evil reputation was greatly exaggerated, probably because visitors there suffered more than did the actual residents. Of the white inhabitants it was said than 10 per cent died each year. This was, roughly speaking, the rate of mortality in Bengal; so that the English had very little ground for self-congratulation in comparing Java with India. It is true that ships calling at Batavia had to moor opposite a pestilent swamp, very likely with an off-shore wind blowing; but then, ships putting into the Hooghli had to do just the same and with very similar results. From the Dutch point of view, the legend about Batavia, partly false as it was, had its usefulness. It remained for many years the city's chief protection against attack. Enemies might make light of the Dutch batteries, but it was long before they could make up their minds to face a tertian ague, knowing how likely it was to become successively a double tertian and a continued remittent. When the English finally took the risk they found Java (Batavia excepted) rather healthier than Bengal.

Batavia was ruled by a council under the presidency of the Governor-General of the Indies. This powerful official, appointed by the Dutch East India Company, lived in very considerable state. 'When he appears in public,' wrote Duclos, 'he is accompanied by guards and officers, with far more pomp than any European monarch.' With one exception, all Dutch possessions east of the Cape were under his control. The exception was the Dutch factory at Canton, which was, and had long been, directly controlled from Holland. Under the Government of Batavia was a host of Dutch officials in the Company's employ. They were all, by the standards of British India, absurdly underpaid. As all Dutch policy was grounded on the determination to maintain a monopoly in the spice trade, and as such a monopoly needed above all for its preservation a set of incorruptible customs officers, it may be questioned whether higher salaries might not have justified themselves. Here it must be remembered, however, that the Dutch (unlike the English) East India Company was a commercial concern and bound to show a profit from year to year. It drew no great riches in the form of revenue from conquered provinces, but had to make its dividend by trade and by trade alone. To this end the Company retained the monopoly of the trade in spices, pepper, opium, tin, coffee, salt and timber. Many of these products were sent to Batavia in exchange for rice grown in Java. A trade was also maintained with Europe, India, America, China and Japan.

From Holland there sailed every year some twenty Indiamen, according to Duclos, laden with European goods, returning in the end with cargoes consisting of the produce not only of the Dutch Indies but of all Asia.

Ships came to Batavia from all over the world, making the city a market in which all kinds of goods were sold. Piece goods, drugs and opium came from Bengal in exchange for spices, coffee and arrack. There was a brisk trade with America, mixed cargoes from thence, including specie, being exchanged for spices, sugar, coffee, rice, and goods from China. In general, the staple exports of Java were pepper, spices, sugar and coffee; while a very important import came in the form of bullion from Europe, amounting, it was said, to upwards of £500,000 a year. Two vital branches of trade were those with China and Japan. Each year, in November and December, junks would arrive from China with raw silk, nankeen, paper, tea and tutenague, loading for their return voyage with arrack, birds' nests, pepper, spices, sandal-wood and sago. The Dutch themselves sent four or five ships annually to China, laden with tin, lead, pepper and spices. The cargoes of these vessels were supposed to value £250,000; half of that amount, however, being in silver, either in bars or Spanish dollars. Realizing on these goods a profit of about £60,000, the Company's agents at Canton bought tea, silks, nankeen and china-ware, the ships returning therewith to Batavia. The Dutch alone were allowed to trade with Japan and, to maintain this privileged position, the nature of the traffic was for long kept a profound secret. In 1790, John Meares confessed to an all but complete ignorance of the details of the Japan trade.

> It is well known that the only European nation which enjoys a commercial connection with the Japanese, are the Dutch. Four Dutch ships are annually dispatched thither from Batavia, and each of them pays an hundred thousand dollars for the privilege of this profitable traffic. . . . The Dutch are too sensible of the advantages of this monopoly, not to clothe the whole in all possible secrecy, or to colour it with every kind of fallacious description. But, however ignorant we may be of their particular imports, exports, and mode of trade, we cannot but know that it is extremely advantageous to them, and would, consequently, prove of equal, if not superior benefit to us. . . .

No other account mentions this payment of 100,000 dollars, nor is it clear by whom and to whom Meares supposed this sum to have been paid. Whatever may be the truth of this, however, the Japan trade, when its nature was revealed, proved to be nothing very extraordinary. Two or three Dutch ships would leave Batavia each year in June or early in July —two ships being apparently the normal—and would make their way to Nagasaki. Arriving about the middle of August, they would sail again after the change of the monsoon, usually before November 25th. On the outward voyage they were laden with a mixed cargo, including spices, pepper, ivory,

lead, tin and piece-goods. On the homeward voyage they carried, principally, copper; and it was said that these returning ships were worth half
a million sterling. In time of war the Dutch sometimes sought to protect
these valuable cargoes, as also those in the China trade, by entrusting them
to neutral vessels. A better protection, however, lay in the doubts prevalent
as to the exact route they took.

In Java the Dutch had one or two garrisons in addition to that of
Batavia, though none of comparable importance. Eastwards of the capital,
along the coast, lay Cheribon, Samarang and, lastly, Sourabaya. Only the
last-named of these deserves particular notice.

> The channel, or strait, of Madura, sometimes called Manara, dividing
> the island of the former name from Java, is from three to six or seven miles
> broad. By the eastern outlet, large vessels have not sufficient depth of water
> to go through; here likewise it is narrowest, and Sourabaya is built. . . .

The straits of Madura, being impossible to enter at the eastern end—as
far, at least, as ships of any size were concerned—formed a sort of cul-de-sac,
narrowing towards the farther extremity very much in the manner of an
estuary. At the highest point to which ships could ascend there was a river
flowing into the straits on the Java side. Straddling this river was the town
of Sourabaya. Fifteen miles below Sourabaya, nearer the entrance to the
harbour, was a smaller town called Griessie or Gressec. Batteries were
mounted there and at Sambelangan on the island of Madura. Defended
thus the Dutch merchantmen commonly anchored opposite Griessie, which
was also the Dutch naval base. At a later period another fort was built,
lower down still, so as to command the approach to the harbour. This
was Fort Lodowic, built in the channel itself on piles and rocks, but only
late in the war and after the Dutch had already learnt by disaster. The
whole strait, from the point where Fort Lodowic was built to Sourabaya,
was a large and secure harbour, with six or seven fathoms of water throughout. At the actual harbour entrance, the channel was much narrower and
little more than three fathoms deep. This depth was, of course, insufficient
for the largest ships, but the mud at the bottom was so light that a way
could be forced through it bodily. Such difficulties as there were about
entering this sheltered roadstead added something to its comparative safety
from attack. Although less fortunate than Batavia in strategic position,
Sourabaya offered at once a better climate and a greater degree of security.

> . . . Sourabaya may be considered the eastern capital of Java, as Batavia
> is the western; for though only of modern date, it is rapidly rising into
> consequence. The distance between these two places somewhat exceeds

500 miles. The new city, however, though much less extensive and populous, is more handsome, healthy and pleasant, than the old: it is, besides, situated on a fine river, and has likewise the very superior advantage of a harbour which may be rendered the best either in this or in any of the neighbouring islands. . . .

The European town lies on the right bank of the river; the Chinese and native Campongs on the left: They are united by bridges, up to which coasters with merchandise may ascend. . . .

(James Prior, *Voyage in the Indian Ocean*, 1810–11.)

Batavia and Sourabaya were the principal Dutch towns in the East Indies. The other possessions there of Holland and their sphere of influence are best understood from a map, and to such a map the reader is referred rather than to any list of names. (See page 24.)

The next Dutch possession to consider is the Cape of Good Hope. The Cape, in those days, was considered mainly as a port of call; and as such, apart from its position, it was not much admired. Of the colonial possibilities of South Africa very little was thought. As late as 1800 Sir Roger Curtis could write thus to Lord Spencer: 'Speaking of the country at large, it is I think physically impossible it can ever be fruitful or produce articles of any consideration, the exportation of which would render it a prosperous and rich colony. . . . To me therefore it appears clearly that this colony, merely as a colony, can never be of any advantage to Great Britain. . . .' Captain Robert Percival's account of the Cape, published in 1804, did much towards correcting this misconception. In the meanwhile, however, partly as a result of the English undervaluing the country, the Cape remained in Dutch hands for a part of the period with which we are concerned.

Regarded almost solely as a port of call, as a source of fresh provisions and a break in the long voyage to the East, the Cape lacked any outstanding advantages. To begin with, there was no real shelter there, and but two places to which ships could go for supplies.

False Bay and Table Bay; the one washing the southern, the other the northern shore of the isthmus, are the usual resort for shipping trading to, or calling for refreshments at the Cape of Good Hope. During the summer season, when the S.E. winds are predominant, which may be reckoned from September till May, Table Bay affords the most secure shelter; and Simon's Bay, a cove or indent on the western shore of False Bay, for the rest of the year, when the northerly or north-westerly winds are strongest. In neither of them is there any sort of security or convenience for heaving down and repairing ships. . . . .

(Barrow's *Travels*, quoted in the *Oriental Voyager*, J. Johnson.)

Seamen were, in general, emphatic in their distrust of False and Table Bays. Captain Basil Hall, for instance, regretted that the 'Cabo de Tormentos' had been given what he called 'its present spoony title.' Captain Beaver wrote:

> The Cape may be a capital colony, but its bay is an infernal one; it is safe against no wind, and its sea is worse than the wind. You have generally a great swell, and even in the fair season, the S.E. winds frequently blow so strong, that you have no communication with the shore for two or three days together. But a north-wester, after the middle of May, shows Table Bay in all its malignancy; and he who is fool enough to anchor there of his own accord, may either part or founder as luck shall befall him. . . .
>
> (Captain W. H. Smyth, *The Life of Captain Beaver.*)

Besides these disadvantages, Table Bay had a very bad holding ground, so that ships were liable to drive on shore in any westerly gale. So little security was there for half the year that vessels at anchor kept themselves in constant readiness to sail at a moment's notice in case of bad weather. Simon's Bay seems to have been a little safer in that respect. On the other hand, its vast extent was littered with dangers, most of them being invisible. Bellows Rock, Anvil Rock, the Noah's Ark, the Roman Rock, Seal Island, the Francis and Whittle Rocks—the navigator had to take all these submerged perils into account. Nor was the entering of either harbour much simplified by the westerly current which sweeps round the Cape throughout the year. It was sometimes proposed that Saldanha Bay should supersede the two existing anchorages, but nothing came of it, partly through the lack there of a sufficient fresh water supply.

To set against the objections frequently made to Table Bay and False Bay, the fact remained that there was no alternative. On the voyage from Europe to the East, especially, there was no other port of call between Madeira or Rio de Janeiro and the Indies themselves.

> . . . No ships, but those of England, can attempt a voyage to the East Indies, on account of its length, without some such convenient place as the Cape of Good Hope to stop at for refreshment. To English sailors, from their habitual hardiness, and from the peculiar advantages which they enjoy respecting the plentifulness and superior quality of their provisions, such a half-way port might not perhaps be of much consequence; but as our ships have frequently a number of Lascars, or unseasoned troops on board, it becomes highly necessary for their relief . . . the mildness of the climate renders the Cape a wholesome and commodious station, for forces that may be destined for the East or West Indies. . . . In a commercial point of view, this settlement is of less consequence, though capable of much improvement. . . .
>
> (*Naval Chronicle*, Vol. 28.)

The only places of importance at the Cape were the two towns corresponding to the two bays, Capetown and Simon's Town.

> Cape Town, the capital, is pleasantly situated at the head of Table Bay. . . . the town, consisting of about eleven hundred houses, built with regularity, and kept in neat order, is disposed into straight and parallel streets, intersecting each other at right angles. Many of the streets are open and airy, with canals of water running through them, walled in, and planted on each side with oaks; others are narrow and ill-paved. . . .
>
> (Tuckey, *Voyage to New South Wales*.)

At Capetown, as at Batavia, the Dutch had been at pains to reproduce the architecture of Holland; the result being one of the handsomest colonial towns in the world, built of brick and kept very clean. The defences of the place consisted of a strong citadel and three forts, made so as to bring their cannon to bear upon the roadstead. Of the public buildings the chief was the palace of the Prince of Orange, the official residence of the Governor, which was surrounded by gardens and approached by fine avenues of trees. This palace was on the landward side of the town and consequently on the lower slopes of Table Mountain. The gardens, which were public, included a menagerie, of which the Dutch were very proud, having stocked it with lions, zebras and many rare beasts and birds. A second spectacle, to which all visitors went, was the famous vineyard called Constantia. Situated between Capetown and False Bay, the Groot Constantia was an object of pilgrimage, partly for its beauty and partly as the only patch of earth at the Cape which would produce a really good wine. The colony as a whole could produce about seven hundred pipes or leaguers of wine (each pipe consisting of 154 gallons) each year. Of this by far the most valuable portion came from the one vineyard of some six acres in extent. The French used to call this wine 'Le vin des têtes couronnés,' the wine of kings. In England it was known simply as constantia.

Simon's Town lay at the foot of the mountains surrounding False Bay. The settlement consisted of about a hundred houses, a barracks and hospital. It had an excellent water supply, of which ships could make use, but offered little otherwise to the voyager. It came to be used, to a certain extent, as a naval base, despite the poor facilities there for refitting and repair.

The last Dutch possession to demand attention is Ceylon. Unlike the Dutch East Indies, unlike the Cape, Ceylon was and had long been coveted by the English. Consequently when it fell into their hands, very early in the war, it was never restored. For nearly the whole of the period we are dealing with, Ceylon is to be considered as an English possession. It need not, therefore, have any very full description here, its importance being apparent from the narrative. Suffice it now to say that Ceylon had never been thoroughly conquered and that successive European forces had succeeded only in occupying a narrow strip of coastline joining the capital, Colombo, with the harbour on the other side of the island, Trincomalee. The interior was still an impenetrable and unhealthy jungle with a native king of Kandy ruling somewhere in the middle of it. The coastal strip and the two strongholds had been held at first by the Portuguese, then by the Dutch. Sir Edward Hughes had taken it in 1782, almost instantly losing it again to the French under Suffren. Restored to the Dutch at the end of the war, it was still a Dutch possession in 1793. From this rather chequered history alone it would be possible to guess at the importance attached to the island. And a study of the map is enough to show where its importance lay. Trincomalee was the only real harbour on the west side of the Bay of Bengal.

The two bays at Trincomalee provided shelter throughout the year. Fort Ostenburg and the adjacent batteries could protect the anchorage, so that, given an adequate garrison, Trincomalee was, in many respects, a perfect naval base. Its defect lay in the barren hinterland of eastern Ceylon. There was an ample supply of water and fuel but a great deficiency of food. This detracted from the value of the place in two ways. In the first place, a squadron could not completely refit there. In the second place, the garrison was always too small, and necessarily so unless regularly supplied from the mainland or elsewhere. As had often been the case in the past, the Dutch garrison in 1793 was wholly unequal to holding what should have been an almost impregnable stronghold. It may be added that the revenue of Ceylon, where there was little trade, could not support any great number of troops; and that, even when inadequately garrisoned, the Dutch settlements in the island failed to pay their way.

Among the European powers in the East, the next in importance to the Dutch were the Portuguese. Although these had been of consequence in the Eastern Seas for a longer period than their rivals, they were no longer taken very seriously in a military or naval sense. The Portuguese capital was at Goa, the settlements subordinate to that Government being as far apart as Macao and Natal. Goa was remarkable in being what might be called a medieval European city.

> The city of Goa, is of all those either on the coast of Malabar or Coro-
> mandel, the most handsome and well built, and approaches most nearly
> to the model and beauty of the city of Venice, than any city in India. On
> the S.W. side of the harbour, stands a stately and conspicuous monastery,

and on the N.W. side, a very large and formidable fort.—It has upwards
of 80 spired churches, many whereof belong to the Protestants. . . .

(Silas James, *Narrative of a Voyage*.)

Silas James visited Goa somewhere about the year 1782 and noticed,
apparently, no particular signs of decay. It is clear, nevertheless, that the
settlement was then declining and was, in the next twenty years, to decline
still more. Later visitors gained from it the impression of a faded gentility,
even going so far as to describe the city as 'almost in ruins.' There was a
trade between Goa and Surat and a certain amount of trade with Macao,
East Africa and Bengal. Some two ships came out from Portugal, it was
said, each year, laden with iron and other civilized necessities, together
with a quantity of specie. Like so many other settlements, Goa was a
losing concern, supported by this annual subsidy. The local produce was
pepper, sandalwood and raw cotton, much of which went to China in
exchange for Chinese goods, and the remainder to Europe. With what
revenue could be derived from this not very enterprising trade, together
with help from Portugal, a garrison was maintained of about two thousand
ill-paid and ill-disciplined Europeans. An anonymous English writer of the
period expressed some wonder that Portugal should take the trouble to
maintain Goa at all: '. . . unless it is as a banishment for criminals,' he wrote,
'of which the Garrison of Goa is mostly composed, it is difficult to account
why the Ministry at Lisbon maintain their Settlements in India.' The plural
is used here because there were two other towns, Diu and Demaun,
subordinate to Goa and in no better state, whether as regards trade or
defence.

In itself a place of no very great importance, Goa was sometimes a
source of anxiety to others. British India relied for its safety on the total
exclusion of foreign European troops. Experience in the past had shown
that the merest handful of French officers, with a battalion or two of
white troops, could stiffen a native army so as to make it as formidable
as the native armies similarly organized by the English. It was therefore
a principle of British policy to hold the greater part of the coastline of
India, with a view to preventing the foreigner landing. Every seaport on
either coast which was not actually in English hands was a potential leakage,
however neutral its Government. Goa was a particularly dangerous gap in
the British harness because it lay perilously close to the Mahratta country,
the last centre of native resistance to British rule. Peace had, it is true,
been made with the Mahrattas just before war broke out in Europe between
France and England; but there was no knowing what the native powers
might do if promised French assistance. And such assistance, if it came,

might easily take the form of a landing at Goa, Diu or Demaun; not with Portuguese connivance but in the absence of effective means of defence. For this reason, the English regarded the Portuguese towns with some suspicion.

Macao was the Portuguese settlement in China, the only European settlement the Chinese would tolerate and a Christian town since 1586. Like Goa, Macao smelt of the Middle Ages. The total population numbered about four thousand white inhabitants, with seven thousand Chinese and a garrison composed of half-breeds and negroes. This slender community contrived to support a bishop, thirteen churches, three monasteries and a convent. To have a settlement in China was a peculiar privilege, but the Portuguese derived no great profit thereby. Two ships arrived each year from Portugal, perhaps calling at Goa or Calcutta in the course of their voyage; that was almost the whole of their China trade. Macao, like Goa, was the object of English fears. In the hands of the French it might have been used to intercept the English trade with Canton. It was looked upon, therefore, with covetous eyes.

In East Africa the Portuguese maintained a number of settlements, and claimed generally to rule the coast from Delagoa Bay up to somewhere in the region of Cape Delgado. In actual practice, they held several isolated points, north and south of their capital at Mozambique, and made no attempt to extend their territory inland. The governor of Mozambique was supreme over these trifling coastal possessions, and also over a subordinate Government at Senna, up the Zambezi. His authority extended no farther, and the interior, like most of the Natal coast, was as unexplored as in the days of Vasco da Gama. Indeed, the country did not invite exploration. Prior, who was there in 1812, described it as being 'low, destitute of vegetation, and faced with sand-hills, having higher land behind. Few places are more repulsive. . . . There are no harbours in the colonial territory, but three roadsteads or bays—Mossel, Plettenberg, and Algoa. . . . They are all insecure for shipping.' Of the Portuguese settlements Prior wrote as follows:

> One or two small settlements on the coast have residents, supported by soldiers, appointed by the Governor of Mosambique. . . . The Portuguese dare not venture far from their own immediate territory, the real traders in the inland parts being people of colour, born in the vicinity of the white settlements, or natives whose nation and language are, perhaps, but little known, who come from a great distance . . . [from Sofala] Slaves, ivory, gold-dust, and rice are annually exported to Mosambique. The port is difficult of access to vessels of burden, on account of sand-banks; the trade,

37

therefore, is confined to small vessels. Refreshments are also difficult to procure, and from these reasons, ships passing through the channel, bound to India, never approach this shore, so that several of the small ports on the coast are less known than might be expected. . . .

(Prior, *Voyage Along the Eastern Coast of Africa.*)

The East African Portuguese were jealous of foreigners to an extraordinary degree. In 1812, the only Englishmen who had ever been up the Zambezi as far as Senna were two officers who had been wrecked in the H.C.S. *Winterton* in 1792. But for this, the English might not have known of that town's existence. As it was, they scarcely knew its exact position. Prior, however, learnt the following facts about the place,

It is said to be a considerable town, well inhabited, protected by some works and native soldiers, and having a governor, second only to that of Mosambique. . . . To this mart the native traders, from the interior, repair in July, August, and September, with slaves, ivory, gold-dust, and medicinal herbs, gums, and roots, taking back in return woollen and cotton cloths, rude trinkets of various species, hard-ware, fire-arms, powder and shot. . . .

(Prior.)

Concerning Mozambique, which he visited in person, Prior is more exact and less dependent on hearsay.

The population of Mosambique, that is, Europeans and their descendants, may be about six hundred; free people of colour nearly as many; slaves, between four and five thousand, besides those kept for sale. . . .

The value of gold-dust annually exported, may amount to about £16,000. . . . But the most valuable branch of trade has been in slaves. Formerly, Mosambique exported about ten thousand annually supplying several parts of South America, and almost all the islands in the Indian Ocean; indeed throughout the East, the common term for an African is Mozambiquer. . . .

(Prior.)

Unlike the minor settlements on the coast, which were sometimes raided by pirates from Madagascar, Mozambique was fortified.

The defence is a square fort, with bastions and outworks on projections of the rock, and, at the time of its construction, must have been formidable; but it is now dilapidated, and has neither bombproofs nor casemates. There were about fifty-seven brass guns mounted, and twenty unanimated embrazures; the ordnance was old, and of all sizes, from a forty-two to a four-pounder, with most of their carriages decayed; nor have they any iron shot for those above nine-pounders, several stone balls being placed near each gun in lieu. The fort is large and roomy, and has good quarters for its garrison; this at present may consist of about five hundred men, of all colours except white; in short the *Nisus* would make nothing of it. But notwithstanding its fallen condition, it retains an air of magnificence, and is a proof that the Portuguese were once a great and enterprising people.

(Smyth, *Life of Captain Beaver.*)

Of the Portuguese in general it may be said that they were, on the whole, friendly with England. In their sympathies, however, there was to be observed a certain divergence; for the Portuguese of East Africa were closely connected by trade with the Isle of France; while those elsewhere were too much in the power of the English to be other than friendly. The Portuguese of Macao, moreover, had trade relations with Bengal, often enjoying English protection—partly, perhaps, because the Calcutta merchants had taken shares in their ventures. In general, the Portuguese of India and China could not afford to quarrel with England; and when they did so it was not through any French sympathies. Indeed, at Macao, the French (not being tea drinkers) were seldom seen in peace time, and never while at war with the English. A French agent, it is true, once sent Napoleon a parcel of tea, but he had to send it in an English Indiaman.

Apart from their own colonies, the Portuguese were to be found all over the East, distinguishable from the natives more by their religion than by their colour. They had permeated the trading classes in a dozen unlikely places, in a way no other European nation had done. They were to be found at Calcutta, Rangoon, Colombo and Muscat. Bombay, in our period, was still a Portuguese town in appearance, owned by Parsees and only incidentally governed by the English. In Ceylon, too, the Portuguese had left their mark. The citadel at Trincomalee belied its Dutch name by enclosing a church, which the English were afterwards to use, characteristically, as a tennis court. Portuguese, again, was the language in which the Dutch of Ceylon addressed their servants. So widely, indeed, was it spoken in India and elsewhere that English chaplains learnt it on their outward voyage to India in preference to any native tongue.

Less extensive than the Portuguese possessions, but as important in their way, were the Spanish colonies; that is to say, the Philippines. Manila, in the island of Luconia, was the capital of the Spanish Indies. The only other town of importance was Cavite, the naval port and arsenal. As for the interior of the island of Luconia, it had never been completely conquered.

The town of Manilla, from its peninsular situation, having on one side the sea and on the other a deep and rapid river, with strongly-fortified ditches across the isthmus, ought to be, with a proper garrison, very defensible, for there are no commanding heights in its immediate vicinity; but their soldiers consist almost entirely of mulattoes and blacks, and seem to be in a very lethargic state of discipline. . . . The Spaniards appear not to be fully in possession of Luconia at the present day. They may be said, indeed, only to be masters of the ground they occupy, in a military point of view; for, by their own accounts, it is not only dangerous to travel without an escort in the country, but it is not safe for a Spaniard to walk out singly after dark about the suburbs of Manilla. . . .

(J. M'Leod, Voyage of the Alceste.)

In Manila itself there was, in 1800, a population, it was said, of five thousand, with another twenty-four thousand in the suburbs; mostly consisting of Indians, Chinese and half-castes. The Spaniards were nearly all creoles; they had been born, that is to say, in the East, though often of white parentage on both sides. They were therefore acclimatized and unlikely to perish from disease. Manila had the reputation of a healthy town, partly for this reason—a reputation none too common among the European settlements in the East.

Compared with Manila, Cavite was of small importance. It had formerly been a place of some size, but an earthquake had destroyed the greater part of it, including the fortifications. As rebuilt, it was an ill-planned town of some three thousand inhabitants, a third of them being Chinese, and another five thousand, mostly Indians, in the suburbs. It was a wooden-built collection of houses, with but small means of defence and a Mexican regiment and some native troops as the sole garrison. Occasionally during the war the Spaniards had at Cavite a strong squadron; at one time as many as four 74-gun ships and five frigates, or so the French asserted. At Manila, for defensive purposes, there was a fleet of thirty gun-boats, flat-bottomed so as to operate near the shore, and each armed with a single 24-pounder in the bows. This flotilla belonged, of course, to the colony, whereas any men-of-war at Cavite would belong to the Spanish Navy. The regular troops at Manila and Cavite amounted only to a few hundred. Thanks, however, to a reorganization carried out by Raphael d'Aguilar, the governor, in 1790, there was a militia of three thousand, capable of expansion to twenty thousand in an emergency. The Indians were said to make very good soldiers, better than Sepoys and without the vices of the Malays. The Europeans in this army numbered rather less than three hundred, presumably all officers.

The Philippines seem to have had comparatively little trade. Chinese junks came there with goods from China, and a Spanish ship was sent each year to Amoy to fetch silks and other goods destined for Spanish America, together with China grass cloth for the use of the Indians. There

40

was in this no very high degree of mercantile enterprise; and, since the Philippines themselves were not remarkably productive of wealth—their cordage manufacturers being still mainly a thing of the future—it is not surprising to learn that the Spanish settlements incurred a heavy annual loss.

The deficit in the revenues of Manila was made up by an annual subsidy from Mexico of at least 1,000,000 dollars. One or two vessels known as 'register ships' or 'galleons' went each year to Acapulco, laden with

piece-goods, chinaware, silk and spices, returning with a mixed cargo of which the most valuable part consisted of silver. The specie—for the silver came in the form of Spanish dollars—was worth far more than the goods exported from Manila; and it was by this influx of dollars that the colony was kept alive. The ships measured from 1,200 to 1,500 tons and were built at Cavite. They generally sailed about the middle of July and reached Acapulco in January, sailing again for Manila three months later. On her return voyage, carrying perhaps a million and a half in Spanish dollars, a register ship was a prize for eighteenth-century seamen to dream of. The ordinary educated man of the present day, seeing the words 'Spanish Galleon,' as for example on a public-house sign, thinks at once of the Armada. But the galleon of English legend does not date from the sixteenth century. The galleon of Elizabethan times was, on the whole, more likely to be English than Spanish. It was not, by any means, a type of ship peculiar to Spain. No, the galleon of ballads and legend, the galleon of the inn-sign and of romance, dates from the eighteenth century. It was not associated in men's minds with hard fighting in the Channel but with easily appropriated booty in the Pacific. Why it should have become the custom in Europe to describe the register ships as 'galleons' is not very clear; but it is manifest, at any rate, that the word and all it connoted had a great appeal to the imagination. Among those to whom the word appealed was the Abbé Raynal, who was at pains to write an account of the galleon and its habits.

The departure of it is fixed for the month of July. After having cleared a multitude of islands and rocks, which are always troublesome, and sometimes dangerous, the galleon steers northward as far as the 30th degree of latitude. There the trade-winds begin to blow, which convey it to the place of its destination. It is generally thought, that if it proceeded further, it would meet with stronger and more regular winds, which would hasten its course; but the Commanders are forbidden, under the heaviest penalties, to go out of the track that hath been marked out to them.

This is undoubtedly the reason that hath prevented the Spaniards, during the course of two centuries, from making the least discovery upon an Ocean, which would have offered so many objects of instruction and advantage to more enlightened and less circumspect nations. The voyage lasts six months, because the vessel is overstocked with men and merchandize, and that all those that are on board are a set of timid navigators, who never make but little way during the night-time, and often, though without necessity, make none at all.

The register ships were not very heavily armed, although commissioned·

as men-of-war; but, in time of war, they normally had naval escort. Considering, however, the enormous value of these vessels, and the fact that their route was perfectly well known, at least in outline, it is surprising how seldom they were successfully intercepted. The English seem to have taken only five in the course of two hundred and fifty years. Cavendish captured one in 1587, Rogers in 1709, Anson in 1743, Parker in 1762 and Rainier in 1807. This comparative immunity of the register ships was due perhaps, partly, to navigational difficulties in the Philippines, partly to the distance of both Manila and Acapulco from any hostile naval base.

One result of the dependence of the Philippines on a yearly subsidy from Mexico was that it rendered the settlements all but immune from foreign conquest. Regarded from a strategic point of view, Manila was a potential menace to the English trade with China. A hostile squadron based on Cavite might, at least temporarily, have put an end to the China trade; and this possibility was present in the minds of English strategists. Their fear was that the Spanish would allow the French to make use of Cavite as a naval base. On strategic grounds alone there was therefore a strong case for conquering the Philippines. What made statesmen hesitate was the thought of the annual deficit incurred by the colony. This was, in fact, Manila's chief defence. A settlement run at such an appalling loss was tolerably safe from annexation. No other country could be eager to take over such an enormous liability. The English, indeed, under Admiral Cornish and Colonel Draper, took Manila in 1762; but they almost instantly regretted it. In Spanish hands, Manila supplied the whole East with its currency—the English settlements included. Following the conquest, this source of specie suddenly dried up. No longer able to depend on Manila for their silver, the governor and Council of Madras found, to their horror, that they were actually expected to furnish that colony with the very article they were themselves beginning to lack. With a fine gesture, not perceptibly spoilt by any unseemly haste, Manila was handed back to Spain. Oddly enough, there was, as we shall see, a scheme to capture the Philippines again in 1797. It was wisely abandoned and, better counsels prevailing, it was never revived.

A peculiarity of the Philippines was that, having been settled originally by an expedition which had crossed the Pacific, the local calendar differed from that of the other European possessions in the East. The fact was significant, for the colony had, in many respects, what might be called a west-about outlook. It had little direct connection with Spain. To the Spaniards the Philippines lay rather beyond the isthmus of Panama than beyond the Cape of Good Hope.

The last European possessions in the East to be considered are those of Denmark. These were very trifling in extent, comprising little more than the town of Tranquebar, south of Pondicherry on the Coromandel Coast, and the factory at Serampore on the Hooghli. Tranquebar had a population of about 100 Europeans and 8,000 natives, with a small garrison of 100 Europeans and 800 sepoys. This town tamely surrendered to the English whenever Denmark found itself involved in the European conflict, being afterwards as regularly restored. The importance of Denmark in the East was not very well represented by the small extent of the Danish possessions, for there was, at various times, a considerable amount of trade under the Danish colours. During the period 1770–84 numbers of Danish vessels traded with China, their return cargoes consisting mostly of tea. The tea was sold to smugglers who found means of conveying it to England without paying the heavy customs duties which the English East India Company had to pay. The demand for tea in England was three times as great as in the rest of Europe put together. This smuggling trade largely died out when the duties on tea were repealed in 1784; and its disappearance was a severe loss both to Denmark and Sweden. Their trade, however, continued both with India and China. The Danish trade with India, moreover, was on the increase because English Civil Servants in India often preferred to transmit their fortunes to England in the form of goods conveyed in foreign vessels. They thus evaded the East India Company's monopoly, while hiding from their employers the full extent of their gains. Danish ships were among those engaged in this business. The trade of the Danes with China fluctuated considerably on the other hand. Until 1784 there had been three or four Danish ships at Canton each year, loading with anything up to 5,500,000 pounds of tea. After the lowering of the duties a single ship was very often the extent of their enterprise. Trade revived for them in 1796, and there were five ships loading with nearly 3,000,000 pounds of tea in the season 1798–99. Then the trade dwindled again in 1800 and was just beginning to recover when war with England put an end to it in 1807. In their better years, as in 1797, the Danish East India Company paid a dividend of as much as 12 per cent. Until 1804–5 the Danish trade was often exceeded by that of Sweden, while there was not wanting a certain amount of competition from Prussians, Hamburgers and Americans. In 1808, however, there were none but English and American ships at Canton, and it does not appear that the Scandinavians recovered their trade until the end of the wars.

In a political sense, Tranquebar had a certain importance during the years when England and France were at war and when Denmark was neutral. At such times the Danes were apt to act as go-betweens. It was from Tranquebar that the French heard the news of India, and it was through that settlement that the French agents communicated with such native princes as they thought to bribe. The proximity of Pondicherry and Tranquebar was of great use to the French, for the former town had French inhabitants even when actually occupied by English troops. In much the same way the English had their news of the Isle of France from the Danish merchantmen returning from thence.

On the whole, the Danes profited by the war until the time came when they were involved in it. Their trade with the French islands was a sort of monopoly, shared only with the Americans and other neutrals. Their trade with Bengal must have been very profitable, judging from the amount of goods they exported from there; although it must be remembered that Anglo-Indian capital was behind most of their undertakings.

The United States had, at this time, no territory in the East. American merchantmen, however, were numerous and ubiquitous and impossible to ignore. It was in 1784 that the first American ship reached Canton, bearing the United States consul. The next year found this number increased to five, laden on their homeward passage with 880,100 pounds of tea. Thenceforward, until 1793, the Americans imported annually about 1,500,000 pounds, this quantity being greatly exceeded as soon as the war began. In 1804 there were thirty-six American ships at Canton, the largest of 600 tons, but the majority of from 200 to 400 tons. Of these, nine had sailed from Boston, seven from New York, and the others from Providence, Nantucket, Salem and Philadelphia. This trade reached its peak in 1806, when the United States' importation of tea amounted to 9,644,667 pounds. As a principal article of export to China, the Americans frequently loaded their vessels with 'ginseng.' This was a root growing wild in American forests and greatly prized by the Chinese for its imaginary medicinal qualities. A trade based on the exchange of worthless rubbish for tea could hardly fail to be profitable.

With India, the American trade began at the same time as the traffic just described with China, in 1784. By the orders of Lord Cornwallis's Government, issued in 1788, ships from the United States were given 'most favoured nation' privileges, and these were confirmed and enlarged by treaty in 1794. The American trade with Calcutta accordingly tripled in extent between 1795 and 1800. The American exports consisted of dollars, with a few coarse goods, wines and spirits, and were so trifling in value that there was an average yearly balance of trade in favour of Bengal of over half a million sterling. This state of affairs was possible because the

Americans were in reality employed to convey private Anglo-Indian fortunes to Europe. For this purpose their ships were well suited, enjoying as they did a neutral status with consequently lower rates of insurance; a status which at the same time gave them access to ports from which the English were excluded. 'These advantages,' Milburn wrote, 'with that of their speaking the same language, and their social intercourse in the British settlements, render them the most formidable rivals of the English in the trade with the East Indies.'

American merchantmen in the East did not trade exclusively with China and India. The encouragement they met with at the hands of the English did not prevent their receiving equal encouragement from the French and the Dutch. Indeed, most of their voyages were triangular and involved dealings with more countries than one. Of the American ships at Canton in 1804, five had called at the Isle of France, three at Batavia, one at Manila, five in the South Seas and two at Port Jackson in Australia. From 1795 onwards a number of United States vessels began to trade in pepper with Sumatra, lading on their outward voyage with brandy, gin, tobacco, iron and dried fish. Others, ostensibly engaged in whaling, smuggled largely among the Spice Islands. The Dutch were always justly suspicious of people found looking for whales off Timor or Ceram. This did not, however, prevent the Americans from trading directly with Batavia. In exchange for the spices, sugar, coffee, rice and China goods they wanted, they would bring cloth, hats, stationery, wine, beer, Seltzer-water and specie. After the wars it was the American trade which largely restored the prosperity of Batavia.

The increase in American trade during the wars was partly due to the safety derived from neutrality. Of that there can be no doubt. But it was also partly due to the function the Americans assumed as receivers of stolen goods. Such piracy as they engaged in was on a small scale, carried on in the Pacific under British colours. Privateering, again, was only possible after 1812. But from the privateering of the French they were able to profit far more than did the privateers themselves. Their route to China or India lay nearly always round the Cape of Good Hope—it was mostly their fur-traders who crossed the Pacific—and it usually led them near the Isle of France. In time of war many of them began to find it more profitable to stop and do their trading there. The privateers were always overstocking the market at Port Louis with their plunder, so that goods there were often cheaper than at Canton or Calcutta. This was of necessity the case in that the cargoes of English prizes were often quite useless to the colonists, who had, moreover, no means of sending them to Europe. This was where the American captain could drive his bargain.

He could buy up the plunder at anything from a third to two-thirds of its cost price, and at the same time save himself the trouble of going farther afield. The goods would sell in America or at Hamburg or Dunkirk, and then would often end up at their original destination—London. The Americans, it will be seen, played an essential part in the French privateering activities. Without their coming to purchase the booty, privateering would scarcely have paid.

In concluding this brief survey of the rivalry encountered by the English in the East, it may be as well to emphasize the factors which underlay the ultimate English success. When comparing the English possessions in the East with those of the other territory-owning powers, it is impossible not to observe two vital differences—differences which were the root and cause of military success or failure. The first point of difference was that England had what no other nation had—a profit-yielding territory. The French Islands barely paid their own expenses. The Dutch profited, when they profited at all, by commerce so that their government and military strength was an overhead charge on the spice trade. When a zealous Governor tried to put Java in a proper state of defence, he plunged the colony into financial ruin, from which nothing but an English occupation could extricate it. The Philippines, as we have seen, were a mere drain on the resources of Spanish America. Even the Government at Goa was unable to pay its way without a subsidy from Portugal. But the English had, in Bengal, a tract of territory which yielded a revenue. This revenue was large enough to support what must have been one of the largest standing armies in the world, and still leave a surplus of tribute. To maintain this army was to be the strongest power in the East. Wherever the French might have established themselves, they could never have afforded to keep a force of that size. It would never have been worth their while to do so, and the same would be true of the Dutch, Spanish and Portuguese. European Governments were not in a position to pay subsidies on that scale. Indeed, no English Government showed very much inclination to spend large sums on the defence of India. Had India been expensive to govern or garrison, the East India Company would have abandoned its territory and confined itself to the China trade. It could at that time expect little help from England, where imperialism had scarcely begun to bud. India, however, was not costly to defend. It paid for its own defence on a scale which dwarfed that of every other European power in the East. During the period with which we are concerned the burden of armament had, it is true, more than swallowed up all surplus revenue. This was a circumstance known only in times of war, however, and the loss in financial stability represented

47

an immediate gain in military strength and an eventual gain in territory. When to this augmented military strength was added an overwhelming superiority at sea, the other European powers could not but feel their comparative impotence.

The second point of difference is less easily explained and less obviously vital; and yet it is, properly considered, as significant as the first. One might put it briefly thus: whereas the French and the Dutch, the Spanish and Portuguese all formed colonies, the English only built forts. It has been said that the English make good colonists. This may be true, but much of the English power in the East plainly depended on their being very bad colonists indeed—or, rather, on their not being colonists at all. It was the deliberate policy of the East India Company to prevent colonization in any shape or form. In Ceylon, indeed, a crown colony, this rule was eventually relaxed. Elsewhere, however, under the Company's rule, and especially in India itself, all colonization, all European landownership, was forbidden by law.

The chief outcome of this policy was that the Englishman in India remained, as he still remains, an exile. He might die in India, and in fact he usually did, but he never settled there. He had always before him the prospect of returning to England. This difference between the English and their rivals is most clearly illustrated by their styles of architecture. To take the Dutch first, it would be true to say that Batavia was a Dutch town, or as near to being one as its situation allowed. It was intersected with canals, planted with rows of trees, and adorned by a Protestant church with a dome. The houses were all gabled seventeenth-century buildings with heavy carved staircases, as if transported bodily from Holland. It was an astonishingly beautiful place. Capetown was built in the same fashion, though not so finely. Goa, again, was a Portuguese town, famous for its cathedral and churches; while Macao, with its own bishop, was as typical on a smaller scale. Manila, with its monasteries and noblemen, was an obvious offshoot of Spain, though all its inhabitants had been born there in Luconia. Port Louis, even, in the Isle of France, is a French town to this day. In all these places the settlers had done their utmost to reproduce the homes they had left, and to which they would never return. They had tried to create their own atmosphere. Paradoxically enough, however, so permanent a settlement is bound to produce a local attachment, and from that there springs a colonial spirit or sentiment fundamentally hostile to any other allegiance. The forces which have tended to reproduce the mother country are the very forces which subsequently tend to sever all connection with her.

In contrast to such cities as Goa and Batavia, the English strongholds had very little resemblance to anything in Europe. Least of all were they reminiscent of anything in England. 'Fort William,' 'Fort St. George,' 'Fort Marlborough'—the names alone are suggestive of anything rather than an English town. In designing these places with their bastions and counterscarps, as in building their houses with verandahs and porticoes, the English provided in some sort for their safety and convenience; but they never tried to convince themselves that the result looked even remotely like England. They were less homesick than other people, simply because they all intended to go home.

This peculiarity of the English possessions in the East may appear trivial. Architecture, however, is seldom without significance. This perpetually alien character of the English, well preserved by the individual's impermanence of tenure, was the secret of their ascendancy. By refusing to settle, the English remained European and therefore formidable. It was what the Portuguese had failed to do, and what the Dutch were failing to do. With the Portuguese before them as a warning, the English were firmly resolved not to make the same mistake. In no circumstances would they marry native women. Half-breeds might come into existence, but that did not matter so long as the half-breed was classed as a native. In thus refusing, in any sense, to make India their home, the English were able to confine themselves almost entirely to the two trades they knew—that of the seaman and that of the soldier.

The decadence produced among white men by a permanent settlement in the East was the constant theme of English travellers and moralists. In this they were not only indulging a national failing; they were also uneasily trying to guard themselves and their countrymen against a similar downfall. The temptation was always present and seldom resisted with entire success. One candid observer wrote, of Bombay, that 'There is languor and lethargy . . . here to which I never elsewhere saw any approach. . . .' Even the English succumbed to a certain extent, it is clear, but never in such a degree as to become altogether unwarlike. With an average service abroad of about ten years, there was always a large proportion of newcomers among them. It is impossible not to distrust the horrified comments made by English visitors to the foreign settlements; and yet a certain contrast there must have been. Captain Beaver, for example, who visited Mozambique in 1812, was assured that the Portuguese governor, Don Antonio Manoel de Mello Castro e Mendoca, had never stirred out of his house during three years of office. Of the same port Beaver wrote that the slave trade was the sole activity. 'Villainous traffic! Every thing else is neglected: all is ruin, and dirt, and devilment. . . .' He also repeated a saying of 'Bombay Jack'—an envoy sent to the Cape by the King of the Comoro Islands: 'Portugee hab too much black wife: he no work, no fight, no do nothing.' Of the Englishman in the East it might at any time have been said that he would not work, but he never at this period reached a state in which he would not fight. The indignation aroused in Captain Beaver by the Portuguese of Mozambique was felt in various degrees by English visitors to other foreign settlements. According to Maria Graham, the officers returning from the capture of the Isle of France said that the inhabitants were 'profligate and immoral beyond even the vulgar notions of French licentiousness.' By other accounts, the Dutch in Java were idle and gluttonous, the Spaniards of Manila superstitious and inert.

There may, admittedly, have been a great deal of prejudice and mere misunderstanding in the English attitude towards their rivals in the East. But what is certain is that, decadent or not, the foreign settlements had all developed a colonial spirit which greatly lessened their effectiveness in war. The Portuguese governor mentioned above astonished Captain Beaver by omitting to ask for news of Portugal: 'one would have supposed that he had forgotten there was a portion of the globe called Europe; or that he was totally indifferent whether the country of his birth yet retained its independence, or was devastated by a relentless enemy.' The Dutch at the Cape, less distant from that portion of the globe called Europe, had so far lost interest in Holland that many of them welcomed the English conquest as likely to improve trade. Such an attitude made the conquest far easier. Similarly, during the early years of the French Revolution, the inhabitants of the Isle of France made it clear that they would sever all connection with France rather than emancipate their slaves. In the time of Decaen, indeed, the settlers so objected to taxation that a considerable party among them wished to surrender the island to the English. Napoleon's victories were too distant and legendary to make much impression on the islanders, who never, in consequence, acquired much enthusiasm for the Empire. It was for this reason that Decaen never counted on the assistance of the local militia; and events proved him right, for the English troops, when they landed, met with no resistance except from the few regular units. The Spanish at Manila showed, on the whole, as little devotion to Spain as the French at Port Louis showed to France. One who visited that town in 1816 remarked that the colony would be an easy conquest for another power, but that 'the Court of Spain, at present, seems to have most to fear from those sentiments of independence which have extended from Buenos Ayres to Manila. . . .' Whether afflicted with decadence, with feelings of profound indifference towards Europe, or with sentiments of independence, all the foreign colonies were but in doubtful alliance with their mother countries. They none of them desired an active share in the war.

A second generation of colonists rarely shows much interest in Europe. This was the weakness of the foreign settlements in the East, and it was a weakness which the English in India did not share. There was no true second generation of Anglo-Indians. They remained English, or nearly so, through having spent their boyhood in England and through planning to spend their later years there. It was to this national spirit, which colonization would have undermined, as well as to the evidently profitable nature of Indian government, that England owed her ascendancy in the East.

PART ONE

PART ONE

CHAPTER I

Cornwallis Returns to England

THE War in the Eastern Seas began with no dramatic overture, no sudden challenge to the English arms. The faintest of rumours, a whispered possibility, a strong expectation; these were the steps which led at last to some tentative hostilities. Perhaps the story should begin on 31st January, 1790, the date on which the news of the French Revolution came to the Isle of France. There were developments, beginning with the election of a Colonial Assembly and ending, for the time being, with the lynching of the naval commander-in-chief. This officer, the Comte de Macnemara, was an unpopular newcomer, suspected of being both an aristocrat and a traitor and guilty, very likely, of being an Irishman. The governor, a M. Conway, having been superseded on similar grounds, though without having been shown to be a Welshman, it became apparent that the colonists were willing to follow the French example, at least up to a point. There was even, later on, some talk of a guillotine. Where a trace of uneasiness crept into the Assembly's discussions was with reference to the institution of slavery. Agreeing, in the abstract, with revolutionary principles and ready to applaud, in a general way, all sentiments about Liberty and Equality, the slave-owners could not but feel that these admirable notions might perhaps be carried too far. Locally, at least, there were practical considerations affecting the issue; considerations that it would be unwise to overlook. In such doubts as these was the seed of future trouble. For the moment, however, minds were set at rest by the decision of the National Assembly—to which the island had sent deputies—that the emancipation of slaves was to be at the discretion of local authorities. All was therefore comparatively quiet when a French squadron arrived in July 1791. The squadron consisted of four frigates, *La Cybèle*, *L'Atalante*, *La Cléopâtre* and *La Résolue*, the first bearing the flag of the Rear-Admiral, M. de Saint Felix. *La Résolue* went straight on to India, followed in due course by Saint Felix himself. During his absence, in January 1792, an epidemic of smallpox broke out in the Isle of France. The infection came with a cargo of slaves brought from Mozambique, and

55

some four thousand inhabitants died during the next three months. For the time being the colonists had other things to think of besides the possibility of war with England. Nevertheless, that possibility was by no means remote and seemed, at one time, in India, even more imminent than it was. To grasp this, it is necessary to consider certain events in India, going back for the purpose to December 1789. It was in that month that Tippoo Sultan attacked Travancore, the capital of one of the East India Company's native allies. The resulting conflict occupied Anglo-Indian attention almost up to the very eve of the war with France.

Eighteenth-century England was governed less by solemn councils and public offices than by casual conversations in the country houses of the great. It was typical of the friendly arrangements thus reached that the Governor-General of the time should have been able to secure his brother's appointment as the naval commander-in-chief on the station. It was again typical that the arrangement worked very well. Commodore William Cornwallis received his appointment in November 1788 and actually sailed for India in H.M.S. *Crown* (64) on 9th February, 1789. With him went the *Phoenix, Perseverance, Atalanta* and *Ariel*; this squadron being joined later by the *Vestal, Minerva, Leopard* (Captain Blankett) and *Thames* (Captain Troubridge). Cornwallis reached Madras on September 3rd and Calcutta—or rather Diamond Harbour—on the 18th. He thus arrived in Indian waters rather more than three months before the storming of Travancore and so was able to blockade Tippoo's coastline almost as soon as the campaign began.

Commodore Cornwallis, who shortly became Rear-Admiral, was generally thought 'an odd fish.' Although undoubtedly a very able officer, he was an eccentric, a woman-hater (so it was said) and given at times to unreasonable favouritism as well as to unreasonable enmity. He had a nickname, 'Billy Blue,' and was more popular with the seamen than with his officers. For a nephew of the Archbishop of Canterbury, his manners were rather uncouth. Hickey, who met him at Calcutta, seems to have taken instant dislike to him; a dislike which he did not fail to record in his memoirs. He wrote

> Commodore Cornwallis, Commander-in-Chief in the Eastern Seas and brother to the noble Governor-General, though very unlike him both in person and manner, came to visit his lordship. The Commodore was a living Trunnion, but more of a brute than Smollett made his hero. After a sojourn of three weeks in Calcutta, during which he abused or found fault with everybody and everything, he took his departure. . . .'

Making all allowances for Hickey's malicious style, it is evident that Cornwallis was out of place in a drawing-room. He practically said as much in a letter to Nelson, remarking that he took every opportunity for exploring, 'which I prefer to being stuck up in a pompous style' ashore. This is a reference, of course, to the custom which prevailed for the Admiral on the East Indies station to spend most of his time at an official residence provided for him at Madras. Having inherited a secure social position as an 'Honourable,' the Commodore was far more averse to pomp than were many of his brother officers.

It was a fortunate circumstance for the East India Company that Tippoo Sultan should have begun the war when he did. For whereas, in the past, he had received help from the French, it was unlikely that he would obtain any active assistance from them at a time when the French were so engrossed in their own affairs. Lord Cornwallis, however, the Governor-General, provided against the possibility of French help by urging his brother to search any French merchantmen found on the Malabar coast. Should he find any carrying troops, arms or military stores 'under pretence of going to their settlement at Mahé,' he was to make it clear to them that they might proceed to Pondicherry but that they might not land on the west side of India. This advice was dated in February 1790, by which time the Commodore was already on the Malabar coast with a small squadron.

The Governor-General's supposition that the French would not assist Tippoo was justified to this extent, that they did, in fact, advise the Sultan against making war at that time. Once he had committed himself, however, they seem to have sent him such supplies as they could spare. During the year 1790 Commodore Cornwallis was continually at sea on one coast or the other, but without intercepting any military stores destined for Tippoo. Any French frigates which appeared were carefully shadowed as long as they remained on the coast. In August 1791, news having come of an American vessel sailing from Ostend laden with arms, a fresh order was issued to the cruisers to detain any vessel found carrying warlike stores, except Dutch or Portuguese ships actually bound for Cochin or Goa. In the course of this year the squadron was reinforced, so that the Commodore was able to spare four ships to cruise on the Malabar coast; the *Minerva* (38), the *Thames* (32), the *Phoenix* (36) and the *Vestal* (28); to which number he later added the frigate *Perseverance* and the sloop *Atalanta*. The searching of French ships caused a great deal of friction, and in 1792 actually occasioned bloodshed.

It will be remembered that, of the French squadron which came out in 1791, one frigate, *La Résolue* (36), went straight on to India while the remainder put in to the Isle of France. On 18th November, 1792, *La Résolue* was at Mahé on the Malabar coast. Two French merchantmen appeared off that port, whereupon the *Phoenix* and *Perseverance* sailed from Tellicherry to examine them. The French frigate sailed simultaneously, apparently to prevent them being examined. The result was a brisk action between the *Phoenix* and *La Résolue*, which ended in the former losing seven killed and nine wounded and the latter hauling down her colours. As this occurred in time of peace, the captain of the *Phoenix*, Sir Richard Strachan, released the French frigate and refused to accept her surrender. It so happened that Commodore Cornwallis was himself at Tellicherry at this time, with his flag in the *Minerva*, and it was he who carried on the subsequent correspondence with the French captain, who refused to re-hoist his colours, claiming to be a prisoner-of-war.

The situation was awkward, and might even have been made an occasion for war. Writing to the French captain Callamand, Cornwallis urged him not to 'carry on the Farce' of considering his ship a prize. 'Whether you hoist your Colours or no,' he wrote, 'seems to be of little consequence.' He ended by pointing out that 'As this must be settled by higher Powers, it is useless for us to write any more upon the subject.' The discussion was not, however, at an end, for a further incident occurred to embitter it. The French Admiral, Saint Felix, was on his way to India in the wake of the *Résolue*. On 4th January, 1792, off Tellicherry, he fell in with Cornwallis himself in the *Minerva*. As a signal that he wished to speak with the Frenchman, the English Commodore fired a gun, afterwards sending a boat on board him. The officer in charge of the boat brought back a message that if another gun was fired, the French would reply with a broadside. A correspondence ensued from which it appeared that the French Admiral denied Cornwallis's right to search French merchantmen, or at any rate such as were escorted by men-of-war. To act on any such pretended right was a 'violation in plain peace to all the Treaties, to all the Customs, and to all regards due to the Flags of Sovereigns' and tantamount to a declaration of war. To this outburst Cornwallis made no reply, merely issuing orders that French merchantmen were to be searched as before, whether with escort or without. At one point in the discussion, Saint Felix actually gave orders, it was said, for beginning hostilities; orders which his men, children of the Revolution, flatly refused to obey, probably because they felt themselves outnumbered.

Curiously enough, it never became clear whether the French merchantmen *were* carrying supplies to Tippoo, or whether they were merely bound, as Saint Felix alleged, for Mahé. About those particular ships the truth remains obscure to this day. On the other hand, that Tippoo did in fact, at some time, receive help from the French seems highly probable.

And the knowledge of this may well have weakened the position of the French diplomats. At any rate, much to the relief of Sir Richard Strachan, the captain of the *Phoenix*, nothing came of the affair. Probably through being otherwise occupied, the French Government allowed the matter to drop.

While Cornwallis was maintaining his blockade and trying to keep the French from overt interference, the campaign ashore was slowly reaching its climax. Throughout 1791 operations continued and then, in February 1792, little more than a month after the arrival of Saint Felix in Indian waters, Lord Cornwallis defeated Tippoo and soon afterwards stormed Seringapatam. Peace was made on February 23rd and the dispatches announcing it reached London on July 25th. Another event which took place in February 1792, was the promotion of Commodore Cornwallis to Rear-Admiral of the White, leave being given him to return home. Simultaneously, his elder brother was to leave India in triumph, his main task at an end, and it was naturally planned that he should take a passage in the *Minerva*. This plan might even have been carried out in 1792, when the two brothers met at Madras on May 31st, had not the Rear-Admiral betaken himself to the Andamans with the object of investigating the possibilities of the group as a naval base to windward of the Bay of Bengal. He was there or in the Straits of Malacca, inspecting the existing base at Prince of Wales Island, during the latter part of 1792. He returned to Madras in December and there heard the first rumours of impending war in Europe, which he entirely discredited. So confident was he that the rumours were baseless that he sent nearly all of his squadron back to England. Some ships, indeed, had gone the year before, as soon as peace was made with Tippoo. 'As the squadron are likely to go home soon,' he wrote on 20th September, 1792, 'I did not think that it was necessary for them to compleat their complements, and I gave orders . . . accordingly.'[1] The *Phoenix* was leaking badly, the *Dispatch* was in a bad state of repair and the *Minerva* herself nearly sank in being heaved over. The *Phoenix* and others were now dispatched home successively, and he himself, with the *Minerva*, went to Calcutta to fetch the Governor-General, meaning to sail with him for England, leaving the Indian Ocean without any naval protection at all. It was his theory that India was a country for the Navy to avoid as far as possible; and it appears that the Admiralty had accepted his views on this subject. What these views were may be gathered from the following letter, written in 1790:

> . . . The seamen are more subject to the scurvy here than in the West Indies. For myself I like it very well, there is a great variety upon this

[1] Ad. 50/31. It is interesting to see that his squadron included, at one time or another, Elphinstone, Troubridge and Blankett, all of whom will figure later in this book.

station, and if the war with Tippoo had not obliged us to go to the coast of Malabar during the whole of the North East monsoon I should have Liked it much better as it would have given me an opportunity of seeing a great Deal more of it, and I think it may be useful to our young folks in future, but except from necessity, or the purpose of exploring I am against keeping men of War in this country, which in general is distructive to officers, and to the Younger part in particular, where nothing is heard of but *making of money*, and Yet I hope it has been Less practiced of Late Years than formerly, there are nevertheless many able and worthy men who would do credit to any country and situation.

(*The Life and Letters of Admiral Cornwallis*, p. 172.)

Cornwallis, as we have had occasion to notice, was a somewhat eccentric officer; and one of his oddest peculiarities was a strict, an almost fanatical honesty where the public purse was concerned. He seems to have worried about his officers' money-making almost as much as about his seamen's scurvy. He had convinced himself, moreover, from either line of reasoning, that India was no place for the Navy in time of peace. He discarded his forces, therefore, with all the more readiness. Writing to the Admiralty, from Calcutta, on 22nd March, 1793, he reported that the *Perseverance* and *Swan* (Captain Elphinstone) had sailed for England from Bombay in January, and that the *Phoenix* had followed on February 23rd. The *Minerva*, his own ship, would follow suit as soon as the Governor-General was ready to embark.

At the date on which Cornwallis was writing the above dispatch the war with France had already begun—had been raging, indeed, for seven weeks. Some rumours of the probability of war reached India shortly afterwards, causing both brothers to postpone their sailing for England. The Admiral must, by this time, have been distinctly anxious. The situation might at any moment become very serious. The French had at least four frigates in the Indian Seas whereas Cornwallis had no ship but his own. There was talk of an impending attack on Pondicherry, and here was the East Indies Squadron practically non-existent. Definite news of the outbreak of war was long in coming. The Admiral, who had gone to the Dutch port of Trincomalee, received there, on June 19th, his first official notification on the subject. This was a letter from Mr. Baldwin, the Company's agent at Alexandria, sent on to him from Madras. This letter was too explicit to leave any doubt about the matter. As England was now at war with Holland as well as France, Cornwallis hastened to leave Trincomalee, where the Dutch were still unaware of the situation, and proceed off Pondicherry in time to capture a French merchantman bound thither with a cargo of ammunition for the garrison. Being in need of supplies, and wanting to concert measures with the Indian Governments, he went on to Madras. What followed may well be given in his own words:

The *Minerva* therefore being the only Ship belonging to His Majesty in these Seas, and the French having by all accounts, four, if not five frigates and a Corvette at the Islands—the being able to prevent succors from being thrown into Pondicherry appeared to me very doubtful;—I had however immediately a communication with Sir Charles Oakley (the President) upon the subject,—He was willing to put three India ships lately arrived from Europe under my directions for the purpose of blocking up Pondicherry and promised to send them to me, as soon as they were ready, with about fifty Invalids, and discharged soldiers on board each Ship.—I sailed in the *Minerva* the twenty ninth the moment the Provisions and water were received on board—On the third of July I took a small Privateer called the *Concorde*; which had been fitted out from Pondicherry, as she seemed to sail pretty well, and having no veſsel of any kind to send in shore after small veſsels which might attempt to land Supplies, to send for Intelligence, or for any purpose whatever.—I put Mr. Manning, first Lieutenant of the *Minerva* to command Her, and sent him to Madras for men, and to join me immediately.

On the Ninth in the evening, I got off Pondicherry, and saw a Ship and a snow at anchor in the Road. On the Eleventh, Captain Whitby having offered repeatedly to go in with the Boats to cut those veſsels out of the Road, he left the *Minerva* about one o'clock, the ship had unluckily sailed in the early part of the night, but the snow was brought out.

Having picked up the Boats, I stood out to look for my Squadron of India ships, which had been seen that morning from the mast head in the South East Quarter.—On the thirteenth in the evening I got hold of them, and brought them to anchor after dark—The next morning at Break of Day, a ship was seen in the offing; I immediately got under sail and chased —The ship had French Colours and appeared to be a large Frigate, at ten o'clock, finding I did not come up with the Chase, although I had dropped the India Ships, which had followed me contrary to my Intention, and were much scattered, and as I had not been able to give them any direction, and I had reason to believe there might be more of the Enemy's ships at hand, besides that which I chased;—I thought it best to join the India ships, and to direct them to anchor off Pondicherry.—I then stood after the Frigate again, in Hopes that seeing only one ship, they might have more confidence, but could see nothing of her—I have since learnt that it was *La Cybèle*, that she had besides Her Complement, three hundred and fifty men, with Stores, Guns, and Ammunition for Pondicherry. I continued to block up that place until the twenty-third of August when it surrendered to the

Army under the Command of Colonel Brathwaite, having made no resistance after our Batteries were opened.

(Cornwallis to Admiralty, 10th September, 1793. P.R.O. Ad. 1/167.)

The surrender of Pondicherry was, on the whole, a tame affair. The French there were outnumbered and without hope of reinforcement. Had the French Admiral known it, though, the game was in his hands. With his four frigates he might not only have raised the blockade but also have done enormous damage elsewhere. He seems, however, to have been unaware of his opponent's weakness. His ship, *La Cybèle*, came alone on the scene, having sailed without any definite information that the war had begun. Finding what she took to be a formidable squadron off Pondicherry, she fled. As a matter of fact, the landing of troops, ammunition and stores could have delayed the fall of Pondicherry for only a few days or weeks. The fate of that unfortunate town was not, after all, a matter of the first importance. It would have mattered far more if the French squadron, coming on the coast in force, had taken the *Minerva* and bombarded Madras, proceeding afterwards to blockade the Hooghli. That nothing of the sort took place was due less to the efforts of the armed Indiamen than to French ignorance of the situation.

Lord Cornwallis originally intended to direct the siege of Pondicherry in person. Realizing that it would be unsafe to proceed there in a merchant ship, he seized a French vessel, the *Bien Aimé*, which was lying in the river, and equipped her as a man-of-war. She was a Bristol-built ship, mounting eighteen 6-pounders, and had once been in the Navy. Despite unfavourable reports that she was not copper-fastened, the Governor-General equipped her and then lent her to the Navy. He made no use of her himself, in the end, because Pondicherry fell before *Bien Aimé* was ready to take him there. On hearing the news, he concluded that there was nothing further to detain him in India. As his brother, the Admiral, thought it his duty to remain on the station for the present, Lord Cornwallis decided to go home in the *Swallow*, packet, availing himself of the *Minerva's* escort for a part of the way. He duly sailed in September, the *Swallow* being convoyed by the *Minerva* and *Bien Aimé* until October 24th, on which date the Admiral headed for Bombay, calling on the way at Diego Garcia in search of French privateers. Finding nothing there but a small brig, he went on northwards and called at Tellicherry on December 4th, for news.

. . . One of the Company's ships was just arrived from England but I could not learn that any of His Majesty's Ships were going to India. I proceeded immediately on to Bombay, where I arrived the 11th of December

—Accounts overland were received a few days after from England, as far as the end of August, and from other parts of Europe of a much later date, by which it appeared, that there was a probability of the War with France being soon over. I determined to get the *Minerva* docked, and the damaged part of Her Bottom repaired, as soon as possible, in the Mean time I sent the *Bien Aimé* to cruize upon the Coast. I could not learn that there were any Privateers out belonging to the Enemy. The French Frigates do not appear to have acted since the Commencement of Hostilities, except the *Cybèle* which had attempted to throw supplies into Pondicherry, as related in my former Letter. To the Eastward about the Straits of Malacca seems to be the only place where the French Privateers have had any succeſs, and it appeared that the Government at Bengal had equipped several ships, and sent them for the Protection of the Trade in that part of India. Such being the state of affairs, as it appeared from Public Reports, for (except a Letter which I found upon my arrival at Bombay, acquainting me, that upon the Departure of Lord Cornwallis, Sir John Shore and Sir Robert Abercromby had taken upon themselves the Stations to which they had been appointed) I did not receive a line from the Supreme Government upon the subject, and having no Naval Force to command in India or Information of any coming out; The *Minerva* having been docked, I sailed from Bombay the 12 of January determined to proceed Home, unleſs I should receive any Intelligence of Importance before I left the Coast. I thought it best to leave Captain King in the *Bien Aimé* with directions, if he should not hear from me before the sailing of the next India Ships, to deliver the *Bien Aimé* up to the Government and repair Home in those Ships with His Officers and Men. . . .

(Cornwallis to Admiralty, 21st April, 1794. P.R.O. Ad. 1/167.)

Thus it came about that India was left without a single man-of-war except such as the Indian Governments could themselves provide. At the time the *Minerva* sailed none but the Admiral knew her destination, even the men on board supposing that he would hardly return home without being relieved. His doing so was a source of some surprise ashore in India as soon as it was generally realized. Sir John Shore provided for the defence of the settlements as well as he could by arming Indiamen as need arose. The *Triton, Royal Charlotte* and *Warley*, the ships present at the siege of Pondicherry, were apparently relieved by three others, the *William Pitt, Britannia* and *Houghton*. These took over the duty of commerce protection, forming a single squadron under the command of the senior captain, Mitchell, who was afterwards knighted for his services. As for Admiral Cornwallis, he passed the Cape on February 25th, called at St. Helena in March and by April was entering the Channel. It was an unhappy voyage,

Captain Whitby proving inexperienced in his handling of the crew.[1] But it was redeemed by a picturesque incident in the Channel where, on April 15th, the officers of the *Minerva* sighted four frigates standing across their bows. These ships were distant and were shortly afterwards hidden by fog.

> Next morning we saw four more, who would not let us escape. The first that came up was the *Arethusa*, Sir Edward Pellew . . . who, seeing our flag, brought to and came on board, and told us the other three frigates were the *Flora*, *Concord* and *Melampus*, all under the command of Sir John Borlase Warren. When he was told we had passed four English frigates yesterday (he very near committed himself for swearing), he said, with an oath that there were not four British frigates together in the Channel but themselves. Therefore the others must be French; so hastening to his ship he gave us a salute, then bore down to his Commodore, gave his news, and off they all set in search of the other four frigates. . . .

What is more, they caught them on the 23rd, taking three of them in a running fight near the French coast, south-west of Guernsey. Cornwallis, meanwhile, after his fortunate escape, pursued his way up Channel and came into Spithead on April 22nd.

---

[1] This, at any rate, was the opinion of William Richardson, who was one of the crew.
'The *Minerva* was under good discipline, and, had we had an experienced captain to carry on the duty, should have been more comfortable; but he was too young—had come out with the Admiral on this station a midshipman, and in the course of three or four years had got made a post captain, when only nineteen years of age; he could work the ship very well, but that was all. Not a word was to be spoken in wearing or tacking the ship except from the commanding officer. . . .' *A Mariner of England*, p. 105.

The Rt. Hon. second Earl Spencer (1758–1834)
by J. S. Copley

PLATE II. The Rt. Hon. Henry Dundas, first Viscount Melville (1742–1811) Secretary of State for War and President of the Board of Control, by Sir Thomas Lawrence

CHAPTER II

Rainier Sails for India

W AR had been waged in India from 1789 and ended in 1792. But these were years of peace in England, of peace disturbed only by news of extraordinary events in France. The news became steadily more grave until it was known, by the end of 1792, that war was imminent. Even then, the naval preparations were not marked by any unseemly haste. They may be traced, day by day, in the Admiralty Board Minutes, which are pervaded with a due sense of dignity, deliberation and calm. The Board Room still exists and it is easy to people it anew, in fancy, with men who used to meet there. The room is panelled with mahogany, part of a consignment from Jamaica in 1719, the rest of it going to the house of the Countess of Suffolk at Richmond—mistress of the future George II, a lady whose garden was laid out by Pope, whose cellars were stocked by Dean Swift. Against this dark background, redolent of Josiah Burchett if not of Samuel Pepys, moved the powdered heads of their lordships. They would sit round the polished table, gaily dressed, cravatted and urbane. There was the Earl of Chatham, Pitt's brother, as First Lord. There was Lord Arden. There were the two naval members, Lord Hood and Captain Gardner, and there was the Hon. Mr. Townshend. There was Mr. Pybus. There was Mr. Smyth. These, or most of them, met daily in the spring of 1793 and it is possible to know what each day they agreed. Thus, on January 8th, they commissioned among other ships the *Suffolk* (74), to be commanded by Captain Peter Rainier. On January 31st they appointed the Rt. Hon. Captain Lord Cranstown to the *Raisonable* (74) and—what was that other man's name?—yes, Captain Horatio Nelson to the *Agamemnon* (64). They took due note, on February 1st, of a discovery applicable to making cordage and ironwork, as also of Captain Pakenham's invention for steering a ship after the tiller in the gun-room had been shot away. But Lord Chatham arrived late on that day and informed the Board of the King's pleasure that the Rt. Honble. Richard, Earl Howe, be appointed to command the Channel Fleet, with the union flag at his main-topmast-head. This was, in fact, George III's own decision and Lord Hood, who had hoped for that command, was furious. On the same date their Lordships applied for an Order in Council empowering them to issue press warrants. At a second meeting, later that day, Lord Chatham signified to the Board that His Majesty had directed certain promotions, including Lord Hood's own promotion as Vice-Admiral and the promotion to Rear-Admiral of, among others, the Hon. William Cornwallis and Captain Alan Gardner.

All this time war had not actually begun. It came nearer on February 8th, when warnings of a probable rupture with France were sent to commanders-in-chief in the Mediterranean, Jamaica, Leeward Islands and Nova Scotia. It began, for naval purposes, on the following day, the 9th, when:

> Accounts having been received that War was declared at Paris on the 2nd inst. by the National Convention of France against Great Britain and Holland; Rec'd, in pursuance of the King's Pleasure signified by Mr. Dundas, one of his Maj.'s Principal Secretaries of State, in his Letter of this day's date, that Orders be sent to the Commanders in Chief of His Majesty's Ships at home and abroad and to the Captains of all the Ships & Vessels in Commission, to seize or destroy all ships or vessels belonging to France, which they may fall in with. . . .

On the 11th was read the King's message to Parliament, notifying the Commons of the war and assuring them that:

> . . . His Majesty has taken the necessary steps to maintain the Honour of his Crown; and to vindicate the right of his People: and His Majesty relies with confidence on the firm and effectual support of the House of Commons and on the zealous exertions of a brave and loyal people in prosecuting a just and necessary war, and in endeavouring under the blessing of Providence, to oppose an effectual barrier to the further progress of a system which strikes at the security and peace of all independent nations, and is pursued in open defiance of every principle of moderation, good faith, humanity and justice. . . . [1]

Thereafter, orders and appointments were made almost daily. Frigates were sent to warn homeward-bound merchantmen. Rear-Admiral Gardner was sent—no doubt on his own advice—to command on the Leeward Islands station. The captain of the *Niger* was ordered (April 18th) to reconnoitre Brest. Captain O'Brien Drury was to proceed to the African coast to protect the slave trade. On May 18th Lord Hood was appointed commander-in-chief in the Mediterranean and given detailed orders, presumably drafted by himself. On July 3rd Admiral Earl Howe was ordered to sea, to the westward, as soon as he had fifteen sail of the line

[1] *House of Commons Journal,* 1793.

in readiness. By September their Lordships were receiving Hood's account of his surprising occupation of Toulon, and of Captain Elphinstone's valuable services there ashore. By November they were ordering Vice-Admiral Sir John Jervis, K.B., to proceed with an expedition to the West Indies. The war, in short, had fairly begun. But there was one possible theatre of hostilities in which members of the Board showed, apparently, no interest. That was the East Indies station.

It is not quite true to say that the East Indies were forgotten. On March 7th, for example, orders were given for the *Thetis* (38) and *Leopard* (50) to meet the homeward-bound Indiamen while the *Powerful* (74) was to escort six of those outward bound as far as Latitude 37° or 38° S., proceeding with Rear-Admiral Gardner's flag as far as the Cape Verde Islands. But these measures of trade protection applied only to the Atlantic. The Indian Ocean was evidently assumed to be safe. For this assumption several reasons can be assigned. In the first place, the French colonies were known to be in a state of disorder. In the second place, the French had no ship of the line east of the Cape and none could sail for the East without being reported. In the third place, war in India seemed unlikely, if only because it had just finished. And, lastly, Admiral Cornwallis was in India and doubtless had the situation in hand. It was not, therefore, until 25th October, 1793, that Captain Smith, of the *Diomede* (50), was ordered to sail for Madras and report there to Cornwallis. Smith was provided with a copy of the H.C.S. *Houghton's* log of 1769–70, evidently the classic example of an East India voyage, and told what to do if Cornwallis were not to be found. A single 50-gun ship was no great reinforcement for a station of such vast extent. It was February 1794, nevertheless, before anything further was done. Action then took the form of the following order addressed to Peter Rainier, Esq., captain (as we have seen) of the *Suffolk*:

25th February, 1794.
You are hereby required and directed to proceed with the Ship and Sloop under your command and the East India Company's Ships under your convoy, as expeditiously as possible consistently with their security towards the Places of their Destination: detaching the *Sampson* and *Argo* to St. Helena at the most proper time for their making the speediest Passage to that Island, and directing the Senior Captain of those Ships to take all possible care to arrive there in the first or second Week in May next or the 20th of that month at the latest, and to take under his Convoy such of the homeward bound ships belonging to the East India Company as may be then and there assembled and ready to come away. . . .

Having detached the *Sampson* and *Argo* to St. Helena as above directed, you are to pursue your voyage with the *Suffolk* and *Swift* Sloop and the East India Ships under your Convoy, making the best of your way off the Cape of Good Hope, where you may expect to find His Majesty's Ships named in the margin which have been sent to cruize off that Cape under Orders from Rear-Admiral Gardner, a copy of which you will receive herewith; and upon joining those Ships, or any of them, either there or elsewhere, you are to take them under your Command (their Captains being hereby directed to follow your Orders) and to prosecute your Voyage to the East Indies, proceeding to Madras and using your best endeavours to see the East India Company's ships thither, or as far as your way and theirs may lie together; and having delivered to the Honble Rear Admiral Cornwallis, Commander-in-Chief of His Majesty's Ships in the East Indies, or forwarded to him wherever he may be on that Station, the Pacquet you will herewith receive bearing his address, put yourself and the ships and sloop which may be with you, under his Command, follow his Orders for your further Proceedings.

Centurion
Orpheus
Resistance

But if on your arrival in the East Indies you shall not find the above-mentioned Rear-Admiral, or any other officer of His Majesty's Ships senior to yourself on that Station, you are in that case to employ the Force under your Command and such others of His Majesty's Ships and Vessels as you may find there, or as may join you afterwards, in such manner as, upon consultation with His Excellency the Governor-General, or the Governor and Council of Madras, shall be judged best for the Protection of the Trade and Settlements of His Majesty's Subjects and His Allies in the East Indies, until you receive further orders.

In case you should not fall in with the *Centurion*, *Orpheus* and *Resistance* off the Cape of Good Hope when you arrive there, you are not to make any delay in looking out for them, but to leave in the Hands of the English East India Company's Agent resident in the Cape Town, Orders for the Commanding Officer of those ships to follow you to Madras with all possible expedition.

Given etc.   Chatham
                                                    Arden
(Ad. 2/1347).   P. Affleck

Here at last was the material for an East Indies Squadron. The partial destruction of the Toulon fleet had increased the margin of British naval superiority and allowed now of measures hitherto thought inadvisable. Even so, the ships sent were those most readily spared. The *Suffolk* (74) had been launched in 1765 and the *Centurion* (50) and *Resistance* (44) were of a class of ships more or less obsolescent. The *Orpheus* (32) was more generally useful, however, being a typical 12-pounder frigate, built as recently as 1780.

The *Suffolk* had been with the Channel Fleet since March 1793, and was still under Earl Howe's command when the above order was written. Rainier was a senior captain and was intended to succeed Cornwallis in course of time. He had thus every motive for escaping from the Channel Fleet as soon as possible. But he could not sail without the East India convoy and that in turn would have to wait for other convoys bound for the West Indies, Quebec and the Mediterranean. They would all sail in approximately the same direction and it would fall to the Channel Fleet to see them out of the Channel—a major operation which in this case led indirectly to the Battle of the First of June. All this took time to organize and Rainier was still at Spithead on 22nd April, 1794, and still armed with the Admiralty letter addressed to Cornwallis at Madras. He must therefore have been mildly astonished to see the frigate *Minerva* entering Spithead under a Rear-Admiral's flag. It was Cornwallis himself who was now saluting the Union Flag with fifteen guns. The Commander-in-Chief, East Indies, and his successor were both at Spithead and India was almost without naval protection. To the directors of the East India Company it all seemed very odd indeed; and most, *most* undesirable. It is probable that Rainier had a few words with Cornwallis, perhaps ashore at the 'George.' But it might not be much more than that for Cornwallis struck his flag at sunset on the 24th and was in London by the 27th.

If the directors of the East India Company expected to hear of Cornwallis's court martial for deserting his station without being relieved, they were disappointed. And indeed a quick reference to their own files might possibly have told them that he was entitled to come home when he liked. The fact is that Cornwallis had explicit instructions dated 7th May, 1791, and signed by Chatham himself, ordering him to leave India when he thought proper.

> In case upon the receipt hereof and after consulting with the Governor General of the British Settlements in India you shall be of opinion that, from the circumstances of affairs your Presence shall be no longer necessary in that Country, you are hereby required and directed to return as soon as possible to this (without waiting to be relieved) bringing with you the whole or such part of the Squadron under your Command as may, under the existing circumstances of affairs in India, appear to you most conducive to his Majesty's Service, and repairing with them to Spithead

where you are to remain till further Orders, sending to our Secretary an account of your arrival and proceedings.

(Adm. Sec. Letters 2/1344.)

If their Lordships were annoyed with Cornwallis—as they may well have been—they had not a leg to stand on. He had had his orders and was very virtuous to have remained at his post as long as he had. Had he consulted the Governor-General (his brother)? Of course he had! Had the war altered the situation completely? Then their Lordships could have cancelled their order of May 1791—which they had never done. Was India exposed to attack? Then their Lordships should have sent him ships with which to defend it. Cornwallis was in a strong position.

Rainier was now more definitely the commander-in-chief designate. He was authorized to hoist a broad pendant as Commodore as soon as he parted company with a flag officer, and appoint an additional lieutenant to his ship at the same time. Lord Howe finally sailed with his convoy on May 2nd, parted from the merchantmen on the 4th, but detached a squadron under Rear-Admiral Montagu to see them past the latitude of Finisterre. There were one hundred and eighty-four sail of the convoy in sight of the *Suffolk* on the 6th. The Straits and Quebec convoys parted company on the 10th and finally Rainier's East Indiamen detached themselves under his guidance on the 11th, the Admiral having made a signal to that effect. With only the *Swift* in company and the Indiamen, Rainier hoisted his broad pendant, simultaneously appointing his nephew (Mr. J. S. Rainier) into the lieutenant's vacancy he was authorized to fill. The other events of the voyage were perhaps less satisfactory. Sailing with Indiamen was all very well from the point of view of hospitality. It meant endless invitations to dinner so long as the weather was fine, and the dinners were good. But it was endlessly irritating in other ways. The commanders of the Indiamen had their own ideas on the best route. Rainier, who had been a lieutenant under Hughes, would of course stand no nonsense of that kind. But two of them wanted to put into Rio de Janeiro for repairs (so they said) and water. This he could not well refuse, but others parted company without permission; four of the big China ships at that. Then a wretched ship called the *Harriet* sailed badly and 'prolonged the passage at least a week,' while the commander of the *Rose* 'twice attempted to leave the convoy' and on the third occasion pleaded the loss of a topmast. These unauthorized separations apart, Rainier successively discarded the Bombay ships (in 37° 46′ S. and 35° 23′ E., on August 8th) and the China ships—or the five that remained—in 36° 27′ S. and 64° 07′ E. on the 15th. With the remaining twelve ships bound for the coast and bay he reached Madras on September 11th, and found the *Orpheus* (32) and *Heroine* (32) already there. He was on his station and his proper task had begun.

No campaign is properly conducted that is not founded on an *appreciation*. Rainier may or may not have recognized this fact, but he was an able and experienced seaman, who had once been in the merchant service; a heavy, middle-aged and unromantic figure, wholly lacking the social position of his predecessor. His appreciation, assuming him to have made one, would be founded, like any other, on information. And, at this juncture, information about his French opponents was plentiful, if confused. It came from exchanged prisoners and 'cartel' vessels which carried them and did some spying at the same time. He thus learnt of the arrival at the Isle of France (in 1792) of the new governor, Anne Joseph Hippolyte Maurès, Comte de Malartic, sent to impregnate the colony with the latest revolutionary doctrines. To have found a man less suited for the purpose would have been extremely difficult. His appointment had been one of the last acts of Louis XVI and it can only have been through oversight that Malartic was not soon afterwards recalled. He seems to have been politically adaptable, serving one Government as readily as another. Apart, however, from this, he personally represented all that was best in the old regime. He was a polished, benevolent and fatherly ruler who talked in a friendly fashion to all and gave away his income in charity. With his old-fashioned sword by his side, he was to be seen going to church each morning and accosting his neighbours in the street. He was conciliatory to the political extremists and scrupulously civil to the enemy. He, more than any other, was responsible for saving the Isle of France from internal disorders.

On landing from the frigate *Fidèle*, on 16th June, 1792, Malartic had found the colony in difficulties. There were financial troubles and the troops were refusing to accept their pay in paper money. A shortage, almost amounting to famine, began in September 1792, and recurred in August and September 1793 and again in March 1794. In the meanwhile, during 1793, came news of the King's execution, of the Terror and the Jacobin triumph. The movement spread, in some degree, to the French colonies and led to the formation in the Ile de France of a Colonial Assembly on more or less revolutionary lines. The Admiral, Saint Felix, fresh from his argumentative encounter with Cornwallis, had returned to the island on 24th June, 1792. It was local political activity which had then prevented him doing anything further. The Colonial Assembly, buzzing with argument and naturally eager to be in the fashion, demanded, and obtained, the arrest of Duplessis, governor of Bourbon, as a suspected royalist. This was in 1794. At the same time the Admiral himself was arrested, being scarcely more popular than his predecessor. A guillotine had been built by this time at the Isle of France, and it looked as if the suspects were likely to forfeit their lives. Malartic could do nothing for them except by delaying the trial. However, on August 29th, a ship from Bordeaux brought the news of the Convention's Decree (16 Pluviose, An 2) abolishing slavery in all French colonies. In the resulting excitement both prisoners and guillotine were forgotten. The latter, having only once been tried (successfully) on a goat, was dismantled; and the former were eventually released. Owing to Malartic's moderation, no great harm was done in these civil dissensions; and the question of slavery did not come to a head until 1796. The tribulations of the Admiral, however, prevented any very enterprising naval operations. Indeed, except for the *Cybèle* and *Prudente*, all the French frigates seem to have returned to Europe. Renaud, who succeeded Saint Felix as commander of the squadron, had thus only a single frigate and a brig. Nor was the colony in a position to assist him very much, as the local paper money was rapidly becoming valueless. The most he could do was to defend the islands against English cruisers; and this, it will later be seen, he did most effectively. All offensive action against enemy commerce was left to privateers. Of these, two, at the outset, fell a prey to Commodore Mitchell in the China seas. The others, unaware of the English weakness, seem to have taken no great advantage of the situation.

Of this political situation Rainier was reasonably well informed. Prisoners taken in the two privateers captured by Mitchell agreed that there were two frigates at Port Louis, together with an armed brig and some six or eight privateers getting ready for sea. Some of the prisoners said that the frigates were destined for a raid on Bencoolen, but others said that the inhabitants of the Isle of France would not let them put to sea at all. All agreed that the island was feeling a shortage of provisions. News came from other sources that the French had captured a Portuguese ship from Lisbon with 600,000 dollars; as also a ship belonging to the Imam of Muscat with half that sum. There was no information of any French activity on the Indian coasts, but the French had 'taken two Junks from the Malays and ill-treated the Crews, by which means they have most impolitically made themselves implacable Enemies. . . .' From all this Rainier concluded that the initiative lay with him. His freedom of action, however, was reduced by the fact that the *Diomede* (44) and *Centurion* (50) had already sailed—by order of Captain Newcome of the *Orpheus*—for blockade duty off the Isle of France, while the *Resistance* (44) had been similarly dispatched to the China Seas. As the blockade of the Isle of France was the only type of offensive open to him, Rainier had perforce to concentrate his remaining ships for the defence of trade.

Rainier's own immediate movements were dominated by the need to leave the coast before the breaking of the monsoon—before, that is to say, about October 10th. His first move was to send the *Orpheus* and *Swift* to cruise off Friars Hood and between Point Pedro and Tranquebar. His next move was to follow with the *Suffolk*, join the other two ships, and take all three with him to Penang. His object was to protect the country ships due about then from China and bound for India by the Straits of Malacca—'which being a very rich convoy and but indifferently protected, may be expected will be attacked.' He expected to return to the coast towards the end of December, in time to protect the homeward-bound Indiamen sailing from Bengal. At about the same period, the *Centurion* and *Diomede* might be expected from the southward—since it was not practicable to blockade the French islands for very long at a time, nor advisable to be there at all during the hurricane months—and the *Resistance* from the eastward, where she had been cruising in the China Seas. These three ships would all probably have to go to Bombay for repairs and refitting.

The above arrangement of his forces gave Rainier the right to claim that he had, at least to some extent, satisfied the many requirements of commerce protection. The Governor-General, Sir John Shore, voicing these various needs, asked for a force to be stationed off Achin, another in the Bay of Bengal, another in the Straits of Malacca and yet another off the French islands.

> From the middle of December until the end of February, the Country Veſsels sail from Bengal to the Eastward with valuable Cargoes of Opium; the China Ships generally enter the Eastern Entrance of the Straits of Malacca early in December on their return to Bengal, Madras & Bombay, and the latest seldom beyond the 10th of Jan'y. The returning Frigate from the China seas will, I conclude, clear the Straits of Malacca of any of the Enemy's Cruisers which may be found there. This protection may be supposed to extend to the end of December, after which the paſsage of the Straits will require farther Protection, the Enterprises of the Enemy have hitherto been made to the Eastward.

> Under these Circumstances I submit to your Excellency the propriety of detaching such force as you may deem fit through the Straits of Malacca so as to arrive at the eastern extremity of them by the middle of December, and after remaining there to the end of the month, to proceed Southerly through the Straits of Dryon or Sunda, and return to Fort St. George by the West Coast of Sumatra, calling at Bencoolin, I cannot but think it probable that such of the French Cruisers as may find the means of leaving

the Mauritius will be tempted to proceed to the Straits of Sunda rather than to the eastern Entrance of the Straits of Malacca, and the Cruise which I have recommended is equally calculated to protect the Straits & the returning Indiamen from China.

Whilst the Season permits, no station appears to me so proper for the purposes of general protection, as one of the French Islands, for the purpose of intercepting their Cruisers either proceeding or returning, as well as supplies of Provisions to the Islands. . . .

(Sir J. Shore to Commodore Rainier, 15th October, 1794. Ad. 1/167.)

In making these suggestions, admirable as they may have been, Sir John Shore had rather lost sight of the actual number of ships at the Commodore's disposal. Rainier, however, did his best, and the Governor-General afterwards approved of what he had done.

Holland was, at this period, on the English side, and Rainier, when at Penang in December, received urgent requests from the Dutch for his protection. Through their subordinates at Malacca, the rulers of Batavia informed the Commodore that their capital was about to be attacked by a fleet of frigates and privateers from the Isle of France. As it was then the sickly season at Batavia, it may be doubted whether anything could have induced Rainier to go there, whatever the emergency. In this case, however, he doubted the whole story. In reply, he said that the French frigates could not come as the French colonists would not let them. He added that, by this time, his ships were blockading the Isle of France and could be depended upon to discourage any such expedition. He ended by asserting that he could not spare the necessary ships. This last plea was the more justified in that the country ships returning from China were giving him a great deal of trouble. They would not keep together, but appeared in groups of two and three despite the efforts of the *Orpheus* and *Swift* to herd them into regular convoys. The last day of December found Rainier still struggling with them and it was not until 23rd January, 1795, that he reached Madras in company with the *Orpheus* and *Swift*. The *Resistance* he left to escort the country trade bound for Bombay.

It was probably before his return to Madras that Rainier had news of the *Centurion* and *Diomede*. These had sailed from Madras on 30th August, 1794, watered at Trincomalee, called at Rodriguez and begun to blockade the Isle of France on October 13th. Being apprehensive of an English attack, and worried at the possibility of a slave revolt, Malartic had by this time put the island into a state of defence. The inhabitants were under arms and all the batteries considerably strengthened. The prospect, however, of a blockade was, at that time, particularly unpleasant because there was a food shortage already. Rice alone was plentiful, and no prizes of any value had recently been taken. Meat was rationed, even as things were, and the cutting off of further supplies was only too likely to produce a famine. With the negroes on the verge of rebellion—twelve of them were executed at about this time—and trouble impending with France over the slavery question, a famine might easily have destroyed the colony. The senior naval officer, Jean Marie Renaud, realized this and decided that, at all costs, the blockade had to be raised. Besides the two frigates, *Cybèle* (40) and *Prudente* (32), he had under his orders the *Coureur* brig (16). To these he added the *Jean-Bart* privateer (22), pressed into service for the occasion. Reinforcing the crews of these ships with soldiers and volunteers, he put to sea with Malartic's blessing on October 19th, by French reckoning. On the 22nd, by the English calendar, he fell in with the *Centurion* and *Diomede* and instantly gave battle. The action which followed was indecisive. Both sides lost heavily, the casualties being mostly in the *Cybèle*, *Prudente* and *Centurion*. These three ships also sustained a great deal of damage in their masts and rigging. The *Diomede* took no very active part in the conflict, and had no casualties. As a result, the French squadron escaped, the crippled *Cybèle* being towed out of action by the *Prudente*, and all four ships returning safely to port. This engagement was fought by the French in a very republican spirit. Thus, Caraud, the commander of the *Coureur*, reported of his crew that 'tous les jours l'hymne de la liberté chantée sur le pont produisait de nouveau Elan,' and in the action he found 'que ne sont plus des hommes mais des furieux que je conduit à l'ennemi.' His seamen cried 'Vive la République' and served their guns 'avec une celerité encroyable.' They could do so without much interruption for they were under fire only from the *Diomede* and were little the worse for it.

As the French had four or five times as many casualties as the English, and as it was they who broke off the action, Captain Samuel Osborn of the *Centurion* might perhaps have claimed a sort of victory. Had he, moreover, been supported by his consort, one or two of the French ships might have been taken. Even with some such loss, however, the French object would have been gained. Whether as victor or vanquished, the *Centurion* needed repairs and so could not maintain her station off the French islands. To have left the *Diomede* alone would have been dangerous, so that there was nothing to do but raise the blockade. The *Centurion* sailed at once for Bombay, the frigate being sent to Madras. Captain Smith of the *Diomede* was court-martialled and dismissed the service for his part in this affair. There was some satisfaction in this, and yet the fact remained that the first encounter of the war between French and English in the East had resulted in what was tantamount to a defeat for the latter. Without the loss of a single ship, and despite a virtual inferiority in force, the French had done what they set out to do. They had driven off the blockading ships and saved the Isle of France from something approaching famine.

On his arrival at Madras, Rainier was met by petitions from the merchants for further naval protection in the Straits of Malacca; petitions which were supported by a request from the Governor-General. He accordingly gave orders for the *Diomede* and *Heroine* to take up a station between Malacca and the north-west end of Banca Island and remain there until all the trade from the eastward had passed. They were then to return, the one by the Straits of Sunda and the other by the Straits of Malacca. These two ships sailed from Madras on February 5th, the *Swift* being sent soon afterwards with a convoy bound for the Arabian Gulf. Rainier himself, with the *Suffolk* and *Orpheus*, remained on the coast, where he was joined in March by the *Resistance*, from Bombay, and at the beginning of April by the *Centurion*.

In these early months of 1795, the Commodore's immediate problem mainly concerned the French islands. Was he to renew the blockade or not? In this connection he had to consider, first of all, the suggestions of the Governor-General contained in a letter dated February 6th.

> The situations of risque from an Enemy during the S.W. Monsoon which prevails from March to August may chiefly be confined to three.
> 1st.   The Island of Ceylon
> 2nd.   The Streights of Malacca
> 3rd.   The Streights of Sunda
> The Island of Ceylon is usually made, I understand, from the month of March to the beginning of August by Veſsels from Bombay to the coast and to China, and in June & July by Ships from the Eastward & those from Bengal to Madras. It is also made by the Ships from Europe to Madras & Bengal. On these grounds this seems a proper Station for a Cruize until August.
> A Station between Acheen and Pulo Penang seems calculated to protect the entrance into the China Seas through the Streights of Malacca, and a Station at the Streights of Sunda is also adapted to secure the paſsage into the China Seas, and the Trade to & from Batavia. It may I imagine be poſsible to establish a communication between this last place and Fort Marlbro'.
> I have already expreſsed my sentiments on the importance of Stationing a Force off the Isle of France as equally calculated to confine their privateers in Port & to cut off their supplies of provisions from Madagascar & communication with Europe. In this Station I think the most respectable Force should be employed as neceſsity will naturally induce every exertion on the part of the French to repel it.
> (Governor-General to Commodore Rainier, 6th February, 1795. Ad. 1/168.)

The Governor-General also proposed that convoy should be given to the Bombay cotton trade, sailing for China at the end of May. Rather unexpectedly, this proposal was rejected by the merchants themselves. Headed by Forbes, Smith & Co., Alexander Adamson and Bruce, Fawcett & Co., they signed a petition on February 22nd, representing to Rainier that 'the sailing of their ships in Convoy is detrimental to their Trade on account of a Glut in the Cotton Market at China.' All they asked was to have cruisers stationed off Ceylon and in the Straits of Malacca.

It will be seen that Rainier's disposition of his forces corresponded fairly closely to the suggestions both of the merchants and the Governor-General. Where he ultimately had to differ from the latter was over the question of the blockade. In this he was influenced by the news, brought by a neutral vessel to Tranquebar, that the French were sending four sail of the line, accompanied by frigates and carrying troops, to strengthen their forces at the Isle of France. With this information, which afterwards proved false, there came the further and more definite news that American ships had been supplying the French islands with provisions brought from Madagascar.

> . . . this news has only probability to support it, however it leads me to be of opinion that sending ships from hence to cruise off those Islands does not appear a measure of expediency, with the small force I have, as their Lordships must know that His Excellency the Governor General who suggested it does not, that I have no authority to stop Neutral Ships entering those ports with provisions only, that it is a Voyage of seven or eight weeks there, as many back again, and dangerous entering the harbour of Diego Royes to water; and but a short time left for Cruising without being able to form a regular relief; besides, in case of distrefs the Cruisers may be obliged to bear up for the Cape of Good Hope, so that I dont think at present of sending Ships that way, as the Service requires Cruisers in the Streights of Malacca, off Achen and Ceylon, for the protection of the trade of the Country which may be pafsing those situations during the SW Monsoon & of the Company's Ships that may be expected from Europe during that Season also.
>
> (Rainier to Admiralty, 19th April, 1795. P.R.O. Ad. 1/168.)

The Commodore's reasons for not continuing the blockade of the French islands were convincing enough. The need remained to capture them. In the meanwhile, however, came the important news of the annexation by France of the United Provinces. If the Dutch were now actual or potential enemies, the whole situation in the East was radically altered. Hearing the news in July, while cruising off Ceylon with the *Suffolk*, *Resistance* and *Orpheus*, Rainier returned at once to Madras to concert measures with Lord Hobart. They would clearly have to act quickly.

CHAPTER III

Danger from the Dutch

RAINIER'S first thought was of Trincomalee. It had once been held by the French in Suffren's time and he did not want to see them there again. His second thought was of Malacca; again, not for its own sake but as a place which must not fall into French hands. Orders came from England to occupy both Malacca and Ceylon, but they were hardly necessary; both ships and troops were in motion before the dispatches could arrive. 'The importance of getting possession of Malacca was so obvious,' Rainier admitted, 'that my idea of it was anticipated by Lord Hobart and Colonel Brathwaite before I arrived.' This evidently showed just how obvious the idea must have been. But even obvious plans are not always easy to execute, and in this instance there was an immediate difficulty in the lack of tonnage at Madras. Providentially, the *Diomede* and *Heroine* had returned from the eastwards, however, and these, with the *Suffolk* and *Centurion*, sufficed, with some country ships, for the expedition to Trincomalee. Captain Pakenham, with the *Resistance* and *Orpheus*, was to occupy Malacca. With hastily chartered transport vessels, both expeditions sailed from Madras on July 21st, parting company the same day. Rainier's three larger men-of-war each carried upwards of three hundred white troops, and the transports carried a further number of sepoys. Flat-boats for a landing were carried, together with field artillery, mortars, shot and shell. The military commander, Colonel Stuart, and his staff were with the Commodore in the *Suffolk*. After calling at Negapatam, the expedition arrived off Trincomalee on August 1st.

It must be understood that the English quarrel was not with the Dutch but with a Holland under French control. The Prince of Orange was an ally, so that this expedition to Ceylon took the form of a peaceful occupation. Armed with letters from the Prince, the English merely asked that the Dutch forts should admit an English garrison to assist in their defence. There was at this time no question of annexation. As for the local Dutch officers, their views were undecided. Those who were loyal to the House of Orange objected, nevertheless, to surrendering their batteries to those who looked uncommonly like enemies. They were in a dilemma. The English proposals had been sent

78

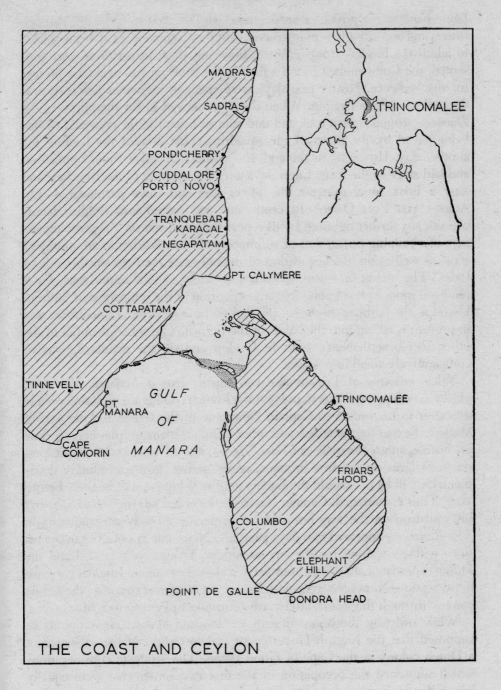

THE COAST AND CEYLON

beforehand to the governor at Columbo who decided to obey the Prince's orders and accordingly sent instructions to the Commandant at Trincomalee to admit the English troops. When, however, these instructions were presented, the Commandant found a flaw in the wording and made it a pretext for disobedience. Nearly two days were spent in argument before it was decided to make a landing. When the ships moved in for the purpose, the *Diomede* grounded on a rock and sank almost instantly, the crew and troops being saved by the boats of the squadron. This delayed the landing for another day. However, in the end, the soldiers landed without opposition and laid siege to the forts. Eight days after the opening of the trenches, and after a brisk bombardment, the lower fort and town surrendered. On August 31st Fort Ostenburg capitulated and passed into English hands without any further fighting. In his report Rainier dwelt on 'the great advantage of obtaining poſſeſsion of so important a fortification in an uninjured state' as well as on 'the acquisition of the only safe Harbour on this side of India.' The taking of Trincomalee was certainly of vital importance, for it rendered more or less impossible any repetition of the campaigns of Suffren. Useful as the harbour might be, the real point in securing Trincomalee was to prevent it falling into the hands of the French. The subsequent fall of the other Dutch settlements, both in Ceylon and on the mainland, was of comparatively small importance.

What was true of Trincomalee was equally true of Malacca. The chief object in occupying it was to prevent the French coming there. Rainier made this clear in his orders to Captain Newcome of the *Orpheus*. After taking Malacca, he was free to attack any other Dutch settlement 'that may, if they are hostile, annoy the trade to China.' He was also to 'lose no time in pushing on to Malacca' in the first instance, remembering 'how exceedingly detrimental it will be . . . should the Enemy get the Whip hand & be there before you.' Thus encouraged, Captain Newcome crowded sail for Malacca, losing his squadron on the way but arriving in person as early as August 15th. The *Resistance* appeared two days later, and Newcome at once began operations without waiting for the last stragglers. Troops were landed and the Dutch capitulated almost without firing a shot. Leaving an English garrison in possession, Newcome went with his two men-of-war to escort the China convoy through the straits, afterwards returning to Penang to refit.

While ordering the occupation of Ceylon and Malacca, it is not to be supposed that the English Government had lost sight of the existence of a Dutch colony at the Cape of Good Hope. The strategic considerations which suggested the occupation of the first two settlements were equally imperative in the case of the last. With the Cape in the hands of the French—

for that is virtually what its continuance under Dutch rule would mean—all communication with India would become hazardous. There was no alternative but to strike swiftly and vigorously before the French could have time to act. This was accordingly done. A squadron under Sir George Keith Elphinstone, consisting of three sail of the line, a frigate and a sloop sailed from St. Helen's on 3rd April 1795, joined forces with another squadron of three sail of the line and a sloop under Commodore Blankett, off the Cape, and dropped anchor in Simon's Bay on June 10th. The squadron carried a detachment of troops under General Craig, but it was hoped at first that no hostilities need take place. As at Trincomalee and Malacca 'liberal offers' were made; offers of alliance and protection against the French. And for some weeks friendly relations were maintained, though with difficulty, between Dutch and English. Negotiations broke down, however, in the end, and a landing was made on August 7th. Skirmishing went on for the remainder of the month, but on September 4th a fleet of Indiamen arrived with General Clarke and a larger body of troops. On the 15th, overawed by these reinforcements, the Dutch governor capitulated and the whole colony passed into English hands. All this took place in what was still technically a time of peace. As Admiral Elphinstone wrote on August 10th, 'The Dutch are obliged to obey the Orders of the National Convention, and we are no doubt at war with them, although I do not know it officially.'

The Cape was not at this time regarded as a particularly valuable acquisition. As a naval base, indeed, it had many disadvantages. Nevertheless, it became necessary to station a considerable squadron there, if only to prevent the Dutch or French retaking it. This squadron was far larger than that based on India. Consequently, when it was decided at the Admiralty that the Cape and the East Indies should form one station under one commander-in-chief, it was naturally agreed upon that the Admiral at the Cape should be the one to command the whole. Accordingly, the dispatch in which Admiral Elphinstone informed Rainier of his success at the Cape contained the following unwelcome passage:

> Agreeable to the directions of the Right Honble Henry Dundas, one of his Majesty's Principal Secretaries of State, on my arrival here upon the 10th I took upon me the Command of His Majesty's Ships & Veſsels employed on a particular service including all the Indian Seas, by which you will be pleased to govern yourself and the ships with you.
>
> All promotions will of course from that date rest with me, and in the mean time you will give Acting Orders when there shall be occasion, aſsuring yourself that your wishes will at all times have great weight with me. . . .
>
> I fear the Season will be too far advanced to get on the Coast with safety,

unleſs you have been so fortunate as to obtain poſſeſſion of Trincomale; but either there, or on the other coast I hope to see you as soon as circumstances will admit—the expectation of a French Squadron will make me inclined to keep all the large Ships as compact as poſsible. I am not without hopes of hearing from you at this place, and request you will not fail to write me by any safe opportunity; you may expect to hear from me as often as poſsible.

(Elphinstone to Rainier, 10th August, 1795. P.R.O. Ad. 1/168.)

The above letter, carried by H.C.S. *Arniston*, reached the Commodore at Madras on September 27th. Any annoyance he may have felt he forbore to express. That the Cape was now in English hands was, of course, good news. What had been 'a feather in the hands of Holland' would have become 'a sword in the hands of France'; and the occupation of the Cape was clearly, therefore, a wise move and well calculated to check any French designs on India. Again, the Cape would not only cease to supply the French islands but would also serve as a convenient base for a squadron detailed to blockade them. On the other hand, grateful as Rainier may have been for this lightening of his task, he must have resented his loss of independence. Moreover, he must have known that the new arrangement was unworkable. It was difficult enough for an officer at Madras or Bombay to dispose his forces in accordance with such information of the enemy as might reach him from the China Seas, the Red Sea, the Straits of Malacca and the Isle of France. But at least his position was reasonably central and reasonably convenient for concerting measures with the Indian Presidencies. At the Cape there was neither of these advantages. To try to direct operations from a station on the extreme verge of an enormous field of activity, spreading into three oceans, was to attempt the impossible. Elphinstone, it is true, approved and defended the scheme; but then it must be remembered what consequence it gave him. There was, in reality, so little to be said for it that the Admiralty very shortly reversed its own decision. In the meanwhile, however, Rainier had to content himself with his subordinate position and report to Elphinstone instead of directly to the Admiralty.

Rainier's position on September 27th, when he received the dispatch from the Cape, was complicated by the recent news from the eastwards. In the course of July the French frigates *La Cybèle* and *La Prudente* 'had dashed thro' the seas between the Streights of Sunda and Western entrance of those of Malacca & took several prizes, English, Dutch, Portuguese & Spanish, about 9 in all' (Rainier to Admiralty, 9th October, 1795). The French frigates, accompanied by *Le Coureur* brig, seem to have made this attack without very much information concerning their enemy. Had they known it, they might have taken, successively, the *Orpheus* and *Resistance*, then bound separately for Malacca on an expedition already referred to. As it was, these ships had, unknown to themselves at the time, a narrow escape. The *Resistance* recaptured one of the French prizes and went on her way. The French frigates, unaware of their opportunity, sailed for their base. On his return to Madras from Trincomalee on September 21st, Rainier was 'agreeably surprised to learn by a Ship lately arrived from the Streights of Malacca that the French frigates had disappeared' and that the expedition to Malacca was likely to succeed. Rainier accordingly determined to proceed in force to exploit any success, carry reinforcements, and 'attack the Spice Islands or otherwise act' as he thought 'most conductive to the execution of His Majesty's Commands.' For this purpose he divided his forces into two parts, one to accompany him and the other to remain on the coast. His force had been augmented by the Governor-General's putting under his orders several of the cruisers of the Bombay Marine. This enabled him to take with him nearly the whole of the King's ships; that is, the *Suffolk*, *Centurion* and *Hobart*, together with the sloop *Swift*. On the coast were to remain the *Heroine* (32), the Company's frigate *Bombay* (32), and the Company's sloop *Swift* (18). Two other sloops of the Bombay Marine, the *Queen* and *Drake*, were to aid the above vessels in what was to be their principal task, the blockade of Colombo, in which town the Dutch were still holding out.

On receiving Elphinstone's dispatch, Rainier did not alter his immediate plans. He felt, indeed, all the more ready to leave India comparatively unprotected, supposing as he did that Elphinstone would presently arrive on the coast. As his orders implied nothing to the contrary, he meant to proceed as planned, strengthened in his resolution by the advice of Lord Hobart and the 'authentick Intelligence that the Dutch at Batavia have armed five of their large ships carrying from 50 to 60 Guns.' Although the activity of the Dutch was due, doubtless, to a fear that Batavia would otherwise share the fate of Capetown, Rainier had to remember that the beginning of the next year would see the Indiamen and country ships returning from the China Seas. He hoped to be able to return to India shortly although, as he wrote, his movements would have to be uncertain. As he expressed it, ''tis not poſsible to say what my detention there may be, which must be regulated by the force of the Enemy in those seas and existing circumstances.' Just before sailing, Rainier received news of the surrender of Malacca in a dispatch from Captain Newcome dated August 31st. He reported this to Elphinstone and left at Madras a number of papers addressed to the Admiral, whom he knew to be on the point of coming to India. In these he described his plans, touched on various administrative matters and finally urged Elphinstone to proceed against Batavia, which might well, he thought, be the next prey. 'Batavia,' he wrote, 'is represented to me as easily to be taken, from the abhorrence the Natives, both Chinese and Malays, have of the Dutch, and the weakneſs of the Fortifications, relying much on the protection of the Ships in the Road. . . .' Rainier sailed for Malacca on October 15th, partly to protect the China trade, partly to further his designs on the Spice Islands.

Elphinstone, meanwhile, as Rainier supposed, was planning to visit India. The Cape was, apparently, in no immediate danger and so he felt justified in taking with him the greater part of his squadron. First of all, on October 27th, the *Stately* (64) and *Victorious* (74) were sent to cruise off the French islands for three weeks and then proceed to Madras. Then, on about November 13th, he sailed for Madras himself with the *Monarch* (74), *Arrogant* (74), *Echo* (sloop) and *Rattlesnake* (sloop). At the Cape he left Commodore Blankett with the *America* (64), *Ruby* (64), *Princess* (26) and *Star* (18). The Admiral reached Madras with his own contingent on 15th January, 1796, and was joined four days later by the *Stately* and *Victorious* and a few weeks later by the *Sphynx* (24)—a newcomer sent on from the Cape. This detachment was completed by the *Prince of Wales*, an armed transport. Some time was spent in refitting the ships, making sails and repairing the *Sphynx*, and then most of the men-of-war sailed 'on various services.' The *Rattlesnake*, *Echo* and *Prince of Wales* were sent to join the *Heroine* off Colombo. The *Arrogant* was detailed to cruise off Point de Galle on January 25th, and the *Stately* sailed for Trincomalee four days later. The *Victorious* was dispatched to Penang on February 4th, leaving the *Monarch* and *Sphynx* at Madras, the former being the flagship and the latter still unfit for service. The ships sent on these various errands, although 'completely stored and victualled for four months' were under orders to return to the coast in the course of a month. Elphinstone was trying to combine trade protection with full control of the squadron. He complained, indeed, that Rainier had made this latter part of his task more difficult; 'another arrangement,' he hinted, 'might have retained the Naval Force more collected and prepared for Services not so remote. . . .'

What other plans Rainier could have made Elphinstone omitted to suggest. Hampered as he was by the need to blockade Colombo and by his orders to occupy Malacca, it is not clear what else he could have done. A weakness, however, in his dispositions; and a weakness which Elphinstone did not correct, was the lack of naval protection in the Bay of Bengal. This lack had already begun to be felt. The French frigates were not active at the moment, it is true, but, as will be seen, there were privateers at sea Elphinstone began to hear accounts of them.

> The Enemy's Cruizers have been troublesome and succeſsful, but the extensive range of Coast requiring protection, the various services on which the ships are indispensably engaged, the expeditions undertaken, some remote, the loſs of the *Diomede* and Defects of the *Sphynx* all unite to counteract the inclination and duty I feel to protect our trade & prevent annoyance. It is my intention as soon as the Season admits the ships return, to collect a force and cruize closely off the Mauritius, the most probable means of intercepting the Enemy's Veſsels. . . .
> (Elphinstone to Admiralty, 23rd February, 1796. P.R.O. Ad. 1/55.)

It will be seen that Elphinstone was not impressed by Rainier's assurances that Java, 'the Bengal of the Dutch,' would be an easy prey. Whether convinced of the fact or not, he evidently thought that the French islands merited prior attention; possibly because of the recent captures, possibly on general principles of strategy. Neither for the first nor last time, the Isle of France was in some danger of a hostile visitation in force. It was saved by a belated Dutch effort to recapture the Cape. Some rumour of the Dutch intention reached Madras while Elphinstone was still waiting for the return of his forces. He waited no longer, but decided to return at once to the Cape in person, leaving orders for some of his ships to follow. Sailing on March 23rd, with the *Monarch* and *Sphynx*, he came into Simon's Bay on May 23rd. Commodore Blankett was there and had seen no sign as yet of a Dutch squadron. On the other hand, he had ample information from Europe that the squadron was to be expected.

Perhaps no force ever went to its doom so inevitably as did the Dutch squadron under Rear-Admiral Lucas. Its destination was known to the British Government about a month before it sailed. It was seen and reported in the North Sea. It was seen again and reported between Madeira and the Canaries. It was sighted once more off the Canaries. The news of its coming was brought to the Cape successively by a fast-sailing frigate and a neutral merchantman. For a part of its voyage the squadron was shadowed by another frigate, which finally outstripped it and arrived beforehand with the news of its approach. Then again, the Dutch ships progressed in so leisurely a fashion that the English Admiralty had ample time to reinforce the squadron at the Cape with two more sail of the line, a 50-gun ship and transports enough for some thousands of troops. Indeed, the forces which Rear-Admiral Lucas ultimately encountered had been collected to receive him from places as remote as the North Sea and the Coromandel coast. A secretly prepared and rapidly developed attack might perhaps have had some effect. It might have reached the Cape at a time when Elphinstone was elsewhere, cruising off the French Islands or Batavia. There was little to be said for the management of an expedition which allowed its object to be known at Madras almost as soon as the squadron had sailed.

On his arrival at the Cape, Elphinstone found there, with Commodore Blankett, the *America* (64), *Ruby* (64), *Princess* (26) and a sloop called the *Hope*. Five days later, on May 28th, there arrived the *Sceptre* (64) and *Crescent* (36) with six transports. On July 21st, there being still no sign of the Dutch, Rear-Admiral Pringle came in with the *Tremendous* (74) and *Jupiter* (50). On the same day the *Moselle* (28) arrived. This was the frigate which had been watching the Dutch. She had fallen in with them off Madeira; four sail of the line, three frigates and a sloop, heading eastwards. Following on this definite news of the enemy's whereabouts came still further reinforcements, the *Trident* (64) and, finally, the *Stately* (64) with the two sloops *Echo* and *Rattlesnake*; these last three coming from India in obedience to Elphinstone's orders left at Madras.

A question which naturally arises is how the Dutch squadron contrived to spend so long on the voyage. James, the naval historian, could find no explanation. 'Where the Dutch admiral had passed the spring and summer,' he wrote, 'no one could tell.' All that we now know is that he spent all those months at sea. He called, it is true, at La Luz in the Canaries, and again at Porto Praya in the Cape Verde Islands; but he made no long stay at either. Nor did he put into any port in Brazil, although he was off that coast by the end of June. Calms and contrary winds and (possibly) bad seamanship seem to have been the sole causes of delay. As remarkable, almost, as this incredible passage was the fact that Lucas received no sort of warning of his danger. Had he, during all those months, fallen in with any friendly outward-bound neutral, he could scarcely have failed to hear of the English preparations. He appears to have heard nothing.

Elphinstone, although fully prepared, had serious doubts as to whether Lucas was really bound for the Cape. He assumed that the Dutch would learn the strength of his squadron and go elsewhere, to relieve or retake Colombo, to attack the Portuguese at Goa, or to recover Malacca and save the Spice Islands. Accordingly, he tried to keep his ships at sea, ready to intercept them. Unfortunately, the weather did not favour this plan. He presently had to report 'the most tempestuous weather' he had ever experienced. Returning, sorely battered, to Simon's Bay on August 12th, he was informed that the Dutch squadron had been in Saldhana Bay since the 6th. The wind rose at this point to 'a perfect tempest' which nearly wrecked the *Tremendous*. There was delay, consequently, in putting to sea; and it was not until the 15th that the English squadron sailed. Elphinstone might reasonably, by that time, have expected to find Saldanha Bay empty. With that fatality, however, which attended his operations, Lucas had been holding councils of war. Despite some military opposition, he had managed to water his ships at least sufficiently to enable him to reach the French islands. Even after having decided to go there, on learning of the strength of the English army ashore, he allowed himself to be detained from day to day, partly out of consideration for the sick men he had been forced to land. He was on the point of sailing, on August 16th, when Elphinstone appeared with seven sail of the line, a 50-gun ship, three frigates and three sloops. Now, the Dutch squadron consisted of the following ships: the *Dortrecht* (66), *Revolutie* (66), *Tromp* (54), *Casthor* (44), *Braave* (40), *Bellona* (28), *Sireene* (26), *Havick* (sloop) and *Maria* (storeship). The force included, that is to say, but two ships of the line, and these of inferior force; scarcely the material, Elphinstone thought, for a naval battle. 'Perceiving,' as he afterwards wrote, 'their numbers very inconsiderable in comparison with the Force under my command,' he sent an officer with a flag of truce. After an exchange of messages during the night a Dutch officer came on board the flagship at daybreak and presented proposals for a capitulation. Terms were agreed upon at 5.0 p.m. that day; terms which amounted to an almost unconditional surrender. The Dutch ships were handed over on the 18th and Elphinstone commissioned them all, asking the Admiralty to send out the necessary personnel. The official reply was to the effect that this proceeding was utterly irregular.

The peerage which Elphinstone received as reward for his part in the capture and defence of the Cape was, on the whole, easily earned. He was, no doubt, a very able officer; but, in this affair with the Dutch Rear-Admiral, his success was mainly due to chance. Only after the surrender of Lucas's squadron was it made clear why the Dutch had put in at the Cape at all. With the French co-operation which had been originally promised, something might have been done; but what could be the point of landing a few hundred men on a shore bristling with English bayonets? Lucas was, as we have seen, more or less ignorant of the English preparations. What caused him, however, to bring his squadron into Saldanha Bay, without even a preliminary reconnaissance, was, more than anything else, shortage of water. He had been at sea for months and could not, in any case, have gone any further without replenishment of supplies. He was also, however, belatedly, in pursuit of the *Sceptre* and her convoy which he had sighted on August 1st. Why he failed to put to sea again sooner than he did is, in some degree, mysterious; but why he surrendered so tamely afterwards became apparent—his men had refused to fight. In many respects, then, Elphinstone can be said to have been exceedingly fortunate; in the ample warning he received, for instance, and in the failure of the Dutch to escape from Saldanha Bay before he arrived.

Oddly enough, dismal as was Lucas's failure from the Dutch point of view, his expedition was of definite use to France. By distracting Elphinstone's attention at a critical moment, Lucas may almost be said to have saved the French islands; no mean achievement, although not exactly what he had set out to do. The fact was that, in July, before Lucas appeared, Elphinstone and General Craig had been discussing the possibility of an expedition against the Isle of France. Indeed, the discussions had taken place even earlier, giving way in July to actual preparations. In a dispatch to the Admiralty, Elphinstone began by pointing out that there were troops at the Cape which might with advantage be employed elsewhere.

> Upon this consideration the Isles of Mauritius offer themselves as most conveniently situated for our operations and the Major General having exprefsed his ability to furnish 5000 men for the purpose with every requisite appendage and the necefsary implements, I have consequently determined in concert with the Major General that no time should be lost in preparing to undertake an Attack against those French Isles, and every exertion is now making for this desirable attempt and I hope little doubt is to be entertained for succefs should it be put into execution.
>
> The Mauritius is the only place in these parts in the pofsefsion of the French, its present utility to them is therefore considerable, and affords every refuge and shelter to their Cruizers in these Seas, by which the British Commerce is greatly annoyed; upon these grounds the subduction of it becomes an important value to His Majesty's Service. . . .
>
> But, altho' the proceeding has been thought advisable, and engages my most sanguine wishes, I have counciled with the Major General on the indispensable duty incumbent on us to suffer no dazzling expectation of conquest to relax our using every endeavour for the certain security of our pofsefsion obtained, upon this Colony, to which every other consideration must yield, and nothing be attempted which could probably afford a distant hazard of its being attacked by the Enemy. . . .
>
> (Elphinstone to Admiralty, 30th July, 1796. P.R.O. Ad. 1/55.)

The Admiral and General agreed that nothing should be attempted unless it were possible to leave the Cape with an adequate garrison and adequate naval protection. The ships were sufficient as soon as reinforcements had come from India and England. The troops were available because the army at the Cape included forces actually destined for India, forming no part of the intended garrison of the colony and easily spared, therefore, for other purposes. There was also agreement between the commanders-in-chief on another point, namely, that nothing should be done until after the Dutch effort to recapture the Cape should have failed. The whole question had to be shelved during Lucas's tedious progress towards disaster. For six wearisome months Elphinstone could do little but wait, spiderlike, for his unpunctual victim. On the other hand, once the prey had appeared, the Admiral had other things to attend to. With a captured squadron of nine ships on his hands, he was busy improvising crews and announcing his success. He was even, perhaps, a little impatient to return home and enjoy his laurels. At any rate, there was no more talk of attacking the French islands; and, indeed, after the middle of September it was getting rather late in the year to undertake any such operation.

One result, and that not the least important, of Admiral Lucas's expedition was the separation of the Cape and East Indies stations. However fortunate the event may have proved, the Admiralty had to observe that, when the Cape was first threatened, its naval defender was at Madras. The decision seems, in fact, to have been made in February 1796, as soon as the Dutch designs were known. In a letter to Elphinstone of the 25th, their Lordships announced their intention, 'not doubting' they added, 'but you will see the propriety of this arrangement when you consider the importance of that settlement and the necessity of employing all your attention in endeavouring to secure to this country that valuable possession.' Elphinstone, in his reply dated June 25th, strongly opposed this arrangement. He argued that it was impossible to keep on both stations a force equal to any the enemy could send. If, he pointed out, the flag-officer at the Cape, with the larger force, knew that an enemy squadron had passed him, bound for Goa or Batavia, he would 'not be at liberty to depart himself or to detach a Force for encountering their Designs'; which designs might very probably include the recapture of any Dutch settlements annexed by Rainier, and the intercepting of the China trade. He begged leave to suggest that the Cape and East Indies stations should remain united and that the Cape should be 'the common Rendezvous for the Superior Commander.' He ended with the words 'as the objects of the Expedition entrusted to my Conduct have been accomplished, my only Wish is now to return to Britain; and on the continuance of hostilities to be employed in my former Station under the Command of Earl Howe.' The Admiralty had given him leave to return home when he saw fit, and it was not long before he availed himself of this permission. Admiral Pringle, it will be remembered, was already there, ready to take his place. Before his departure,

Elphinstone made his final arrangements. The plan for the conquest of the Isle of France having been abandoned, he thought it best to institute a blockade, which was to continue until the approach of the hurricane months. For this purpose, he sent a detachment under Captain Losack, consisting of the *Jupiter, Braave, Sceptre, Sybille* and *Sphynx*. The *Braave* was one of the captured Dutch ships, of 40 guns. The *Sybille* was another 40-gun ship, which arrived on September 18th with troops from Gibraltar. The *Trident* and *Fox* (32) sailed to strengthen the East Indies squadron, then weakened by the disablement of the *Orpheus* and the *Heroine* during bad weather in the Bay of Bengal. On October 5th Elphinstone addressed to Pringle a long letter of instructions and advice, and then, on the 7th, sailed for England with the *Monarch* and *Daphne* (20). His departure restored Rainier to his former independence.

CHAPTER IV

Sercey at the Ile de France

COMMODORE RAINIER returned to Madras (September 21st) after the capture of Trincomalee, without waiting for the fall of Colombo. In fact, operations in Ceylon continued, with naval co-operation, well into 1796. It was not until February 15th that Colombo capitulated—not for nothing is its present shopping centre called the Fort —with profit to the captors amounting to £300,000. The naval commander was Captain Alan Hyde Gardner—the Admiral's son—and the *Swift* sloop (16) was commanded by Captain James Sprat Rainier who had just been appointed to a death vacancy. But the elder Rainier, in September 1795, had already been planning the next move. With no news as yet of the success of the expedition to Malacca, but assuming its success, the Commodore was thinking of the Spice Islands. Troops might be lacking for an assault on Batavia itself, but what of (say) Amboyna? The Dutch had always been very secretive about their eastern empire. The time had come, perhaps, to inspect it. The result of discussion with Lord Hobart was a Letter in Council to Rainier dated September 29th.

To His Excellency Commodore Rainier,
    Commander-in-Chief, etc.
Sir,
       In consequence of the communication our President had with you, upon your arrival from Trincomalee, and a conversation from Colonel Brathwaite upon the same subject, we have given orders for two Companys of Europeans and a Battalion of Sepoys to be in readiness to embark immediately and to consider themselves under your orders. We conceive that the first object which will engage your attention will be that of proceeding to Malacca with a view to inform yourself of the situation of affairs there, and, if that place should not have been subdued, to give such aid as may appear to you necessary for its speedy Reduction. The orders from home having particularly directed that we should, in the first instance, turn our attention to Trincomalee, and afterwards progressively to the Molucca Islands, we shall take the liberty of submitting to your consideration the advantage that would result from an early possession of Amboyna, which

we understand to be one of the most valuable; but as we are extremely deficient in point of information with respect to the strength or value of the Dutch Spice Islands; and as so much must depend on the Intelligence you may receive either at Prince of Wales's Island or at Malacca, we should not wish to dwell on any particular object—Satisfied as much of your Prudence and Discretion as we are of your Gallantry and Zeal, we are persuaded that every Exertion that is practicable will be made, and that in whatever way the Troops under your Command may be employed it will equally redound to your credit and the advancement of the Public Service. . . .

   We have the Honour to be
    With great regard and esteem
     Sir
    Your Excellency's most obedient humble Servants,
         Hobart
         Edward Saunders
         E. H. Fallofield

Fort St. George,
29th September
1795.   (Ad. 1/168.)

This was, from Rainier's point of view, very satisfactory. The troops were put under his command and he could do very much as he liked with them. It is observable that the emphasis has now moved from strategic dangers to a question of which islands were 'most valuable.' No one, after all, could pretend that Amboyna was a threat to the China trade or a likely centre for French intrigue. There is no mention, even, of the possibility of the Dutch at Amboyna turning out to be adherents of the Prince of Orange and therefore allies. The object of the expedition was, manifestly, loot. The fly, however, in the ointment was in the superscription 'Commodore . . . Commander-in-Chief.' For Rainier was *not* commander-in-chief. He was Commodore and since May 6th—though he only knew it on the date of the above letter—had been authorized to appoint a captain under him. But two days before, on the 27th, he had received the unwelcome news of Elphinstone's assuming the command. To make matters worse, Elphinstone had been commander-in-chief since August 12th and so would share even in the prize money for Trincomalee—let alone for Colombo and the Moluccas. There *were* flag officers who would have renounced the Admiral's share in such circumstances but Elphinstone—a Scotsman—was not one of them. It was all very exasperating. Consolation came before very long in the shape of his promotion as Rear-Admiral, although it was months before he heard of it.

One advantage resulting from the operations against Trincomalee was

that Rainier's squadron was well concentrated on the coast. The loss of
the *Diomede* was partly made good by the purchase of a French-built 400-ton
ship which was renamed *Hobart* and commissioned as an 18-gun sloop,
with seamen from the *Diomede*. The rest of the frigate's crew was divided
between the other ships from which fifty-eight seamen and marines had
recently been invalided, many from scurvy. On October 11th Rainier
reported to Elphinstone that he was about to sail for Malacca with the
Suffolk (74), *Centurion* (50) and *Swift* (16), expecting to find there the
Resistance (44) and *Orpheus* (32). For trade protection in the bay he left
only the *Heroine* (32), the *Hobart* (18) and the Company's cruisers *Bombay
Frigate* (32) and *Swift* (18). Of these last he had, incidentally, the poorest
opinion. ('There is something in the management of those ships that
disgusts British Sailors'.) He was running rather a risk, but had heard
nothing of the French frigates since the beginning of August and now
learnt (October 12th) that they had been seen in Lat. 10° S. on their way
back to Mauritius. This account was in fact true—they had been frightened
away by a copy of the *Madras Gazette* in which mention was made of the
expected arrival of the *Sceptre* (64). Malacca had fallen, meanwhile, to
Captain Newcome, news of which reached Rainier on October 15th, the
day on which his expedition sailed.[1]

Rainier did not expect any resolute resistance from the Dutch. They
had only two men-of-war (as he knew) and were divided among themselves
on the political issue. His main opposition would come from uncharted
waters, short supplies and disease. He reached Penang on November 14th
with his men-of-war, three transports, troops totalling 317 Europeans and
596 Indians and artillery comprising four 18-pounders, two 8-inch mortars
and two 6-pounder field guns. There he made careful inquiries about the
Dutch Indies and decided to approach Amboyna via the 'Straits of Sinca-
pour.' He next went to Malacca, where he found, to his annoyance, that
the Dutch governor had been left in office by the military commander,
Major Brown. Rainier dissolved the Government at once and appointed
Brown as governor; but finding him too lenient in confiscating public
stores, allowed him to resign the office. He reported to Elphinstone
(27th December, 1795) that he was sending the former Dutch governor
to Madras

> . . . which was becoming necessary from the great influence the Dutch
> had acquired, and were allowed to go on to increase in the plan of Govern-
> ment Major Brown seemed disposed to adopt. The removal of the Governor,

[1] See *Journal of a Voyage through the Straits of Malacca* by Captain W. C. Lennon, 1796–97.
Journal of the Straits Branch of the Royal Asiatic Society, June 1881.

tho' oppressive to my own feelings, appears to me a measure of unavoidable expediency to convince the Inhabitants, particularly the Chinese and Malays and the traders from the Eastward, that the Settlement is under his Majesty's Dominion. . . .

Allow me with all due respect to suggest that should circumstances admit, there is little doubt but the Island of Java, the Bengal of the Dutch, will be an easy capture. . . .

(Ad. 1/168.)

However other people might view the matter, Rainier regarded himself as at war with the Dutch; and there can be no doubt that, for all practical purposes, he was right.

No account seems readily available of the means by which Rainier reached Amboyna. That he had Dutch pilots seems more than likely, and he is known to have had valuable assistance from Captain Page of the *Hobart*, and a pilot called Mr. Shaw. He certainly chose the right season for his expedition when the north-east monsoon would help him, and chose the right time again for his return. He must, nevertheless, have been relieved to find himself off Amboyna on February 16th with his squadron intact and ready to avenge the massacre which took place there in 1623. He found, as he had expected, that the Dutch were in no position to resist him. They had received no reinforcements from Holland for some years and little news, even, since 1794. The European population of Java was said to number about two thousand, a third of them sick. To them in December had come the news of peace with France, brought simultaneously by an American brig from Europe and by messengers from the Ile de France. The governor had shut himself up and failed to appear in Council for over a year, it was said, and then came down heavily on the French side. There was endless quarrelling among the higher officials, ending in the governor's removal. But the pro-French party came into power with the news of the peace. At one stage they were sending envoys to the Sultan of Java with the unhopeful mission of explaining to him the principles of Equality and Fraternity. Their crestfallen return did not perceptibly damp the democratic ardour of their friends but left no one in any doubt as to what the Sultan thought of liberalism. He was, it seems, against it.

Upon this disorganized Dutch Empire Rainier fell on 16th February, 1796, landing and taking possession of Amboyna, capital of the Moluccas. The occupation was complete by the 18th. Having thus cornered the bulk of the world's supply of cloves, Rainier went on to Banda which he reached on March 7th and occupied by the 9th after some slight resistance. The garrison of Amboyna numbered 841, that of Banda 432, with no less than

260 cannon. The booty came to about 184,000 rix-dollars, apart from the spices at Banda. The Banda warehouses were chiefly stored with nutmegs and mace but Rainier now learnt, to his surprise, that there were more nutmegs and cloves on Ternate. He was planning how to secure these when news came (about the first week in April) 'of an almost general Insurrection among the Natives . . . [in Amboyna] . . . not without the stimulus of some opium sold by the *Armenia* Transport.' Rainier quietened this revolt but immediately heard of the intended rebellion of a Moslem Rajah whose general intention was to exterminate the Christian Rajahs, 'particularly the one most attached to us of any.' Rainier found himself becoming involved in commitments which he had not foreseen. He could not simply destroy the Dutch power, collect the booty and sail for India. He had, besides, trouble in procuring supplies and sent to Canton for, among other things, cordage, sugar, rice and cocoa. He offered to pay for them, as well he might, in spices. The upshot was that he was detained among the islands for nearly the whole of 1796, not sailing from Amboyna until December 1st. On the 8th he issued his final instructions to Captain Pakenham of the *Resistance*, a ship which had recently been crammed with nutmeg and mace but was now to remain with the *Amboyna* brig and the H.C. Frigate *Bombay*. Pakenham was to defend the captured islands and add Great Timor to them. He was to do surveying work and see whether the shoals were as laid down in the Dutch charts. He was to watch out for any hostile armament. Rainier, meanwhile, would call at Macao and collect the homeward-bound Indiamen before returning, via Penang, to Madras. It was none too soon for, other considerations apart, the *Suffolk* had 200 men sick out of 481, and the *Swift* 41 men sick out of 107. To set against that, the captains' prize money was reputed to be about £15,000 each and Rainier's more in proportion. For the first time, moreover, since the seventeenth century, England had a footing in the Malay Archipelago.

Rainier had left Madras on 15th October, 1795. He returned there on 13th February, 1797, to find himself once more commander-in-chief and now, in addition, a Rear-Admiral of the Blue. It was a long period of absence and much might have happened in the meanwhile. Much, indeed, *had* happened. It is fair to remember, however, that Elphinstone made a brief visit to Madras on 15th January, 1796, with the *Monarch* (74), *Arrogant* (74), and the sloops *Echo* and *Rattlesnake*. He remained there refitting his ships and arranging for trade protection until March 23rd, when he sailed for the Cape. He left orders for two ships of the line and two frigates, when available, to blockade Batavia and protect the homeward-bound China trade. For the rest, he was chiefly interested in plans for blockading, or ultimately capturing, the French islands. He was back at the Cape by May 23rd. Six days later he heard that a French frigate squadron had entered the Indian Ocean. The information was quite definite, for the *Sphynx* (28) had been chased by them off the False Cape. More than that, the French ships had taken the whaler *Lord Hawkesbury* on May 15th in Lat. 31° S. and Long. 8° E. A prize crew of thirteen men was put on board and only two of the English crew retained. These, Robert Morrow and David Laing, being allowed to take their spell at the wheel, put the vessel on shore about 150 leagues to the eastward of Simon's Bay.

> The information from the several Persons saved from the wreck of the *Lord Hawkesbury* does not afford a certainty of the present Track of the Frigates, or I should have dispatched some of His Majesty's Ships in pursuit of them, and the very tempestuous weather prevailing has also tended to prevent the attempt; but I shall use every endeavour to counteract their Designs, and if they remain in these Parts I hope to be able to transmit welcome accounts of them.
>
> (Elphinstone to Admiralty, 24th June, 1796. Ad. 1/55.)

Elphinstone was still, it must be remembered, waiting for his unpunctual Dutch opponent, and so unable to weaken his own squadron materially. Rainier was out of touch. Of his disposition Elphinstone had written plaintively: '. . . the object of the Rear-Admiral will doubtless be conducive to the British Interest; but another arrangement might have retained the Naval Force more collected and prepared for Services not so remote' (23rd February, 1796, Ad. 1/55). This was profoundly true, but the fact remained that the French had possibly eight large frigates and two corvettes in the Indian Ocean, with very little (if they but knew it) to oppose them. Of the two English flag officers one was at the Cape and the other in the Moluccas. Elphinstone considered the idea of attacking Mauritius. Then he abandoned that plan and reverted to the idea of a blockade. But how could he maintain a blockading squadron superior to the force they were now to blockade? He asked the Admiralty for reinforcements but was well aware that the damage might be done before they could arrive. The next move lay with the French.

Fortunately for Elphinstone and Rainier the settlers at the Isle of France were not at this moment pondering how best to attack British India. They were rather planning how to defy Republican France in the matter of the abolition of slavery. Developments were slow, however, and it was not until 21st September, 1795, a year after the first news came of the threatened change, that the colonists had any definite orders to defy. The orders, moreover, when they came, were easy to set aside as irregular in not being addressed to the Colonial Assembly. They were accompanied by fervent appeals signed by the colony's own deputies in the National Convention and directed to the troops and the national guard. The brave citizens were urged, in these appeals, to enforce the Decree of 16 Pluviose, An 2. There would be opposition, it was admitted, from slave-owners and from the rich generally; but, in that case, all the citizens had to do was to treat them as public enemies. As it happened, these appeals never reached the people to whom they were addressed. The Colonial Committee of Public Safety read the documents and arranged that they should go no farther than the Colonial Assembly; first trying, indeed, to prevent them going as far. It was then decided to ignore the Decree and shelve for the present all the papers relating to it. In view of the fact that both the Committee and Assembly were mainly filled by the wealthy slave-owners who were to be dealt with so severely, this decision was not surprising. As a conciliatory step, however, and to soften their opposition on the main point, the colonists agreed to abolish the trade in slaves, as opposed to the ownership of those already in the islands.

The Convention which originally passed the Decree might perhaps have overlooked the colonists' inactivity in this matter, but the Committee of Public Safety was made of sterner stuff. It was decided to follow up the Decree by a mission sent to see that the settlers obeyed it; a mission to consist of two fully-empowered agents and an escort of troops. The agents chosen were MM. Baco and Burnel. Baco was an honest man and an ardent, if not particularly tactful, republican. Burnel was the Directory's authority on the affairs of the Isle of France, he having lived there for four years as editor of a local newspaper. He had the reputation of a local politician given to intrigue. The two agents, with their secretary, sailed from Rochefort on 4th March, 1796. With them went four frigates under Rear-Admiral Sercey and a body of troops under General Magallon de la Morlière. It was fortunate for the British that this squadron was as small as it was. The frigates were originally to have numbered six. Then, in May 1795, Rear-Admiral Kerguelen suggested that the frigates should be followed up by two 74-gun ships, a suggestion which was negatived (Archives Nat. BB⁴ 86). Possible commanders whose names were put forward were Vanstabel, Bouvet and Lacrosse. But the Marquis Pierre-César-Charles-Guillaume de Sercey was, on the face of it, a better choice. He had been born in the Ile de France, to begin with, and had served in the Indian Ocean in 1767–70. He had become captain in 1791, Rear-Admiral in 1793, and had been at St. Domingo during the risings there, being instrumental in saving six thousand colonists. After a period in prison he had been reinstated (on

Robespierre's fall) in 1794 and was now chosen as a rising officer and a native of the island he was to save from the enemy.

It was, no doubt, disconcerting for Sercey to learn from the Minister of Marine and Colonies (Vice-Admiral Truguet) that he was virtually under the orders of the two agents.

> 'Cés agents' [wrote Truguet firmly] 'étant revetus d'une autorité superiure, je leur ai communiqué les Instructions qui vous ont été expediees afin de leur faire connaitre l'objet et les details de la mission dont vous etes chargé —Vous vondriez bien sommettre à leur approbation les mesures que vous croiez convenable prendre, non seulement sur l'emploi des forces navale qui vous sont confieés mais encore sur les differents objets de service que vous devez remplir. J'attend de votre zéle et de votre patriotism . . . a executer leurs ordres, vous donnerez l'example des égards et de la deference qui sont dus á leur caractere et á l'autorité que le Directoire leur a déléguée.'

(Archives Nat. BB⁴ 86.)

Sercey had been too recently under the shadow of the guillotine to look too dubiously at orders like these. He looked perhaps with more concern at the agents themselves. He hoisted his flag, nevertheless, in the *Forte* (44), and assumed command of a squadron comprising the *Régénérée* (36) and *Seine* (36), with two corvettes, *Bonne-Citoyenne* and *Mutine*. The *Vertu* (40) was to follow and did so. With General Magallon went eight hundred troops, two companies of artillery and a quantity of munitions and equipment for the Ile de France. As Malartic pointed out, the colony had received no men, money, supplies, arms or ammunition since January 1793; so this aid was, if anything, overdue. The squadron sailed on 4th March, 1796.

The voyage was not, from Sercey's point of view, a particularly happy one. He rather liked Baco but found Burnel extremely tiresome. The former used to explain to him that his colleague was very good-hearted, really, but that authority had gone to his head. Later in the voyage the two agents quarrelled with each other in 'scenes bien scandaleuses' and all too public. From verbal abuse, on one occasion, they went on to fisticuffs and ended by trying to throw each other overboard. Sercey, who would by then have been glad if they had both succeeded, separated them with difficulty and vented his annoyance in a private letter to Truguet (Archives Nat. BB⁴ 86). In reality, the Admiral would have had more cause for anxiety if the agents had been more dignified. For he thoroughly disliked their mission and wanted, if he could, to procure its failure. For a raid on the Bay of Bengal Sercey was well chosen. For assisting to abolish slavery in the Ile de France he was unsuitable. For one thing, he was an aristocrat and a native of the island, brought up among a slavery in which he thoroughly believed. For another, he had seen, at St. Domingo, exactly what was likely to happen when the slaves should be freed. Those scenes he did not wish to see again. From this point of view, the agents' behaviour (which he possibly exaggerated) was playing into his hands.

Both Sercey's sloops parted company from him, crippled by bad weather in the Bay of Biscay, and both were captured by a British frigate squadron, the *Mutine* while on her way back to France. The three frigates, however, reached the Canaries where the *Vertu* (40) joined them. Sailing thence, Sercey captured the *Lord Hawkesbury*, as we have seen, followed by a Portuguese Indiaman, chased the *Sphynx*, took another prize, the *Montrose*, and, on June 18th, reached Port Louis in the Ile de France. The *Prudente* (36) and *Cybèle* (40) were there and the British ships which had been blockading them had withdrawn. It was a 'decadi,' the republican sabbath, and the principal inhabitants were mostly out of town. They reassembled, however, in Port Louis as soon as the news came, and three delegates were sent on board the flagship as soon as the squadron dropped anchor. Ascertaining something of the purpose of the agents' coming, these delegates sent one of their number ashore, ostensibly to arrange for an official reception. The other two tried to gain time by raising intricate points of etiquette. The Colonial Assembly, they insisted, liked to do things with all proper solemnity. In point of fact, the arrangements for the official reception included the drawing up of troops along the shore, and the sounding them as to their willingness to fire on the squadron. It seems more than likely that it was Sercey who warned the delegates of the agents' intentions and hinted at his own sympathy with the colonists. He and Malartic moved very circumspectly. Sercey may, however, have persuaded Magallon to place himself under Malartic's orders and so avoid taking sides. The attitude of the troops proving ambiguous, the envoys were, very reluctantly, allowed to land. The troops from the squadron were also allowed to land on the following day. Baco and Burnel, once ashore, lectured the Assembly, disclosed dictatorial powers and threatened the Colony with dire penalties for disobedience. After talking of dissolving the Assembly, deposing the governor and deporting all who opposed them, the agents heard of a plot to assassinate them and hastily took refuge in the barracks. The Assembly having flatly refused to obey the Decree, the agents tried to persuade Magallon to use force. That astute officer referred them to General Malartic, his senior in rank. As for Malartic, his conduct appears to have been non-committal. Events then followed swiftly. Narrowly escaping being shot, Baco and Burnel were hustled on board ship amidst scenes of tumult, while the troops in barracks were surrounded by the National Guard and threatened with cannon. The corvette *Moineau*, in which the agents had taken refuge, received orders from Malartic to sail at once under sealed instructions. These instructions, when opened, directed the captain to proceed to the Philippines. Under threats from the agents, however, the captain disobeyed orders and took his two passengers back to France. They fully expected to be able to return at the head of an army. Instead, however, they found the political situation altered, and a new Government in office which felt no inclination to interfere further in the matter.

Elphinstone had early information of the above events, if only in outline, for the *Moineau* fell in with and pillaged a vessel belonging to the East India Company called the *Lady Shore*. This vessel was released and reached the Cape on July 21st, bringing the news of the agents' discomfiture. It was this news which filled the Admiral with ideas about conquering the French islands, for he and General Craig were partly convinced that the inhabitants would, at this juncture, welcome British protection. Some such offer seems, in fact, to have been sent to the islands; only, of course, to be refused. Nevertheless, while in no mood to admit an English garrison, the colonists were for a time very anxious about their relations with France. They were, moreover, expecting an attack from the Cape, as Elphinstone learnt from prisoners. From the same source he gathered that the settlers might accept British rule 'if their property were secure,' but that they 'did not much like accounts of what the English did at the taking of Martinico.' Altogether, this was an anxious period at the Isle of France. There seems even to have been a certain shortage of provisions there; a shortage which would have been more serious but for the frequent arrival of American merchantmen. Many vessels, it may be added, came from India 'under the Colors of various Eastern Country Powers and other disguised pretensions.' These were often commanded by British seamen and, very probably, it was thought, owned by British merchants, who were always apt to do business 'to the Destruction of their Country's Interests.'

Sercey, now rid of the two deputies, turned his attention with relief to his proper business of commerce destruction. He now felt the loss of his two corvettes and requisitioned, in their place, a privateer schooner called *l'Alerte*. With this vessel to do the scouting, he sailed on 14th July, 1796 (after refitting) with a squadron of six frigates—*Forte* (44), *Prudente* (40), *Seine* (44), *Régénérée* (36), *Cybèle* and *Vertu*. The *Preneuse* and *Brule-Gueule* (32) he sent to cruise in the Mozambique Channel and *Coureur* (20) apparently left behind, perhaps as being too slow. The French squadron steered for Ceylon before the monsoon and sighted it on August 14th. It does not appear that Sercey had any inkling of his opportunity. He could, had he known it, have raided Madras or blockaded the Hooghly. He was heading for a vast gap in the English defences and could have safely swept the Bay of Bengal for a month. It was natural, however, for him to assume that the bay must be defended and his first need was to find out where its defenders lay. He sent the *Alerte* to find out, cruising off Ceylon to await her return. Drieu, however, the commander of the *Alerte*, was a born privateersman and wanted not information but prize money. On the night of August 19th he attacked a supposed Indiaman, which turned out to be the *Carysfort* (28). The presence of this frigate was more or less accidental —she had just brought out dispatches from England. The *Alerte*, when taken, was found to contain papers giving full details of Sercey's intended cruise; papers which Drieu had not the sense (or perhaps the time) to destroy. It was, for Sercey, an extraordinary misfortune. As for Captain Alexander, of the *Carysfort*, he had a difficult problem and no Admiral nearer than Capetown to whom to report. His solution was as good as any. He 'planted' on Sercey, presumably in some native vessel, the information that there were four ships of the line at Madras. As a result, the French Admiral ventured no farther north than Tranquebar—which two of his frigates raided—and presently sailed for the Straits of Malacca.

Sercey's object was to raid Penang. Given a stronger squadron and some troops, he would have been glad, no doubt, to capture the island and use it as a base. Francis Light had been nervous in 1794 that such an attempt would be made.[1] But Sercey was not in Suffren's position. He had no ships of the line and, much as he might have desired a forward base against India, he had no means of holding it. Penang was in no state, however, to resist a raid, being almost unfortified at this period and far from any other settlement. As for naval protection, Rainier was still in the Moluccas, as Sercey no doubt eventually realized. Sercey was off Sumatra on September 1st and took several prizes in the roads at Acheen. He had just added a country ship, the *Favourite*, to his score and was relieving her of stores when, on the 8th, two large ships were sighted to leeward. That Sercey was unlucky must be allowed. They were two 74-gun ships, the *Arrogant* and *Victorious*, and their presence there was almost by chance. Admiral Elphinstone, in quitting India, had made arrangements (see page 90) for blockading Batavia and protecting the China trade. These had coincided with Rainier's demands for supplies, with the result that the *Victorious* had sailed to escort a transport round Acheen, bound for the eastwards, and the *Arrogant* (one of

[1] See *Malay's First British Pioneer*, H. P. Clodd, London, 1948.

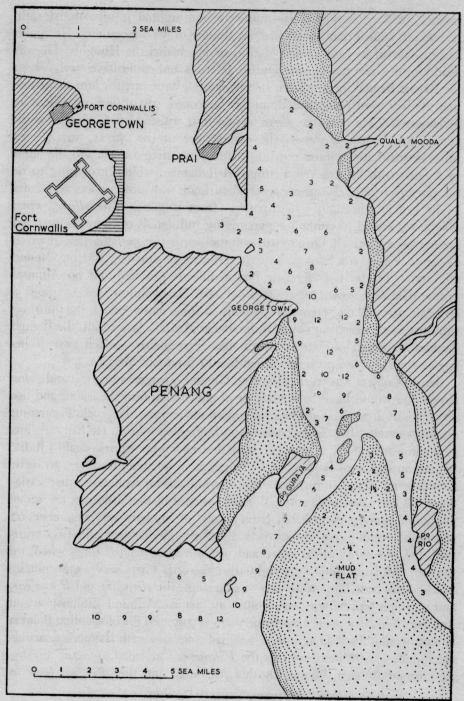

Elphinstone's ships from the Cape) sailed from Madras on July 31st, partly to escort transports and partly to protect ships bound to China from Bombay. Captain Lucas, of the *Arrogant*, had reached Penang on August 3rd, to find there the *Centurion* and *Orpheus* but not the *Victorious*, which was escorting a transport back to Madras. The *Orpheus* had been crippled in a gale. Lucas, acting apparently on some rumour of the French approach, succeeded in recalling the *Victorious*, 'Thinking it of the greatest consequence to collect all the Force I could,' but did not think himself justified in detaining the *Centurion*, which was wanted to escort the China ships. On August 25th the *Hobart* sloop arrived from Bengal with dispatches from Elphinstone and the Governor-General, addressed to Rainier. These Lucas opened and learnt of the danger, or as he put it, 'found the situation I was in with so small a Force.' The *Orpheus* at that moment was without fore-mast, mizzen-mast and bowsprit, and the *Hobart* scarcely to be kept afloat in harbour. Lucas had accordingly decided to sail for Trincomalee and Madras, hoping to refit, revictual and return with reinforcements. He had sailed on September 1st, and now sighted Sercey's squadron at daybreak on the 8th.

It would probably be true to say that neither side was very keen to fight. The issue of an action between two 74-gun ships and six frigates would be doubtful, depending much on the weather. Sercey was bent on commerce destruction and did not want to see his frigates crippled. He would have avoided action if he could. Lucas, on the other hand, was aware of what might happen if Sercey sailed on his way unopposed. He went in pursuit, explaining afterwards.

> The critical situation I now found myself in and the advantage they might take, it being doubtful my falling in with them again, and the probability of their meeting the *Centurion* on her return thro' the Streight and believe me, Sir, Rear-Admiral Rainier's critical situation to the Eastward was not forgot: nor the protection of the different Settlements in this Country, all these circumstances determined me to risque an action. . . .
> (Lucas to Elphinstone, 17th October, 1796. Ad. 1/168.)

The settlement immediately to be considered was Penang, with the crippled *Orpheus* and *Hobart*. Given such full information as the French might obtain, say, at Malacca (after capturing it), there was nothing to prevent them going eastwards and catching Rainier with his sickly crews and dispersed ships in the Moluccas. Lucas had no alternative but to fight. He followed the French frigates throughout the 8th, watching for a favourable opportunity; attempted to cut off their two rear ships (without success) on the morning of the 9th, and shortly afterwards (at 7.20 a.m.)

engaged the enemy squadron at an opening range of 240 yards. The *Victorious* was then close astern of the *Arrogant* and their immediate opponents were the four heaviest frigates (*Vertu, Seine, Forte* and *Régénérée*) sailing in line ahead.

In considering the accounts of the action which followed, two factors seem so far to have been insufficiently stressed. First, the French flagship, the *Forte*, was an exceptionally large frigate—in fact, an 80-gun ship cut down, mounting thirty 24-pounders with fifty-two guns in all (enough, Sercey found, to strain her timbers). She was something equivalent to the British *Indefatigable* and Lucas, in fact, mistook her at first for a ship of the line. The second factor to be noted is the mishandling of the *Victorious* as apparent from the *Arrogant's* log.

> . . . at 6 the Enemy showed their colours, same time showed ours, the Enemy wore and stood towards us forming the Line of Battle ahead—10 Ms. past 7 perceiving the *Victorious* lower Deck Guns not run out, hailed Captain Clarke 'and desired him to run them out as the Enemy had attempted to fire several Guns but they would not go off.' His answer was 'that he wished to wear and stand in shore upon the other tack to examine him, as he was afraid they were in the same state'—assented to it, but 6 Ms. after hailed Captain Clarke and informed him we should not have time to wear . . . therefore desired him to haul his, wind again upon the Starboard Tack and keep close under our stern, which he did—at 20' past 7 four of the Enemy's Ships being with their heads towards us, we began to engage, dist. about 1 cable length and fired two broadsides into them before they could get a gun to bear upon us . . . received several shots from the *Victorious*, one of which was between wind and water. At ½ past 7 it fell quite calm. . . .

Now, it is understandable that powder should become moist in the Straits of Malacca. But the *Victorious* had been in the presence of the enemy since the day before. Thus, the *Arrogant* had cleared for action soon after 9.0 a.m. on the 8th—as soon as the private signal was not answered. Here, however, was a ship with her lower battery unready for action ten hours later. Note, too, that the accidental hits scored on her consort were not in the heat of a confused action but almost before the battle had begun. At about 8.0 Captain Clarke was wounded and Lieutenant Waller, taking command, allowed the *Victorious* to become separated from the *Arrogant*. As Captain Lucas reported of Waller 'he wore without any Signal or Order, by which means he got the ship raked by most of the Enemy's ships as they passed.' Worse than that, the *Victorious* was becalmed in the midst of the enemy squadron and the *Arrogant* unable to help her. Indeed, at 9.30, the *Arrogant* reopened fire at a range of one mile and was still at extreme range when Sercey broke off the action at 11.0. The *Victorious* was too crippled to pursue and Lucas ordered Waller to steer for Penang.

'... am sorry to add' [concluded Lucas] 'by that officer's imprudence in getting her head a different way from the *Arrogant* exposed the ship to the whole of the Enemy's Fire, which rendered her incapable of renewing the action when every advantage might have been taken; the enemy having got their sweeps out and making off by every possible means they could use.

In bringing the said ships to action, I am happy to say, it proved so far fortunate as to oblige them to give up their expedition and quit the Straits of Malacca and I have every reason to suppose they were sick of the business. Two of them were so much disabled as to be obliged to steer with sweeps, they afterwards were taken in tow and appeared to make a great deal of Water; they made all the sail they could to get off.'

(Ad. 1/55.)

It was an unsatisfactory action from the British point of view and the *Victorious* had suffered fairly heavy casualties (17 killed and 55, including two officers, wounded). On the other hand, the French frigates had 42 killed and 104 wounded between them, with enough material damage to compel them to refit. For this purpose Sercey went to the Mergui archipelago and did not sail again until early October. His immediate mission had failed.

The French Admiral could obtain only a partial refit at Ile-du-Roi, his Mergui anchorage. He managed there to replace masts and spars but two of his frigates needed docking. When he sailed again, therefore, in early October, he made but a short visit to the Bay of Bengal—during which he took nothing—and then made for Batavia, arriving there at the end of November. He expected to find there a Dutch squadron with which to co-operate. He also wanted still more urgently docking facilities, cordage and sailcloth. Dutch naval co-operation was not forthcoming, but he did obtain at Batavia the stores he needed with a promise of rice for the Ile de France. He was there for two months altogether and then on 4th January, 1797, sailed to intercept the homeward-bound China fleet. On January 28th he met his prey off the east end of Java. The Select Committee of Super-cargoes at Canton had heard, of course, of the French Admiral being at Batavia and had decided not to let the returning Indiamen risk the Straits of Sunda. Their precise orders for the ships to use the Straits of Sapi or Allas were addressed to Captain Lestock Wilson,[1] who is not mentioned, however, in James's account (Vol. II, p. 89) of the sequel, perhaps because of a change in plan. It was Charles Lennox, it seems, who led the Indiamen

[1] H. B. Morse. *Chronicles of the East India Company Trading to China, 1635–1834*, Vol. II, Oxford, 1926, p. 291.

through the Straits of Bali. This decision was forced on them, to some extent, by Rainier, who called at Macao on December 30th, with the *Suffolk* and *Swift*, and collected there four East Indiamen and two other ships. These he escorted through the Straits of Malacca, without waiting for the other six Indiamen expected. This may have been because his ships needed refitting or because the six East Indiamen preferred their own route. It seems more than probable that Rainier expected trouble, if any, in the Malacca Straits and thought the Bali route safe. Unfortunately, Sercey heard of this plan and, while Rainier escorted one small convoy through the Straits of Malacca, Sercey was waiting for the others off the east point of Java. He was none too sure, however, of the intelligence he had received, and half-expected Rainier to appear, after all. Having had one encounter with two 74-gun ships, the French Admiral was in no mood for another. The sequel was an instance—and not the last to be here recorded—of an intelligent plan being ruined by an excess of imagination. Apart from that, however, Sercey had no orders to seek and destroy the enemy—quite the reverse—and he had just seen his squadron immobilized for three months as the result of an action forced upon him. He was, therefore, in cautious mood.

Captain Lennox may have sensed what Sercey's anxiety would be likely to be. At any rate, on sighting the French, he formed a line of battle, hoisted a Rear-Admiral's flag and ordered the other Indiamen to hoist blue ensigns and naval pendants. When Sercey detached the *Cybèle* to reconnoitre the enemy, Lennox followed suit with two ships—which would, of course, prevent the French frigate having too close a view of the *Woodford* and *Ocean*. In rough weather and a bad light they sufficiently looked the part, and Captain Therouart reported to his Admiral that he had recognized two ships of the line and four frigates. Sercey believed this report and made sail away from this evidently superior force. Nor was his action altogether unreasonable. He would have learnt at Batavia all about Rainier's operations in the Moluccas. There was nothing, he knew, inherently unlikely about finding a British Rear-Admiral in the Straits of Bali. If Rainier had completely ignored the duties of commerce protection, he might have returned by that route. In fact, however, on January 28th, Rainier was at Penang. By February 13th he was at Madras. Sercey, meanwhile, returned to the Ile de France, closely pursued by the story of how he had been chased by the merchantmen. That had certainly been a wasted opportunity and a source of mirth to the enemy. But his whole cruise had been, in a sense, a wasted opportunity. He had approached India when most possible naval opponents were off the Cape or in the Moluccas. He had been driven from the Coromandel coast by a false report, driven from the Straits of Malacca by two 74-gun ships and finally driven from Java by a piece of bluff. The Dutch empire had been ransacked while he was fighting with shadows.

When compared with that of the French privateers, Sercey's achievement appeared even more meagre than it was. For the opportunity afforded in 1796 was not neglected by everyone. It was not overlooked by Robert Surcouf, for example, of St. Malo. Whereas, in general, any detailed account of privateer activities must be deemed impossible, to ignore Surcouf is equally impossible. Of his contemporaries one may say that the facts about them would be difficult to verify; and, once established, more difficult to present. It would be like chronicling the morning's activities of eight or ten blue-bottles; and rather secretive blue-bottles at that. But more is known of Surcouf than the rest. We know, for example, that he was born in 1773, the son of a Breton noble and a descendant of Duguay Trouin. He came out to the Ile de France as a boy of sixteen, and served in a slaver called the *Aurore*, which stowed as many as six hundred slaves. Four years later he was commanding a small slaver called the *Creole* and continued to do business after the trade was officially abolished. The resource he displayed in evading punishment for this offence so impressed two local ship-owners that they offered him the command of a ship called the *Modeste*. This vessel, mounting fifteen 6-pounders and manned by thirty men, had apparently been built originally as a privateer. Although measuring only 180 tons, she had performed successful voyages under Guerroniere of Nantes and Le Vaillant of Bordeaux—the latter being now one of her owners. She came out from France before the war began and, after refitting, was eventually renamed *l'Emilie* and equipped once more as a privateer. Seven or eight letters of marque seem to have been issued early in the war, and Malartic refused to issue any more, explaining that applications were numerous and that some must be refused if the island were not to be left defenceless, without male inhabitants of military age. Surcouf sailed, nevertheless, without letters of marque, partly in order to fetch supplies for the Ile de France, then suffering from shortage. This was on 3rd September, 1795. Calling at the Seychelles early in October, he sailed from there for the Bay of Bengal, making his way northward by coasting the Nicobars and the shores of Pegu. Taking an English vessel called the *Penguin* laden with timber, which he sent back to the Isle of France, he went on and arrived off the Sandheads in January 1796.

In contrasting, as one cannot avoid doing, the comparative success of cruiser and privateer, one must remember that a man like Surcouf had great opportunities for gaining information. Formerly a trader himself, he knew by what routes merchantmen would pass and when. He knew whom to question and how much to believe. It was more probably from design than luck that he arrived off the Hooghly when Elphinstone was at Madras but shortly due to sail for the Cape. It was certainly no accident that brought him there during the north-east monsoon when no French privateers were expected. And, once there, he did not waste his opportunity. He began by taking two merchant ships, the *Russell* and *Sambolasse*, together with a pilot brig. Transferring himself with twenty-three men to the brig, which he renamed the *Cartier*, he sent *l'Emilie* home with the prizes.

In the brig *Cartier* Surcouf had the perfect privateer; perfect, at least, for the station on which he was now cruising. It was the privateer's object to avoid fighting, it must be remembered, and especially to avoid cannonading. A prize with her masts and rigging shot to pieces was not easy to remove from the scene of the capture. It was by boarding, therefore, that the privateer captain liked to seize his prey; and boarding necessitates either a stealthy approach or an approach in disguise. In a pilot brig off the Sandheads, Surcouf was disguised to perfection. Not only was his appearance above suspicion, he could also be sure that his victims would seek him out. The *Cartier's* first prize was a Bengal rice-ship, the *Diana*, taken off Point Palmyras on January 28th. On the following day the H.C.S. *Triton* appeared, bound from Madras to Bengal. What followed may best be gathered from two contemporary accounts which appeared in the *Calcutta Gazette*. The first, from Captain Tapson, of the *Diana*, relates in turn the capture of that ship, and then the affair with the *Triton*. The second is based, apparently, on first-hand evidence taken from the Indiaman's crew.

> On the 28th ultimo, about half past seven P.M., we were on larboard tacks (wind at south south-east), and discovered a 'Snow' on the weather-bow close to us. I took no notice of her, as she passed without hailing; about twenty minutes after, it was perceived that she had tacked, and was close under our lee quarter. I consequently concluded it was an enemy, and immediately altered my course to north-west with the intention to run the ship on shore, if possible, and began trimming the sails to that course.
>
> She then hailed me in broken English, 'What ships that hoa?' I answered in English 'Man of War.' I was then told with harsh language to haul down my colours and strike. I desired them to wait a little, and I would tell them a different story, on which she gave us a volley of musketry and guns from the side next us and passed ahead. The shot went through our sails and topmast rigging. That myself and two mates were left to ourselves is not to be wondered at, as I had a most wretched crew. Whilst the privateer was

veering, I prevailed on a few to come on deck, and by the time she came abreast of us again, we had the sails trimmed to a fine breeze. My people then went below. I asked the chief mate M. Strange whether he or I should take the helm; he went to it cheerfully, and I pointed out to him a prospect of our reaching the shore. She then gave us the other broad-side and the musketry: the second mate and myself stood by the capstern; the shot came pretty thick, several struck our sides, and one lodged in the capstern.

She dropped so far astern before she wore the second time; that if the *Diana* had been a better sailor, we should have escaped.

Before she came near us again, I sounded in twenty-seven fathoms, got a light and a compass in the gun room, and cut the tiller ropes; as we could steer and manage the ship below, we all left the decks.

When they got alongside us again, they hailed us, and threatened to put every man to the sword if we did not strike. I went on deck, but gave no answer; perceiving them close under our lee bow, we had nothing left but to give them the stem: and disable both ships. I consequently called to the mate below to put the helm hard a-port, and we ran on board her abreast the main mast. We had not weight enough to run her down, but carried away our jibboom.

Our bowsprit was then lashed to their main mast, and they came on board, on which I told them not to commit murder, the ship was theirs. I was at the juncture particularly fortunate in talking French. The Frenchmen behaved gallantly to a man, and did not offer to ill-treat us.

As soon as the ships were disentangled from each other, the Captain desired the man that had charge of the *Diana* to send me and my two mates to him: we accordingly went and found her to be the *Cartier*, a prize to the enemy's privateers of the Mauritius, and commanded by M. Sieurcouff.

He received us well, told us we had given him much trouble: but that he did not blame us.

His and his Surgeon's behaviour to us was very brave and honourable, as indeed was that of his officers, and people in general, whilst I remained his prisoner.

At four a.m. the two vessels tacked and we immediately discovered a sail which they gave chase to.

About seven o'clock the ship hoved too, and as she had a jack at the fore, I concluded it was meant as a deception, and that they knew of the Pilot Schooner's being taken, particularly as we were at least forty miles to the southward of pilot's water. I, however, found, to my mortification, that the Indiamen's people were deceived by the appearance of the snow, and being off their guard, were made an easy prize of.

By what I learn of this extraordinary circumstance, the people were so much terrified on board the Indiaman, under a supposition of their deck being full of armed men, and that the other ship was also about to attack them, that they could not be prevailed on by their officers to rally, and go on the upper deck. Captain Burnyeat and Lieutenant Pickett were entirely deserted and shot, and several of the people wounded. Two of the Frenchmen were wounded, one by a random shot from their own vessel, and the other by a cutlass.

11th February, 1796.

On Friday last accounts were received in town of the capture of the Hon'ble Company's Ship *Triton*, Captain Burnyeat, off Juggernath Pagoda, on her passage from Madras to Bengal. The particulars of this unfortunate event we understood to be as follows:—

Early on Friday morning, the 29th ultimo, a Pilot Schooner was seen from the *Triton* on her larboard bow, on which Captain Burnyeat ordered the ship to be hove too. The schooner approached till within fifteen or twenty fathoms, and Captain Burnyeat was in the act of hailing her, when she fired a volley of musquetry immediately on the people on the *Triton's* deck, on which Captain Burnyeat called his men to their quarters, but unfortunately all who were on deck, the Captain, Lieutenant Pickett, Mr. Agnew, Midshipman, the man at the helm, a quartermaster, Mr. Jackson, Purser and one of the Captain's servants excepted, precipitately went below. The schooner had put her helm a-port, and fallen directly on the *Triton's* quarter, and boarded from the bowsprit.

The Captain, and the few who with him remained on deck, were almost instantaneously either shot or cut down by the assailants. The men who had retreated to the gun deck being panic struck, made no attempt to resist, but soon calling out for quarter, delivered up the ship to the enemy.

This unfortunate capture, which appears to have been the consequence of a sudden surprise, will be a warning to all commanding officers during war never on any occasion whatever to be off their guard.

(W. S. Seton-Karr. *Selections from Calcutta Gazettes of the Years 1789–1797*, Vol. II, Calcutta, 1865, p. 444.)

Although the apprentices in an Indiaman were properly called midshipmen, it was unusual to call the chief officer 'Lieutenant.' Apart from this, it will be noted that the *Cartier* was described indifferently as brig, snow and schooner. The difference between these rigs was not very fundamental and it is probable that Surcouf was at pains to alter his vessel's appearance as her description became known. For the rest, these two captures present a contrast between two ways in which a capture might be effected. The country ship *Diana* had no real means of defence but her captain acted very correctly. He recognized the enemy in time and successively tried to escape, to run his vessel ashore and finally to ram his assailant. By compelling the privateer to fire her guns and by disabling both ships he had done his best to improve his chances of recapture. He could do no more. The Indiaman was feebly handled and fell a prize in just such a way as a privateer would prefer, quickly, cheaply and with little damage on either side. The *Triton's* ports were closed and her arms in the gunroom. There were only six men on deck when she was boarded and all the firing was with muskets: mostly those fired down the hatchways until the crew surrendered. An Indiaman was supposed to be fully equal to any privateer and this capture made a deep impression, especially on Admiral Elphinstone, who wrote on February 24th from Madras:

> The Hon'ble Company's Ship *Triton* has been disgracefully captured by a small Pilot Vessel, manned only with twenty-five Frenchmen. The number on board the *Triton* was one hundred and forty, she was going from hence to Bengal. The circumstance is unparalleled in the history of surprizing events, and scarcely to be credited, but the fact is confirmed and the commander killed.
>
> (Ad. 1/55.)

Lacking the men to navigate both the *Triton* and *Diana*, Surcouf sold the latter to her commander, accepting ransom to the amount of Rs. 30,000, and put all his prisoners on board her. He then sailed for home in the *Triton*, reaching the Ile de France on March 10th. The Government naturally confiscated his prizes, he having sailed without letters of marque. Surcouf took passage for France in order to lodge his appeal, which partially succeeded. The result was his absence from the Indian Ocean until 1798. The *Cartier* never reached the French base, being retaken on the way.

Surcouf was not the only privateer at sea off India in 1796. In June a 'small crazy vessel,' carrying twelve 9-pounders and manned by 150 men, took three prizes and put into Coringa. Her first prize had been a pilot schooner and she had used Surcouf's trick, employing the pilot vessel to attract and capture the other two. One of these was, rather surprisingly, recaptured by her lascar crew under the leadership of the serang. There were a number of privateer successes at this period, tending to show that the opportunity offered by the British disposition of forces was put to better use by the privateers than the men-of-war. It is known, for example, that in September 1796 some thirteen American ships sailed from Mauritius, laden with English prize goods shipped on French account—sugar, sugar-candy, indigo and piece-goods (i.e. cotton cloth)—ostensibly bound for America or Hamburg and actually destined for Bordeaux. But now the situation changed again with the Spanish entry into the war. The British interest in the Moluccas could now be transferred to the Philippines. Dreams of Spanish treasure could now become a reality.

CHAPTER V

The End of Sercey's Squadron

WAR with Spain was inevitable as from 19th August, 1796, the the date on which the treaty of alliance between France and Spain was signed. It was not, however, declared until October 5th and it was not known for certain in India until April 1797. At that period Rear-Admiral Rainier was on the Coromandel coast in some force. 'In the present state of affairs,' he wrote on February 27th, 'it appears to me to be a measure of prudence to keep as many of the King's Ships together as possible.' He had with his flag at about that period, or within easy reach:

Suffolk	74	Captain Peter Lambert
Arrogant	74	Captain Richard Lucas
Victorious	74	Captain William Clark
Trident	64	Captain Edwd. Osborn
Dordrecht	64	Captain J. S. Rainier
Centurion	50	Captain Samuel Osborn
Sybille	38	Captain Edwd. Cooke
Heroine	32	Captain A. H. Gardner
Fox	32	Captain Pulteney Malcolm
Carysfort	28	Captain Charles Adams

In addition there were at Bombay under repair:

Orpheus	32	Captain Newcome
Hobart	Sloop	Captain Will. Hills

At Amboyna there were:

Resistance	44	Captain Pakenham
Amboyna	Sloop	

Presently bound for Malacca and Macao was:

Swift	18	Captain Thomas Hayward

There had been, in addition, a vessel called the *Suffolk's* tender, but Rainier sold her 'as I don't know what she is fit for if she won't sail.' Of the

Company's vessels, the *Bombay* was with Pakenham in the Moluccas, and the *Seahorse* and *Fly* under repair at Calcutta.

As regards the captains there were certain changes, apart from the dismissal (after court martial) of Captain Mathew Smith. Alan Hyde Gardner was invalided home and his place taken by the Hon. John Murray. John Sprat Rainier exchanged duties with Samuel Osborn, and John Halstead (lately of the *Swift*) became governor of the naval hospital at Madras. The genius among Rainier's officers was Edward Cooke of the *Sybille*, who had (as a lieutenant of the *Victory*, Hood's flagship) carried out a confidential mission ashore at Toulon in 1793. The worst captain, according to Rainier, was Lucas. His 'injudicious arrangements' after the action with Sercey had included bringing his damaged ships to Madras when they should have been docked at Bombay. But, apart from that, Lucas was guilty of inattention to discipline 'owing in some measure to an ill state of health.' William Clark was far from brilliant, one supposes, but it was Lucas whom the Admiral was anxious to supersede. It proved unnecessary; he died in 1798.

Rainier was now in considerable strength and the existence of a squadron of seventeen ships at the Cape—under Pringle, after Elphinstone's departure —relieved him of the task of blockading the Ile de France. He had evidently no great opinion of Sercey, or else concluded that he would be immobilized by political dissensions at his base. Rainier concluded, at any rate, that he was free to attack the Spanish and that India could look after itself. His last information about Manila had been obtained in January from the country ship *Sylph*, then at Penang. The *Swift* was sent to discover more and Rainier consulted with the Indian Government to find what forces would be available. The Governor-General, Sir John Shore, had been told to make preparations for an expedition to Manila in a dispatch from the Secret Committee of the Court of Directors dated 11th November, 1796. Rainier was approached by Lord Hobart on the subject and on March 21st expressed his willingness to co-operate, urged the necessity for speed and warned the Supreme Government that he could leave only one frigate in India for trade protection. Shore exonerated him in advance (May 26th) for anything that might happen in the squadron's absence, and Rainier made his plans accordingly. He described the position in a letter to Pakenham dated from Trincomalee, 15th April, 1797:

> Sir—I send the *Swift*, Captⁿ Thomas Hayward, herewith to acquaint you that I have received official Intelligence from Mr. Secretary Nepean, that the King of Spain has declared War against His Majesty, and by the same conveyance I am commanded by their Lordships to co-operate with

the Commander-in-Chief of the British Forces by Land, and the several Presidencies in India, in an expedition against Manilla, the outlines whereof are sketched, but wait the concurrence of the above authorities from Bengal. If this expedition should be determined upon, shall endeavour to give you timely notice thereof, in the mean time you are to keep yourself in readiness to join me—have nothing further to say on this subject at present, only informing you that if it takes place, it ought to leave the Coast by the beginning of August at farthest.

Capt. Hayward is to call at Macao to deliver dispatches to the Select Committee there and get information respecting the forces and designs of the Spaniards at Manilla. . . .

Our overland dispatches are dated Nov. 11, 1796—have not received positive orders for reprisals on the Spaniards, but think you will be fully justified in seizing all Ships and Property by land belonging to Spanish subjects—am in hourly expectations of receiving His Majesty's Proclamation to that effect by a Frigate or Packet. . . .

(Ad. 1/168.)

As three months or more would pass before the expedition could sail, Rainier busied himself with preparations. The *Suffolk*, *Centurion* and *Carysfort* were under repair at Trincomalee while the Admiral went in the *Victorious* to Madras. He sent the *Fox* to patrol the Straits of Malacca and the *Orpheus*, which had been damaged, to dock at Calcutta. The *Trident* came out of dock at Bombay, and the *Sybille* and *Centurion* sailed to join the *Fox*. Expecting no reinforcement from England, Rainier persuaded the Governor-General to equip for the purposes of the expedition a fireship (the *Goonong Assi*) and a bomb vessel (the *Vulcan*). By August preparations were so well advanced that the first eight transports were able to sail with the *Victorious* and *Trident* for Penang. The *Heroine* was sent to convoy other transports sailing directly from Calcutta, and the fleet organized as follows:

Order of Battle

Frigates etc.			Guns	Men
Fox	First or	*Victorious*	74	590
Hobart	Starboard	*Resistance*	44	295
	Division	*Trident*	64	491
Carysfort	to repeat			
Vulcan				
Goonong Assi		*Suffolk*	74	590
Heroine	Second or	*Centurion*	50	343
Swift	Larboard	*La Sybille*	44	300
	Division	*Arrogant*	74	590

Order of Sailing

1st or Starboard Division		2nd or Larboard Division
1. *Victorious*		1. *Arrogant*
2. *Resistance*	*Suffolk*	2. *La Sybille*
3. *Trident*	*Amboyna*	3. *Centurion*
4. *Fox*		4. *Heroine*
5. *Goonong Assi*	*Carysfort*	5. *Vulcan*
	to repeat	
6. *Hobart*		6. *Swift*

To the men-of-war were added five Indiamen from the outward-bound fleet, armed with additional cannon and destined to transport the 33rd Regiment from Bengal. These were:

			Guns	Tons
Lord Macartney	12 pdrs. her own	20	36	796
	12 pdrs. from Arsenal	6		
	6 pdrs. her own	6		
	6 pdrs. from Arsenal	4		
Lord Camden	9 pdrs. her own	20	36	776
	9 pdrs. from Arsenal	6		
	6 pdrs. her own	8		
	6 pdrs. from Arsenal	2		
Lord Hawkesbury	12 pdrs. (Iron) from Arsenal	25	36	803
	12 pdrs. (Brass)	1		
	9 pdrs.	10		
Phoenix	12 pdrs. her own	22	34	800
	12 pdrs. from Arsenal	4		
	9 pdrs. from Arsenal	8		
Sir Stephen Lushington	9 pdrs. her own	20	36	608
	12 pdrs. Brass, from the Arsenal	16		

The 33rd Regiment to embark on the above ship

VIZ: Europeans 948
      Native Followers 362

Total 1,310

Three other ships were to carry the Bengal Marine Battalion of Natives—the *General Goddard*, *Nancy* and *Abercrombie*. The troops and their followers, including the 33rd Regiment, numbered 2,059 all told.

For the historian of this period, the interest of this expedition centres on the fact that the 33rd Regiment was commanded by the Hon. Colonel Arthur Wesley (later spelt Wellesley), the future Duke of Wellington. He might have commanded all the land forces but preferred to command, under Doyle, the troops from Bengal. The Commander finally chosen, however, was Major-General Sir James Craig. In April 1797, while still at Fort William, the Colonel wrote an outline plan for the conquest of Java as a preliminary to the later attack on the Philippines. He estimated the Dutch garrison at 2,000 men, very scattered, and considered that Batavia might be easily destroyed. That done, he envisaged the fleet concentrating afresh at Tanjonan (Tanjong Patani?) on the eastern coast of Malaya before attacking Manila in October, after the change of the monsoon.

'I do not conceive' [he concluded] 'that any danger is to be apprehended from the six French frigates which are said to be cruising in the China Seas. I conceive the frigates and armed Indiamen to be more than equal to them; and besides them, the three ships going as transports carry guns.

Upon the whole then, seeing that the place is so weak and that it would fall so easily, and that a force sufficient to destroy it can be sent there without any inconvenience, danger, or much additional expense, I consider that it would be an expedition honourable to the Governor-General, and to those employed upon it, and useful to the country, as it would deprive the enemy of his only remaining port in the Eastern Seas, and of one of which he has lately made the greatest use; and as such I offer my plans.'

(*Supplementary Despatches and Memoranda of Field Marshal Arthur Duke of Wellington, K.G., India, 1797–1805*, Vol. I, 1858, p. 4 *et seq.*)

The future Field-Marshal was still a young man and inclined to over-simplify—as he soon realized—the problems involved in destroying the Dutch East Indies. He dabbled in the navigational problems affecting the date of sailing but reflected (on May 20th) that:

. . . as the decision upon that subject depends upon the Admiral, who is the only independent and uncontrolled man in these parts, it is impossible to say what he will do; and as an attempt of the Government to influence him, or convince him, might be attended with bad consequences: they don't seem to me to have given sufficient attention to that part of the question. Ships cannot lie in Manilla Bay in safety during the south-west monsoon. They cannot get there after the north-east monsoon will have set in, and being in the China Seas at the time of the Change from the south-west to the north-east is attended with much danger, so that there is much difficulty in coming to a proper decision about the time of attack. This difficulty would be removed if they would determine to attack a fort (Cavité) which commands the entrance of a bay in Manilla Bay, which is sheltered from the south-west monsoon; but in that case they must be stronger both in men and stores, as they will have two sieges instead of one. . . .

(*Supplementary Despatches, 1797–1805*, Vol. I, p. 6. Letter from Colonel Wesley to Lord Mornington.)

With his brother hardly yet installed as Governor-General, the younger Wellesley was not, at this period, as influential as he was soon to become. The operational plans lay between General Harris, the Admiral, and Major-General St. Leger; and the Colonel of the 33rd Regiment was not even supposed to know whither the expedition was bound. He thought his seniors 'guilty of great neglect in suffering a ship under Danish colours to go out of the Ganges . . . avowedly bound to Manilla,' but further consideration led him to write (July 12th), 'The destruction of Batavia would ruin the Dutch; but it may be a question whether it would be right completely to annihilate them, and it is probably that consideration which has prevented from attacking them. . . .' It probably was. Colonel Wesley was on firmer ground in drawing up his admirable regimental orders governing the daily routine of his men while on board ship. Hammocks must be numbered, properly rolled and regularly scrubbed. Men are to be divided into watches, guards mounted and sentries posted, troops paraded morning and evening, men exercised with dumb-bells, parade states rendered, kit inspected once a week, smoking prevented and cleanliness ensured. Soldiers were to be exercised with great guns and small arms, sixty rounds per man to be allowed for musketry practice during the voyage (*Supplementary Despatches*, page 19). There can be no doubt that Indiamen with additional cannon and carrying troops so disciplined and trained would have been, as the colonel claimed, more than equal to the French frigates.

The Manila expedition met its first check in the late arrival of the second division of transports supposed to sail from Madras. The first division had sailed and so had the division from Bengal, but the transports from Calcutta, due at Madras, had mostly failed to appear. On August 10th Rainier thought that the expedition might proceed by the north of Borneo with a rendezvous at Balambangan, or might alternatively wait until November and then make the eastern passage through the Moluccas. Lord Hobart, at Madras, with whom the final decision lay, objected that this latter plan would leave India unprotected for a very long time. Rainier explained this to the Governor-General in a letter of August 10th, concluding:

I am therefore necessarily led to conclude that the Expedition will be laid aside, and all that remains will be the execution of the secondary plan of operation, my attempt to destroy the Ships of War at Manilla. . . .

(Ad. 1/168.)

This secondary plan involved troops and Craig, on August 17th, was wanting to know what he was to do if unable to reach the Philippines—attack some other place, or what? Hobart was opposed to any change in destination and thought the destruction of the Spanish ships a great object in itself as safeguarding the China trade. He reminded himself of the Secret Committee's letter of 4th August, 1796, which ended with the words 'even conquests may be inconvenient if they tend too much to scatter our Troops or to expose them to great mortality in unhealthy climate.' It was accordingly decided by Lord Hobart, on August 25th that the expedition, if unable to reach the Philippines by either the direct or the Mindoro route, should return at once to India. On the 27th Rainier wrote to the Admiralty 'expecting now to sail in a day or two' despite the difficulty over the transports. He added, however, that 'in the prosecution of so distant a military enterprize the way whereto lies thro' so perilous and perhaps intricate a navigation, and consequently exposed to a variety of casualties, adverse and unforeseen circumstances may interfere and disappoint the wisest measures. . . .' They may indeed. On the 28th the whole expedition was abandoned.

The causes for this change of policy are best given in Rainier's own words, contained in his report to the Admiralty.

Suffolk, Madras Road,
September 3rd, 1797.

Sir

I beg leave to acquaint you for their Lordships information that on the 28th ultimo, almost on the instant of my quitting this road with His Majesty's Ships and the last Division of Transports, an express was received from His Majesty's minister at Constantinople by this Government and immediately communicated to me, announcing the important intelligence of the Emperor of Germany having concluded a Peace with the French Nation, an event so extremely favourable to the interests of the latter as cannot, we think, fail to draw their attention to the execution of their long projected plan of attack on the British Possessions in this Country in concert with Tippoo Sultan with whom they have had much friendly intercourse of late. In order to guard against the consequences of so formidable an alliance it has been thought advisable by the Right Hon'ble the President in Council of this Government to relinquish in toto the Expedition to Manilla, in support of which determination such forcible arguments were adduced by his Lordship, as put it out of my power from a principle of zeal for His Majesty's Service, to withhold my consent to it—The chief point of discussion turned on the great risque the Possessions and acquisitions we now hold would be exposed to, after so large a part of the troops and most of the King's Ships were detached on a service so distant, if attacked by two such formidable Powers. . . .

(Ad. 1/168.)

The news from Constantinople was of the preliminaries at Leoben in July which led to the Treaty of Campo Formio in October. The effect in India was instantaneous and inevitable. It was, however, a sad moment from many points of view. While it is clear that the surprise achieved in 1762 would not have been gained in 1797, the destruction of the Spanish squadron was not impossible. The squadron was supposed to include three 74-gun ships and four frigates—a fifth having been lost in a typhoon. This would have been a useful success and Rainier and Craig may have remembered wistfully that Admiral Cornish and Colonel Draper had each, in 1762, made over £122,500 in prize money—even the seaman or marine receiving £3 14s. 9¼d. The captured colours would not, in 1797, have gone—as had Draper's—to King's College, Cambridge. But Rainier might have been made a baronet and his sailors (in the year of the Mutiny) would have appreciated some ready money. On the other hand, the expedition might quite possibly have failed. The Spanish squadron, dismasted (except for one frigate sunk) in a typhoon, had been laid up at Cavité, as floating batteries, their sides protected by fascines of rattan, 18 inches thick. They were supposed to have 150 gunboats with 8,000 regular troops, 10,000 militia and 2,000 cavalry. An informant at Canton predicted complete success for an invading force of 10,000 or 12,000, but it is fair to remember that no such army was to have been sent. The attempt, anyway, was never made. Events in Europe had saved Manila from attack. It should be noted, however, that events in India had played their part—how large a part will presently be shown.

With the situation suddenly altered, Admiral Rainier was thrown on the defensive. The Spaniards, he realized, would soon hear of the expedition being abandoned. That would leave them free to join forces with Sercey and attack the China fleet in overwhelming strength. Sercey, even without the Spanish, might gain contact with Tippoo Sultan. There were all sorts of dangers to be averted and no excuse now for failing to avert them. Rainier began a rapid redeployment of his forces, beginning with a recall of the ships already at Penang. Captain Clark was ordered on August 30th to bring the King's ships and transports back to India, and detain or recall the *Fox* until the *Svbille* and *Trident* arrive as escort for the China trade. A by-product of the transports being collected at Penang was the Memorandum on that settlement which the younger Wellesley took the opportunity to write—'Memorandum on Pulo Penang'[1]—probably cut short by this hasty recall. Captain Cooke of the *Sybille* was to proceed with the *Fox* and *Trident* to Macao and thence return with convoy. The *Hobart* was to escort some supply ships to Amboyna. Pakenham was to be relieved of his duties at the Moluccas and transferred to the *Trident*. Rainier himself, with the *Suffolk*, *Arrogant* and *Carysfort* would cruise between Trincomalee and Negapatam until the middle of October and then sail for the Malabar coast so as to prevent, if possible, any French contact with Tippoo. The *Orpheus*, with probably the *Heroine*, was ordered to cruise off the Sandheads and the *Resistance* would have to be docked at Bombay. All offensive plans had been tacitly abandoned.

The English instinct in thus cancelling what seemed a promising enterprise in the autumn of 1797 was essentially sound. The year 1797, with the naval mutinies and the threat to Ireland, had seemed full of peril. But the threat to India, made possible by the British withdrawal from the Mediterranean in 1796, coupled with the French success in Europe of 1797, was to develop in 1798. The men who then ruled England and India sensed the danger even before they had evidence of it. Dundas was warned by the Chairman of the East India Company, Stephen Lushington, in February 1796, that India might be attacked overland via Egypt.[2] Dundas kept the possibility in mind and was able to take swift action when the moment came—his best work, as some believe, throughout the war. In arousing the suspicions and the caution of the authorities in India, the French of Mauritius played a certain part. Guiltless in this respect was Admiral Sercey. To have saved Manila, had that been thought an object, his best policy would presumably have been to appear near Mangalore and attempt to open negotiation with Tippoo Sultan. He did not do that, and indeed his operations in 1797 were mostly defensive, and governed by the idea that the French islands might be attacked. His problem was, in the first instance, one of supply. For the Ile de France was still rent by political conflict, and a majority in the Colonial Assembly was opposed to allowing the squadron any provisions. Apart from that, there was a shortage of seamen; few came from France and those in the island all preferred privateering. First victim of these circumstances was the *Cybèle*, which Sercey sent back to France in March or April, partly no doubt for repairs. For the rest, his operations involved little more than taking the *Forte*, *Vertu* and *Seine* to the Seychelles in May while the *Régénérée* and *Brûle-Gueule* reconnoitred

[1] *A Selection from the Despatches, etc., of the Duke of Wellington*. Ed. by S. J Owen, Oxford, 1880, p, 487.

[2] C. H. Philips. *The East India Company, 1784–1834*, Manchester, 1940, p. 101.

India to gain information. The *Seine* and *Vertu* now proceeded to Batavia with three hundred men sent to reinforce the Dutch, then indirectly threatened by the British expedition concentrating at Penang. The Admiral returned to Port Louis on 20th September, 1797, bringing with him the *Forte*, *Preneuse* and *Brûle-Gueule* and finding there the *Prudente* and *Régénérée*.

Complaints now began afresh about the difficulty of supplying the squadron. Opportunely, from the colonists' point of view, came a request from the Spanish Government at the Philippines for naval assistance. Two ships were to proceed to Spain with treasure (presumably from Mexico) and the Spanish offered 300,000 livres for an escort of two frigates. Since the colony wanted the money, and did not want the frigates, Sercey agreed to send the *Vertu* and *Régénérée* to France—both ships needing repair. Later he was persuaded to send home the *Seine* with three hundred troops on board. While the squadron was thus being destroyed piecemeal, its vital task was performed for it by Ripaud de Montandevert. This person was an officer in the privateer *l'Apollon*. Being given charge of a prize, he arrived, probably by accident, on the Malabar coast. Seized at first and imprisoned, he was presently taken from Mangalore to Tippoo's camp. There he improved his position by announcing himself as an envoy from the French Republic. He gained still warmer hospitality by talking glibly about the French aid which Tippoo might reasonably expect. The result was that Tippoo decided to send two agents (secretly and incognito) to discuss the possibilities with Malartic. These two embarked with Ripaud and sailed with him to the Ile de France. Misled, no doubt, by Ripaud (who was enjoying this, his first and almost his only appearance in history) Malartic mistook the nature of this mission and greeted the secret agents, when they landed on 19th January, 1798 (masked, doubtless, and furtive) with a salute of a hundred and fifty guns. He simultaneously issued a proclamation inviting brave Frenchmen to volunteer for Citizen Tippoo's army and join in destroying the British Empire. Some eighty-six men volunteered for this congenial task, but the secrecy of the whole transaction seemed somehow to have fallen short of the ideal. The need now arose to send the two envoys, with their new French allies, back to Mangalore.

Sercey appointed *La Preneuse* (36) for the service and the frigate, commanded by L'Hermitte, sailed on 8th March, 1798. L'Hermitte caught two East Indiamen, the *Woodcot* (802 tons) and *Raymond* (793 tons) at Tellicherry, capturing both and drawing fresh attention to his mission before landing the envoys and volunteers at Mangalore on April 24th. A reinforcement of eighty-six was not of vital importance to Tippoo's army, which numbered seventy thousand. The same number of men forming a military mission—officers, instructors and technicians—would have mattered; but these were just volunteers. They were enough, nevertheless, to cause alarm at Madras. Ripaud alone had caused a stir—it is presumably to his visit that Rainier refers in his letter of 3rd September, 1797 (see page 118)—and his escapade might be included in the reasons why the Manila expedition was abandoned. But the stealthy arrival of Tippoo's emissaries at Port Louis—known at Madras in a flash—caused consternation. Colonel Arthur Wellesley refers to it in a paper dated 28th June, 1798.

> The reasoning upon the proclamation of the Governor of Mauritius, and upon the evidence of the persons who were there at the time it was issued, is conclusive.
>
> There is not a doubt but that Tippoo offered to conclude, and that he, in fact, has concluded with that Government, an alliance offensive and defensive against the British nation, and that the immediate object of that alliance is to drive us out of India. . . . The consequence of that alliance has been an addition to the forces of Tippoo of 150 men at most, and a certainty that he can receive no more assistance from the island of Mauritius. . . .
>
> (*Supplementary Despatches*, etc., p. 52.)

There was at that time no war between Tippoo and the Company and the younger Wellesley was against provoking one. But this ineffective aid from Mauritius brought such a war, in the circumstances of 1798, appreciably nearer. As a gesture, it was significant. There was a sequel when Tippoo tried to send his envoys to France in 1799. These were 'a Monsr. De Buque self appointed General and Ambassador Extraordinary to the French Directory, with two Mussalmen under the same character,' two secretaries, two lascars and fifteen servants. These embarked in a French armed ship called *La Surprise*, which was caught at the Seychelles by H.M.S. *Braave*. The ambassadors, retrieved from the shore, where they had hidden, were told of Tippoo's death.

With the *Preneuse* on her way to Mangalore, Admiral Sercey's force was reduced to the *Forte*, *Prudente* and *Brûle Gueule*. That he was weak in yielding, as he had, to the local feeling in Mauritius is certain. But it was the dawn of democracy and Sercey liked the colonists, being one of them by birth. More than that, he had recently married in April 1797 Louise Victorine Caillean, a wealthy creole and a relative of the former governor, René Magon. This was no time for making himself unpopular ashore with his wife's friends and relations; among whom, incidentally, he was to live after his retirement from the Navy. He was not blamed in France, the

Minister reporting favourably on him to the Directory (Archives Nat. BB^4 117; 21 Thermidor, An. 5). For a man, however, whose squadron had acquired for the island 700,000 piastres and 4,000,000 pounds of rice, he was treated locally with small consideration. Influenced by the weakness of his squadron, by the possibility of being relieved (perhaps by Kerguelen), and maybe by his recent marriage, Sercey now decided to remain ashore and send the *Forte* and *Prudente*, under Ravenel as Commodore, to cruise on the Malabar coast. The cruise was mainly remarkable for a mutiny—which Ravenel suppressed—among the troops which the *Forte* carried as marines. The frigates made, however, a number of captures off Ceylon, in the Straits of Bali and then in the Bay of Bengal.

Sercey had achieved little in 1797, partly because the preparations for the Manila expedition had kept him away from the China Sea in which Dutch and Spanish co-operation might have been expected. If he was to achieve more in 1798, he would have to rely, with his weakened forces, on these allies. He contemplated the idea of a joint Franco-Spanish inter-ception of the China Fleet. Having thought out the plan, Sercey sent the corvette *Brûle-Gueule* to convey orders for Ravenel to bring his two frigates to Batavia. The *Brûle-Gueule* reached Tranquebar on 13th September, 1797, having taken the East India Company's extra ship *Thomas* off Ceylon on the 9th. The *Brûle-Gueule* narrowly missed (without knowing it) an encounter with Rainier in person and so went on to deliver Sercey's orders. These orders were evidently received but not acted upon, for the *Forte* and *Prudente* returned instead to Port Louis. Knowing Ravenel's intention, perhaps from the corvette bringing his reply on about October 5th, Sercey sailed in the *Brûle-Gueule* for Batavia, leaving orders for the two frigates to follow. They reached port four days after the Admiral had gone and would have obeyed their instructions. Once more, however, the Colonial Assembly intervened and compelled Malartic to disarm the *Prudente* and sell her to a commercial firm. She was taken, cruising as a privateer, in February 1799. When Sercey heard of this at Sourabaya he wrote (19th November, 1797) that Malartic had exceeded his powers. He wrote bitterly to the Minister on December 15th, complaining of how he was opposed by the colonists and explaining the impossibility of basing his squadron on a place where he was refused all supplies (Arch. Nat. BB^4 117). Nor was the Admiral wholly reconciled to this loss by the soothing letter from Malartic (received December 26th) to say that the *Forte* should be sent to him in due course. Sercey himself reached Batavia in June 1798, and was joined there by the *Preneuse*, her crew having been so mutinous that five of them were court martialled and shot. It was no moment for keeping her in port and the Admiral sent her for a month's cruise off Borneo, hoping at that time that the *Forte* and *Prudente* would have appeared before the month ended. Disappointed of this reinforcement but promised Spanish help in a letter from the Governor of the Philippines, dated 21st January, 1798, Sercey remained ashore at Sourabaya and sent the *Preneuse* and *Brûle-Gueule* to Manila with orders to co-operate with the Spanish against the China Fleet. This they did (arriving 18th October, 1798), sailing from Manila with two Spanish ships of the line and two frigates. So bad was the Spanish seamanship, according to the French, that nothing could be done. Spanish inactivity in 1797 had been due, apparently, to all their men-of-war being dismasted in a typhoon in April. Perhaps this made them the more cautious in 1798. They returned, at any rate, to port and L'Hermitte rightly refused to intercept the China Fleet single-handed. He sailed instead for Batavia and arrived on 6th April, 1799, where he found Sercey in a bad temper—furious with Ravenel for not obeying orders, furious with Malartic and the Colonial Assembly, furious with the commander of the *Prudente* for yielding up his frigate, and now (on hearing L'Hermitte's story) furious with the Spanish as well. He hoisted his flag in the *Preneuse* and on 17th April, 1799, sailed, with the *Brûle-Gueule*, for the Ile de France. Approaching the island on 9th May, 1799, he was chased by a blockading squadron, but took refuge in the Riviere Noire and landed guns to make a shore battery. He finally reached Port Louis on May 22nd, probably hoping to find there his former flagship *La Forte*. She was not there. She had been taken.[1]

It was Malartic who sent the *Forte* on her last cruise and Sercey's annoyance at this encroachment was increased when he heard that Ravenel, who was ill, had been relieved in the command by Beaulieu le Loup, who was old and worn out. Ravenel had protested to the end, urging Malartic to send the *Forte* to Batavia as Sercey had ordered and as Malartic himself had promised. Instead, she had sailed from Mauritius towards the end of 1798 with orders to raid the Bay of Bengal. The time of year was well chosen, being later than the season during which French cruisers were expected there. The year itself was well chosen because—as we shall see—attention was fixed on the Red Sea and Malabar coast. But the Bay of Bengal was not wholly without protection, for Rainier had told the *Sybille*, Captain E. Cooke, to remain there. An order of 3rd January, 1799, had approved Cooke's proposal to give a passage, in fact, to Lord Mornington,

[1] For these operations, see *Histoire des Marine Français sous la république, 1789–1803.* Charles Rouvier, Paris, 1868, p. 435, and *L'Ile de France. Esquisses Historiques. 1715–1810.* Albert Pitot, 1899, p. 212.

the Governor-General, who wanted to visit Madras. It was while there that Captain Cooke heard of the havoc being wrought among the country ships. *La Forte* captured, in rapid succession, the *Recovery, Yarmouth, Earl Mornington, Chance, Endeavour* and *Surprise*. The *Endeavour* was commanded and largely owned by Robert William Eastwick, from whose published memoirs[1] may be gained a vivid picture of all that happened. He had recently had as a passenger the future Duke of Wellington and it was fortunate that Colonel Wellesley was no longer aboard. The *Endeavour* was off Balasore Roads when intercepted and Eastwick did his best to run into shallow water but was dissuaded by accurate fire from *La Forte's* bow-chasers, so that 'at 9 p.m.,' as he writes, 'on the last day of February, 1799, I was forced to haul down my colours and surrender my ship.' It was the flash of these guns (captured English 24-pounders) which was seen on board the *Sybille*, arrived after a quick passage from Madras and soon standing towards the scene of the capture. Eastwick and his two mates were taken on board *La Forte*, which went on to capture the *Mornington* (Captain Cooke) on board of which ship was a passenger called Mackerel. Cooke and Mackerel now joined Eastwick in captivity.

> There were several other English prisoners on board the *La Forte*, from whom we learnt the treatment we might expect. Their food was salt beef, boiled in vinegar, to which was added boiled peas, as a substitute for bread. Only one quart of water was allowed *per diem*, and not a glass of wine or spirits.
>
> As for the discipline of the ship, it was very slack. It was not at all unusual to see one of the foremast men, with his beef in his hands, eating it while walking the quarter-deck, and claiming an equal right to do it with the commanding officer, thus, I suppose, demonstrating the claims of liberty, equality and brotherhood. Nor was any scruple made of playing cards on the quarter-deck. The lieutenants generally came on deck with only trousers and an open shirt, often a check one, so that it was almost impossible to distinguish them. The men, however, went through their duty with alacrity, and were obedient to orders.

The succeeding part of Eastwick's narrative is rather surprising because he describes an interview with Admiral Sercey, 'a fine old man and a very distinguished officer.' Sercey was not, of course, on board. *La Forte* had for long been his flagship and that is presumably why Eastwick mistook the elderly Beaulieu le Loup for the Admiral. The mistake originated, no doubt, among the prisoners. It was repeated in the local press after the

---

[1] *A Master Mariner, being the life and adventures of Captain Robert William Eastwick.* Ed. by Herbert Compton, 1891, p. 130 *et seq.*

action and led finally to an account of Sercey's death in battle appearing
in *The Times* with a few words of obituary. Sercey actually lived to be
a Vice-Admiral, a Commander of St. Louis and a Peer of France in 1830;
honours which he continued to enjoy until about 1835.

The *Sybille* first sighted *La Forte* at 9.30 p.m. (February 28th) and,
according to Eastwick, by moonlight. It may be doubted, however, whether
the *Sybille* was sighted by her opponent so soon. For she was able to
manœuvre for position and still secure a certain measure of surprise. The
French officers mistook her for some merchantmen 'with the watch
asleep.'

> Nearer and nearer came the strange sail, as calm and stately as if she had
> the entire Ocean to herself, and no other vessel in sight. Such confidence
> amounted to audacity, for the display of lights marked her as a man-of-war.
> As the approaching ship continued her cruise and came within range, the
> Captain of the *La Forte* began to exhibit some doubts about her, and ordered
> a few shots to be fired at her. But these eliciting no response, he commanded
> the firing to cease, observing in my hearing, 'she will prove another Bon
> Prix!' Still, as a matter of precaution, every man was kept at his quarters,
> though in a careless way, and the guns were all loaded and pointed at the
> stranger.
> We prisoners were now ordered to retire below, and were shown into
> the officers' berth-place, the door of which was locked upon us. . . .

It was presumably the first lieutenant whom Eastwick overheard, but
he afterwards saw no more of the battle than he could glimpse through
a port-hole. The affair began when the *Sybille* put her helm up at 12.45 a.m.
and fired her port broadside into the *Forte's* stern at very close range. She
then came close alongside to leeward and had fired a second broadside
before the Frenchmen were sufficiently organized to reply. Then an
engagement began which lasted for one hour and forty minutes. Eastwick's
account deserves quotation as evidence from an unusual point of view:

> I had rather be in a dozen actions face to face with belching cannon, and
> exposed to the full fury of the tops, than experience again such another
> hour as we passed through. The din and noise were awful; the great ship
> shook and quivered under every discharge of her guns; a suffocating smell
> of gunpowder smoke pervaded the whole vessel, we being to leeward;
> and every second or third minute there came a great crash, most startling
> in the dark, and we heard a shot go in, and did not know whether the next
> might not carry us all off. From overhead came the trampling of feet, the
> cries of the wounded, the crashing sounds of falling spars and top-hamper,
> heard between the thundering of the cannon and the lesser roar of the

small arms. And added to all was the terrible sense of uncertainty as to what was happening, with whom we were contending, and whether the *La Forte* was winning the day or losing it.

After the tenth or twelfth shot had penetrated the berth-room, Captain Cooke swore he could stand it no longer, and that it required more courage than he possessed to sit still and be shot at, like a rat in a hole. He therefore began groping about to find a means of exit, and came across an aperture in the bulkhead, made by the starting of the timbers consequent on a shot striking the place. Through this, being exceedingly spare in person, he managed with great difficulty to squeeze his body, and so got further below to a place of comparative safety, from whence he called to us to join him.

The advice was excellent enough in its way but the thing was to carry it out. Mr. Mackerel attempted the task first, I, at his request, aiding his exertions. But unfortunately he was a very fat man, and got fairly wedged when half-way through, so that he called out violently to be hauled back. This was no easy matter, and accomplished with such difficulty that the ludicrous effect of the scene has never passed from my memory, and critical as our situation was, I could not refrain from laughing aloud, when, in my endeavours to pull him back by the legs, his pantaloons first began to peel off, and when I transferred my grip to his feet, one of his boots gave way in my hand, and sent me sprawling backwards.

Mr. Mackerel was mightily indignant at my levity, and upbraided me for it in solemn and measured language, after I had at last managed to extricate him. He then very soberly laid himself down flat on the floor, observing, with a groan, that it was safer than standing; and as this seemed sensible, and I did not like to desert him, I followed his example, jestingly thanking him for the extra protection his ample person afforded me—a joke he was in far too much consternation to relish.

There we lay for half an hour, Mr. Mackerel saying not a word, but breathing very hard, and whenever a crash was heard, turning instantly on his side, so as to present his back to the attack if it should come, and then giving vent to a groan, by way of thanks-giving, when he found himself unhurt.

At last the action began to draw to a close. The discharges of cannon were less frequent, and the *La Forte's* men being all engaged in trying to set sail, the rattle of musketry on the quarter-deck above our heads almost ceased. Very nearly the last shot fired was one which, in penetrating the berth-place, was so checked, that it came rolling slowly towards us; upon which Mr. Mackerel jumped up and made a clean bound over it with an agility that would have done credit to a goat. As I scuttled out of its way, its size showed me it came from a twenty-four pounder, and I knew it must have been fired by a Man-of-war. . . .

From a 24-pound shot Eastwick might properly have inferred that *La Forte* was engaging a ship of the line—there were only three 24-pounder frigates in the English service and none of these was in the Indian Ocean. In fact, however, he was mistaken, the shot being more probably from an 18-pounder. The *Sybille*, although a captured French 40-gun frigate, was far from being a match for *La Forte* and had no 24-pounder guns on board. The comparative broadsides were as follows:

(Ad. 1/169.)

	La Sybille		La Forte		Weight (English)
24	18-pdrs.	Main Deck	30	24-pdrs.	27 lb.
6	12-pdrs.	Quarter Deck	6	8-pdrs.	9 lb.
8	32-pdrs. Cannonades	Quarter Deck	6	36-pdrs. [1]	40½ lb.
4	12-pdrs.	Forecastle	4	8-pdrs.	
2	32-pdr. Cannonades	Forecastle	2	36-pdrs. [1]	
		Gangways	2	8-pdrs.	
		Gangways	2	36-pdrs. [1]	
44		TOTAL	52 and 8 swivels		

The two ships compared otherwise as follows:

	Length of Gun Deck	Beam	Burthen	Guns	Men
La Sybille	156	40½	1,050	48	370
La Forte	169	44½	1,360	52	403

La Forte was an exceptionally large frigate and had sailed with about 510 men, of whom, however, 100 (including several officers) were absent in her prizes. The crew of the *Sybille* had been reduced by sickness to 240, but she carried a party of soldiers and some volunteers shipped at Madras, which gave her a total of 130 supernumeraries.

The result of the action was to leave *La Forte* a wreck, surrendered by a junior officer after the rest, including the captain and first lieutenant, had fallen. All three masts had been shot away (18, 3 and 10 feet above the deck), the bowsprit taken off close by the figurehead, her bulwarks and chains gone, her cables, booms and boats cut to pieces and 300 shots in her hull. She had 93 killed and 80 wounded, of whom 20 afterwards died. *La Sybille*, by contrast, had 5 killed and 17 wounded, two masts damaged, all her rigging and sails shot away (which enabled the French

[1] Brass

PLATE III. Two-decked man-of-war shortening sail

The Honourable East India Company's ship *Pitt*

prizes to escape) and no more than six shots in her upper works and hull. It was a curious result of a duel in which the French ship was so much more heavily gunned. It is explained, in part, by the fact that *La Sybille* was a crack ship, her crew trained by the best captain on the station and her handling masterly up to the moment when Captain Cooke was badly (it proved fatally) wounded. It is explained, on the other side, by Beaulieu le Loup's relative incompetence and his bad relationship with Vigoureux, his first lieutenant. His unreadiness for action—some guns not mounted, some masked by the cable, the powder damp and no drinking water for the guns' crews—was manifest. And apart from that, he had an obsession about gunnery and had, a few days before the action, ordered his gun layers to withdraw their quoins and so elevate to a commencing range of 2,000 yards. They were mostly firing at that range during the action and so clean over the hull of a smaller opponent. *La Sybille's* shooting was, as Mr. Mackerel had occasion to notice, extremely accurate. And Captain Cooke's monument stands to-day in Westminster Abbey, in lieu perhaps of that wider fame which, had he lived, would certainly have been his.

With the capture of the *Forte*, Sercey had only the *Preneuse* and the corvette *Brûle-Gueule*. The *Preneuse* was commanded by Captain L'Hermitte, Sercey's most distinguished officer. He shares the laurels with Surcouf, Lemême and the other corsairs. But the normal difficulty about ascertaining all that took place among these French heroes is greatly enhanced by the existence of a book called *Voyages, Aventures et Combat* by Louis Garneray. This work and *Mes Pontons* has been published and republished in France, often with illustration but never (it would seem) in a critical edition. It is a popular adventure story and no one has troubled to test its truth. Thus Mr. H. C. M. Austen translates pages of it in his otherwise valuable book on the naval history of Mauritius,[1] and remarks (p. 71) that 'the testimony of an eye-witness is irresistible.' This is not strictly true. Eye-witnesses can be mistaken—as Eastwick, for example, is mistaken about occasions on which he was unquestionably present. But the value of an eye-witness depends, after all, on his having been there. And no one, so far, has taken the trouble to discover who Louis Garneray was—whether he was the painter or his brother or whom—and in what ships he served and when. When his narrative has been checked by the muster rolls of ships, we shall know better what to believe. For present purposes it may suffice to point out that the highly-coloured and unlikely story of L'Hermitte's reception by Sir Edward Pellew in 1799 is open

[1] H. C. M. Austen. *Sea Fights and Corsairs of the Indian Ocean, being the Naval History of Mauritius from 1715 to 1810*, Port Louis, Mauritius, 1935.

to the mild objection that Pellew was not then on the East Indies station. Whether Garneray was there either remains to be proved. In the meanwhile, his works are most safely classed as fiction.

L'Hermitte sailed from the Ile de France on 4th August, 1799, to cruise, by Sercey's orders, on the African coast. Shortly afterwards, on September 26th, Sercey was persuaded to send the *Brûle-Gueule* to France. There had been a small rebellion at Mauritius in October–November 1798, and some of the ringleaders were sent home soon afterwards. Other arrests followed later and the suspects were sent to France for trial—a death sentence, as it turned out, for the *Brûle-Gueule* was wrecked on the Point du Raz, most of those aboard being drowned. The *Preneuse*, meanwhile, reached the African coast and the Mozambique Channel and, on September 20th, entered Delagoa Bay towards nightfall. The vessels at anchor there included the *Camel*, storeship (24), the *Rattlesnake* (18), a schooner and possibly a brig. English and French versions of what happened are somewhat at variance, the French having invented two Indiamen and a shore battery to enliven their tale and the English practically calling L'Hermitte a coward, which he certainly was not. There was, at any rate, an indecisive night action, which ended, by one French account,[1] with the *Preneuse* escaping from the brig, which was on fire and drifting towards her, and being afterwards prevented by the wind from re-entering the bay. By another account,[2] L'Hermitte had suffered forty casualties and broke off the action to avoid further damage. He put to sea, at any rate, and his late opponents sent a message to the senior naval officer at Table Bay. The result was that the *Jupiter* (50) went in pursuit of the *Preneuse* and overtook her on 9th October, 1799. L'Hermitte, however, beat off his pursuer during a high sea and was able to continue his cruise, although without any particular success.

During the absence of the *Preneuse* two of the King's ships, the *Tremendous* (74) and the *Adamant* (50) were sent to blockade the French islands. They arrived off Port Louis on about December 7th, just in time to intercept the *Preneuse*, which appeared on the 11th. Trapped between the *Adamant* and the coast, L'Hermitte ran his frigate ashore near some batteries. When within range, the *Adamant* opened fire and L'Hermitte lowered his ensign. When the boats from the English ships reached the *Preneuse* they found Captain L'Hermitte, his officers and a handful of men,

[1] Albert Pitot. *L'Ile de France Esquisses Historiques* (1715–1810), Port Louis, Mauritius, 1899, p. 216, *et seq.*

[2] Charles Rouvier. *Histoire des Marins Français sous la Republique, 1789–1803*, Paris, 1868, p. 442, *et seq.*

the rest having escaped ashore. Having removed these few prisoners, who were later released on parole, Lieutenant Grey of the *Adamant* set fire to the frigate, which was completely destroyed. This was the last of the French squadron. Admiral Sercey was with the nearest shore battery and saw with his own eyes the fate of this, his last frigate. Now, having no squadron to command, he decided to return to France. On arrival there he was given an administrative post ashore and later offered another command. This he refused, asking leave instead to retire. This being granted, he returned to the Ile de France, which he helped later to defend. One might almost wonder why.

CHAPTER VI

The Threat from Egypt

ERCEY'S operations in 1797–99 had not given Admiral Rainier much cause for anxiety. He received, it is true, inaccurate information about the French from time to time, mostly from Danish vessels. He thus heard in the autumn of 1797 that a fleet was expected from France, but commented "tis doubtful how far the Dane's intelligence was to be relied upon, as the account he gave of the French Frigates we know to be erroneous.' Writing to the Admiralty on 15th October, 1797, Rainier gave the latest news about the Dutch East Indies and added 'The French Frigates, there is reason to suppose, are lurking somewhere in these seas.' He was not unduly concerned about them. 'We have also late information,' he added, 'of a Privateer or two being on the Malabar Coast . . . the only mischief they have hitherto done has been the plundering of some Arabian Dows, and as 'tis said to a considerable amount.' Here again he was only mildly interested. It was, in point of fact, a period during which the French privateers were extremely active. Robert Surcouf appeared with the *Clarisse* (14) in 1798. Houdoul with the *Appollon* (16) was the privateer to whom Rainier refers as on the Malabar coast and Malroux with the *Iphigenie* did some damage in 1798. Lemême was at sea with *L'Uni* in that year, which also saw Vaillant's career brought to its sudden close. *L'Uni*, Lemême's ship, was described as 'from Europe, mounting 26 nine-pounders on her gun-deck, besides her quarterdeck and forecastle guns, 220 men, she is reckoned a very fast sailor, has much the appearance of a London-built ship, painted with yellow sides and white mouldings.' *L'Uni* was at Mocha, disguised as a Dutch merchantman, in 1798, having left the French islands on July 16th. She took a number of prizes off Socotra. But the fact is that Surcouf was almost the only privateer who would attack an East Indiaman. And the captures of his contemporaries (there were perhaps eight of them, all told) were, many of them, not at the English expense. Surcouf's more notable prizes included the Portuguese ship *Nostra Signora de la Conception*, with 116,000 piastres on board. Houdoul's best capture was the *Bader-Bux* bound from Mocha to Surat.

Of the country ships with English names many were owned by Bombay Parsees. Rainier, incidentally, suspected many of them of trading with the enemy, either by a collusive arrangement at Tranquebar or by a fictitious sale which gave them Danish colours. Losses among these ships, causing annoyance among the Calcutta underwriters, did not arouse speechless indignation either at the Admiralty or at the India House. For the war was at a critical stage and statesmen had other causes for anxiety. Chief of these in 1797 was the Naval Mutiny at Spithead, which spread from there to the Nore and so, after some delay, to the foreign stations.

Had the mutinies been what some people said they were, the results of a sinister plot between French Jacobins and United Irishmen, the French would have been ready to take advantage of them. Instead, they scarcely knew of the mutinies until after they were over, and they gained from them little or nothing. That year saw, however, the military successes which brought the French armies to Venice and Genoa and Corfu, thus setting the stage for the great blow of 1798 at Malta and Egypt. A recurrence of mutiny on the foreign stations in 1798 would therefore have been peculiarly dangerous. It has sometimes been said that the East Indies station, as contrasted with the Cape, was free from mutiny. This is not quite true. There was the beginnings of a mutiny and it was owing to Rainier that no more came of it. He had in some measure forestalled it by care for his men's welfare, and his firmness did the rest. He believed, indeed, that he had averted trouble altogether by distributing copies of the Act which provided for increases of pay and provisions, and reported accordingly on 7th January, 1798:

> I have the satisfaction to acquaint you for their Lordships' information that there has not appeared the least disposition to mutiny on board any of the Ships of the Squadron, though the circumstances of that at Spithead and the consequent measures adopted had been known from the Newspapers some time before. (Ad. 1/169.)

Rainier was then at Madras, having been on the Coromandel coast or off Ceylon after the Manila expedition was cancelled, meaning then to proceed to the Malabar coast. He had, however, changed his mind and sailed instead for Penang, which he had reached on November 18th, returning to Madras on 2nd January, 1798, with the *Suffolk* and *Arrogant*. From there he sailed for Colombo, arriving on the 13th. On the 25th he was rather sadly reporting to the Admiralty that his seamen had mutinied at Colombo, the trouble beginning in the flagship while the Admiral was on shore.

. . . They [the seamen] came aft and demanded of Captain Lambert his acquiescence in several extravagant propositions nearly similar to those made by Parker at Nore and presenting several trivial complaints of ill usage from the officers, insisted on Lieuts. Batt. and Dobbie being put on shore. Captain Lambert in vain reasoned with them on the irregularity of their conduct, but judging my presence would have a better effect on them, accordingly sent for me, having gone on shore but the evening before; when I came on board it was near dark, observed everything to be quiet in the ship, and in the morning the usual duty carried on without any interruption, or disorder. After breakfast I ordered all hands to be turned up, and harangued them on the unreasonableness and impropriety of their demands, acquainting them that they had been misinformed as to any further gratification made by Government to the seamen on board the fleet at home, except such as had already been read to them, (the contrary whereto forming one part of their complaints) and in confirmation shewed them the impossibility of it from the dates of Mr. Nepean's Letters than which nothing later had arrived, that as to the Lieutenants, of whose ill usage of them they had complained, they should be tried by a Court Martial if they could produce a charge with sufficient evidence against them—I then recommended to them the serious consideration of their conduct, how unlike anything I had ever observed in them before, and that it was but the other day I had wrote the Secretary of the Admiralty to express to their Lordships my sense of their dutiful behaviour. Therefore I hoped they would return peaceably to their duty and by their future good conduct, efface as far as it was in their power their very reprehensible proceedings of the preceding day, but assured them in the strongest terms that I was determined to regulate my conduct towards them by the Terms of the Articles of War, their Lordships' orders and those of the King in Council, and took my leave; on which they quitted the Quarter Deck in a sullen discontented manner, and not long after as I was walking the Quarter Deck with Captain Osborn and Turner, we heard a loud hooting below which was followed by 20 or 30 men running up the Fore Rigging and giving 3 cheers towards the *Arrogant*. I immediately ordered the officers to push forward and seize them, on which the men ran down the shrouds precipitately, not being answered by the *Arrogant's* Ship's Company, while Captain Lambert attended by his officers armed followed them to the lower Gun-deck, and secured the most culpable, eleven in number, whom I ordered into a boat alongside to be carried on shore and there secured till sent for, which was complied with, my Lord Hobart being then at Colombo and apprized of what had happened, giving orders for that purpose. There was a man on board the *Carysfort* who endeavoured to excite a similar disturbance, and was afterwards sent on shore likewise. Nothing material has happened since, save that the Ship's Company of the *Suffolk* came aft the second day after to Capt. Lambert, to assure him of their readiness to do their duty, and that they would inform him of any of their Shipmates who should hereafter attempt to excite any disturbance amongst them. Previous to this they had requested the enlargement of the men confined, which Capt. Lambert informed them could not be complied with, but that they might depend upon it justice would be done them. 'Tis some satisfaction to me to acquaint you, that the main deck petty officers in general, and several of the best of the crew, appeared to have no hand in this business, and except one man who is secured, there was nobody offered to interrupt the Captain and his officers in apprehending the prisoners, tho' 'tis imagined the principal ringleaders are not among the number. Capt. Osborn, who was on board the *Suffolk* when the cheering happened, went on board his proper ship, and inquired of the Ship's company if they had any complaints to make, which they answered in the negative. He took occasion at the same time to observe to them how attentive the Admiral had always been to them, and instanced it in the goodness of their provisions, the procuring them the indulgence of the allowance of Tea from their Lordships which they had found so gratifying, and also the commodious provision I had made for the sick in the lately established Hospital at Madras: they all replied they were very sensible of it. The disturbance originated as far as I am able to judge with some men impressed from the Indiamen lately arrived, by his Majesty's Ship *Victorious*, whom I had ordered to be discharged into the *Suffolk*, and who perhaps found some mutinous disposed persons on board ready enough to join them, of which I fear there are not wanting some in all ships. . . .

The mutineers were tried by court martial and sentenced, but the Admiral celebrated the news of the Battle of Camperdown by pardoning them. To judge from his portrait, Peter Rainier was not an inspiring leader. He was fat, spectacled and perhaps a little solemn; an excellent officer and one who knew the Indian Ocean better than most, but not a vivid personality. Granted that the germ of mutiny came out from England, the *Suffolk's* crew were probably predisposed to mutiny from boredom. Life in the flagship must have been almost as tedious as in the Channel fleet. The only time—three months before—when they had been even *near* any prize money, the whole thing had been cancelled. If the *Arrogant* and *Victorious* were free from mutiny, it was probably because they had been in action in September 1796 and their seamen had had something to talk about ever since.

The mutiny in the ships of the line was short-lived, in the frigates non-existent, and the Admiral could devote all his attention to the war. Early in 1798 his thoughts were chiefly with Captains Pakenham and Cooke, respectively in the Moluccas and the China Seas. When Rainier had extricated himself from the complex problems inherent in ruling the Moluccas, he had left Pakenham to take his place. Pakenham had with him the *Resistance* (44), and the three sloops, *Hobart*, *Vulcan* and *Amboyna*. For a time Pakenham was chiefly occupied with a rebellion in Amboyna itself, but by July 1797 he was able to report the conquest of the Dutch settlement at Copong on the island of Timor. This was followed, however, by a Dutch plot to kill Pakenham by treachery. The town had surrendered and been occupied by a small garrison, mainly sepoys, under Lieutenant Frost. The fort was found difficult to defend, easily entered from the sea side and overlooked by houses nearby. On the day of the rising the lieutenant visited the Dutch governor at his office. The Dutch were evidently disappointed and asked particularly whether the Commodore was coming ashore. Leaving the governor's the lieutenant heard a tumult and saw one or two of his sentries being killed. Realizing that the Malays (probably armed by the Dutch) had burst into the town, he ran for the fort, with one or two survivors, and there found himself under heavy musketry fire from the neighbouring buildings. The situation was momentarily saved by some marines, landed from boats, who climbed into the weak embrasures on the sea side. It was clear, nevertheless, that the fort was in no condition to stand a siege and that the marines were too few to defend it even if it had been. It was decided, therefore, to burn the whole town and blow up the fort, which was done after the marines had been re-embarked. Some three hundred of the rebels were killed and sixteen of the seamen and sepoys.

The relatively easy occupation of Amboyna and Banda had encouraged Rainier, it will be remembered, to order (before he left in 1796) the further conquest of Ternate. But Ternate, northernmost island of the Moluccas, had been well fortified and was held by the obstinate Governor Budach. He did not surrender to Pakenham's summons and held out, in fact, until 1801.[1] In the meanwhile, certain ships of Rainier's squadron had to remain in the Moluccas and more would have been needed had not the East India Company's cruisers been there to assist. It was an awkward commitment, but it is fair to recall that Rainier regarded the Moluccas as a permanent conquest and a part of the British Empire. In accounts of the expedition to Java in 1811 it is too often forgotten that the way had been prepared by a previous occupation of the Moluccas and by the naval operations which, extending over years, had gradually familiarized the Navy with a region from which the Dutch had for generations excluded all European rivals.

[1] See *Commodore Sir John Hayes, his voyage and life, 1767–1831*. Ida Lee. London, 1912. (Chapter XIV.)

Farther to the eastward, the problem was to ensure the safety of the China fleet at a period when the Spanish at Manila were actively at war, with ships admirably placed to waylay the trade. Rainier's first measure of trade protection, taken while the Manila expedition was still in preparation, had been to send the *Sybille* (38), Captain Cooke, and *Centurion* (50), to escort the outward-bound China trade (i.e. from Bombay to Macao) through the Straits of Malacca. This was on 12th July, 1797, and by August 21st he had sent the *Victorious* (74) and *Trident* (64) in the same direction. The *Sybille* and *Trident*, with the *Fox* (32) were to go on to Macao and escort the China ships homeward. The danger to the China trade was increased by the cancellation of the Manila expedition, the threat of which, while it lasted, was enough to keep the Spaniards in port.

> The necessity I shall be under of sending a strong convoy to China every season whilst the Spaniards are in so much force there, will naturally occur to their Lordships' observation, and as they may be expected to put to Sea again when they receive information of our Expedition being laid aside, which must have reached them by this time, I am apprehensive it will delay Capt. Cooke's return with the ships under his command to a later period than I had calculated, as it may be conjectured the Supercargoes will apply to him to wait to take under his convoy the whole of the homeward bound ships then in port by the different routes they may be directed to take, as far as their courses lie together. . . .
>
> (Rainier to Admiralty, 25th November, 1797. Ad. 1/168.)

Captain Edward Cooke duly brought his convoy to Macao on 13th December, 1798, his crews much enfeebled by sickness, especially that of the *Trident*. As Rainier had expected, Cooke was asked, and agreed, to remain until all the Indiamen were loaded. To be more exact, he agreed to escort one division of the fleet as far as the latitude of Manila and then return for the rest, or for such as were ready by the end of March. The supercargoes wanted to fix an even later date but the necessity for this would be apparent only if the Spaniards were at sea. This Captain Cooke decided to learn by personal reconnaissance as soon as he had parted with the first group of Indiamen. The information received through Swedish intermediaries seemed to him, no doubt, too vague and contradictory. There can be no doubt that Cooke had an additional motive in hoping to intercept two of the Spanish treasure ships, which he believed to be at Manila and due to leave. Sailing with the *Sybille* and *Fox* (Captain Malcolm) on 5th January, 1798, Cooke rid himself of his Indiamen and was off the Philippines by the 11th. He learnt from a coasting vessel that only two of the Spanish men-of-war were ready for sea. Thus encouraged, Cooke proceeded to disguise his two frigates, probably modelling the *Sybille* on the *Seine* and the *Fox* on the *Prudente*. The transformation must have been very complete, extending even to uniform—one imagines the sailors glee-fully learning to shout 'Vive la République' from time to time. Thus disguised and rehearsed the two frigates entered Manila Bay after dark on the 13th, passed Corregidor and anchored before midnight. At sunrise they hoisted French colours and worked up the bay until within sight of the Spanish squadron in Cavita road—three ships of the line and two frigates. The *Fox* was leading and it was that frigate which the Spanish guard-boat approached. Answering the inevitable question, a linguist on board the *Fox* explained nonchalantly that the two frigates were part of Sercey's squadron and had put in, hoping for supplies and Spanish co-operation. A Spanish naval officer then promised them supplies, but explained that none of the men-of-war could be prepared for sea in less than two months; which was perhaps just as well. Captain Cooke now came on board (to the tune, one hopes, of the *Marseillaise*) and was introduced as Commodore Latour. The party then adjourned to Malcolm's cabin for a glass of wine, drunk to the downfall of England. There they were presently joined by some more officers, rowed out in Rear-Admiral Don Martin Alaba's barge. A second boatload arrived with messages from the Admiral, brought by his A.D.C. At that point the guests had to be undeceived; if only perhaps to save the *Fox's* crew from hysteria. The episode ended with the bloodless capture of three Spanish gunboats, the prisoners taken, about two hundred, being all released.

There can be no doubt that a slightly stronger squadron, given the same measure of surprise, could have destroyed the Spanish squadron at its moorings with probably the dockyard as well. As it happened, the squadron might easily have been reinforced by the *Resistance* (44), which Rainier had ordered to Macao from the Moluccas. She had been off Manila—by mere accident, of course—a few days before. Instead, however, of capturing the richly-laded *Marquesetta*, she had merely frightened the Spaniards into unloading that ship. The *Marquesetta* was now lying, with the *Rey-Carlos*, in Cavita, well out of reach, and the *Resistance* had put back to the Moluccas after sustaining such damage in a gale that she very nearly foundered. Had her visit coincided with that of the two frigates, Pakenham would have been in command—a man without Cooke's touch of genius—and the *Resistance* did not, of course, resemble any of the French frigates. Apart, however, from these material considerations, it is evident that Cooke did not want to carry matters too far. He had learnt, in great detail, all he wanted to know. The Spanish had the *San Pedro* (74), *Montanes* (74) and *Europa* (74), the *Maria de la Cabeya* (36) and *Lucia* (36), all in port, and another 36-gun frigate expected back in two months. None of the ships in port was fit to sail. They were all fairly harmless and ill-equipped, and no real threat to anyone. It was just as well to let them alone. Rainier evidently thought the same for he reported Captain Cooke's adventure to the Admiralty as follows:

> . . . Captain Cooke in *La Sybille* and *Fox* during the lading of the Indiamen at Canton made an alert into Manila Bay, January 13th last and by hoisting French Colours completely deceived the Spaniards till he had obtained every useful information . . . and then dismissed the Spanish officers and crews with the boats that brought them off; a conduct much to my satisfaction, as the Governor of Manila behaved so very honorably towards his Majesty's subjects on the breaking out of the war. . . .

Anglo-Spanish relations fell something short, it is evident, of total war. A year later, as we have seen, Edward Cooke lay mortally wounded at Calcutta while his prize the *Forte* was towed by the *Sybille* into port.

During the latter half of 1798, Admiral Rainier had more important things to worry about than the safety of the China fleet. On May 19th, the expedition under General Bonaparte sailed from Toulon. On July 1st his troops were landing in Egypt, and on the 2nd they captured Alexandria. A month later his fleet was destroyed in Aboukir Bay. That Bonaparte was bound for Egypt Rainier knew on September 17th, if not before. More detailed information he lacked. He knew enough, however, to understand the chief factors in the situation and he must have had, for the moment, sufficient food for thought. As regards the invasion of Egypt, neither he nor Dundas nor the authorities in India were taken wholly by surprise. They had, as we have seen, expected something of the kind. On the other hand, they were mostly (Dundas excepted) sceptical of Bonaparte's chances of reaching India. Supposing him firmly settled in Egypt, with all Turkish opposition neutralized, the choices open to him were, broadly, two: to proceed by sea or by land. The march overland would imply, in the first instance, an understanding with the rulers of Persia and Arabia, and, in the second place, a solution to a supply problem which seemed insoluble. The voyage from Suez would imply ships. These could be either sent from France, sent from the Mauritius or acquired somehow (built, for example) at Suez. With the French ports closely watched, there seemed no likelihood of a squadron leaving France without being so closely pursued as to be foredoomed to disaster. The squadron at Mauritius had ceased to exist, or nearly so, and neither Dutch nor Spanish allies had so far proved effective. The privateers, if requisitioned, were mostly quite small. As for the Red Sea, the local craft to be found there were smaller still, and the materials for building anything larger were conspicuously absent. This, nevertheless, seemed the most hopeful line of approach, for Tippoo Sultan was the obvious ally and the Red Sea led in his direction. Mangalore was the obvious place of disembarkation and the Governor-General knew that, say, three thousand French soldiers landed there could do enormous harm. It is not clear that Bonaparte ever contemplated thus sacrificing a brigade, but Wellesley had to bear the possibility in mind. And granted that the tonnage to embark his whole army might seem unobtainable, the craft needed to carry a brigade might just possibly exist. Tippoo himself might strive to send some ships and, once given a few, these might scour the Red Sea for more. Dundas seems to have expected Bonaparte to follow Alexander's route to India and took diplomatic means to impede him, while not ignoring the Red Sea alternative. His more energetic measures included ordering the Bombay Government to occupy the island of Perim, at the southern entrance to the Red Sea. He also instructed Wellesley to deal with Tippoo before French help could reach him. 'If Tipu has made preparations of a hostile nature . . . do not wait for actual hostilities on his part . . . attack him!'[1] This was sound policy, whatever Bonaparte's plan might be.

Apart from the wisdom he may or may not have shown, Dundas is given much credit, and no doubt rightly, for the speed with which he acted. His suspicion of Bonaparte's destination had become conviction by June 13th and his orders followed at once. One essential, he decided, was to have a squadron in the Red Sea at the earliest possible moment. One way to ensure this would have been to send orders to Rainier, possibly followed by reinforcements. But it was a moment of crisis and to Dundas, at his most Napoleonic, this procedure seemed too slow. He decided to send a squadron directly there from England. It would come eventually under Rainier's command—that was inevitable—but with orders from the Secretary of State it could go straight to Suez and cut out the delay which might result from an attempt to give orders to Rainier. One project urged by Dundas at this time was countered by Grenville with an unkind suggestion that he should consult a large-scale map of Asia: his Red Sea project would have lost none of its effect had he also had time to consult a chart and sailing directory. Be that as it may, he chose Captain J. Blankett for this service and instructed the Admiralty to send him to Suez at the earliest

[1] See *The East India Company, 1784-1834.* C. H. Philips. Manchester, 1940, p. 101, *et seq.*

possible moment with the rank of Commodore. By June 30th Blankett was at the Fountain Inn at Portsmouth and urging the Commissioner of the Dockyard to hasten the victualling of the *Leopard* (50) in which he was to hoist a broad pendant. A Captain Blair was to have gone with him, but a change of plan sent this emissary off 'to pursue his journey overland to Jedda and other Ports in the Red Sea, as also to Aden for the purpose of furnishing you with such Intelligence as he may be able to collect.' This representative of an M.I. Branch vanished (no doubt in Arab disguise) while Blankett chafed at the maddening deliberation with which stores were being supplied to the *Orestes* (13) and *Daedalus* (32). 'I have now served more than forty years,' he confided to Nepean, 'and find impatience still prevails. . . .' By July 5th he was at Spithead and wondering what the Navy was coming to.

> It appears to me that the manners of our service is much changed, particularly the officers, who seem to have lost much of that vivacity we used to see formerly, and as for respect it seems almost lost. We sent away 200 women yesterday and reserved none. The fashion of carrying women to sea answers no good purpose, but introduces many bad ones. . . .
>
> (Ad. 1/169.)

On July 6th the *Leopard* was at St. Helen's but the *Daedalus* was still without captain, first lieutenant, master or surgeon. To make matters worse, Captain Surridge and Captain Ball had been summoned to sit on a court martial. 'Could not they be excused?' begged Blankett of Admiral Waldegrave; but he begged in vain. The idea! What would he be asking next? One may imagine Waldegrave expressing his surprise to a contemporary 'The manners of the service are sadly changed, Sir—as for respect, it seems almost lost!' Blankett was able to sail soon afterwards and was at Torbay on the 12th, renewing his water supply, but 'I shall put to sea again without a moment's loss of time.' That interview with Dundas had had its effect; Blankett had been breathless ever since.

John Blankett had been made captain in 1780 and was now, in 1798, very near his flag. He was known to Jeremy Bentham, who described him (in 1781) as:

> . . . One of the most wrong-headed blockheads I think I ever met with; putting in his oar on every occasion, talking *à tort* and *à travers*, and spoiling every discussion that is started. Yet he is connected with many of the first people in opposition and, in particular, has the ear of the *maitre de la maison* (i.e. Lord Shelburne) to a degree I am sorry to observe. His great merit is the having been a lieutenant to Keppel, whose *âme damnée* he is, and has

written paragraphs and pamphlets on his side. Before he went, he took me into confidence, and consulted me about a nonsensical project of his for discovering polished and commercial nations where Cooke had been, and found none: the most absurd idea, supported by the most absurd arguments, in the most confused method, and in the most slovenly and awkward style. He it is who brought home the *Rippon* from the East Indies. He is personally acquainted with Rumbold and defends him without argument and without shame. *Sed de hoc plus satis.*

(*Works of Jeremy Bentham,* ed. by John Bowring, Vol. X, Edinburgh, 1843, p. 95.)

On another occasion Bentham said:

Blankett was a retainer of Lord Shelburne, one of the numerous hangers-on who were tale-bearers to my lord and was familiar with the Whigs. He was an ignorant, confident, amusing fellow, an object of great aversion to the Bowood ladies from his coarse manners. But he was employed by Lord Shelburne to repeat to him what passed among the Whigs, and especially to report the conversations at the Admiralty. . . . We had a dispute about the relative size of Sicily and Ireland. He would have it that Sicily was the biggest. But though ill-read and assuming, and addicted to falsehood, rather from temerity than mendacity, he was a necessary instrument to Lord Shelburne. . . .

(*Ibid.*, p. 116.)

Blankett had professional virtues which could hardly be appreciated by one who had met him only at Bowood. He had been in the East Indies but not in the Red Sea. Indeed, to have found an officer acquainted with the Red Sea would have been extremely difficult; it was a region rarely visited, almost unsurveyed, and generally but little known. Owing to bad weather in the Atlantic, Blankett did not round the Cape until October 1st. He was harassed by easterly gales, in which his two consorts parted company, only rejoining him at the Comoro Islands. It was the wrong time of year for the voyage he was attempting, and he spent all November and December on the East African coast struggling against adverse winds and currents. On December 10th he captured the French privateer *Apollon* (12 guns, 125 men), the corsairs having every reason to be surprised and hurt at finding British men-of-war where, in all conscience, they had no business to be. Writing to the Admiralty on 16th January, 1799, Blankett reported:

I have now been eight weeks on this Coast, hitherto little known (if at all) to the English, in the course of which time, I have endeavoured by standing both to the Northward and Southward, to find the means of proceeding on my voyage, hitherto without success, and have crossed the Line fourteen times, but have found the Winds invariably to the Eastward and a strong current setting to the S.W. so as to have made it impossible to get off the Coast. I am now anchored in about 4° 5′ North, with an intent to send the *Daedalus* to the Cape for a supply of salt provisions and spirits. . . .

The *Daedalus* went off, with orders to rejoin him at Aden, and Blankett pushed on doggedly, his men on reduced rations. He learnt from native craft that 'the French had landed at Alexandria and were got to Cairo' which spurred him on afresh. Still delayed by gales in February, and running short not only of food and water, but of fuel and candles and everything else, he put into Zanzibar 'altho',' he wrote, 'I do not know that an English ship has ever been there,' and managed to obtain there rice, beef, wood and water. So fortified, he was enabled to reach Mocha on April 13th. There he found Captain Wilson of the Company's Marine and learnt from him that Admiral Rainier had sent two ships up the Red Sea already, the *Centurion* (50) and *Albatross* (18), and that these had sailed from Jidda for Suez a fortnight before.

It is sad to think that all this frantic hurry should have ended, after a ten months' voyage, in this horrible anti-climax. The idea of sending a small squadron to watch Suez was not (when one pauses to consider it) as brilliantly original as all that. Rainier had thought of it for himself—as of course he would, and as he was paid to do—and had acted early in December with calm efficiency. It would have been quicker, for that matter, to have sent him an order direct. Blankett may have reflected on these depressing facts. There, however, he was, as senior naval officer in the Red Sea, and he had to decide what to do next. He turned to Captain Wilson for information. The officers of the Company's Marine were a rather embittered set of men, without the prestige of the Navy or the profits of the Indiamen. Apart from prize-money they had no legal means of making a fortune and no very obvious prospects of advancement. One may picture Wilson as probably a man who knew the Red Sea, the Arabs and the Royal Navy and disliked them all. His replies would be laconic. Blankett wanted to reach Suez? It was too late in the year. The northern monsoon would set in before he could arrive there. What about the *Daedalus*? If she did not appear within a month she would not be able to enter the straits. Would the *Centurion* be likely to return? She couldn't—not until the monsoon changed. Were any supplies to be had locally? No. Any water? Oh, yes—at three dollars a cask. Was there any news of Bonaparte? Nothing to be relied upon—it was mostly invented by Arab chieftains to serve their own

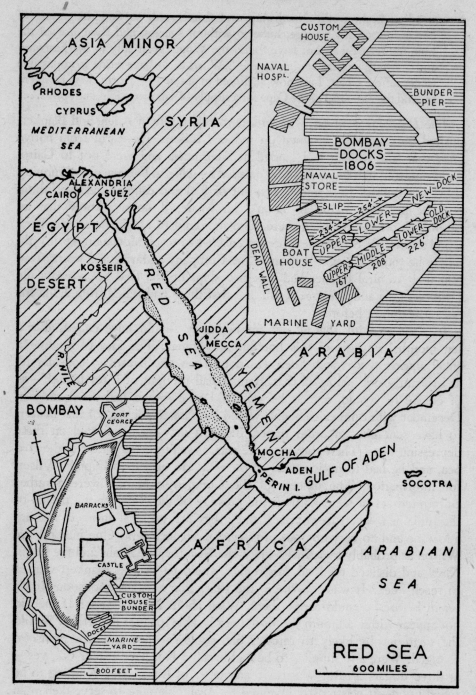

ASIA MINOR

RHODES
CYPRUS
MEDITERRANEAN
SEA

SYRIA

ALEXANDRIA
CAIRO SUEZ

EGYPT

KOSSEIR

DESERT

R. NILE

RED SEA

JIDDA
MECCA

YEMEN

MOCHA
ADEN
PERIM I. GULF OF ADEN
SOCOTRA

ARABIA

AFRICA

ARABIAN
SEA

CUSTOM
HOUSE

NAVAL
HOSPL

BUNDER
PIER

BOMBAY
DOCKS
1806

NAVAL
STORE

SLIP

NEW DOCK

OLD DOCK

UPPER LOWER

254'

234'

226

DEAD WALL

BOAT
HOUSE

UPPER MIDDLE

LOWER

208

167

MARINE YARD

BOMBAY

FORT
GEORGE

BARRACKS

CASTLE

CUSTOM
HOUSE
BUNDER

DOCKS

MARINE
YARD

800 FEET

RED SEA

600 MILES

devious ends. Blankett found that he could do little but wait. He found, however, a certain grim satisfaction in realizing that Bonaparte had chosen the worst sea in the world for the sort of operation he apparently intended. For three months no ship could enter the Red Sea and for the following three months no ship could leave it! For a squadron to dash into Suez and dash out again with troops on board would imply staff-work of a superhuman order.

'In a month from this' [wrote Rainier on April 16th] 'the Northern Monsoon will set in, during which time no ships can enter the Straits (as I am told) so that I shall have then no apprehension from without. In this Monsoon Buonaparte, if he move at all, must make his push, and I hope in that case to give a good account of him.'

When the monsoon was over, Blankett intended to go to Bombay to repair his ships. That they needed repair may well be believed.

What had Bonaparte been doing all this time? It had taken him two or three months to deal with local resistance in Egypt and it was not until November 1798 that he ordered an advance on Suez. Even then, because of the Turkish threat, the column sent was quite small and the orders only for a reconnaissance in force. General Bon marched from Cairo on December 3rd, with six hundred men and two guns. With him went a naval man called Collot, with ten sailors. Bon's task was to see all the cisterns filled and arrange with the Arabs at Tor to keep up the supply of water. He was to build a battery to face seawards and secure Suez from molestation. He was to prepare one or two local craft to act as cruisers, assure the merchants of Yambo and Jidda that their trade was safe, fortify Suez on the landward side, and gain all possible information about Jidda and Mecca.

General Bon reached Suez on December 7th, occupied the town without difficulty, and found in the harbour four unarmed merchantmen and five or six small craft. He reported that the place was easy to defend against naval attack, being protected by sandbanks stretching seawards for miles and approachable only by a narrow channel having a depth of two and a half fathoms at most. No man-of-war could get within range. On the 11th, hearing that all was well, Bonaparte sent off a supply column with fifty more sailors, seven or eight shipwrights, thirty-five engineers, and another gun.[1] On December 24th, Bonaparte set off to visit Suez in person,

[1] On December 18th Bonaparte ordered General Bon to survey the anchorage and ascertain 'si des frégates de l'île de France, que j'attend, pourraient, étant arrivées à Suez, s'approcher de la côte jusqu'à 100 toises de manière à etre protegées par les batteries de côte.' See *L'Expedition d'Egypte*, Vol. III, p. 444 *et seq*.

accompanied by a small escort, together with Rear-Admiral Ganteaume and a motley following of antiquaries and Egyptologists, geologists and surveyors. Arriving on December 27th, he questioned such Arab seamen as could be found, inspected the town, and issued a number of characteristic orders. The Admiral was told to equip three gunboats and use them to reconnoitre Tor and other neighbouring ports. Leaving subordinates to carry out these orders as well as they might, Bonaparte hurried off again on 3rd January, 1799, to explore the traces of the canal dug by the ancients. He was back in Cairo on the evening of the 6th. At this period he was evidently considering the construction of a Red Sea squadron, and had even begun to draw up plans for naval operations in the near future. These would have been more realistic if Admiral Sercey's frigates had been at hand. Instead, the *Preneuse* and *Brûle-Gueule* were far to the eastward, attempting to co-operate with the Spanish, and the *Forte* was on her way towards the Bay of Bengal and capture. It does not appear that Sercey was even ordered to co-operate with Bonaparte; if he was, the orders came too late, after his squadron had virtually ceased to exist. As for the ship-wrights at Suez, they managed to build not only the three gunboats but a brigantine constructed from the timber of two dhows. They were still so busied when, on April 27th, two ships were seen approaching from the south. They were not Sercey's frigates. They were the *Centurion* and the *Albatross*. To anything of a flotilla which anyone could conceivably build at Suez, they were the answer; the finish; checkmate.

In the crisis occasioned by the invasion of Egypt, Dundas, as we have seen, acted with great vigour. But the Governor-General of India and Admiral Rainier were fully as resolute, both before and after their instructions arrived. On the 17th June, 1798, while Bonaparte was at Malta and about to sail for Egypt, Rainier was assuring the Admiralty 'that all His Majesty's extensive Dominions in this Country are in perfect safety and tranquillity, which as far as lies with me no exertions shall be wanting to preserve.' He had been busy organizing the protection of trade and had been, in person, on the Malabar coast from April until his arrival at Trincomalee in June. While on the west side of India he had heard from Calicut 'of the warlike movements in the dominions of Sultan Tippoo, indicating a sanguine expectation of being joined by a French force,' but the fact that the *Suffolk* and *Arrogant* were far more in evidence than the French had a sobering effect. On July 9th, Rainier outlined his plans for the benefit of the Governor-General. He proposed to send the *Arrogant* (74), *Fox* (32) and *Carysfort* (28) to the Straits of Malacca, while retaining the *Suffolk* (74), *Victorious* (74), *Trident* (64) and *Virginie* (38) on the Coromandel coast.

He explained that (with several under repair) he lacked the ships for offensive action and added:

> There is no reason at present to apprehend any hostile equipment being in motion in Europe to attack the British settlements in this country; and the fears of any from the French Islands, which so lately existed and took their rise in the events that followed the appearance of *La Preneuse*, French frigate, on the Malabar Coast may from very recent intelligence received from the Mauritius be looked upon as entirely removed; and therefore am of opinion there will be no occasion for the services of His Majesty's ships during the S.W. Monsoon on that coast . . . altho' I shall ever regard it as an object to prevent as far as lies in my power, the Enemy's cruisers from molesting the Trade of that Coast and affording a confidence to their friend Tippoo Sultan. . . .
>
> (Ad. 1/169.)

Bonaparte had captured Alexandria a week before Rainier wrote the above letter, news of which reached India rather slowly. But Lord Mornington acted before the news came, warning Rainier on August 31st in a letter to which the Admiral replied as follows:

> *Suffolk*, Madras Road.
September 17th 1798.
>
> My Lord
> Influenced by the consideration of the several circumstances so ably detailed in your Lordship's letter of the 31st ultimo respecting the apprehensions that may be reasonably entertained of the inimical designs of Tippoo Sultan, and the co-operation that may be afforded him on the part of the French, affecting the safety of British possessions in India, I purpose proceeding to the Malabar Coast with his Majesty's Ships *Suffolk* and *Trident*, leaving the *Victorious* for the protection of this Coast 'till the Homeward bound Indiamen are loaded. . . .

By September 27th, ten days later, in giving orders to the captain of the *Arrogant* to proceed to China and then rejoin the flagship, Rainier was able to include a warning:

> As 'tis apprehended part of the French armament said to be destined for Egypt may be coming this way, if they can escape Lord St. Vincent, it will behove you to approach the Malabar Coast with great caution. . . .

It was November before Rainier seems to have had any precise information about Egypt, and even that was accompanied by many baseless rumours. He knew enough, however, in September to begin re-deploying his squadron to the westward, mainly in order to blockade Mysore. He was thus able to report (in cypher) on December 2nd that he had received his orders from the Admiralty and, with them, information about Commodore Blankett's mission.

Centurion, Bombay 2nd Dec.

... The present disposition of His Majesty's Squadron under my command, is as follows, *Suffolk* and *Victorious* on the Malabar Coast near Mangalore —the *Trident* preparing to dock; *Centurion* has docked, and proceeds to Mocha with the *Belvidere* Indiaman in five days, to reinforce Commodore Blankett, a situation of the greatest alarm at present—The *Sybille* is or was at the mouth of the Ganges, but ordered to join me. The *Arrogant* and *Virginie* in the Streights of Malacca but may be gone to convoy the Trade from China—The *Carysfort* and *Fox* at China; daily expected to return to Prince of Wales Island. These last four ships are also ordered to join me, but uncertain when they may receive the order; the *Resistance* missing— The *Orpheus*, *Hobart*, *Vulcan* Bomb and *Amboyna* Brig stationed at the Spice Islands.

Certain intelligence, VIZ. Buonaparte getting possession of Cairo— Admiral Nelson's Victory—the French had not reached Suez the 25th of August last, nor was there the least apprehension of their penetrating through Persia in the middle of last month, on the contrary, the attempt is deemed utterly impracticable.

Intelligence received from Bussora [Bushire] but not authenticated; burning of the Ships at Alexandria by Captain Trowbridge; successive defeats and massacres of the French Army in Egypt by the Arabs—Buonaparte determining to get to the East Indies, had reached Suez with 8000 men. . . .

(Ad. 1/169.)

Without committing himself to belief or incredulity, Rainier felt justified in planning to reinforce Blankett and patrol the Persian Gulf. A week later, on the 9th, the Admiral had no further news, save that the *Centurion* had sailed (without the *Belvidere*) and that

I have ordered the Senior Captain of His Majesty's Ships on the Malabar Coast cruizing off Mangalore, to treat Sultan Tippoo as His Majesty's Enemy, whenever he shall be informed by proper authority, in my absence, that the Supreme Government of India have commenced Hostilities against that Prince.

(Ad. 1/169.)

The Supreme Government was taking no risks as far as Tippoo was concerned. It might be satisfactory to know how difficult it would be for Bonaparte to make contact with his potential ally in India. But it would be far more satisfactory to be certain that he would find no ally there to contact. The campaign against Tippoo began in February 1799 and ended with the storming of Seringapatam in May. As Rainier had assured the Admiralty in January, the East India Company was 'ready to take the field in such force as, from intelligence received, the Sultan is little able to cope with, without the assistance of the French, whose junction it will be my duty to prevent; and of which at present there is no great apprehension entertained.' It was General Baird—once Tippoo's prisoner in that very place—who commanded the army. But when they found Tippoo's body it was Colonel Arthur Wellesley who felt the heart and rose to tell the General that their enemy was dead. Afterwards, had any more French troops found their way, by any means, to Mysore, they would have found Arthur Wellesley there to meet them. All chance of an Indian alliance was a thing of the past.

The measures taken to block Bonaparte's route to India—measures naval, military and diplomatic—were held to be incomplete unless some bases were occupied at the mouth of the Red Sea. The orders from Dundas provided for such a base being seized—the island of Perim being specified. The Government of Bombay prepared to carry out instructions but without excluding the island of Melun as an alternative. The idea was to secure, if possible, a position from which the straits—or at least the navigable channel —might be covered by shore batteries. Informed by Government of this intention, Rainier sent orders to Commodore Blankett to co-operate. These reached Blankett soon after his arrival at Mocha and were brought by a much-needed storeship. This was followed by a number of transports and, going over to the island in early May, Blankett found a Lieutenant-Colonel Murray with 'all the apparatus for a large settlement.' The troops had been landed, and fortifications were being put in hand. If that rocky and forbidding island had a defect, however, it was in the total lack of any water supply. The chief concern, therefore, of the garrison was in the digging of reservoirs and the fetching of water-casks from the Arabian coast or from Abyssinia. Blankett looked on the whole business with the strongest disapproval. In the first place, he held that the straits could be blocked perfectly well by men-of-war based on Mocha, near which port all shipping had to pass. In the second place, he had not been consulted. And, in the third, he did not want to see his ships tied to Perim by the necessity of fetching water for the garrison.

The expedition actually comprised the *Fox* (32), the H.C.S. *Princess Charlotte* (armed—36), the H.C. bomb ketch *Strombolo*, two gun-boats and several transports including the *Baker*, *Jehangeer* and *Upton Castle*.

The European troops were of the 84th Regiment and numbered two hundred, the native troops six hundred. In reporting (31st March, 1799) the early departure of this convoy from Bombay, Rainier wrote complacently of the preparations made:

> The cannon for the Batteries are twelve thirty-two pounders, besides lighter guns. Proper materials are embarked on board the transports both for erecting Batteries and constructing Barracks and Storehouses. This convoy will sail in a day or two, and there is no doubt entertained of making the passage in good time . . . it may be reasonably conjectured there is fresh water on the island. . . .

As so often happens, however, the expedition made a smaller impression when it reached its destination. Blankett reported from Mocha on June 6th, to Rainier, that he had co-operated according to orders.

> In consequence of the orders you sent me, as soon as I could be supplied with Provisions from the Storeship, I proceeded to the Isle of Perim, in the Straits of Babelmandeb and in my passage met the *Fox* who had previously landed Lieut-Col. Murray and his suite on that island and was on his way to join mé in Mocha Road; on my arrival at the Island on the 7th [May] I found the troops landed—soon after which I wrote a letter to Lieutⁿ Col^l Murray. . . . I soon found that they were come on a great scale to build batteries in the Sea, that should command the Straits, but that they were unprovided with Water, without casks to procure it, without tools for their carpenters, caulkers or Coopers and even without shovels or spades and without money to purchase any of those wants—in short so helpless an expedition *perhaps* never left India before—Whenever they wished the assistance of the Navy it was given them, but they would neither consult or allow an opinion from the officers on the most practicable mode of pro- ceeding. . . . From this persisting, their work has been ill done, their tanks are badly put together, and they have been doing and undoing ever since their arrival. . . .
>
> I cannot think after the unprecedented manner in which the Bombay Presidency have treated me, that it was my business to enter into speculative opinions, how the force at the island could be better applied. It is possible for folly to defeat a Plan wise in itself, by making its prosecution impracti- cable.
>
> I shall always think that the possession of this island was highly eligible, practicable and even necessary at the present moment, but to set down a large body of men unprovided and helpless without a previous consideration, speaks too plainly for itself to need any illustration of mine.
>
> Whether the Island affords Water or not is still problematical. . . .
>
> (Ad. 1/169.)

Problematical it was to remain. Blankett, however, remained at Mocha and tried to recall the *Centurion* (Captain J. S. Rainier) from Suez. This order was based on a belief, fostered by Arab reports, that the French army had been defeated and 'completely surrounded.' He cancelled it later and promised to reinforce the *Centurion* instead. He considered, however, that the straits were the point to defend in force and the place to which a desperate Bonaparte would eventually be driven. On May 19th, the *Daedalus* at length arrived from the Cape, with stores no longer wanted but having taken the *Prudente* off the Cape on February 9th. Also, on June 6th, the *Centurion* arrived at Mocha, having left the *Albatross* to cruise for six weeks off Tor. Captain Rainier's report was reassuring—Bonaparte had no flotilla at Suez. And now, with the setting in of the northern monsoon, there was little chance of any vessels reaching Suez from the Indian Ocean. Blankett remained at Mocha, however, and was presently joined by the *Albatross*, with definite news that the French had occupied Kosseir and a letter from Sir Sidney Smith giving news of the successful defence of Acre. This information was quite correct. The French General Desaix had been chasing the Mamelukes up the left bank of the Nile, and, towards the end of May, he sent a small force to garrison Kosseir and its semi-ruined fort. This port was thought useful as a means of intercepting any help which the Mamelukes might otherwise draw from Arabia: while, at the same time, facilitating negotiations with the Shereef of Mecca.

Had the French been still intent on invading India (which they were not) the attitude of the Shereef would have been an important factor in the situation. Jidda was the nearest port at which the French could have found any quantity of shipping and the Shereef, with a doubtful claim to his office, was following a tortuous policy of his own, having probably been bribed by Tippoo Sultan. As Blankett wrote in August:

> The Sheriffe is considered as extremely arbitrary and avaritious, practised in various deceits, seldom avowing any reason for his actions and jealous of the encreasing power of the Turks, from whose hands he has now almost wrested the whole authority they were used to exercise in his territories. . . .

Blankett considered that the French capture of Kosseir was done 'by connivance from Mecca' and that the time had come for resolute action. By now Blankett was worried chiefly about the possibility of a permanent French occupation of Egypt.

> From the judgment I have been able to form, I should conclude that Buonaparte meditates at present a firm establishment in Egypt, a system

far more formidable to our interests than the visionary atempt of passing to India, in which he must according to all probabilities, have failed. . . .

(Blankett to Bombay Government, 17th August, 1799. Ad. 1/169.)

Perhaps chiefly to impress the Shereef, Blankett ordered the *Daedalus* and *Fox* to visit Jidda and then go on to Kosseir and—supposing it were in enemy hands—destroy it. This feat would be doubly impressive as performed against the monsoon; which, for a frigate, was found to be possible. The two frigates left Mocha on July 7th, left Jidda on August 2nd and reached Kosseir on the 14th. Seeing the tricolour flying on the fort, they anchored at a suitable distance and opened fire. They went on firing 'day and night' until the fort was in ruins and the colours shot away. The bombardment lasted three days, with occasional and unsuccessful attempts to land, and ended only from shortage of ammunition after the expenditure of about three thousand rounds. Blankett's motive in this was to impress the Arabs (before the days of Mahan) with the possibilities of sea power. As he wrote to Lord Spencer, 'Your Lordship will naturally suppose it was not an old Arab castle I considered of consequence,' but rather the moral effect in Arabia, and especially at Mecca.

Following up his line of reasoning about the danger of a permanent French hold on Egypt, Blankett was now intent on making Egypt less valuable to France. Suffering badly from the heat, and by now a little shrill, Blankett propounded a scheme for interrupting all trade connections of Egypt and Arabia. Towards this the first step was to reduce the Shereef to reason. Trusting that the bombardment of Kosseir had left the Shereef in a receptive mood, Blankett determined to visit Jidda in person. Fortunately, on the very eve of his departure, Blankett (a Rear-Admiral now by the promotion of February 15th which made Rainier a Vice-Admiral of the Blue) received two important pieces of news. One was of the death of Tippoo Sultan, the other of the departure of Bonaparte from Egypt in August 1799. With these two events, the danger to India was virtually at an end. The result was that when Blankett took his squadron to Jidda he had no difficulty in persuading the Shereef to forbid all intercourse between his ports and Suez. On his return to Mocha, he found that Colonel Murray had in early September transferred the bulk of his force from Perim to Aden. This move was the result of an invitation from the Sultan of Aden, who was willing and indeed anxious to surrender the town as a dependency with himself a pensioner. Taking this offer with him, Blankett went with the *Leopard*, *Centurion* and *Daedalus* to winter and refit at Bombay. He left the *Fox* and *Albatross* at Mocha, where they were joined for a time by the *Braave* (38) and *Amboyna* (14).

At Bombay, from which Rainier had recently sailed, Blankett settled down to discuss with the Bombay Government the merits of Aden which Colonel Murray extolled. It had few, by his account. Perim was now ruled out as impossible because the water found, by boring to 24 feet, had turned out to be salt. Mocha was more useful but could not become a British possession. The question was too important to decide at Bombay, and the same could be said of Blankett's proposals for discouraging trade with Egypt. By careful inquiry, Blankett had established the fact that Arabia depended partly on the export of coffee but more on the pilgrim traffic. With the money derived from these services, the inhabitants bought corn from Egypt and European goods from Cairo. It was, therefore, a simple matter to cut off their food supply by naval blockade, as a means of political pressure. But, apart from that, Blankett, turned economist, pointed out that Aden, while useless to the Navy, might have commercial possibilities. Why not, he asked, deflect to Aden all the trade now carried on between India and Mocha and Jidda? The Bombay Government was sufficiently intrigued with this idea to submit it to the Governor-General in Council. The decision of 4th February, 1800, made by Lord Mornington and his advisers, was eminently sound. They would do nothing to interrupt or deflect a pilgrim traffic which was of interest to every Moslem in India, and the disturbance of which would justify the belief that the Company was the enemy of Islam. 'On the whole,' they concluded, 'we are perfectly satisfied that the proposed measure is in no respect eligible—We therefore direct that the overture of the Sultann of Aden be declined in as conciliatory terms as possible' and Colonel Murray's force withdrawn. They were opposed to Blankett's plan 'for reducing the commerce and consequence of Jedda and Mocha,' and opposed equally 'to the interruption of the corn trade between Egypt and Arabia' except in so far as India could offer an alternative source of supply.

Rainier returned to Bombay in January 1800, conferred there with Blankett and on February 3rd gave him orders to return to the Red Sea 'for the purpose of frustrating and defeating the hostile designs of the French on this Country from Egypt.' For this purpose Blankett was to have the *Leopard* (50), *Forte* (38), *Fox* (32), *Orestes* (18), *Albatross* (18) and *Amboyna* brig. The *Orestes*, however, foundered at sea and never joined him. Rainier and Blankett were not on the best of terms, the latter being ill, irritable and quick to resent any hint of criticism. He confided his troubles to the First Lord of the Admiralty—as even more junior officers were in those days encouraged to do—in a letter dated from Bombay on January 17th:

My Lord

    . . . I have found Vice-Admiral Rainier here, who being of opinion that my presence was still necessary in the Red Sea, I have not declined to go, being willing as long as I am able to perform the duty entrusted to me to the best of my endeavours; but my health has suffered from the climate, and my situation is sometimes made very irksome. I cannot act from myself, and the distance and difficulty of intercourse with a commander-in-chief on the other side of India is attended with too many inconveniences to be proper for me to describe in a private letter. . . . In dealing with the Arabs I have to do with the most artful and deceitful scoundrels in the world. . . .

    . . . should circumstances change, and that my presence in the Red Sea should be no longer requisite, I hope you will forgive me if I return home and leave Admiral Rainier in his sole command in these seas. A second flag officer in India can gain little profit or honour, and is amenable more than the chief and most exposed to censure of all sorts. . . .

J. Blankett.

(Spencer Papers, Vol. IV, N.R.S., pp. 210, 217.)

Blankett thus sailed rather reluctantly for the Red Sea, reaching the straits on 30th March, 1800, and finding both Aden and Perim evacuated and Colonel Murray gone northward. He also found dispatches from Sir Sidney Smith reporting the convention of El Arisch (4th January, 1799) by which the evacuation of Egypt had been agreed. He sailed at once for Suez expecting to find Murray in possession and, arriving on May 1st, was disappointed to find the French still there. The convention had been annulled by Elphinstone—Lord Keith as he had become—and Colonel Murray had withdrawn to Tor. The truce lasted long enough for Blankett to invite several French officers to dine, and so gain information from them about Suez. Then he retired to Jidda and sent a report to the Admiralty in which he advised that Suez was hardly worth capturing or even bombarding. He ended with a note on the climate:

> When we first arrived off Suez the weather was pleasant and to our feeling *cold*, the thermometer at Day and by Night being from 64° to 78°. But the latter part of the time when the Northern Monsoon set in about 2 o'clock in the afternoon it began to blow strong, the wind bringing with it such quantities of Sand, Flies and Mosquitoes etc. as to darken the sky like a thick winter fog, altho' we were three miles from the land. The air was hot and suffocating as if from the mouth of an oven, with a bad smell, and the thermometer rose to 100° and continued so till at night. . . .

On June 15th Blankett had a satisfactory conference with the Shereef of Mecca, whom he urged to resist the French 'as the Invaders of the rights of Mankind and as destroyers of every principle of Morality and Virtue.' All went well on this occasion, but two dhows from Suez presently arrived with letters from General Kleber, telling of the retreat of the Turkish army. This caused an abrupt change in the atmosphere and it became evident that the Shereef's main object was to gain complete independence of the Porte, then a British ally. But Blankett blockaded Suez and kept the Shereef outwardly friendly. 'Jidda is so much exposed,' he wrote wistfully, 'that I could easily fire the Town and the whole of the ships and vessels attached to it.' Of this the Shereef was made aware and the summer passed away without the French gaining much advantage from his vacillation. Towards the end of August Blankett saw that nothing more remained to do. He sailed for Bombay, leaving *La Forte* with the Company's cruiser *Comet* at Mocha, and withdrawing the remainder of his squadron. As he did so the French privateer *Clarissa* (16 guns, 148 men) sailed into his clutches, her commander seeking a mild revenge by telling an unfounded story of French frigates bound for the Red Sea. Blankett reached Bombay on August 31st after a ten days' passage from Mocha, destined to return, after refitting his squadron, to his thankless task. Still viewing the French as the permanent rulers of Egypt, he was becoming prophetically obsessed with the possibilities of the Red Sea route.

> We have held almost exclusive trade with India by the Cape of Good Hope, which appears to me to be more owing to the ignorance and weakness of the Turkish and Arab Governments than to any manifest superiority of our own. Surat or any of the other Northern Settlements are so well situated to carry on trade thro' the Red Sea that it would be dangerous to make them sensible of all the advantages that would arise from it.
>
> From Surat to Suez at the proper season of the year is a voyage of six weeks and from Suez to Cairo that of three days, from thence down the river to the ports of France is too well known to mention, so that it is possible a Surat cargo to be landed at France in the course of eleven weeks. This always alarmed me, and I have constantly been of opinion that it is more our policy positively to check the present existing trade to the Red Sea than to encourage [it]. . . .

Despite these memories of Albuquerque, this foreshadowing of De Lesseps, the danger from Egypt was dwindling to nothing. The Indian Governments were passing over to the offensive and the question was no longer 'Are the French coming?' but 'Where shall we attack them?' To this question, it will be seen, the answers were prompt and emphatic; energetic but diverse.

CHAPTER VII

Java Reprieved

Left to his own devices, Rainier would have gone back to the point at which the offensive of 1797 had been broken off. The danger from Egypt having diminished, there was no longer any reason why Manila should be spared. The Spanish, it is true, had now had ample time in which to strengthen their defences. But secrecy had not been the chief characteristic of the 1797 expedition, and there was now an additional reason for the stroke then planned. For the Spanish squadron had of late shown an enterprise of which their former inertia had given no warning. The China fleet was, of course, a standing temptation—a convoy of the largest merchantmen in the world, richly laden and adhering to a time-table (fixed by the monsoons and the tea crop) which was known, in outline, to everyone. Had there been a more prolonged emergency in the Red Sea, the China fleet might have been unescorted in 1799, which would have made the temptation greater still. Actually, Rainier was able to spare the *Intrepid* (64), the *Fox* (32) and *Carysfort* (28), the first of which arrived at Macao, or rather Anson's Bay, on or before 16th November, 1798. The *Fox* and *Carysfort* sailed on December 10th with the country ships for India, and the Indiamen for Bengal sailed without escort on 6th January, 1799. This left only the *Intrepid* to protect the Indiamen sailing for England. But Admiral Rainier had foreseen the difficulty. Hearing that the Spanish had two sail of the line and two frigates ready for sea, with the French *Preneuse* (36) and *Brûle-Gueule* (32) eager to co-operate, he sent the *Arrogant* (74) and *La Virginie* (38) to reinforce the escort. It was regarded as something of a feat for these last two ships to reach China when they did by the Eastern Passage, and Captain Oliver Osborn was commended afterwards for his exertions.

Subsequent events are represented rather differently in the English and Spanish accounts. Rainier's report, based on the report he received from Hargood of the *Intrepid*, the senior captain, ran thus:

> Captain Osborn had arrived in Macao road but 3 or 4 days after a passage of some length wherein both ships had suffered considerable damage from

156

tempestuous weather and high seas in the Pacific Ocean, the *Virginie* having carried away her mizen mast and was laying without one when the combined force of the Enemy under Rear-Admiral Don Alaba appeared suddenly in that road, consisting of two seventy-four gun ships, two large frigates, Spanish, and two French Frigates, and approached His Majesty's ships *Intrepid, Arrogant* and *La Virginie* in Line of Battle; Captain Hargood of the *Intrepid*, the senior officer, slipped his cables per signal and sail'd immediately in pursuit of them, being followed by the other two ships. Both squadrons were obliged to anchor among the Ladrones in the night, and in the morning to their surprise the Enemy were not seen.—The ships of the enemy appeared in very good order, and the Spanish Admiral's ship sail'd remarkably fast—their running away from a force so much inferior to their own is no otherwise to be accounted for, but from their dread of a conflict that would in all probability have terminated in their disgrace and added another trophy to the Naval Atchievements of the War. It is proper to notice that none of the Convoy had then come down from the Tigris to alarm them by their doubtfull appearance.

The *Arrogant* arrived at Macao on 21st January, 1799, and the Spanish appeared on the 27th, probably without knowing of her arrival. Their account of it appeared in the *Manila Gazette* of February 11th. From this it seems that the *Europa* (74) and *Montanes* (74), the *Lucia* and *Fama* frigates, together with the *Preneuse* and *Brûle-Gueule*, sailed from Manila on January 9th on a cruise 'which from circumstances could not exceed 30 or 40 days.' He heard that the English convoy would sail on about January 20th–30th and tried to time his arrival to coincide. He knew about the *Intrepid* but was rather vague about other escorting ships. He arrived among the Chinese islands on the 26th, anchored overnight and sailed with the flood on the morning of the 27th. The English, when sighted, ran away, although the *Europa*, having outsailed her consorts, was alone. Don Ignacio de Alava gave up the chase in order to rally his squadron. By the evening he had his ships in line of battle, intending a night attack, but the captain of the *Montanes* reported that his main-yard was sprung 'which rendered it impossible for him to make any effort whatever.' It was getting dark but Alava suspected that the enemy 'were going on the opposite tack without shewing any light.' So he showed poop lanterns and mast-head lights to let them know where to find him. He was prevented from further pursuit by the accident to the *Montanes* and had to be content 'with seeing two English Ships of the Line and one Frigate run and abandon the Port before two Spanish Ships of the Line and three Frigates with whom they do not choose to measure their strength—which was less inferior to the Spanish squadron than were the Spanish gunboats to the English frigates in Manila

Bay, which they reconnoitred when they knew that 'there was no ship in a state to oppose them.'

It is perhaps fair to conclude that neither squadron was spoiling for a fight. Captain Horsburgh of the *Bombay Anna* wrote, 'The general opinion was, that the surprize and disappointment of the Enemy must have been great, on their finding three English ships of war at Macao'—Danish ships having assured them there was only one. Captain Hargood had a convoy to protect, and Admiral Alava's men were showing an appalling lack of seamanship. When they were parted by weather and darkness, each went his own way. Hargood sailed with his convoy on February 7th and the Spanish Admiral returned to Manila, where the two French frigates left him in disgust. With Hargood gone, however, the *Europa* (74) and *Fama* (36) reappeared off Macao and indeed anchored there on May 19th. The super-cargoes wrote anxiously to Rainier on the 26th, and the Admiral responded by sending a strong detachment to cover the convoy of 1799–1800. This was ensured by an order given to Captain Josias Rowley of *L'Imperieuse* (38) on August 21st, directing him to proceed with convoy to China. The *Trident* (64) and *Providence* schooner went on the same service and the *Arrogant* (74) was ordered in September to strengthen still further the homecoming China fleet. Captain Rowley's convoy was delayed on the way and then caught in a typhoon on October 22nd, *L'Imperieuse* losing her foremast, mizzen-mast, bowsprit, main-topmast and rudder. Once at Macao with the badly-damaged *Imperieuse*, Captain Rowley had fresh trouble in seeking to secure the use of a regular man-of-war anchorage at Anson's Bay. The Chinese would not admit men-of-war into the river if they could help it and they threatened to stop the trade if the *Imperieuse* did not leave. Although the Spaniards did nothing more, they had certainly, at least indirectly, caused trouble enough.[1]

For the above reasons among others, Rainier would probably have liked to attack Manila. The defeat and death of Tippoo, however, had left the Governor-General with troops to spare and his own ideas of how to employ them. It had also left him with a fire-eating General in Baird and an extremely able military adviser in his own younger brother, the Hon. Colonel Arthur Wellesley. The Governor-General, left to himself or to his brother's advice, would probably have preferred to attack Mauritius. Whereas the Admiral's responsibility was maritime, the Marquess Wellesley's responsibility was for British India as a whole. If an invasion overland were impracticable, as now seemed almost certain, the only possible threat to

[1] See *The Chronicles of the East India Company trading to China, 1635–1834.* H. B. Morse, Vol. II, p. 332.

India must come by sea. But no one supposed that an army could sail from France to India without calling anywhere for supplies and water. With the Cape in English hands, the necessary halfway house must be Mauritius. With that captured, a large-scale expedition to India would be almost physically impossible, even without naval opposition. As Colonel Wellesley had written in 1797, 'Mauritius ought to be taken. As long as the French have an establishment there, Great Britain cannot call herself safe in India.' Apart from that, the French islands were a nest of privateers. Merchants and shipowners in India were complaining of their losses and a Governor-General at Calcutta could not help but hear them. He heard more about their troubles than did the Admiral at Madras and far more than anyone at India House or in Whitehall.

The French privateer vessels in 1799–1801 may have numbered as many as a dozen. Nine of them, at least, are known by name. These were:

Name	Guns	Men	Commander	Remarks
Clarisse	14	140	Robert Surcouf	Chased by *Sybille*, 30th December, 1799. *Took* the *Jane*.
„ „	20		François Lemême	Took *Armenia* in 1800.
„ „	—	148	Pinaud	Taken by H.M. Ship *Leopard*, 3rd September, 1800.
Confiance (490 tons)	20	250	Robert Surcouf (From April 1800)	Took numerous prizes. Chased by *Sybille*. Took the H.C.S. *Kent* in October 1800. Returned to France in 1801.
Malartic	12	110	Jean Dutertre	Took numerous prizes in 1800. Taken by the *Phoenix*.
Adele	12	60	Nicolas Surcouf	Made eight captures. Taken by H.M. Sloop *Albatross*, May 1800.
Iphigenie	18	200	—— Malroux	Took the *Pearl*. Destroyed in action when H.M. Sloop *Trincomalee* blew up, 10th October, 1800.
Grand Hirondelle	—	—	François Lemême	Taken by H.M. Ship *Sybille* in 1801.

Name	Guns	Men	Commander	Remarks
Gloire	18	183		Took six prizes. Taken by H.M. Sloop *Albatross*, 23rd March, 1801.
L'Uni	30	216	—— Houdoul	Took *Henriette*. Taken by H.M. Ship *Arrogant* 4th August, 1800.
Courier	—	—	Joseph Potier	At sea, 1801.

This list is sufficiently complete to gain a general impression of these craft. *L'Uni* was exceptional and probably uneconomic. She was described as a small frigate, armed with 18-pounders and 9-pounders, nearly all of which had been thrown overboard by the time the *Arrogant* overtook her. Normally, they carried 12–20 guns, a very large crew (to allow for manning prizes) and were either exceptionally fast or else cleverly disguised as country ships. They were usually taken in the end—1800 was a good year for the privateer-hunters—but that did not necessarily terminate their career. Unless bought for the Navy, they were sold by auction and so often purchased (through an intermediary) by their original owners, to begin their career again, perhaps under another name. Robert Surcouf was the best-known of the privateers and the one whose efforts were most likely to bring down vengeance on the Ile de France. The following account, by Captain John Stewart, gives a fair picture of Surcouf's methods. Stewart commanded the *Jane* belonging to the well-known firm of Bruce, Fawcett & Co. of Bombay. Outward-bound from Calcutta on 30th December, 1799, he was warned by an American ship, the *Mount Vernon*, that a French privateer was off the Sandheads. He decided accordingly to keep in company with H.C. Ships *Manship* and *Lansdowne*, thinking the Indiamen sufficient protection. On the 31st he spoke H.M. Frigate *Sybille*, returned from chasing the privateer off her cruising ground.

> . . . at day light on the 1st of January the Indiamen were 5 or 6 miles ahead, at the same time we saw a strange sail to the windward, standing to northward who on perceiving us bore down with great caution, because as Monsieur Surcouf afterward told me, he took one of the Ships to be either the *Sybille* or *Nonesuch* seeing the other two ships safe into the Sea. When I saw the strange sail altered her course, I took it for granted that she was the Privateer which the American had given intelligence of and immediately ordered a gun to be fired as a signal to the Indiamen. We continued the signal till about 8 o'clock when the Privateer saw that the Ships a-head paid no attention to our firing, she hoisted English Colours—up studding-sails and royals and came on with more confidence—at ½ past 8 she gave us a shot, hauled

down the English Colours and hoisted the French National Flag. We returned her fire from a six-pounder which we got off the deck into a stern port in the great cabin, at the same time carrying every sail after the Indiamen, anxiously hoping that the constant firing would bring them to our assistance, but we looked in vain, for they never made the smallest movement to assist us. At 9 the Privateer having got very near us, they began to fire grape shot from 2 brass 36-lb. cohorns which they had mounted forward. At this time it came on a light squall from the southward which brought the Indiamen directly to windward of us. During the squall we carried on press of sail and the firing ceased on both sides [but] the superior sailing of the Privateer soon brought her up again when she commenced a smart fire from musketry and grape shot from one of the 36-lb. cohorns—the other having been disabled early in the action; At 11 our powder was wholly expended, the last gun we fired being loaded with musket cartridges. The Frenchman then prepared to board us. They triced up graplins to their main and fore yardarms, and Surcouf gave orders to board, animating his men with a promise of liberty to plunder. Seeing that we were incapable of resisting the force that was ready to be thrown on board of us, I was under the necessity of ordering the Colours to be hauled down and we were taken possession of by an officer from the *Clarissa* French Privateer, Mons. Surcouf Commander, formerly mounting 18 guns, but now mounts no more than nine 4-pounders, one 9-pounder and two cohorns already mentioned, one of which is incapable of further service, one of the nulls being broke off close to the piece. She has likewise several bell-mouthed blunderbusses in each top which we saw them sending down after [we] were on board. Her reduced force is owing to her being chased by the *Sybille* frigate. At that time she threw overboard 4 12-pounders, three 9-pounders with their carriages, and all her spars, sawed thro' a bulkhead which runs across abaft the mainmast and separates the officers from the crew, knocked down all the stantions and got the axes and saws up to cut off her poop, when unfortunately it fell little wind and they found they could save themselves without having recourse to the last resource. Her crew consists of M. Surcouf, his brother, four officers and a surgeon, sixty Europeans of several nations, ten caffries, eleven lascars who entered when he took the *Albion*[1] and a few Malays. Surcouf sent on board the prize one officer (by trade a taylor), sixteen Frenchmen, and ten lascars. They were employed untill sunset shifting prisoners, and so refitting the rigging of the prize, which had been shot away during the action, and cutting out a double-headed shot which had entered near the stern post just above the waterline. All this time the Indiamen were

---

[1] This was a common practice. But when the *Prudente* was taken by the *Daedalus*, and an English deserter (Thomas Tring, alias Thomas Spinks) found among the Frenchmen, he was condemned to death by a court martial and promptly executed. Maltese deserters from the French army at Suez were enlisted in the King's ships as marines.

F

in sight to the S.W. At sunset when Surcouf was viewing them from the poop thro. a telescope he requested I would tell him upon my honor whether they were Indiamen or not. I repeated what I told him before that they were two Company's ships with whom I had kept company ever since we left the pilot. He replied they were two *Tritons*, alluding to the easy capture which he made of that ship, and said the commanders deserved to be shot. This was the universal opinion of the French officers. I fear their conduct will be attended with bad consequences to the Hon'ble Company's ships as it has given the Frenchmen a very contemptible opinion of them and will subject them to many attacks which a spirited behaviour would have freed them from. . . . We landed at Bemblepatam yesterday . . . [having been released]. . . . Surcouf does not mean to come any more near the Sand Heads, being very much afraid of the *Sybille* and *Nonesuch*, but intends to cruize in the latitude of 19 and 20 degrees, and should he be joined by *La Constance* [*Confiance?*] as he expects, the trade of Bengal will be entirely cut off until they have surfeited themselves with prizes and returned to the Mauritius to recruit their crews. I have written to Lord Mornington a similar letter to this. . . .

(Ad. 1/170.)

Lord Mornington received many such letters, not all written as philosophically. As for what Stewart says about the encouragement given to Surcouf to attack Indiamen, he was perfectly right. This incident led directly to the capture, on October 9th of this same year, of the H.C. Ship *Kent*, of 26 guns, off the Sandheads. The *Kent*, it is true, put up a fierce resistance before being overpowered by boarding, her casualties including 14 killed (her captain among them) and 44 wounded. Of a crew of about 90 to 100, with 38 male passengers, this represents a high proportion. And the fact that the action continued for one hour and forty-seven minutes proves that the *Kent* was far from being 'a *Triton*.' On the other hand, had Surcouf expected such a struggle—he had sixteen casualties of his own—he might have hesitated to attack the *Kent* at all.

The capture of the *Kent* made a sensation at Calcutta, but Bombay was more shaken by the fate of H.M. Sloop *Trincomalee* (16). The privateer *Iphigenie* (18), Captain Malroux, from the Isle of France, intercepted a packet called the *Pearl*, on 7th October, 1799, at the entrance to the Persian Gulf. Captain Fowler was killed and his chief mate could do no more than sink the mails and surrender. The *Pearl* was carrying treasure, which was transhipped, and Malroux meant to quit the gulf with his prize and make for his base. The *Iphigenie* was chased, however, by the *Trincomalee* and the *Comet* schooner. Overtaken on the 12th, the privateer engaged her pursuer, which was in fact less heavily armed. A duel with cannon ended with the privateer attempting to board the *Trincomalee*. That sloop lost her lieutenant, master and boatswain during the first attempt, her captain and carpenter during the second. The third attack found her with twelve survivors resisting, headed by the purser. At that moment she blew up and sank, destroying the *Iphigenie* in the process, which sank four minutes later. The privateer lost about 115 men, some thirty to thirty-five survivors being picked up by the *Pearl* prize (which had beaten off the *Comet*). The *Trincomalee* went down with all hands but two. This, again, was the sort of event which would lead some people to conclude that the capture of the Ile de France should not be long delayed. When an East Indiaman could be taken by a privateer off the entrance to the Hooghly, and when a man-of-war could be sunk while engaging another privateer in the Persian Gulf, the time for stern measures might be thought to have come.

While Admiral Rainier might dream of capturing Manila with the 'galleon' in port; while the Marquess Wellesley might plan to add Mauritius to the Empire, the Cabinet in London had different ideas. The 'Cabinet' meant, in practice, so far as India was concerned, Mr. Henry Dundas. And Dundas, as bellicose as Wellesley could be, wanted to complete the overthrow of the Dutch East Indies by the capture of Java and Surinam. The Admiralty orders to that effect were dated 21st October, 1799, and were received by Rainier on May 5th. Parallel orders had gone to Wellesley 'from Mr. Secretary Dundas, conveying His Majesty's commands to the same effect.' These commands were not so emphatic as to deprive the Governor-General of the right to cancel the operation if need arose, and the likelihood of its taking place was lessened at the start when Lord Clive at Madras protested against having to provide the troops. On hearing, however, from Wellesley, Rainier decided to blockade Batavia as a preliminary measure. Wellesley approved this policy and decided to base the expedition on Calcutta, where it could be assembled under his own eye. November 20th was the provisional date by which the expedition should be ready to sail, and Rainier agreed to lead it in person. On the military side the Governor-General had chosen his brother to command, junior as he was, and now braced himself to receive the protest of the Generals.

Rainier was on the Malabar coast early in 1800 but at Madras on April 29th when he assured the Admiralty that 'affairs continue in a tranquil state on this station.' After May 5th he issued his orders for the blockade of Batavia —the *Daedalus* (Captain Ball) to sail under sealed orders with the *Centurion*, *Braave* and *Sybille*. In the manner of more recent years their destination would have been veiled under a code name (Operation ANTI-MACASSAR, perhaps), but in 1800 they were simply described as cruising off 25670.

The final orders were drawn up on June 28th—it was not until then that the squadron could be assembled—and before that, on June 21st, Rainier ordered Rear-Admiral Blankett to take command at Madras, 'His Majesty's service requiring my absence from this coast on a particular service of importance, not proper to be divulged.' On July 2nd Rainier informed Sir Roger Curtis at the Cape that he intended to keep *L'Imperieuse* and *Braave* for the present, although not of the East Indies squadron. So the preparation went on until, on July 5th, Rainier received a dispatch from the Governor-General to say that the expedition was to be postponed. The Marquess was considering the possibility of attacking Mauritius instead. The Admiral reported this to the Admiralty on August 25th, remarking that he personally had received no countermanding orders and would continue to blockade Batavia until told to desist.

> ... with regard [he concluded] to the object on which the Noble Marquis's reasons were founded for postponing the Expedition, I conceive any such equipment to be totally impracticable, unless considerable reinforcements had arrived in this Country. You will please inform their Lordships 'tis my intention to continue the blockade 'till I receive orders to the contrary from their Lordships or other competent authority.
>
> (Ad. 1/170.)

He resisted the temptation to underline the word 'competent' and waited patiently for the next change in policy. It came on September 16th and to the Admiralty he reported that:

> *Victorious*, Madras Road, 26 Sept. 1800.
>
> ... I have, after a silence of some weeks, received His Excellency the Governor-General's assurance of his entire and unqualified concurrence with the step I had taken in dispatching Captain Ball to institute the blockade of Batavia, pursuant to my letter to you of 28 June last. His Excellency has also avowed to me his determination to renew the preparation for the expedition against it. ...
>
> You will please inform their Lordships that I am come to the determination of proceeding with His Majesty's Ships *Victorious* and *Intrepid*, as soon as they can be got ready, to Prince of Wales Island and Malacca. ...
>
> *Arrogant*
> *Suffolk*
> *Trident*
> armed vessels
> *Prudence*
> *Mongoose*
> The ships and vessels as per margin will have orders to follow me with the least possible delay after their arrival in this road, one of whom will be detached to proceed to the Sandheads of Bengal River to take charge of the Transports. .....

Wearied by this apparent vacillation, Rainier followed this up with a personal letter to Lord Spencer, dated September 30th, which ended sadly:

Feeling the caducities incident to the decline of life I think it a duty encumbent on me to acquaint your Lordships therewith, that I may be superseded by a more active officer for the good of His Majesty's Service. Sensible how much I am indebted to your Lordships' goodness for continuing me so long in so honourable an employment, and trusting my humble services have had the merit hitherto to merit your Lordship's approbation, I have the honor to remain with great veneration and the most profound respect,

My Lord, Your Lordship's
most obedient & most humble servant,
Peter Rainier.

It is not apparent that Rainier wished his resignation to be taken too literally. It was timed, besides, to take effect after the Batavia expedition should have taken place. Supposing it cancelled again, the Admiral might well have had enough of the Indies.

On the eve of his departure for Penang, the Admiral had deployed his squadron (September 28th) as follows:

	Guns	Captain	
La Virginie	38	Astle	Molucca Islands under former orders
Hobart	20	Elphinstone	
Vulcan	Bomb	Straton	
Imperieuse	38	Rowley	To Moluccas and the Cape
St. Thomé		Lt. Blair	To Amboyna and Madras
Leopard	50	Rear-Adm. Blankett, Capt. Surridge	At Bombay, in the harbour or in dock. Blankett's squadron
Fox	32	Stuart	
Albatross	18	Waller	
Amboyna	14	Sheldrake	
La Forte	38	Lt. Hardyman	Red Sea
Orpheus		Lieut. Evans	To Bombay, to dock
Daedalus	32	Ball	Blockading Batavia
Centurion	50	J. S. Rainier	
Braave	38	Alexander	
Sybille	38	Adam	
Victorious	74 (Flag)	Clark	With the commander-in-chief's flag, or to proceed to the Straits of Malacca
Suffolk	74	Malcolm	
Intrepid	64	Hargood	
Trident	64	Turner	
Prudence	Armed Vessels		
Mongoose			
Arrogant	74	Osborn	To refit and join C.-in-C.

Of Rainier's squadron, the *Resistance* (44) had been lost at sea and so had the *Orestes* (18). *La Forte* was lost in the Red Sea, from 'downright neglect' as Rainier suspected. The *Hobart* was condemned by survey, the *Carysfort* (commanded by Lieutenant William Goate) sent back to England and the *Heroine* (Captain Murray) had left Rainier almost speechless with indignation by going home without orders to do so.

Before sailing for Penang, Admiral Rainier reversed his earlier orders to Admiral Blankett, telling him now to remain at Bombay, ready to return to the Red Sea if the occasion should arise. He evidently sensed further trouble in that direction, even to the point of leaving the Bay of Bengal almost unprotected. Sailing from Madras on October 1st, with the nucleus of his squadron, he reached Penang on the 19th. On the 30th he was joined by the *Trident* from Madras, which had sailed ten days after he had, bringing the unwelcome news (from Vienna, via Bushire)

> . . . of the unfortunate reverse the affairs of the Austrians had experienced in Italy, in having been obliged in consequence to capitulate for an armistice with the French General Buonàparte in terms highly disadvantageous. . . .

Rainier heard also that 'the French General in Egypt had determined to keep his ground,' and concluded (a little wearily) that the Governor-General would cancel the expedition again. No news came, however, to that effect and the Admiral went in the *Victorious* as far as the Straits of Dryon, sent her on with supply ships to join Captain Ball, and returned in the *Intrepid* to Penang, expecting to find there the *Suffolk* with the transports from Bengal. Instead, he encountered on December 2nd the *Cornwallis* packet with a dispatch (dated October 22nd) from the Governor-General to say that the expedition against Batavia must be postponed, if not cancelled. Instead, the forces collected for that operation should now concentrate at Trincomalee 'to act on any emergent service of defensive or offensive' character, 'but principally pointing to a co-operation with any Armament that might be embarked in the Mediterranean for the purpose of compelling the French to abandon Egypt.' To this Rainier was more or less resigned, aware though he was that he would have to redeploy his entire squadron again. But an accompanying letter, of slightly later date, delivered by the same means, left the Admiral more or less stunned.

> . . . His Excellency [he told the Admiralty on 27th December, 1800] roundly offers to my concurrence the Plan of an Expedition against the Isle of France, the particulars whereof I defer sending to another opportunity, contenting myself for the present in acquainting you, that I refused the co-operation of His Majesty's Squadron, as being decidedly of the opinion

that His Majesty's Command officially signified to His Excellency and the officers commanding the land and sea forces were indispensably required to authorise an undertaking of that importance, quoting in justification thereof the three several instances of the kind that had occurred during my present command and of others within the compass of my experience: I have accordingly acquainted his Excellency with this determination. . . .

(Ad. 1/171.)

Wellesley's dispatches in the *Cornwallis* had been entrusted to Mr. Stokes, perhaps the person who had originated the plan and one certainly conversant with Wellesley's ideas about it.[1] It is evident that Stokes made the worst impression on Rainier, who discussed nothing with him and waited until the 24th before handing him his sealed reply. Wellesley afterwards made this delay a principal ground for complaints; of which again Rainier took little notice. The Admiral privately thought Wellesley's plan 'utterly impracticable . . . from the various glaring inconsistencies and inaccuracies observable in it. . . .'

Wellesley's arguments for abandoning the expedition against Batavia were convincing enough. Bonaparte's successes in Italy would lead him to attempt the relief of the French in Egypt and then perhaps renew his threat to India. Lord Elgin's correspondence suggested that the British troops in Minorca might very probably be used to expel the French from Egypt, with Turkish help, before such a threat could develop; in which case a diversion from the Red Sea would be called for. Apart from that, the French menace made it unwise to disperse the forces needed for the defence of India, for 'the pursuit of any foreign conquest, however easy, must always yield to the necessity of self-defence.' These arguments, as Rainier pointed out, were equally valid as objections to the attack on Mauritius. He refused, therefore, to co-operate.

What motives underlay Wellesley's vacillation at this time? He was genuine, no doubt, in his concern for the safety of India, but he was also swayed by concern for his brother and by the persuasive tongue of Mr. Stokes. Arthur Wellesley was in command of the troops at Trincomalee and responsible for organizing the expedition, 'deep,' as Guedalla remarks, 'in demands for vinegar, tea, sugar, beef, Staff officers and rum.'[2] Still only a colonel, Arthur (the best officer in India) was eligible to command the

---

[1] On December 1st Wellesley urged his brother to be attentive and kind to Stokes. 'He is a very honourable and honest man, of considerable knowledge in his own line, and of very uncommon talents. His ardour will not displease you, but he is sometimes inclined to a little too much magnificence. . . .' Stokes was to be secretary and commissary to the expedition and *intendant* of the island when it fell. *Supplementary Despatches*, p. 315.

[2] Philip Guedalla. *The Duke*, p. 97.

three thousand men thought sufficient for capturing Mauritius but too junior to lead the probably larger force which might be needed in Egypt. As for Mr. Stokes, 'a seafaring gentleman,' he had been prisoner in the French islands and was prepared to swear that they were poorly garrisoned and easy to capture by surprise. Of these influences Rainier was partly aware. Writing personally to the First Lord, on the same date as his official letter, he ended by assuring Lord Spencer that he was actuated only by his sense of duty:

> . . . sensible of the delicacy of the situation I have placed myself in by opposing one of his Excellency's exalted ranks and deservedly high estimation in the eyes of His Majesty's Ministers, entirely confiding in your Lordship's candour for giving full credit to the truth of my assertion.

In thus refusing his co-operation, Admiral Rainier was taking, as he well knew, a grave responsibility. He had, however—perhaps without being aware of it—an ally in Admiral Sir Roger Curtis, the commander-in-chief at the Cape. Mauritius had been blockaded intermittently by cruisers from that station and it was on Curtis that Lord Spencer relied for his information about the island. While agreeing that the inhabitants were 'rather inclined to Monarchy in France than the present order of things,' Curtis did not think that they would surrender tamely to England. Privateering suited them too well. A force of 3,500 or 4,000 effectives, he thought, would be needed to subdue the island and it would be folly to count on local sympathy.

> . . . a good deal of stress is laid on the temper and jarring interests of the inhabitants. I put no confidence in such ideas, and I think that in very many instances during the war we have seen the fallacy of such expectations. The indulging such hopes has often occasioned to us disappointment and distress in quarters nearer home than Isle France. . . .
> (Curtis to Lord Spencer, 28th November, 1800. *Spencer Papers*, Vol. IV, p. 238.)

This was, of course, profoundly true and more recent experience has illustrated the principle afresh. But Curtis was further worried about the fate of the troops if the expedition should fail, with the men sickly, with supplies short and with no neighbouring base to which the transports could return. In the event, moreover, of success, the Ile de France would itself be difficult to supply, being normally dependent on the more fertile Bourbon for corn and, in part, for cattle. Bourbon would also, therefore, have to be captured, but Curtis believed it 'next to being impregnable' from having no harbour. Curtis ended his letter rather acidly:

... I have not presumed to say a word as to the political expediency, or inexpediency of making an attempt upon it. I have confined myself to stating facts, perhaps not generally known, or if known, not sufficiently reasoned upon; it being the usage of projectors when enamoured of a scheme, not to touch upon, or to speak lightly of such things as may be deemed impediments. ...

(Ibid.)

Adamant as he was about Mauritius, and supported in this by Curtis and ultimately by Lord Spencer, Rainier had no alternative to abandoning operations against Batavia, nor to concentrating his squadron as the Governor-General suggested. He issued orders on December 5th for raising the blockade of Batavia and rallying his ships at Trincomalee.

On January 27th the squadron was deployed as follows:

	Guns	Captain	
Centurion	50	Admiral C.-in-C. Capt. J. S. Rainier	
Victorious	74	W. Clark	Penang Squadron with commander-in-chief
Arrogant	74	E. O. Osborn	
Braave	38	T. Alexander	
Sybille	38	C. Adams	
Amboyna	14	W. Sheldrake	
Intrepid	64	W. Hargood	To Sandheads and Madras
Daedalus	32	H. L. Ball	To Madras, then to refit at Bombay
Mongoose	—	Lieut. J. Duval	Malacca
Suffolk	74	P. Malcolm	Sandheads
Providence	—	Lieut. Mayo	
Albatross	18	W. Waller	
Leopard	50	Rear-Adm. Blankett Capt. T. Surridge	Red Sea
Fox	32	H. Stewart	
La Forte	38	L. F. Hardyman	
Orpheus	32	R. Evans	To dock and refit at Bombay

The *Victorious* rejoined him at Penang, as did the *Daedalus*, and on 21st February, 1801, Rainier sailed with the *Centurion*, *Victorious* and *Arrogant* and reached Colombo on March 7th. There, as he informed Lord Spencer on May 10th:

I received a letter from Lord Wellesley expressive of much chagrin at my refusal to co-operate with his Majesty's squadron in the project His

Excellency had proposed, and suggesting a variety of arguments tending to prove me in the wrong, and to impress me with the idea that his public consequence and intimate connection with His Majesty's Ministers were more than sufficient to shelter my conduct from any degree of responsibility in the issue. I must confess to your Lordship that I am not in the least convinced by his Excellency's reasonings, and have therefore forborne to make any reply to them, having neither inclination or leisure to enter into such tedious discussions, the necessity whereof was happily suspended by the alteration in public measures that soon after took place and was announced to me by his Excellency at the same period. But I discovered his Excellency had for the third time (though none could have been so appropriate as the first) determined on the prosecution of the 5670 [Batavia] business, with a more considerable force than was first proposed. . . . In the case of my refusal to attend it, or give protection to it, it was nevertheless to have gone forward; but fortunately for the security of his Majesty's possessions in this country, after orders were issued for the final departure of the expedition from Trincomalee, which was on the 5th of last February, on the 10th the dispatch of the 6th October, 1800, from the Right Honble Secretary of State arrived. . . .

(Ad. 1/171.)

In short, Wellesley's vacillation and Rainier's own preference were alike overruled by a direct order from England to send a force up the Red Sea. In fact the transports collected at Trincomalee had already sailed for the Malabar coast, having passed Colombo on February 20th under escort of the *Suffolk*. The emphasis of the war was swinging back from the Dutch islands to Suez, from Captain Ball to Admiral Blankett. Colonel Wellesley would now be superseded by General Baird and the Mauritius left immune for another year at least. Rainier naturally decided to sail for Bombay, base for the operation now ordered, and there he arrived on the 15th April, 1801.

Futile as the campaign of 1800 may seem, in retrospect, to have been, it would be wrong to suppose that it was altogether without result. The expedition never reached Batavia, it is true, and the troops went no nearer the place than Trincomalee. But the naval part of the operation had made some progress before the expedition was cancelled and the results cannot be wholly ignored. Captain Ball of the *Daedalus* (32), with the *Sybille* (38), *Centurion* (50) and *Braave* (38) under command, appeared off Batavia on August 23rd, detained two American ships which he found leaving the port and approached the islands of Onrust and Kuyper which were practically undefended. They were garrisoned by some forty native troops and a German officer. 'There was but three guns on Onrust, old, and carriages out of repair. The storehouses had nothing in to speak of. . . .' These harbour defences having fallen, the Dutch vessels in the port mostly ran themselves on shore. These numbered about forty ships, brigs and sloops. Three others were towed into an inner harbour. Eight were taken and destroyed, mostly laden with rice or in ballast. The neutral ships then or subsequently detained comprised four American, four Danish and five Moorish vessels. Native prows taken later, laden with rice, firewood and coffee, numbered thirty. This effectively put an end to the trade of the port and Ball now settled down to blockade it, ordering the *Sybille* off the River Maroondah and the *Centurion* off Edam Island, which was occupied.

Ball expected Admiral Rainier to appear in October at latest, but was disappointed. Finding his supplies running short, he finally abandoned the blockade on November 9th–12th, his last acts being to release the neutral vessels, destroy the buildings on Onrust, Kuyper and Edam Islands and remove the Malay Chief (who was pro-British) from Maroondah. In his report dated 16th December, 1800, Captain Ball expressed something of the anxiety he felt during the period:

> As I am not versed in fortification and indeed know very little on the subject, I cant speak of the different works erected near the town of Batavia, and the lowness of the land prevents a good view of them. They were but badly prepared for the reception of an Army and Fleet on our first arrival there, but we could see them throwing up fresh works every day. To the eastward of the town there are six batteries flanking the sea and three to the westward, besides the one on the West side of the Pier and some heavy guns on the East side of the Pier Head.
>
> The little information obtained from such unintelligible people which made their escape from the town was not worth noticing. All which amounted to the great distress of the slaves, and that there was no Rice, that they were starving and that if we once made a landing, the whole of the Malays would join the British and would not leave a Dutchman alive, they could get at.
>
> From an anxiety of mind hardly to be expressed during the whole of our stay, I am not so well prepared to relate the various events in a letter as I otherwise should have done & the diabolical climate preventing all the mental faculties taking their due course. . . .

Although he does not explain it, Ball was chiefly worried about disease. Batavia lived up to its reputation at this time and the fever was taking its toll. The casualties in action numbered only three killed and twelve wounded, mostly in the *Sybille*, but the loss from disease was heavy, amounting to 151 officers, seamen, marines and soldiers. No less than twelve naval officers and midshipmen died, and there were no less than fifty-seven deaths in the *Centurion* alone, all from what Rainier called 'the direfull epidemic of that unhealthy and fatal climate.' How many were ill and recovered is not stated, but it is evident that sickness was widespread and that Ball himself was probably ill when he wrote his report. At the period when he was raising the blockade for lack of supplies, the *Victorious* was on the way to join him with transports carrying provisions for four months. Captain Clark's orders were countermanded, however, on December 5th, and he did no more after meeting (and superseding) Ball, who was junior to him, than to lead the sickly squadron back from the Straits of Banca to Malacca on December 19th.

Further to the eastward the Dutch governor Cranssen was still holding out in Ternate and *La Virginie* (38), one of Rainier's ships, with the *Hobart* sloop, replaced by *St. Thomé*, was co-operating with the East India Company's ships and troops in a siege which did not end until the Dutch finally surrendered on 20th June, 1801. Apart from that, operations among the islands were over and Java left, for a time, to enjoy its reprieve.

CHAPTER VIII

The Red Sea and Peace

IN retrospect it is difficult to understand why the threat to India via Egypt was taken seriously after Tippoo's defeat. It is equally difficult to acquit Dundas of indecision. For just as the troops collected at Trincomalee were destined now for Batavia, now for Mauritius and now for the Red Sea, another and larger army concentrated at Gibraltar was destined now for Portugal, now for Ferrol and now for Teneriffe. It seemed, in fact, in the spring of 1800 that a concentration had been made at Gibraltar without any definite object in view.[1] As peace negotiations were already, however, in prospect, Dundas gradually became convinced of the need to expel the French from Egypt. To have the French established there in time of peace was obviously undesirable, but their removal by negotiation could only be gained by a sacrifice of territory elsewhere. Egypt was not furthering French aims in the war, but it was an undeniable asset in negotiating peace. Dundas pointed this out on September 28th and suggested that the Turks might expel the French if the latter were driven from their ports; Alexandria, Damietta and Rosetta on the Mediterranean side, and from Suez and Kosseir on the Red Sea. 'The first of these objects can only be attained by a force sent from the Mediterranean, the second by a detachment from India.' Although there was opposition from the King and from several of his colleagues, Dundas had his way and signed the necessary orders on October 6th. The military command was given to his friend and relative by marriage, Sir Ralph Abercromby, and orders for the Red Sea expedition were sent (as we have seen) to India.

As regards Rear-Admiral Blankett's detachment, the Government's decision was anticipated, to some extent, by the Governor-General. Writing directly to Blankett on October 16th, Wellesley said that news from Europe suggested the need for 'reducing the power and resources acquired by the Enemy in Egypt and on the shores of the Red Sea.' He recommended the destruction, if practicable, of Suez, the seizure of vessels trading (under any

[1] Cyril Matheson. *Life of Henry Dundas*, London, 1937, p. 284, *et seq.*

173

flag) with ports in French possession, and the interruption of the corn trade between Upper Egypt and Arabia. This last measure Wellesley had previously opposed but the circumstances had altered.

> Recent events in Europe and in Egypt now impose on the British Government in India, the duty of impairing by every possible means the resources of the French in Egypt as well as those of their adherents in Arabia.
>
> I shall direct the Governor and Council at Bombay to comply with every requisition for troops, vessels, gun boats, or any other supply you may require for the execution of the services suggested in this dispatch.
>
> *My expectation is that the Government of France will make an early effort to assist the French Army in Egypt thro' the Red Sea,* and under this impression I shall advise Vice Adl. Rainier to endeavour to reinforce your squadron.

Lord Wellesley's fears and Dundas's strategy were not identical, but both implied a naval force in the Red Sea. On 22nd December, 1800, Blankett was on the point of sailing again with the *Leopard* and *Fox* to join the *Forte,* which was still at Mocha. Urged by Wellesley, the Bombay Government had provided him with additional strength in the *Bombay,* frigate, the *Antelope* and *Fly* (Company's sloops), and the *Strombolo* and *Drake* (bomb vessels). To his squadron were attached, furthermore, eight small vessels to use as fireships or blockships, and three hundred soldiers, 'besides followers.' 'This has been a great effort,' Blankett pointed out, 'for Bombay in its present state.'

At the same time Blankett was not over-optimistic:

> I cannot profess myself very sanguine on the advantages that may arise from my little expedition. It may serve effectually to check those who wish to assist the Enemy and it is probable that a shew of force which the nature of the Arabs will undoubtedly lead them to magnify may be the means to draw off some part of the French force for the protection of Suez, and it is possible that the garrison of that place, finding themselves liable to be constantly annoy'd, may be tempted to desert.
>
> (Blankett to Admiralty, 22nd December, 1800. Ad. 1/170.)

Blankett was at Jidda on or before 26th February, 1801. Through sheer carelessness (as Rainier thought) the frigate *Forte* (38) struck a rock in entering the harbour and sank in six fathoms. Her crew, guns and anchors were saved, but the divers could not recover the ten months' provisions she carried, which proved a serious loss. Her hull was given by Blankett to the Sheereef, who could salve the timbers and ironwork when she broke up. At Jidda, Blankett received orders from the Secretary of State to occupy Suez or Kosseir as a landing place for troops which were to be sent to invade Egypt. This altered the nature of Blankett's task. His plan had been to make a night attack on Suez with mortar and gun-boats, using that as a feint to cover the destruction, by a landing party, of the town's water supply and the simultaneous blocking of the river by sinking vessels in it. This had to be abandoned, as the port might be wanted. He was thwarted as regards Kosseir by a different circumstance. 'Had Cosire been in the hands of the Enemy, I should certainly have again knocked it down,' but there was no longer a single Frenchman in the neighbourhood. So Blankett began negotiating afresh with the Shereef of Mecca. These conferences were at first vague and contradictory but Blankett, who needed Jidda as his base, could not afford to quarrel, as he pointed out on 26th February, 1801.

> The necessity of having the use of this Port at present will be too obvious to you, for me to speak more on the subject. After leaving Jedda no refreshment of any sort to be found, except water at Tor, which I doubt would fail in a dry season. From Tor to Suez, there is not a leaf to be seen, nor a blade of grass. All is a dreary, inhospitable, barren rock, sometimes varied with patches of sand, which serves to retain the heat reverberated from the surrounding mountains.

> The Sheriffe in one of his letters says justly: *Christians can never make war in my country, it is full of mountains, has little water, and has too great heat for their complexions.*

Leaving Jidda on March 9th, Blankett struggled against northerly winds and finally reached Tor. His object there was to present to various Arab chiefs the letters he had extorted from the Shereef. This he accomplished after holding a preliminary meeting of townsfolk. 'I summoned the People at Tor,' Blankett reported proudly, 'read the letters *in Arabic* to them, gave them presents, promises and threats' with the object of persuading them to provide camels for the expected army. Blankett then entered Suez on the 22nd, having lost one of the transports on a coral reef and saving only her crew and soldiers. He found that the French had evacuated the town, which he found ruinous and desolate. This was because the main expedition had landed under Abercromby at Aboukir on March 8th, compelling the French to concentrate in northern Egypt. Taking possession of Suez and hoisting the flag, Blankett waited for the expedition to arrive. In the meanwhile, realizing from letters which arrived from the Turks and from Lord Keith that even a token movement from Suez would have a moral effect, Blankett considered sending forward the three hundred and twenty soldiers he had with him under Lieutenant-Colonel Lloyd. Lloyd was eager to march but Blankett detained him until the necessary camels should arrive, as promised by the Turks. Blankett's supplies were running short in May and as the wind was north-westerly, he could see little likelihood of the troops arriving in time. By the 17th he had decided to withdraw, even if it should dispirit the Turks, but postponed doing so until June 6th. On that day he received a letter from General Hutchinson (Abercromby had been killed) asking that Lloyd's detachment should join him. Lloyd marched that evening into the desert and the *Leopard* fired an 11-gun salute as he did so. Lloyd was destined to reach General Hutchinson's camp but only after twenty-three men, including three officers, had died of thirst, and the remainder had suffered great hardship. As the northern monsoon had set in, there was no possibility of further troops reaching Suez. Blankett accordingly sailed for Kosseir, supposing (rightly) that the expedition might have arrived there.

In point of fact, there were two separate forces concerned in the main landing; the troops from Bombay and Captain Sir Home Popham, with the *Romney* (50), *Victor* (18), and *Sensible* (36), from England. The *Sensible* was acting as a troopship and two others were supposed to be in company but may have separated on the way. For the Admiralty, with that same sense of urgency which had originally brought Blankett on the scene, were now repeating the procedure by sending Popham. He was sent to relieve Blankett, at the latter's request, but was also chosen as a navigational expert and a man of known ingenuity. His was an independent command and Rainier wrote rather stiffly in May that 'Captain Sir Home Popham's appointment precludes the necessity of my interference in affairs in the Red Sea, as he is not placed under my orders.' It seems that Popham left the Cape about February 21st, but Blankett had no news of him or of any other part of the expedition until May 17th when he heard of the arrival of five transports at Jidda together with the Company's frigate *Marquis of Cornwallis*. This division received Blankett's orders, left at Jidda, to follow him to Suez, but acted on other orders they had received at Bombay. 'There appears,' wrote Blankett plaintively, 'a manifest impropriety in sending out a squadron of ships to an unknown sea where an Admiral commands, without ordering them at least to follow his advice. . . .' Had they done so, those transports might have reached Suez. That was not, however, what they had been told to do, and there can be little doubt that the decision to land at Kosseir was wise. Lloyd's march, with a larger force, would have involved more than proportionate hardship, and the remainder of the army would, in any case, have had to land elsewhere and advance down the Nile.

Admiral Rainier played little part in the Red Sea expedition. When he reached Bombay on April 15th in the *Arrogant* he found there the *Suffolk* and *Orpheus* in dock, the *Trident* recently docked and getting ready for sea. He was presently joined there by the *Victorious*, *Sybille* and *Daedalus*, the last two from Madras. He learnt at Bombay that two divisions of transports had sailed from thence on April 1st and a third with General Baird had followed soon afterwards. Other transports had sailed from Goa, and there was then no prospect of overtaking any of them. Captain Malcolm of the *Suffolk* would have escorted the General's division as far as Mocha but dared not defer the docking of his ship. Indeed, when Rainier arrived, the shipwrights were discussing whether she was worth repairing at all. Rainier decided to remove some of her guns, reduce her spars and alter her rating to that of a 64-gun ship. The *Orpheus*, *Daedalus* and *Sybille* were all needing extensive repair, and the squadron had been further weakened by the loss of the *Forte*. Rainier decided, accordingly, not to send any ships to the Red Sea. He thought it unnecessary and doubted whether the transports, sailing so late in the season, would not have to return. Besides, it was now Home Popham's responsibility—who was he, the mere commander-in-chief, to interfere? He was more intent on withdrawing from the Red Sea such ships of his squadron as were already there. He thus wrote to Blankett on May 16th:

> As their Lordships make no provision, for your Flag being flying in the Red Sea at the time when Captain Sir Home Popham would arrive, you are on receipt hereof to make the best of your way to join me with His Majesty's ships *Leopard* and *Fox* unless Sir Home Popham should make application to you for the latter . . . and you are to bring with you all the crew of *La Forte*. . . .
>
> (Ad. 1/171.)

He anticipated that Blankett would probably forestall this order by withdrawing when Popham appeared. Blankett had no instructions to take Popham under his command, and Popham was junior even to Captain Surridge of the *Leopard*.

Feeling that he could do no more, Rainier sailed for Madras with the *Arrogant*, *Victorious* and *Trident*, leaving orders for his other ships to follow when repaired. He could not resist the temptation to point out to Lord Spencer (on May 10th) how fortunate it was that the expedition to Mauritius had not taken place.

> . . . had the whole armament proceeded on the distant Service I have intimated to your Lordship the consequences could but have been serious. . . . I feel no small degree of satisfaction in the reflection that my application

to Your Lordship to be superseded, preceded the period when this difference of opinion on Publick Service appeared.

Lord Spencer did not accept Rainier's resignation but did decide to relieve Blankett, who was sick and obviously worn out. An order to Rainier to allow Blankett to return to England in the *Leopard* was received in India before 10th May, 1801, but came, as we shall see, too late.

Rainier had been troubled at intervals during the year with reports of a French squadron coming out to the Red Sea from France. Ganteaume's squadron which escaped from Brest in January 1801, might conceivably have been bound for the Indian Ocean, and Rainier was sufficiently impressed to keep a part of his squadron concentrated. He hardly supposed that a large force could leave Europe for the East without being closely pursued, but he thought it possible that isolated raiders might attempt to interfere with Blankett's or rather Popham's line of communications. The problem for any such raider would be one of supply and Rainier concluded that the only possible base for French operations would be in the Seychelles. He gave orders, therefore, on July 7th, for the *Sybille* to proceed, after repairs, to the Seychelles, cruise in that vicinity, and return to Madras by October 1st. This was, as it turned out, an astute move. For the French did what Rainier had expected, sending to the Seychelles from Nantes the brand-new frigate *Chiffonne* (36). Her initial errand was to land there thirty-two persons suspected of plotting against the First Consul, but she had taken two prizes on the way out and had, no doubt, plans for further operations. The *Chiffonne* was at Mahé in the Seychelles when the *Sybille* (38) found her. She was no match for her heavier opponent and, being attacked (with some difficulty) while at anchor, surrendered after a brief action and the loss of twenty-three killed and thirty wounded. She was purchased into the Navy as a 12-pounder frigate, virtually replacing the *Forte*.

As for Admiral Blankett, his remaining career was brief. Arriving at Kosseir on June 15th he found Sir Home Popham with the *Romney* (50) and *Victor* sloop. The first division of troops under Colonel Murray had landed a month before and gone inland to the Nile. General Baird was still there, preparing to follow, but Blankett on the 20th announced his departure for Mocha, mainly to procure supplies. He sailed on the 24th, called at Jidda and sailed for Mocha, then intending to return to Kosseir. But he died, worn out, on July 14th, as the *Leopard* entered Mocha, having written his last report to the Admiralty on the 5th and having lent the General sixty seamen to help in his voyage down the Nile. Baird reached that river on May 30th, but did not join Hutchinson until after the fall of Cairo. It is not apparent that Baird's march made any material difference to the campaign. His force, comprising two divisions and over ten thousand men, was strong enough to affect the result and appeared from a direction which might be thought unexpected. Rainier considered the plan a good one but left, as indeed it was, too late in the year. 'According to my idea, they will be very successful if half the troops from hence reached Cosire.' Blankett was aggrieved at having been left to suppose that Suez, not Kosseir, was to be the point of disembarkation. He pointed out in his last dispatch that he could, if warned, have done something to prepare the way. At the same time he admitted that 'no other obstacle will be in the way of General Baird's progress except the difficulties of the march. . . .' Actually, Baird's march (largely waterborne) was remarkably swift, the delay being rather over the departure from Bombay, and that possibly inevitable.

Baird's march was spectacular, if not brilliant in results, and attracted much popular acclaim in England. In the services the operation was regarded more critically. Baird's appointment to command, itself a cause of delay, had left Colonel Wellesley furious at being superseded and scarcely on speaking terms with his brother. He was ill, in any case, with the 'Malabar itch'—an ailment which had again been a source of delay. Rainier was irritated by the way in which Popham was placed beyond his control, and Blankett hurt to think that his hard-won knowledge of the Red Sea (purchased, as he must have begun to suspect, at the cost of his life) had been put to so little use. Back in England, Blankett's Whig friends (to whom he was still Keppel's lieutenant) were offended at the way he had been treated while other officers were still shocked to think how Rainier's authority had now twice been set aside. To others who might be critical of Dundas's moments of strategic inspiration the appearance of Popham would be the finishing touch—so junior a captain, with so little experience of command and so much the pet of the politicians! Dying, Blankett might reflect that it was only Lloyd's detachment which could arrive in time to be of service. Dying, Abercromby knew that any diversion from Suez was bound to come too late. Most ironical of all must have been the reflections of Sir Sidney Smith, who could recall that the Treaty of El-Arich in 1800, if ratified, would have secured without bloodshed all the objects for which this costly campaign had been fought.

The war was nearly over and little else of moment occurred in 1801–2. Rainier was at Madras in the autumn of 1801 but finding the weather threatening, he put to sea on October 29th with the *Victorious* and *Arrogant* and, after searching in vain for a rumoured privateer, dropped anchor at Penang on December 11th. There he was joined by the *Centurion* from

China and, on the 24th, by Sir Home Popham in the *Romney*. Popham was escorting two transports with native troops which were landed to relieve those stationed at Penang and Malacca. What purports to be the inner story of what followed is given in the autobiography of Captain D. Macdonald:

> There existed at this time a very serious misunderstanding between the commander-in-chief of H.M.'s naval forces in India and the Governor-General...(who had no control over H.M. Ships).... To show the impolicy of the system, and the dangerous lengths to which it might be carried, I will cite one instance. ... It happened that, late in the year 1801, after the final expulsion of the French from Egypt, H.M.S. *Romney*, bearing the broad pendant of Commodore Sir H. Popham, came from the Red Sea to Calcutta ... and while the *Romney* was undergoing repairs, intelligence reached my Lord Wellesley of the projected invasion of Portugal by the French; and he came to the resolution of sending a force to take military occupation of their settlement at Macao, for the protection of the Chinese trade, and applied to Sir H. Popham to undertake its direction. As soon therefore as the equipment was complete he sailed; but, arriving off Prince of Wales's Island, was met by the Admiral who, with a large portion of the squadron, had gone thither to intercept him: he was taken into port, made to deliver over charge of the armament, with all surplus stores and supernumeraries, to Capt. Osborne of the *Arrogant*—and with seemingly undue severity, remanded back to the Red Sea for presuming (though at the request of the Governor-General in Council) to undertake any operation within the limits of his (the Admiral's) station. All this, doubtless, the Admiral had power to enforce, but the consequences in this case might have been most disastrous. Sir Home Popham was *alone* in the confidence of Lord Wellesley and in possession of his views, as far as related to the ulterior objects of the expedition, all of which were to be jeopardized, if not sacrificed, to the caprice of one individual: as it happened, however, the peace of Amiens luckily intervened and rendered this precautionary measure of his Lordship's government unnecessary.[1]

This fairly represents the East India Company's point of view. But Rainier had some excuse for being tired of Wellesley's vacillation, and more for being irritated by the presence of Popham. If, moreover, he was opposed in principle to the occupation of Macao, events were ultimately to prove him right.

Fighting in Europe had stopped on 1st October, 1801, but Rainier had no definite news of this until some months later, February 1st being the

---

[1] *A Narrative of the Early Life and Services of Captn D. Macdonald, I.N. Weymouth,* n.d. *Circa* 1842.

date by which the war was, for him, to end. But he had preliminary warning no doubt, that peace was likely and took no offensive action in the meanwhile. He did take proper steps to protect the China trade, but was partly relieved of that responsibility by the knowledge that the *Belliqueux* (64) had come out from England with the Indiamen and had remained with them at Canton. When details of the peace treaty were known, the provisions of most interest in India were those which restored all her Indian settlements to France. 'His Britannick Majesty restores to the French Republick, and her Allies, namely, His Catholick Majesty and the Batavian Republick, all the possessions and colonies which belonged to them respectively, and which have been occupied or conquered by the British forces in the course of the war, with the exception of the island of Trinidad, and the Dutch possessions in the island of Ceylon. . . .'

France thus regained Pondicherry, Chandernagore, Yanaon, Balasore, Foul Point and the other villages she had lost. Nothing was said of the trading rights conceded in 1783, which had not indeed proved very valuable. The Netherlands recovered Malacca, Amboyna, Banda and Ternate, as also the Cape. Ceylon was the sole eastern conquest to be retained: and this became a crown colony, being denied to the East India Company as firmly as it was denied to the Dutch.

It cannot be said that the naval war in the Indian Ocean from 1794 to 1801 had been a brilliant success. There was little French opposition in the early stages when the French settlements in India were occupied; and the Dutch, becoming enemies in 1794, were relieved without much difficulty of Ceylon, Malacca and the Cape. Their attempt to retake the Cape having failed, Rainier went on to conquer the Moluccas in 1796. No naval effort was made by the French until 1796, when Admiral Sercey tried to raid Penang and then tried, with as little success, to intercept the China fleet. His squadron was so ill-supported by the colonists of Mauritius that it had become ineffective by 1797 and was henceforward ignored. But Spain too had become an enemy in 1796 and the expedition was now prepared to capture Manila in 1797. With little naval opposition to be expected, the success of this raid was fairly certain. It was abandoned, however, when news came of the Treaty of Campo-Formio and of the relations established between Tippoo and the French. With the landing in Egypt in 1797, British attention was transferred to the Red Sea and remained fixed there until 1799, leaving the Spaniards free to threaten the China fleet in two successive years. As Tippoo was crushed and as the danger from Egypt seemed to lessen, a new British expedition was prepared, primarily to subdue Java but with Manila and the Ile de France under discussion as alternative or subsequent objectives. This was abandoned on the news of a fresh Austrian defeat and orders came from England for an expedition to expel the French from Egypt before peace should be made. The expedition took place in 1800–1, as part of a larger operation in the Mediterranean, and played some small part in ensuring that Egypt should not become a French colony. And so the war came to an unsatisfactory, and as it proved temporary, end.

From the French side, two general conclusions suggest themselves. First and foremost, French colonial methods had combined with the effects of the Revolution to make the Mauritius almost useless as a naval base. It was a poor source of supplies in any case but the colonists were, apart from that, acting in their own interests and not in those of France. What supplies they had went to their own privateers, not to Sercey's squadron, and French naval efforts died away for lack (after 1795) of a base any nearer to India than Brest. British sea power was thus almost unchallenged from 1794 to 1797, which circumstance led to the successive capture of the Dutch colonies other than Java. In the ordinary course of events, Java, Manila and the French islands would have fallen in turn. But British sea power had been stretched to the uttermost in the effort to cope simultaneously with the French, Spanish and Dutch fleets, and the result was that withdrawal from the Mediterranean in 1796 which made Bonaparte's counter-stroke possible. What followed is a striking demonstration of what can be done by an army against a fleet. For the remaining enemy settlements were saved by Bonaparte and by his indirect threat to India. With Tippoo's help, he saved Manila by the military successes which led up to the Treaty of Campo-Formio. He saved Mauritius by landing in Egypt. He saved Java by threatening to retain Egypt. In assessing the relative failure of his Egyptian campaign, these indirect results should be borne in mind. To put British India on the defensive from 1797 to 1801 was, in itself, no mean achievement.

What is more doubtful is the question of whether the British reaction to Bonaparte's threat was not exaggerated. It is manifest that the British operations in the Red Sea, naval and military, produced no great result. As against this, it might be argued that the mere presence of these forces had a deterrent effect, in itself decisive as apart from anything they did. This is true enough but much still depends on whether Bonaparte's advance on India was in fact feasible. The Governor-General evidently considered that it was; and was especially sensitive to the threat so long as Tippoo was in the field. Grenville and Lord Spencer were less credulous, but the final verdict lies with Bonaparte himself, whose actions may be thought to represent his views. Of him it would be true to say that, although planning an invasion of India in 1801, he was not concerned with Egypt as a stepping-stone. His later plan depended on his alliance with Paul I of Russia and involved a French army descending the Danube, crossing the Black Sea in Russian ships to Taganrog, marching to the Volga and so by that river to Astrakan, and thence with a Russian army into India. Masséna was admittedly to cross Persia and Afghanistan, but equally without making use of Egypt. The assassination of the Tsar finished this particular scheme but it went far enough to demonstrate Napoleon's lack of interest in the Red Sea route.[1] On the British side it is proper to remember that Dundas united in himself the offices of Secretary of State for War and President of the Board of Control. From long association with Indian affairs, he had acquired a proprietary interest in India which may have influenced unduly his conduct of the war. Lord Wellesley's anxiety is less open to criticism—defending India was his main responsibility—but that it was excessive in 1800 seems clear. Perhaps it would be fair to acquit the Indian Government of any needless caution up to and including 1799. Then again, in 1801, with negotiations for peace in contemplation, Dundas can hardly be blamed for wanting to evict the French from Egypt. It was perhaps in 1800 that the chance for offensive action was culpably let slip. One cause of this misfortune was, no doubt, the appointment of Arthur Wellesley to govern at Seringapatam which, by depriving the Marquess of his brother's advice, contributed perhaps to that vacillation of which Admiral Rainier justly complained. This was at its worst in 1800 and was perhaps attributable, in part, to the exhaustion of Dundas and the excitable temperament of Lord Wellesley. The peace, in leaving France in possession of Mauritius, left her with the means to renew the war in the Indian Ocean. Towards this the first step, as Bonaparte realized, was to bring the colony under effective French control. It remained only to find a man capable of doing it.

[1] See *La colonisation Française pendant la periode Napoleonienne* (1799–1815). J. Saintoyant, Paris, 1931, p. 426.

PART TWO

PART TWO

CHAPTER IX

Decaen and Linois

At the time of the Peace of Amiens, the French Minister of Marine and Colonies was Forfait, but he was replaced in 1802 by Denis Decrès. The change involved no reversal, however, of policy. Forfait had argued that the French factories in India were, since Tippoo's defeat and death, militarily valueless. He thought it useless to fortify Pondicherry afresh and his successor thought the same, urging that the town would be captured in any case in the event of war and questioning whether the English would even allow it to be fortified. But if agreed on that point, Forfait and Decrès were different in outlook, and from this point Decrès becomes important. Generally speaking, France had no coherent colonial policy between 1793 and 1801. But France had latterly acquired a ruler and one whose mouthpiece was to be Decrès. Born in 1761, a noble, Decrès entered the Gardes-Marine in 1779 and saw service in the West Indies. In 1791 he was a lieutenant in the *Cybèle*, St. Felix's flagship in the Indian Ocean. In the early days of the revolution Decrès was in some danger of being hanged by the *Cybèle's* crew. He avoided that fate but, sent by St. Felix to France to ask for help, he was arrested and not reinstated until 1795. He served in the expedition to Ireland and was later promoted Rear-Admiral. In the *Guillaume-Tell* he fought at the Battle of the Nile and escaped; only to be taken later, off Malta, in 1800. The action between her and the *Penelope* (36), *Lion* (64) and *Fondroyant* (80) became famous in French naval annals, ending as it did with the *Guillaume-Tell* dismasted, twenty guns silenced and two hundred casualties.[1] Decrès, who had himself been wounded, was given a sword of honour and made, successively, Prefect-Maritime at L'Orient and Minister of Marine. He is said to have done extremely good work in connection with the dockyards at Venice, Antwerp, Flushing and Cherbourg.

Whatever virtues Decrès may have had as an administrator—and they were considerable—he was not the man to revive and inspire the French Navy. Napoleon was unfortunate in his Admirals, as he himself recognized.

[1] See Rouvier, *Histoire des Marins Français sous la République* (1789–1805), Paris, 1868.

J'ai passé mon temps [he wrote at St. Helena] a chercher l'homme de la marine sans avoir jamais pu le recontrer. Il y a dans ce métier une specialité, une technicité qui arretaint toutes mes conceptions. . . . Sous mon régne, il n'a jamais pu s'elever dans la marine quelqu'un qui s'ecartât de la routine et sur créer. J'aimais particulierement les marins. J'admirais leur courage, j'estimais leur patriotisme, mais je n'ai jamais pu trouver entre eux et moi l'intermediaire qui sut les faire agir et les faire meriter. . . . Oh! pourquoi Suffren, n'a-t-il pas vécu jusq' à Moi? Ou pourquoi n'en ai-je pas trouvé de sa tiempe? J'en aurais fait notre Nelson, et les affaires eussent pris une autre tournure.[1]

Emigration and the guillotine had removed most of the senior officers of the previous war, and even though many officers of the old regime rallied to Napoleon, it has been said that only two—Bruix and Latouche-Treville —proved capable of commanding a fleet. Decrès never had the opportunity of command but it seems generally agreed that his appointment as Minister was a catastrophe.

'Je n'hesite pas a dire,' a écrit l'auteur des Souvenirs d'un marin, l'amiral Jurien de la Gravière, 'que dans mon opinion, le long règne de cet homme d'esprit fut une calamité pour la marine.

'Cet administrateur si habile, ce coutisan si fin, si ingénieux, était, pour l'epoque surtout ou nous vivions, le pire de tous les ministres.'

Cette opinion de l'amiral Jurien etait celle de tous les marins de l'Empire.

Absolu dans ses ordres, dur avex ses inférieurs, partial pour ses favoris, souple vis-à-vis de maitre, crainte et detesté, le ministre Decrès etait peu propre a relever la Marine de l'Empire. . . .[2]

If Decrès showed partiality towards his favourites, the inhabitants and seamen of the Ile de France were not numbered among them. His experiences there had been unfortunate and the colonists firmly believed that governmental neglect of them was due to his hatred. Be that as it may, Decrès was certainly unsuitable for his post in one respect—he had no belief in Napoleon. His unspoken disdain for the upstart must have affected the whole Navy, in which the best officers seem all to have been quite junior.

After the peace, on the 7th May, 1802, Decrès submitted a memoir to the First Consul suggesting weak garrisons for the settlements in India— 400 at Pondicherry and only 1,200 for the Ile de France. He urged that any large force sent might be made by the English an excuse for making war. In fact, he distrusted all plans for expansion in the East. This was a subject

[1] P. J. Charliat. La Mer et l'Empire, 2e Serie. Ligue Maritime et Colonial Française. La Marine de l'Empereur, p. 262.
[2] H. Moulin. Les Marins de la Republique, Paris, 1883.

on which Napoleon felt very differently, but he too was influenced by the fear that the English would declare war—as they actually did—before he was ready. Decrès went further and urged a policy, in India, of self-effacement. Although not, in general, much given to self-effacement, Napoleon was partly convinced by his Minister's arguments. He agreed that the force sent should be small, and that it should be led by someone unlikely to alarm the British. But he did not fall in with Decrès's views to the extent of sending nearly all the troops to the Ile de France. And he differed again in his choice of an officer to send. The man he chose was not at all the tactful, obscure and diffident type of person the Minister had in mind. The man he chose was Decaen.

Decaen was a man of middle-class origin, born in 1769. As a youth he served in the Marine Artillery for three years (1789–90). After quitting that corps, he settled down to study law as the articled pupil of a provincial lawyer in his native town of Caen. He was still a law-student when the wars demanded his services—a student, but also a sergeant-major in the National Guard. This served as a starting point; and, once on active service, he soon displayed a gift for organization. He was, in consequence, promoted swiftly, but without seeing much service as a regimental officer. From the beginning, something in the quality of his mind, added to a literacy none too common in the armies of the Revolution, marked him out as a specialist and staff-officer. He reached the rank of captain while in Klèber's battalion, but his work seems mainly to have been the organization of the transport in La Vendée. Transferred to the Army of the Rhine, he was employed in the Intelligence Department. Rising quickly, he became Adjutant-General in September 1795. With the rank of brigadier, he served under Moreau at Ingolstadt. Then he commanded a detachment of the 'Army of England' at Cherbourg. Afterwards, he was sent to the army at Mayence, but, quarrelling violently with Jourdan, he was transferred to the Rhine. Under Moreau once more, he commanded a division at Hohenlinden. This gained him some distinction. He was thought of as a coming man.

Although he had served under Hoche and Klèber, he was regarded in the Army as a follower of Moreau. And so he regarded himself. It is essential to grasp this, for it is the key to his subsequent career. Being in a position to know something of Moreau's dislike of Bonaparte, and being able to guess at Bonaparte's jealousy of Moreau, Decaen realized what the fate of his chief was likely to be. He saw that his own position, as a follower of Moreau, was not without its dangers. Noted as he was for sincerity and bluntness, he had quite sufficient acumen to change sides before it was too late.

His first meeting with Bonaparte took place early in 1801, just after the Peace of Luneville. He was presented by Dessolles at Malmaison and very graciously received. Succumbing readily to a little flattery, he became from that hour an admirer of Bonaparte. Failing, subsequently, to bring Moreau into a similar frame of mind, he decided that his safest course would be to seek a command in the colonies. He foresaw what was going to happen and, like other followers of Moreau, had no desire to be involved.

In thus deciding to go abroad, Decaen was only, in fact, anticipating what would certainly be his fate. The First Consul naturally wished to disperse Moreau's friends before he dealt with the man himself. The boughs were to be lopped off before the tree was felled. All this Decaen foresaw. Chiefly in order to avoid being sent to the West Indies to serve under Leclerc, he went boldly to Bonaparte and asked to be sent to India.

'Have you been there before?' asked Bonaparte. No, Decaen admitted, he had not. But he was still young, and he had a particular hatred for the English. He would not mind waiting ten years for the chance of a blow at them. Bonaparte probably interpreted Decaen's motives correctly enough. Without making any direct reply to this, he ended by saying something which led Decaen to hope for the best. He went away, or rather was sent away, in the belief that his request would be granted. He was sent to the Midi on a tour of inspection which kept him occupied, and also perhaps kept him out of harm's way, for the whole winter of 1801–2. The preliminary treaty of 1st October, 1801, had already been signed, by which French possessions in India were restored; but nothing could be done towards taking possession of them until the final agreement.

Meanwhile, Decrès was urging the First Consul to make his choice of a Captain-General to command in the East. Like most subordinates asking for a decision, he had a very definite idea of what decision he wanted. It was his, Decrès's, choice that the First Consul was to make. Almost certainly with a friend of his own in mind, he began to indicate what sort of man should be sent. The Captain-General, he suggested, should be a man of intelligence, a man of the most austere patriotism; but prudent also, modest and even reserved. Bonaparte had other ideas.

On his return from the Midi, Decaen went to report at Malmaison. He was asked to lunch. He ate expectantly, waiting for the magic words to be spoken. They were spoken. Presently Bonaparte inquired whether he was still thinking about India. Decaen assured him quickly that he was. 'Then,' said the great man, 'you shall go there.' 'In what capacity?' 'Captain-General,' came the reply. 'Go to the Minister of Marine and ask to see the papers relating to the expedition.' A jubilant Decaen went off to seek

Decrès. Moreau, arrests, trials, firing parties; all these already seemed a long, a very long way away.

The reasons underlying Bonaparte's choice are fairly clear. Added to the need for getting rid of Decaen was the desire to annoy Decrès; and overshadowing both was an Indian policy quite distinct from that which Decrès was so persistently advocating. For the furtherance of this policy—the trend of which will appear from the orders which Decaen subsequently received—his choice was well advised. Decaen was a good intelligence officer, as Bonaparte knew. The birds, in fact, which a single stone slew were three in number. A man Bonaparte wished to exile was exiled. A vacancy he wished to fill was filled. A minister he wished to snub was snubbed.

Even the snub was threefold. It marked, in the first place, a partial rejection of a particular policy. It asserted, secondly, a determination to keep all patronage in consular, in Napoleonic hands. And it had, lastly, a personal aspect. Decaen had already quarrelled with the naval department. His appointment was a missile, an elaborate retort, a thing certain to be ill received.

Decaen's first interview with Decrès, following that luncheon with the Consul, was somewhat painful. The Minister was aghast. Why had he not been consulted? Why Decaen of all people? Such questions, if unspoken, were evidently implied. Decrès finally refused to produce the relevant documents. Decaen went. He came once more, armed with fresh and positive orders. He bore away the papers in triumph.

The danger in compelling a subordinate to carry out what he does not approve lies in the possibility of his thwarting the general scheme by a manipulation of the details. Decrès, before the expedition sailed, had contrived to hamper its leader in more ways than one. And it may be supposed that the making of the necessary arrangements was attended by a good deal of friction.

The Definitive Treaty was signed at Amiens on 27th March, 1802; and it was thereby agreed that the restitutions to take place in the continent and seas of Asia should be within six months as from that day. Decaen was appointed to his command in June 1802. But he did not sail until March 1803. The intervening period was spent partly in waiting for the proper time of year for the voyage, partly in preparation and discussion. The original proposal was for a force of some six hundred and fifty men. Bonaparte increased this to rather over a thousand; and then added another battalion, composed of creoles from Guadeloupe. This last addition proceeded from an inability otherwise to dispose of them—an attempt to sell them to the United States having failed. The coloured troops were to go in transports, the rest in ships of war. The expedition was to include civilian officials and the ships were to carry provisions for a year as well as large sums of money and valuable presents for the native princes of India. There was certainly much to arrange.

Decaen received his orders from Decrès on 8th February, 1803—orders to proceed to Pondicherry and demand the cession of the place under the terms of the Treaty of Amiens. In these instructions the possibility of a speedy outbreak of war was not forgotten. The most important point, however, concerned Decaen's relations with the naval commander-in-chief. As a revenge for the various occasions on which Decaen had seemed to score over him, Decrès made the naval command independent of the military, instead of being subordinate. The two commanders-in-chief were merely urged to co-operate. Decaen's naval colleague was Rear-Admiral Durand Linois.

Charles Alexandre Léon Durand de Linois—so ran his full title—was born in 1761, and was thus Decaen's senior by eight years. He was of the smaller Breton nobility which often supplied the old regime with officers for the Navy. Entering in 1776, he saw his first service in the East Indies, under Suffren; a fact of significance, largely explaining his appointment. He was captain of the *Formidable* in 1795, when he was taken prisoner. Being soon exchanged, he commanded a ship in the Bantry Bay Expedition of 1796. Promoted Rear-Admiral in 1799, he served first as Captain of the Fleet to Bruix and afterwards as second-in-command to Ganteaume in 1800. Then, in the following year, came the great moment of his life. This was the action at Algeciras. On this occasion Linois, with three sail of the line, contrived to inflict a reverse on Sir James Saumarez, with six. One of the English ships surrendered to him. It was a defensive action, and one in which Linois had the powerful aid of shoal water and shore batteries. But such details are trivial compared with the central fact that the English had, somehow, been beaten. The phenomenon was not altogether unknown. Nevertheless, the French Navy at that time had no superfluity of victorious Admirals, so that Linois came to be regarded as a hero and a rising man. He was to go to the East Indies where, it was hoped, he would prove another Suffren.

In character, Linois is best understood as the opposite of Decaen. Whereas Decaen was a man of the revolution, promoted from the ranks, Linois was of the old regime and a man of birth. While Decaen retained the ardour of youth, Linois had already, in middle life, the caution of age. Where Decaen failed was in lack of patience. Where Linois failed was in

PLATE IV. Action between H.M. frigate *La Sybille* and the French frigate *La Forte* (28th February, 1799)

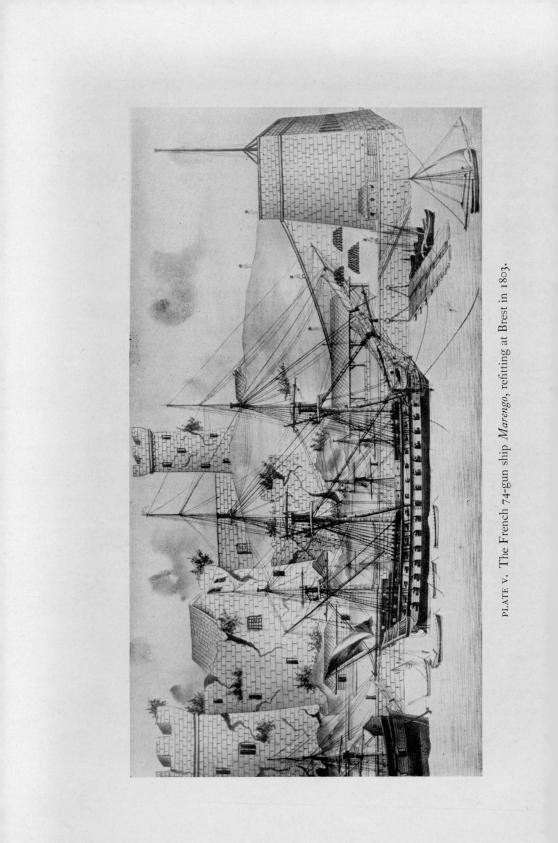

PLATE V. The French 74-gun ship *Marengo*, refitting at Brest in 1803.

lack of enterprise. Decaen was lavish in money matters and given to display. Linois was economical and inclined to be avaricious. Decaen had ability without reputation, and Linois had reputation without ability. Decaen was hot-tempered but Linois was always calm. Decaen was a Norman, Linois a Breton. They were utterly and completely different. They disliked each other at sight. And these were the men who were to travel together, work together, and together plan the ruin of the English in India.

In a sense, friction began even before the two men met, for Linois was writing to Decrès on February 15th on the subject of authority and precedence.

General Ministre

J'ai recu hier au soir mes instructions. Je n'ai encore pu que les parcourir. Je les mediterai et me penderai des intentions du Gouvernment afin de justifier autant que mes moyens me le permettront la confiance done il m'honore.

Je suis convaincu que le succes de ma mission exige que mes operations concordent avec celies du Capitaine General, et que conformement aux expressions enoncées dans mes instructions je les concerte avec cet officier superieur; mais je dois prevoir ce qui est dans l'ordre des possibles, le cas ou je me trouverais par des motifs majeurs en opposition d'oppinion avec le Cap^n General, il ne manqueroit pas de se prevaloir de l'article I^{ier} de l'arrete du 24 Fructidor An 11, qui dit formellement 'le Capitaine-General commandera immediatement les forces de terre et de mer etc.' Mes instructions du I^{ier} Consul et les votres, General Ministre, sont evidement en contradiction avec cet article, puisquelles mettent immediatement sous mes ordres les forces navales, en me prescrivant seulement de concerter mes operations avec le Capitaine General.

Je pense que l'esprit de l'arrete mettent les forces de Mer sous l'autorite du Cap^n General, ne comprend que les moyens maritimes de la colonie et non la station dans les Mers de la colonie.

J'ai cru pour toute discussion que mon caractere, mes principes et le bien du service me servent toujours prevenir devoir vous soumettre mes observations qui ont pour objet de ne pas compremettre l'autorité importante que vous m'avez devolue.

L'arrete relatif aux honneurs a rendre au Capitaine General dans l'Inde ne faisant pas mention du Pavillon qui doit etre arboré á bord du Batiment ou il se trouvera et ayant été a meme d'observer a St. Domingue que le Pavillon Amiral au Grand Mat avoit été hissé sur tout Batimens ou etoit le Capitaine-General, je vous priez instruire, General Ministre, si je dois tolere qu'il soit arboré une marque distinctive superieure a la mienne dans ma division. . . .[1]

[1] Archives Nat. BB^4 185.

It is not apparent what Decrès replied or what flag was hoisted, but Linois evidently considered himself in independent command.

Before proceeding to Brest, where the troops and ships were being collected, Decaen had two more interviews with the First Consul. The first was an official farewell, a luncheon party at Saint-Cloud. The rather recently married Decaen had the honour of presenting his wife to Madame Bonaparte. It was all very flattering and agreeable. Then, the next day, came another interview; this time at the Tuilleries, Decaen and Bonaparte alone. Decaen asked for further, and written, instructions from the First Consul himself. Bonaparte was at first unwilling. He said he could see no point in it. 'What instructions can I give you that will be of any use at such a distance?' he demanded. 'You must act for the best according to circumstances.' Decaen persisted, and with eventual success. He left the palace bearing a document of which the following is a translation:

INSTRUCTIONS FROM THE FIRST CONSUL
In the name of the French People

The Captain-General has received from the Minister of Marine his instructions relative to the administration in India and the various rights and privileges to which the French settlements and commerce are entitled. But the First Consul thinks proper to add to these some additional instructions by which political and military affairs are to be guided.

The Captain-General will find himself in a land in which our rivals hold sway, but with a rule which weighs equally heavily upon all. He must take care, then, to avoid giving them any cause for alarm or ground for complaint. He will disguise as far as possible the intentions of the Government. He is to uphold the diplomatic relations essential to the safety and maintenance of our settlements. He must study to maintain a cordial connection with the Peoples and Princes groaning under the yoke of the East India Company. The English are the tyrants of India; they are suspicious and jealous. It is necessary to treat them with smoothness and deceive them with apparent innocence. . . .

Six months after his arrival at Pondicherry, Decaen is to send an officer to France, entrusted with full knowledge of the situation, of the strength of the English and of the possibilities of a campaign in India. Decaen is subsequently instructed to report on these topics every six months, each report correcting and amplifying those preceding it.

In considering how to sustain a war in India over a period of years, it is necessary to work on the assumption that we shall not have command of the sea; and that considerable reinforcements are not, therefore, to be expected.

It would be difficult for an army-corps to maintain itself in face of the strong English forces without allies and without a fortified base. Such a base would serve, in the last event, as a fortress in which to hold out for terms of capitulation; terms allowing of a return to France with arms and baggage. . . . The base should be a place of strength with a harbour or road-stead capable of protecting frigates and merchantmen.

After the question of alliances and of a base, the next things to be considered are supplies and munitions. The Captain-General will give both these subjects his most careful attention. He will report on each in the most detailed manner. . . .

Should war break out between France and England before September 1805; and should the Captain-General hear of it before any orders reach him from the Government, he is free to act as he thinks proper. He may fall back on the Isle of France and the Cape. On the other hand, he may remain on the mainland if the situation admits of it, provided that the troops are not thereby exposed to the risk of having to make an unconditional surrender. It is important that the army should not play a part calculated to lower our prestige in India, or, by its annihilation, weaken the potential resistance of the Isle of France.

It is not to be supposed that Holland could remain neutral in the event of war with England. One of the first duties of the Captain-General will be to ascertain the state of the Dutch, Portuguese and Spanish settlements and discover what resources they can offer.

The Captain-General's mission is, first and foremost, one of reconnaissance. With a handful of troops, he will watch the political and military situation, while at the same time occupying our factories for the protection of trade. But the First Consul, aided by information received from him as well as by the exact observance of these instructions, will some day be able to place him on the road to a fame outlasting the memories of men and the passing of centuries.

Given by the First Consul

(*Signed*) Bonaparte.

Decaen showed a right instinct in demanding separate instructions from Bonaparte. He had sensed the divergence in policy between the First Consul and his Minister.

Armed with his orders, and attended by relatives, Decaen made his appearance at Brest on 22nd February, 1803. Caffarelli, the Préfet Maritime, reported his arrival to the Minister (23 Frimaire, An. 11). His forces were already there and he inspected them on board ship soon after his arrival. His staff consisted of General Vandermaesen, Brigadier Sainte-Suzanne,

Brigadier Penmarch-Mainvielle and Brigadier Montigny; Engineer-Colonel Richemont, and two aides-de-eamp, Binot and D'Arsonval. Binot had instructions to go ahead in one of the frigates and make arrangements for the reception of the troops at Pondicherry. A number of civilians accompanied the expedition, headed by Decaen's colleague, the Colonial Prefect Leger, and including several envoys bound for Persia or the Philippines. It was arranged that Leger should accompany Binot, bearing letters for Fort William and Fort St. George and empowered to take over the territory which England had agreed to restore. This, it was thought, would facilitate an immediate landing of the troops on arrival.

In one respect, Decaen's appointment had already proved a success. It had served to disarm English suspicion. He was so junior an officer that his appointment excited little attention. The English had never heard of him. Lord Whitworth, the ambassador, wrote vaguely that Decaen was a man of good character but without striking talents either as a soldier or a statesman. He concluded that so young a man—Decaen was not quite thirty-four—would be sent rather to maintain than increase the French power in the East. Leger seemed to be an equally innocuous character, chosen for having served at Pondicherry under the old regime. A nephew of Dupleix had been rejected for this post on the ground that his name might create alarm.

The one thing about the expedition likely to attract attention was the number of general officers. It was excessive and unnatural. There were too many of them for the number of troops carried. The obvious conclusion was that it was intended to raise sepoy battalions in India. And this was indeed the case. Lord Whitworth was not unduly alarmed. He might have been more anxious had he known that some 80,000 francs had been spent in gifts for the Indian princes. And he might have been still more anxious had he known the gist of Decaen's secret instructions.

On February 24th, Decaen met his naval colleague. He and Linois then went on board the *Marengo*, the ship that was destined to carry them both. She lay in the outer harbour, all but ready for sea, a fine 74-gun ship. The *Marengo* had been built at Toulon in 1794-95, doubled and coppered in 1796 and extensively overhauled in 1800-1. She had originally been called *Jean Jacques Rousseau* and was renamed, shortly before sailing, on 8th December, 1802.[1] Her burthen (1,926 tons) exceeded that of many an English second-rate; so that, according to English ideas, she mounted too few guns for her size. Her weight of metal, however, was more than respectable. She was pierced for 86 guns and mounted 84, including 28

[1] Arch. Nat. BB3 196. Caffarelli to Minister of Marine, 17 Frimaire, An 11.

36-pounders on her lower deck. In English weights these would have counted as 39-pounders, and were heavier than any English lower-deck guns. Her broadside weighed 907 pounds. She measured 172 feet long in the keel, with an extreme length of 198 feet 11 inches, and a beam of 44 feet 6 inches. There was rather more space between decks than English ships had, her lower deck having a height of 6 feet 10 inches and her main deck 4 inches less. She was a roomy ship, not unfitted to carry the large numbers that were to sail in her. The crew alone numbered nearly 700, while the passengers and troops numbered little under 450. The official report on her sailing qualities ran as follows:

> Gouverne superieurement, vire bien, ne cule presque pas, porte bien la voile. Excellentes qualités. Marche superieure.[1]

She was virtually an 80-gun ship, exceptionally well-armed and exceptionally fast.

The *Marengo* was at this time painted as follows: The sides of the ship were painted black above the line of the copper. The tiers of ports were painted yellow, the port-lids being of the same colour. The topsides were black again, and she was painted internally the usual blood-red. All her spars were yellow, or else perhaps left their natural colour and varnished. Her figure-head is shown in the pictures of her as a winged figure of a woman, wreathed and classically draped in white, bearing a wreath in her hands; a figure, presumably, of Victory. Her stern was decorated with a carved and gilded trophy of arms and standards, as well as with a normal amount of scroll work. Her four boats were all smartly painted green and white.

The general colour scheme was somewhat altered during her refit at the Isle of France following her grounding on the Ile de Passe. Perhaps with an idea of making her look more like an Indiaman, the yellow stripe of her lower tier was painted out. From then until her capture she is shown as black from her main-deck port-sills down to the copper.

After duly admiring the ship, Decaen followed Linois below to inspect the cabin accommodation. Leger was with him, and Vandermaesen; also Caffarelli, the Prefect of the Marine at Brest. The Admiral showed them the state-room; then his own cabin, to starboard; and then the captain's cabin to port. Decaen was wondering where *he* was to go when Linois solved the problem by showing him the second cabin to starboard; this, he gathered, was to be his own. Now, Decaen was sailing as Captain-General of the French East Indies, and he quite properly regarded himself

[1] Archives Nat. BB5/6. Batiments de l'Etat. Matricule 1801 à 1807.

as the most important person in the ship. Yet he was apparently relegated to the third place. This was bad in itself, but something in the way the thing was done made it infinitely worse. He discovered, next, that no furniture had been provided for him, although Decrès had told him that he would find everything prepared. He would there and then have to purchase his bedding, furniture, linen, plate, utensils and crockery. The whole situation was a deliberate insult. He announced that he would not sail in the *Marengo* at all. He would rather go in a transport.

A hectic scene followed this outburst. The little group fluttered round the fuming General, begging him to see reason. He could not go in the *Côte d'Or*, they told him. It was, they said, unprecedented. The Prefect said that he would not hear of it. He would be blamed if he allowed anything of the sort to happen. Linois said that he was only following custom in allotting the cabins as he had. He was only doing, he said, what was always done.

Decaen quelled the tumult with a word. He would appeal to the First Consul. Needless to say, he had his own way in the end. Caffarelli did not want Bonaparte to hear of it, and so settled the question by making Linois give way. Decaen should have the first cabin to port, with half the state-room if he preferred not to mess with Linois. The partition of the state-room, however, did not take place. Some sort of peace was made between them, and Linois gave a dinner party on the 26th to which Decaen and his staff were invited. Linois wrote to Decrès:

> Le Capitaine de Vau Delarue ayant bien voulu offrir a Madame Decaen sa chambre pour la traversée le Capn General paroit flatté et satisfait du logement qui lui est destiné et de sa famille. Je la reunis aujourd'huy pour diner a Bord avec les autorités civiles et militaire de ce departement. . . .

The incident was closed. Or was it?

The final arrangements were made. Binot and Leger embarked in the *Belle Poule* frigate, the ship destined to go ahead of the squadron. General Vandermaesen went in the *Semillante* frigate and Montigny in *L'Atalante*. Colonel Sainte-Suzanne went in the despised *Côte d'Or*. The other transport, *Marie-Française*, carried a few passengers but was laden chiefly with provisions and stores. The creole troops were to follow later in transports under convoy of the corvette *Belier*. One of these, the *Malabar*, was loaded with biscuits, flour, oil, wine, vinegar and lard, mainly for the hospital at Pondicherry. There was a great deal of overcrowding in all the ships.

The East Indies squadron consisted of the following ships:

Ships	Guns	Captain	Crew	Troops
Marengo	74	Delarue	593	418
Belle Poule	44	Bruilhac	266	209
L'Atalante	44	Beauchene	264	183
Semillante	36	Mothare	215	164
Côte d'Or	2	Dufresne	87	361
Marie-Française	2	Le-Bourg	18	12
	202		1,443	1,347

(Note: Accounts vary as to the numbers, both of seamen and soldiers. The crew of the *Marengo* was probably much larger. This *Belle Poule*, second of her name, had been launched at Nantes not long before, in 1802, being built in a private yard after a design by Sané. Her commander, Bruillac de Kerevel, was an old 'officier bleu' who had served in a French East Indiaman and was Sous-Lieutenant at the time of the Revolution. Moizeau was his First Lieutenant at the age of twenty-five, the other officers, except the purser, being younger still. The *Semillante* had been built at L'Orient in 1791.)

The squadron put to sea on 6th March, 1803, and ran at once into bad weather, which lasted until Finisterre was passed. Nearly everyone was seasick, both Linois and Delarue being confined to their cabins for twenty-four hours. Decaen, by his own account, was immune. And he was certainly well enough to resume his feud with Linois at an early stage of the voyage. The chief source of dispute was the food. Although handsomely paid beforehand, Linois proved a very economical host. A solitary thin and diminutive Breton cow had perished in the gale; and a few fowls had shared the same fate. So the cabin fare was at once reduced to beef and haricots, salt bacon and beans. And even this unambitious scale was not maintained for long. The passengers shortly found themselves eating almost exactly what was served out to the crew. The wine, too, was execrable, undrinkable; but Decaen was enough of an old campaigner to have brought his own. Linois assured his guests that fresh provisions would be obtained at the Cape.

The *Belle Poule* parted company on March 15th and went straight on to Pondicherry, calling only at Madagascar. The rest of the squadron put into the Cape, arriving in False Bay on May 8th. *L'Atalante*, which had parted company by accident early in the voyage, and had since been on fire, arrived two days earlier. The *Côte d'Or* arrived a few days later.

According to Decaen, a somewhat biased critic, the *Marengo* nearly went ashore at the Cape. By his version, Delarue blundered by moonlight into the head of False Bay under the impression that it was Simon's Bay, and then woke up next morning with a start to find himself almost on the beach. Decaen, in fact, thought very little of Delarue. Perhaps with some reason, he ascribed the slowness of the *Marengo* to the incompetence and timidity of her captain. In this view he was loudly supported by the commander, Vrignaud, who was at daggers drawn with his superior officer.

Few of the passengers had taken much trouble to conceal their disgust at the meals provided, but they took heart on sighting the Cape, confident that there would be some improvement. Eggs and radishes graced the festive board on the day of their arrival, and Linois announced that he was laying in a plentiful stock of provisions at enormous expense. Nothing, however, materialized beyond some fowls, some bushels of onions and a few pumpkins hung up in the stern gallery. The Admiral's unpopularity intensified. He quarrelled again with Decaen about whether or not to call at Bourbon, as previously on whether or not to reduce the water allowance. All these matters of dispute were trivial enough in themselves, but they were fatal hindrances to any effective co-operation between the naval and military forces.

The squadron sailed again on May 28th, passed within sight of Bourbon and Galega, and made Ceylon on July 7th. Pondicherry was sighted on the 10th. Before, however, following the further proceedings of Admiral Linois, it is necessary to see what had happened meanwhile in India.

The Governor-General, Lord Wellesley, had received three successive dispatches on the subject of Pondicherry. The first of these, dated 5th May, 1802, was simply an order to restore the French and Dutch settlements. The second, dated October 17th, countermanded the first and ordered him to delay restitution without in any way committing himself. The treaty was not, of course, to be broken; but the expected outbreak of war was to find Pondicherry still in English hands. These instructions arrived on 30th March, 1803. Finally, on May 8th, the Governor-General received Lord Hobart's third dispatch, the effect of which was to annul the second and reiterate the injunctions of the first. Doubtless, these contradictory orders were moves in some complex diplomatic game. Each dispatch may well have been founded on some fresh piece of information. But Wellesley thought otherwise. He regarded his orders as representing mere indecision. Preferring his own judgment to that of a Cabinet which did not know its own mind from one week to another, he decided to ignore the third dispatch. The arrangements made in accordance with the second were allowed to stand.

These arrangements were as follows: The Governments of Madras and Bombay had been instructed to send him all documents relative to the execution of the Treaty of Amiens. If restitution was demanded of them, they were to plead lack of instructions and refer the matter to Fort William. While awaiting his reply, they were to treat the French with all possible civility. What his reply was to be does not appear. Perhaps he hoped to find a flaw in the wording of the treaty; or perhaps he had already found one. Again, he may have intended to be elsewhere when the dispatch should arrive. Delay is always easy. There were a dozen ways in which he could postpone restitution, and he probably meant to resort to each in turn.

The *Belle Poule* parted company, as we have seen, on March 15th; the intention being that this fast-sailing frigate should reach Pondicherry in time to complete arrangements for the landing of the troops. Leger and Binot, who sailed in her, were authorized to take over the settlement. They had with them letters from Decaen to the Governor-General and the Governor of Madras, demanding the surrender of the French settlements under the terms of the Treaty of Amiens and naming Binot as the officer empowered to receive them. The frigate also carried two companies of infantry and the sum of 200,000 francs—or the equivalent in piastres—to cover the initial expenses.

The *Belle Poule* arrived at Pondicherry on June 15th, and Binot presented his letters to the English Commandant—a certain Colonel Demeuron. Demeuron sent them on to Madras, explaining that he himself had, of course, no power to hand over the territory in question. But he was naturally very anxious to help the French in any way he could. He would take it upon himself, he said, to allow both civil and military officers to land. He offered to help the surgeon of the *Belle Poule* to establish a temporary hospital on shore. He had already had a lodging prepared for Binot himself.

The reply from Madras came on June 19th. The Governor, Lord Clive, was politeness itself. He promised to proceed without delay in the restitution—as soon, that was to say, as he had received orders from the Governor-General. Meanwhile, Colonel Cullen was the Commissioner for the handing over of Pondicherry. He and Demeuron would do their utmost to find accommodation for the French troops. Let them land, by all means.

On the day that Binot heard from Lord Clive, he saw some English newspapers which were filled with rumours of war. Somewhat alarmed, Binot consulted with Leger and the captain of the *Belle Poule*, Bruilhac. Binot and Leger were in favour of landing the troops, Bruilhac strongly against it. After some hesitation it was decided to land the greater part of them. A hundred and eighty men were accordingly landed on June 31st, while eighty-two remained, for the time being, on board the frigate. Cullen and Demeuron received them warmly and asked all the officers to dinner. At the first toast, Cullen proposed the health of the First Consul. Binot then proposed that of George III, afterwards presenting his host with a medallion of Bonaparte. Cullen said that he would keep it and value it as the portrait of one of the greatest men the world had seen. He was, in short, enjoying his part.

A week passed, ten days, a fortnight; and there was still no word from Madras or Bengal. Then came the news that the English squadron had sailed from Trincomalee and come to anchor on July 5th off Cuddalore —some twenty miles down the coast from Pondicherry. Binot became still more anxious. Bruilhac was definitely frightened. The English flag was still flying at Pondicherry. There were rumours at Madras of an alliance between France and Russia. The French commercial agent, Bruix, was refused permission to go to Tranquebar. Leger noticed that no mention was made in the *Madras Gazette* of the *Belle Poule's* arrival; an insignificant fact which somehow added to his anxiety. In the light of other events, even Cullen's hospitality began to seem rather sinister. In retrospect, had he not been a shade too polite? Not without some misgivings, Binot allowed the rest of the troops to land. Meanwhile, the English men-of-war *Trident* (64) and *Rattlesnake* (18) sailed from Cuddalore and dropped anchor close to the *Belle Poule*. Retreat now seemed impossible. Binot could do nothing but wait; and he was still waiting when the French squadron arrived.

CHAPTER X

New Outbreak of War

PETER RAINIER had now been on the East Indies station for over eight years. Nothing had come of his previous resignation but he was now more definitely expecting to be relieved. He was more elderly now and probably looked it, still spectacled and stouter than ever. His prize money, chiefly from the Moluccas, had made him a rich man and his property at his death was valued at nearly a quarter of a million— a tenth of it rather oddly bequeathed towards the reduction of the national debt. He did not long enjoy his wealth for he died some three years after his return to England. Gossip (of which India had plenty) said that he was too much addicted to the pleasures of the table; which was very likely true. His experience of the Indian Ocean was now unrivalled, and his sense of his own importance by no means diminished. Nearly worn out as he was, he was quite unfit to direct another naval war in the Indian Ocean. On the other hand, his presence at the outbreak of war was an advantage and he could do much to advise whoever came to succeed him.

The custom had grown up for the bulk of the English squadron to remain at Bombay, or anyway on the Malabar coast, during the north-east monsoon; at Madras or anyway on the Coromandel coast during the south-west monsoon. The rumours of war, therefore, which preceded Decaen's arrival in India, found Rainier in the act of moving round from his winter to his summer base. He accordingly stopped half-way, at Trincomalee. It was a good place to await events, and his presence there would serve to protect the port, which was valuable and ill-defended. The forces with his flag consisted of the *Centurion* (50), *Tremendous* (74), *Trident* (64), *San Fiorenzo* (36), *Terpsichore* (32), *Fox* (32), the sloops *Albatross* and *Rattlesnake*, and the troopships *Sheerness* and *Wilhelmina*. With these he came to anchor at Trincomalee on about June 4th; and there he was joined by the *Concorde* (36), *Dedaigneuse* (36), and the *Lancaster* (64)—all from Madras; and ultimately by the sloop *Victor*, from Bombay. This comprised the whole force then on the station.

In April and May, Rainier, anticipating war, seemed chiefly anxious to prevent Goa from falling into French hands. This Portuguese port was a weak place in the defences of India, and it offered the easiest access to the Mahratta country, where France would presumably look for allies. But news came that there were no forces collected at the Isle of France in March, and this, with the setting in of the bad weather season, convinced the Admiral that his best plan would be to concentrate all his forces at Trincomalee.

When the news came that the *Belle Poule* was at anchor off Pondicherry, and that a squadron from France was due to arrive there shortly, Rainier moved his squadron to Cuddalore roads. There was still no news from England to justify apprehensions of an immediate outbreak of war. As late as May 19th, Wellesley wrote that he thought an early renewal of hostilities improbable. But, shortly after the arrival of the *Belle Poule*, some information arrived at Madras which strengthened the determination of the Indian Governments not to surrender Pondicherry. This was the news of the King's speech of March 10th, or rather his message to Parliament, which came by the overland mail. The news reached the Governor-General by July 6th, in the form of a letter from Castlereagh stating that the fleet was being equipped for sea, that press warrants had been issued, and that the whole of the militia had been called out.

While at Cuddalore, Rainier received an application from Cullen for naval support to overawe the French troops already landed 'who had become rather disorderly and impatient at the delay in the restitution of the place.' And it was to comply with this request that the *Trident* and *Rattlesnake* had been sent to anchor near the *Belle Poule*. When Linois appeared, Rainier moved his whole squadron up to within four or five miles of the French ships, and recalled the *Trident* and *Rattlesnake*. He was now within striking distance and only waited for news of the outbreak of war. Linois was trapped and the news might arrive at any moment.

On first sighting Pondicherry, on July 11th, Linois simultaneously made out Rainier's squadron, which was then making sail in order to prevent his escape. He at once prepared for action, thinking that war had already broken out—which indeed it had, but not in India. He was reassured by a ship outward bound from Pondicherry for the Isle of France, and accordingly came to anchor in the roads. The captain of the *Belle Poule* came on board the *Marengo* to report.

On learning the situation, Decaen's first move was to write a letter of protest to the Governor of Madras. He demanded that he should surrender Pondicherry on his own responsibility. The letter was conveyed by the *Belle Poule*. But before any answer could arrive, the whole situation was changed. For, on the 18th, the brig *Belier* appeared. As soon as she was signalled it was obvious that she carried news of importance—she was not expected to come out so soon; nor, as the escort for the transports to follow, was she expected to come alone. As soon as she dropped anchor, her commander came on board the *Marengo* with dispatches for Decaen and Linois. She had sailed some ten days after the squadron and the dispatches were dated March 15th. The orders were made out in the expectation that the *Belier* would overtake Linois at the Cape. In view of the English preparations for war, the squadron was not to go to Pondicherry but to the Isle of France, there to await further orders.

Decaen was in a difficult position. With war clearly impending, he dared not land at Pondicherry. Nor could he remain where he was. The English were almost certain to hear the news of war, by overland mail, before he did. And their first move would be to annihilate Linois. It was essential to go at once. But would Rainier allow him to go? There was always the disquieting possibility that the English would treat his departure as an act of war; as they might also treat the re-embarking of the troops landed from the *Belle Poule*. They would suppose that the *Belier* brought news of war, and act accordingly.

Decaen asked Linois if it would be possible to avoid sacrificing the troops on shore. The Admiral promptly refused to risk his ships in the attempt. He suggested calling a council of war. Decaen derided this proposal and ended the discussion by saying 'Can you sail at midnight? If so, make your arrangements for doing so.' And so it was decided that the squadron should slip away in the darkness, leaving Binot and his men to take over the French settlements if there was peace, to capitulate in the event of war. Binot had three months altogether at Pondicherry which he spent in making contact with the Rajahs of Tanjore and Travancore and in establishing an agent in Danish Tranquebar for intelligence purposes. He discovered that French troops landed between Goa and Bombay would find Mahratta allies. That possibility led to Decaen's plan for invading India with four thousand men in January 1805. It did not, however, settle the immediate problem of escaping from Pondicherry.[1]

Elaborate precautions were taken to ensure secrecy. Only three men were present at the inception of the plan—Leger being the third—and no fourth person was to be informed until the last moment. It was only after sunset that Decaen and Linois rowed round the squadron and told the chief officers of the change of plan. At 8.0 the order was given to hoist in the boats quietly, clear for action, and heave the cables short. Soon

---

[1] J. Saintoyant. *La colonisation Française pendant la periode Napoleonienne* (1799–1815), p. 426, *et seq.*

after midnight, cables were cut and the whole squadron made sail to the north-north-east—a direction no pursuer would be likely to take. The anchors were buoyed and some boats were left behind at these buoys, with lights burning in them. The ruse succeeded, and by dawn there was not a sail in sight. So course was altered to south-east, as direct a course for the Isle of France as the monsoon would allow the ships to steer. The squadron made the island of Roderigue on August 14th, and reached the Isle of France on the 16th.

It is not clear whether the French squadron actually escaped unobserved.

> . . . About Midnight the French Admiral slipped and put to sea, with the two Frigates and corvette, and as we observed had left boats on their anchors with lights on them, obviously for the purpose of concealing their motions. At Daylight I sent ships out in different directions to observe what course he had steered, but none of them were able to get sight of him. . . .
>
> (P.R.O. Adm, 1/173. To Admiralty, July 24th.)

This is Rainier's version of the affair, and it reads as if the departure of the French was noticed. Had it not been reported, Rainier would have been more doubtful, one would think, as to when it took place. Duclos,[1] moreover, states that alarm rockets were fired on shore. In that case, it seems odd that there was no immediate pursuit, if only to ascertain the direction they took. But Rainier may have been rather afraid of overtaking them. He was probably in some doubt as to what he should do if he did come up with any of their ships. The departure of the French, however secret and hurried, could hardly be construed as an act of war. Rainier was evidently in something of a quandary. When the *Belle Poule* returned from Madras, to find Linois gone, she seems to have been chased by English ships, though without success. She reached the Isle of France before Linois arrived there. The *Côte d'Or* transport appeared on the 16th. She was fired on and detained, but eventually released. The *Marie-Française*, another transport, came in on August 25th. She also was detained for a few days, and actually taken to Negapatam. When released on the 31st, she did not sail at once, and the result of this was that she did not sail at all. News of the outbreak of war reached the coast on September 6th.

Following the disappearance of the French squadron, Rainier remained on the coast until the end of the month and then took his forces to await developments at Trincomalee. At the end of August came the news of war, which decided the Admiral to proceed with the strength of the squadron to protect Bombay and Goa. Captain Bathurst was ordered, on

[1] MS. Memoir in the National Maritime Museum, Greenwich. See Appendix A.

August 30th, to take command of a detachment, consisting of the *Concorde* (36), and the sloops *Victor* and *Rattlesnake*, with which to patrol the Sandheads, protect Madras and convoy the China trade back to India. To this detachment the two troopships *Sheerness* and *Wilhelmina* were annexed, chiefly at first for the purpose of rushing troops and guns to reinforce Trincomalee, threatened at that time by the Kandians with whom Governor North was in conflict. Both, however, were armed with heavy carronades from the arsenal at Bombay, and were to be reckoned with as ships of war. The China trade needing protection consisted of country ships, twenty of them being bound for Bombay and expected to sail by way of the Straits of Malacca between November and February. Bathurst was to meet them, presumably, at Penang. Having made all these arrangements, Rainier sailed for Bombay in the *Centurion*, with three sail of the line, two frigates and two sloops. He was there in November, with his smaller ships watching Goa and the Malabar coast. Arriving on the 7th, he had at once to put the *Trident* and *Tremendous* in dock, both being much in need of repair.

Trident, Bombay Harbour.
10th December, 1803.

Sir

Triplicate of my last of 14th ultimo (Original and Duplicate whereof were forwarded by Overland Dispatch on the 14th ultimo and 5th instant) accompanies this, since which have dispatched Ships to Cruize for the protection and defence of this Coast, and to scour the Gulf of Persia, for the security of the Trade, and particularly the conveyance of the Overland Dispatch between this Port and Bussorah [i.e. Bushire]. . . .

The intelligence from the Mauritius of the arrival of the French Squadron there from Pondicherry, has been fully authenticated. . . . From the best information it has fell in my way to procure from Batavia, the strength of the Dutch Squadron in those Seas appear to consist of three sail of the Line as pr. margin, five large Frigates, and three stout Corvettes, one of the large frigates, 'tis reported has been lost among the Moluccas.

Bato
Pluto
Kortenaar

I have no account of the strength of the Spaniards at Manila but expect intelligence from thence soon. . . . The Governor-General of Goa has admitted a British Garrison into Alguada Port and I have directed Captain Bingham in His Majesty's Ship *St. Fiorenzo*, Senior Officer of the Cruisers employed as above-mentioned, to pay particular attention to the defence of Goa. . . .

(Rainier to Admiralty. P.R.O. Ad. 1/173.)

Decaen had come out to the East dreaming of a great campaign to recover India for France. After his escape from Pondicherry he realized that there was no chance of an immediate invasion of India. The task devolved upon him of ruling the Isle of France instead. He found plenty to do. The political sentiments of the colonists were of an obsolete kind, and his first duty was to explain to them how unfashionable their views had become. The previous Governor-General, Malartic, had died in July 1800 and the Colonial Assembly had invited the military commander, General Magallon de la Morlière, to take his place; which he did.[1] This appointment, like the Colonial Assembly itself, was irregular, and the removal of a Governor who had been there since 1796 was obviously essential. Orthodox Bonapartism could hardly be expected of a man who had left France as long ago as that. Another step was to rid the island of its Assembly and other anachronisms. Decaen transferred Magallon to Bourbon, with a suitable force, and himself took over the government of the Isle of France.

Military operations being out of the question, Decaen could make war only by giving advice to Linois. He urged him to proceed with his squadron to Java, and that for several reasons. To begin with, the Dutch at Batavia had to be informed of the outbreak of war. It was advisable to reinforce them at the same time, for which purpose Decaen planned to send them the same battalion, by this time rather depleted, which had protected them during the last war, and for which he had no particular use. Then, it was well known that the English China fleet always sailed from Canton early in the year. The French squadron could arrive in the China seas in time to intercept it. There was a chance of there being no naval escort there so early in the war. Finally, Decaen was anxious that Linois should go, and as soon as possible. He disliked him personally, and the stay of his squadron was a heavy burden on the colony, which was not too well provisioned.

The actual news of the outbreak of war was brought to the Isle of France by the corvette *Berceau*, which came in on September 25th. By that time, Linois had agreed to go to Batavia. He had wanted at first to send the *Marengo* back to France, but it was pointed out that she would probably fall in with the English on the French coast. His next proposal had been to cruise on the Malabar coast, which was what the English Admiral expected him to do. When he had at last been persuaded to sail for Java, every effort was made to complete the refitting and recruiting

[1] J. Saintoyant. *La colonisation Française pendant la period Napoleonienne* (1799–1815), Paris, 1931. (Chapter VIII.)

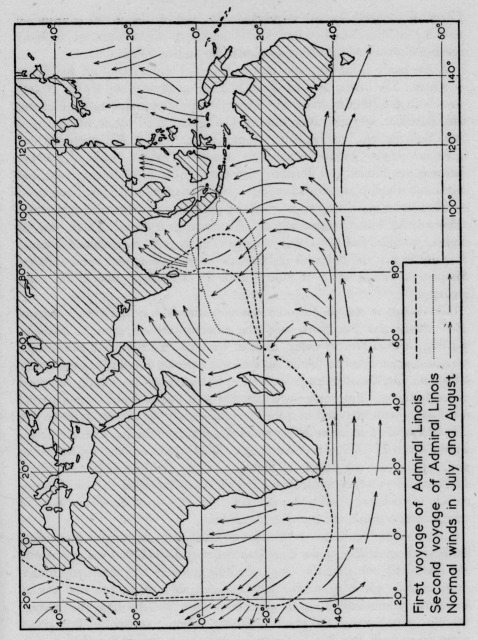

First voyage of Admiral Linois
Second voyage of Admiral Linois
Normal winds in July and August

of his squadron. His force had, however, to be weakened by the departure of *L'Atalante*, which was dispatched on a mission to Muscat. She was expected to rejoin him before the probable date of his encounter with the

China ships; and, in the meanwhile, she served the useful purpose of drawing off the *Centurion* and *Fox* in pursuit of her as soon as the news reached Bombay of her being seen near the Gulf of Persia.

L'Atalante's actual mission was to take a French envoy to the Court of Oman. The Imam Seid of Oman reigned at Muscat and owned twenty vessels in the Pilgrim trade. His state monopoly extended to the Red Sea and Zanzibar. On arrival at Muscat, Cavaignac could obtain no interview with Seid Sultan, but the latter's representative, Sheik Ali, explained that a French envoy would be welcome in time of peace. News of the war had reached Muscat (via Bushire) two days before *L'Atalante* arrived, and Sheik Ali asked pointedly what forces Napoleon had in the neighbourhood —whether he had a seaport nearby, and generally what protection he could offer to the Sultan supposing an alliance were agreed? There was no answer to this, and a fruitless voyage is now only remembered because Cavaignac was the father of the General of that name, and because Pierre Bouvet—a future sailor of note—made in *L'Atalante* one of his early voyages.[1]

Linois put to sea on October 8th with the *Marengo*, the two frigates *Belle Poule* and *Semillante*, and the recently arrived corvette *Berceau*. Calling at Bourbon in order to land General Magallon and his troops, he sailed again from St. Denis on the 14th, steering roughly for the Straits of Sunda. On November 21st he took the *Countess of Sutherland*, described as an Indiaman, but evidently a country ship out of Calcutta and bound for China with rice and cotton. She was sent with a prize crew to the Isle of France. Linois probably owed this prize to the fact that she sailed before the news of war reached Bengal. This would account for her being on a course for the Straits of Sunda, perhaps with the object of calling at Bencoolen—which settlement Linois himself intended to visit. Unprotected merchantmen seldom went near the Straits of Sunda in time of war; it meant going too near the Dutch base.

Linois made Sumatra on December 2nd, and sailed into Bencoolen harbour the next day, under English colours. A French raid was apparently the last thing the garrison expected. The gunners at Fort Marlborough were entirely taken in by the false colours and a pilot was sent out to bring the supposedly English ships into port. By the time the mistake was discovered, it was too late to make any effective resistance. Two prizes were taken and five English merchantmen were burnt by their crews. Landing parties set fire to the warehouses on shore, which were filled with

[1] See *Revue Maritime et Coloniale*, Vols. 75 and 78, "La Guerre Maritime dans l'Inde," E. Fabre.

rice, opium, pepper, camphor and spices, and the squadron sailed again on the 6th, well satisfied with the damage done.

> . . . d'apres les renseignmens que j'ai obtenus depuis, la perte que l'ennemi a eprouvée doit etre beaucoup au dela de dix millions que nous avions estimee d'abord. Les deux Bricks qui ont été brulés etaint charges de munitions de guerre et quatre proas aussi incendies en outre des cinq Batimens etaint tres richement chargés. . . .[1]

It may, however, be doubted whether the raid was altogether wise. It advertised the presence of the raiders at a time when much depended upon secrecy. The results might have been—and nearly were—disastrous.

Linois entered the Straits of Sunda on December 10th, and anchored in Batavia roads on the 12th. Mistaken at first for the enemy, his arrival spread consternation among the Dutch shipping. He reassured them by firing a salute, and his men were soon busy watering and landing the troops. He told the Dutch authorities of the outbreak of war and asked for naval co-operation against the China fleet. But here he was disappointed, and that for several reasons To begin with, the Dutch squadron was not there. Rear-Admiral Dekker had on October 20th sailed for the Isle of France in order to discover whether war had begun; and, if so, to ask for reinforcements. He had in fact quitted Batavia a few days after Linois quitted Bourbon. Even more final, however, than the temporary absence of Dekker was the attitude of the Dutch officials. They greeted the French without enthusiasm, were disposed to be critical of the troops Linois had brought them, and seemed ill-disposed to co-operate in any way. Linois managed to obtain some supplies from them, but the only vessel they would allow to join in his enterprise was a small brig called *L'Aventurier*. They evidently wished to keep out of the conflict as far as possible.

Meanwhile, what was Admiral Rainier doing; and what, in particular, had he done for the protection of the China ships? His first instinct, as we have seen, was to protect what he considered to be the weak points in the coastline of India—Goa, Bombay and Trincomalee. Being uncertain as to whether Linois was likely to be joined by reinforcements from France, he was anxious to keep his squadron together. Indeed, he half-apologized to Wellesley for detaching Bathurst's squadron, saying that the step was justified by the Kandian war and the consequent necessity for having some naval force on that side of India. As it was, however, he kept together his three—or, counting the *Centurion* (50), his four—ships of the line. By December he had been induced to allow the *Centurion* to go in chase of

[1] Archives Nat. BB4 185.

L'Atalante, and had also been compelled to dock the *Tremendous* and *Trident*. The *Tremendous* had a weakened frame and decayed sternpost, and 'the most serious consequences would certainly have taken place had she continued much longer afloat.' The *Trident* was at first docked merely to stop some leaks, but it was then found that, being iron-fastened, many of her bolts were corroded. She appeared to be falling to pieces. After pondering the problem for several seconds, Framjee Monakjee and Jamsetjee Bomanjee recommended exactly what their remote predecessors would have recommended to Marco Polo. They thought, on consideration, that the best thing to do would be to give the ship an extra layer of wood sheathing. Rainier agreed, and the *Trident* was thus put out of action for some time to come. He was thus left with only one ship of the line at his disposal, and that was the *Lancaster* (64).

On 14th November, 1803, the exact disposition of the English squadron was as follows: *Trident* and *Tremendous* in dock at Bombay; *Lancaster*, *Dedaigneuse*, *Albatross*, *San Fiorenzo* and *Arrogant* at Bombay, some in need of refitting and docking, one or two available for watching Goa; *Dasher* and *Caroline* on their way to Bombay; *Centurion* at Bombay, but about to proceed to the westward; *Wilhelmina* on her way to Bombay from Madras with provisions for the squadron and troops to land at Point de Galle, Ceylon. Then there was the detachment under Bathurst; the *Terpsichore* and *Concorde* on their way to Penang to meet the homeward-bound country trade; the *Sheerness* and *Rattlesnake* to follow them; the *Victor* on convoy duty, gone to Bengal. The *Caroline* (36), was expected from England, and had in fact arrived, but the Admiral did not know where she was.

The first mention of the China fleet was in a dispatch from Lord Wellesley to Rainier, dated 17th September, 1803, immediately after the news of the outbreak of war had reached Fort William. He states that the renewal of hostilities does not, in his opinion, require any material change in the distribution of the squadron, 'excepting such arrangements as Your Excellency may think fit to adopt for the protection of the Company's trade with China. . . .' Rainier says nothing of any arrangement for this purpose in his dispatch to the Admiralty of December 10th. After the event, however, in his dispatch of 17th May, 1804, he claims that he had provided for the protection of the China fleet by sending Bathurst to Penang. He adds that Bathurst, with the *Terpsichore* and *Concorde*, would have been there to protect the China ships had he not deviated from his orders, which were 'to wait till the whole Country Trade was arrived from China.' He had so deviated from his instructions in accordance with the wishes of the Governor-General, as expressed in a dispatch addressed to Rainier at Madras, which Bathurst, as senior officer there, had opened.

To grasp how lame these excuses are, it is only necessary to glance at a chart. Penang is four hundred miles from the obvious place for intercepting the China fleet. What Bathurst had done, in fulfilment of the Governor-General's wishes, was to give escort to the first or earliest division of the country ships, not waiting to collect the remainder. He had not waited until the *whole* country trade was arrived. Had he done so, he would have been there to protect the China fleet. But *where* would he have been? At Penang. There was nothing in his orders to authorize him to go any farther south than that. And what use would he have been at Penang? True, he might have heard of the French squadron being at Batavia and then gone to meet the China fleet as a stroke of initiative. But it would have been a very bold stroke. For what if he met Linois before he found the China fleet? Besides, an Admiral has no business to rely on strokes of initiative.

The truth Rainier was trying to disguise was that he had done nothing for the protection of the China fleet. The object of Bathurst's visit to Penang was simply to escort the country ships bound from China to India, in compliance with the petition of the Bombay shipowners of August 29th. This much is clear from the instructions given Bathurst on August 30th. He was not told to concern himself with the China fleet proper, the Indiamen carrying the tea from China to England. Therefore—apart from the chance of his acting on his own initiative—it made no difference to the China fleet whether he was at Penang or not; for it was highly improbable that the French would lie in wait anywhere near that settlement. And the question of his deviating from his orders—even if important in itself— had nothing whatever to do with the unprotected state of the company's ships. To have been of the slightest use to them, Bathurst would have had to do more than deviate from his orders. He would have had to ignore them.

Rainier, then, did nothing to protect the China fleet, but was afterwards ashamed of the fact; so ashamed that he pretended otherwise and put the blame on a subordinate. Why did he do nothing? Wardroom gossip had it that he was so addicted to eating mangoes that he refused to leave the Malabar coast during the season for them, which begins in May; and that he should have gone to meet the China fleet himself. Granting that his taste for mangoes may have overridden every other consideration in his mind, and that he might have lost his share of them by going eastwards at that time of year (both of which suppositions seem a little improbable), it is still not quite clear why he could not send someone else. As a matter of fact, his reputation as a mango-lover probably originated in his efforts to make his seamen eat fruit as a preventive of scurvy.

In finding a more tenable solution to the problem, one fact to bear in mind is that he did not know that the China fleet was going to be attacked. This may sound sufficiently obvious. Nevertheless, the knowledge of what did happen is apt to blind us to the fact that other things might have happened. Linois, we assume, was bound to make an attempt on the China fleet. Because he did so, we think that it was the obvious thing to do. It was not obvious to him, as we have seen. His first proposal was to send the *Marengo* back to France; his second, to cruise on the Malabar coast. It was only Decaen who induced him to go eastwards at all.

In the nature of things, Rainier could have no information as to what Linois was doing. On December 10th, it must be remembered, he was writing to say that the intelligence of Linois's arrival at the Mauritius had been 'fully authenticated.' By that date, Linois was passing the Straits of Sunda, leaving Bencoolen a smouldering ruin. That raid provided the earliest news of his whereabouts. And when did Rainier hear of the raid? In February 1804. There was, in short, very little possibility of Rainier receiving information in time for it to be of any use to him. His only hope was to guess where the French were going and be there before them. And yet the chances were heavily against his guessing aright. There were plenty of rumours to misguide him. There was a report, which reached England via Bordeaux in April, that 'Admiral Linois had sailed for the Cape of Good Hope, for the purpose of preventing its falling into the hands of the English.' This was only one, probably, of a dozen rumours then being repeated. One of them—it reached England by way of Philadelphia—happened to be correct. But how could Rainier know which was correct?

On 7th January, 1804, Rainier was writing to Lord William Bentinck, the new governor at Fort St. George, to say that such ships as were available were distributed between Dondra Head and the vicinity of Bombay. The letter goes on—

> Various have been the reports of a Force of the Enemy having been seen on the Coast of Guzerat, and near the Gulf of Kutch, a very late one (as pr. Copy of intelligence herewith enclosed) that was considerable enough to occasion an alarm in my own mind, that it might consist of the whole of Rear Admiral Linois' Squadron. . . .

Such a rumour as this originated, of course, in some ignorant native mistaking *L'Atalante* for a ship of the line. The Admiral may not have believed it for long, but he was careful to transmit the news to Bentinck. Why? Simply because rumours of the same type were reaching him from the other side of India. Here is an extract from his letter to Governor North, of Ceylon, dated February 27th:

Trident, Cananore Road

Honble Sir

Your Excellency's Secret Dispatch of the 18th Ultimo, reached me in Goa Road, via Bombay, the 18th instant.

A report similar to that your Excellency mentions, of an expected attack by the combined Forces of France and Holland, was communicated to me by Lord. W. Bentinck, only differing in the object, as it was there given out to be the Coromandel Coast. I dont know a better situation the Squadron can occupy at present, than about this part of the Malabar Coast, to be as near at hand as possible, to afford your Excellency's Government any assistance if needful, or eventually to oppose the effects of the intrigues of the Enemy with the Court of Portugal, with regard to Goa, and other settlements belonging to the Portuguese to the Northward as from intelligence suggested by the latest news papers to 21st October last, the crisis of that negociation, was daily expected to discover itself in terms inimical to the British interests, particularly in this Country. Your Excellency can forward a Dispatch to me in a few days by sending it to Anjango, whereas was the part of the Squadron now with me at Colombo, it would require a fortnight or three weeks to beat up to Goa. . . .

Each Indian Government, it is clear, thought itself threatened.

The next point to emphasize is that the Admiral's ignorance extended not only to the French whereabouts but to their strength. He had seen Linois's squadron, and he knew how formidable the *Marengo* was. What he did not know was whether the French were to be reinforced, and whether the Dutch intended to act with them. He had heard something of a second and a third division due to arrive from Brest—with troops, it was believed. These might have arrived for all he knew to the contrary. He knew, again, something of the Dutch strength; but he did not know that Dekker and Linois had failed to meet. Still less did he know that it was the Dutch policy to avoid active co-operation with the French. Failing such knowledge, he had to consider the possibility of being called upon to face an allied squadron of a strength at least equal—and perhaps superior—to his own.

Knowing, then, that his strength was lessened through several ships being in dock or in need of repair, and that an enemy of uncertain—but possibly considerable—force was roaming at large in the Indian Ocean,

Rainier wished to keep his squadron together. His attitude is apparent in a letter he wrote to Lord Wellesley on 11th January, 1804:

> . . . adverting to the strength of the combined Force of the Dutch and French Squadrons, I shall be extremely cautious of trusting single Frigates to Cruize at any distance from the Strength of the Squadron, on Stations where they may be liable to be attacked by a superior Force. . . .
>
> (P.R.O. Ad. 1/175. *Trident*, Bombay Harbour.)

This fear of allowing isolated frigates to run the risk of falling into Linois's hands accounts for the fact that Bathurst was not ordered to go further south than Penang. It was also another factor in deciding Rainier not to send an escort for the China fleet. He would not send frigates while there was a possibility of their meeting the *Marengo* on the way. And he had only one ship of the line at his disposal; and that was the *Lancaster* (64). Now, apart from his other reasons for wishing to keep the *Lancaster*, it is obvious that the argument against exposing frigates to capture applied also, in a lesser degree, to a 64-gun ship. With every allowance for innate national superiority, the issue of a conflict between an English sixty-four and a French eighty-four would be, to say the least of it, doubtful. The risk was one which only certain conditions could justify.

Lastly, it must be observed that Rainier had reason to hope that the China fleet could do without his help. It had sometimes been the practice, during the previous war, for a ship of the line to accompany one of the outward-bound convoys to China and then return with the whole fleet to England. He had received no news from Canton for some time, and he was not certain that this precaution had been neglected. It was at least possible that a ship or ships might have been sent to bring the China fleet home, even without giving convoy to any portion of it on the outward voyage. Some reinforcements were expected for the East Indies squadron. It was quite possible that they would be sent out with orders to proceed first to China and then see the tea ships past the Straits of Sunda. If, on the other hand, no escort was sent, Rainier supposed that the Committee of Supercargoes at Canton would have the intelligence to send the fleet back by one of the eastward passages—Bali, say, or Lombok. There was little risk in returning through these straits, for the enemy would not know which to guard; and the route they were to take was always kept secret, in any case, during a war—even the commanders being kept in ignorance until after the homeward passage had commenced.

Rainier's opinion on these possibilities may be gathered from two of his letters. The first, to Lord Wellesley, is dated 11th January, 1804:

. . . The protection of the Trade of the Company to, and from China, I apprehend will be provided for by the Admiralty, agreeable to the mode generally adopted during the late war; by sending a line of Battle Ship direct from England; and am disposed to think that one of the Ships of the Line seen off Madeira by the *Tygress*, was destined for that Service, if not two, and the other for St. Helena, or one for China and two for St. Helena. I did not conceive myself authorized to detail any part of the Squadron on that Service as things were circumstanced when the intelligence of the commencement of Hostilities was first received, or even on the first alarm of that event.

(P.R.O. Adm. 1/175. *Trident*, Bombay Harbour.)

The second, to Lord William Bentinck, is dated 21st March, 1804:

. . . And with regard to the Company's Homeward bound Ships, I never knew an instance during the last War, of their proceeding through the Streights of Sunda but with Convoy, even when the force of the enemy was so trifling in these Seas, and never through the Straits of Malacca but once, and then at my instance, having taken them under my Convoy at Macao. But when without Convoy they always had recourse to some one of the Eastern passages, as I trust they have now done, and the remaining Bombay Ships with them, part of the way. . . .

. . . No communication whatever has been made to me from England, or China, as to any expectation of Convoy from me, and for the last four years of the late War, a line of Battle ship had been constantly dispatched direct to China with the Convoy, to wait and conduct them Home again. . . .

(P.R.O. Adm. 1/175. *Trident*, off Cochin.)

The Admiral, it is evident, was worried about the China ships. He confidently asserted they were safe, and hoped, while convincing Wellesley and Bentinck, to convince himself. He failed. His arguments are sound enough as far as they go. But he was crediting the supercargoes with an intelligence of which they never seem to have shown any symptoms. They were capable of assuming, as they apparently did assume, that the Navy would 'do something.' To admit the entire validity of the Admiral's arguments would be to leave unexplained his own anxiety, which took the form of querulous complaints that no one had told him any details about the China fleet, and more especially its time of sailing—as if that would have made any difference. The situation was that he was more or less unable to do anything to protect the China ships, but would probably be made the scapegoat if they came to grief. The calamity of their capture would involve his ruin. His subsequent self-contradictions are the proof of it.

Curiously enough, Rainier was something of a hero at this time in the eyes of the public in England. The rumour was that he had detained Linois's squadron at Pondicherry on his own responsibility; and no news had come, in December 1803, of the French ships' escape. On the 17th of that month the following paragraph appeared in two newspapers, the *True Briton* and *Sun*:

> The detention of Linois's Squadron becomes daily more credited . . . we think that little doubt ought to be entertained upon the fact. If such an event then has really taken place, how much is the country indebted to Admiral Rainier for the promptitude, spirit and energy of his conduct! for it is a fact, which, if it were not well known, would hardly be believed, that it was two months after the commencement of the War before any orders were dispatched from the Admiralty to the Naval Commandant in the Indian Seas . . . our Officers abroad have been left pretty much to their own discretion, from the criminal negligence in certain public departments. . . .

After the fall of the Addington administration, Lord St. Vincent employed his leisure in prosecuting the proprietors of these newspapers for libel. Their criticism was, as a fact, rather oddly misplaced. St. Vincent's crime was rather in the brutal haste with which he sent reinforcements to sea. One at least of the two 74-gun ships dispatched to the East Indies in June 1803 was ordered away in the midst of refitting, without enough provisions, without money and without medical stores. Considering that the war began only on May 16th, this reinforcement was fairly prompt. The two ships were the *Sceptre* and *Albion*.

The *Sceptre* was sent off at the end of June. The *Albion*, Captain Ferrier, followed soon afterwards, with convoy; as did also the *Grampus* (50) and, apparently, the *Russel* (74). They were all at Rio de Janeiro in the last week of September 1803. There they found a Dutch squadron under Admiral Hartsinck, consisting of the *Terrible* (60), *Resistance* (60), *Pallas* (36) and *Scipio* (18). There was said to be another 68-gun ship belonging to the squadron. These Dutch ships had slipped out of Ferrol on June 16th, just as Sir Edward Pellew, captain of the *Tonnant*, came to blockade the port in company with the *Mars*—a seventy-four like the *Tonnant*—and a sloop called the *Aigle*. Finding the birds flown, he followed them for three weeks without overtaking them; and at Rio de Janeiro, of course, they were protected by the neutrality of the port.

The English ships sailed from Rio de Janeiro on October 15th, but parted company soon afterwards, the *Russel* and *Grampus* remaining to bring the convoy along, the other two ships pushing on ahead. The *Albion* and

Sceptre came into Madras roads on 8th January, 1804, both their crews being 'extremely sickly and highly scorbutic.' Rainier was then on the other side of India, as we have seen, and he could not know for some time of their arrival. They stayed off Madras for the next three weeks, partly to await his orders. They were still there when the news came of the raid on Bencoolen. Lord William Bentinck instantly sent for Captain Ferrier and strongly urged him to take his two ships to the eastward. They might yet arrive to save the China fleet. The chances were that they would be too late, but there was a bare possibility of their being able to effect a rescue. It seemed, at least, the only hope. Ferrier agreed to make the attempt. He put to sea on February 8th and made sail for the Straits of Malacca. He might have made a quicker passage to the Straits of Sunda, but that would have put him hopelessly to leeward of where he wanted to be. Bentinck saw him go and then sat down to make his apologies to Admiral Rainier.

An Indian Government could not, of course, give orders to a captain in the Navy. But it could 'requisition'; and an officer with no previous orders to the contrary to plead, was taking a grave responsibility if he neglected to comply with a requisition. Rainier's wrath fell, therefore, on Bentinck and his colleagues in the Madras Government. It was they who were responsible rather than Ferrier.

> *Trident*, Mangalore Road.
> 14th March, 1804.

My Lord

 I must confess myself at a loss to express to your Lordship the deep and sensible regret impressed on my mind since I received the information that His Majesty's Ships *Albion* and *Sceptre* were detached to the Eastward, at the suggestion, and with the concurrence of your Lordships Government, without my Knowledge, on a distant Service so far from my reach. . . .

(To Lord William Bentinck. P.R.O. Adm. 1/175.)

Rainier was thoroughly annoyed. He did not like other people ordering his ships about. He felt as if he was losing control of the situation. And it would be months before he had the *Albion* and *Sceptre* under his orders. The news of the raid on Bencoolen put him in no good mood for hearing of such happenings. The disaster impending at the eastern end of the Straits of Malacca was likely to be the ruin of his reputation. Nor did there seem to him the slightest probability of the *Albion* and *Sceptre* doing anything to avert the catastrophe. The news of the raid took two months to reach Madras. It would probably take Ferrier five or six weeks to get even as far as Penang. That left Linois with nearly four months at his disposal in which to deal with the China fleet—which he knew now to be unprotected and heading for the Straits of Malacca. He wrote that 'before Captain Ferrier could reach the Streights of Singapore, the business must have terminated one way or the other.'

'They answered me with some chagrin' was the Admiral's comment on the reply to his letter to Madras of March 14th. But before the reply came he had somewhat changed his mind about the matter. He was joined by the *Concorde* frigate, returned from the Straits of Malacca, on March 19th, and Captain Wood was able to give him some information as to Ferrier's progress. On February 24th he had seen what he took to be two sail of the line, to leeward of him, close together and standing to the eastward under a press of sail. This was about fifty leagues north-west by west of Penang. Rainier at first doubted whether these could have been the *Albion* and *Sceptre*. For, to be as far east as that, they would have had to make an impossibly quick passage, considering the time of year. But Wood, however, reassured him on this point. The winds had been northerly for the whole time of his voyage. Such a passage from Madras was, he thought, quite practicable. This gave Rainier a ray of hope. If the China ships had sailed very late, Ferrier might just be in time to be of some use. On March 21st he wrote to Lord William Bentinck that 'This information has almost induced me to retract the dissatisfaction I had expressed, in my letter to your Lordship in Council of the 14th inst.' And yet, in the end, the Admiral's first emotions were more or less justified. Despite an exceptionally quick passage, the *Albion* and *Sceptre* did not arrive in time.

CHAPTER XI

The Battle of Pulo-Aur

THE first information Admiral Linois obtained concerning the China fleet was from the officers of the *Countess of Sutherland*. They said that the country ships bound from Bengal to China had been accompanied by two frigates. This was probably true. Bathurst's two frigates had certainly gone in that direction. The officers did not say—indeed they may not have known—that this escort went no farther than Penang. This intelligence left Linois free to suppose that these two frigates might be returning with the convoy from China. He next heard, at Batavia, that Rainier had been reinforced, his squadron now consisting of eight sail of the line, besides frigates and armed Indiamen.

> J'ai ete informé qu'il etait arrivé d'Europe a L'Amiral Reinier deux vaisseaux de 74 et une fregate. Ainsi son escadre est composée de huit vaisseaux, un grand nombre de fregates, sans compter les vaisstaux de compagnie qu'ils peuvent avoir armés. Mais comme ils ont beaucoup de points a garder, leur forces doivent etre necessairment divisées. Cequi me laisse l'espoir de pouvoir leur faire beaucoup de mal en me portant successivement a de grandes distances dans les diverses parties des mers de l'Inde.[1]

An American ship at Batavia, lately arrived from Canton, had brought news that the Indiamen at Whampoa numbered seventeen, with six country ships and a brig expected to sail in company, making twenty-four sail in all. By this account, if it was true, there were no men-of-war in Canton river; although the two frigates or some of the recently arrived ships of the line might, of course, be on their way there. If no escort arrived, Linois knew that he might expect to see twenty-four sail. If more appeared, he would have to act with caution.

Now, this question of numbers is the more important in view of the difficulty of distinguishing between Indiamen and ships of war. Something has already been said about this, but the point cannot be over-emphasized. It was not as if there was any line to be drawn between them. A 1,200-ton

[1] Archives Nat. BB4 185.

Indiaman could be turned into something like a frigate by leaving her hold empty, adding a few guns and doubling her crew. An 800-ton Indiaman could be made as formidable by the same process. A 1,400-ton Indiaman could be turned into a 64-gun ship in the like manner, putting guns in her lower-deck ports and trebling her crew. These were not mere technical possibilities. Early in 1804 the Government of Bengal was actually equipping two Indiamen for war, the *Calcutta* (40) and *Lady Castlereagh* (40). Linois had heard something of this, but he could have no certainty that the Indiamen so equipped would be stationed, as they were in fact stationed, at the head of the Bay of Bengal. They might quite easily have been sent eastwards. Then again, certain Indiamen had been bought into the Navy. These only differed from armed Indiamen in being better manned. In appearance, they can have differed very little from their former consorts. Lastly, Linois had to remember that there were such things as men-of-war disguised as Indiamen. The English frigates were disguised as often as not. At least two of them were so disguised at that very time—the *Sheerness* and the *Caroline*. A French privateer was actually taken by one of them on February 4th. Another shared the same fate, through chasing what appeared to be a merchant ship, on May 5th. The *Concorde* was playing the same game in 1805. What is more, the mistake might be made even where there was no effort at disguise. Even while Linois was at Batavia, on December 21st, a French 12-gun privateer was crowding sail in reckless pursuit of the two 74-gun ships *Albion* and *Sceptre*. She had even the mortifying experience of catching them. The French Admiral, in short, had a difficult problem. He had to do more than distinguish between merchantmen and ships of war. There were merchantmen trying to look like Indiamen. There were Indiamen trying to look like men-of-war. There were Indiamen armed as men-of-war. There were men-of-war which had once been Indiamen. There were men-of-war trying to look like Indiamen. And, to complete the circle, there were men-of-war trying to look like ordinary merchantmen.

As it happened, there was, as we have seen, no escort with the China fleet. Nor were any of the ships armed for war. They had sailed from England before the war began. It seems, however, just possible that the ships which had come out via Bombay had taken the opportunity to take in some lower-deck guns from the arsenal, as ballast. There is no mention of this, however, in the *Earl Camden's* log, and none but the Bombay ships had the opportunity. China ships did not call at Calcutta, the only other place where guns could be obtained. Perhaps as many as three ships might have been able to muster a few lower-deck guns. They need not necessarily have been the Bombay ships, for there was a certain amount of refitting in Canton river. This much is clear, that three Indiamen were rumoured to have been armed as 64-gun ships—a rumour which might have had some slight basis of truth.

It would be interesting, on this point, to know exactly what had been done and discussed at Canton. It seems that, early in January 1804, the commanders of the seventeen Indiamen met in council and resolved, by a majority, to advise the supercargoes to dispatch the ships in a single fleet via the Straits of Malacca. A minority advised sending the fleet home in two divisions, one by the Straits of Allas or Lombok, the other (later) by Dampier's Straits. The supercargoes took the advice of the majority but they were worried and produced at this time, oddly enough, a scheme for arming Indiamen more heavily and increasing their crews by eighty or a hundred men.[1] It is an odd coincidence and just conceivable that a rumour of a supposedly secret discussion might have represented as done what was merely, in fact, proposed. It was, of course, quite impossible to find any additional men at Canton (or, indeed, anywhere else). Guns might have been procured there from any country ships which agreed to spare them. Lacking, however, any specific evidence of this having been arranged, and finding no mention of extra guns in any ship's log, there is a strong presumption against a laden Indiaman having any guns on her lower deck.

To set against this the French reported afterwards that several of the English ships fired from two decks. Their reports varied, it is true, as to the exact number of Indiamen with lower batteries; but that can hardly serve to discredit the report altogether. It is admittedly absurd to state, as does one French author, that the China ships, twenty-seven of them, each mounted fifty guns with a crew of at least 150.[2] The truth possibly is that two or three of the 1,400-ton ships had cleared a little space on their lower decks and mounted half a dozen real guns and perhaps as many dummies. A precaution of this kind might easily have been taken at Canton as soon as the danger was realized; so long, that is to say, as the guns were procurable. If none came with the Bombay or country ships, on the other hand, the whole story must probably be rejected. The commanders would not have had much success looking for cannon in China.

The China fleet sailed on 31st January, 1804, under the command of

[1] H. B. Morse. *Chronicles of the East India Company trading to China, 1635–1834*, Vol. II, Oxford, 1926, pp. 408–9.

[2] C. F. Tombe. *Voyages aux Indes Orientales, 1802–1806*, Paris, 1810. Two vols. Vol. I, p. 296.

the senior captain, or Commodore, Nathaniel Dance. He was aged fifty-six and chiefly noted for his persistent ill-luck in his private ventures. He was a very resolute man in an unimaginative way. He had with him as a passenger a naval lieutenant called Fowler, who was on his way home after the wreck of the armed vessel he had been commanding, the *Porpoise*. It was said afterwards that Dance received some instruction in tactics from Fowler, which is likely enough, and that a plan of action was arranged between them beforehand. It must be remembered that all commanders of Indiamen were tolerably expert in performing ordinary fleet movements. From constant sailing in convoy they knew how to obey the commoner signals, even if they often did so in their own time. In making signals and knowing what signals to make they were less proficient. They were not much given to drilling when left to themselves.

Commodore Dance had with him sixteen regular Indiamen of the 1,200-ton class, eleven country ships and the *Ganges*, a fast-sailing brig, to be used for scouting and carrying orders. Two other vessels, a Portuguese ship and the *Rolla*, Botany Bay ship, were to have been in company, but failed to join the fleet when it sailed. There were, therefore, twenty-seven ships and a brig. The fleet was off Macao on February 6th, and clear of the land on the following day. Linois had sailed long before from Batavia, on December 30th. With his squadron he had worked laboriously up the Straits of Banca. It being the wrong time of year for that voyage, he had a succession of calms and contrary winds, only arriving off Pulo-Auro (Pulo-Aur was the French way of spelling it, Pulau Aur is what it is now called) on January 28th. He was nevertheless well up to time. The *Berceau* was sent to reconnoitre while the other ships watered. Then, on February 1st, Linois sailed again and took up a position near the mouth of the Straits of Malacca. Being astride the trade route, he had only to wait for his prey to arrive.

At this point it is interesting to observe that the north-east monsoon, which had hindered the French Admiral's progress up the Straits of Banca (or Banka, as now spelt), was now serving his purpose very well. For all the traffic was going one way, from east to west or from north to south; that is, *from* Dance and *towards* Linois. Linois could therefore obtain plenty of information about Dance, but Dance could obtain no news of Linois. The French ships could straddle the path for weeks, secure in the knowledge that there was no one to give their position away. Had Dance known exactly where the French would be he could have gone another way. He might, for instance, have made directly for the Straits of Sunda. But he had no news and was well aware that he could expect none. Linois, on the

contrary, had almost daily intelligence of Dance's movements. He took
a Portuguese ship, a suspect, on February 1st; an English brig from Macao
on the 2nd; another Portuguese, also with papers out of order, on the 3rd;
a Danish ship from Manila on the 6th; another Portuguese ship, which
was not detained, on the 7th; an English ship from Bombay on the 11th.
Oddly enough, none of these gave him any better information as to the
numbers of the China fleet. He retained the impression that it numbered
about twenty-four sail, and from the Government of Batavia he received
a list of the sixteen Indiamen, correctly named. He learnt, of course, their
date of sailing. And he heard some tale, from a Portuguese ship, that three
of the Indiamen were fitted out as 64-gun ships—or so, at least, it was
afterwards said. It would be interesting to know whether these neutrals
had been primed with this story and indeed persuaded to reiterate the
number 'twenty-four.' Bribery was possible with vessels due to be at
Canton again in 1805.

On the 14th, at daybreak, the French scouts, the *Berceau* and *Aventurier*,
made the signal for four, then for eight, and finally for twenty-eight sail.
There had been a gale during the night and dawn found the two French
frigates somewhat separated from the flagship. It took Linois some hours
to collect his forces. The convoy was sighted soon after 5.0 a.m., and he
had not formed his line of battle until 11.0. In the meanwhile, the sight
of five sail approaching to reconnoitre him was enough to make him come
into the wind. He was already a little anxious. He had expected to see
twenty-four ships, and here he was faced with twenty-seven and a brig.
He remembered what he had heard about there being two English frigates
somewhere to the eastward. He remembered the story of the three 64-gun
ships—the exact number in excess of what he expected. He decided to take
no risks. Sending the *Berceau* ahead, he approached the convoy cautiously.
Then he detached the *Belle Poule* to reconnoitre. She returned to report
at about 5.30, the *Berceau* coming in, presumably, at about the same time.
The captain of the *Belle Poule* reported that two of the enemy carried
lower-deck guns, and that fifteen or sixteen more were of the same size
but seemed to have no lower batteries. Four or five of the ships, he said,
appeared to be intended for the defence of the convoy; but he thought
that they could not be very strong. Halgan, of the *Berceau*, seems to have
reported in much the same strain. Neither he nor Bruilhac could perceive
any men-of-war among them. Linois was still doubtful. He decided to
delay his attack until the following morning, and signalled accordingly.

The English were rather slow in sighting their opponents, possibly
because they were not expecting to see them. The *Royal George* made the

signal for four strange sail at 8.0 a.m., and Dance thereupon signalled for her and three other Indiamen—the *Alfred*, *Bombay Castle* and *Hope*—to go ahead and reconnoitre. Lieutenant Fowler volunteered to go too, and was sent after them in the *Ganges* brig. These vessels presently signalled an enemy squadron consisting of one ship of the line, three frigates and a brig. Dance then recalled them. This was at 1.0 p.m., and he was still striving to put his forces in order. He had not quite succeeded by 4.0 p.m., and indeed the country ships were not properly in position, covered by the Indiamen, until after dark. Lieutenant Fowler, who stationed them, returned with a few volunteers who did not wish to miss the battle.

The China fleet lay to during the night, in line of battle, with the country ships on the lee bow, that is, the side farthest from the enemy. Three ships, detailed to play the part of the escort—probably the *Earl Camden*, *Royal George* and *Hope*, the first being the Commodore's ship—kept lights burning all night. In the morning the same three ships hoisted blue ensigns, as did also the *Ganges* brig. The rest apparently hoisted the red ensign. And so the convoy offered battle.

Linois spent the night in working to windward so as to have the weather gage in the morning. One of his main objects in delaying the conflict was to see what the convoy should try to do under cover of darkness. If the ships tried to escape during the night, that would settle the question as to whether there was an escort or not. It was with some disappointment that he saw the convoy in line of battle next morning. The determined aspect of the enemy thoroughly disconcerted him. What he failed to realize was that nobody but a fool, in Dance's position, would have attempted to run away—escort or no escort. Those heavily laden 'tea wagons' would have been overtaken in a few hours. Incidentally, a less cautious tactician might have drawn the opposite conclusion from Dance's behaviour. Had the apparent ships of the line been what their colours seemed to portend, they would hardly have left Linois undisturbed during the night. They would, in fact, have attacked him headlong the day before.

> If the bold front put on by the enemy in the daytime had been intended as a ruse to conceal his weakness, he would have profited by the darkness of the night to endeavour to conceal his escape; and in that case I should have taken advantage of his manœuvres. But I soon became convinced that this security was not feigned; three of his ships constantly kept their lights up, and the fleet continued to lie-to, in order of battle, throughout the night. . . .

At 6.0 a.m. on the 16th, Linois was two or three miles to windward of the convoy. He hoisted French colours when the Indiamen hoisted English, but did not at once accept the challenge. At 9.0 Commodore Dance tired of waiting for him, and made sail, steering his course as if the French had not been there. Linois then made sail and edged down towards him. His delay in doing so was due to lack of wind in the early part of the day, and he took the opportunity to call his captains together and explain to them what he intended to do. His plan was to bear down on the enemy's line, threaten the centre and then cut off the rear. He was still in doubt as to his opponent's force, as the following extract from his report will show:

> At half-past seven, the enemy hoisted their colours; the squadron imme-diately did the same. Though near enough to distinguish the vessels of the fleet, the Admiral could not ascertain their real force. Twenty of the vessels had the appearance of two-deckers. We thought we could dis-tinguish a frigate. A brig of war and three ships had blue ensigns. The latter formed part of eight ships which seemed to be more particularly appointed for the protection of the convoy. . . .
> (Paraphrase of Linois's report, as transmitted by Decaen to Bonaparte.)

As Linois came down towards the English rear, meaning to cut off the two sternmost ships, Commodore Dance was in some perplexity as to what he should do. Fortunately, the *Royal George* and the *Earl Camden* were close together, and the first-named ship was commanded by Captain John Timmins. Timmins, who had begun life in the Navy and was one of a notable family in the Company's service, was the genius on the English side. It was he who first sighted Linois on the 14th. His ship was with the detachment sent to reconnoitre. He afterwards did most of the fighting. And it was he—and not Fowler, as it was rumoured in the Navy—who now saved the situation. Dance stepped to the rail and shouted across to him 'What shall I do now?' or words to that effect. Timmins shouted back 'Tack in succession'; and suited the action to the words.

> At noon perceiving the enemy bear up to attack our rear, made the signal to the headmost ships and tacked towards them. At 12.10 the enemy opened their fire on the *Royal George*, *Ganges* and ourselves, which we all returned. . . .[1]

More by example than in obedience to signal the five leading Indiamen tacked and, led by Timmins, went to succour the threatened rear. The other ships cheered them as they passed. Seeing this movement, Linois abandoned his original plan and steered to meet them. A brisk action followed, lasting about forty minutes, in which the *Marengo* fired three

[1] *Log of the Earl Camden*. India Office Library.

hundred and eighty rounds, receiving two shots through her foresail and another through her fore-topsail, while two of her fore-topmast backstays were shot away at the mast-head. The *Royal George* bore the brunt of the fighting 'and got as near the enemy as he would permit him,'[1] but was well supported by the *Ganges* and *Earl Camden*, the two ships astern of her.[2] No other ships were engaged. The first broadsides were not very effective on either side, and Timmins was boldly trying to close the range when the action ceased. It ceased becaused Linois at about 1.0 p.m. hauled his wind and stood to the eastward under all sail. Faithful to the rules of war, Dance signalled for a general chase, and the whole convoy made sail after the retreating foe. After two hours of this ineffective pursuit, Dance made the signal to tack. The Indiamen obeyed, some of them taking the opportunity to fire their broadsides after the enemy; who was, of course, well out of range. Dance then rallied his forces and shepherded them towards the Straits of Malacca. 'As long as we could distinguish the enemy, we perceived him steering to the Eastward under a press of sail.'

Dance was not without his vanity. As soon as he had recovered from his astonishment, his swelling pride gave an unwarrantable colouring to his version of the affair. He says nothing in his report about blue ensigns and bluff. With an obvious and innocent motive, he rather preferred to attribute his victory to hard fighting and *esprit de corps*. 'We soon gave them all they wanted,' one can imagine the captains telling each other. But this interpretation will not, of course, bear examination. As a battle the affair was negligible. There was hardly any real fighting. None of the ships engaged was appreciably damaged. There were no casualties on the French side and but two on the English. Linois was not defeated. He was deceived.

Duclos, in his journal, makes out a case for the French Admiral by adding up what he chooses to believe were the numbers of the English guns and men, showing that the French were heavily outnumbered. Such arithmetic is uncalled for. Of course they were outnumbered; much as wolves might be outnumbered by sheep. The case would not be convincing even if the statistics were correct, which, as a fact, they are not. Duclos proves too much. Even granting his Indiamen their bristling artillery, no one, not even Linois, thought them capable of withstanding the frigates, let alone the *Marengo*. Linois was not unnerved by the contemplation of some such list as Duclos presents. Had he been certain that the enemy was no stronger than that, he would have continued the action for days. If he

---

[1] Dance's report, quoted in *Hardy's List* of 1760–1812.
[2] The log of the *Royal George* states that 'a hot action was kept up for half an hour.'

was to be frightened by Indiamen, it might well be asked what he had crossed the ocean for, if not expressly to look for them.

What Linois actually feared was that some of the ships opposed to him were men-of-war, or else Indiamen on the footing of 64-gun ships. At first merely suspicious, he eventually became convinced that this was the case. The first stage by which he reached this conclusion was attained on the 14th, when twenty-eight sail were counted from the masthead. The second stage was reached when Bruilhac reported that two of the English ships carried guns on two decks. The third stage was gained as a result of the convoy's resolute aspect; and the fourth as a result of its confident behaviour in the action. The final stage in the deception was reached when the English actually pursued him for two hours. That tactical error was justified in its psychological effect. Linois could not doubt the presence of an escort after that. He broke off the action from fear of being surrounded. It may well have been the pursuit which decided him not to renew it.

Linois, in his report, did not commit himself to any particular view. He merely insisted on the strength of the enemy.

> During the action the Admiral observed that seven or eight of the ships fired from both their decks. It was obvious that they wished to induce him to attack them, as they did not show their lower-deck guns until after the action began. . .

'The superiority of his force was ascertained'—that is the burden of Linois's narrative. The lower-deck guns of at least four or five out of the 'seven or eight' ships credited with them were an illusion, due to the smoke and to the excitement of battle; an illusion, moreover, which other French officers did not share. Neither Bruilhac nor Halgan saw any such number of two-deckers, and Van der Sande, commander of *L'Aventurier*, said Linois and Delarue were alone in their belief. Motard afterwards declared that he had seen men-of-war, but said nothing of it in the report he made at the time. He, like the other officers, began to defend his chief only when he was attacked. That his officers should later have tried to justify him shows that Linois inspired a certain loyalty. Some attributed the fiasco to Delarue's cowardice and to his influence over the Admiral.

The weakness of Linois's case lies in his failure to ascertain his opponent's strength. The *Belle Poule* reported that two ships had lower-deck guns. The *Berceau* reported that several were so armed, eventually making the number eight. The *Semillante* reported that four Indiamen had two batteries with an estimated number of sixty guns. Delarue of the *Marengo* said that more than half of the Indiamen had two tiers and that each of the others was at least equal to a frigate. Linois himself stated that six or eight of his antagonists fired from their lower decks with guns which were not disclosed until they opened fire. These estimates were made afterwards, but those made at the time were conflicting enough. All depended on the question of these lower-deck guns, for if there were none, the English were exactly the opponents that Linois had been seeking and armed in exactly the way he must have had reason to expect. Now, granted this measure of doubt, the only remedy was to approach near enough to see. Linois tried to gain the needed information by sending the *Belle Poule* to reconnoitre, but she had evidently kept her distance and may have been partly foiled by the ships which Dance had used for a similar reconnaissance. It remained, therefore, to draw the enemy's fire and see what it amounted to. The disadvantage of this policy lay in the likelihood of being unable, through damage, to break off an engagement with a force found to be superior. Uneasily aware of this, Linois led his ships into battle. He fought, according to Tombe 'pendant plusiers heures a mi-portie de canon.' But was that the range? Was Linois really able to see his opponent?

On this point the evidence of Captain Van der Sande of *L'Aventurier* is perhaps relevant. His brig was fourth in the line, just astern of the *Belle Poule*:

> ... L'ennemi arriva aussitot a l'exception de 6 à 7 v^{aux} dont 4 à 5 me parurent armée de deux Batteries, formant une Ligne les amures a tribord pour couvrir le reste de leur flotte. Je n'ai pas distingué parmi eux aucun vaisseau du Roi....
>
> ... A midi ¼ *Le Marengo*, *la Semillante* et *La Belle Poule* s'engagaient avec deux Vaisseaux ennemis mais à une distance que les Corvettes ne furent pas prendre part au combat. Pour m'en convaincre je fis tire un coup de Carronade dont le Boulet n'atteint pas la moitie chemin de son but.... Le cannonade ayant durée a peu près une demi heure, *le Marengo*, faisant force de voiles cessa son feu et diregea sa route à L'E.N.E. repetant de nouveaux le signal 133....

The Dutch commander is definite here in his statement that his opponents were out of range.[1] He does not say that they were out of effective range or just out of extreme range. He says that the only shot he fired failed to carry *half* the distance. *L'Aventurier* mounted sixteen guns, possibly 8-pounders, but his carronades might have been larger and indeed presumably were so as he used one to try the range. How far would his guns carry? Fifteen hundred yards? Call it, however, a thousand yards. In that case Linois engaged at upwards of two thousand yards. That would

---

[1] They were also out of range from the *Berceau*, according to Duclos; and Dance reported that the enemy were 'in a very close line.'

sufficiently account for the little damage done. It would also explain why he never made out whether Indiamen were firing from one deck or two.

Dance entered the Straits of Malacca on the day after Linois's retreat. Thinking it not impossible that there might be ships of war at Penang, he sent the *Ganges* brig on from Malacca to ask their protection. There was none stationed there at this time, but on February 28th, in Lat. N. 4°30′, the convoy fell in with the *Albion* and *Sceptre*, arriving about a fortnight too late for the fray. Captain Ferrier was persuaded to escort the convoy as far as St. Helena, where he arrived on June 9th. There were men-of-war there to protect the China fleet on its voyage to England.[1] It would be interesting to speculate what might have been the result had the *Albion* and *Sceptre* come via the Straits of Sunda.

Having lost a prize worth eight millions sterling, Linois sailed for Batavia by the Straits of Gaspar. On February 22nd he was joined by *L'Atalante*, just returned from her unsuccessful diplomatic visit to Muscat—where the French agent was not allowed to land. Coming into Batavia harbour on the 25th, Linois found a Dutch squadron composed of two 70-gun ships and a frigate. This was part of the squadron Ferrier had seen at Rio de Janeiro, and was under Vice-Admiral Hartsinck. At a more leisurely speed, Hartsinck had passed the Straits of Malacca. Linois asked him to co-operate in a raid on Balambangan, the English settlement in North Borneo, or else in a second raid on Bencoolen. Hartsinck refused. He had been ordered to stay near Java. Onrust had been raided during the last war and the Dutch wanted their naval forces at hand to prevent future insult. Linois doubted whether Hartsinck's presence would be much protection. He argued that Batavia was open to attack in any case, and that none of the other ports was any safer, except Sourabaya, which could float nothing larger than a frigate. These arguments had no effect. The Dutch Admiral had his orders.

Meanwhile, all sorts of rumours were current in Batavia as to the cause of Linois's failing to take the China fleet. There had been an escort, it was said, of two frigates; or, by another account, of six sail of the line. Each Indiaman, the story went, had been armed with fifty guns and two hundred men. The more sceptical, however, refused to believe this. Allowing the fifty guns, they doubted whether the crews amounted to much more than a hundred and fifty. Linois, it is clear, was not very communicative on the subject. While at Batavia he took the opportunity to dispose of his two recent prizes, the *Henrietta* and *Admiral Rainier*, the latter a brig, the former an opium ship, with thirty-five chests of opium on board, worth 1.600

---

[1] Ironically, the *Earl Camden's* lading included, it was said, some chests of tea intended as a present for Napoleon. (*Naval Chronicle*, Vol. 12, p. 238.)

piastres each. The shabendar, or harbour-master, bought the cargoes of both ships for 133,000 piastres; thus acquiring the opium which was probably destined for him in any case. The Admiral had to be paid, of course, in specie.

Linois sailed from Batavia on March 4th, three days after Hartsinck sailed, apparently for Sourabaya. The French squadron then split up, the *Belle Poule* and the *Atalante* being sent on a cruise, while the *Marengo*, the *Semillante* and *Berceau* returned to the Isle of France. Here an important decision was taken, for the separation of his force committed Linois to an unambitious strategy for the immediate future.

It was April 1st when Linois reached the Isle of France; Easter Day. Decaen was at Mass when word came that the Rear-Admiral was in sight. All impatience, he can hardly have stayed to the end. One of his staff came on board as the flagship anchored. To this officer's discreet inquiry as to what had happened, Linois made no direct reply. He merely remarked that the convoy had teeth. To this extent was Decaen prepared for the worst when Linois presented himself on the following day.

Decaen began the interview with some civility. In the presence of the Admiral's staff and his own, he made some attempt to hide his anger and disappointment. But Linois's story of failure and the calm assurance with which he told it had the worst possible effect. When Decaen expressed some surprise at the Admiral's early return, he was told that the squadron had done very well. A large sum had been made in prize-money and honour had been done to the French flag. At this, Decaen's annoyance fairly boiled over. 'Your profit is the last thing I take any interest in. As for the honour of the flag, to that I attach rather more importance. But the Government of the Republic will judge how far you have honoured its flag in the China Seas.' In his description of this interview Delarue describes Decaen's behaviour in terms which may be accurate:

> . . . la contraction violente et les mouvemens decomposés de ce chef a son premier abord; son insultante reception, ses doutes et ses soupcons injurieux. . . . Je dois . . . attester a votre excellence que le Cap^n Gl de Caen a blessé, dans cette facheuse conjointure, la delicatesse des officiers present a cette conference, que sa conduite étrange a offert aux yeux de tous le spectacle vraiment scandaleux d'un homme qui foule aux pieds toute espece d'ordre et de convenance et qui sans egards, comme sans sujet et sans raison, se laisse entrainer a des mouvemens que l'ont de phisionomie morale que la haine et l'envie et pour caractere que la fougue et la violence la plus bizarre et la plus extraordinaire.

(Archives Nat. BB^4 185. *Precis historique de la Campagne de l'Inde.* Capitaine de Vaisseau Delarue (Delarue de la Gréardière).)

This ended the interview, but Decaen wrote to Linois that afternoon, again expressing astonishment at his return. He pointed out that the squadron's stay was a burden on the colony, and ended by advising him to put to sea within forty-eight hours. A cruise, he thought, in the vicinity of St. Helena might lead to the capture of the convoy which had escaped at Pulo-Aur.

In reply to Decaen's letter, Linois refused to do anything of the kind. His men, he said, wanted resting. Besides, as he explained in a second interview, his station did not extend west of the Cape. And, for that matter, his forces were insufficient. He proposed to send the *Marengo* to Europe, for repairs. Decaen prevented this with some difficulty, and it was finally agreed that the *Berceau* should return to France for fresh instructions. The Captain-General and Admiral then began to compose their dispatches.

Decaen wrote a fairly moderate dispatch to Decrès, asking only that the naval forces should be subordinated to himself. He entrusted this to the commander of the *Berceau*. Then he heard that Delarue, the captain of the *Marengo*, was being sent home also—obviously carrying the Admiral's complaint against himself. So he wrote another letter, addressed to the First Consul, containing an account of his quarrels with Linois; and to this he added his own impression of what had happened at Pulo-Aur. This he gave to his aide-de-camp, Lefebure, who also embarked in the *Berceau*. Of the two messengers, Delarue carried the more violent missive. Linois recommended that Decaen should be superseded by Magallan. In defence of his own conduct, he estimated the strength of the enemy at Pulo-Aur as eight 64-gun ships, twelve of twenty-six guns and one armed brig. He could well, he said, distinguish the enemy ships but

> . . . Je ne pouvois connaitre sa force reele. Vingt de ces Batiments avaint l'apparence de vaisseau à deux Batteries; on crut avoir reconnu une frégate. Le Brick de Guerre avoit Pavillon Bleu ainsi que trois Vaisseaux; ceux ci faisoint partie de huit V^{aux} qui paroissoient plus particulièrement chargés de la protection du Convoi. . . .
>
> Je pus remarquer pendant l'action que six à huit vaisseaux avoint fait feux de leurs deux Batteries, il n'est pas douteux qu'ils n'objent en le desir d'etre attaqué ce n'est qu'au moment de l'engagement qu'ils ont ouvert les sabords de cette Batterie.
>
> Cet engagement a duré 40 minutes. Les Boulets de l'ennemi dirigés generalement a dégréer ne firent aux Batiments de la Division que de legé Dommage. Personne ne fut blessé.
>
> (Archives Nat. BB^4 208. Linois to Decrès. Much of the rest of this dispatch is printed in James, *Naval History*, Vol. III, Appendices 20 and 21.)

By landing at Pontavinda in Spain, Lefebure contrived to reach Paris

H*

before Delarue. But the English accounts of the action had reached Paris even sooner; and these did more for Decaen than the superior speed of his messenger. Bonaparte never saw Linois's dispatches and he was furious long before he read Decaen's. He was particularly angry with the captain of the *Marengo* for quitting his ship in the middle of a campaign, and with Linois for sending him. He expressed his feelings in successive letters to Decrès.

> The conduct of Admiral Linois is miserable, and that of Captain Larue is worse. How can a captain lower himself to perform the duties of a midshipman? How can a captain desert the ship he commands? Do not let Captain Larue remain longer than twenty-four hours in Paris. Tell him that I refuse to see him. Send him back to the Indies. Tell him to find some boat at Bayonne. I have entrusted a ship to him, for which he is responsible. Make it known at all the ports that I refuse to see him because he has quitted his ship.
>
> . . . I have explained already what I think of Admiral Linois's conduct. He has made the French flag the laughing-stock of the Universe. The very least one can say in criticism is that he has shown too much caution in handling his squadron. Fighting ships are not merchantmen. It is our honour I wish to guard—not just so many ships and so many men. . . . Rather than have had this happen, I would have preferred to lose three ships of the line.
>
> Write to Linois. Make him realise what he has done. Show him his mistake in thinking himself the only hope of the navy in the Indies. No man can call himself that while there is timber in our forests and men on our shores. With his rotten ship and five or six hundred men, it is absurd for him to reason as if he were Villars at Denain or the Archduke Charles on the Mur. . . . You will tell him that he showed a lack of moral courage— the courage I value most in a leader—and so great a lack of it that I now think much less of his physical courage. Also tell him that I hope he will have done something for the honour of the flag before he returns to France.

It was some time before the substance of these remarks reached the Isle of France, in a form which Decrès had very greatly softened.

> Vous avez combattu pendant quarante minutes, selon votre rapport, et vous n'avez pas eu un homme blessé. D'un autre cote, celui de l'ennemi annonce qu'il n'a pas eu plus de trois hommes hors de combat. A cette manière d'attaquer, la resistance ne pouvait qu'etre longue; en la faisant au contraire de tres pies, pas un de ces vaisseaux de la Compagnie (et il n'y en pas d'autres) n'eut soutenu votre feu pendant trente minutes.
>
> (Decrès to Linois, 7th October, 1804. Quoted in *La Colonisation Française pendant la periode Napoleonienne*. J. Santoyant. Paris, 1931.)

But the effect was the reverse of what Bonaparte intended. The reproof went a long way towards breaking Linois's spirit. It entirely failed to spur him to action.

It is unlikely that Napoleon even saw the long report drawn up by Delarue in defence of his chief—the *Précis historique* quoted above (see page 232). It is a deplorable document. It described, however, a quarrel between Decaen and Linois at the Cape, on the outward voyage, not recorded elsewhere. In it Delarue praises Linois's diplomacy at Batavia and gives an account of the action at Pulo-Aur in which 'nous avions a combattre des forces au moins triples de notres,' but in which Linois made up in skill and sangfroid for his small strength and so cheated his opponents of their expected triumph. He compares the strength of the two sides thus:[1]

Division Française		Flotte Anglaise	
Le Marengo	74 canons	Huit v'aux de 64	512
La Belle Poule	42 canons [18 pdrs.]	Douze v'aux de 26	312
La Semillante	36 canons [12 pdrs.]	Un Brick de Guerre	18
Le Berceau	22 canons [8 pdrs.]		
L'Aventurier	16 canons		
Total des Bouches á feu	190		842

He ends with a description, quoted earlier, of Decaen's reception of Linois, and of the 'systeme de calomnie at de diffamation perfide organizé contre le Commandant des forces navales' by Decaen's toadying staff: a collection of ignorant, self-seeking, malicious nonentities. Delarue could show (if that were any use) that Linois was a gentleman and that Decaen was not. But his report is chiefly valuable in revealing himself, and little, as it happens, to his advantage.

The rewards showered on the victors of Pulo-Aur are well known. The Government, the Company and Lloyd's were all in a generous mood. The underwriters of Bombay were more especially munificent to Captain Timmins. Silver vases and presentation swords were the order of the day. And in the midst, as it were, of the buzz of congratulations, Admiral Rainier's voice was faintly to be heard making lame excuses for himself. Fortunately for him, no one was disposed to be critical. His disingenuous explanations were allowed to pass. Excuses apart, Rainier seems to have heard of the affair with mingled relief and astonishment. He referred to the 'fortunate escape made by the China fleet' as a 'most extraordinary circumstance.' An almost equally bewildered posterity can find no better word for it.

[1] Duclos, more moderate, allows Dance only 652 guns. He had, probably, between 500 and 550.

CHAPTER XII

Cruise of the *Marengo*

Admiral Rainier was still on the Malabar coast in April and May 1804, and still impressed with the necessity for guarding India against a possible French invasion. He was at Goa on May 4th— in the mango season, as his detractors doubtless remarked—when he wrote to Governor Duncan at Bombay, doubting whether he could provide all the convoys the merchants were petitioning for.

(P.R.O. Adm. 1/175.)

. . . I conceive it will behove me to act with great caution in detaching Ships for Convoys, so as not to reduce the Squadron too much to allow it to face that of the Enemy, should they make a push this way, whose united force is from the best intelligence in my possession, superior to that of His Majesty's under my Command, nor yet to appoint Convoys of too little strength to meet such Force as the Enemy may naturally be expected to have cruizing for them, and thereby expose the whole to capture; in which remark I have an eye particularly to the China Trade, who must necessarily navigate in a known direction, and unavoidably arrive at certain points. Other parts of the navigation of the Trade of His Majesty's Subjects in these Seas nearer at hand will also require attention and protection from the Squadron, and particular inconvenience attending the Convoy to China is, that the Ships employed on that Service cannot be recalled, but must necessarily wait the return of the Season; from others they may be recalled in a certain time. . . .

. . . Reflecting on the critical situation of Public affairs at Home, by the latest Accounts, in the threatened invasion daily expected to be attempted, there exists a strong probability the Company's China Ships may not be able to get out of the Channel. . . .

When he wrote the above, Rainier had not received sufficient information to enable him to grasp the vital factor in the situation. He was still on the defensive, as Decaen guessed he would be when he advised Linois to operate to the eastwards. But a defensive strategy was no longer necessary. For the whole situation was altered by the Dutch refusal to co-operate with the

French. Rainier had before him a list of the allied ships opposed to him, from which he could see that he was slightly outnumbered. There was the *Marengo*. There was Vice-Admiral Dekker and his three sail of the line. And there was Vice-Admiral Hartsinck, with two or perhaps three more. Linois was presumably back at the Isle of France. But there was no news of Dekker. And Hartsinck, last heard of at Rio de Janeiro, was also at large. These facts were enough to suggest the need for caution. But if the Dutch were committed to a policy of inaction, most of the forces opposed to Rainier could be ruled out with a stroke of the pen. Dekker and Hartsinck could be ignored and the English squadron could assume the offensive against Linois. Rainier, however, knew nothing of this as yet. Nor did he know of a curiously improbable event which was then taking place—an event on a par with 'the unaccountable timid retreat' of Linois at Pulo-Aur. This was the disappearance of Admiral Dekker.

Dekker, it will be remembered, sailed from Batavia for the Isle of France at about the same time as Linois sailed from the Isle of France for Batavia. He had sailed, to be exact, on 25th October, 1803, arriving at Port Louis on November 18th. His squadron consisted of the *Pluto* (74), *Bato* (74) and *Kortenaar* (64). In a pleasantly seventeenth-century fashion, all three ships had their lower-deck guns struck into the hold to make room for cargo. It must, of course, be borne in mind that Dekker sailed before news had come of the war. Indeed, it was chiefly in order to obtain news that he went, as if the Batavian Government had a premonition that the brig carrying the dispatches from Holland would be taken on the way, as in fact she was. So that the cargoes of rice and sugar, to be disposed of at the Isle of France, were not deliberately shipped in time of war; nor were they the sole object of the voyage.

Decaen was not very pleased to see the Dutch squadron. He thought that Dekker might have been of some use to Linois, had he remained at Batavia. Incidentally, it was not easy to find provisions for the Dutch squadron so soon after refitting the French. Dekker thought himself fully entitled to all that the island could supply, remembering that Admiral Sercey had refitted at Batavia in 1798. To Decaen's suggestion that he should return to Java and join forces with Linois, Dekker replied that it was too late, that he required stores which Port Louis was apparently unable to furnish, and that he was going to the Cape: now once more, of course, in Dutch hands. To the Cape he went, arriving fairly early in the year. He was there in June. Then, sending his other two ships back to Batavia, still miserably equipped and with crews reduced by sickness, he himself returned to Holland in the *Bato*. His motive for quitting the station was a jealousy of Hartsinck. That officer, under whose orders he was placed, was junior to him, it seems, in years if not in service. Rather than serve under him, Dekker returned home without orders. For this he was court-martialled and condemned to death, though afterwards reprieved. His departure weakened the Dutch squadron in numbers but hardly altered its fighting potentialities. While the orders were that nothing should be done, it scarcely mattered how many ships and men there were to do it. Masterly inactivity was clearly the best policy and the promises to abandon it made to Napoleon by the Grand Pensionary were never fulfilled. The Dutch were unfortunate in being unable to maintain their virtual neutrality in the East. Had they been able to do so, their colonies might have been left undisturbed throughout the war.

Admiral Rainier left the Malabar coast in the middle of May 1804, accompanied by a part of his squadron. The remaining ships, including those in dock or else about to enter dock, were directed to follow him shortly. Some of them were appointed to convoy the country trade from Bombay to Madras, where it was arranged that all the ships bound for China should rendezvous. The flagship, *Trident*, was at Trincomalee on May 30th and at Madras on June 7th.

Meanwhile, information was being received which enabled the Admiral to appreciate the situation more justly than had so far been possible. The Dutch, it was becoming apparent, were playing a passive part in the war. Some of their ships were evidently unfit for service, and the rest were acting on the defensive. The French, too, had not been reinforced. This intelligence convinced Rainier that Linois would confine himself to commerce destruction. India, therefore, needed no particular defence against invasion, and the squadron might presently assume an offensive role. It was Wellesley, it seems, who now proposed that the Isle of France should be blockaded, as during the last war. With the Cape in Dutch hands, the blockade was difficult to organize, and Rainier was inclined at first to object, but in the end he came round, with reservations, to the Governor-General's point of view. While the squadron was being collected, however, and before any decision was reached on the policy of blockading the French islands, the immediate problem was how to thwart the French Admiral's next move.

In attempting to guess what the French plans were, Rainier was either unimaginative or over-subtle. Or then, again, he may simply have been misled by rumour. At any rate, he came to the conclusion that Linois was likely to make a second attempt on the China fleet, with perhaps a second visit to Bencoolen or else a raid on Padang. As far as one can judge, Linois seems to have been by no means incapable of repeating himself in this way. And as he did once propose revisiting Bencoolen, Rainier's supposition was not as wild as might at first appear. He was mistaken, but it is easy to understand why he should have been determined at all costs to avoid any further anxiety on behalf of the China trade. He had come very near losing his reputation over the Pulo-Aur affair and was in no mood to take any more risks such as he had then been forced to take.

Having made his guess as to what Linois would do, Rainier made his arrangements accordingly. While leaving ships to patrol various parts of the coast of India, he sent, or planned to send, his strongest detachments to the eastwards. Owing to the slowness of the Bombay ships, the country vessels bound for China, over twenty in number, did not sail from Madras until August 13th. The escort consisted of the *Caroline* (36) and *Grampus* (50), and Captain Page, who was in command of the convoy, was to take the first sloop he came across and add her to the force. The *Dasher* was thus picked up in the Straits of Malacca. At Penang the convoy was to be joined by the three Indiamen from Bombay, escorted by the *Dedaigneuse* (36). The four men-of-war were then to proceed to Macao with the convoy and wait there until the China fleet should sail. Captain Page was urged to look out for traces of the enemy 'as 'tis suspected the French Admiral may be gone that way.' In case the Admiralty had sent no men-of-war with the Indiamen sailing direct to China, a part of this escort was to convoy the China fleet, if necessary, to England. As the Admiralty had sent a 64-gun ship, the total force at Macao was considerable.

Captain Page was sent on a purely defensive errand. Other arrangements were made for the pursuit of Linois should he appear in the China Seas. First of all, Captain John Osborn was sent off with a strong detachment to call at Bencoolen. He was given his orders on June 26th. They were to the following effect:

By Peter Rainier Esq.,
Vice-Admiral of the White,
and Commander in Chief of
His Majesty's Ships and
Vessels in the East Indies

SECRET

Whereas information has been received that the French Admiral was ready for Sea with two Frigates on the 8th ultimo at the Mauritius; and tho' industriously given out to be about to sail for Europe, was generally supposed to be going on a cruise against our Trade in these Seas, or probably to attack the Settlement of Bencoolon.

You are hereby required and directed. . . .

The gist of the instructions were that Osborn was to go to Bencoolen with his ship, *Tremendous* (74), *Lancaster* (64), *Phaeton* (38) and *Terpsichore* (32). If he found no trace of the French squadron in that direction, he was to proceed to the Isle of France and blockade it as long as his victuals lasted. The orders included directions for retaking the settlement at Bencoolen, should he find it in French hands. By a subsequent order, dated July 3rd, Osborn was empowered to add the *Albion* and *Sceptre* to his force, supposing he fell in with them and supposing they were fit for service after their voyage to St. Helena.

Osborn sailed from Trincomalee on July 8th. Rainier had heard that Linois had sailed from the Isle of France on June 22nd, and he calculated that it would take the French ships from four to six weeks to reach Bencoolen or the Straits of Sunda. Osborn would be there in ten days or a fortnight. Hunter and hunted would therefore arrive simultaneously. It was excellently timed.

No sooner had Captain Page departed than Rainier was wondering whether he had been wise to detach him with so small a force. 'I have been somewhat uneasy almost ever since you sailed,' he wrote, 'from a suggestion of my own fears, that Mons'r Linois may have stationed himself & Squadron to Cruise for you. . . .' So, to be on the safe side, Rainier sent the *Russel* (74) and the *Victor* sloop to Penang. The orders were that these vessels should reinforce Page's detachment in case of need. If, on the other hand, the convoy had passed safely, and if there was no news of the French, they were to cruise until further orders from Achin Road to the Nicobars.

To make assurances doubly sure, and to complete this concentration to the eastwards, the Admiral resolved to proceed there himself in October. He would take the *Trident* (64), the *Centurion* (50) and the *San Fiorenzo* (36), sail with them to the Straits of Malacca, collect the *Russel* (if she was there), and appear in the vicinity of Pulo-Aur between December and March.

The plan was to treat the Malay Archipelago as a sort of trap. The bait was the China fleet, due to arrive at the eastern end of the Straits of Malacca at a certain time of year. Should Linois feel tempted, he would enter the trap by the Straits of Sunda. Osborn, close at his heels, would close the exit. Still followed by Osborn, the raider would gradually approach Pulo-Aur. Then, as the bait came within reach, the trap would close with a snap. Page would disclose himself to the eastward, Osborn to the southward, and the Straits of Malacca would suddenly disgorge Admiral Rainier himself. The unfortunate Linois would be overpowered by as many as sixteen men-of-war, and so his career would come to an abrupt conclusion. Of course, things do not happen quite like that in real life. But it would certainly be odd if the French Admiral could roam the China Seas for long without encountering one of the squadrons sent in search of him. Sooner or later, the end would come.

Just as Rainier was putting the finishing touches to this admirable scheme—oiling the mechanism, as it were, and pausing to admire the effect—the news came that the *Marengo* had been seen, with two frigates, about forty leagues due east from Dondra Head. The effect of this bombshell may be imagined. Instead of going to the China Seas, Linois had placed himself in the track of the trade outbound from the Bay of Bengal. Complete as Rainier's arrangements were, they were based on a mere guess. And it now proved that the guess was utterly and completely wrong.

After more than two months of refitting and wrangling with Decaen, Linois had sailed again on 20th June, 1804. He had with him the *Marengo*, *Semillante* and *Atalante*. His plan was to cruise on the west side of India and intercept the trade with the Red Sea and Persian Gulf. He expected to be joined in the Gulf of Oman by the *Belle Poule* and by the *Psyche*, a 32-gun privateer which Decaen later commissioned as a national frigate. Both these ships were then at sea. Linois sailed, first of all, to St. Augustine Bay, Madagascar, where he arrived on July 6th. Sailing again on the 18th, he next called at the Comoro Islands. From there, he should, by the original plan, have gone on to the Maldives. But some information he had received, perhaps from Portuguese vessels out of Mozambique, and perhaps relative to the disposition of the English squadron, caused him to change his mind. Passing instead through the Eight Degrees Channel, without calling at the Maldives, and then passing to the south of Ceylon, he made for the Coromandel coast. On the way, on August 19th, he took two Bengal rice ships, English vessels bound for Bombay, one having just called at Madras. Then, having gone well to the eastward of Ceylon, he fell in with a couple of Portuguese ships, the first on September 7th and the second on the following day. This second ship was the *Gran Para*, of Lisbon, last from Rio de Janeiro. After her captain had been called on board the *Marengo*, the ship was released. She at once put into Madras, and it was from her that Admiral Rainier heard of the *Marengo's* whereabouts.

Linois parted from the *Gran Para* on September 8th, in Lat. 8° 30' N., and Long. 82° E., and Rainier heard the news on the 13th. He was in an awkward position. Had Linois appeared in that latitude a year before, he would have found six men-of-war posted to protect Trincomalee and three more off Dondra Head. But now that the Kandian war had somewhat subsided, and fears abated of an attempt on Ceylon or on the mainland, there was no force near at hand. All the strength of the squadron had been dispatched to the eastward. Fortunately, however, not all the ships destined for that service had actually sailed. The *Albion* and *Sceptre*, returning from St. Helena, had not fallen in with Captain Osborn. They were therefore at Madras, though hardly in a state for any immediate service. The Admiral himself, though about to proceed to the eastward, was still on the coast. With his flagship, or somewhere within reach, there were two or three ships which he had intended to take with him, as well as those to be left for the protection of trade. The *San Fiorenzo* and *Rattlesnake* were to hand, as also the troopships *Sheerness* and *Wilhelmina*, which could be used as men-of-war though hardly as frigates. The *Centurion* was farther up the coast on convoy duty. With these not very promising materials Rainier had to devise some scheme for dealing with the intruders.

In making his plan of action, the Admiral had once more to guess at the enemy's intentions. And in making his guess, he took into account a fact which he might have done better to forget. His period on the station was nearly at an end, and his successor, he knew, was on the way out to relieve him. Sir Edward Pellew was to be the new commander-in-chief— a newly promoted Rear-Admiral and the same officer who had chased Hartsinck across the Atlantic—and he would be coming out with a convoy. Linois, when last seen, was not only in a position to intercept the country trade but also in a position to waylay the expected convoy. Rainier concluded that this was a deliberate move on the French Admiral's part, who could accordingly be relied upon to remain on his cruising ground. The mistake here was in over-estimating Linois's knowledge as well as in imputing to him a love of glory of which that officer was innocent. To encounter Sir Edward Pellew and a convoy of Indiamen more or less in ballast was not one of Linois's ambitions, even had he known where Pellew was to be found. And indeed, as it happened, the new commander-in-chief took a different route. However, Rainier had to make some decision, and the decision he took was not unintelligent.

> *Trident*, Madras Road
> 14th September, 1804

My Lord

    In consequence of the Intelligence received yesterday from the Commander of the Portuguese Ship *Gran Para*, who was on board the French Admiral the 8th instant . . . I purpose proceeding as expeditiously as possible to the Southward, as the Station he appeared to be cruizing in borders nearly on the Track of the outward bound ships; whether I shall be able to beat round the Basses is extremely doubtful, as it is whether the French Admiral will be able to preserve his station to windward of them, the consequence of his getting to leeward from the effects of the Winds and Currents, or of chasing, will leave him no option but that of facing me, if I am fortunate enough to reach the Basses in time, or steer to the Eastward out of my way, probably, of returning to the Mauritius.

I have no other Ship to take with me but the *Albion*, the lower yard of the *Sceptre* being found in a State not fit for Service, and the new one will not be ready in less than eight days. When it is finished that Ship will follow me, and I expect to fall in with the *St. Forenzo*.

I am in hopes the *Centurion* will by the time the *Sceptre* leaves the Road be not far off (with Your Ship the *Princess Charlotte* from Vizagapatam) who will be ordered to remain for the protection of the Road, and eventually to proceed with the Homeward bound Convoy, and to see them well on their way, at least to the distance of the French Islands.

I have the Honor to be
My Lord
Your Lordships
most obedient
Humble Servant,
Peter Rainier.

(To Lord W. Bentinck)
(P.R.O. Adm. 1/175.)

After thus informing the Governor of Madras of what he intended to do, the Admiral put to sea. He fell in with the *San Fiorenzo*, cruising on the trade route eastward of Madras, and sent her to fetch the *Sheerness* from Pondicherry. Both these were to rejoin him at Trincomalee. Orders were sent to the *Rattlesnake* to do the same. Then, sailing on the 15th, the *Trident* and *Albion* arrived in a day or two on the spot where Linois had been seen. After cruising for a few days without seeing anything of the enemy, Rainier gave it up. He sailed once more for Madras.

Rainier's failure to fall in with the French ships off Ceylon was not unnatural. They were not there. On parting from the Portuguese ship, Linois made straight for the coast, sighting the Madras mountains on the 14th. He missed Rainier by a hairbreadth, being off Madras on the very day that the English ships put to sea. He seems to have crossed their wake, just out of sight. An hour or two's difference would have brought on a collision between the two Admirals. Indeed, they would have met in any case, had Rainier been bound to the southward. As it was, Rainier steered eastwards in order to pick up the *San Fiorenzo*, which greatly reduced the chances of their meeting. And once they had missed each other, the chance was gone; for they were bound in opposite directions.

243

On the evening of the 16th, the French squadron was off Masulipatam, where a native coasting vessel was found. From this craft the information was obtained that the *Princess Charlotte* Indiaman, referred to in Rainier's letter to Bentinck, had left that road a few days before for Vizagapatam, under convoy of the troopship *Wilhelmina*.

There were, as a matter of fact, three Indiamen then on the coast, destined to proceed to England with piece goods and cinnamon. But two of them, the *Bengal* and *Asia*, had first to ship saltpetre and sugar at Calcutta, to serve as deadweight to the finer goods. There they accordingly went. At the last moment, the Admiral ordered the *Wilhelmina* to escort them, sending the *Centurion* to protect the *Princess Charlotte*. Thus it came about that Linois found a 50-gun ship where his information led him to expect a vessel 'en flute,' not much more formidable than a sloop.

Linois passed Coringa during the night of the 16th, which was fortunate. In daylight he would probably have made out the *Albatross* sloop, at that time being docked there for repairs under the superintending care of Mr. Roebuck. Then, on the 18th, he sighted the *Centurion* and other vessels at anchor off Vizagapatam. In Rainier's words, 'Mons'r Linois dash'd into that Road in the forenoon of the 18th, and commenced a furious attack with the *Marengo* and Frigates on His Majesty's Ship the *Centurion*.' The *Princess Charlotte* hauled down her colours without firing a shot. A country ship, the *Barnaby*, ran herself on shore. The *Centurion* was thus left free to protect herself as best she could. She was normally commanded by John Sprat Rainier, but he, being dangerously ill, had been temporarily replaced by Captain James Lind. He in turn was ashore and the *Centurion* was at first commanded in this action by Lieutenant Phillips. After three hours of confused fighting, in which the English ship took advantage of the shoal water to keep the *Marengo* at a distance of about a mile, the French ships retreated. Unaware of the extent to which the Bay of Bengal was denuded of naval protection, Linois was afraid that an English squadron might arrive at any minute. He launched his attack on the *Centurion* in the belief that she would soon be overpowered. When he found that this was not the least likely, and that his own sails and rigging were beginning to suffer, he discontinued the action. The *Marengo* might have sunk the *Centurion* outright had they been near each other, but the former ship could not close the range to less than a mile. Fighting of that kind might continue all day without decisive injury to either side. To have sunk or taken an English man-of-war—'a two-decker' as Duclos described her with more accuracy than candour—would have done something for Linois's reputation. But such a success could be bought too dearly. Dismasting on that hostile coast might have serious consequences. As it was, the *Marengo* came very near to losing her fore topmast. Only the heel was struck, as it happened, but two or three more such lucky hits would have crippled her. The French Admiral decided to haul off before it was too late. Contenting himself with the captured Indiaman, he left the *Centurion* in possession of the field.[1]

After this skirmish, Linois stood away to the northward, his prize disappearing, on the other hand, in a south-easterly direction. This was merely a ruse, for Linois altered his course immediately afterwards, rejoining the prize and steering for the Isle of France. He thus avoided his last pursuers. These were the men-of-war *Sceptre* and *Sheerness*. The *Sceptre*, it will be remembered, was left at Madras when Rainier sailed, with orders to follow as soon as her new yard could be finished and sent off to her. This would be in about eight days, it was expected. When she was almost ready to sail, on the 23rd, news came of Linois having been seen off Masulipatam a week before, heading northwards. The captain of the *Sceptre*, Sir Archibald Dickson, then very properly disobeyed his instructions. Putting to sea, and collecting the *Sheerness*—also somewhat slow in joining in the wild-goose chase to the southward—he made straight for the Sandheads. He knew, as Linois did not know, that there was not a single man-of-war at the head of the Bay of Bengal, and that it was in the power of the French squadron to play havoc among the shipping there. He was, of course, too late to intercept Linois by steering that course. He started five days after the *Centurion's* action. Hearing nothing of Linois at the Sandheads, he returned despondently to Madras. It was not until then that he heard of the affair at Vizagapatam. Rainier was already there. He had heard the news off Negapatam on the 29th, when on his way to Madras, where he arrived on October 2nd. 'I learned to my great regret that I had erred in my conjecture of the French Admiral's designs,' he wrote to the Admiralty. 'How unfortunate I was in my conjecture,' he wrote to Lord Wellesley, 'your Excellency has been some time since fully apprised of. . . .' Rainier was in a dejected mood. The war was not developing as planned.

Those with the longest experience in such matters tell us that a single mosquito, once inside the net intended to exclude him, will effectually prevent his victim from gaining any sleep for the remainder of the night. When the would-be sleeper first hears that high-pitched buzzing close to his ear, he will—so they say—make such violent gestures as may seem most likely to dispose of his enemy. On composing himself, however, for

[1] Thomas Colby was serving in the *Centurion* and his journal describes this action. See *Mariner's Mirror*, Vol. 13, p. 259.

sleep, the same noise will again be heard, calling for renewed exertions. And so, they say, the whole night will pass. In the morning, they conclude, the insect will be found to have won. It is by means of some such simile that a war of commerce destruction can be understood. Linois knew, as he said, that the forces opposed to him would of necessity be scattered; and that he could deceive them by appearing successively at widely different points. This is, presumably, the mosquito's idea of strategy. The effect, at any rate, is the same. With the first news of the raider's approach, the naval defenders swung their forces hither and thither, making wild grabs and wilder guesses at his supposed position. First there is a swift clutching movement towards Pulo-Aur, then a snatch in the direction of Ceylon, and lastly a feeble slap on the brow at Calcutta. In the meanwhile the sprawling English possessions have been stung in quite a different place. Dawn comes to find the damage done. An Indiaman has been taken at Vizagapatam.

It would be easy to censure Rainier for predicting so ill what his opponent would do; and indeed he may at times have shown too little imagination. At the same time, it is evident that he had to make some sort of guess. And if his guesses were unfortunate, it does not appear that anyone else had proved a better prophet. In one of his letters he begins a paragraph with the words, 'As I may without presumption pretend to as much knowledge of the navigation in these Seas as most people. . . .': and it is quite possible that he knew the ground better than any other man alive. He had served under Hughes just as Linois had served under Suffren. In correspondence with the Admiralty he would casually refer their Lordships to his memorandum submitted in 1783. There was no disputing with him about the monsoons or the currents. And yet, despite his knowledge, the enemy had made his escape. In a game of hide-and-seek it sometimes happens that imagination is more needed than experience.

Curiously enough, although they operated in the same waters, Linois never fell in with the *Belle Poule*. He was aware of her presence through falling in with one of her prizes on October 14th, a country ship she had taken off Madras called the *Pearl*. But they did not meet until they regained the Isle of France. His failing to come across the *Psyche*, privateer, was more understandable. Her cruise ended early in the year, in April, when she fought an indecisive action with the *Wilhelmina* and returned in a damaged condition to the Isle of France.

Before Linois himself had finally reached safety, he had to avoid a last danger in the shape of Osborn's small squadron off the Isle of France itself. Osborn's orders had been to proceed to that station if there was no news of Linois at Bencoolen. He had sailed from there accordingly on August 12th, arriving at Rodriguez on the 24th, and being off Port Louis on the 27th. Apart from merchantmen, the battered *Psyche* was the only ship in port. During the first few days he caught two or three slavers coming from Madagascar, and sent them to be disposed of at Penang. Then he sent the *Phaeton* and *Terpsichore* to cruise off the south end of the island, stationed the *Lancaster* off Port Louis, and went with the *Tremendous* to his post off the Gunner's Quoin. The blockade was not very effective, but it was as efficient as the number of his ships allowed of. Osborn had been employed on the same service during the last war and knew all there was to be known about blockading. Unfortunately, however, the inhabitants of the Isle of France knew all there was to be known about being blockaded. Their experience was very wide indeed and their arrangements correspondingly complete.

Osborn was Admiral Rainier's last card. If all his other plans failed—as they did fail—there was still the chance that Linois would approach his base a little too carelessly, and so perish on the threshold of safety. It was a very slim chance. Linois had little opportunity, it was true, of hearing of Osborn's presence beforehand; but then he was not much given to rashness of any kind. He arrived off the island on October 30th, hove-to until it was dark, and then got in touch with the shore by signals. In this way he learnt that Osborn was off Port Louis. He accordingly steered for Grand Port, which he entered the following day. In entering, the *Marengo* grounded on the Ile de Passe, carried away her rudder and scraped off part of her false keel. However, damaged or not, she and her consorts were safe in harbour. And Osborn at once raised the blockade, in which there was no longer very much point. He sailed almost at once for Bombay, where he took command in Rainier's absence. As soon as he had gone, Linois moved his ships round to Port Louis, which he entered on November 13th.

While the *Marengo* was being careened and repaired, the feud broke out afresh between Linois and Decaen. Prize-money was the chief source of dispute. Linois and his officers were not content to have their money paid them on their return to France. They took their share at once, as soon as the prizes were sold, and invested the money at high interest with local capitalists at Port Louis. Decaen objected to this practice, as the revenue of the island was not improved by it. To such objections Linois replied that he would send his prizes for sale elsewhere if the system was interfered with. Linois would not remain at sea for more than five months. When criticized by Decaen on this score, he claimed that the colony profited from his cruises. To this Decaen replied that the cost of refitting and repairing the ships of the squadron exceeded the value of the prizes sent in.[1] Other disputes arose on more trifling points, and renewed appeals to Decrès and Bonaparte were the result. Linois asked to be recalled, on account of the ill-feeling between him and Decaen. Decaen asked that his authority over the naval forces in the Indies might be defined.

On reading the correspondence forwarded to him by Decrès, Bonaparte replied to the Minister as follows:

(May 8th, 1805)

> I return you the letters from the Isle of France. I see nothing in them but disputes and vulgar squabbles between Linois, who is thoroughly second-rate, and fire-eating Decaen, who is utterly devoid of tact. The result of these disputes will be that Linois will stay at the Isle of France no longer than he can help. This will keep him at sea. And if he loses a frigate or two, it will be a loss I fully expect; and, anyway, the enemy will pay dearly for it. . . . Write and tell Linois to show a little more energy. Activity and boldness, that is what is wanted in the East.

In noticing the absence of co-operation between Decaen and Linois, Bonaparte made no attempt to make one of them the culprit. In a sense, he blamed both; but then he had no very high opinion of either. He had reasons, however, for wishing to encourage Linois, and the dispatches sent out in 1805 tended rather to put the blame on Decaen.

Napoleon's motive for encouraging Linois sprang from two considerations. The first was a general change in policy. Decaen had been sent out with orders to report on the possibilities of a campaign in India. Now, in 1805, all plans for such a campaign were, for the time being, laid aside. Indeed, Napoleon had virtually abandoned the project the year before. Decaen's reports had all been sanguine enough, of course. But Napoleon did not believe them. The author had too obvious a motive. Lefebure, who had been granted the interview denied to Delarue, duly urged Decaen's point of view. He spoke of native allies to be expected and of the scattered nature of the English power. The proposal, as discussed, was for twenty-three thousand men to land in India from a squadron of twenty-eight sail of the line. Lefebure was closely questioned, and all the possibilities of the scheme were carefully weighed. And the result was that the proposal was rejected. Napoleon said that he could not spare twenty thousand men and would not spare a lesser number. To send five or ten thousand would be to run the risk of a serious reverse. It was in view of this decision that

[1] Arch. Nat. BB4 239.

interest shifted from Decaen to Linois. For a systematic campaign of commerce destruction was now the most that could be attempted in the East. More would have been possible had the Dutch co-operated. Decrès and Napoleon's foreign minister made strong representations at The Hague and was assured by the Grand Pensionary of Holland that steps would be taken.

> Personne n'est plus mécontent que moi, Monsieur, de l'inactivité absolue de l'escadre Batave dans l'Inde et personne n'est plus pénétré de la necessité de faire cesse aussitot que possible cet état de choses. . . .
>
> Le Gouverneur de Batavia devait être changé. Je viens de nommer a cette place importante Monsieur Grasveld. . . .
>
> (13th September, 1805.)

At a moment when, as Decrès told Linois (13th October, 1805) 'l'Empereur etait prêt à passer en Angleterre à la tete de son armée, qui deja etait embarquée sur la flotilla' the Grand Pensionary was not inclined to resist French pressure. But it does not appear that Hartsinck was in fact spurred into activity.

The second consideration in Napoleon's mind was the want of a naval officer more fitted for the task than Linois, the man already on the spot. Linois was second-rate, but he could think of no one better. In criticizing Linois, he could not help criticizing all the other admirals in the same breath: 'All the naval expeditions which have been undertaken since I came to be Head of the Government have failed, partly because the admirals see double, and partly because they have found (I don't know where) that you can make war without taking risks.' Supposing that the other admirals were no better, Linois had this in his favour, that he had once won a battle. It was more than the rest could boast.

[1] Archives Nat. BB4 239.

CHAPTER XIII

Pellew and Linois

ADMIRAL RAINIER did not persevere for long in his fruitless search for the enemy. As we have seen, he soon returned to Madras. It was near the change of the monsoon and he had to complete his provisions before quitting the coast. The convoy for England was also due to sail, and he intended to escort it for a part of the voyage. After that he intended to be off Pulo-Aur, as originally planned, in case Linois or Hartsinck, or both, should have designs on the China fleet. He was not yet convinced of the deliberate inactivity of the Dutch; and Linois, of course, had still plenty of time in which to make some further attempt in that direction. Rainier, it seems, had not received the information, sent him by Osborn, that the French squadron had been provisioned only for three months, and was therefore likely to return soon to the Isle of France. Even had he done so, however, there remained the possibility of Linois being in time, despite his necessary call at Port Louis. He might even, for that matter, obtain provisions again at Batavia. It was essential, at any rate, to be on one's guard. The tea ships might not always be saved by a fluke. Rainier sailed with the convoy on October 22nd, twenty days after his return to Madras.

Trident at Sea

1st November 1804.

Sir

You will please acquaint their Lordships that pursuant to the plan formed and communicated to His Excellency the Governor General for the Employment of His Majesty's Ships for the approaching N.E. Monsoon as hereafter detailed with His Majesty's Ships as pr margin, the *Centurion* having charge of 3 Homeward bound ships. On the 23rd I ordered His Majesty's Ship *Sheerness* to return to Madras Road for a particular purpose, and from thence the Captain is to make the best of his way to Trincomalee, agreeable to an application I had lately received from His Excellency the Governor General, to be in readiness to take charge of a Convoy of transports His Excellency was on the point of sending there to embark native Troops for Prince

Trident
Albion
Sceptre
Sheerness
St. Fiorenzo
Victor
Rattlesnake
Centurion &
Convoy

of Wales Island and Calcutta. On the 27th inst. I dispatched His Majesty's Ship *St. Fiorenzo* to cruise off Point Negrais and the Sand Heads.

When I part with Convoy, [I] purpose making the best of my way to Achin and the entrance of the Streights of Malacca where I expect to be joined by the *Russel*, and if I find necessary, to proceed to the northward as far as Negrais, taking care to be between the Eastern entrance of the Streights of Malacca & Pulo Auro by the time the Trade from China may be expected thereabouts, as 'tis highly probable the combined force of the French and Dutch may be induced to make another effort to intercept them.

For the protection of the Malabar Coast, I have appointed the *Concorde* and *Fox*, the latter but lately returned from the Red Sea, the former I conclude to have arrived there by this time, after having seen the Homeward bound Ships into the S.E. Trade from Bombay; the Captain of the *Fox* has my directions to defer docking till the Senior Officer thinks proper, as she will require a great repair, and her Services in the mean time may be wanted to protect the Trade till more of His Majesty's Ships arrive on that Coast.

Captain Osborn having the option to repair to either Coast according to the Season when he leaves his Station off the Mauritius, I conclude he will make choice of that of Malabar and I have sent orders to meet him on his arrival at Bombay to act for the good of His Majesty's Service. . . . According to the letter I have received from him dated the 14th ultimo off Port Louis, he might be at Bombay in the Course of the first ten days in December at farthest. . . .

Please to inform their Lordships that I have thought proper to order Captain Rainier to proceed all the way to Spithead with the Convoy, as the *Centurion* will soon require an expensive repair if detained any longer in this Country; in her present state she may be converted by the Navy Board to some usefull inferior establishment, and I know of no other means of effectively getting rid of the White Ants on board her, who have at times discovered themselves by serious depradations in her timbers aloft. And there is no reason to suppose they have been exterminated. . . .

(Rainier to Admiralty. P.R.O. Adm. 1/174.)

This dispatch is quoted in full, or nearly so, because it gives, as well as any paraphrase could do, the situation of the East Indies squadron at the period when Rainier's term of office was coming to an end. His successor was already on the scene, although Rainier did not know of it. One symptom of his approaching departure was the damage done by the white ants on board the *Centurion*. Admirals liked to have their sons or nephews with them on a foreign station, and it often happened that the son or nephew returned home when the Admiral did. It was a type of coincidence the Admiralty usually overlooked. In this case, however, the younger Rainier returned again to India. He may too have had a taste for mangoes. He certainly resembled his uncle in another respect—namely, that he made a fortune there.

Rainier's successor in the command, as already noted, was Sir Edward Pellew, Bart., Rear-Admiral of the White. He had been one of the most noted frigate captains of his day. Then, latterly, he had been dragged unwillingly into serving with the Channel fleet. His promotion to flag-rank represented his escape from blockade duty. With promotion had come the appointment to the East Indies station. This was given him, at his own request, as a reward for political services to the Addington administration. His title, however, had this flaw in it, that his claim to the gratitude of the outgoing ministry was no merit in the eyes of the former opposition, now in power. Scarcely had he been appointed than his friends went out of office. It was in doubt for some time whether the appointment would not be cancelled. As a result, apparently, of a bargain by which he surrendered his seat in Parliament to one of Pitt's followers, he was ultimately, though grudgingly, confirmed in his command. He left England in the knowledge that his tenure was insecure, and would have felt little surprise to hear that his recall was decided upon on the eve of his sailing.

Pellew's flag was hoisted in the *Culloden* (74) on 4th July, 1804, at Spithead. He sailed on the 10th, being joined off Culver Cliff by nine of the ten East Indiamen he was to convoy. He reached Madeira on the 23rd, leaving again three days later. In passing the Isle of Amsterdam on October 11th he learnt that a convoy of nine sail with a ship of the line had passed the day before. These were the Indiamen bound for China direct under the escort of the *Athenienne* (64). Pellew's convoy consisted of the last ships of the season, bound for Madras and Bengal and crowded with the men of the 17th Regiment. To reach Bengal at that time of year, during the north-east monsoon, it was necessary to keep well over on the east side of the bay, passing probably through the Ten Degrees Passage and then through the Passage of the Andamans. The ships for Madras could not go there until the change of the monsoon and were to have waited at Penang for that to happen—that being also the port for which Pellew was bound—but Pellew heard some news which induced him to alter his plans. Meeting a ship from Madras off the coast of Sumatra, he learnt that the army had taken the field against Holkar, the Mahratta chief. Thinking that the 17th Regiment might be needed, he sent the Madras ships along to Bengal with the rest of the convoy, parting with the whole off Cape Negrais on November 20th. Then he turned south and went down the Straits of Malacca in the hope of finding Rainier at Penang.

Pellew was not unreasonable in expecting to fall in with Rainier at Penang at that time of year. Rainier had himself expected to be there. But chasing after Linois had unduly delayed his departure from the coast, delayed it indeed until a dangerous season, long after the proper time for sailing. Rainier had long since put to sea, but he was escorting the homeward bound convoy for the first part of its voyage, and was not, therefore, going to Penang by the shortest route. Sir Edward arrived there before him, was disappointed, and instantly set sail for Madras, which he reached on December 10th. There he found a letter, left in the hand of the naval officer, in which Admiral Rainier gave him a rendezvous at Penang, or rather off Pulo-Aur. The two Admirals were off Achin Head at the same time and had only failed to see each other owing to the thick and squally weather usually met with at that season. Rather exasperated, Pellew sailed once more for the Straits of Malacca. In a letter to a friend in England Pellew wrote at the time:

> We have reached our destination without accident and have felt the glowing heat of a Thermometer at 88°, how I shall hold out against such melting I know not, hitherto my health continues and I think it will if I am prudent, and when I tell you that I still continue flannel next my skin and have not yet tasted Curry or any made dish you will give me credit for my intention of being so. I cannot say I am much struck with the Country, and am often very angry with myself for being instrumental to my leaving England and think I did not act wisely; however, here I am and will do the best I can until I am relieved and I hope that will be according to the usual rotation, for I dare say I shall have been fully gratified before that—dont however mistake me and think I mean money. I declare to you that is not my object. I long to deserve well of my country and I came in the hope of giving a blow to the inveterate and restless Enemies of Mankind. . . .[1]

Rainier, meanwhile, had parted with the *Centurion* and convoy on November 8th in Lat. 3° 3′ N., Long. 92° 42′ E., and arrived at Penang on December 9th, some five days after Pellew's departure. He had with him the *Trident*, *Albion*, *Sceptre* and *Seaflower*, cutter. Sailing again almost immediately, he fell in with four country ships from China under convoy of the *Dasher*, sloop. By this early and imprudently small convoy he received letters from Captain Page and from the Secret Committee of Supercargoes.

[1] *Edward Pellew, Viscount Exmouth*, p. 327.

From these he gathered that the direct China ships had not yet arrived, but that the others, 'with several Country Ships would positively be ready to leave Whampoa for the Streights of Singapore, sometime between Christmas day and the New Year.' Undismayed by blowing weather, Rainier proceeded to Pulo-Aur, which he reached on 4th January, 1805. On the 14th the convoy appeared, Captain Page with the *Caroline*, *Grampus* and *Dedaigneuse*, eight Indiamen, one Botany Bay ship and seven country ships. The direct ships, with the *Athenienne*, had reached China on the very eve of the convoy's sailing, it was reported, and they would not be ready to leave for another two months. There was no possibility of forming a single convoy when ships were delayed to that extent.

Returning to Penang with the convoy and the united escort which was reinforced by the *Rattlesnake* off Malacca, but not by the *Russel*, which should have been there, Rainier found Pellew waiting for him. The two Admirals greeted each other with the thunder of cannon, and then settled down to the long and complicated business of handing over the command. Rainier did not relinquish his responsibility at once, for he had to return to collect the homeward bound trade at Madras before he quitted the station. He spent some time, however, in explaining the situation to his successor. This was essential in that they would not meet again. Pellew explained that he had orders to purchase ships into the Navy, and as this transaction necessitated a visit to Bombay, he and Rainier would have to part company. Pellew's tenure of office would begin, then, at Bombay, on the day that Rainier sailed from Madras.

Taking into consideration their Lordships' Order of 29th May and 7th June last for the purchase of six Ships for His Majesty's Service . . . which I conceived would be best effected at Bombay, as supplying the best built Ships in India adapted to the King's Service and as the principal part of them would be in Port on their return from China by the time the Rear Admiral would reach that Island and the present being a very favourable part of the Monsoon to make the quickest passage there, I therefore advised the Rear Admiral . . . to proceed to Bombay to make the purchases required on his own Authority, disposing of such of His Majesty's ships as he might fall in with as he thought most for the good of His Majesty's Service, taking with him the valuable Trade from China bound for that Island together with His Majesty's Ships *Grampus* and *Victor*, Sloop, which both required to be docked. . . .

(Rainier to Admiralty, 21st June, 1805. Adm. 1/176.)

This matter being settled, another question arose. The senior commander of the Indiamen wished to know what was being done to protect the convoy for the rest of the voyage to England. Now, ordinarily, with the whole China fleet united, there would have been a man-of-war to escort them all the way. But the *Athenienne* could not be with both divisions, so that the first group was unprotected. Rainier replied that he would take the Indiamen with him to Madras, and there they could join the convoy of coast and bay ships destined to sail with his flag. The senior commander agreed to this plan, but the other commanders strongly objected to it. Five out of the seven ships, they said, were not in a condition to meet bad weather off the Cape. Three of them were leaky—so much so that they were floored with gruff goods to protect the cargo—and their crews were composed of foreigners and Chinese, few of whom were to be relied upon in rough weather.

Rainier said that the best he could do for them was to dispatch them with the *Culloden*, to remain in company as long as their courses lay together. After that they would have to take their chance. He disclaimed all responsibility for the consequences. Perhaps wisely, the commanders of the Indiamen preferred risk of capture to risk of foundering; or perhaps they were moved by personal considerations—fear, for example, of losing a favourable voyage in the following season. This would account for the senior commander's attitude, as he was very likely on the eve of retiring. At any rate, the Indiamen sailed with Pellew on January 27th, and boldly parted company with him the same evening. This was just a week after their arrival at Penang.

Pellew having departed, with the *Grampus* and *Victor* and the country trade bound for Bombay, Rainier detailed the *Dedaigneuse*, *Albatross* and *Seaflower* to remain in the Straits of Malacca for the protection of trade and to look out for the *Athenienne* and convoy. The *Albatross* came in just as Pellew left, escorting two transports from Ceylon and bringing the news of the loss of the *Sheerness*, which had driven ashore in a gale. Rainier, it may be remarked, had received information which led him to believe that the Dutch contemplated some action in the immediate future.

It is proper I should acquaint you for their Lordships' information that when I arrived at Prince of Wales Island on the 9th of December as before related, I received Intelligence from an American Ship recently arrived there, who had left Batavia only six weeks before (26 October) that at that time Vice Admiral Heartsingh was lying there with a Squadron consisting of Four Ships of the Line, Two or three Frigates and Five or Six Armed Vessels. One of the Line of Battle Ships was refitting at Onrust, all the other Ships with the Armed Vessels were ready for Sea—it seems he had been lying some considerable time before at Sourabaya to recover their crews who had suffered severely from the unhealthiness of Batavia Road . . . and had only returned to it the 6th of that Month.

The American's Intelligence confirmed me in my former conjecture of the enterprise the combined force of the Enemy would undertake early in the N.E. Monsoon, it being absolutely necessary the Dutch Squadron should from its Windward situation be in Batavia Road for their more convenient junction with the French Squadron of whose movements I had received no Information since the Attack on the *Centurion* in Vizagapatam Road on the 29th September. . . .

(Rainier to Admiralty, 21st June, 1805. Adm. 1/176.)

It is not very easy to understand Rainier's attitude towards the Dutch. He knew what strategic use might be made of Batavia if the Dutch should choose to turn their position to account. That was in itself a sufficiently rational ground for anxiety. On the other hand, his own actions do not imply any fear of what Hartsinck might do. For he sailed for Madras on the 29th two days after the departure of Pellew, and took with him the *Trident, Albion, Sceptre, Caroline* and *Dasher,* leaving only a frigate and two sloops to reinforce the *Athenienne* as her convoy came to the danger-point. The *Russel* arrived later, it is true, crippled by a gale, but this was not Rainier's arrangement. And even if it had been, and the *Russel* was repaired in time, the force was quite unequal to the Dutch squadron. Rainier's real opinion can probably be judged better from what he did than from what he wrote.

Before leaving India the Admiral was guest of honour at a farewell party of which the details were recorded in the *Madras Gazette* of March 2nd.

On Tuesday evening, the Civil Servants of the Hon'ble Company gave an elegant entertainment at the Pantheon to His Excellency Vice Admiral Rainier, on occasion of his departure for Europe.

The Admiral was received by the Stewards who were appointed for the occasion, in the front room of the Pantheon, and the Right Hon'ble the Governor, accompanied by His Excellency Sir John Cradock and the Hon'ble Sir Arthur Wellesley, arrived shortly after.

A trumpet announced dinner being on the table, and was followed by the band striking up the popular tune of God Save the King; the company now passed through the theatre, and descended to a building which had been erected for the purpose.

On entering the pavilion, the eye was immediately attracted by the elegance and splendour with which it was fitted up; the whole was covered with fine white linen, richly embossed with stars of gold and fringed with variegated colours, to which were attached small reflecting globes which

PLATE VI. Captain Sir Home Riggs Popham (1762–1820)
by M. Brown

PLATE VII. Rear-Admiral Sir Edward Pellew (1757–1833), Commander-in-Chief
on the East Indies Station, by James Northcote

presented the most grand coup d'oeil the imagination can conceive; the superb pillars by which the whole was supported, were alternately gold and blue and white, the whole evidently displaying the taste of the gentlemen who had the management of this part of the entertainment.

The chandeliers and lamps which illuminated this spacious and grand building, were distributed with an equal degree of simplicity and elegance.

The Dinner.—The Admiral was conducted to the centre of the table on the right hand of the Senior Civil Servant, the Governor and Sir Arthur to the left, and the Commander-in-Chief and Mr. Petrie to the opposite side. At regulated spaces, two Stewards were placed throughout the whole length, by which means the utmost regularity prevailed, and notwithstanding the number of visitors that were present, a private entertainment could not have been conducted with more order and regularity.

The tables were covered with every luxury that munificence could produce; every thing was of its best kind, and what is scarcely to be paralleled, was quite hot. The wines were cool, excellent, and in great abundance, and the other wines were of the best importations. . . .

(After the King, and the Navy and Army, Admiral Rainier's health was drunk with three times three and the tune of Hearts of Oak. The Hon. Company was toasted to the tune of "Money in both pockets" and the Marquis Wellesley to the tune of "St. Patrick's day in the morning.")

The company were obligingly entertained by several gentlemen of the Presidency with many select and choice songs, and the gallant Admiral sung three or four during the evening. . . .

The Right Hon'ble the Governor did not rise from the table until past twelve, and it was nearly three o'clock before the Admiral departed from this well supplied and hospitable board. . . .

Any faint suggestion here that the Admiral's songs were neither select nor choice must be, surely, inadvertent. And one would like to think that someone had been able to procure some mangoes for the dessert.

After collecting the homeward-bound trade at Madras, Rainier sailed for England on March 10th, taking the *Albion* and *Sceptre* with him as far as Lat. 4° 10′ S., Long. 84° 22′ E. from whence he dismissed them on April 4th, with orders to proceed to Trincomalee. He reached St. Helena on June 20th.[1] There he found the China ships which had parted from him at Penang, with the exception of one of the leaky ships, the *Brunswick*, which had been sent to be docked at Bombay. Why they were still there is not clear, but it is probable that they were detained by the governor until a naval escort could be found for them. Rainier took them on to England, brought them in

[1] Sir Arthur Wellesley was with him. At St. Helena the Admiral 'gave public breakfasts every morning,' and contributed £100 to a fund for consoling a whaler skipper whose ship had been captured.

I

safety and struck his flag on 10th September, 1805. His services were over, and he retired to live ashore until his death in 1808. His will was peculiar.

> The late Admiral Rainier has left property to the amount of nearly 250,000l and after providing amply for his near relations, has made the following bequest:
> "I bequeath one-tenth part of my personal property to the Chancellor of the Exchequer for the time being, towards the reduction of the national debt, in acknowledgment of the generous bounty of the national establishment of the Royal Navy, in which I have acquired the principal part of the fortune I now have, which has exceeded my merit and pretensions."
>
> (*Naval Chronicle*, Vol. 10, p. 382.)

Pellew, on his voyage out to India, had apparently had all the convoy duty he wanted; for, on parting with the Indiamen, immediately after quitting Penang, he left the *Grampus* and *Victor* to escort the country ships while he himself went on alone. He reached Bombay on February 23rd, finding Captain Osborn gone, he and the other captains being employed in protecting trade farther up the coast. The only ships in port were the *Lancaster*, *Terpsichore* and *Fox*, all three being in dock and the last-named frigate being hardly worth repairing, according to Pellew. As he was to add six ships to the squadron by purchase and had already heard of several ships suitable for the service, Pellew planned to spare sufficient forces to keep up a continuous blockade of the Isle of France by a system of alternate reliefs. Osborn was to be sent back to blockade duty almost as soon as he should appear.

While the *Marengo* lay inactive during the winter, other French men-of-war were afloat, and it is now necessary to follow their movements. The *Belle Poule* and *L'Atalante* went to cruise in the Bay of Bengal, but without a great deal of success. They returned directly to the Isle of France in order to join Linois in his next cruise. The *Semillante* was sent on a different kind of service. In February 1805 news had reached the Isle of France of the probability of war between Spain and England. The master of a Danish vessel had seen some German newspapers in which there were accounts of the taking of the four Spanish treasure ships on their way to Spain. This was sure to mean war, and the *Semillante* was accordingly sent to warn the Spanish Governor-General at Manila, Don Mariano Fernandez de Fulgueras; and also perhaps to see in what way the Spaniards might be willing to co-operate. Manila, like Batavia, was a place of great strategic possibilities, supposing that an active naval force were based on it. The *Semillante* sailed on March 8th and, having gone three or four degrees southward, into the westerly winds, reached the Straits of Sunda by 18th April, 1805. Then, with difficulty, against contrary winds, she managed to arrive at Manila on May 30th. Her captain, Motard, had intended, after warning the Spaniards and landing there a French commercial agent, to cruise in the China Seas. But he found the Spanish in difficulties and was induced to alter his plans. The governor, Raphael Maria Deguilas, explained that the subsidies from Mexico were three years in arrears because of a royal order closing the ports. The colony was in need of specie and there was no ship of war to escort the galleon from Mexico. Motard agreed to cross the Pacific with the object of convoying this all-important vessel, and sailed accordingly on July 21st. With the aid of a Spanish pilot, the *Semillante* reached the entrance to the Straits of San Bernadino. There, while waiting for a favourable wind, she was attacked by the English men-of-war *Phaeton* (38) and *Harrier* (18). The first, it will be remembered, was one of the detachments left by Rainier at Penang. The second was a new arrival. Motard, with the aid of batteries on shore, succeeded in beating off his assailants. His ship, however, was damaged, and he abandoned all idea of going to Mexico, partly because he realized that the English would be lying in wait for him on his return. Entering the Pacific, he turned southward and avoided further molestation by a complicated passage south of the Celebes and out into the Indian Ocean near Timor. It was a feat of navigation even if it concluded a more or less futile voyage. The *Semillante* did not arrive at the Isle of France until November 5th.

The *Psyche* is the fourth frigate to be dealt with. She has already been mentioned as a privateer. Decaen bought her into the Navy for 340,000 francs at the conclusion of the voyage during which she fought an action with the *Wilhelmina*. A noted officer, her former owner, Captain Bergeret, was given the command of her on 18th June, 1804. He sailed for the Bay of Bengal, a favourite hunting ground, on November 9th and cruised there with some success. There were hardly any ships of war in the bay at that time, and the consternation at Calcutta was out of all proportion to the damage done. As Rainier said, the merchants were 'more apprehensive of depredations on their Trade from Captain Bergeret's abilities and activity, than from the whole remaining Force of the French Navy at present in these Seas united.' The *San Fiorenzo* (36), being sent to deal with the intruder after the news had reached Calcutta of her being seen off Vizagapatam, managed to come up with her on 13th February, 1805. There followed a long chase and a murderous conflict, which ended in the surrender of the *Psyche* to her much heavier opponent. Bergeret would not haul down his colours until fifty-seven officers and men were killed and seventy wounded; until, that is to say, rather more than half his men were casualties. On returning to the Hooghli, Lambert, the captain of the *San Fiorenzo*, received a present of 5,000 rupees from the merchants and under-writers, with which to purchase a piece of plate. Captain Bergeret was an old friend of Admiral Pellew, having been his prisoner before in 1796. Their meeting at Trincomalee was an affecting scene. They were close enough friends to plan, later, to live near each other in France. The plan came to nothing, but the Admiral's descendant in the present century went to live in the part of France where these two 'enemies' talked of living as neighbours.

The unprotected state of the Bay of Bengal, to which was due the impunity of the *Belle Poule* and *L'Atalante*, could only be attributed to an error on Rainier's part. Pellew was careful to point out that it was none of his doing.

> Their Lordships will long since have heard of the departure of Vice-Admiral Rainier on the 10th Ultimo from Madras Road with eleven Sail of Indiamen. . . . The Admiral took with him from Madras the only Ships there, namely the *Albion* and *Sceptre*. The *Caroline* was ordered to Colombo, so that the Bay was left without a Ship of War, nor did the Admiral communicate to me what his intentions were respecting them.
>
> He had scarcely sailed before I received information of two small Captures made by the French Frigates *La Belle Poule*, and *L'Atalante*, near the head of the Bay of Bengal, in Lat. 19°20′ North, Long'de 85° East. The Admiral had information of the two frigates having been spoken a month before by a Dane in Latitude 3° North, Long 93° East. Their Lordships will perceive that I had no means from this side of India and at this Season to send after them for some time, and I trust any mischief they may do, will not therefore be charged to me. . . .
>
> Nothing more has been heard of the two Frigates since, and I conjecture, from learning the fate of the *Psyche*, that they proceeded down the East Coast, and if so, it is not improbable but they may fall in with the *Russel* and *Dedaigneuse* off that Coast. . . .
>
> (Pellew to Admiralty. 23rd April, 1805. Adm. 1/176.)

Pellew's first concern while at Bombay was the purchase of ships for the strengthening of the squadron. When he arrived he could find no vessel suitable, but when all the China ships had come into port, his advertisements in the *Bombay Courier* produced several tenders. The ships offered included the *Carron*, of 1,072 tons, belonging to Messrs. Bruce, Fawcett & Co., and the *Shah Kaikuseroo*, of 1,048 tons, owned by a Parsee called Sorabjee Muncherjee. Pellew bought these for £41,000 and £43,000 respectively, in rough figures. The prices were exorbitant, but there was no choice. Each of these ships could mount fifty guns.

Besides these two frigates, renamed by Pellew (to placate his enemies?) as the *Duncan* and *Howe*, and besides any further ships he was to purchase, there were several vessels handed over by the East India Company. There was the frigate *Cornwallis* of the Bombay Marine, 'a prodigious fine ship' which Pellew altered to suit naval prejudices by opening her spar-deck amidships—the Navy was not yet converted to the flush deck. He also increased her spread of canvas, for her spars had been designed for a lascar crew. Then there was the *Sir Edward Hughes*, an Indiaman, already acquired, which Pellew loathed at sight. 'She sails uncommonly bad in all points,' he lamented, and went on to say that her decks were too weak for heavy guns and that she had only four feet between decks. Before long, Wellesley was offering him the other frigate of the Bombay Marine, a ship called the *Bombay*; as also a smaller vessel, the *Mornington*. Finally, there was the recently taken *Psyche*, much in need of repair after her terrific battle with her captor. She was bought into the service on account of her good sailing qualities.

The chief difficulty, of course, was to find men for these newly acquired ships. The *Cornwallis* and *Hughes* brought their crews with them from the Company's service, but were much under strength. The two country ships, *Howe* and *Duncan*, heavily armed by Pellew, a gunnery specialist, with 18-pounders and 32-pounder carronades, had to be manned with drafts from existing men-of-war, with soldiers borrowed from the Company as marines and with lascars to fill up the gaps. However, the squadron was growing in numbers, and reinforcements were expected from England. Pellew could hope before long to undertake some decisive action against the enemy.

Behind this growth of the squadron were three active forces. The first was the realization at the Admiralty that the East Indies station, since the renewed outbreak of war, had many of the responsibilities which had been borne in 1796–1801 by the squadron based on the Cape. There was a case, therefore, for making it equal the two squadrons combined. The second was the policy of Pitt's last administration, which had begun just before Pellew left England. When in opposition, Pitt had made vigorous attacks on the Admiralty for not increasing sufficiently the strength of the Navy. Lord St. Vincent was accused of exposing the country to invasion. On coming, therefore, into office, Pitt and Dundas felt obliged to show what a little energy could do. While ordering ships right and left, they felt it especially desirable to be able to point to an *immediate* increase following their accession to power. From that point of view, the purchase of ships in India was an excellent move. By a mere order to Pellew, six men-of-war came at once into theoretical existence. These could be added to the paper strength of the Navy. Then the Ministers could turn to an admiring House of Commons and say 'When we came into office there were so many ships. And *now. . . .*' At a later period, the policy was modified.

The third motive underlying the growth of the East Indies squadron was Lord Wellesley's earnest wish to abolish the Bombay Marine. That force was a source of continual trouble. It was amenable, certainly, to the Indian Governments in a sense in which the Royal Navy was not. But there was endless difficulty in manning it and preserving its personnel from impressment. And at the end of it, the force was thoroughly despised.

> The merchant ships of the Company are men-of-war; the men-of-war of the Company are—what shall I call them? By their right names—they are all *Bombay Marine* . . . the vessels and the crews are equally contemptible.

This is the opinion of the Navy, as reflected in the pages of Captain Marryat; and it was an opinion which Wellesley had come to share. In time of war, at any rate, the larger cruisers were clearly better in the hands of the naval commander-in-chief. More money would be spent on them, better crews would be found for them, and their movements would be co-ordinated with those of the other ships on the station.

Leaving out of account these various additions to the squadron, the force handed over to Pellew from Rainier consisted of the following vessels:

Tremendous	(74)	Phaeton	(38)	Rattlesnake	(18)
Albion	(74)	Terpsichore	(32)	Albatross	(18)
Sceptre	(74)	Concorde	(36)	Victor	(18)
Russel	(74)	Fox	(32)	Dasher	(18)
Lancaster	(64)	Pitt	(36)	Seaflower (Cutter)	
Grampus	(50)	Sheerness	(32)	Arrogant (Hulk)	
		San Fiorenzo	(36)		
		Dedaigneuse	(36)		
		Caroline	(36)		
		Wilhelmina	(32)		

To which must be added:—*Culloden* (74)
And subtracted:—*Sheerness* (32)—wrecked.

The *Wilhemina* had been re-armed as a frigate, and was no longer 'en flute.'

With a force of this size, including six sail of the line, it was obviously possible to deal with such ships as the French and Dutch—to whose strength must now be added the Spanish—could muster to the eastward of the Cape. With military co-operation, indeed, the bases of the allies could be captured and annexed. And, even without military help, an effective blockade could be instituted such as would restrain all enemy action. Pellew's first strategic move was to send a detachment to cruise off the French islands. Osborn accordingly sailed on 25th March, 1805, with the *Tremendous*, *Grampus* and *Terpsichore*. His orders were to proceed from Bombay and cruise in Lat. 2° N., Long. 80° to 90°E. —across the line of approach to the Bay of Bengal—until joined by the *Pitt*. Then all four ships were to take up their stations round the Isle of France. The *Pitt*, a new frigate, was dispatched from Bombay on April 14th. Thus, Pellew provided for the temporary protection of the Bay of Bengal until he should be able to proceed to Madras in person and carry out the plans he had in mind for a system of flying squadrons.

Pellew quitted Bombay on April 30th, accompanied by the *Concorde*, *Cornwallis* and *Howe*. The last-named ship had been chosen by Wellesley for his accommodation on his return to England. He called at Trincomalee on May 21st, and arrived at Madras on the 24th, where he found the *Albion*, *Duncan*, *Rattlesnake*, *Harrier* and *Albatross*. The *Howe* was at once sent on to Bengal. Then Pellew began to make his arrangements for a scientific disposal of his squadron.

To provide for the security of the Eastern Side of India, with a view to contribute every protection to the Ships of the Honourable Company and those of Individuals trading thither, has occupied my most serious attention. As a preliminary to the arrangement which it is my intention to make for this important purpose, I have directed Captain Wood in H.M. Ship *Phaeton* to sail in company with the *Cornwallis* and *Harrier* under his Orders for the immediate protection of the Trade on the Coast of China, to reconnoitre the Port of Manilla in their way to China, and to prevent the predatory views of the Enemy Cruizers in that quarter. H.M. Ships *Dedaigneuse* and *Albatross* will be stationed in the Straits of Malacca and its vicinity, and the *Lancaster* and *Sir Edwd Hughes* . . . will convoy the Convoy from Bombay and from this Coast towards the close of the month of July & early in August.

I shall in person move towards that side of India towards the fall of the year, and whatever purposes I shall hereafter have matured for the further effectual defence of the Company's Trade and Settlements will be unfolded from time to time. . . .

(Pellew to Admiralty. 1st June, 1805. Adm. 1/176.)

Pellew tended to scatter his forces more than Rainier had done. In June 1805, when the above was written, he had eight ships on the coast, four at Bombay, four with Osborn, six to the eastward, and two off Ceylon. The sending of the *Phaeton* and her consorts to reconnoitre Manila—with unfortunate results, as we have seen, for the *Semillante*—was a result of the Admiralty's orders to detain all Spanish vessels. These orders, dated 4th December, 1804, arrived at Madras about 30th May, 1805, soon after Pellew himself arrived there, and he acted at once. There was nothing to fear from the Spaniards at the moment, but there was some hope of plundering them. All naval officers had heard of the Acapulco galleon, the ship the *Semillante* was to have convoyed, and war with Spain was always popular. One of the objects of Captain Wood's mission was to make direct inquiries as to the route taken by this desirable vessel, as to its time of sailing and as to its exact value. It transpired, when his report was made, that there were distinct possibilities. The reconnaissance was not fruitless.

In warfare one is seldom given the chance to develop one's plan of operations. Events intervene and the scene changes faster than plans can be made. In this instance, Pellew was not allowed to develop any strategic ideas he may have formed. Hardly had he made his initial moves when news came that a French squadron had escaped from Rochefort, possibly bound for the East Indies. The Admiral had therefore to make distracted efforts to recall and collect his line of battleships, as also to inform Osborn. Conditions were changed again when information arrived enabling him to appreciate better the intentions of the Dutch.

> By authentic intelligence recently obtained from Batavia I learn that the Dutch Squadron were then lying at Samarang in a very inactive and sickly Condition, and it may not be expected that they will be induced to undertake any service of importance or act offensively at present. I am not so well apprized of the motions of the French at the Isle of France. . . .
>
> (Pellew to Admiralty. 27th June, 1805. Adm. 1/176.)

About three weeks later the situation was changed again by the news that the squadron from Rochefort was not bound for India at all, and had indeed been located in the West Indies. Then came the news of the operations of Admiral Linois, a fresh complication which dwindled into insignificance shortly afterwards in comparison with a final thunderbolt which had the effect of turning a temporary muddle into a semi-permanent state of chaos.

To follow these developments it is necessary to return to the period at which Pellew left England. He had been allowed to retain his appointment, it has been noted, although his friends went out of office immediately after the appointment was made. But he had earned the enmity of the existing Government, and was aware when he sailed that his recall might be decided upon at any time. Instead, however, of recalling him, Lord Melville decided to send a second flag officer out to India with orders to take over half the squadron. The command was to be split in two, and the two commanders-in-chief were to be almost entirely independent of each other. The dividing line between the separated commands was to be a line due south from Point de Galle. And Sir Thomas Troubridge, junior to Pellew and chosen to supersede him in part of his command, was to have the eastern half.

This arrangement is not wholly attributable to malice. The dispatch of a second flag officer, indeed, had much to commend it. It was not even an innovation. Rainier had Rear-Admiral Blankett serving with him in 1799–1800. This precedent was not encouraging, it is true, as the two did not remain on good terms. Blankett ended, as we have seen, by asking to be relieved, saying that 'A second officer in India can gain little profit or honour, and is amenable more than the chief and more exposed to censure of all sorts.' Nevertheless, the precedent existed and the possibility was discussed before Melville's time. Where personal rancour entered was in making the junior flag officer independent of the senior—obviously a fatal arrangement—and in giving the junior officer the more important part of the command.

Pellew had sailed in July 1804, and what was for all practical purposes his ruin was under discussion within two or three months. Troubridge was actually appointed in February 1805, and he was on board his flagship by the end of that month.[1] He sailed on April 24th, his flag in the *Blenheim* (74) accompanied by a convoy of eighteen sail. With him was the frigate *Greyhound*. Concerning his voyage out to India, and the trouble he had with the ships he was convoying, something has already been said; from which it may be gathered that he was distinctly difficult to deal with. It is sufficient now to say of his voyage that he detached the *Greyhound* with the Bombay ships at the southern entrance to the Mozambique Channel in July, and continued his voyage with the remainder. Parting with the Bombay ships reduced his convoy from eighteen to fourteen sail. Three other Indiamen succeeded in being left behind by accident, and August found the *Blenheim* with eleven Indiamen in company. Of these, six were China ships. Troubridge was then in the middle of the Indian Ocean, in the latitude of the French islands, and bound for Madras.

[1] There came out with him the officials appointed by Dundas to what was now the fourth presidency. They came to be known collectively as the 'Scotch invasion' of Penang.

After his long period of refitting at the Isle of France, Linois sailed for his third cruise on 22nd May, 1805. The *Semillante* having gone to the Philippines, and *L'Atalante* having gone to cruise off the Cape of Good Hope, the *Marengo* had the *Belle Poule* as her only consort. Captain Osborn was attempting to blockade the Isle of France at that time, but Linois, having ascertained his exact position from an American ship, had no difficulty in avoiding him. The French ships then proceeded to the Seychelles, where they watered, sailing again from Mahé on June 11th. They were in sight of the Laccadives on the 30th.

When nearing Ceylon, Linois fell in with the ship *Prime*, a cartel out of Bombay. Pellew had sought to arrange a general exchange of prisoners almost as soon as he arrived on the station, and the *Prime* was bound for the Isle of France with a shipload of Frenchmen. She was sailing, of course, under a flag of truce. The French Admiral stopped her and compelled the officer in charge to give up seventy-five of the prisoners. This was utterly irregular in that an exchange needed to be arranged and ratified by accredited agents, and could not take place like this in mid-ocean even if the English officer had been ready to consent to it; which, in fact, he was not. Decaen expressed his disapproval—he usually did where Linois was at all concerned —and Pellew afterwards declared the whole proceeding void, whatever that may have meant. In the meanwhile, however, the deed was done. Forty-eight men went to the *Marengo* and twenty-seven to the *Belle Poule*, and this very likely brought their complements up to strength. Another, and unforeseen, result was the taking of the H.C.S. *Brunswick*.

The *Brunswick* was a China ship and one of the fleet present when Rainier met Pellew at Prince of Wales Island. She was then in a leaking condition, having grounded on Second Bar while on her way up to Whampoa. It was in the evening when the fleet had got under way, and the Chinese had marked the channel with a hundred boats carrying lights. At one point, one of the two Chinese pilots on board the *Brunswick* had called out 'port littee' at the same moment as the other said 'starboard littee.' The disaster had not been caused by that, but by Captain Grant kicking one of the pilots overboard, which led the Chinese to extinguish their lights. Next morning had found three Indiamen aground. All three were damaged, and it was this which caused the dispute at Penang. The commanders of these three ships refused to accept convoy to Madras as it would entail rounding the Cape at the worst time of year; or so, at least, they said. The *Brunswick* was more seriously damaged than the other two, and, not long after they sailed, her leaks increased so much that it was thought necessary for her to go to Bombay. There she was docked and her cargo transhipped to homeward bound Indiamen. As it was then too late for her to proceed to England, it was decided to send her back to China.

This decision of the Bombay Government was highly gratifying to Captain Grant. He thus accidentally achieved what was for many the ambition of a lifetime. He not only had the coveted privilege of a voyage from Bombay to China, but his was also the first ship of the year. He determined to sail as early as possible. He was unfortunate, however, in being at Bombay during the period when Pellew was doing his utmost to find crews for his newly acquired frigates. Practically the whole of the *Brunswick's* crew was impressed. Captain Grant was therefore 'obliged to hire French sailmakers out of the prison to repair our sails.' The cartel put to sea shortly afterwards with these same Frenchmen on board. It was from them that Linois learnt all he could wish to know about the *Brunswick*. They knew the date of her sailing, her destination, and the fact that she would be without naval protection. They could also, of course, be relied upon to recognize her at a glance.

Captain Grant sailed on July 1st, in company with three country ships, and laboriously worked his way down the coast in the teeth of the monsoon. Two of the country ships lost touch with him in the dark, so that only the *Sarah* was present on the 11th when the *Marengo* appeared. The *Brunswick* was manned mainly by Chinese and lascars and could do nothing but surrender. Linois reported afterwards (23 Messidor, An. 13) that the Indiamen mounted 30 guns but with ports for 60 or even 64. Some of her guns were struck down in the hold as ballast and there were only twenty white seamen aboard. The *Sarah* ran herself on shore near Fort de Galle, for it was off Ceylon that the incident took place. Grant would have done the same with the *Brunswick* but was overhauled too quickly. Satisfied with his prize, and afraid to linger in search of the other two country ships, Linois made sail to the southward so as to avoid pursuit.

News of this capture quickly reached Colombo and Madras.

> On the 20th of May last the French Ships *Marengo* of 80 guns and *Belle Poule* of 44 sailed from the Isle of France in consequence of receiving Intelligence by an American Ship which had passed through the Squadron of Commodore Osborn, of his situation to windward out of sight of the Island, & who by this means avoided him.
>
> By a dispatch received express from His Excellency the Honble Fred'k North, Governour of Ceylon under date of the 12th instant, I learn that these ships had appeared off Point de Galle, where they unfortunately

intercepted and captured the Honourable Company's Ship *Brunswick*, laden with Cotton from Bombay to China. She left that port on the 1st Instant, in company with the *Sarah* and two other Country Ships. The *Sarah* was run on shore by her Commander a little to the North West of Point de Galle in order to prevent her falling into the hands of the Enemy. The Cargo will be saved, and there are hopes of getting the ship off. The two other Ships I have reason to believe have made their Escape.

It should be observed that the Sailing of these Ships without protection was totally in contradiction of my purposes, and had their Commanders thought proper to avail themselves of the Convoy appointed to sail from Bombay early in the approaching Month with the regular Ships, this loss would have been effectually prevented, and it is still less excusable when it is known to result from considerations of Individual profit arising from an early market.

The further operations of the Enemy's Ships are at present altogether Conjectural, and I shall make such a Disposition of the Force, as I trust may succeed in intercepting them. His Majesty's Ships *Albion* and *Duncan* were on the Coast of Ceylon at this time, but altho they subsequently received Intelligence of the Enemy's appearance they were unable to gain a position sufficiently weatherly, owing to the Strong Gales which constantly prevail at this Season.—His Majesty's Ships *Russel* and *Concorde* were also dispatched from hence on the receipt of this information with a similar want of success. It is my intention to send H.M. Ship *Albion* to unite with the *Dedaigneuse* and *Albatross* in the Straits of Malacca without loss of time, under an expectation of Captain Ferrier's falling in with them in that quarter should the Enemy have proceeded to the Eastward, and a Frigate will be dispatched tomorrow to apprize Commodore Osborn of their motions, who I trust may yet fall in with them should the disposition of the several ships fail in the accomplishment of this desirable object. His Majesty's Ships *Sceptre* and *St. Fiorenzo* will be placed to receive them off Vizigapatam should they appear in that Quarter, while the *Culloden* and *Caroline* will be held in readiness to move on the first Intelligence from this Fort.

(Pellew to Admiralty, 22nd July, 1805. P.R.O. Adm. 1/176.)

Pellew's plans were made, of course, with a knowledge of the Rochefort squadron's destination. He would not otherwise have been able to disperse his ships of the line in this fashion. And, without dispersing ships of the line, there could be no pursuit. The arrangements made, it will be observed, did not show the Admiral as committed to any one view of what the enemy might do. He had provided for the obvious possibilities, and now waited for further news. None came for the next five weeks. Instead of attempting to do further damage, the French Admiral had fled southwards and was soon far beyond the reach of his opponent at Madras. It was well for him that he did so, for Pellew had already shown himself a far more formidable strategist than Rainier. Instead of rushing all his forces towards the scene of the crime, he more or less took it for granted that whoever also might be off Ceylon after the taking of the *Brunswick*, it would not be Linois. His orders were designed to checkmate possible movements towards other points of vantage. He thus showed a just appreciation of what Linois was trying to do. 'As they have many points to guard,' Linois had written in 1803, 'their force must necessarily be divided, and I hope to be able to do them considerable mischief by directing my course successively to very distant points in the different parts of the Indian Seas.' Pellew had grasped the essence of the mosquito's strategy as well as if he had read this sentence —which, by the way, he very probably had. Where his sagacity began to fail was when the mosquitoes multiplied.

In making off to the southward, Linois had thrown off any immediate pursuit. But, although he did not know it, he was running into the arms of yet another adversary; and that was Sir Thomas Troubridge. The *Blenheim* and her convoy, bound for Madras, were on a course to the northward in Long. 81° E.; that is, on the meridian, roughly speaking, of Point de Galle—from whence Linois was steering due south. It was not altogether unnatural that they should meet, and so they eventually did, in Lat. 19° 09' S., Long. 81° 17' E. on August 7th, nearly a month after the taking of the *Brunswick*.

In the action which followed it would probably be true to say that the *Belle Poule* was the decisive factor, although neither side mentioned it. Had the *Marengo* been alone, Troubridge would very likely have left his Indiamen and hurled himself on the French Admiral. It would have been a very even battle and might have ended in mutual destruction, which would have been an ideal result from Pellew's point of view. But Troubridge could not leave the convoy while the *Belle Poule* was there, for the frigate might easily snap up two or three Indiamen while the duel was in progress.

Troubridge's first shots were fired at his own side in an effort to make them form line of battle. They ultimately did so, and the *Blenheim* brought up the rear. Linois, having sent the *Brunswick* away, made a half-hearted attack on the convoy, keeping at long range. He discontinued the action as soon as a few shots from the *Blenheim* had convinced him that he had an escort to deal with. 'I fancy he thought we were all Indiamen,' wrote Troubridge, 'for the moment he made the *Blenheim* out through the Haze, he bore away. . . .' Little damage was done on either side, for it was evening

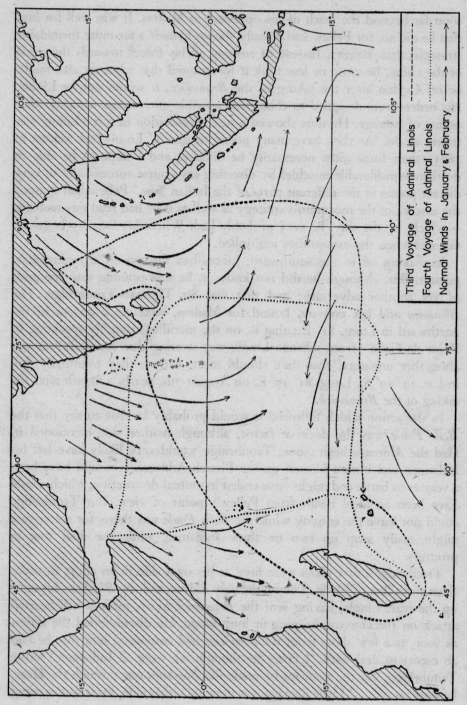

Third Voyage of Admiral Linois
Fourth Voyage of Admiral Linois
Normal Winds in January & February

when the encounter took place and the weather was too rough to allow the two flagships to make much use of their lower-deck guns. The *Blenheim* shipped so much water in trying to fire her 32-pounders that she had three feet of water in her hold after a few minutes of it. Linois drew off for the night, reconnoitred the convoy throughout the following day, and finally 'took himself off' as Troubridge expressed it. The *Blenheim* continued on her way to Madras.

At this period the *Marengo* had on board an unsympathetic witness in the person of Captain Grant of the *Brunswick*. In his subsequent report Grant describes the encounter with the *Blenheim* and convoy and continues thus:

> . . . Thus did this valuable convoy bid defiance to the *Marengo* and her consort, and I take the liberty of remarking that while the Honorable Company's ships are sufficiently manned, and have the support of one line of battle ship, there is little to be apprehended from the force that is at present under the command of Rear Admiral Linois, who has often confessed to me, that not having any port open for him to resort to in case of any accident happening to his ships, and no possible means of replacing a mast, should he unfortunately lose one, he is under the absolute necessity of acting as a privateer, and that it is therefore equally impolitic for him to risk the chance of an action with an equal force.
>
> As I have been two months at sea on board the *Marengo*, I have had full opportunity to confirm these ideas and to judge of the internal state and condition of the ship. . . . She sails uncommonly fast; but her ship's company, though strong in number, there being 800 men now on board, does not possess 100 effective seamen, and is generally composed of a variety of characters of all nations, in which are included 200 Lascars and natives from the Isle of France. There does not appear to be the least order or discipline amongst their people; all are equal, and each man seems equally conscious of his own superiority; and such is the sad state and condition of the *Marengo* that I may with safety affirm, she floats upon the sea as a hulk of insubordination, filthiness and folly. . . .

(H.E.I.C. *Proceedings Relative to Ships*, Appendix No. 4229.)

Although bound to the southward, Linois was not heading for the Isle of France. As Napoleon had anticipated, that base had become intolerable owing to his quarrels with Decaen. And he was now resolved to base his further operations on the Cape of Good Hope. He arrived at Fort Dauphin, Madagascar, on August 21st, hoping to find the *Brunswick* there. Hearing nothing of her, he sailed again at once. On the 24th he fell in with a Danish ship from the Isle of France and was informed that the English squadron off the island now consisted of two sail of the line and two frigates. This may have confirmed Linois in his determination not to return there. His decision, however, to go to the Cape—which was, strictly speaking, outside his station—had been taken before the cruise began.

The Cape was sighted on September 10th and the *Marengo* and *Belle Poule* came to anchor in Simon's Bay on the 13th. There they took in provisions and water, expecting to be joined before long by *L'Atalante* and by the *Brunswick*. Both of these ships arrived. The *Brunswick* came in on the 18th, in the midst of a gale, and instantly went ashore, becoming a total loss. The frigate appeared on the 22nd, and the whole squadron moved round to Table Bay a month later. On November 3rd, during another gale, *L'Atalante* went ashore. She was floated again but, being found in need of repairs which could not be carried out at the Cape, her day of usefulness was judged to be over. Captain Beauchene tried to save *L'Atalante* but was ordered by Linois (supposing *L'Atalante* to be beyond repair) to see whether the Dutch *Bato* (74) left there by Dekker two years ago, could be taken to Europe. Finding that this could be done only at a colossal expense, Linois distributed seventy of *L'Atalante's* men between the *Marengo* and *Belle Poule*. The remaining one hundred and sixty took part in the defence of the Cape and afterwards became prisoners of war. Some or all of these are said to have fought under their captain at Blauenberg.

With a squadron reduced once more to two ships, Linois sailed on November 9th, in order to cruise on the west coast of Africa. It was a futile proceeding, resulting in nothing but the capture of two or three English slavers. Having gone as far north as the Gulf of Guinea and the latitude of Fernando Po, Linois went as if to cruise in the region of St. Helena, with the intention of returning ultimately to the Cape. Some distance south-west of the island, he fell in with the American ship *Ganges*, sixty-two days out of Canton and bound for Philadelphia. This chance encounter was the first event of importance—apart, that is to say, from the loss of *L'Atalante* and of the *Brunswick*—that had taken place during the cruise. For the master of the *Ganges*, a certain Mr. John Philipps, gave Linois the news of the Cape having been taken by the English. The decisive action was fought on January 8th, and Linois heard of it from Mr. Philipps on the 27th.

The taking of the Cape meant for Linois the loss of his base. He had taken in but four months' supplies before he sailed, and he had already been at sea more than ten weeks. He would have to sail for the Isle of France at once. But at this point destiny interfered in the person of Mr.

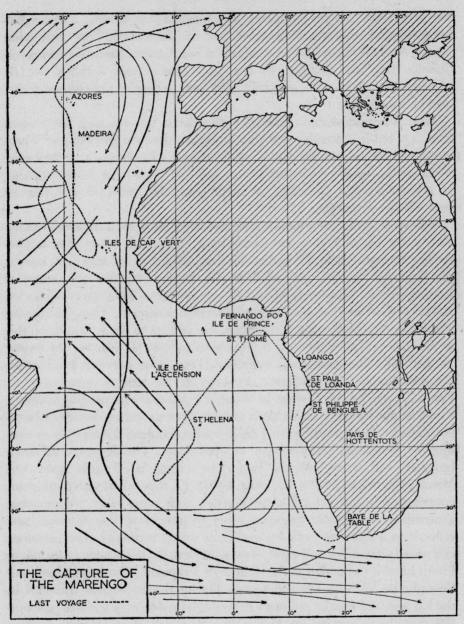

THE CAPTURE OF
THE MARENGO

LAST VOYAGE ....

Philipps. Having told the truth about the Cape, which he had heard from one of the English men-of-war engaged in its reduction, he went on to elaborate his story. There were, he said, three English men-of-war at St. Helena, besides the squadron at the Cape. Admiral Pellew was off the

Isle of France, and the *Semillante* was blockaded at Manila. The English knew where Linois was, he asserted, and the ships at the Cape were lying in wait for him. They had a squadron on the Agulhas bank and another in Simon's Bay. After dealing with him, they were to make a dash at the Isle of France, he concluded—probably with some enjoyment of the consternation he was causing.[1]

Most American seamen disliked both sides in the war with fairly equal intensity, but it is possible that this American hated the English less. There seems to have been more than a touch of malice in his story. At any rate, whatever his motive, whether it was love of mischief or casual impulse, he evidently began by telling the literal truth and ended off with hearsay or deliberate invention.

Believing all this information, true and false, the French Admiral decided that, as the Isle of France was immediately threatened, it would be unwise for him to return there. He had at this time bread for fifty days at 12 ounces per head per day, but he had little else, having obtained only water at Port-au-Prince. Supposing, he argued, that the Ile de France was blockaded and itself short of food, his return there would weaken it. Then, his rigging was worn out. Supposing it damaged, his voyage to Java, Manila or Rio de Janeiro would be prolonged beyond fifty days. 'Je n'ai vu,' he wrote, 'de parti plus convenable aux interets de l'état, pour parvenir a sauver les batimens qui m'etoient confiés, que celui de me rendrer directement en France.' Even for that voyage he thought it necessary on meeting contrary winds to put his crew on reduced rations of water and 10 ounces of bread per day. In thus returning to France without orders, Linois was risking disgrace, dismissal, imprisonment or even death. The desperate decision, however, was taken, and the two ships steered northwards again. On March 13th, in Lat. 26° 16' N., Long. 89° 26' E., they fell in with a squadron commanded by Sir John Borlase Warren, both being taken after making a strenuous resistance. Engaged by a 98-gun ship, the *Marengo* was reduced to a shattered hulk before Linois would surrender. The casualties comprised sixty killed and eighty-two wounded, the latter number including Linois himself (wounded in the right leg), Vrignaud (who lost an arm) and Enseigne de Vaisseau Durand Linois. Duclos the diarist was wounded in the left arm and legs by splinters of wood. The *Marengo* was brought into Portsmouth as a prize on May 14th.[2] So ended Rear-Admiral Linois's

---

[1] Information given in letter from Linois to Decrès, 20th May, 1806. Arch. Nat. BB⁴ 252.

[2] She was dismasted in a gale and nearly foundered on the way. The action and the voyage to England are described in two letters written by a midshipman of the *Ramillies* who was one of the prize crew. (*Naval Chronicle*, Vol. 15, p. 407.)

campaign in the East Indies.[1] His next letter to Decrès was dated from Bath.

Linois remained a prisoner of war until 1814. He was made Governor of Guadeloupe under Louis XVIII, to whom he remained loyal during the 'Hundred Days.' He retired in 1816 and died at Versailles in 1848. His naval career was not without distinction and its less creditable episodes were redeemed, in part, by the obstinacy with which he fought his last battle in 1806. Like Decrès he was never, probably, a believer in the Napoleonic Empire. And he evidently derived from the old regime a tactical caution which his own parsimonious nature tended, perhaps, to reinforce. His anxiety, as shown in the words quoted above, to save the vessels committed to his charge, extended to their rigging and sailcloth. He hated to see waste and damage and tended to regard an action mainly in the light of expended stores, the value of which had to be set against a possible gain in prize-money. This is the privateer's approach to war, with ledger to balance the profit and loss, and it was too prevalent in the French Navy. But Linois's interest in prize-money sprang, at least in part, from a care for his men, who were otherwise unpaid. His thought for their welfare is always apparent and they repaid him with loyalty and something like affection. More happily circumstanced, he might have had more success. It is difficult, however, to imagine any circumstance which could have made him a useful ally of Decaen.

---

[1] Much information concerning this last voyage is to be derived from the journals of Thomas Addison (*The Naval Miscellany*, Vol. I, Navy Records Society, Vol. XX, ed. J. K. Laughton, 1902). Addison joined the *Brunswick* as midshipman in 1803 and was present when Captain Grant surrendered to Linois, 'not having twenty effective European seamen on board.' He describes his life as a prisoner of war in the *Marengo*. 'They had 1,000 French sailors on board, including, by the way, a good many Yankees among them, with about a hundred Lascars. . . . We soon discovered the looseness of their discipline, officers and men mingling, hail well met. Liberty and Equality was a motto indeed stamped on the guns. I frequently saw the ship's barber . . . walking arm in arm with the first captain, chatting intimately together on the quarter-deck. . . . They have a poor idea of cleanliness; neatness is out of the question. . . . Our living was wretched. Only two meals per diem; both put together would hardly make a good English breakfast, with a purser's pint of sour Bordeaux claret, and half a pint of water. . . .' Addison was present at the action with Troubridge and he saw the *Brunswick* wrecked at the Cape. He was there released and so missed the action in which the *Marengo* was taken.

CHAPTER XIV

The Command Divided

W ITH the departure of the *Marengo* there was a profound change in the character of the war as waged in the East. Linois, in his three cruises, had not succeeded in any one major enterprise, apart perhaps from the raid on Bencoolen. Nevertheless, the presence of the *Marengo* had been a factor in the situation, and one which the English could not ignore. By a series of accidents, the French flagship never showed her formidable fighting qualities until the day she was taken. The calibre of her guns, however, was known, and there was always a risk of some isolated English man-of-war falling a prey to her. The *Centurion* was very fortunate to escape capture, and would hardly have so escaped but for shallow water, an improvised battery on shore, and Linois's anxiety to be gone. In the skirmish with the *Blenheim*, it happened that lower-deck guns could not be used. And yet, although little used, the *Marengo's* 36-pounders had always to be reckoned with. In her last action, by an extraordinary accident, the *Marengo* was caught as we have seen by a three-decker. Judging by the terrific conflict that ensued, and the courage shown both by Linois and his crew, it may be doubted whether any English 74-gun ship could have taken her. With so formidable an enemy at large, the English had to be cautious.

Once rid of the *Marengo*, the strategic problem resolved itself into mere commerce protection. There was no longer much risk of the English cruisers being taken. The difficulty was to ensure that they should be everywhere at once. There remained, of course, the possibility of a fresh squadron coming out from France. But of this Pellew was fairly certain to receive warning beforehand. The blockade of the French naval bases was never effective enough to prevent the enemy from sailing. What it did do was to prevent them sailing unobserved. The ships blockading a French harbour might not see the enemy go, but they could hardly fail to notice the fact that he had gone. And the news would get to India by overland mail long before the squadron itself was likely to arrive. False alarms, however, were to be expected and we have already seen that they were not unknown.

From the French point of view, the departure of Linois was no great loss. He had not been a success. Had he waged war against English men-of-war and settlements, he would have served a useful purpose. Instead, he had chosen to play the part of a corsair. It was a part for which he was unfitted. And, in any case, there was a disproportion between the means and the end. To use the *Marengo* as a privateer, to chase merchantmen in an 80-gun ship, was like employing a steam-hammer to crack a nut. Printed in Appendix C will be found a list of vessels taken or destroyed by Linois's squadron. It includes the ships taken by the frigates when cruising independently. And even so, it is not impressive. Three Indiamen were taken altogether: the *Princess Charlotte*, the *Brunswick* and the *Althea*, extra ship. Another extra ship was taken by the *Psyche* —the *Admiral Aplin*—but that was in her privateering days. Five large country ships were taken, the *Countess of Sutherland*, *Henrietta*, *Eliza Ann*, *Pearl* and *Hope*; the *Upton Castle* and the *Charlotte* should perhaps be added to the number. These, then, with eight smaller vessels and the damage done at Bencoolen, were all Linois could show as the results of between two and three years' cruising.

Estimates as to the amount of the damage, as made by Duclos and Flinders, are more or less valueless. There is an inevitable confusion between the cost price and the sale price of both ships and cargoes, and more confusion between the expected and the actual sale price of goods. There was always, and of necessity, an enormous difference between the amount lost by the English and the amount gained by the French. The thing stolen is seldom worth to the thief what it was to the rightful owner. The *Brunswick*, for example, was loaded with cotton, the value of which depended on the fact that it was destined for China, where there were Chinamen who wanted it. Taken by Linois off Ceylon, the *Brunswick* was sent in the opposite direction. And the farther she went from China the less valuable did the cotton become. Tea, again, was chiefly in demand in England. Once taken from an English ship, its value sank at once, for it was no longer on its way to the best market. Where there are so many uncertainties, little reliance can be placed on French boasts or English lamentations. Only the amounts paid by the underwriters would give any certain clue to the damage inflicted.

Duclos's statement, on the other hand, of the amount of prize-money recovered by the squadron is almost certainly accurate. It is a fact he may be supposed to have known, if only from calculating beforehand what his own share would amount to. His totals for the whole campaign add up to 1,821,500 piastres. Allowing the piastre to have been worth five shillings, this comes to rather more than £455,000. As a quarter of the proceeds went to the Government, the actual sale amount of vessels and goods must have been in the region of £600,000. This may have been as much as a third of the value of what the English lost.

Now, £600,000 was quite a respectable sum. Yet the fact remains that what Linois did was no more than any resolute privateer might have done; and indeed it was no more than one privateer actually did. Linois had to divide his profits between four ships. The resulting average of £150,000 per ship is exactly what was made by *La Henrietta*, privateer, during the first sixteen months of the war. If Linois had been made to deduct his expenses from his gross profits, he would presumably have found himself confronted with a deficit.

As Linois's discomfiture left but one French man-of-war in the Indian Ocean, it was now to be expected that some vigorous action would be taken by the English against the French and Dutch headquarters. Plans for such an offensive were, indeed, already under discussion. But all such schemes were shattered by the division of the command, which fatal arrangement left the English naval forces all but incapable of effective action for twelve months to come.

We left Troubridge pursuing his voyage to Madras after his encounter with the *Marengo*. He arrived at his destination on 23rd August, 1805, and hastened to show his orders to Pellew. The orders were to take over the command of half the squadron—fourteen ships, to be exact, two being of the line. His station was to be to the east of a line drawn due south from Point de Galle. He was to be independent of the commander-in-chief of the station to the west of the line; but in case a superior squadron of the enemy should approach, a saving clause allowed the senior flag officer to resume command of the whole or part of the ships of the line assigned to serve on the eastern station.

Pellew had heard something of the Admiralty's plan of dividing the command as early as July 22nd. Knowing that the proposal was insane in itself, and intended chiefly to bring about his ruin, he had already decided to evade his orders by every possible means. His first move was to take Troubridge under his command. Troubridge, according to an eye-witness, 'protested strongly against it and was very violent.' What followed is best told in Troubridge's words.

Blenheim, Madras Roads
1st September, 1805.

Sir

Be pleased to acquaint the Lords Commissioners of the Admiralty that on my arrival at Madras I met Sir Edward Pellew. I communicated to him my orders, the tenor of their Lordships' Commission and Instructions to me as Commander in Chief on the district of Coast which their Lordships had been pleased to assign me, requesting him to proceed to an arrangement of the several points therein contained, to establish under the existing circumstances, places of Rendezvous, and also others, under events which might possibly arise; begging him at the same time to place under me the ships and vessels pointed out in the margin of their Lordships' Orders, or such part thereof as were then in the Roads, when to my astonishment, he gave me for answer, that he did not understand by their Lordships' Commission to me, or the instructions thereon, which I gave him to read, that I was authorised to take the Command on the Coast of Coromandel or the Bay of Bengal, and that what he conceived to be their Lordships' intention was, the Coast due East from the South Line (named in their orders and Commission) from Point De Galle, which will embrace Prince of Wales's Island and the entrance to the straits of Malacca only, and consequently I am not allowed to consider Madras or Bengal within the limits of my station: such a decision, and the Captain of the *Blenheim* as well as myself having previously received his orders to put ourselves under his Command, is, I conceive, in direct opposition to their Lordships' directions. . . .

. . . I must request that you will be pleased to move the Lords Commissioners of the Admiralty speedily to afford such further explanation of their Lordships' orders to Sir Edward Pellew as *he* seems to require. . . .

I most cheerfully proceed under the command of Sir Edward Pellew, because it is my duty to yield obedience to a senior officer, and because I hope the result may prove beneficial to His Majesty's Service; but I am persuaded that their Lordships will agree with me in opinion, that as effectual Co-operation might have been given by me as Commander in Chief agreeably to their Lordships' appointment, as under the present circumstances, by which, in defiance of their Commission I am placed as second in Command of the Squadron only. . . .

(P.R.O. Ad. 1/176.)

Pellew's reading of the instructions was remarkably adroit. By confining Troubridge to the south of a line due east from Point de Galle as well as to the east of a line due south, he kept most of the station in his own hands; and, more especially, he kept Madras and Trincomalee. On the other hand, it was an obvious quibble. For one thing, it did not make sense. What could be the point of making Troubridge responsible for defending the trade off Ceylon, if he had no base nearer than Penang? And then again, if Pellew was to keep two-thirds of the station why was he to be left with only half the ships? The excuse was ingenious, but it was too flimsy to uphold. Pellew changed his ground eventually. Indeed, he had to. The argument was a sound opening, as it took the wind out of Troubridge's sails and shook his self-confidence generally. But it left Pellew no pretext for retaining any of the ships assigned to Troubridge. The instructions were explicit as regards the ships, having a list of names in the margin. The only way of withholding compliance on this point was to play for time.

As soon as Troubridge had recovered from the astonishment he naturally felt at his rival's coolness, he asked Pellew to explain his point of view in writing. In answer to his note—they were not on speaking terms by that time—he received a carefully worded non-committal reply. There was no hope of using it against Pellew later on, for there was no obvious method of discovering what it meant. Pellew had not decided where he was to make his stand, and so would not as yet commit himself in writing. The same caution is apparent in his letter to the Admiralty of September 8th. There he merely states his intention of escorting the whole China convoy to Prince of Wales Island, and of waiting there to protect the homeward bound trade. He goes on to say that he will afterwards 'proceed to the completion of their Lordships' arrangement agreeably to their Instructions already noted, *according to the existing circumstances*, both in relation to the Enemy's force now to the Eastward as well as the general state of this part of His Majesty's Empire at large, always keeping in view the high responsibility with which I am invested, and *acting to the best of my judgement and discretion*. . . .' The words underlined are not so emphasized in the original, and they would not, in themselves, excite much comment at the Admiralty. But, laid alongside Troubridge's letter, they would be enough to prepare their Lordships for what was to come.

The movement to the eastward to protect the China fleet was a following of precedent, and it was natural that Pellew should take Troubridge with him. The convoy actually proceeded in two divisions, one on September 6th, with Troubridge, and the other on the 10th, with Pellew. The escort consisted of the two flagships, the *Sceptre* (74), *Greyhound* (32), *Concorde* (36), *Dedaigneuse* (32), *Rattlesnake* (18) and *Albatross* (18); or, at any rate, it did so by the time they reassembled at Penang on the 23rd. There, while waiting for the division from Bombay, with the *Sir Edward Hughes*, and for two other ships from Bengal, the two Admirals resumed their discussions. Pellew proposed a compromise. He would allow Troubridge to have the ships assigned him, but the dividing line between the two commands should be $82\frac{1}{2}°$ E., which would have the effect of bringing Madras and Trincomalee into the western station. He suggested that the commanders-in-chief should share patronage and emolument equally between them. On Troubridge refusing to agree to this, Pellew informed him that he intended, nevertheless, to divide the command on these lines. A final interview on the 30th brought the two Admirals no nearer an amicable agreement; and, on the same day, the rubicon crossed, Pellew wrote his memorandum on the division of the command. It was sent to the Admiralty, together with copies of his correspondence with Troubridge. The following extracts contain the gist of his argument.

At this extreme distance from England, on a Station so far removed from their observation, I conceive their Lordships may not have been fully apprized of the various local considerations which will operate against the proposed Division of the Command, and that when these circumstances shall be laid before them, and reviewing the subject with additional Lights, their Lordships' opinions may experience an essential change, and it will appear distinctly that should the proposed arrangement be carried fully into adoption, it cannot fail of being attended with prejudicial consequences and extreme inconveniences to those entrusted with its completion.

Upon an Attentive examination of their Lordships' Instructions for the separation of the Command, I observe that I am still vested with the weighty responsibility of providing for the general protection of our Possessions in this Country, by the authority given to me of resuming command of the whole number of line of Battle ships, so often as present impending danger shall render such a measure necessary, although I am restricted by those Instructions within a Line of Division which does not afford any eligible station where I could meet with effect the hostile operations of an Enemy's Squadron.

The danger of wintering at Bombay and the consequent practice of removing to the Coast of Coromandel during the South West Monsoon has uniformly prevailed. The Harbour of Bombay affords no adequate shelter during that Season for Ships of the Line—upon several occasions Merchant Ships which from their lesser draught of Water are able to take a station nearer to the Shore, have been driven from their anchors and wrecked during the prevalence of those tremendous Gales. Should the Squadron assigned to the Western Division remain at Sea during the continuance of that Monsoon, unless it proceeds across the Line it must be exposed to the severest weather with the probability of being crippled, without having a safe Port to resort to, and while thus disabled from active operations, no impediment to the hostile views of the Enemy could be afforded for the security of the Company's Possessions.

Madras has from a variety of considerations been hitherto established as the chief Station of the Commander in Chief in the East Indies. Its centrical situation for the purposes of ready communication with the several Presidencies, and the receipt of intelligence from Europe, is obvious. It is the point where the Fleet may be most readily assembled upon emergency, and upon almost every occasion its vicinity has been the Theatre of those Actions which have heretofore distinguished His Majesty's Naval Service in these Seas. From its great advantages of obtaining the several Articles of Supply from other Ports of the Bay of Bengal, Madras has been long established as the principal Depot of Naval Stores; The Victualling of the whole Squadron and the only Naval Hospital for the ships of His Majesty's service in the East Indies, have been fixed at this Presidency from considerations of obvious Utility and convenience.

Under their Lordships' Instructions of the 24th September last, I had given every consideration to the means of continuing the Blockade of Port Louis in the most effectual manner. Many difficulties presented themselves in carrying on that Service without interruption as well from its extreme distance from our Settlements as from the inexpediency of keeping the Crews during so protracted a period on Salt Provisions, who, from long Service in this Country, are very generally affected with Scorbutic and Ulcerous Complaints, which have increased to an alarming degree, as will appear from the Hospital Reports. The limited number of ships now assigned to my Command will not possibly permit of my relieving the Force which may hereafter be employed off the Isle of France so frequently, as from these considerations, I have previously proposed.

The necessity of preserving a constant Force of Line of Battle Ships concentrated for the Protection of the Company's Possessions, is sufficiently manifested by the Instructions of their Lordships of old date to my Predecessors, which have been reiterated on a late occasion to me, in the month of June last when a French Naval Force was expected to proceed to India from Rochefort and which established the principle as a Point of indispensable Policy. . . .

. . . I have determined to adhere to the precise letter of their Lordships Instructions in every point consistent with my sense of the public interests, reserving only the Fort of Madras within my own direction, from a deliberate Conviction of the necessity of making that coast the Principal defensive Station in case of Emergency, until upon reference to their Lordships' consideration of the Arguments I have done myself the Honour to submit to them in the foregoing paragraphs, I shall receive their final judgement on the Question. . . .

I take the liberty of offering to their Lordships a deliberate opinion that the Public Interests will be most effectually secured by placing under the Charge of the Senior Admiral the protection of both the Coasts of the Peninsula of India, and the island of Ceylon, who, thus vested with a comprehensive charge, inseparably connected in all its bearings may be enabled to reconcile the various contending Interests and provide an adequate Security to the Commercial and Territorial possessions of the Honourable Company. . . .

Concurring fully in their Lordships' Sentiments, I am well satisfied that more than one Flag Officer may be employed with very essential advantage on a Station so extended as that of the India Seas, and especially that a separate Command may be allotted to the Eastern side of India. The protection of the rising Colony of Prince of Wales Island, and the security of the important and rapidly increasing Trade carried on by the Country Ships between India and China, together with the observation of the Enemy's possessions in that quarter, would engage all the attention of a distinct Command, while the charge of the Coasts of the Peninsula and Ceylon and the protection of the Convoys passing between the Ports of India and Europe, would furnish the more important Duty of the Senior Admiral.

The Defence of the Honourable Company's Principal Possessions when threatened by any hostile Attack from an Enemy's Squadron would require that the Chief part of the Line of Battle Ships should be placed under his immediate Authority to enable him to arrange them at all times with a view to their ready co-operation, as otherwise, when employed in two far distant quarters of India, and acting under the Orders of different Commanders, as at present, many months would necessarily elapse before they could be assembled, and an Enemy's Fleet arriving in these Seas, would have leisure to execute any views of hostility before the equivalent Force could possibly be collected to defeat their designs. . . .

(P.R.O. Adm. 1/176.)   Ed. Pellew.

Instead of looking for flaws in Troubridge's commission, Pellew had wisely taken his stand on higher ground. In the above memorandum he did not fail to point out the injury done to himself in confining him 'to the Presidency third in rank,' but his main contention was impersonal and sufficiently convincing. It is possible that he did rather less than justice to Bombay as a place of shelter during the south-west monsoon. On the other hand, he omitted an argument which was almost equally conclusive against leaving a squadron there. For even if ships of the line ran no appalling risk while at anchor in the harbour—and it is only fair to say that such ships had survived the experience, even during the worst gales[1] —their presence there could serve no useful purpose. For at that season there was, speaking generally, no trade to protect and no enemy to fear. It would be a pitiful economy of effort to leave half the squadron idle for half the year.

[1] The example to the contrary was in the storm of 4th November, 1799, when over a hundred vessels and five hundred lives were lost, H.M. Ship *Resolution* going to pieces under the castle walls. *See Glimpses of Old Bombay.* James Douglas.

The effect of Pellew's memorandum was to postpone the complete execution of the Admiralty's orders until some further instructions should arrive to enforce or modify those originally sent. On another station this would have seemed a far less desperate proceeding. In the East Indies it meant, in effect, disobeying orders for a year. If, moreover, the new instructions left any loophole, it was in Pellew's power to apply respectfully for further explanation, and so gain another year. To Troubridge, at least, it seemed possible that Pellew would thus continue to raise objections indefinitely, 'go on quibbling for ever,' and so remain in supreme command until definitely recalled. As regards the personal conflict between Pellew and Troubridge, it is perhaps fair to remember that Pellew's personal papers have survived while Troubridge's were lost. We thus know exactly what Pellew thought of his rival but rather less of what Troubridge thought of Pellew. 'Sir Thomas is more outrageous than ever,' wrote Pellew to Sir Evan Nepean, 'and from a public correspondence full of invective and low insinuation, has now commenced a private one of no less scurrility and abuse. Language which degrades the Gentleman is ever flowing from his lips. . . . I wish to God I was out of it. I would rather command a Frigate with her Bowsprit over the rocks of Ushant all my Life, than command here on such terms: for Heaven's sake call one of us home. . . .' To a friend Pellew wrote, 'Sir T. Troubridge . . . is I fear a weak man— entirely commanded by his passion; who is every week dishonouring himself by striking some of his Midshipmen or anybody else who comes in his way. . . .' But writing to Admiral Markham, in a more reflective mood, he wrote, 'We are both warm enough, God knows; but brothers could not agree as we are placed.' And that is very near the truth of the matter. Troubridge evidently intended to challenge Pellew at some future date and only death prevented him.

It will be observed that Pellew did not go so far as to suspend their Lordships' orders touching the division of the squadron. Troubridge was to have the ships he had been assigned, although not immediately; for it was Pellew's intention first to reconnoitre, and probably attack, the Dutch squadron at Batavia. Before anything could be done, however, the situation was altered by the arrival of the *Russel* from Madras on October 1st. Pellew had been waiting for her, meaning to sail for Batavia as soon as she should arrive. She brought a dispatch which had come by overland mail, 'their Lordships' Secret letter in Cypher of the 7th May,' which conveyed the warning that a considerable French force might arrive very shortly in the Indian Seas. The danger was real, for in January 1805 Napoleon had in fact ordered squadrons to be equipped at Brest, Rochefort and Ferrol to carry an army to India. Decrès talked him out of it, but the threat meanwhile had its effect.

Pellew at once decided to abandon the attack on Batavia and return to India. He also concluded that the emergency was such as would justify him in retaining command of all ships of the line, including those assigned to Troubridge. Indeed, he was fairly obviously glad of the excuse. He had also a certain satisfaction in keeping his rival in the dark as to what news exactly the *Russel* had brought. It was, he hinted, a matter of weighty importance; something, evidently, which a mere Rear-Admiral of the Blue could not be expected to understand.

After some hesitation, Pellew decided not to take the *Blenheim* with him. Instead, he detached her to guard the convoy on its voyage to China. Troubridge was left to hoist his flag in the sloop *Rattlesnake* (18), while Pellew sailed for Madras with the *Culloden*, *Albion*, *Russel* and *Sceptre*, leaving orders for the *Lancaster* to follow. During the voyage, on October 22nd, Pellew wrote another disquisition on the subject of the division of the command, without, however, improving very much on the first. Arriving at Madras on November 1st, he sent a report of his proceedings to the Admiralty. Parts of it seem worth quoting.

> . . . I trust their Lordships will approve of my not having taken the *Blenheim* under my command upon this occasion, the presence of which Ship to the Eastward will now afford a sufficient protection to the China Fleet, as from authentick intelligence obtained whilst at Fort Cornwallis I learned that the Dutch Force is not in a capacity of active operation, and that the measures of that Government are solely directed to the protection of their own Coasts.—My former expectations of a combined operation of the French & Dutch have been in consequence entirely relieved for the present, and no intelligence of the *Marengo* being on this Coast having reached me, I am satisfied M. Linois must have returned to the Isle of France.
>
> It is my intention to establish Trincomaley at present as the most eligible Station to await the arrival of the Enemy's Fleet, both as considering it the most Centrical point for affording protection to the different Coasts and for the receipt of Intelligence as well as from a persuasion that should the Enemy have matured any plan of hostility against our Eastern possessions that Port will become the first object of his attack from the peculiar advantages it would furnish to the hostile Squadron, its great and very improveable means of defence, its being calculated to afford the most effectual annoyance to our Commerce, and from whence hereafter he might most readily extend his views of Territorial requisitions on the Continent of India.
>
> The present state of the internal defence of Trincomaley is by no means calculated to resist the force of a premeditated and powerful attack, without

the cover of a defensive Squadron and should such a Force as that stated to be preparing for the East Indies at Brest be directed against it with an adequate body of Troops they might unless deterred by the presence of His Majesty's Ships, rush into the Fort, and probably carry the Garrison by Coup de Main. At this momentous Crisis when it is known that one considerable Expedition has been directed against our Colonies in the East Indies and, from their Lordships Information another of greater magnitude is preparing at Brest as supposed for this Country, it behoves me to use every caution to take the best possible measures for the security of the British Possessions in India, more especially when I reflect upon the State of Politics in Europe, and the operation of the Intelligence which will have been received relative to the military Events which have taken place in the Interior of India, which though now wearing a more favourable aspect may have excited in the Enemy strong expectations of success in any attempt of this nature. The purpose of invasion may perhaps have been at present abandoned for the more feasible design of a General Attack upon our Colonial possessions, and occasioning a necessity for detaching largely from home defence.

(P.R.O. Adm. 1/176.)

As soon as the state of the weather enabled Pellew to communicate with the shore at Madras, which was by no means always possible at that time of year, he received a further dispatch dated June 4th, confirming the contents of the earlier one. He also heard of the peace made with the native powers, news of the death of Lord Cornwallis coming simultaneously. Then, as it was unwise to linger on the coast in November, he sailed on the 3rd for Ceylon. Before he sailed, however, and perhaps as a result of his consultation with the Government at Fort St. George, his views seem to have changed on the subject of Trincomalee. He wrote, at any rate, on the 2nd, saying 'My attention will be carefully directed to the safety of the Coasts of the Peninsula and Ceylon, viewing Bombay, Goa and Trincomaley as the most important objects of Defence.' And it was in this order of importance that he seems to have viewed them henceforth, to judge fom his movements. For, with but a short pause at Trincomalee, he proceeded directly to Bombay.

Arriving at Bombay, with a part of the squadron, on December 14th, Pellew received the news of 'the defeat of the combined fleet by Sir R. Calder.' He had still no assurance, however, as to the destination of the expedition from Brest. He therefore thought it best to keep the line of battleships on the Malabar coast, venturing to detach the *Lancaster* only, which he sent to protect the homeward-bound China fleet off Pulo-Aur. He felt more confident in detaching this ship because he was now reinforced by the *Tremendous*. Osborn had quitted his station off the Isle of France in the middle of August, leaving the frigates *Pitt* and *Terpsichore* to continue the blockade. The *Tremendous* was worn out and due to return to England, with convoy, in March 1806. On December 20th Pellew had the following ships within call, ready for emergencies: *Culloden*, *Tremendous*, *Albion*, *Sceptre*, *Russel* and *Grampus*. At this period the squadron was strengthened by the purchase of another country ship, the *Asia*, bought at Bombay for £28,000 and renamed *Sir Francis Drake*. At this time also, on December 27th, the news came of Linois being at the Cape and expected to cruise between there and St. Helena. More news followed which laid at rest all immediate fears of an expedition from Brest. Pellew was thus left free to consider the problem of how to deal with the privateers from the Isle of France.

The French privateers at this time were thought to number about ten. Four had from 30 to 36 guns, one had 24, three had 16 or 18, and there were one or two smaller ones. The best-known at this time were:

Napoleon	Le Nouvel	8 guns	1805–6
Amélie	Le Nouvel	14 guns	
Henriette	Henri	8 guns	1803–6
Deux Soeurs	Desjean Hilaire		1806
Fortune	François Lemême	12–24 guns	1804

The *Revenant*, Robert Surcouf, of 18 guns and 192 men, was even better known, but operated rather later, in 1807. This was the period of Surcouf's spectacular return to his old cruising ground, described in a later chapter. Exact figures about these privateers are unobtainable, either of their numbers or the numbers of their victims. Nor is it possible to follow their movements. The Bay of Bengal, however, was their usual hunting ground, and Pellew heard of five prizes falling to them while he was at Bombay. The division of the command was entirely favourable to their activities, for merchants did not know to whom to apply for convoy. A number of the English cruisers, incidentally, were to the eastward with Troubridge when they might perhaps have been employed more profitably in the bay. The merchants began to complain, and the substance of their lament duly found its way into the pages of William Hickey's memoirs.

> ... With such eminent nautical men as Pellew and Troubridge the merchants flattered themselves that the Indian Seas would be kept quite free of French privateers or cruisers of any description, in which expectation, however, they were sadly disappointed. The two rival Admirals, jealous of each other's line of command, soon began to dispute and actually to

quarrel, mutually upbraiding and taxing each other with neglect, during which dissensions the British trade, instead of being protected from the attacks of the enemy, suffered in a far greater degree than at any former period, more ships being captured in one twelvemonth than during the four preceding years. . . .

Hickey cannot be relied upon for facts but he usually conveys a sufficiently convincing idea of atmosphere. His account of British losses may not be strictly accurate, but it is probably what the merchants and underwriters were telling each other. There was no real naval remedy, short of a strict convoy system or a strong expedition against the Isle of France. And to a convoy system the Bengal merchants —unlike those of Bombay—were opposed. As far back as 1799, Rainier was writing that he had 'frequently taken occasion to point out to the merchants the security that would result to their trade from their ships sailing with convoy. . . .'; but he had sagely added 'I am, however, induced to believe 'tis a plan not very compatible with the nature of the trade they carry on. . . .' Indeed, it was not. You cannot go on a smuggling expedition with naval escort. And even the rice trade admitted of no waiting for a convoy to collect. The habit of putting the blame on the naval commander-in-chief was also of some antiquity. There was a complaint in the *Bengal Gazette* of 1781 of the bay being infested with French privateers, reigning unmolested to the great impediment of trade; 'But the A——l seems deaf to every complaint of this kind . . . however if he so barefacedly neglects this part of his duty. . . .' etc., etc. The problem was no new one.

Pellew was convinced that the oft-discussed expedition to the Isle of France was the only means of putting an end to the French privateering activities. On 4th January, 1806, he sent a proposal for such an expedition to the Governor-General. Sir George Barlow, who had automatically succeeded to the office on the death of Cornwallis, was not the man to listen to such a project. According to Hickey, he was 'a compound of meanness and pride without a particle of genius'; and, whether this description is accurate or not, he was certainly filled with a fanatical parsimony where the Company was concerned. It was a rare quality, with much to commend it in domestic affairs; but in war a rigid economy is apt to defeat its own ends. When the Hon. Philip Dundas wrote from Prince of Wales Island in 1805, asking for funds with which to improve the defences of Fort Cornwallis, and especially for more troops and more artillery, he received a reply which may be taken as typical of Barlow's mood. The Governor-General began by stating his fears that 'the utmost exertion of public Credit, added to the whole of our Resources, will not enable us to meet even these Demands which we know to be certain and unavoidable' and ended by refusing to send reinforcements *until peace was made*. It is hardly to be wondered at that Pellew should receive a similar reply a few months later. There was no money for such enterprises, and there was an end of it.

Barlow was exceptional in his anxiety for the Company's finances. Most officials in India were quite content to let things slide; and most would have agreed in the policy of attacking the French islands—if only through being personally interested in the country trade. But Barlow had the support, and indeed the positive orders, of the Court of Directors, with which to repel all warlike proposals. And here it must be observed that the Company, as such, suffered little at the hands of the privateers. Indiamen could usually look after themselves where mere privateers were concerned. On 28th November, 1805, for example, the *Admiral Gardner* beat off the *Jeune Adele*, privateer of 32 guns, after nearly two hours' fighting. It was among the country trade that the havoc was wrought. The directors were not altogether deaf to complaints from Calcutta, but they were sufficiently cool on the subject to delay action in the hope that the expedition might be undertaken by the home Government. And what, after all, was more likely, considering that the Cape of Good Hope was sure to be attacked sooner or later?

On receiving from Barlow a reply in which financial difficulties and the orders of the Court were pleaded, and the suggestion made that the islands should rather be attacked by an expedition from England, Pellew did not fail to pass on the idea to the Admiralty. He enclosed a copy of his own original proposal with his dispatch of 12th February, 1806, and declared himself well assured that,

> . . . altho the limitations under which the Governor General is placed, may not permit of his accepting of such an offer of co-operation, the dispossession of the French from the Isles of France and Bourbon, can alone secure the safety of the British Commerce in the Indian Seas from these depredations which it is otherwise so difficult to restrain, and to which, from Considerations of Commercial Insurance, the Country Trade is voluntarily exposed, by the eagerness of the Owners to anticipate early Markets for their Cargoes, at the hazard of Capture.
>
> (P.R.O. Adm. 1/177.)

Thwarted in his desire for a combined expedition, and well aware that no purely naval attack could make any impression on the French base,

Pellew did his best to maintain the blockade. To this end, he sent the *Russel*, *Duncan* and *Psyche* to relieve the *Pitt* and *Terpsichore*. It was a hopeless enterprise, for what Osborn failed to do with four ships was hardly to be done by his successor with three. A squadron of six sail was necessary, if, indeed, the islands could be blockaded at all. And, as such a force would have to be relieved periodically by another squadron of equal strength, Pellew could have made the blockade effective by devoting his entire squadron to the task but in no other way. It may be doubted whether his reduced force would have been sufficient, even had there been no other duties to perform. Taking into account the continual need for refitting and docking, a squadron of fourteen or fifteen sail can seldom have had an effective strength of twelve. As it was, there were other duties to attend to, and it was as much as Pellew could do to keep three ships off the Isle of France, with another three in readiness to relieve them.

At Prince of Wales Island, meanwhile, Troubridge was striving to collect his squadron. His minor grievances included, at first, an ignorance of where Pellew had gone and why. He also complained that all his ships had been dispatched elsewhere, and he himself left stranded without his flagship and without his squadron. He occupied himself in studying Penang's resources as a naval base. This was the period when Penang, or Prince of Wales Island, was being developed as the eastern base of the divided East Indies command. The idea originated from Henry Dundas. who in 1805 had influence over both Admiralty and India House. The settlement was made a presidency and was also to be made a dockyard.[1] Thus, in February 1806, Philip Dundas, the governor, informed the Court of Directors of his intention '. . . of laying down the keel of a large Frigate, without delay' with expectation of a 74-gun ship to follow. On 29th March, 1806, Troubridge wrote to Lord Sidmouth:

> I am still shut up here by Sir E. Pellew . . . but I have not been idle. . . .
> I have just returned from a *thirteen hours* row and sail along the Coast and
> up the River looking at Timber; by *way of treat*, I took the Governor
> with me—the Thermometer 93. I am so well season'd that it does not

[1] *Journal of the Malayan Branch of the Royal Asiatic Society*, Vol. XXIII, Part 2, March 1950. *Early Penang and the Rise of Singapore*, 1805–1832, C. D. Cowan, pp. 26, 29 *et seq.* Although the whole episode savours of jobbery, the appointment of Mr. Philip Dundas was not unreasonable. He had been a sailor and had commanded the H.C.S. *Melville Castle* —a significantly named ship—for three voyages between 1787 and 1790. His uncle, Henry Dundas, had then secured his appointment as Master Attendant at Bombay where (according to Farington) 'he had £10,000 a year and accumulated £70 or £80,000.' After making a good marriage in England he was sent out to the Penang governorship which was created for him. But for the building up of a naval base he was not ill-qualified. See *East Indiamen*. Sir Evan Cotton, pp.178–9.

effect me. I see nothing to hinder us from launching 74-gun ships, frigates and sloops. . . .

There were in fact several hindrances he did not see; and the joke of taking Philip Dundas in search of timber was rather spoilt by the latter's death in 1807. The plans for shipbuilding were shelved in 1809 and the Government at Penang eventually placed on a less ambitious and more economical establishment.

While Troubridge explored Penang, the *Blenheim* meanwhile reached Macao on 16th December, 1806, having gone with her convoy by the Straits of Macassar. The *Cornwallis*, *Phaeton* and *Harrier* operated in the China Seas and the *Lancaster* arrived to act as escort for the China fleet on its voyage to St. Helena. This convoy was very much delayed in 1806, and it was not until April 2nd that Troubridge sailed to protect the last division of Indiamen. By that time he had recovered the *Blenheim*, and sent the *Lancaster* off with thirteen of the China ships. There were four more to come, and Troubridge determined to meet them off Pulo-Aur with the *Blenheim*, *Sir Edward Hughes* and *Harrier*. He intended to proceed afterwards to the Coromandel coast, but all his plans were upset on April 6th. For on that day the *Blenheim* grounded on a sandbank in the Straits of Malacca. As luck would have it, this disaster took place at high water, on a spring tide. Troubridge and his crew worked for days, trying to heave her off at every flood, and in the end they succeeded. The ship's water was started soon after she went ashore and the heavy stores heaved overboard soon afterwards. A raft was made to take other stores to the *Sir Edward Hughes*. Then the guns and shot were jettisoned. The ship still lay inert, and, by the third day, the situation seemed hopeless, with the ship heeling over in but seven feet of water at low tide with an equal depth of water in her hold. Her masts were next cut away. This righted her, and she was floated again on the 10th, to return, crippled, to Penang. The indomitable Troubridge saved what he could of her stores and then set to work to carry out repairs.

There was a certain fatality attending Troubridge in his last years. It so happened that the *Blenheim* had been built as a 90-gun ship in 1761, and reduced to a third-rate only in 1801. She had still the under-water dimensions of a three decker. She was consequently some few inches too long to enter the old dock at Bombay—a fact which was known.[1] The new dock would have taken her, but was not yet completed. It was only in a state of forwardness, as Pellew reported at about that time. The only way to repair the *Blenheim's* hull was to heave her down where she was,

[1] See p. 144.

at Penang. The difficulty had been foreseen to the extent of sending out the necessary tackle for the purpose. But careening does a wooden ship no good after she has been at sea for forty-five years; that is to say, it may stop the leaks but will also weaken the frame. To Troubridge, a man of St. Vincent's school, the word 'cannot' was unknown. His motto was not to make difficulties, and he duly set to work. But Pellew wrote to the Admiralty 'I much doubt whether the *Blenheim* can be considered fit for any Active Service.' It was a conclusion which events were to justify.

Pellew quitted Bombay on February 23rd, and was off Point de Galle on March 16th, supervising the departure of the convoy for England. He was joined by the *Pitt* and *Terpsichore*, returning from the Isle of France, the one with a hundred and twenty men on the sick list with scurvy, the other damaged by going ashore and lacking most of her guns, which had been jettisoned. Sending them to Bombay to refit, he came into Madras roads on March 22nd. There, on April 17th, he received a reinforcement in the shape of the *Powerful* (74). Sir John Duckworth, cruising with a squadron off the C. de Verde Islands, had sighted, without being able to overtake, a French squadron of six sail of the line. Judging that they were bound for the East or West Indies, he had at once detached the *Powerful* to warn and reinforce Pellew, while he himself intended to sail for Barbados. On the 22nd a convoy arrived from England with the *Belliqueux*, a 64-gun ship which came to take the place of the *Tremendous*. She brought no news, but on the 30th a gun-brig appeared from the Cape of Good Hope, bearing the tale of the capture of that settlement, together with further but more doubtful intelligence of the French squadron from Brest. Pellew made his arrangements for meeting the danger. The detachment off the Isle of France already had orders to fall back on Madras if threatened by superior forces, and it was there that Pellew meant to concentrate. Not having heard of the *Blenheim's* misfortune, he hoped to add her to his strength as soon as she should arrive.

No further news arrived of the French danger, but on July 29th a dispatch arrived which interested Pellew as much as could any intelligence of the enemy. It was from the Admiralty, acknowledging his various memoranda on the division of the command. It conveyed no decision, but the mere fact that judgment was suspended was wholly in his favour. If the Cabinet were considering the question, his arguments were fairly certain to carry the day. The risk had been that the matter should be treated, first and foremost, as a breach of discipline. St. Vincent, for example, had he been in power, would have refused to discuss the points at issue. He would have said that the question was, whether orders were to be obeyed or not; and this was a question on which he had made up his mind at an early stage in his career. Events, however, were shaping themselves in Pellew's favour. Melville was ruined and Pitt was dead, and from impartial minds Pellew knew what kind of decision was to be expected.

During the summer of 1806 an event occurred which might have seemed to postpone indefinitely all chance of an expedition from India against the French islands. This was the mutiny at Vellore. During its crisis, the marines of the squadron were landed to occupy Fort St. George while the regular garrison hastened to the scene of the massacre. The outbreak itself was soon suppressed, but the anxiety which resulted from it, and the possibility of the French being encouraged thereby to attempt an invasion, were enough to impose a policy of caution for years to come. So Pellew had to maintain the blockade of Mauritius as well as he could. The *Russel* was relieved by the *Albion* and the *Albion* by the *Sceptre*. Nevertheless, the news was not good. Two new French frigates had arrived at the Isle of France, the *Piémontaise* (40) and *Cannonière*. The *Piémontaise* was a fine new frigate built in 1802–3. Epron, her commander, said of this ship, 'il est impossible d'avoir de meilleur qualités que cette frègate.' The *Cannonière* (48) had been the English *Minerve* captured after grounding near Cherbourg in 1803—originally a French ship, however. These, the *Semillante* (32), and the privateers continued to enter and leave port, and there seemed no way of preventing them. An Indiaman, moreover, the *Warren Hastings*, was taken by the first-named frigate and brought into Port Louis with impunity.

As for the privateers, four of the most formidable were taken during the period 1805–6. But it was already clear that taking them did little to reduce their numbers. The men who manned them had to be exchanged in order to obtain the release of English prisoners, who were ill-treated at the Isle of France and could not in humanity be left there. The ships themselves, if sold, were bought by neutrals and resold to the French 'armateurs.' Discovering this, the Admiral bought into the service such larger ships as the *Bellone*; while the smaller craft were sometimes sunk or burnt. But this was no final solution to the problem. Captured English merchantmen were turned into privateers and specially built vessels sent out from France. There was no method of discouraging them. Indeed, the men of Port Louis were, in a manner, forced to engage in this kind of enterprise. There was nothing else for them to do. The English blockade was at least effective enough to prevent much trading, except through the neutrals. And it may be added that the neutrals, who were also the receivers of stolen goods, were always ready to supply information as to where the richest prizes were to be found. Port Louis, again, was a slave-trading port, and the history of Liverpool shows how readily the slaver turned into a privateer. The two occupations were alike in demanding courage; and, of the two, privateering was perhaps the less dangerous.

October 1806 found Pellew still at Madras and still in ignorance as to the Admiralty's final decision, or at any rate without any official communication on the subject. But he was confident now that his action was approved, and was making his plans accordingly. Rumour was still rife of the approach of a French squadron from Europe.

> A report which was now prevalent throughout the British possessions in India occasioned considerable anxiety and alarm, especially amongst the mercantile people. This was that Jerome Bonaparte, brother to the tyrant of France, with a powerful squadron of ships of war, had escaped the vigilance of the British Fleet and had arrived in the Indian Seas, being at that time in the Dutch port of Batavia; it was further said that the fleet had brought out upwards of two thousand military men! The whole, however, turned out to be utterly without foundation, probably fabricated by some of the French emissaries resident in Calcutta, of which description of persons it was well known there was a great number. . . .

The above is Hickey's account, more valuable as gossip than history. The ubiquity of enemy spies is presumably well known in every war. To detect espionage is a sport beloved of the civilian mind. But, as far as is known, Decaen relied for information on the French agent at the Danish colony of Tranquebar. Hickey is again at fault in stating that the rumour was utterly baseless. Two French squadrons had in fact escaped, and one (under Willaumez, not Jerome) had gone as far as St. Helena. This was not on the usual route to the West Indies, and it is not to be wondered at if rumour would have it that the squadron was bound to the eastwards.

These reports made a certain impression on Pellew, the more so because the news he had received officially was, in the main, corroborative. It would also be true to say that he was very willing to be impressed. Rumours of a threatened French offensive were enough to constitute that state of emergency which justified his retaining the ships of the line under his command; a state which he had held to exist ever since Troubridge arrived. He was eager, again, to find some excuse for an attack on Batavia. His career demanded that his name should appear prominently in the *Gazette* from time to time, and Batavia offered the best opportunity for a certain and easy success. It may be asked what Batavia had to do with the expected French squadron; to which the answer must be that such a squadron might seek the co-operation of Hartsinck. It is not a very convincing answer.

Nevertheless, Pellew did not hesitate to use this argument when writing to the Admiralty. The Dutch, he held, should be dealt with to prevent them joining actively with the French. And the French, he thought, if they came out to the East, would begin their campaign by attacking the China fleet. This would necessitate a call at Batavia. Hence it behoved him to be there before them.

How far Pellew was serious in suspecting the Dutch must remain in doubt. In March of that year he had written that 'unless effectual support shall be given to it from Europe, and the nature of that officer's orders be very essentially changed, a reasonable assurance may be entertained of no Active Operations being undertaken by the Dutch Admiral from Batavia. . . .' This conclusion was supported by local information and intercepted letters between Hartsinck and the Dutch Government, and there was no apparent reason why he should change his mind on the subject. Moreover, his anxiety for his own fame was open and undisguised. When abandoning the idea of attacking Batavia in October 1805 he took credit for his lofty motives: '. . . altho impressed with the most sanguine expectation of success, I hesitated not a moment to surrender every anticipated prospect of personal reputation. . . .' On the other hand, a phrase in one of his letters to Admiral Markham—'I shall take the chance of Batavia and act accordingly. If the French squadron should be there, don't be alarmed for us. . . .'—seems to indicate a real belief in the French menace. It was a subject on which he was perhaps willing to be credulous.

Pellew sailed from Madras on October 22nd, with the *Culloden*, *Powerful*, *Russel*, *Belliqueux*, *Terpsichore* and *Seaflower*. At Trincomalee the homeward bound convoy was collected, fifteen of the smaller Indiamen and extra ships, which Pellew intended to protect on the first stage of the voyage. He saw them across the line as if he had been intent on making a southern passage to Bombay, and then, leaving them to the care of the *Woolwich*, a man-of-war sent out from England for the purpose, he turned eastwards and made for the Straits of Sunda. He was, in a sense, invading Troubridge's province, even as defined by himself, but news had come before he sailed which made it safe to do so. The news was that Troubridge was to be transferred to the Cape, which was to be a separate station as it had been under Curtis during the last war, and that he, Pellew, was to be restored to his full command. This intelligence was authentic, though not official, and it was very much what Pellew had been expecting for some months. It was a sound solution of the problem, doing justice to the one Admiral without disgracing the other. The establishment, moreover, of a Cape squadron was clearly a step towards blockading the Mauritius from the Cape and not from India; an admirable plan, according to Pellew's ideas. Troubridge showed somewhat less enthusiasm.

The Dutch squadron Pellew was bent on destroying consisted of the following ships, or had done so until recently: *Revolutie* (70), *Schrikerrwekker* (70), *Pluto* (70) and *Kortenaar* (70); *Pallas* (36), *Maria Riggersbergen* (36) and *Phoenix* (36); *Aventurier* (18), *William* (14), *Maria Wilhelmina* (14), *Zee Ploeg* (14) and a number of armed vessels belonging

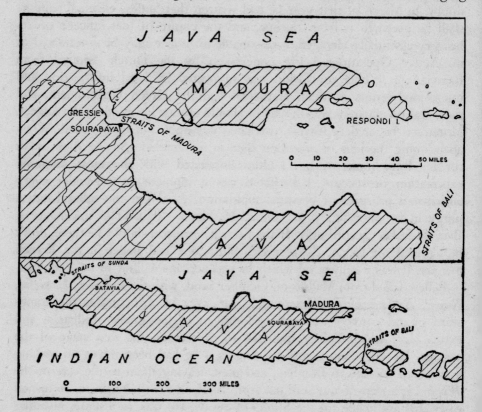

to the Dutch East India Company. On paper the squadron looked formidable enough. But various circumstances had somewhat modified Hartsinck's real strength before Pellew arrived. Of the ships of the line, the second had been wrecked and the fourth turned into a sheer-hulk. The remaining two were not at Batavia but, like the *Kortenaar*, at Gressie. They lay there undergoing repairs, partly because they needed repairs and partly to be out of harm's way in case the English should raid Batavia. Of the frigates, the first and second had been taken by Troubridge's squadron, the one in July and the other in October, and the third was dismantled. The smaller craft, used for police work among the islands, were tolerably effective but too small to be of much use in warfare. Altogether, there were materials for a theoretical naval victory but not for a genuine struggle.

Being joined by the *Sir Francis Drake*, Pellew swept through the Straits of Sunda, caught the *Maria Wilhelmina* off Bantam, and came into Batavia roads on November 27th. Practically all the ships in harbour instantly ran on shore. The boats of the squadron then went in and set fire to them. The corvette *William* remained afloat and was taken, but she was afterwards destroyed as valueless. The *Phoenix, Aventurier, Zee Ploeg*, five armed vessels of the Company, and some twenty merchantmen were burnt, as was also the dockyard and the establishment on the island of Onroost. The attack was led by Pellew's younger son, Fleetwood, made post-Captain (aged seventeen) in the *Terpsichore*. A proud father wrote afterwards to a friend:

He led the squadron thro' Sunda and to Batavia with the greatest judgment, was never at fault. . . . He placed his ship ag't the Dutch Frigate and Batteries with equal skill . . . upwards of 100 pieces of Cannon were opened at once on the boats—and in three minutes after they boarded the *Phoenix* of 36 Guns, she was in full action ag't her old friends and protecting his boats while firing at the ships. He fought her until the water overflowed her magazine, as they had scuttled her. I assure you, a prettier exploit I never saw. You will say, Aye, Aye, here is the Father. I have therefore done— but I assure you I say not half what others say of him. And so let it rest; it is great comfort to see that one has not reared a bevy of Pigeons. I assure you that my Eyes ran over and my heart swelled when I heard a general shout on board the *Culloden* from the lookers on when the Dutch frigate opened her fire under British Colours over Dutch—Well done, Fleetwood— well done, bravo—was the cry all around me. What Father could have kept his Eyes dry? I was obliged to wipe them before I could look again thro' the Glass. . . . It was a pretty Command, 24 boats in three divisions towing each other until just within reach of Grapeshot, where they all rested to take breath and cast off, and with three cheers off they set thro' shot and shells of all sorts, flank'd by two ships of 20 Guns on each side, the spare bowman standing erect waving his cutless over his head, all the officers standing with drawn swords—I never saw such a rush. . . . Now you will ask, what have you got by this. I answer little or nothing. I think if we had had 500 Troops we should have carried Batavia. We burnt about half a Million or more— bro't off scarcely anything—£500 may be my share, and that I shall present to my dear Fleetwood—he is a nice boy to do this at 17; but don't mention his age for your life, he is full 30 in discretion, sense and manners. . . .

. . . You will naturally conclude I am in high spirits, and have nothing to do. That latter is true, for this day: When walking in the stern gallery and bringing to my mind all my dear friends at Home, I thought I would sit down, broiling as I am with heat, and write you a long letter, and here it is, puffing as I go, pens dried up, ink scarcely to be moved upon paper and a hand half shaking. . . .[1]

Pellew afterwards ascertained where the missing ships were, the *Revolutie* and *Pluto*, collected what information he could concerning the state of the Dutch possessions in general, and then sailed again on December 1st. He left the *Powerful* in the vicinity to make further inquiries, sent three ships to Trincomalee and two to cruise to the eastward, and proceeded in person to the Straits of Malacca.

While off Malacca itself on 1st January, 1807, he at last received the order reappointing him to the sole command in the East Indies. He was instructed to detach two ships of the line, one to be of 64 guns, for service under Troubridge. He at once proceeded to Penang in the hope of finding Troubridge there, with whom he could make the necessary arrangements relative to his departure. He was disappointed. Arriving at Penang on January 11th, he found that Troubridge had gone. It was scarcely to be wondered at. After their period of bitter rivalry the loser had no wish to meet his successful enemy. Troubridge had not even written to Pellew. He had no sooner received his orders to go to the Cape than he went off in a fury, hoping never to see Pellew again. He never did see him again.

Troubridge sailed from Penang on December 7th, and arrived at Madras on the 19th. By his own account, he had expected to find Pellew there, and only decided to proceed to the Cape on hearing that he was not expected for two or three months. The need for haste which he put forward was the absence of any naval protection at the Cape, most of the ships from there having been taken to Buenos Ayres. That his real motive was a fear of meeting Pellew seems more than probable, for the manner of his departure verged on the insane. The *Blenheim* was utterly unfit for the voyage and leaking so badly that the pumps were kept going even as she lay at anchor. Her captain protested against going to the Cape at that time of year, which would necessitate being off the French islands during the hurricane months. The ship was almost falling to pieces. Troubridge had his way, however, and sailed on January 12th. He took with him the *Harrier* and *Java*, the latter ship in little better case than the *Blenheim*, and left a letter for Pellew explaining that he did so in order to have the means of communicating with India and Europe.

---

[1] *Edward Pellew, Viscount Exmouth*, p. 374, *et seq.*

Pellew did not linger at Penang, but sailed at once for Madras in search of Troubridge. Had he arrived in time, he would almost certainly have prevented the *Blenheim* sailing. He would have compelled Troubridge to delay his voyage or go in another ship. But Troubridge sailed on the day after Pellew went in search of him and ten days before the *Culloden* arrived. When he did arrive, Pellew presently wrote to Troubridge, informing him that the *Lancaster* and *Sceptre* were under orders to join him, but that the latter would need to refit at Bombay after returning from her station off the Isle of France. He also promised to send the *Greyhound* to the Cape—that being the frigate commanded by Troubridge's son—as soon as the *Java* should return to India. His intention was kindly, but it was kindness thrown away. For Troubridge was caught in a heavy gale off the south-east end of Madagascar on February 1st, the *Blenheim* and *Java* sinking with all hands and the *Harrier* having a narrow escape. The last-named vessel was able to report having last seen the *Blenheim* on the evening of the 1st, when she was visibly settling in the water, with a signal of distress flying.

Considering this last circumstance, it is curious to note how persistent were the rumours of the *Blenheim* having survived the gale. The state of the *Harrier*, which had several ports stove in, her rigging blown to pieces and gear washed overboard, and had been compelled to jettison four of her guns, would hardly have seemed to encourage such a belief. Pellew heard in June that the *Blenheim* and *Java* were still missing as late as May, and he accordingly sent Troubridge's son to make inquiries—under a flag of truce—at the Isle of France and the settlements in Madagascar. Meanwhile, it was confidently reported in England that the *Blenheim* was already in port: 'We are happy to state, that the safety of the *Blenheim*, Admiral Troubridge's flagship, has been ascertained' (*Naval Chronicle*). And again, in the *Calcutta Monthly Journal* for January 1808, it was very definitely stated that the *Blenheim* and *Java* had survived the gale and afterwards touched at the island of St. Mary's, near Madagascar. Natives there were said to have described them with some accuracy when questioned by the officers of the *Greyhound*. This, in turn, gave rise to the legend that the disappearance of the *Blenheim* was due to the subsequent mutiny of her crew. It is this legend which is enshrined in the more or less libellous pages of the novel called *The Port-Admiral*. However, whatever may have been the fate of the unfortunate Troubridge, his removal had solved a difficulty. The year 1807 saw the East Indies Command once more united under a single Admiral, and the good effects were soon apparent.

CHAPTER XV

Pellew and Decaen

ON being restored to the sole command, Pellew found himself with some twenty-eight men-of-war under his orders, apart from those he had to send to the Cape. In February 1807 they were distributed as follows: The *Powerful* (74), with the frigates *Drake* and *Terpsichore*, was near Batavia; the *Belliqueux* (64) was at Penang and the *Victor* (18) on the coast of Sumatra; the frigates *Caroline*, *Cornwallis*, *Hughes* and *Phaeton* were in the China Seas. There were thus nine ships to the eastward. The *Culloden*, *Psyche*, *Wilhelmina*, *Macassar*, *Dasher*, *Rattlesnake* and *Seaflower*—the flagship, three frigates, two sloops and a cutter—were stationed at various points round the Bay of Bengal. The *Bombay* (32) was off Point de Galle. The *Albion*, *Russel*, *Grampus* (50), the frigates *Pitt*, *Bellone*, *Concorde*, *Duncan*, *Dedaigneuse* and *San Fiorenzo*, and the sloop *Albatross* were all either at or near Bombay or else bound thither. The frigate *Fox* was busy taking the Persian envoy back to Bussorah. This was an even distribution of force—nine to the eastward, eight in the Bay, eleven to the westward—and was intended for purposes of cruising and trade protection. There was no longer any fear of invasion.

Pellew returned from Batavia full of plans for the conquest of Java. He had been impressed by the feeble resistance he had encountered and was confident that, with a small military force, he could speedily add the Dutch possessions to the British Empire. He accordingly sent a long memorandum on the subject to Sir George Barlow. It was dated from Madras, January 28th, and had probably been written on the voyage there from Penang. The chief point he emphasized was the danger of Batavia coming directly under French control.

> My attention has been more especially directed to this object from the recent establishment of a French Sovereignty in Holland and the expectation of a New Government being formed at Batavia under the principles of the present rulers of that unhappy Country, which may probably place the affairs of the Dutch in India upon a very different footing, and give a more active disposition to their measures than heretofore.

The system of Military inactivity so long persisted in by the Batavian Government, from political considerations of Commercial security, promise to be exchanged for those of Active hostility against our China Trade. The attention of the Government, henceforward directed by the authority of France, will be doubtless turned to that object, and the situation of Batavia will afford such opportunities of threatening the Commerce of the China Seas, as to endanger the safety of the Honble Company's Ships employed in that Trade, and considerably embarrass the British interests in that quarter.

A new Governor General was then daily expected at Batavia from Europe and much anxiety was entertained on that account by the old Inhabitants of the Settlement, who, I confidently learn, are extremely averse from the French Interest. . . .

It appears to me worthy of our particular attention to consider the expediency of dispossessing the Dutch from Batavia before the measures of the New Government shall have given vigour and Activity to their authority there, and before any active operations against our Trade, probably even now in contemplation in Europe, shall have actually commenced.

(P.R.O. Adm. 1/178.)

The memorandum dwells on the Dutch jealousy of the French, on the recent rebellions of the natives at Samarang and elsewhere, and on the feebleness of the garrison of Batavia. The objections answered include that of the unhealthiness of the place, which Pellew thought had been exaggerated, and the cost of an expedition, which he thought would be inconsiderable. The force to be sent need number no more than two thousand, half to be Europeans; so that the objections to the expedition to the Mauritius did not apply. Finally, if the scheme were rejected, it would surely be possible to send troops sufficient for a landing to destroy the two ships up the river at Griessie.

Pellew was a very able officer; but he was not a born advocate. What he failed to see was that the two parts of his argument tended to cancel out. If the Dutch were so feeble, so distracted by native risings, and so ill-affected towards the French that a handful of troops could subdue them, there was surely nothing to be feared from their hostility. Where, on the other hand, he was certainly in the right was in contending that Java should be attacked at once if it was to be attacked at all. The impending French Governor-General could not do much offensively unless he brought a squadron with him; and that he could hardly do without Pellew receiving warning in good time. But he could clearly improve the defences of the island, so as to make its capture more difficult in the future.

The reply from Fort William was dated February 14th, and was very much what Sir George Barlow might have been expected to write. In questioning the reality of the dangers Pellew described, he was probably right; but it was the financial aspect which aroused his eloquence.

> Our perfect reliance on your Excellency's distinguished judgement and discretion preclude any hesitation in confiding to your Excellency's knowledge the actual condition of the Company's finances in India, the burthen upon which still presses with such accumulated weight that no consideration inferior to the utmost supposable emergency could justify the adoption of any measure involving even a temporary augmentation of Expenditure to any considerable amount, or relieve us from the obligation to prosecute with unremitting solicitude the reduction of the public charges. . . .
>
> The rumour of a distant expedition might materially impair the public Credit and frustrate the Efforts now in progress for the relief of our financial difficulties. But any considerable Expenditure beyond the extent of the ordinary demands of the publick Service, would not only be inconsistent with the principles of Economy and reduction which we are indispensably required and pledge to pursue, but would in its immediate operation be highly embarrassing. . . .

Another potent reason Barlow had to urge was the Vellore mutiny or rather the possibility of a fresh outbreak if any considerable number of white troops were withdrawn from India. And, last of all, there were the orders of the Court of Directors prohibiting any such expedition, which were still in force. The dispatch ends, however, with an offer to co-operate in the destruction of the ships at Griessie.

If the question had been merely whether the French menace was such as to justify an expedition to Java, there can be no doubt that Barlow was right. But there was also involved the more general problem as to whether it would be worth while to turn the Dutch out of the Spice Islands. Nor can much weight be given to Pellew's opinion on the subject. His motives were too obvious. He wanted fame and he wanted money. Rainier, when only a Commodore, had made his fortune in dollars, cloves and nutmegs when he took Amboyna and Banda in 1796. Pellew had so far made practically nothing—some £4,000, to be exact, which barely covered his outfit expenses. As for the widening of the bounds of Empire, he probably cared not a farthing one way or the other. One of his first comments on coming to India was that we seemed to be doing there exactly what we hated Napoleon for doing in Europe. Barlow, on the other hand, cared a great deal. With the mind of a merchant, he thought that the Company had far too much territory as it was. There was something to be said for his point of view. And there was also something to be said for the point of view of his critics who repeated Clive's maxim 'To stop is dangerous, to recede is ruin.' But there seems to be nothing whatever to say for the course actually adopted; which was, to alarm the Dutch by a futile raid, give them three or four years in which to improve their defences, capture their islands with four times the force originally needed, and finally hand them back at the end of the war.

If Pellew was at all cheered to have gained his point about destroying those two wretched ships at Griessie, he soon had a better cause for self-congratulation. He left Madras in February in order to pay a visit to Bombay, where he arrived on the 28th. He was still there in April when the great news came that the *Caroline*, Captain Rainier, had taken the Spanish register ship *San Raphael* in the Straits of St. Bernadine. She was out of Lima and bound for Manila with half a million in dollars and a valuable cargo, mainly of copper. Pellew deserved his share, about £26,000, at least as much as most Admirals can have done. For the trap was of his setting, and the galleon would have fallen to some other frigate if she had not encountered the *Caroline*. As for the actual captor 'Rainier of 22 who took her was 13 Months ago a Mid—he has since married, taken very handsomely a frigate, and now pocketts full 50,000 l.' The price paid for this cruising to the eastward was in scurvy. At least one of the frigates returned with hardly enough men on deck to work her. Four of the ships lost a hundred men between them, and more invalided afterwards.

It was unusual for an Admiral to be at Bombay in April, but Pellew could not very well omit his annual visit, for there was much for him to do. A brig was purchased, a prize to the *Sceptre*, and named the *Diana*. The *Albatross* was condemned and sold to be broken up. A new frigate was hauled out of dock and named the *Salsette*. Having attended to the various affairs requiring his decision, Pellew sailed again for Madras at the end of the month. His forces now comprised:

Culloden	(74)	Cornwallis	(44)	Wilhelmina	(32)
Albion	(74)	Phaeton	(38)	Macassar	(32)
Russel	(74)	Duncan	(38)	Terpsichore	(32)
Powerful	(74)	Drake	(36)	Fox	(32)
Belliqueux	(64)	Modeste	(36)	Bombay	(32)
Arrogant		Salsette	(36)	Dedaigneuse	(32)
(sheer hulk)		St. Fiorenzo	(36)	Bellone	(28)
		Psyche	(36)	Dasher	(18)
		Caroline	(36)	Rattlesnake	(18)
		Hughes	(36)	Victor	(18)
		Concorde	(36)	Seaflower	(14)
		Pitt	(36)	Diana	(12)
		Greyhound	(32)		

In June 1807, when Pellew returned to Madras, four ships were laid up for repairs at Coringa or Bengal. The chief detachments were to the eastward; one, consisting of the *Russel*, three frigates and a cutter, was assembling by degrees at Macao; another, consisting of the *Albion* and *Belliqueux*, a frigate and two sloops, was based on Penang. The *Psyche* and *Caroline* were reconnoitring Java. Eight ships were stationed round the Bay of Bengal, four being at Madras. Three frigates were to the westward, and two, sent to the Cape with convoy, found some excuse to return to England. The *Greyhound* was still seeking traces of the *Blenheim*. It will be noticed that there was now no squadron off the Isle of France. That thankless task had been assigned to the senior officer at the Cape, pending the arrival of an Admiral to take Troubridge's place.

Pellew had now to make preparations for his second visit to Java. Barlow, superseded by Lord Minto in July, was no longer standing between India and bankruptcy. It was probably too late, however, to alter any plans, even had Minto felt so inclined. In discussions between the supreme Government and the Government of Fort St. George, it was eventually decided that five hundred troops of the 30th Regiment should be embarked at Madras, together with some artillery, for the purpose of co-operating in the attack on Griessil. During the summer of 1807, Pellew did what he could to persuade Lord Minto to authorize a bolder plan, but without success. Minto replied that the Government in England was against it, and that any considerable scheme of operations would upset the conversion of Government loans in India. By October the expedition was ready to sail.

His Majesty's Ship *Culloden*
Madras Roads
18th October, 1807.

Sir

  Their Lordships will have been already informed by my Communication under date of 1st February, 1807 of my proposals to the Supreme Government of India, in relation to the Dutch Force in the Island of Java. . . .

  The troops have been embarked in good order yesterday and this morning, the Honble Company's Ship *Worcester* having been taken up for the transport of the Chief part of the Troops, the remainder being put on board His Majesty's Ships *Culloden* and *Powerful*.

Culloden
Powerful
Victor
Samarang (18)

  It is my intention to get under weigh this Evening, or to-morrow morning with the ships named in the margin, augmenting my force by a junction at Prince of Wales Island with His Majesty's Ship *Russel* and two frigates.

In conveying to their Lordships the proposed operation herein mentioned, I cannot forbear from expressing my sincere regret that the want of a sufficient authority from His Majesty's Ministers at home prevents the undertaking of an Expedition of more importance, being entirely satisfied that had the supreme Government of India felt itself at liberty to enter into my original proposal of an attack upon Batavia, that that Capital and every subordinate Settlement of the Dutch on the Island of Java, would have fallen a very easy conquest to a force little superior in comparison to that which has been thus allotted for the execution of a more limited Service. My latest intelligence from that quarter, brought by Captain Fleetwood Pellew, represented the situation of affairs at Batavia as extremely favourable to such an undertaking, the disunion of the French and Dutch Interests being very greatly augmented by the late innovations in that Government, occasioned by the Elevation of Louis Bonaparte to the throne of Holland, as well as by the very sanguinary insurrections which have taken place among the Native Inhabitants, who are extremely averse to the domination of either the French or Dutch Nations.

In making my original proposition to the Governor General I had in view the ultimate destruction of the works, and the abandonment of the City of Batavia, had it fallen into my possession, and the creation of a more healthy establishment at Grissey, or some point to the Eastward. . . .

The Port of Grissey has been carefully reconnoitred by our Frigates, and trust such measures have been taken, as will provide for the assistance of Pilots and other persons of Experience to lead the force to the attack of the place and effectually secure us from disappointment. . . .

(Pellew to Admiralty. P.R.O. Adm. 1/180.)

The sloop *Samarang* mentioned in the above letter as destined to sail with the expedition was a corvette taken from the Dutch by the *Psyche* in the course of her reconnaissance of Java. She was called the *Scipio* when taken, and Pellew bought her into the service for £4,725, paid to the captors. The *Jaseur*, French brig, was bought for £1,794, at about the same time. They were to replace the *Harrier* and *Albatross*.

Sailing from Madras according to plan, Pellew arrived at Penang on November 10th. There he found the *Albion*, *Russel* and *Belliqueux*, with the *Caroline*, *Fox*, *Seaflower* and *Jaseur*. He had changed his mind, however, about adding the *Russel* to his force. With some fear perhaps of what the French cruisers might be doing in his absence, he sent her instead to the Bay of Bengal. The *Belliqueux* was at the same time directed to cruise off

Point de Galle. The *Albion* was in need of docking, and had to go at once to Bombay. Adding the other vessels to those he had brought with him, Pellew reached Malacca on the 19th, and sailed for Griessie on the following day. His squadron consisted now of the *Culloden* (74), *Powerful* (74), *Caroline* (36), *Fox* (32), *Victor* (18), *Samarang* (18), *Seaflower* (14), *Jaseur* (12) and the *Worcester*, transport.

The concealment of the *Revolutie* and *Pluto* up the River Sourabaya might be compared to the concealment in our century of the *Konigsberg*; with this difference, however, that the two Dutch ships had never done any harm, even in their most active days. There seems, also, every reason to suppose that they would have died a natural death if left alone. But the practical problem was not dissimilar, for in either case the difficulty was in reaching the enemy after he had been located. Pellew was at the eastern end of Java by December 5th, and soon discovered that his two ships of the line were prevented by shoal water from ascending the river as high as Griessie. He hopefully summoned the Dutch to surrender. They correctly interpreted this as a sign of weakness and refused. He then lightened the *Culloden* and *Powerful*, heaved them through the shallows and managed to reach Griessie with his whole force, silencing the batteries *en route*. The Dutch promptly asked for terms, first taking the precaution of scuttling the ships under dispute. Terms were thereupon agreed to, under which the *Revolutie*, *Pluto*, *Kortenaar* and *Rusthoff* (Indiaman) were burnt, the batteries destroyed, and water and provisions found for the squadron. In returning to the mouth of the river, it was found that the difficulty experienced in ascending it was due to ignorance more than to any defect in the navigation. Pellew hastened to write his dispatches and 'congratulate their Lordships upon the entire destruction of the Naval Force of Holland in the East Indies.'

His Majesty's Ship *Culloden*
off Grissee 15th Dec. 1807.

Sir

Their Lordships will be informed by my letter of yesterday of the circumstances under which the Dutch Ships of War lying at Grissee have been destroyed. The Government of Sourabaya having furnished me with pilots, the whole of our Squadron have returned in safety to the mouth of this Harbour from whence it is my intention to proceed immediately to Madras by the Straits of Malacca.

The observations which I have had an opportunity of making during my continuance at this place lead me to a very favourable opinion of the value and importance of this Settlement should it hereafter be in the contemplation of His Majesty's Ministers to obtain establishment on the Eastern extremity of Java. The Harbour is perfectly safe and Commodious; well protected from the violence of the periodical Winds, and has no dangers whatever within its limits, the bottom being throughout a soft mud.

I have obtained possession of a very exact Chart of its whole Extent, and the adjacent Coast, the accuracy of which has been fully ascertained by our own experience. . . .

Grissee is capable of being made an excellent Station for the refit of Men of War, where every accommodation might be formed with facility for heaving down. . . .

The Climate of Sourabaya, Grissee, and the circumjacent Country is remarkably healthy, and as such is made the resort of persons sent from Batavia for recovery. The soil is very productive and excellent Teak timber grows in abundance throughout the whole district. Supplies of every kind of provisions are readily obtained from the neighbouring Country. . . .

(Pellew to Admiralty. P.R.O. Adm. 1/180.)

On the subject of Java, Pellew was a little apt to become lyrical; and even his official dispatches read rather like the prospectus of some emigration agent. He seems to have had a fellow enthusiast in Stamford Raffles, from whom, indeed, the idea may have originated. The two men certainly knew each other. But whether Grissie could ever have become of much importance in a modern world which has lost most of its desire for cloves and nutmegs, may well be doubted.

The squadron reached Malacca on 25th January, 1808, to find there the first division of the China fleet, eight Indiamen with the *Cornwallis*. The second division, the direct ships and the *Jupiter*, was not expected to sail from Macao until March. Pellew did not linger in the straits, but pushed on for Madras. The expedition had been, in the main, a disappointment. It was a tame affair. And, what was worse, the Dutch ships from Japan had again somehow escaped him. These vessels shared the celebrity of the *Acapulco* galleon, with an added touch of mystery in that no one seemed to know exactly what they were laden with. Pellew had discovered when they usually returned to Java and had timed his visits accordingly. Each time, however, he missed them by two or three days. They would have been caught on this occasion if Pellew had not allowed the Dutch to pilot him so efficiently (and eagerly) out of Sourabaya River. To obtain more exact information on the subject, Pellew hit on the expedient of sending one of his sons to Japan. By this means, he at least discovered where Nagasaki was. He incidentally founded the Japanese Navy, which had its origin in a fervent desire to prevent anything of the sort ever happening again. The young Pellew's visit, if short, was eventful. (See Appendix F.)

The squadron arrived at Madras on February 10th, and Pellew was at once greeted with two alarming items of news. The first was that a large French army was about to march through Persia to co-operate with a powerful squadron then on its way to the Persian Gulf. This had started, it seems, as a popular rumour which the supreme Government began by contradicting. Its persistence, however—which is not difficult to understand, since it had a substratum of truth—eventually won over the highest officials. The result was that Captain Ferrier, senior officer at Bombay, had been persuaded into sailing for the Persian Gulf on February 6th, with the *Albion*, *Phaeton* and *Dedaigneuse*. And Pellew was met with an urgent demand that he should proceed forthwith to the western side of India, there to await the threatened invasion. Perhaps a little wearily, Pellew agreed. He had been resisting French invasions ever since he arrived in India, and must have been getting a trifle tired of them.

The second item of news concerned the activities of the French cruisers in the Bay of Bengal. It is best told in his own words.

> The Enemy's Cruisers have of late been very successful in their depredations on the Country Trade passing thro' the Bay, tho' they have fortunately not intercepted any of the Company's Ships; their successes are to be attributed in a great measure to the Circumstance of the Masters of these Vessels being in the constant practice of running without Convoy, tho' it has been always afforded upon application, and which has hitherto secured the Company's Ships from Capture. Although not less than six of my ships have been constantly cruizing in the Bay for the protection of the Trade, and intersecting it in every direction, none have had the good fortune to fall in with the Enemy's Cruizers excepting the *Russel*, which captured the *Adele* privateer on the 5 December.
>
> The Isle of France being no longer within the limits of my Station, no information can reach me but by very uncertain Channels respecting the arrival and sailing of the Cruizers, and for the most part, the first Intelligence of their appearance in the Bay is announced by their successes. . . .

(Pellew to Admiralty, 22nd Febuary, 1808. Adm. 1/180.)

With regard to the invasion scare, it is interesting to note that Napoleon was actually considering something of the sort at that time. Seyd Sultan of Oman had died in 1806 and Napoleon may have hoped for better things from the new ruler, Seyd-Said.[1] Apart from that, he was in close touch

[1] Dr. Rouire. 'La question du Golfe Persique,' *Revue des Deux Mondes*, Vol. 16, Paris, 1903, p. 889.

with Persia, and this led to an alliance concluded on 4th May, 1807, following the Battle of Jena and also following Duckworth's repulse in the Dardanelles. Russia and Persia were then at war in Georgia and General Gardanne's mission was to arrange military co-operation between Persia and Turkey. This phase ended when Napoleon came to terms with the Tsar at Tilsit and new plans were made for sending help to Decaen, still with an eye on Persia. On 22nd June, 1807, Napoleon wrote to Decrès from Tilsit:

> Je recois votre mémoire sur la Perse. J'attends, pour faire cette expedition dans le golfe Persique, que j'aie réponse de mon ambassadeur, le général Gardanne, qui est parti avec des officiers de l'artillerie et du génie, et qui doit etre rendu dans ce moment a Constantinople. Je desire que vous envoyiez un ingenieur de la marine qui soit un peu marin, pour lever les plans des cotes. . . . Faites-le partir sans delai. . . . Mon intention est d'envoyer, a le fin de septembre, 2 frégates neuves a l'ile de France; elles auront des instructions pour se rendre dans la golfe Persique, ou elles prendront les depêches de mon ambassadeur. Ecrivez au général Decaen par toutes les voies possible, pour instruire de l'arrivée de mon ambassadeur en Perse, de de mon traité d'alliance avec cet empire, et de la necessité de se mettre en correspondance avec lui.[1]

In some moods he was more than inclined to treat Decaen and his dispatches as something of a joke. One of the many emissaries sent to him from the Isle of France was greeted cheerfully with the words, 'Well, how is Decaen? Bored down there, I suppose?' When he treated the proposals seriously, it was only to reject them. He came nearest, however, to accepting such a scheme in the early months of 1808; that is, at the very time that the Persian scare was at its height. This was partly due to the personality of René Decaen, the General's younger brother.

René was sent off from the Isle of France in September 1807. His mission, like that of previous messengers, was to convince Napoleon of the possibilities of a campaign in India. But he brought knowledge, and complete knowledge, of his brother's plans; which was more, perhaps, than other messengers had done. And, more important still, he carried the news of the sepoy mutinies of 1805–6. Sailing towards the end of the month, he reached Paris by 9th January, 1808. He had an interview with Napoleon on the 27th.

René had been transferred by his brother to the Navy, and had been serving as an officer in the *Piémontaise*. He was probably, therefore, in naval uniform. Napoleon, at any rate, laughed at his appearance and said,

---

[1] *Correspondance de Napoleon avec le Ministre de la Marine 1804–1812.* Extracte d'un portefeuille de Sainte-Helene. Two vols. Paris, 1838. Vol. I, p. 204.

'Hallo, I thought you were your brother's aide-de-camp! And to what regiment of cavalry do *you* belong?' After René had given some explanation, Napoleon asked where the vessel was in which he had come. 'At St. Cyprien? Good. I'll send you back at once.' Then he asked for news of the frigates, remarking that he had sent out two more last October. Satisfied on this point, he suddenly asked, 'Why haven't the English taken the Isle of France?' 'I think,' said René, 'that they have not attacked it so far because, each time they have been about to do so, something has happened to distract their attention in India or Europe.' He added something about Napoleon keeping them so busy elsewhere that they lacked the forces. He supposed that they were waiting for an opportunity. They were not, he thought, still in error as to the strength of the place. An attack would come if the English in India were given time to breathe. 'Oh, that's it?' said the Emperor, 'I have never been able to understand why they didn't take it. It's sheer idiocy on their part. . . .'[1]

In the course of the conversation, Napoleon returned to this point three times, still wondering at the English stupidity. At last he said, 'Come now, tell me frankly, without boasting, how many men would be needed to take the Isle of France? Exactly how many, I mean.' René replied that four or five thousand Europeans, with a few sepoys, could do it easily. Decaen had only twelve or thirteen hundred men—for the militia and black troops were almost worthless. Napoleon said that he really must send Decaen five hundred more men. Two frigates, he thought, and, yes, another five hundred men.

Then it was that René broached the subject of India. Napoleon said that he stood well with the Porte; that he was friendly, too, with the Persians. He might send an army corps overland. . . . True to his new uniform, René pointed out that an attack by sea would arrive sooner, and the English would be unable to concentrate to meet it. 'And where do you think I am going to get the ships?' demanded the Emperor. 'You know very well that I have none. . . .' Many more questions followed. Supposing he was able to find the ships, how could the troops be fed on the voyage, now that the Cape had fallen? René answered all objections so well that he went away thinking the matter settled and the expedition decided upon. It is curious to remember how thoroughly Lord Minto shared this belief.

Although not completely convinced, Napoleon was certainly thinking seriously of a stroke at India. At length, on May 13th, he went so far as to write to Decrès and ask him whether a squadron of three sail of the line and six frigates could be fitted out by September; a squadron to carry four

[1] Henri Prentout. *L'Isle de France sous Decaen*, Paris, 1901.

thousand five hundred men to the Isle of France. Fifteen thousand men were to follow later; and then the whole force was to land in India, perhaps to co-operate with another twenty thousand coming through Egypt. Napoleon begged Decrès not to raise objections and make difficulties. Would he, for once, try instead to suggest expedients? Decrès would not. But it did not matter, for news came almost at once of the risings in Spain. By July Napoleon had decided not to send any considerable force out of Europe. When a small reinforcement was eventually sent, it arrived too late.

As regards the losses in the Bay of Bengal, many of them were due to the arrival in the Indian Seas of the famous privateer Surcouf. It has not been found possible to give here any distinct account of the activities of the French cruisers, whether private or national. The subject is one on which books have been written, but it is not one which lends itself for compression into pages, or even chapters. Some mention, however, must be made of Surcouf; for his successes had certain results which it will be necessary to deal with later.

Surcouf sailed from Saint-Malo on 2nd March, 1807, in a specially designed 18-gun ship called the *Revenant*. He sighted Bourbon on May 31st, evaded the blockading squadron and entered Port Louis on June 10th. Few merchantmen had run the gauntlet for some time past, and the inhabitants were experiencing some mild degree of famine. Surcouf was enthusiastically welcomed, and Decaen suggested that he should try to intercept some of the Bengal rice ships. The corsair agreed and, sailing on September 3rd, arrived off Ceylon a fortnight later. He was soon on the trade route between Bengal and Madras, and successively took the *Trafalgar*, *Mangles*, *Admiral Aplin*, *Susannah* and *Hunter*. All these were rice ships. Having advertised his presence too much—there was by that time an embargo on the shipping in the Hooghli and a price on his head of a lac of rupees—he went to cruise on the Pegu coast for a fortnight. Then, when the scare had a little subsided, he suddenly came back to his old station off the Sandheads. He now took the *Success*, *Fortune*, *New Endeavour*, *Colonel Macaulay*, *William Burroughs*, *Oriente* and *Jean Labdam*. This was a more mixed bag, the last two being neutrals detained for some irregularity in their papers. Some of these craft he released or destroyed. One, the *Admiral Aplin*, went ashore after her capture. The rest were sent to the Isle of France where they all arrived safely, Surcouf himself coming in afterwards on 31st January, 1808.

The *Revenant* was not the only French cruiser operating in the bay in 1807–8. There were others, and notably the frigate *Piémontaise*, which was still cruising successfully when Surcouf returned to his base. Altogether, the damage done was considerable. Pellew, of course, was held to blame for every vessel captured. All the merchants agreed that their losses were entirely due to his negligence. If, they said, he refrained from wasting his time in futile expeditions to Java, he might have ships to spare for the protection of trade. Surcouf had, as a matter of fact, been chased repeatedly during the whole time he was in the bay. His impunity was not caused by an absence of English cruisers, but by the fact of his sailing in one of the fastest vessels afloat. Nevertheless, a scapegoat there had to be. If Pellew could have added to his unpopularity at Calcutta, it was by saying, as he did say, that the merchants were themselves to blame for not accepting convoy.

While Pellew was still at Madras digesting the highly unwelcome news about Persia and about Surcouf, he was pleasantly surprised by the arrival of Rear-Admiral Drury. This was on February 17th. Drury had received orders to go to the East Indies as long ago as August 1807. With instructions to seek Pellew and put himself under his orders, he had hoisted his flag in the *Monmouth* (64) at Spithead on September 8th. With seven Indiamen bound for the coast and two for Bombay, he had touched at Madeira on the 27th, seen the *Piémontaise* in the distance on the 20th January, 1808, and now came to report at Madras, bringing his convoy with him.

Drury's arrival had two pleasing aspects from Pellew's point of view. In the first place, he had asked to be relieved, and was glad to have his successor at hand. He had as yet received no orders to hand over the command, however. The Admiralty's intention was apparently that Drury should learn his business under Pellew before being appointed to succeed him. In the second place, Drury brought with him the news of the impending war between England and Denmark. The dispatches he brought, dated in August and September 1807, directed Pellew to detain and bring into port all ships and vessels belonging to the Crown of Denmark, treating their crews 'with all possible civility and attention and not by any means as Prisoners of War.' The Governor-General had heard the news a few days before, sending troops to occupy the Danish settlements as early as the 12th. Tranquebar capitulated at once without any resistance. It was not for the first time. News of the actual outbreak of war does not seem to have come until about May 16th, but as the Danish shipping, both in Bengal river and at Tranquebar, was detained in the meanwhile, it was a simple matter to make the detention permanent. 'That sturdy dog of Denmark has given me by his obstinacy about fifty thousand pounds,' wrote Pellew on June 1st. He began to feel that he had not come to India in vain.

His Majesty's Ship *Culloden*
at Sea, 22 Feb. 1808

Sir

You will be pleased to state to the Board my arrival at Madras on the 10th instant and that the whole of the ships which accompanied me to the Coast of Java, have safely returned to that Anchorage.

The arrival of Rear Admiral Drury in His Majesty's Ship *Monmouth* to serve under my Flag has afforded me an advantageous opportunity of providing for the Services of this part of my Station during my absence on the Western side of the Peninsula.

The Intelligence which has reached me from the Communications of the Governor General has rendered it advisable to move round without delay to Bombay in readiness to act upon any Emergency which may arise in that quarter.

I have received no Instructions from their Lordships as to the views of the French in Persia by the latest opportunity nor of any projected Naval Expedition towards that Gulph. Accounts very variable and often Contradictory have been circulated in this Country for some time past, and of late have gained considerable strength by the most recent information from Constantinople. The Eyes of the Supreme Government of India have been long directed with much solicitude to the situation of our Affairs in the Gulph, and to the Intrigues of the French Emissaries employed in the promotion of their views at that Court.

A Communication lately received from Captain Hallowell of His Majesty's Ship *Tigre* at Alexandria, announcing the arrival of General Menou with 12000 Men at Constantinople in his way to Persia (whither an advanced number of French Officers had previously proceeded and are stated to have actually arrived at the Capital of Terehann) has greatly augmented the anxiety with which Lord Minto in Council had received the former accounts of their progress. . . .

The Supreme Government having resolved to send Colonel Malcolm on a political mission upon this important juncture to the Gulf of Persia, I have, at the request of the Governor General, received him on board the *Culloden* for a passage to Bombay, from whence he will prosecute his voyage thither, and on my arrival at that Port I shall adopt such immediate measures as may be necessary to meet any future designs of the Enemy, or to co-operate with the wishes and measures of His Lordship in Council. Rear Admiral Drury will meanwile take charge of the Bay of Bengal and communicate with me overland to Bombay during my absence. . . .

(Pellew to Admiralty. P.R.O. Adm. 1/180.)

Drury's flag was transferred from the *Monmouth* to the *Russel*, the former ship being directed to accompany the homeward-bound convoy then about to sail. Drury then went over to Achin and so to Penang, the arrangement being that he should return and meet Pellew at Madras in May or June. The commander-in-chief evidently did not intend to be kept for long by all this nonsense about Persia.

Meanwhile, the homeward-bound convoy was collecting at Point de Galle, detachments of Indiamen arriving there with naval escort from Bengal, Madras and Bombay. Until the Madras contingent arrived, with the *Monmouth*, the convoy was protected by the *Belliqueux*. But three of the Indiamen, from Bombay, sailed for the rendezvous without escort— apparently through being delayed. The *Piémontaise*, French frigate, then cruising in the vicinity, learnt of their sailing from one of the half-dozen prizes she had taken. She therefore lay in wait for them off Cape Comorin. Unfortunately for the French ship, the English frigate *San Fiorenzo* arrived from the opposite direction just as the Indiamen at last appeared, on March 6th. A terrific conflict ensued between the two frigates, which lasted for three days and ended with the surrender of the *Piémontaise*. The *San Fiorenzo* and her prize, both in a shattered condition, came into Colombo on the 12th.

The *Semillante* was also cruising at this time, in the Bay of Bengal. She fell in with the *Terpsichore* between Ceylon and Madras, but escaped after an hour's fighting. As such an encounter was bound to put an end to her cruise, the English squadron had, altogether, done fairly well. Of the three largest French cruisers haunting the coasts of India, one had been taken and one so badly damaged that she had to return to France. Nevertheless, one of the Indiamen waiting at Point de Galle carried a memorial to the Admiralty from the merchants, agents, underwriters and shipowners of Calcutta, complaining bitterly of the way in which commerce was left exposed to the enemy.[1] It was entrusted to Alexander Steward and Michael Prendergast, passengers in the *Castle Eden*, who showed it to their fellow passenger, William Hickey.

Of this memorial there were other copies about besides the original document which Hickey inevitably transcribed as material for his memoirs. More will be said of these later. For the present, Pellew was unaware of the insult intended. He reached Point de Galle on March 8th, together with the *Powerful* and two other men-of-war, and went on at once towards Bombay, leaving the convoy to sail as soon as the *Belliqueux* should be relieved by the *Monmouth*.

[1] 'The favourite expeditions against the Dutch . . . a prostrate, a fallen and passive foe, are attended . . . with no national or public advantage, while at the same time they leave the whole Trade of India exposed to the depredations of an active and enterprizing Enemy.'

Pellew was at Bombay in April, where he seems to have found the threatened invasion through Persia already somewhat discredited. There was, in fact, no further reference to the subject. Colonel Malcolm having been sent to stem the onrush single-handed, the incident was regarded as closed. Its place was at once taken by another matter of equal urgency. This was the Portuguese question. So far, Portugal had been regarded as a friendly neutral power. The occupation of Goa had been ordered in an apologetic spirit. It had taken the outward form of military assistance lent to the Viceroy in order that he might more effectually preserve his neutrality. But now the news came of French designs on Portugal and of the flight of the Portuguese royalty to South America. The English Cabinet was already regarding Portugal as a potential ally of France, as just such another vassal State as Holland. With the news, therefore, came the order to occupy the remaining Portuguese settlements. Preparations were also to be made for turning mere occupation into actual annexation, should need arise. The orders were addressed, of course, to the Supreme Government. The instructions sent to Pellew, which he received on April 24th, were simply to the effect that he was to co-operate with the Indian Governments in taking possession of the settlements in question.

The object of this apparently aggressive policy was mainly defensive. In subordination to France, certain of the Portuguese colonies would be highly dangerous. Those in East Africa, for example, if turned into bases for the French cruisers—which the Portuguese alliance would multiply—would close the Mozambique Channel to English trade. This is the more easily understood when it is recalled how completely the Dutch alliance with France had closed the Straits of Sunda. In the case of East Africa, certain difficulties presented themselves and the matter was still under discussion when the danger disappeared, Portugal becoming the ally of England instead. East Africa, however, though important, was not nearly so obvious a danger as Macao. The French could never seize Goa. They could be ejected if they occupied Diu or Demaun. But Macao was a different matter altogether. To have the French there would end the China trade at a blow.

All that Pellew did at first in response to his orders was to offer his assistance to the Governor of Bombay and send the *Albion* and *Dedaigneuse* to cruise off Goa in case they should be required to overawe the town. On May 26th he was writing to say that he thought Macao could be left alone for the present. He knew its importance, and he also knew that the frigate *Cannonière* was at that moment in the China Seas, operating from

Manila. He knew, for that matter, that there was another French frigate, the *Caroline*, which might easily be sent in the same direction. And other ships might arrive, of course, from France. But, despite all this, he doubted whether the French would ever get possession of Macao. The Chinese, he thought, could be trusted to prevent this.

It was while at Bombay that Pellew heard of the memorial from the merchants of Calcutta. A copy had been sent there with a request that the merchants of Bombay would add their signatures. The Bombay merchants, so far from doing so, brought it to Pellew instead. Soon afterwards, another copy arrived, sent by the Calcutta merchants to Pellew himself with the somewhat unreasonable request that he would take it home with him and deliver it to the Lords of the Admiralty. As he knew from his Bombay friends that the original was already on its way to England, he refused to do anything of the sort. He began to collect materials for his defence. He wrote to the Admiralty, enclosing a resolution in his favour passed by the Bombay merchants. Lord Minto wrote independently to bear witness to his good character. His friends even managed to work up a slight reaction in his favour at Calcutta.

This memorial from the Bengal merchants produced a great deal of controversy and a mass of correspondence. The statements and counter-statements are too bulky and far too complex to be dealt with here. They sufficiently show that the willingness of the Bombay merchants to accept convoy, and the extreme unwillingness of the Calcutta merchants to follow suit, both arose from the character of their business, and not from the character of the merchants. Another fact made apparent in the course of the dispute is the influence wielded by the Calcutta business men in London. Pellew was definitely anxious to justify himself. Although clearly innocent, he began to draw up papers to show where all his ships were in the autumn of 1807. He seems to have been quite worried about the possibility of pressure being brought to bear on the Admiralty by Lloyd's and the India House. Both did, in fact, make some pronouncement against him, the Court of Directors afterwards apologizing, however. It must be remembered in this connection that Pellew was a self-made man. Lord Wellesley once wrote that 'No additional outrage which can issue from the most loathsome den of the India House will accelerate my departure when the public safety shall appear to require my aid.' This is the language of an independent nobleman. But a man like Pellew could not afford to ignore the India House, or even Lloyd's. Fortunately, his case was strong. Lord Minto, moreover, was on his side. The result was that the memorial was ignored. 'I have never heard,' wrote Hickey, 'that this Memorial produced the smallest effect. . . .'[1] It is to the credit of the Admiralty that it did not.

Pellew sailed from Bombay early in June, captured a small French privateer off Point de Galle on the 10th and reached Madras on the 12th. His presence there was now highly necessary in that Lord Minto had finally decided on the occupation of Macao. In his letter of May 9th, he proposed to send the same type of force as contemplated in 1802; five or six hundred sepoys, two companies of European infantry and a company of artillery. He did not anticipate any resistance, and the supercargoes assured him that there would be no trouble with the Chinese. He was in doubt as to whether he should inform the Chinese before or after the deed was accomplished. He wanted to obtain an order from the Viceroy of Goa for the governor of Macao, directing him to admit the garrison on the same terms as at Goa; but this he would have to leave to the last moment, to avoid betraying his intention. Pellew agreed to co-operate, as a matter of course, and proposed to put Rear-Admiral Drury in command of the expedition, having under him a ship of the line, two frigates, and two small craft. At first it was arranged that the expedition should assemble at Madras. On Lord Minto's desiring that Bengal should be the rendezvous instead, Penang was decided upon as a compromise.

As soon as Pellew arrived at Madras, events moved swiftly. He found Drury already there, together with the ships he intended to send on the expedition. By June 17th the Madras Government informed him that the white troops were ready to embark. On the 18th, Pellew gave Drury his orders, which were as follows: His Majesty's Ministers having ordered the occupation of Macao, in order to thwart French designs on it, and he himself being ordered to co-operate, Drury was to take the *Russel*, *Dover*, *Greyhound*, *Diana* and *Jaseur* under his command, and embark the troops at Madras. He was then to proceed to Macao and assist in the occupation, in close conjunction with the Select Committee of Supercargoes. If the Select Committee wished it, and if it should appear advisable, he was to assist in the suppression of piracy at the mouth of Canton river, where the Ladrones were said to be increasing in numbers and activity. Should he find that there was nothing to be done, he was to return to his station at Prince of Wales Island. Pellew wrote on the same day to the Government of Fort St. George, stating that Drury was to sail on the 23rd and requesting that the troops should be embarked at once.

Drury actually sailed on the 24th, the *Dover* sailing two or three days

[1] See *Memoirs of William Hickey*, Vol. IV, p. 410 *et seq.* Also Adm. 1/180 Pellew to Lord Minto, 21st April, 1808, and underwriters to Lord Minto, 7th March, etc.

later and proceeding to Bengal to escort the two Indiamen, *David Scott* and *Alnwick Castle*, in which the sepoys were to embark. These ships rejoined or joined the expedition at Penang, the whole then proceeding to the eastward.

Pellew's time in India was now nearly finished. He had not fared badly in the end. 'My objects here,' he had written in 1806, 'were my two sons.' Both were now post-captains; the elder, Pownall, having made £3,000, the younger, Fleetwood, £5,000, from prize-money. He had probably made £100,000 himself and had the satisfaction of seeing Pownall Pellew married to the eldest daughter of Sir George Barlow, a good match. He was, lastly, promoted Vice-Admiral and could return to England as the successful raider of Java—a coming man. Having thus made his fortune, as his detractors remarked, he was eager to go home. On June 1st, he had written to the Admiralty, stating his intention to proceed to England in October. He was, as he said, beginning to wear. 'My floor timbers are very shaky.' He was, as he complained, 'Grey as a badger and fat as a pig, running to belly.' In more official language he told the Admiralty that 'the state of my health renders it expedient for me to proceed to England for the benefit of a Change of Climate.' This dispatch crossed with one from the Admiralty, dated April 26th, directing him to resign the command to Drury. The Macao expedition, however, combined with the failure of the mission to Persia, caused him to abandon his original intention. When he received the Admiralty's dispatch, towards the end of September, he replied that he would retain the command until Drury should return. On quitting Madras, he would proceed to Penang, hand over the command as soon as Drury appeared, and then return with the China ships. The October convoy from the coast and bay would have the protection of the *Albion*, also due to return to England.

Although no Persian crisis occurred during Drury's absence to the eastward, Pellew had quite enough to do in organizing a convoy system for the country trade in the Bay of Bengal. To the merchants' complaints he had invariably replied by saying that they could have avoided their losses by accepting convoy. He had repeatedly drawn their attention to the fact that hardly any Bombay ships had been captured. This so exasperated the merchants that they ultimately tried to silence him by proposing a convoy system, very much as if they had been wanting it all along, being thwarted only by naval slackness. Anxious to pacify these potentates—Trail, Palmer & Co., Fairlie Gilmore & Co., Hogue Davidson & Co., and the rest—Pellew rather weakly consented to their scheme. Their proposal was that there should be four convoys a year to the eastward and four to the westward, with cruisers to patrol off Cheduba, Negrais, the Andamans, the Nicobars and Achin Head; as also off Ceylon and eastward of the Straits of Singapore. Wholly to comply with this demand would have been impossible, but Pellew did his best for them. He formed a detachment of one frigate and four sloops, destined for convoy work in the bay and confined to that service. He appointed the dates of sailing for. the convoys, as desired, and he tried to provide other ships for the defence of the head of the bay, and also for patrolling the various points indicated, or at any rate some of them. The reply of the merchants was to the effect that they had now changed their minds about the dates of sailing, and that the sloops were not strong enough; they demanded frigates instead. . . . A system of some kind was in working order when Pellew quitted the station, but it did not long survive his departure. In Rear-Admiral Drury the merchants met their match.

CHAPTER XVI

Drury in China

THE expedition destined for Macao assembled at Prince of Wales Island in August 1808. Drury himself arrived there about the 23rd, and was joined presently by the transports from Bengal. These were now guarded by the *Dedaigneuse*, the *Dover* having been detached on another service. The *Phaeton* also joined at some period, perhaps because of the *Greyhound* being lost on the coast of Luconia on October 11th. The expedition proceeded to the eastwards and reached Macao early in September.

Before describing the events which took place, something should perhaps be said about Rear-Admiral O'Brien Drury himself. The clue, possibly, to his character lies in his claim, when commander-in-chief, to hold 'the highest official situation in India.' The claim was characteristic both in its accuracy and unreality. Strictly speaking, the Governor-General and the governors of Madras and Bombay were the servants of the East India Company and therefore bound to yield precedence to an Admiral, who was the servant of the King. By the same wild logic they might be expected to yield precedence to a midshipman. It was a trivial claim, and even Drury failed to support it in practice. But there is a significance in the fact that the claim was made, for it shows the extent to which Drury was out of touch with life.

Self-importance was a common failing among the senior officers of the Navy. It was the natural product of the deference of subordinates, heightened by an insufficient contact with men of equal eminence in other callings. But Drury's failing was not quite of this type. His pride was in his profession and his office as such. He may not have thought meanly of himself, but he reserved his real reverence for the thing that was to become in time 'The Service.' Now, an officer can hardly think too highly of his responsibility or the honour due his colours, but it is as well if he can do so without disparaging the position of other people. The white ensign gains little by any disrespect shown to the red. Drury was, in this respect, a little before his time. The naval officer had quite recently become a

320

PLATE VIII. Rear-Admiral Sir Thomas Troubridge (1758?–1807), Commander-in-Chief on the East Indies Station, by Sir William Beechey

PLATE IX. Captain Peter Rainier (*d.* 1836)
by John Hoppner

gentleman, and many of the officers of Drury's generation hardly regarded themselves as such. Ashore, they were liable to be treated as parvenus. Pellew and Troubridge were both of this type, and so probably was Rainier. But Drury had come to regard his profession as a superior caste, above the criticism of ordinary mortals but infinitely responsible in the sight of heaven; a chosen aristocracy with a special standard of honour, worthy therefore, of a very special respect.

There is much to admire in Drury's attitude. But there is also much to admire in the attitude of Don Quixote. A high notion of honour does credit to any man. To be of use, however, it should have some relation to the world about us. In Drury's respect for his calling there was that trace of insanity apparent in Lord St. Vincent's respect for discipline. Like Sir Sidney Smith he united much that was admirable with much that was fantastic. A more prosaic person—Pellew himself, for example—might have quarrelled less violently with the Company's officials and the commanders of Indiamen. A hearty and unconcealed contempt for all the Company's concerns was no very good qualification for an officer sent to co-operate with the Indian Governments and the supercargoes at Canton. That he was sent, however, can hardly be regretted; for the expedition was futile in any case, and but for him it would not even have been romantic. There is a poetry in his dispatches which must go far to console one for the complete absence of times and dates.

It must be remarked, first of all, that Lord Minto apparently failed to persuade the governor, or rather the Viceroy, of Goa, to send suitable orders to the governor of Macao. Neither, in the end, did he see fit to inform the Chinese beforehand of what he intended to do. So that Drury's arrival at Macao was a surprise for all but the Select Committee, the members of which had done nothing to warn or conciliate either the Chinese or Portuguese. And here it must be remembered that the super-cargoes had no experience of government. They ruled no territory. They controlled no troops. A situation in which they had to wield political power was utterly novel to them. They had made their first mistakes before Drury arrived, but these were very far from being their last and farther from being their most disastrous.

Drury had his first interview with Mr. Roberts, the President of the Select Committee, on September 12th. He at once proposed to send a message to the governor of Macao, stating his intention of occupying the town with British troops, which were to be regarded as auxiliaries assisting in its defence. He would make it clear that, unless they were admitted as friends, the town would have to be taken by force; 'the necessity then existing of occupying Macao by British Troops to prevent it falling into the hands of the French, which would involve in it the destruction of our Commerce with China.' He also proposed that a similar message should be sent to the Viceroy of Canton, and to the Emperor, asking permission

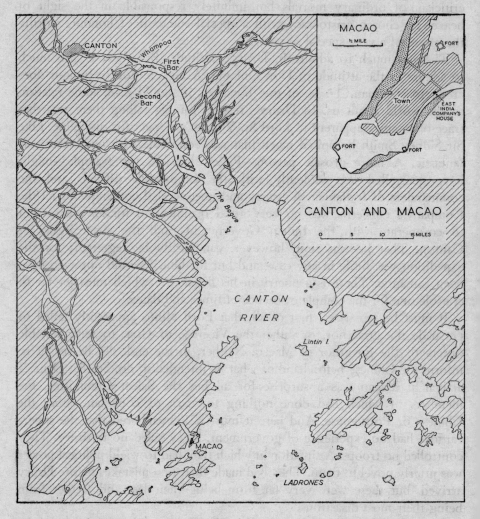

to occupy the town until peace should be restored. The Select Committee agreed to the first proposal, recommending, however, that Drury should go and see the governor in person. As to informing the Chinese, they thought it would be 'productive of much mischief.' They preferred, apparently, to confront the Viceroy with a *fait accompli* and leave him to inform the Emperor if he saw fit.

Drury went, as requested, to speak with the governor, Sr. Bernado Alexe de Lemos e Faria. This gentleman seems to have been altogether worthy of his office, dignified, courteous and intelligent. In a long conversation, he consented to admit the troops, find accommodation for them, and try to conciliate the Chinese; but only on condition that Drury would wait for the orders to come from Goa—orders which he said were daily expected. As the Select Committee said that such a delay would be of no consequence, Drury agreed to wait. He added, however, a proviso to the effect that he might have to occupy the town in the meanwhile if it became necessary. He hoped that in that case there would be no opposition from the Portuguese garrison. But the governor was firm on this point. He would resist if anything was done before the orders arrived.

To Drury the governor's attitude seemed perfectly reasonable, and he thought that the consent of the Portuguese was worth some trouble to obtain. Their resistance could only be trifling but their value in negotiating with the Chinese would clearly be immense. Macao was not their absolute possession. They held it by permission from the Emperor. It was one thing for them to request leave to admit English auxiliaries, and quite another for the English to force an entry and then ask the Emperor's approval. Nor would matters be improved by their omitting to ask the Emperor's approval.

The Select Committee agreed at first to the principle of securing Portuguese consent, if it were possible, but changed their minds on the following day. The whole China fleet was at that time discharging, or beginning to discharge cargo at Whampoa. Drury mentioned their number as fifty-seven, but a printed list of the period contains only forty-two names. According to the latter authority, there were fourteen Indiamen, all but one of 1,200 tons nominal burthen; fifteen large country ships from Bombay, one of 1,250 tons and the rest averaging about 700 tons; six country ships from Bengal, mostly of 500 tons, more or less; five country ships from Penang, one from Madras and one from Negapatam. Whatever the exact number may have been, the property at stake was enormous. Now, this fleet in the river complicated the negotiations. For one thing, the Chinese could imprison it by blocking up Second Bar. For another, they could more simply render it valueless by a mere refusal to trade. A permanent stoppage of the tea supply would practically ruin the East India Company at a blow. That was the one aspect of the situation. The other aspect was that the stoppage of the cotton supply, and the trade generally, would equally ruin Canton and its Viceroy, the officials and the Hong merchants. The stoppage, moreover, of the customs duties would surely be unwelcome at the Imperial Court. If, finally, it came to blows, the China fleet was, in relation to the Chinese, a formidable force in itself.

For some reason, the supercargoes took the view that the trade was more important to the Chinese than to the English. They knew what effect its cessation would have on the Viceroy, and they reckoned on his being amenable to pressure. They accordingly decided that the time to negotiate was before the cotton had been landed and the duties paid. The prospect of there being no cotton and no duties would, they thought, compel him to see reason in the matter of Macao. In this belief they were partly justified. That they should, for the moment, have quite forgotten the existence of the Emperor was natural enough. He was a personage they never saw and rarely heard of. He was a dim and distant figure of whom they were but vaguely aware at any time. But they were unwise to ignore him, for two reasons. First, he was bound to hear of a landing at Macao. Second, he had very little interest in the trade at Canton. It is known that the Viceroy retained most of the customs revenue for his own use. The extent to which he did so made the trade more important to him; but it also made it proportionately less important to the Emperor. The Imperial Court was admittedly at a very great distance; but its mere remoteness made it matter less to the Emperor whether Canton were ruined or not. In ignoring him the supercargoes made a great mistake.

When the Select Committee informed Drury of the change in their views, strongly recommending him to occupy Macao without delay, that officer began to show signs of impatience. 'I endeavoured to show these Gentlemen,' he wrote, 'that 24 Hours had scarcely elapsed since I had agreed to delay the occupation of Macao until the orders daily expected from Goa should arrive, and that it would be a breach of faith with the Governor. . . .' Drury tried to dissuade the supercargoes, but in vain.

> Requisitions were, however, so pressed by the Committee on me to occupy Macao, that I at length consented to take forcible possession of it and prepared to storm it; but having assured the Governor that I would not surprize him, and that I would give him notice before I landed, I accordingly sent him a Summons to allow the Troops to land—or I should do so at the point of the bayonet.
>
> After many hours consultation he gave a half assent, and I landed the Troops. The extraordinary convulsions this step occasioned, and the highly agitated and irritated state of both Chinese and Portuguese, with the reiterated entreaties of the Supra Cargoes, that I should go on shore, and by my presence restore tranquillity, I was induced to do so, and assumed an authority at Macao which gave me very great pain, being so insulting

to the Governor, who readily acquiesced in every requisition I made, as did all the authorities, especially the Bishop, to whom I gave my most solemn assurance of Protection.

It may seem strange that Drury should have given way in this manner, but it must be remembered that the troops were not under his command. He was the King's officer. The troops were the Company's. They were under the orders of the President of the Select Committee, just as they might be under the orders of the governor of Madras. If the Committee wanted them to land, Drury could not refuse to land them. His landing in person did not affect the issue. By that time the town was occupied. He went on shore merely to restore order, which the military commanding officer was apparently unable to do. Once there, he took command by mere force of character.

About 70 or 80 of the Mandarine Junks with about 5000 men having enter'd the Harbour, I saw the necessity of interfering and collecting the Handfull of men I had on shore to guard against surprize; By the most earnest solicitations of the Select Committee I almost forced the poor Governor to let the British Troops occupy La Monte Fort (the Governor's only secure retreat). This point being gained the Committee appeared very much pleased and at their ease, but no sooner had the fermentation of loaded Stomachs begun to operate than their minds changed, and at 6 o'clock next morning Mr. Roberts and the Commanding Officer of the Troops came to request of me that the Troops should not occupy Monte.

The Mandarine Vessels and Men having now withdrawn, and perceiving the most impotent indecision in the Committee, I told them it was so derogatory to my situation that I should immediately embark, having been on shore 3 weeks or a month, tranquility being restored and provisions supplied the Town. I went on board my ship to proceed to Cheunpu to water, and in the idea of the Select Committee to intimidate the Chinese by moving upwards towards the Bocca Tigries.

Eight hundred additional Troops now arrived under Colonel Wiguilem, from Bengal, when the President of the Select Committee sent off an express to me, to know if I had any objection to the Transports going into the Typa near Macao, and landing the Troops under Portuguese Colours, my reply was, the proposal was so contemptible, so unworthy of an Englishman, to land British Troops as a Portuguese Banditti, I would if it were done withdraw myself altogether from so scandalous a set.

Mr. Pattle, the second of the Select Committee, now went to Canton, and opened what he called a negotiation with the Chinese, pressing each day my sending men of War into the Tigriss. Mr. Roberts, the president, proceeded also to Canton, and in the expectation that each day would terminate the business, I was induced to send two Frigates up the Tigriss to Whampoa, in order to intimidate, as well as to receive specie, which was promised to a great amount, both public and private (a very small proportion of which was at last received).

Perceiving we were infringing and trampling under foot every moral law of Man, and of Nations, and the poor defenceless Chinese infuriated to Phrenzy, calling forth their feeble means of defence and offence, and still trusting in the superior local knowledge of the Supra Cargoes, that all would be suddenly ended well if I appeared at Canton, I was at length induced to hoist my Flag in a Frigate, and, by reiterated entreaties, to go to Canton to demand an audience of the Viceroy, which I am now convinced the Supra Cargoes did every thing to prevent, and which I certainly could have had, from the dreadful alarm of the Chinese at my appearance at Canton with near a thousand armed men in my retinue, were it not prevented by the Supra Cargoes.

A Chinese was now privately sent to me by the Hoppo, and I suppose the Viceroy, proffering me 400,000 Dollars to evacuate Macao, or as much more as I pleased, and that the Troops should be permitted to land again in small parties and remain there.

The incident shows that the supercargoes were right in believing that the prospect of a cessation of trade—and of course no cargoes were being discharged at this time—would frighten the Viceroy more than any one else. He was ready to offer an enormous sum as a bribe to bring about even a sham evacuation of Macao. Why? Obviously, the affair had come to the ears of the Emperor. There was no other person for whose benefit the sham evacuation could be intended. To avert the abolition of the trade by an Imperial decree, the best thing the Viceroy could do was to make some show of compelling the English to depart. He probably knew, as the Emperor did not, that there was no hope of ejecting them by force. But his experience apparently led him to suppose that any Englishman could be bribed.

This old Chinese (who spoke English very well) was sent to me without the knowledge of the Supra Cargoes, whom I informed of the circumstances, and who I was well informed by Gentlemen present when the old Chinese delivered my note to Mr. Roberts, that he appeared exceedingly chagrined, Mr. Pattle petulantly declaring 'By God, Roberts, this has marred all, and we will immediately embark the Troops.' A letter was witten by Mr. Roberts immediately to me, declaring the old Chinese to be every thing that was bad, and that the Hong Merchants believing me the ostensible person would do great mischief, which I replied to by saying I would withdraw from the business altogether; and the *honor* and *advantages* should be entirely the Select Committee's.

Reiterated entreaties (that all would be lost if I withdrew) induced me to remain, and still appear the ostensible person.

Something so extraordinary and mysterious was now so evident to me, in the conduct of the Supra Cargoes, that I could not but suspect some secret transaction was going on, of which I was totally ignorant. My message to the Hoppo, and Viceroy, was 'An English Officer is insulted by offering him a Bribe and Merchants would be punished for taking it, but as a proof of my sincerity that the protection of Macao and our Commerce was my only object I would withdraw one half of the Troops, but cannot receive any reward.'

This plan was agreed to by the old Chinese, and I am persuaded, had it been followed up by the Supra Cargoes with common sense and justice, every matter would have been at that time settled and our Troops allowed to remain at Macao. . . .

With a single inspired phrase, Drury tried to convey to the Chinese the social gulf yawning between him and the East India Company's servants. 'An English Officer is insulted by offering him a Bribe and Merchants would be punished for taking it. . . .' Perhaps the Chinese saw the point of this. But they had sensed the cleavage between Drury and the supercargoes at an earlier stage. That is why they tried to bribe him without telling them.

The narrative from which the above quotations are taken is Drury's report to Pellew (P.R.O. Adm. 1/181). In the absence of dates, it must be explained that the events described covered nearly three months. The crisis came on November 27th–28th. On the first of these days, Drury addressed a sort of ultimatum to the supercargoes.

Whampoa, 27th Nov. 1808.

Sir

Having for nearly three months acceded to every admissible requisition of the Select Committee of Supra Cargoes, in the faint hope of conciliating the Chinese Government to the aggression of occupying Macao by British Troops, and as I cannot but behold with regret and alarm, that the Great and Advantageous Commercial Monopoly which England has enjoyed, is in danger of being lost for ever to the Country.

However Highly the superior local knowledge of the select Committee may be esteemed by the Honble Court of Directors, experience, the least fallible of human knowledge, evinces me it has failed in every instance throughout this arduous and most complex transaction, and as the crooked, left handed, winding mode of proceeding, is so opposite to the Summary straight line, prompt and vigorous common sense, prudence, justice, and Dignity marked for an Officer to pursue, I can no longer waste the Services of His Majesty's Ships, so much required in India, in negotiating where neither party gives the other Credit for a sentence of truth being uttered. . . . I feel myself called upon to fulfil my duty by warning you against the mischiefs likely to arise from a continuance of your proceedings, at the same time to offer my opinion how the great pending Evil may in some degree be remedied.

You have scarcely left a mean between peace and War, the sword is nearly half out of the Scabbard. . . .

However completely one's sympathies may be with Drury, it must be confessed that his solution of the problem, as propounded at this juncture, was as wild a scheme as could be conceived. His lecture to the Select Committee is admirable, but its effect must have been spoilt by its constructive as opposed to its critical aspect. He wanted the supercargoes to abandon the factory at Canton and turn Macao into the depot for the Company's trade. This, as he was careful to explain, would have the pleasing effect of ruining 'the Mandarin and infamous Hong Merchants.' As the Hong merchants were heavily in debt to the East India Company, their ruin was not as desirable as Drury seemed to think. The Mandarins, also, and the Viceroy, were standing alone at that time between the English and an Imperial decree abolishing the China trade. As for Macao, it would obviously be given back to Portugal sooner or later, whereupon the Company would find its depot under foreign jurisdiction, and far less conveniently situated than at Canton.

The crisis on the 28th had little to do with the above ultimatum. It was simply caused by a number of armed ships' boats being sent up to Canton to fetch stores from the English factory there. Drury at first intended that these launches should be under the command of Captain Dawson of the *Dedaigneuse*. At the last moment, however, he decided to accompany the boats himself.

> . . . fearful of the consequences of the immense mob at Canton provoking our men, and considering the too great responsibility I was putting on the Shoulders of so young a man as Capt'n Dawson, with express orders not to risque anything which could endanger an hostile act on our part, and fearing Seamen and Marines, if attacked, might not be withheld by his authority; and viewing the immense Stake we were playing for, suspended by a thread, a single musquet would have broken, and the greatest monopoly England and India has in the World would be lost for ever! I determined to accompany Capt'n Dawson in my Barge, as my controul would be more than his possibly could.

It may be doubted whether Drury was quite honest in his report of this boat expedition. He speaks as if the fetching of stores (liquor mostly for the frigates) was the sole object in view; and yet he also says that he 'assented' to it. Now, if the wants of his men were all he had in mind, he would surely have initiated rather than approved the scheme. And, again, if the China trade might have been brought to an end by the firing of a musket, why did they take their muskets with them? The most certain method of preventing a shot being fired would have been to leave all firearms behind. Granted that a Rear-Admiral might have more authority than a junior captain, a physical impossibility might be supposed to have more authority than either. It is fairly obvious, in fact, that this boat expedition was not quite what Drury afterwards tried to make it appear. It must have been suggested by the supercargoes as a final, though half-hearted attempt at intimidation. They probably had some vague hope that the Chinese would collapse as soon as they heard of Drury's approach. And Drury himself must have shared in this expectation to some extent. Otherwise, he would not have agreed to send the boats together and armed. The fetching of stores was a mere pretext, to be used in explanation if anything went wrong; a thin pretext, as the stores could have gone in single unarmed boats, at night.

> On approaching Canton, their armed Junks were drawn across the River and myriads of People on board of them. Apprehending they might fire their little guns (which were pointed in the air) I ordered Capt'n Dawson to remain behind with all the Boats while I advanced in my Barge with a man in the Boat who spoke Chinese, in order to explain to their Admiral my peaceable intentions.
>
> When within about a hundred yards of them they fired a shot over the Boat. I still advanced, and one or two shots more passed over us, untill I got within about forty yards, all this time endeavouring to speak, but in vain. Now all the Junks opened their fire on my Barge, with stones and God knows what, untill one of the Marines in the Boat was struck, and the Seamen in all the other Boats, seeing me fired at so furiously, no longer were under control, but pulled close up, when I saw the necessity of ordering them all back, or the total annihilation of their poor Junks and Canton must have been the inevitable consequence, had I permitted a single Musquet to be fired, which was most impatiently looked for by every one. The Launches and boats anchoring out of reach of their little Junks, thousands of People came down in Boats shouting, and on the beach close to us, not in the least apprehensive of us or our guns; and when the tide turned I ordered all back.

Fortunately for the Chinese, and still more fortunately for the East India Company, Drury was at once exceedingly brave and remarkably humane. It was not every officer who could reason in that pitying way while confronted by a howling mob of Chinese, and under a heavy fire of 'stones

L*

and God knows what.' If it originated in folly, the incident at least closed with a scene showing European forbearance, chivalry and discipline at its best. It is, perhaps, worth mentioning that the Chinese claimed a naval victory and erected a large war memorial to commemorate it. There is no striving against ignorance.

To continue the narrative:

> I thought this was a pretty strong proof that the Supra Cargoes could have no serious Idea that these People were to be intimidated into their measures, whatever they were; and as every step they had taken since I left them at Macao was in direct violation of their orders from the Supreme Government, I made Mr. Roberts read his instructions, and told him, if peace and Commerce can only be had by war, in two hours every Junk they have shall be destroyed, but if neither peace nor commerce is to be obtained by War, I never will sanction the slaughter of those defenceless multitudes, yet if my Seamen, or one of them, is killed, I will destroy Canton; therefore recollect what you will have to answer for. I gave you quiet possession of Macao with 300 men, you have there 1,100 with a regular staff at your Command. I never will give you an opinion in regard to what you are to do in Macao. I tell you no hostile act shall be committed against the Chinese, unless a man is killed, which nothing but the most singular accident has prevented. The Seamen under my controul have borne to be fired at, but if once let loose no power on Earth can stop them.

After his encounter with the Chinese Navy, Drury wrote an account of what had just happened for Pellew's benefit. In describing the situation he made it clear that, if the Select Committee should decide on war, he would not lend his sanction to it. He refused to be the murderer of 'this strange and almost totally defenceless Rabble.' He ends by saying 'I hope for the honor of the Service and the Welfare of our Country, that neither you nor I may ever be again employed on a Jean bon St. André Expedition. I never will.' On the same day, either before or after his interview with Mr. Roberts, he wrote officially to the Select Committee, which was apparently assembled by that time on board the *Walmer Castle*, Indiaman, at Whampoa. After a suitable amount of abuse and admonition, the letter goes on 'The Select Committee are directed to be the sole Arbiters in this transaction; and I hope and expect that their next requisition to me may be firm, wise, and final.'

The supercargoes may have been the sole arbiters on the English side, but this hardly gave them a complete control of the situation. There was another arbiter to consider, and that was the Emperor of China. The now distracted Viceroy had played his last card in sending word to the Emperor, and it was at this juncture that the answer arrived. It was worded with the firmness to be expected from the ruler of the world when addressing the chiefs of some insignificant but occasionally troublesome frontier tribe. The English had offered their assistance in excluding the French from Macao, and also in suppressing the Ladrones. The Emperor, however, was quite capable of guarding his own dominions against the French; and, as for the pirates, there were none. He did not believe a word of what the English said in excuse for seizing Macao. They had taken it because they wanted it for themselves. Having thus summed up the situation, the Emperor pronounced his judgment. The English were to leave Macao at once. If they failed to do so, not only would they lose their trade, but an infinite number of soldiers would be sent to seize them. This admirably moderate decree was translated and sent on by the Viceroy, with a covering letter of his own, urging the English to submit.

The Imperial letter was apparently addressed to Drury, for he replied to the Viceroy on December 5th, asking him to send some Mandarin of rank to confer with him. At the same time he informed the Select Committee that the Chinese ultimatum seemed to him to be 'dictated by Wisdom, Justice and dignified Manhood in support of those Moral Rights of Man, of Nations, and of Nature, outraged and insulted.' He ended by saying, though not for the first time, 'I shall therefore no longer degrade my situation by the further continuance of a Negotiation which has long appeared to me so mysterious and extraordinary.' This message resulted in a requisition from the Select Committee, dated December 8th, for Drury to withdraw his ships from Whampoa and embark the troops at Macao. This requisition being as 'firm, wise, and final' as he could have wished, the Admiral gladly obeyed. He wrote again to Pellew from off Macao on December 23rd.

> . . . And thus has finished the most mysterious, extraordinary and scandalous affair that ever disgraced such an Armament, seven Months employed on this Service, but which will be, I trust, a lasting memento and, for the Honor and welfare of the Country, prevent placing great National concerns in the hands of Merchants or Supra Cargoes, or any others whose individual views and Interests must be deeply involved in the Transaction . . . vesting such men with exalted authority, to be supported by British Ships and British Troops, was offering a mighty sphere to the small and feeble hand; which recoiling at every effort to grasp, it at length falls and crushes vain and impotent presumption.[1]

[1] The Select Committee of Roberts, Pattle, Bramston and Elphinstone was replaced on 6th December, 1810, Elphinstone alone being retained. On the Chinese side the Viceroy and Governor were both cashiered and degraded two steps in rank.

In regard to the Ladrone Pirates which you ordered me to act against, as was advisable, according to suggestions of the Select Committee, I beg leave to observe all offers to assist the Chinese with British Seamen, *in the total extirpation of* 50,000 *Ladrones* have been treated by the Chinese Government with the most dignified contempt, as I trust it will in future be by you, as a *Tale* told by the Supra Cargoes of Canton, full of sound signifying nothing. The Ladrones have ever existed, and I do firmly believe, are a most necessary Component part of this almost indefinite Empire. . . .

As the Ladrones are still flourishing in some degree, the necessity for their existence may perhaps be allowed. Drury's attitude towards them was explained by himself with more emphasis than lucidity. He apparently thought that piracy was useful to the Chinese as an outlet for bad characters and a natural defence of their coasts against strangers. He also said that the idea of British seamen being used 'to murder these defenceless myriads' was 'repugnant to common sense and decency.' Without attempting to follow this line of reasoning, it would be safe, probably, to admit that the extermination of the pirates was impracticable. That they were as numerous as Drury states them to have been was, at any rate, the common belief of the time. Other accounts make the pirate vessels number between five and six hundred. How the trade should have been of a volume to support so many thieves is not apparent. However, whatever their exact number, there was no obvious way of dealing with them, and Drury was clearly wise in leaving the problem alone. The Admiral's final report on the whole affair ends as follows:

They [the Supercargoes] still continued from indecision to something more absurd, till finding I was not to be driven from the Tigriss thro' want and that I would not allow the Chinese to be slaughtered nor their little Forts to be destroyed, and the Gentlemen at Macao taking fright, a requisition was at length made that the Ships should quit the Tigriss and the Troops withdrawn.

Viewing the whole transaction at the moment, since giving it my best consideration, and being convinced the Select Committee had no just ground to found their letter to the Supreme Government of the 9th of March, that if the Troops were landed at Macao, the Chinese would not make any serious objection to it (or words to that amount) and as their representation of the danger to be apprehended from the Ladrones is totally void of Common Sense, and without foundation, as also their representations of the hatred, and malignancy of the Portuguese Government towards them, is, I firmly believe, most groundless: I can only conclude from the immense sum offered me to withdraw the Troops from Macao, that the object of the Supra Cargoes was by intimidating the Chinese, to have forced them to a Liquidation of the immense debt due by the beggarly Hong Merchants to the Honourable Company—as I cannot attach to Gentlemen standing so high for liberality and honour, any thing so unworthy as selfish motives.

I judge it proper to mention that my appearing as the Ostensible Person during this transaction was a matter of necessity in consequence of the entreaties of the Select Committee who assured me (which was true) the Chinese would neither correspond or communicate with them, and the Portuguese Governor at Macao could only communicate with me.

When Mr. Elphinstone, one of the Select Committee, accompany'd by the Portuguese Judge of Macao came on board the *Russel* to inform me it was determined by the Committee to evacuate Macao immediately; with the declaration of the Commanding Officer of the Troops that Macao was not tenable with 1100 men, and requesting my assistance to reimbark the Troops, I assured the Judge the Portuguese Trade should experience the same protection it had ever done, and that I had no reason to find fault with any part of the Governor's conduct.

I informed Mr. Elphinstone that when the Ships were laden and had sailed, as the same motives for the Select Committee wishing to occupy Macao might still exist, if they made the requisition, the same three hundred men that gave them before the possession should do so again, and maintain it, provided the Select Committee were not to interfere with the Officer left in the command of the Troops.

(P.R.O. Adm. 1/181. Report and correspondence sent by Drury to Pellew.)

The same opinion regarding the impregnability of Macao is expressed in Drury's letter of the 23rd, in which he says that he could hold it with a British regiment against all China 'provided no Merchants or Supra Cargoes, India Captains, Parsees, Portuguese Priests or Governors have any thing to say to the execution of the plan.' The truth of this contention, however, was never ascertained. Macao was henceforth willingly left in the possession of Portugal. It is curious to note that the Portuguese, compelled to suffer such indignities at the hands of the English, were at the same time suffering actual losses at the hands of the French. One of their most valuable ships had long since been intercepted on the voyage from Goa to Lisbon. In time of war it is dangerous to leave the combatants in doubt as to which side one is on.

Owing to the long delay in discharging cargo, there was no hope of the China fleet sailing at the usual time of year. Drury accordingly left the *Dover* and *Dedaigneuse* to assist the *Lion* in escorting it, and left Macao on about December 24th. He was at Pulo-Aur by the 31st, and reached Penang two or three days later. Two days after his arrival, Pellew appeared in the *Culloden*. It will be recalled that Pellew had intended to escort the

China ships to England. He was now assured that they would certainly not be sailing before March. As he did not intend to wait until then, he at once handed over the command to Drury. The two Admirals sailed on the same day, Drury bound for Madras and Pellew bound for Point de Galle, where the *Terpsichore* was assembling the spring convoy of Indiamen from the three Presidencies. The convoy sailed with the *Culloden* and *Terpsichore* on 15th February, 1809. Off the Isle of France a very heavy gale was encountered, the *Culloden* herself being considerably damaged, and the convoy dispersed. The Admiral waited in Table Bay for the ships to reassemble, sending some of them on to St. Helena as soon as they arrived. Four of them did not arrive. After waiting for ten days, Pellew proceeded to St. Helena, where he waited another ten days. The missing Indiamen did not appear; and, in short, they were never heard of again. The rest of the convoy sailed from St. Helena on May 9th, and arrived in the Channel two months later. The *Terpsichore* escorted the Indiaman into the Downs, while the *Culloden* put into Plymouth on July 10th. Four days later, Pellew struck his flag and went ashore. He had made his fortune at the price of a five years' exile.

PART THREE

CHAPTER XVII

The Navy in India

At the period when Sir Edward Pellew left India, the East Indies station was organized on a pattern which survived for the rest of the war. With the limits of the station restored to what they had been in Rainier's time, but with the Cape established as a separate command; with the squadron in considerable strength, and with the last French efforts impending, it may not be out of place to describe the administrative problems which underlay the strategy of the Indian Ocean. How did this station compare with others? What were its peculiarities? Its first characteristic was its remoteness. The naval commander-in-chief in India was too far away for effective control. Thus, the Admiralty was perpetually trying to assert some kind of authority in India and as perpetually finding itself thwarted; largely by mere distance. To official orders to appoint an officer to a ship, to appoint a firm as agents, to promote a midshipman, the Admiral was apt to reply that the ship was wrecked, the firm bankrupt and the young gentleman dead.

From the flag-officer's point of view, this comparative freedom from effective control was one of the principal attractions of the East Indies. More especially was it valued as the means of promoting friends and relations. Rainier's nephew took less than a year to rise from the rank of midshipman to that of post-captain. Sir Edward Pellew made one of his sons a post-captain at the age of seventeen. Sir Thomas Troubridge did much the same for his son. Officers were apt to die in the East Indies, and the commander-in-chief could shuffle the vacancies round in such a way as to leave the Admiralty eternally out of date in its information. Prizes, too, were taken from the enemy, and it was for the commander-in-chief to purchase them into the Navy if he thought fit. When he did so, he named them, commissioned them, and appointed officers to them. Again, when ships were worn out, it was he who had them sold out of the service. In patronage and administration, he was very much a despot.

The administration of the squadron's finances, and the purchasing of its non-edible stores, was entrusted to the naval officer at Madras and the naval officer at Bombay. The former had a subordinate agent at Calcutta

337

and, after 1807, another subordinate agent at Penang. The first characteristic of a naval officer was that he was never a naval officer; he was never, that is to say, an officer in the Navy. He was a civilian and the representative of the Navy Board. When there was a vacancy, the commander-in-chief would sometimes appoint his secretary to the post. Otherwise, these officials may have been promoted from the dockyards in England. At the beginning of our period, the naval officers also acted as agents to the Sick and Hurt Board, but this latter office was abolished in 1806.

The duty of a naval officer was to take charge of the specie sent out from England in dollars for the use of the squadron, to check all expenditure and keep accounts of all supplies purchased. As storekeeper, it was his duty to hire storehouses and, at Madras, an office as well. If, as was often the case, there was no money to carry on the business, he had to dispose of bills on the Navy Board, signed by the commander-in-chief. When these could not be sold at any reasonable discount, he had to borrow money from the Company's treasury. One of his duties, in the absence of the commander-in-chief or a senior officer appointed to command in his absence, was to open dispatches from the Admiralty and decide whether to forward them; and if so, how. It was a responsible post.

The stores which a naval officer had to purchase and supply on requisition to the ships of the squadron were chiefly items such as canvas, cordage, ground-tackle, tar, paint and so forth. Sometimes the Navy Board would send out quantities of canvas, cordage, and the like in the East India Company's ships—the Company took out stores freight free for the squadron in India. But at other times it was necessary to make purchases in India, often of country canvas and other local products in the absence of European supplies. The greatest purchases were in connection with ships bought into the Navy—country ships as well as prizes—which might occasion the drawing of bills up to £90,000 at a time.

Ordnance stores, strictly speaking cannon, shot and gunpowder, were supplied by the East India Company through the arsenals at Bombay and Madras. The Navy Board repaid the Company afterwards. This was a transaction which did not affect the civil department of the Navy in India. The victualling, again, was a separate affair. This was done by contract for bills drawn on the Victualling Board in London. The building of men-of-war in India, as apart from the carrying out of repairs, was arranged in London between the Navy Board and the Company.

As a result, apparently, of the activities of the Commission of Naval Inquiry, the system under which the naval officers drew their emoluments was entirely altered in 1806. Until then the officer at Madras, Mr. Hoseason, who had been secretary to Admiral Rainier, drew £600 a year as naval officer, £300 a year as Agent to the Sick and Hurt Board, with an allowance for house rent and a percentage on all disbursements. As purchases were at that time extensive, the post was considered lucrative. Under the new regulations, the total salary was reduced to £200 a year, and the purchases on which 1¼ per cent was allowed were to be cut down, stores being sent out from England instead. Under this system the emoluments were reduced to about £600 a year. As Sir Edward Pellew calculated that £3,000 a year was the least on which a respectable man could live with credit at Madras, it is not surprising that both naval officers instantly resigned. The Hon. B. Cochrane, the victualling contractor, retired at the same time. Sir Thomas Troubridge attributed this exodus to fear of investigation. Had he ever assumed command at Madras, he would have sifted the whole matter and exposed the culprits, if there were any. Pellew was more lenient.

Following the resignation of the naval officers, there was a period of something like chaos. Pellew's secretary, Mr. Hawke Locker, filled the post at Madras for a time. He stated, however, that the salary was insufficient, and was glad to be relieved by an Admiralty nominee. A Mr. Hall was induced to act until the new official should arrive. At Bombay, Pellew appointed Sir Miguel de Lima e Souza, a Portuguese resident who had held the post under Sir Edward Hughes. The Admiralty sent out Mr. T. J. Williamson to supersede him in 1807. On arriving, Mr. Williamson found the emoluments insufficient, the stores in disorder and the staff inadequate. A staff of four was allowed by the Navy Board—a native clerk, two watchmen and a labourer. Sir Miguel was actually employing sixteen people in all, a European clerk, nine native clerks and six watchmen and labourers. Mr. Williamson said that the post was not what he had been led to suppose. He declined to accept it and embarked for England three weeks after his arrival. Hawke Locker had already refused it, so that Sir Miguel was left to carry on. The Navy Board was still, however, intent on introducing reforms and economies. The next move was to send out two commissioners, one to each port. Commissioner Inman duly landed at Madras in 1809. He had become a lunatic in the course of the voyage, and died almost as soon as he came on shore. Commissioner Dundas arrived at Bombay and instantly became involved in a feud with Admiral Drury. Something was done, nevertheless, to reduce expenses; for, while detesting each other, Drury and Dundas were both reformers, and the former could do more than would have been possible had Inman been alive.

Drury's ambition was to establish Negapatam as the chief refitting port, with Trincomalee both for refitting and supplies. The chief advantage of Negapatam was that it was not Madras. It was possible to establish there a new civil department, untainted with the expensive ideas of the old. Trincomalee had obvious advantages but was handicapped by the absence of a town, and by the absence even of a sufficiently productive countryside. Efforts to introduce settlers could not have instantaneous effect.

Bombay was the only port capable of repairing ships of the line in dock. For frigates, however, and smaller craft, there were two alternatives: Calcutta and Coringa. Whereas Bombay dockyard was the Company's property, the docks at Calcutta and Coringa were in private hands. The Navy had to pay, and heavily, for the use of any one of them. The objection to the Calcutta dock was that it involved an appalling loss of life from disease to enter the Hooghly at all. To keep ships constantly in the neighbourhood—as Pellew had been frightened into doing—was to decimate their crews. To dock a vessel there was worse, for it kept the men idle as well. The objection to the Coringa dock was the muddy bar which had to be crossed in reaching it. Bombay was not free from disease, but it was, in the main, preferable to the other two. Nothing came of the plans to make Penang a refitting port. One or two men-of-war were built there at considerable expense, and after protracted delays.[1] Finding the master builder idle in 1807, Pellew appointed him to act as agent to the naval officer at Madras. Like the agent at Calcutta, he was given the care of certain hired storehouses. There were no docks even in course of construction, all the schemes for developing Penang having been shelved, mainly owing to lack of funds at Fort William.

Equal in importance to the building, repairing and refitting of ships was the supply of men. Ships were not always fully manned when they came out to India, more especially if they sailed in peace time and therefore on a peace establishment. And, whether fully manned or not, they very soon found themselves in want of men. The only way in which men could be procured was by impressment from the Indiamen. The country ships had, of course, no European seamen to impress, and their officers were all

---

[1] It appears that a frigate was laid down at Penang in 1805, called the *Malacca*, and completed in 1809. Her copper fastenings, guns and other stores were sent out from England but no orders that she was to be handed over to the Navy. She seems, therefore, to have gone to England as a merchantman. Meanwhile timber was being collected towards building a ship of the line. It took three years to assemble the timber for half the frame and Admiral Drury then poured scorn on 'the wasteful and ridiculous Idea of ever building Men of War at this Island where neither timber or workmen can be procured without immence expense' and the timber was then sold again.

exempt. About the impressing of men from Indiamen there was endless trouble. It was decided very early in the war that the crews of the Company's cruisers should be exempt; and thenceforward the ground of dispute was as to whether men could be received from them as volunteers. Naval officers claimed that they were bound to receive all seamen who should offer themselves, the East India Company maintaining that the men were under contract and were not free to volunteer. This problem never seems to have been solved. Neither was any satisfactory solution arrived at on the subject of impressment from Indiamen. Here, the law was entirely on the side of the Navy. The Company's ships were only merchantmen with something of the status of privateers. They had no valid claim to any degree of exemption. However, there were continual and bitter complaints from the Company, culminating in the inquiries made into the foundering of Indiamen in 1808 and 1809.[1] Perhaps partly as a result of these disasters, which were widely—though probably wrongly—attributed to under-manning, the admiralty eventually issued a code of regulations under which most of the petty officers as well as the officers and apprentices of Indiamen were protected. This was only the last of a number of attempts to solve the problem. Most of the previous efforts had been made by the commanders-in-chief in the East Indies. They had failed for various reasons, one being the tendency of individual captains to disobey orders on this topic, another being the tendency of admirals to issue orders which they did not mean to enforce. It was always an easy matter to draw up one set of instructions to show the Governor-General, and give out slightly different instructions over the port. Whether the Admiralty's regulations would have been very effective at such a distance must remain doubtful. After 1810 the question began to solve itself as the strength of the squadron was reduced.

In this question of impressment, one's sympathies must usually be with the Indiamen. Their officers had to put up with insult as well as injury. The case mentioned by Hickey of the lieutenant who impressed twenty-two men from the *Castle Eden*, replying to all remonstrances with the words 'Orders, Captain, orders! I am bound to be obedient to my superiors! Let them look out that's got the watch!' was not unusual except in the civility shown. There was an affair on board H.C.S. *Asia* in 1809 which nearly led to blows, which actually led to pistol shots, though none happened to take effect. It was almost entirely due to the bad manners

[1] See *Naval Chronicle*, Vol. 26, p. 214, *et seq*, and p. 305. The case is cited of the *Asia* from which Drury agreed to impress only thirteen men, but which yielded thirty-three men altogether to the ships of his squadron.

of an acting lieutenant—aged about fourteen—who began the interview by ignoring the chief mate's bow, and calling out rudely 'Call your hands out. I am come to press your men.' As he held no commission and showed no press warrant, some dispute then followed, in the course of which one of the boat's crew shouted, 'You —— of a Chief Mate, I know you well and I only wait for orders to blow your brains out.' The first lieutenant of the sloop, on the same occasion, on being 'touched gently on the shoulder and desired to keep calm'—this was after the exchange of shots— shouted 'Don't touch me. You're poisonous. You are no gentleman. . . .' until the chief mate threatened to kick him over the side. The details of such an incident are childish enough, but the upshot is not. The Indiaman had given up her proper quota of men and received a 'protection' for the remainder from Admiral Drury. Despite this, she was boarded in an irregular manner, and eventually forced to give up thirty-three more. On her officers showing their resentment—more at the incivility than the injustice—a scuffle ensued; and the result was that the first, second and fourth mates of the *Asia* were suspended from office for armed resistance to His Majesty's flag.

Leaving aside the rights and wrongs of that particular case, it is evident that the Company's officers had much to complain of in a state of affairs which exposed them to such treatment. The comments of Captain Tremenhere, the commander of the *Asia*, are worth quoting in this connection. 'The young men in the Navy are too often impressed with such high notions of the honor and consequence which attach to them from being in His Majesty's Service that they are very apt to forget what is due to the Officers in the Company's Service, of equal respectability with and possessing as nice a sense of honor as themselves, and imagine they may just speak and act towards them as they think proper. . . .' A commander of an Indiaman was something of a personage in India, the equal of a colonel when ashore. To lose all his best seamen was bad enough without his being ordered about in the process by an offensive little boy with a blue coat as his only warrant.

Impressment from Indiamen was practically the only method of obtaining recruits for the Navy in India. Occasionally a few foreign seamen, taken in French and Dutch prizes, would volunteer for the service. Ships' companies were always rather cosmopolitan in those days; in the *Blenheim*, for instance, fifteen of the marines were Dutch and one of the lieutenants Russian; so that foreign seamen did not come amiss. Then, the Marine Society used to send out parties of boys from time to time, both in men-of-war and Indiamen. If they came in Indiamen, the mates usually managed to shuffle them round in such a way as to make sure that the Navy had only the worst of them. Parties of boys coming in ships of war were therefore preferable, as not being adulterated in this way. As a final resort, when all else failed, there were lascars and Malays. These were never shipped when it was possible to avoid it; but it is probable that most ships had four or five of them. Had the war continued much longer, all ships would have had a considerable number. They were not so particular in the French service; the *Marengo* had two hundred of them at one time. There do not seem to have been many negroes in English men-of-war. Many French slavers were caught in the early years of the war, but the slaves seem to have been sold in the ordinary way for the benefit of the captors. There is mention at the end of our period of officers buying negro boys at 10 dollars apiece. But these were probably good for nothing except as servants. Lascars, it may be added, were useless in action. The French frigate *Piémontaise* carried nearly 200 lascars in a total crew of about 500, but they were merely in the way when it came to fighting. Finally, even after Indiamen had been robbed of their last man, after foreigners and natives had been enlisted, men-of-war were often undermanned. The *San Fiorenzo*, at the time of her famous action, had only 186 men on board, including the sick.

A problem akin to that of the supply of men was that of the supply of officers. The solution of this problem was found in the turning of boys into men. There were always a fair number of midshipmen, and they were promoted as fast as vacancies occurred. Lieutenants, therefore, might be very young indeed—sometimes as young as fifteen. They might also be fairly old, for the promotions from lieutenant to commander were very capricious. Luck and interest were the keys to promotion from a lieutenancy. It was a rank more easily gained than quitted. It sometimes happened that a specially favoured officer was posted at the age of eighteen or twenty. In such cases, the Admiral usually appointed a 'dry nurse'—that is to say, a capable and experienced first lieutenant, aged perhaps about forty. The fate of such an officer was hard, for his chances of promotion were in inverse proportion to his usefulness.

To fill up the depleted ranks of the midshipmen there was but one method, apart from receiving fresh supplies in the ships newly arrived on the station; and that was to entice apprentices from the Indiamen. Sometimes a few assistant surgeons could be obtained in the same way, and there was often a greater shortage of these than of midshipmen.

The payment of officers and men employed on a foreign station was always a trifle erratic, but the East Indies had local peculiarities as well.

Officers were paid, as elsewhere, in quarterly bills drawn on the Navy Board. To convert these into cash, they had to be negotiated at a considerable discount—about 20 per cent. As, however, the East India

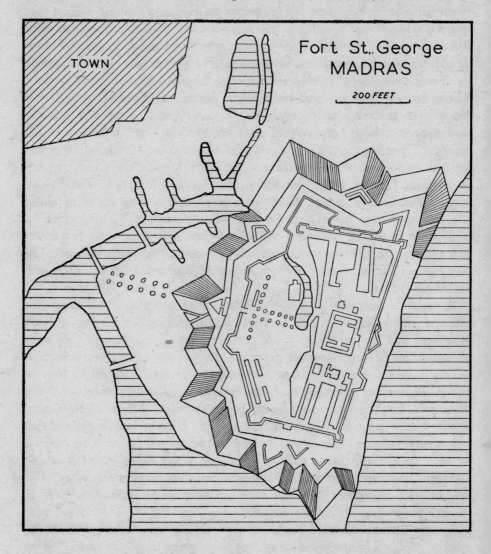

Company was beholden to the squadron for any safety its shipping enjoyed, it expressed its gratitude by making certain allowances both to officers and men. Commanders-in-chief were naturally considered first. In Admiral Rainier's day the commander-in-chief had, besides an allowance of £3,000 plus table expenses, a furnished country house provided for him, with servants, at both Madras and Bombay.[1] The Company was in a more economical mood when Sir Edward Pellew arrived. Nevertheless, his comfort was not overlooked. The allowance made to post-captains was £500 a year, to commanders £250 and to ward-room officers £24. This was called 'batta' or table money, and it was theoretically intended to make the officers' pay equal to that of the Company's officers of equal rank. The allowance made to the rest of the crew took the form of tea and sugar —enough for breakfast every day. This was a peculiarity of the station; elsewhere the men had cocoa for breakfast, tea being confined to the

ADMIRAL'S HOUSE MADRAS

officers. Payment of 'batta' was not, it will be noted, on a reckless scale where lieutenants were concerned. In fact, as their pay was only a trifle over £100 a year, the 'batta' did little more than make up for what the officers lost in discounting their bills. Lieutenants were thought to fare badly in India, as clothing was expensive and palanquin hire a necessity whenever they went on shore.

As regards the payment of 'other ranks' the theory was that they could only be paid at a 'King's Port'—which meant in practice Portsmouth or Plymouth. Trincomalee was a 'King's Port,' but it does not seem that

[1] The Madras 'Admiralty House'—where Robert Clive had lived—still exists, or existed at least in 1921. See *The Story of Madras* by Glyn Barlow, p. 85.

ships were ever paid there. In fact, they do not appear to have been paid at all until they returned to England. As both ships and men were liable to remain in the East up to ten years, the hardship is apparent. It did not attract much attention at the time. Dundonald once raised the point in the Lower House, but the matter was not taken up—if only because it was he who brought it to light. In this connection there was a problem which remained unnoticed for an incredibly long time: the problem of how native seamen were to be paid—men who could not return to England (never having been there) and whom the voyage would probably kill if they undertook it. The problem was first realized in 1809, when two native seamen meekly petitioned for fourteen years' pay. Only then did it dawn on a British Admiral that the lascars in the squadron had never been paid, and apparently never would be paid.

Besides pay there was prize-money, which sometimes eased the situation for needy officers and which was the only money the men ever saw while on the station. From this point of view the squadron's greatest blessing was the Vice-Admiralty Court established at Colombo in 1804, under the jurisdiction of the governor of Ceylon. So convenient a place made for the speedy adjudication of prizes, and that in turn made for the early payment of prize-money.

Prizes were fairly numerous. On quitting the command, Sir Edward Pellew thoughtfully provided the Admiralty with a list of his recent achievements. He was able to boast of the capture or destruction, in about four years, of 223 sail. The list includes 2 French frigates, 2 corvettes and 13 privateers; 2 Spanish armed ships; 3 Dutch sail of the line, 2 frigates and 17 of the Company's ships. The remaining 182 vessels were merchantmen of various nationalities. Of course, many of the merchantmen were worthless. The men-of-war which were destroyed would bring in 'head-money' only after a return to England. Still, there was a certain profit to be made. And here it must be observed that the squadron enjoyed an advantage in the complete absence of privateers on their own side. When on other stations there were valuable prizes to be taken, and there were privateers about, it was not to the Navy that the prizes fell. This was what the French soon discovered. Naval officers made next to nothing and a few—a very few—corsairs became millionaires. There could be no English privateers in India simply because none but the Company's ships might round the Cape. To fit out a privateer in India was impossible for lack of men. So the absence of English letters of marque does not prove that there was no profitable cruising to be done. What it does show is that the East Indies squadron had a clear field.

When a ship of war was taken, she was brought straight into harbour and offered by the captor for purchase into the Navy, without reference to a prize court. The official report sent to the commander-in-chief almost invariably ended with the words 'she is a fine vessel, nearly new, copper-fastened, and admirably suited for the service' or something to that effect. It was always the captor's object to persuade the Admiral to buy his prize, for a ship of war was often of little value except for the purpose of war. She was therefore unlikely to be bought except by a combatant; that is, by the commander-in-chief, or else—through a few middlemen—by the other side. And the commander-in-chief was likely to pay more in the Government's name, if only to prevent the other side getting the ship back. Here are some instances of the prices paid. The Dutch corvette *Scipio* was bought into the Navy for £4,725. *La Jaseur*, a smaller vessel, was purchased for £1,794. The Dutch frigate *Pallas* was purchased for £15,000, the *Maria Riggersbergen* for a little over £12,000. These prices were arrived at as the result of a survey by impartial committees of builders and carpenters. The Navy Board accused Pellew of paying over £2,000 too much for *La Bellone* privateer, and tried to charge him with the amount—thus ignoring the nature of the valuation by survey.

When a merchantman was taken, she was sent with a prize crew to Ceylon, where her case came before the Vice-Admiralty Court. If released, the cost of her detention might have to be met by the captain who sent her in. If condemned as a lawful prize, which was more usual, she then became the property of the captor or captors. More than one ship, it must be observed, might be present at her taking; and all ships present shared equally. It was usual for ships sailing together on a particular service, such as the blockade of the Isle of France, to agree beforehand to share all prizes taken, whether all the ships were present or not. A condemned prize was next sent to one of the big ports. There she was put in charge of the captor's agents. One agent might be an attorney and the other the Admiral's secretary; or else the whole agency might be vested in a single firm. Agency, however, was highly profitable—the *San Raphael* brought Pellew's secretary £10,000—and it was frequently given as a compliment to the secretary of the commander-in-chief. The agents then immediately arranged for the sale. On page 348 is a typical notice, from the *Bombay Courier* of 2nd March, 1805.

In this instance, another auction was held for the disposal of the ship's stores 'at Mr. Adamson's Warehouses, on the 7th, in small lots to suit purchasers.' The stores thus sold were cables, canvas, tarred marline, lead line, twine, paint-brushes, copper nails, sheet lead, futtock plates, hammock stanchions, iron hoops, medicine chest, etc. The cargo, of course, when there was any, would be sold at yet another sale. But there was sometimes a difficulty about this if the goods fell within the Company's monopoly. Much depended on the business acumen of the agents. In this case, for instance, care was doubtless taken to send the ship to Bombay. It would have been hopeless to try to sell a 750-ton ship at Calcutta.

To be sold
By Public Auction
on account of the
Captors
in the
MARINE YARD,
On Monday 4th March next
precisely at noon, the
Dutch East Indiaman
ELIZABETH
a prize to
His Majesty's Ships
Tremendous   *Lancaster*
Phaeton and *Terpsichore*
with all the
ordnance stores
as she now lies
at her Moorings in this Harbour

The ship is between 3 and 4 years old, of about 750 Tons burthen Carpenter's Measurement. Copper fastened, built at Liverpool by one of the first Mercantile Houses in London, by which she was sold to the Dutch during the late peace, is in very high condition, and well calculated from her construction for the trade from this Port to Canton.

From the gross selling price of ship, fittings and cargo, was deducted the expenses of condemnation, the agents' commission and the expenses of the sale. The remainder was then divided into eight parts. One-eighth went to the Admiral, a quarter to the captain or captains, an eighth to the lieutenants, an eighth to the warrant officers, an eighth to the petty officers, and a quarter to be divided among the remainder.[1] Captains very rightly had the lion's share, as it was they who were responsible if the vessel sent in were not condemned. When not under a flag-officer's orders, they had the Admiral's share as well. This was never the case in the East Indies, however. Apart from the remote possibility of a prize being taken by the escort of the direct China ships, the Admiral might claim a share in every capture. It was he, on the whole, who benefited most under the system. His share might be small, but it was universal, and he had not to divide it with anyone else. Thus, Rainier and Pellew were both supposed to have made about £300,000 during their service afloat, the former entirely in the East Indies. Pellew probably made about a third of his fortune there. He would have made a great deal more if Troubridge had not taken £30,000 out of his 'Birds nest,' as he expressed it. Admirals had, of course, to live on a very expensive scale. What they gained was not all clear profit. Pellew said that his outfit, on being promoted to his flag, cost £3,250—most of this, perhaps, being spent on the silver plate which guests expected to see on an Admiral's table. Captains scarcely ever made fortunes, or met expenses, on quite this scale. In twenty years as a captain, Pellew did not make much more than £50,000.

In the East Indies, occasional windfalls in the form of prize-money probably meant most to young commanders and ward-room officers. The seamen, it is true, had no other pay; but neither had they many opportunities of spending. Officers, on the other hand, had continual expenses. To the newly promoted captain of a frigate, an unexpected £500 may have made a great deal of difference. Prize-money was not the only profit made by captains. There was also the freight charged on the specie or bullion sometimes entrusted for greater safety to ships of war, both by the Company and by private merchants. The former, after 1805, paid no more than 1¼ per cent. A clue to what had formerly been paid may lurk in Pellew's complaint that the new regulation reduced his income by £2,000 a year. Although the Admiral shared in the profit, it may be doubted whether the lower grades received anything. Merchants had presumably to drive their own bargain with individual officers. There is evidence that the captain of a frigate escorting the country ships to Canton might make as much as £2,000 on the voyage.

The victualling of the squadron was done, as we have seen, by contract. This department never fell into the disorder which afflicted the naval offices

[1] The proportions are laid down in the proclamation of 7th July, 1803, quoted in *Naval Chronicle*, Vol. 10, p. 77.

at Madras and Bombay. When the Hon. Basil Cochrane withdrew from the active duties of contractor, he appointed Messrs. Balfour, Baker and Hart to act as his attorneys. Whether his return to England was due, as Troubridge thought, to dread of investigation; or whether it was due to regret at losing his friend Admiral Rainier; or whether, again, it was due to his fortune having been made, Cochrane at least left a system in working order. In return for a specified sum, the contracting firm supplied the squadron with provisions of certain kinds. It did so through agents appointed at all the ports frequented by ships of the Navy, who would deliver the provisions only on receipt of a proper demand, signed by a captain. The victualling of six thousand men for one year—this was the strength of the naval personnel on the station in 1810—cost the Government £150,000. The chief items were beef and bread. Beef was usually to be obtained without much difficulty; but bread, by which was meant biscuit, had a tendency to give way to rice. It was never possible to keep rice out of the menu for long at a time. For the seamen, rice was simply boiled dry and so brought to table. For the officers, rice took the form of curry, in which form it appeared even at breakfast. The ubiquity of rice is shown by Pellew's demand in 1805 for sets of copper boilers for all ships in the squadron, as the iron ones did not answer. He explained that 'the constant boiling of Rice, which must be well dried to be eatable, wears the Cast Iron very fast—The Frigates will want at least six sets, by the time they arrive. . . .'

Just as wheat was apt to give way to rice, so was cocoa sure to give way to tea and rum to arrack. Vinegar and pease seem to have been obtainable in India, but there was never any beer except during the early part of the voyage out from England. Some ships carried essence of malt, spruce and yeast with which to brew a further supply, but this can never have lasted for long. In 1808, Sir Edward Pellew issued orders that 'vegetables of the country' were to be provided daily for a month after a ship came into port, provided she had been at sea for twenty-eight days or more—for the first fortnight, to the amount of a halfpenny a day per man, and afterwards to half that amount. There were also certain rules about lemon-juice, but it may be questioned whether lemons were often to be had. In this connection, it may be noted that the victualling contractor supplied only the staple articles of diet. Each ship was allowed a certain sum of money in dollars, called 'necessary money,' with which the purser might buy fresh meat, vegetables, etc., as the need arose. The cost of watering ships at Madras, Bombay and Penang was borne by the Company.

There seems to be no direct evidence as to what the normal diet was in a man-of-war on the East Indies station, but the contract for the victualling of the hospital ship at Penang, in 1809, is at least suggestive. The full diet may be taken as being much the same as what a seaman would have in an ordinary ship when in harbour and commanded by a thoughtful captain, with the addition of certain luxuries usually confined to the officers. By the contract, then, every patient on full diet was to have a pint of tea for breakfast, the tea to be 'real good Souchong' in a stated quantity, with a fixed proportion of brown sugar and milk. For dinner, each was to have a pint of stew composed of a pound of beef or mutton, with barley or rice, onions or pumpkin. With this the patient was entitled to a pound 'of the best wheaten Bread' and two-thirds of a pint of 'good sound wine.' For supper there was an allowance of rice, boiled as congee with some milk added. Patients on low diet were to be given sago, vegetables, milk, eggs and arrack in lieu of meat and wine. All patients, whether scorbutic or not, were generously dosed on arrival with lemons or limes so as to be on the safe side. The full diet, with salt beef usually substituted for fresh, and omitting the wine and milk, was probably not unlike the ordinary fare in a sea-going ship.

As regards clothing in the East Indies squadron, the men seem usually to have worn some kind of tropical kit. The crew of the *Blenheim*, for instance, were supplied by contract with 'coarse and inferior' duck frocks and trousers; the frocks costing 4s. 10d. and the trousers 4s. 3d. a pair. There is mention in other ships of straw hats and canvas caps. Strictly speaking, the officers were supposed to wear their proper uniforms when on duty; and they always did so at dinner. Even in the strictest ships, however, they changed into white jackets as soon as they came off duty. Midshipmen were at such times content with nankeen trousers and an open shirt; they also very probably wore straw hats, even when on duty. With regard to dress, it is clear that things were tolerated in the East and West Indies which would not have passed muster at Spithead. In his *Naval Adventures*, Bowers describes joining a smart ship at Plymouth in 1807, as midshipman. Having served only in the East Indies, he arrived on board in a Flushing greatcoat and a 'Leadenhall-street-cut' jacket—amidst roars of laughter from the young gentlemen on the quarter-deck, who were all dressed in uniform coats, silk stockings or Hessian boots with tight pantaloons, and gold-laced cocked hats. In such matters the East Indies were probably more careless than the West, as being farther away. And when the attire of a frigate's officers at Madras might be a little faded and frayed, it may be supposed that midshipmen of a sloop at Malacca would scarcely be distinguishable from the men. There was never quite the slovenliness in the English squadron as was to be seen in the French frigates, where lieutenants appeared in check shirts without cravats. But smartness was hardly even aimed at except under the eye of the commander-in-chief. The acting lieutenant (aged fourteen) who came to impress men from the H.C.S. *Asia*, as mentioned on an earlier page, was described as 'dirty and ragged in his dress' with a midshipman's coat and 'dirty trowsers.' On a second visit, he had rectified his appearance by donning a lieutenant's coat, the effect being spoilt, however, by his having no stockings. That this was not exceptional is shown by the fact that the observant Hickey once mistook the first lieutenant of the *Belliqueux* for a midshipman.

In general, the East Indies squadron must be thought of as eternally struggling to keep up appearances. The main object of the struggle was to remain European. That is why 'Bombay Marine' was the insult used in place of the more usual 'regular privateer'; the point of the sneer being to insinuate that the ship referred to was 'going native.' This was a tendency to which all ships were, in fact, exposed. Despite every effort, lascars and country canvas, coir cordage and boiled rice, arrack and ghee would find their way on board. What was worse, many a frigate had to disfigure herself at a blow by assuming the appearance of a country ship and the function of a 'plain clothes' policeman. Altogether, we must picture the ships as totally unlike the contemporary prints of them. We know what a frigate was supposed to look like. It was not thus that she was seen in India. The cloud of snowy canvas gave place in the East to an odd collection of grey and yellow sails, patched and worn and discoloured with age. The awnings were stained and streaked with tar from the rigging. The paintwork was dingy and blistered and the pitch had run from every seam. Half the crew looked like natives, some of them because they were natives; and the rest looked ill, chiefly because they were ill. The marines would be reduced to a handful, their tattered uniforms faded to a sort of pink. Officers and midshipmen had lost all resemblance to the fashion-plates, and there was a strong tendency for everyone to hold acting rank. There might be two or three soured and elderly lieutenants, ruled with some difficulty by a very young and anxious commander, blessed with an acting commission and a load of debt. This is the kind of ship we must imagine; and at the end of it we must recall, with something of a start, that she was practically invincible.

PLATE X. Captain Fleetwood Pellew (1789–1861) in the raid on Batavia
harbour in 1807, which he led at the age of seventeen, by George Chinnery

CHAPTER XVIII

Health and Sickness

FROM an administrative point of view, perhaps the greatest difficulty encountered by the Navy in India was that of keeping seamen alive in sufficient numbers to carry on the duty. There were few means of replacing them and the wastage was terrible. It was not unusual for a frigate to have 50, 60 or even 80 men on the sick list at a time; and there was at least one case of a frigate coming into port with only 30 men on deck. Still more significant are the statistics of men invalided by survey. It does not appear that men died on board ship in very alarming numbers, except when ships were anchored off such pestilent marshes as those of Bengal or Batavia. The steady and constant wastage was rather represented by the long list of men discharged as either totally unfit for further service, or else needing a change of climate. The following figures are not complete, for a number of reasons; but they may serve to indicate the extent of the evil.

	Invalided	Remarks
September 1806 (at Madras)	100 men	Including a captain, five lieutenants, a master and a captain of marines.
January 1807	30	Including three captains, three lieutenants, a surgeon, four midshipmen and two boatswains.
September 1807 (at Madras)	27	
April 1807 (at Bombay)	24	Including a lieutenant and a master.
June 1807 (at Bombay)	49	Including a captain and a lieutenant. In 1807 four ships lost a hundred men between them—died of scurvy.
February 1808 (at Madras)	62	Including two officers.
July 1808 (at Madras)	100	Including three lieutenants, two masters and a lieutenant of marines.
August 1808 (at Madras)	16	Including a lieutenant.
December 1808 (at Bombay)	41	

	Invalided	Remarks
December 1808 (at Macao)	48 men	
January 1809 (at Penang)	50	
February 1809 (at Madras)	10	
February 1809 (at Penang)	27	Of seventy-four men invalided at Madras, Bombay and Penang, from February 28th to June 2nd, five were lieutenants.
June 1809 (at Bombay)	29	
July 1809 (at Madras)	15	
September 1809 (at Madras)	100	Including four lieutenants, a surgeon and two masters.
October 1809 (at Penang)	27	Including a lieutenant.
October 1809 (at Bombay)	9	
December 1809 (at Penang)	63	
January 1810 (at Madras)	51	

The above lists are incomplete because they omit the numbers invalided at Penang during the period of Sir T. Troubridge's command there, that officer having sent no communications on the subject to the Admiralty. They are incomplete, again, as regards officers, and perhaps in other respects. Even so, here we have little under nine hundred men invalided in something over three years. Add to this the probable number invalided at Penang in 1807 and 1808, another hundred at least. To the thousand so obtained, add the hundreds who died of disease or were killed in action and the scores drowned or killed in falling from aloft. Then add the further numbers who died while prisoners at the Isle of France, or who died afterwards from wounds received in action. Going merely on the probabilities, and leaving out the eight or nine hundred men who went down in the *Blenheim* and *Java*—as men who were quitting the station in any case—it would be safe to say that the squadron lost between fifteen hundred and two thousand men in three years, mostly died or invalided from disease.

Now, what were the prevalent diseases? Scurvy was probably the commonest, and the one causing most loss of life. It hardly appears, however, in the invalid lists, except as a complication in some other disease. Men with scurvy either died or recovered. They were either buried at sea or sent back to their duty. And the same applies to the common fevers and fluxes. The diseases for which men were invalided were various. Officers, on the other hand, were nearly always invalided for the same complaint—'Chronic Disease of the liver.' Sometimes they combined this with dysentery, spasms or bowel complaints. The liver disease was very common on shore at Madras, and was often connected with various forms of excess. Seamen had hepatitis instead. Of the 92 men invalided at Madras in September 1806, 19 had ulcers, 13 suffered from hepatitis, 12 from debility and 6 from dysentery; 5 had lost a leg by amputation, 11 were lame, and others were epileptic, ruptured or insane. Of nearly 100 men invalided in July 1808, 19 had ulcers, 15 suffered from debility, 12 had dysentery—scorbutic or otherwise—and 7 had hepatitis. These are roughly the proportions found in most lists. Other diseases which were fairly common were consumption, phthisis, diseased viscera, gravel, asthma, rheumatism, vertigo, paralysis and venereal disease. The average age of the men invalided works out at about 33, and the average number of years in the service at 7 or 8. Very few of the men invalided were as old as fifty and many were under twenty-five. Admiral Drury was guilty of no exaggeration when he referred to the 'frightful Invalided Lists' he had to submit.

The principal naval hospital was at Madras. It was first established by Admiral Rainier on his own authority, to meet a growing need. The Admiralty approved, and the Commissioners of the Sick and Hurt Board sent out a surgeon and other officers. This first and temporary establishment consisted of three detached buildings, not designed for the purpose, but apparently built originally as private houses. As no instructions were sent out by the Board responsible, these buildings were used for some years, being repaired and added to as appeared necessary. Pellew, soon after his arrival, appointed a naval officer as governor, a fourth building being added as an official residence. The post was, of course a sinecure; but the Admiral found it a convenient method of securing the promotion of favoured lieutenants. The appointment, as created by himself, carried with it the rank of commander, and lay in his own gift. The holder of the office was automatically given the first sloop that fell vacant, his rank giving him a superior claim. So matters continued until December 1807, when a violent gale destroyed part of the hospital and rendered it necessary to reconstruct the whole. Pellew accordingly asked the Government of Fort St. George to allow their civil engineer to design and submit an estimate for a new building. Hospitals, by this time, had been transferred from the

Sick and Hurt Board's care to that of the Transport Board; but Pellew received neither encouragement nor blame from either department. The matter was too urgent to admit of any delay in waiting for orders. Left to his own devices, Pellew accepted the estimate and told the builders to proceed. The new hospital was finished by October 1808; an impressive edifice with Ionic columns and a T-shaped ground plan. There was accommodation for some three hundred patients, and various detached buildings served to house the staff. The grounds were adorned by a large

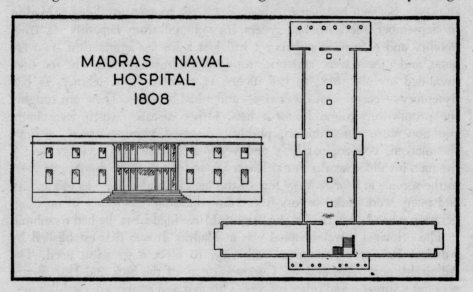

MADRAS NAVAL
HOSPITAL
1808

tank, and a rope walk was constructed in one of the verandahs, providing employment for convalescents. The old hospital buildings were demolished.

At Bombay the naval hospital consisted of some buildings in the dock-yard, formerly used for stores. It was not a very satisfactory arrangement, Bombay itself having no great reputation for healthiness. Admiral Drury went so far as to write 'the Grave of our Seamen is Bombay Hospital.' The only alternative to it was a building on Butcher's Island, which proved little better. A solution, however, was found in 1810. In that year the *Arrogant* (64), which had been used since 1804 in the triple capacity of receiving ship, sheer hulk and floating battery, was condemned as unfit for further service. The *Ardaseer*, country ship, was purchased at this time to serve as a man-of-war. Admiral Drury, thinking little, apparently, of her qualities, resolved to turn her into a floating hospital. For this purpose she was renamed *Arrogant*. She presumably served as sheer hulk as well. The duties of a receiving ship were transferred to some ranges of barracks on Butcher's Island, and for a floating battery there was, it seems, no further occasion.

The idea of establishing a floating hospital at Bombay was suggested by the success attending a similar experiment at Penang. Since 1804 the practice had been to put all the sick and wounded which had to be landed at Penang under the care of the Company's chief surgeon, a certain Dr. Hunter. Early in 1808, however, the *Wilhelmina* was reported as worn out, and Pellew decided to send her to Fort Cornwallis to act as hospital ship. She was a 32-gun frigate, it will be remembered, and had formerly been used as a troopship. She began her new duties in January 1809 when the contract already mentioned—for victualling—was entered into with the surgeon in charge. For half a dollar a day per patient he undertook to supply victuals, bedding, night gowns, night caps, lamps, bed pans, etc.; which was thought a great reduction on what had formerly been paid for the patients under the Company's surgeon.

As regards the skill of the medical men, little can be said. When a crew was infected with contagious ulcers, the surgeons offered no remedy except amputations all round; and these did not necessarily save the life of the patient. They were defeated, again, by malignant fevers. When some seamen in the *Tremendous* were poisoned with fish caught off the Isle of France—just as Boscawen's men had been poisoned a half-century before—the surgeon's remedies seem to have been sufficiently drastic. Beginning with ipecacuanha emetics, purgatives of Cl. Ricini, Natron Vitriolat, and the common purging powder (Pulv. Jalapii and Cremor Tartari), he went on to administer large doses of opium, Peruvian bark, warm fomentations, more Cl. Ricini and an electuary of sulphur in particular cases. The men recovered, whether because of or in spite of the treatment it is for the learned to decide. It seems improbable that the surgeons had attained any very great degree of skill in their art. On the other hand, when Pellew wrote that 'the Invalids and Sick from the several Ships in general, are gradually diminishing in their number under the attention they receive from medical treatment. . . .' he probably intended his words to be interpreted in the best possible sense.

More important than the efforts made to cure disease were the efforts made to prevent it. The art had been more or less founded by Captain Cook, who, on his voyage of 1772, which lasted three years, lost but one man out of a crew of a hundred and eighteen—the one man having had his lungs affected before he embarked. His method involved the frequent use of sweet wort (malt), sour-krout, and portable soup, but it is possible that his success was more due to his force of character. It is not everyone who can compel sailors to eat sour cabbage. In the same way, he insisted on having a clean ship. The desirability of cleanliness, like the antiscorbutic properties of sour-krout, was known before Cook's time. His innovation was in seeing that the ship was cleaned and the cabbage eaten. Although, however, he had laid the foundations of a system of naval diet and hygiene, its instant adoption throughout the service was hardly to be looked for. In the first decade of the nineteenth century a great many officers were still ignorant in regard to the preservation of health afloat. The days of 'spit and polish' were just beginning, and there was already a routine for keeping the decks, the galley and the cooking utensils spotlessly clean. This was very well so far as it went; but shining decks were perfectly compatible with dirt below the waterline. Captain Cook's care in ventilating, scrubbing and drying the underwater parts of a ship was by no means universally imitated. Captain Smyth, the biographer of Captain Beaver, relates how, as an officer in a ship of the line in the East, he discovered the cause of the disease which had decimated the crew. The ship referred to must have been either the *Powerful* or *Russel*, in 1806. On clearing her hold at Bombay, after the return from Batavia 'the ground tier of casks was found imbedded in a feculent mass of putrid mud! This palpable source of remittent fever did not excite much remark at the time. . . .' That it was not thought in any way remarkable is significant, but what is especially worth noticing is that the evil was wholly preventable by washing the shingle ballast before stowing it and thenceforward flushing and pumping out the bilgeways at regular intervals. If these precautions could be neglected on board a ship of the line, it may be supposed that frigates and sloops, often commanded by mere boys, were frequently in at least as bad a case.

It would not be too much to say that the vast majority of the seamen who lost their lives in the East Indies were the victims, not of the climate, but of the ignorance of their officers. The older captains, who had sometimes learnt something from their own blunders, sighed over the inexperience of youthful commanders. Their error was in believing that experience was necessary. Actually, the methods of avoiding disease were all laid down in print. Where officers failed was simply in neglecting to read it.

Besides dirt and occasional errors in diet, a frequent source of debility in a crew was that described by Captain Basil Ball in the following passage:

> It is a most painful thing . . . and exceedingly destructive to the health of a ship's crew, who have been for some time in that country, when she falls under the command of an inexperienced officer, just arrived from Europe, and who, from being himself at first almost entirely insensible to

the disagreeable effect of the heat, considers the objections which other people make to exposure as mere fancies. Under this impression, he admits of no difference being made in the hours of work, but employs his people aloft, and in the boats, when sailing through the Straits of Sunda, or moored in Madras Roads, with as much unconcern as if he were navigating the British Channel, or lying snug at Spithead. The officers, and especially the surgeon, remonstrate in vain; poor Jack of course can say nothing; but in a few months, or it may be in a few weeks or days, half the ship's company find themselves in the doctor's list . . . a judicious captain, under exactly similar circumatances, will not, perhaps, lose a man. . . .

From half-past nine or ten, till two or three o'clock, an officer of experience and consideration, if he can help it, will never allow a seaman's head to appear above the hammock-railing, but will discover some employment for the men on the main and lower decks. If the ship be at anchor, he will lay out a line, and warp the ship broadside to the sea breeze, that the cool air may sweep freely through all parts of the decks, and render everything fresh, sweet, and wholesome. No boats will be sent away from the ship during that fiery interval; or if any duty absolutely requires exposure, it will be got over with the utmost expedition. In the event of the men getting wet by a shower of rain, it is always right to make them shift their clothes instantly, and to muster them afterwards, to see their things are dry and clean . . . the fatal effects of a hot climate on the European constitution, unless very carefully watched, are inevitable. When I have seen regiments reduced to mere skeletons, and ships so weakened in their crews that they could scarcely weigh the anchor, I have often thought of Dr. Johnson's words . . . etc.

The failure to guard against the effects of a tropical sun was not confined to the young and inexperienced. In 1806 Sir Thomas Troubridge was writing to Lord Sidmouth from Penang, 'I have just returned from a *thirteen hours* row and sail along the Coast and up the Rivers looking at Timber; by *way of treat*, I took the Governor with me—the Thermometer 93. I am so well season'd that it does not effect me.' The heat may or may not have affected Troubridge; but what about his boat's crew? And, as for the governor, we know that he died shortly afterwards. It is quite possible that this futile expedition cost half a dozen lives one way and another. Troubridge was neither young nor inexperienced, and he should, in fact, have known better.

Another point to notice in Troubridge's letter is that he shared the common heresy about the possibility of becoming 'seasoned' to the climate. This may have been possible ashore, but it was repeatedly shown that the effect of the climate on seamen was cumulative; and that no men were so liable to sickness as those who had been in the East for four or five years. Johnson, the surgeon of the *Caroline*, wrote some remarks on this point which he included in his *Oriental Voyager* and which are worth quoting.

> And here let me most sincerely bewail the cause, whatever it may be, that can induce government to keep ships such a length of time on the East India station before they are relieved!
>
> The prevailing idea, that men, by remaining a long time in India, become seasoned to the climate, and thereby better able to bear its effects, is, in my opinion, erroneous and uncharitable. It is true, that most Europeans on their first arrival here, as well as in other hot countries, experience a slight fit of illness, which probably renders them less obnoxious to disease for the next three or four years; but after this period we may, in general, expect that the constitution is imperceptibly giving way before the effects of the climate, which is rendered still more evident by the first serious illness that happens; when the debilitated state of the constitution gives them a much smaller chance of recovery, than if the disease took place within the above-mentioned period. It is well known, that the depressing passion of 'Hope deferred' is highly injurious to the constitution in any country; but in this one it is peculiarly so; many of the sailors looking entirely to the gloomy side of the picture, and considering themselves as sacrificed to the climate, when they see their messmates gradually drop off, with little other prospect before them than that of sharing the same fate! Men of this description are the very first to feel the baleful influence of the climate . . . men stand a much better chance of enjoying good health during the first three years in India, than they do afterwards. This was strongly instanced in the *Caroline* frigate; for though we were in the most sickly parts of India, we lost fewer men, in the same space of time, than any of those frigates whose crews had been a long time in the country. . . .

Johnson's recommendations for preserving the health of seamen in India, while including the above plea for a shorter period of service there, are also interesting in other respects. He urges the frequent washing of lower decks, the keeping of the crew under the awnings between 11.0 and 4.0, the substitution of wine for arrack whenever possible, and the withholding of liberty to go ashore. On the subject of cold baths, he is less drastic than the Duke of Wellington. The latter made his men have a cold bath every morning while on board ship in the East, whether they liked it or not. Johnson merely advises that the officers should encourage the men to bathe by example and precept—a bath to consist of a few buckets of water thrown over the head, in the chains. He is less keen on allowing the men to swim about the ship, or in a sail over the side, owing to the risk of sharks or excessive fatigue.

James Prior, the surgeon of the *Nisus*, left no dissertation on the subject of preserving health at sea, but the system observed in that frigate was recorded by Captain Smyth. When at anchor, especially in any unhealthy locality, no boats were allowed to leave the ship after sunset, and nobody was allowed to sleep on shore. 'During the hours of rest, the men were kept strictly to their hammocks, from an impression that the night dews of the tropics are frequently productive of disease; for seamen, sooner than endure the heat below, will, if left to themselves, run any risk by sleeping in the open air.' Every morning the 'tween decks were washed, and then kept clear for the rest of the day, so as to be cooled by ventilation and ready for when the hammocks should be piped down in the evening.

On this question of keeping the men to their proper berths at night, Johnson was somewhat heretical. In his view, it was best to allow the men to sleep on the forecastle, booms, hammock nettings or quarter-deck. He maintains that, in harbour, this was their only chance of getting a night's rest. If kept below they merely sweated and fidgeted, making excuses to come on deck as often as they could. He recommends that the awnings should be left standing at night, and the men—despite the regulations—allowed to sleep where they would; except, that is, when off rivers or swamps or at seasons when a heavy dew falls.

Considering how intelligently Johnson writes about the general domestic economy of a ship, it is rather astonishing that he had so little to say about diet. His assumption was that all that could be done was already being done. As a matter of fact, the best remedy for scurvy and hepatitis was available in his day and yet utterly neglected. It came into use only in 1808, as a result of the efforts of Dr. Anderson of Madras. This remedy was the nopal.

Dr. Anderson came out to India in 1758, as surgeon in an Indiaman called the *Drake*. Scurvy broke out on the voyage, and Anderson found that he could not check or cure it with any of the conventional remedies —that is, by the unlimited use of portable soup, claret, port, madeira, beer, porter and elder. On a return voyage in 1760 he made the still more interesting discovery that lime juice was utterly useless. It is curious to see how early its uselessness was proved, if only because of the nineteenth-century legislation which compelled all British ships to carry it in quantities which gave them the name of 'limejuicers.' It was only the experience of arctic explorers which eventually shook the official doctrine on the subject. Dr. Anderson, then, had his attention drawn to the subject of scurvy by his own failure to cure the crew of the H.C.S. *Drake*. He discovered that lemons could do what limes could not; but lemons were not obtainable in the East Indies, and he set about looking for another remedy. In the course of his experiments he tried, and apparently failed, to transplant the cultivated cochineal from Mexico. Applying, however, to Sir Joseph Banks, the President of the Royal Society, he was given a nopal plant from Kew gardens. He was living, by that time, at Madras. The plant was sent out to him and he started to cultivate it in his garden. This must have been a great many years after his first voyages, for it was not until 1796 that a trial was made of the nopal's antiscorbutic properties. In that year, having sailed in 1795, the supercargo of the ship *Two Brothers* wrote to Dr. Anderson to say that the nopal was 'equal to any vegetable I ever eat in soup, famous in curries, and very good boiled,' and that it was, moreover, an excellent antiscorbutic. Dr. Anderson published this letter, but without attracting the slightest attention. He continued, however, to cultivate the plant, someone sending him a better specimen from China. Although he offered to supply ships with it gratis, and frequently wrote and spoke in its praise, nothing was done until 1808, which must have been near the end of his life. In that year he was able to write to Sir Joseph Banks to say that several men-of-war were now using the nopal with good effect, so that there was 'a fair prospect of abolishing scurvy from the marine service.'

The first ship to make use of Dr. Anderson's discovery was the *Russel*, Mr. Charles Edmund being the surgeon. He reported in March of the year 1808 that he had begun by giving it to his patients in its raw state; that they liked it, comparing it with sorrel, but instantly had diarrhoea afterwards. Thenceforward he had only used it in soup, putting some in the coppers every day so that the whole crew should have it. His letter to Dr. Anderson ends with a request for a further supply. The next officer to experiment with the plant was Captain Tucker, of the *Dover*. He and his surgeon, Jeffreys, dosed forty selected men with a leaf a day, and noted that not one of them had scurvy while all the rest of the crew was more or lest tainted with it. After this, the plant came widely into use, Dr. Anderson circulating a paper of directions for its preservation and offering to supply the leaves to all who applied. The particular virtues claimed for it were that it would keep indefinitely, that it was always procurable, and that it was wholesome, nutritious and palatable whether raw or cooked.

Although the nopal was a useful discovery, it was still possible to combat scurvy without it, in the same way as Captain Cook had done. This was demonstrated by Flinders, the explorer, who sailed in 1801 to survey the shores of Australia, and who preserved his men merely by cleanliness, ventilation, sour-krout, oatmeal, portable soup and plenty of fresh water. More significant still was the voyage of the *Belliqueux* from China to England in 1811. The ship had been in the East for five years, and, of the 491 men on board, some 50 were exchanged from other ships as invalids needing a change of climate. Most of these had been in the East for ten years but had not actually been invalided. Thirty-two more of the total complement were sent on board as unfit for duty. Despite all this, Captain Byng contrived to land his seamen in England, alive and well. Partly through the captain's generosity, there was purchased in China 12 dozen capons, 2,000 pounds of potatoes, 200 pounds of carrots, 800 pounds of pumpkins, 500 pounds of dry onions and 2 catties of rusk. The nopal was not forgotten, being introduced as an ingredient of a pickle of which the basis was formed of onions and vinegar, nutmegs, mace, cinnamon, ginger and pepper. It played, however, but a small part in the triumph. Fresh supplies of livestock and vegetables, particularly watercress, were obtained at St. Helena, and the voyage ended without the loss of a man.

CHAPTER XIX

The French Islands Blockaded

FROM the time of the *Marengo's* capture, Decaen was in effective command of the naval forces based on Mauritius. From 1806 to 1808, however, these amounted to very little. The *Piémontaise* cruised with some success until taken, as we have seen, in 1808. The *Semillante*, after her action with the *Phaeton* in 1805, returned to refit at Port Louis. She cruised the year following in company with the privateers *Bellone* and *Henriette*, both of which were taken. Motard of the *Semillante* was more fortunate, took numerous prizes and brought them safely to port. Damaged in action, however, with the *Dedaigneuse* in 1808, the *Semillante* returned that year to France. This left Decaen with only one frigate, the *Canonnière* (40) which had come out in 1806, and one corvette, the *Jena* (18), a purchased privateer. To this force was added the British sloop *Laurel* (22), taken by the *Canonnière* in 1808, but this gain merely offset the loss of the *Jena*, taken by the *Modeste* (36) off the Sandheads. Soon afterwards the *Canonnière*, found to be worn out, was disarmed and sold as a merchantman, only to be captured on her way back to France.[1] The naval force at Port Louis was reduced almost to nothing.

As against this dwindling of resources, the Ile de France was experiencing an increasingly effective blockade. Pellew had been able to blockade the French base only intermittently from India. But the recapture of the Cape in 1806 and its re-establishment as a separate command altered the whole situation. Troubridge was succeeded by Rear-Admiral Stirling and he in turn by Rear-Admiral Bertie. Before the latter's arrival in the *Leopard* (50) in August 1808, the squadron was commanded by Captain Josias Rowley and comprised the *Raisonable* (64), *Grampus* (50), *Nereide* (36), *Laurel* (22), *Otter* (18), *Harrier* (18) and *Cormorant* (20). The duty of these vessels resolved itself into a blockade of the French islands which Bertie directed from the Cape and Rowley commanded off Port Louis. The capture of the *Laurel* was an early incident of a blockade which became effective in the autumn of 1808, and increasingly so as the squadron was reinforced.

[1] Worth about £150,000, she was chased fourteen times in ninety-three days and finally taken off Belleisle by the *Valiant* (74), Captain John Bligh.

The Ile de France was now in real danger of famine and Decaen lacked any naval means of breaking up the blockade. His appeals, however, to Napoleon were not wholly ignored. In 1808–9 there reached Port Louis successively the *Manche* (40) Captain Dornal de Guy, the *Caroline* (40) Captain Billard, the *Bellone* (44) Captain Duperré, the *Vénus* (44) Commodore Hamelin and the *Mouche No. 6*. These four frigates formed the 'Division Hamelin' but sailed from different ports—Cherbourg, Nantes and Flushing—the Commodore on 12th November, 1808. All four reached Port Louis in safety, despite the blockade, the *Manche* and *Caroline* being fired on by the *Raisonable* but without effect. Putting to sea again in February 1809, the *Caroline* cruised off the Sandheads and captured two East Indiamen, the *Streatham* and *Europe*. Commodore Hamelin himself with the *Vénus* and *Manche* and a corvette, the *Creole*, raided and destroyed the East India Company's small settlement at Tappanooly, off the west coast of Sumatra, and then captured three East Indiamen, the *Windham*, *United Kingdom* and *Charlton*. The *Bellone* also appeared in the Bay of Bengal and there captured the sloop *Victor* (18), and later the Portuguese frigate *Minerva* (52). The success of Hamelin's squadron was due partly to surprise—there had been hardly any naval opposition in 1806–8 and Hamelin appeared without warning—partly to Drury's disdain for trade protection, and partly to luck. At any rate, there was consternation in India, and eventually in Leadenhall Street. There was also a growing realization that nothing short of the capture of the French islands could make such a raid impossible.

Just as the arrival of Hamelin altered the whole situation for Admiral Drury, so did it alter the whole position at the French islands. Whereas the blockade could previously be maintained by a 50-gun ship or frigate with two sloops, the autumn of 1809 found the French islands watched by the *Raisonable* (64), *Leopard* (50), four frigates and two sloops. Even in this strength the squadron had failed to prevent the *Bellone* (44) breaking out on August 17th. The blockade had never, in fact, been very effective as regards men-of-war, although a sufficient discouragement for the slower kind of merchantman. Some of the British officers had great experience of blockading but the French islands were not and had never been easy places to blockade. The problem was to watch three widely separated ports— Port Louis, Grand Port and St. Paul's in the neighbouring island of Bourbon —and guard each with a force equivalent to the force inside or likely to arrive from elsewhere. In practice, the French men-of-war were normally at Port Louis. It was open to them, nevertheless, to put in, on arrival, at one of the other ports, both of which were adequately defended. They could also obtain by signal, when approaching from to windward, the exact position of the blockading ships. Generally speaking, duty off the Mauritius was an unpopular and unrewarding task. Early in 1809 it was made slightly easier by the occupation of Rodriguez (or Roderigue) by Lt.-Col. Keating and a small force from Bombay. Rodriguez provided wood and water, with occasionally a few vegetables and poultry.

One result of a closer blockade by a larger force was that British naval officers became more familiar with the French islands. The idea that they were impregnable began to be modified as a result of intensive reconnaissance. This may be said to have begun when the boats of the sloop *Otter* (18) cut out a lugger from under the batteries of Riviere-Noire, Ile de France, on the night of the 14th–15th August, 1809. Unimportant in itself, this affair served to show what could be done. What was a mere raid might have been a landing. Apart from that, it served to bring into local prominence the name of Nesbit Willoughby, the *Otter's* commander. As a quarrelsome lieutenant he had been dismissed his ship, and then dismissed the Navy. He had thereafter regained his commission by service as a volunteer, and then gained promotion on appointment to the *Otter*. He was to be in the forefront of events which followed—a man of courage and resource, able, cruel and—although repeatedly wounded—apparently immortal. Contemporary with him on this station was Captain Robert Corbet, another very active officer and even less popular among the men.

Next stage in the reconnaissance of the French islands was heralded by the arrival of the *Caroline* after her successful cruise in the Bay of Bengal. Being warned of Rowley's presence off Port Louis, the *Caroline* put into St. Paul's, Bourbon, with her two prizes, the H.C. Ships *Streatham* and *Europe*. Rowley pursued the *Bellone*, which escaped from Port Louis on 17th August, 1809, failed to overtake her and returned to find the *Caroline*, as reported, at St. Paul's. Thoroughly exasperated, he now decided to repeat, on a larger scale, Willoughby's raid on Riviere-Noire. He sent Corbet with the *Nereide* (36), *Otter* and *Sapphire*, sloops, to Rodriguez, with a request for the loan of some troops. Keating decided to come in person, embarking about 368 of his 600 men on board the frigate, sloops and *Wasp* schooner. This was on September 16th, and Corbet's ships joined the *Raisonable* (64) and *Sirius* (36) off Port Louis, where the final arrangements were made. The team was an exceptionally strong one for the purpose in view. With Rowley to direct, Corbet to carry out the disembarkation, Keating to plan and command the attack on land, and Willoughby to dash in with the seamen who would man the captured batteries, the success of the operation seemed certain. The plan involved, first, a threat to the Ile de France. Then the whole squadron sailed after dark on the 19th, and so timed the voyage as to be off St. Paul's, but unseen, by sunset on the 20th. The squadron then hove to and the *Nereide* went in alone, carrying all the troops and equipped with barges and cutters from other vessels, hoisted on temporary davits all round the ship.

Lieutenant Samuel Walters in the *Raisonable* reported the landing, which took place seven miles from St. Paul's, as follows:[1]

> Very light wind, all the first watch: by midnight the *Nereide* had not run above one third of her distance towards Galet point. But soon after daylight [when] we were about to telegraph to know if the troops were disembarked, that ship was laying within a quarter of a mile of the beach, sails all furl'd, and it is believed that she had never been discovered by the enemy from her anchoring to her making sail from it. Before we had time to hoist the second number, she made the whole at once, as follows 'troops on shore and near the first battery.' At that moment the frigate's anchor trip'd, and she was in [under] a cloud of sail. [She] joined the squadron and took her station in succession in the line, and sent the boats to their respective ships, with a celerity peculiar to the gallant Captn. Corbet. Very soon after, the report of several guns were heard, and about 6 o'clock we had the pleasure of observing the Union Jack planted on the first or Eastmost battery—a great success in such a short time. . . .

The anchorage at St. Paul's was defended by a series of seven batteries mounting over a hundred guns, and forming a wide crescent. The first three were captured more or less by surprise but the centre battery had to be stormed. The squadron meanwhile could not close on the anchorage, partly because the western batteries were still firing, partly because their own fire had to be withheld until the position of the troops ashore was more exactly known. When the last battery ceased fire, the squadron stood in to the bay and anchored near the *Caroline* and shipping, which quickly surrendered. By 8.30 a.m. the affair was over and the town captured.

> Thus was executed [writes Walters], in less than four hours by the superior skill and judgment of a few clever men, plans that treble the force would have failed in under inferior commanders. . . .'

There was no question at that time of attempting the conquest of the island, which had a considerable, although mainly militia, garrison, and Rowley withdrew his forces on the 28th and took the troops back to Rodriguez, thereafter resuming the blockade as before. The question was now whether the squadron would succeed in intercepting the French

[1] *Samuel Walters, Lieutenant R.N.* Ed. by C. N. Parkinson, p. 78, *et seq.*

frigates when they returned from their cruise. It was a question soon settled, for on 2nd January, 1810, Duperré appeared with the *Bellone* and *Manche*, the captured men-of-war *Minerva* and *Victor*, and the prizes *Charlton* and *United Kingdom*. Hamelin had previously, with the *Vénus*, lured Rowley away from Port Louis and now a freak of wind allowed the French frigates to enter port while the British were becalmed. A month later Rowley returned to the Cape, leaving Captain Lambert of the *Iphigenia* to continue the blockade, with Captain Pym of the *Sirius*, the *Magicienne* and *Sapphire*, and other vessels. The reputation of St. Paul's as a haven of refuge had been rudely shaken, but Port Louis remained as formidable as ever. The blockade, moreover, had to be abandoned as the hurricane season approached, and Decaen seized the opportunity, on March 14th, to send Duperré to sea again with the *Bellone*, *Minerva* and *Victor*.

One fact that emerges from accounts of the French operations at this time is that the French Navy was recovering. A new generation of officers was coming to command, many of them extremely capable. Napoleon had never found his ideal sailor in the generation of Decrès and Linois. Officers who remembered the Navy of the old regime mostly despised the Navy of the Republic and Empire. The best of them, if alive, were in exile or ashore. Of those who served, many were time-servers, glad to achieve swift promotion over mediocre competitors but without any belief in the France of Napoleon. Eastwick describes seeing the sailors of the *Forte* eating their beef or playing cards on the quarter-deck. What sort of discipline was that in the eyes of le Marquis Pierre-Cèsar-Charles Guillaume de Sercey? Or of Charles-Alexandre Leon, Comte Durand de Linois? When the time came they hailed Louis XVIII with relief. In the meanwhile, they went through the motions of naval warfare without enthusiasm for the cause or belief in the outcome. But the new generation of younger officers were of a different kind, brought up in France of the Revolution and with few regrets for what they had hardly known. They appeared in the Navy after 1800 and now, by 1810, were coming to command corvettes and frigates with increasing efficiency. Such men were Pierre Bouvet of the *Minerve*, Duperré of the *Vénus*, Roussin and Baudin, the future Admirals. In the *Marengo*, even, there had been some good junior officers, especially the navigators who charted the coast from Cape Frio to Cape Lopez.[1] The result was seen in such an action as that of *L'Arethuse* and *Amelia* in 1813, as well as in the actions now to be described.

---

[1] In the *Belle Poule* was Bonnefoux, later to be the author of the *Dictionnaire de marine à voiles et à vapeur*. The *Belle Poule*, which crossed the equator twenty-six times in three years, certainly offered her officers some experience of navigation.

What was happening, meanwhile, on the East India Station proper? The blockade of the French islands was not so stringent as to save India from the French commerce raiders whose safe return we have noted. It is natural to ask what the East Indies Squadron was doing about it. The station was, from 13th February, 1809, under the command of Rear-Admiral Drury. That was the date, at least, of his arrival at Madras following Pellew's departure for Europe. Drury found the squadron reduced in strength, three sail of the line and two frigates having been sent home and a frigate and two sloops lost or taken. French cruisers were at sea and Drury wrote to Lord Minto on the 26th to explain that he would do what he could to check their activities. His immediate grievance, however, concerned their present deployment.

The memorial signed by the Calcutta merchants had been ignored at the Admiralty, but it had not failed to have its effect on Pellew. Although one of the ablest men in the Navy, Pellew had his weaknesses. He had but just become a Vice-Admiral, and he was not much over fifty. The best part of his career was only beginning and, if all went well, the highest honours might be his. Nor did he despise such things as rank and fame. He looked forward to the peerage he was afterwards to obtain. On the other hand, he was far from certain of it. He knew what had happened to Duckworth and Strachan; and he was the last man to take any risk with his reputation if he could avoid it. He was thus always sensitive to criticism, always thin-skinned. Even in later days, when immortal fame as well as peerage seemed almost within his grasp, he was often on the brink of resigning because of some slight put upon him by the Admiralty. In sending that memorial to England, the merchants had in fact found the joint in his armour.

It is not surprising that a man with Pellew's special weaknesses should have taken pains to ward off further criticism. Instead of pigeon-holing all complaints with an Admiralty official's nonchalance, he had tried in all seriousness to remedy what the merchants found amiss. He may thereby have earned their gratitude. He certainly did not receive it. As for his unfortunate successor, it was left for him to undo the mischief and face the abuse. Luckily, Drury was the reverse of Pellew. With his supreme contempt for all 'Merchants or Supra Cargoes, India Captains, Parsees. . . .' etc., he was quite impervious to any criticism in the Calcutta newspapers. In fact, he probably enjoyed it. What he did object to was having to spend months in making a better disposal of the force left to his care.

. . . my predecessor by his disposal of the squadron had compromised the high and ostensible situation of a Commander in Chief by placing the whole effective force almost out of my reach. . . .

(P.R.O. Adm. 1/181. 8th May, 1809.)

When applied to for convoy by Lord Minto, he replied, on April 25th, that he had not a single ship to spare. Pellew had allotted three-quarters of the squadron to the Bay of Bengal—6 frigates and as many sloops. There were 3 frigates and 5 sloops based on the Hooghli, a frigate between Cape Negrais and Junkceylon, another between Achin and the Nicobars, and yet another, with a sloop, on the west coast of Sumatra. As for the rest of the ships, there was a ship of the line with the China fleet, and a frigate to escort the Bombay country ships. There were three frigates lending dignity to Brigadier-General Malcolm's mission to Persia. Five other ships were in dock. This left only the *Russel* and *Modeste*; and now the latter ship, a frigate, had gone in chase of two of the enemy's cruisers in the China Seas. The situation was the worse because the ships in the Hooghli were rendered almost inactive through loss of men by disease.

Pellew's system for the defence of the Bay of Bengal—in the establishment of which he made the same mistakes as Rainier had once made—would not have survived for long in any case. But several events took place to hasten its end. The capture of Rodriguez had been decided upon, as we have seen, as a means of maintaining a closer blockade of the Isle of France. The *Belliqueux* had therefore to be detached to escort the transports thither, sailing from Bombay on June 28th. Earlier than this, before June 13th, the orders came for Java to be put under a strict blockade. Finally, the *Cornelia* frigate had been chased off Achin by a French squadron composed of two frigates and a corvette. This had the immediate effect of sending Drury to sea with the *Phaeton* and *Cornelia* to look for them—the *Russel* having gone to fetch troops from Ceylon to suppress a fresh mutiny at Madras. It had the ultimate effect of imposing a new strategy in which frigate squadrons had to be allowed for.

The search for the three French ships, which was not successful, carried Drury as far as Penang. He was there in August, making arrangements for the blockade of Java. The *Modeste*, *Barracouta* and *Procris* were the first vessels detailed for the service, others being later substituted. When first informed of the orders Drury had received, to intercept Arab and Malay trading vessels, Minto protested, as the merchants in the country trade feared reprisals. Drury agreed to modify the blockade, though making it clear that he resented the Supreme Government's interference. 'Their Lordships will perceive,' he wrote to the Admiralty, 'from the tenor of the remonstrance that propensity which is met throughout this Country to direct the Navy as a machine, which never can be permitted, nor shall it ever be left to the disposal of any one but the Commander in Chief so long as I may have the honor to hold that situation.' This was a sentiment he often found occasion to express. Leaving his cruisers to blockade Java and deal with the new fleet of corvettes which the Dutch had, from necessity, brought into existence, Drury returned to Madras, arriving there on September 10th.

Before the Admiral left the coast, at the change of the monsoon, news came of the taking of the Indiamen *Europe* and *Streatham,* the sloop *Victor*, the Portuguese frigate *Minerva* and a number of country vessels in the Bay of Bengal. Almost simultaneously came the news of the plundering of the small settlement at Tapanooley, in Sumatra. The bay had not been left defenceless—far from it—and yet, for the hundredth time, the raiders had escaped. It was 'singularly unfortunate,' as Drury observed. While the *Bellone* made her captures, many English cruisers were crossing the bay, but none had fallen in with her. With the news of the French successes, or hard upon it, came the complaints of the Calcutta merchants. As before, they were sent to the Admiral with a request that he would forward them to the Admiralty. Assuming that they were also communicating direct to England, Drury took care to mention the matter in his next dispatch.

> . . . I am naturally induced to apprize their Lordships of circumstances, as well as to guard them against the deceit practised on the face of the business, by a detail of imaginary distresses, made up, apparently supported by a very large body of Merchants and Agents for the Insurance Companys, which upon a close examination will be found to bear their signatures both collectively and individually. . . .
> . . . To satisfy the Caprice of the Commercial part of Calcutta is utterly impossible: the multifarious interests and views of speculative men, whose minds are only directed to gain their own end, cannot altogether accord with the Commander in Chief, who must judge of the means as well as the result. . . . The Gentlemen of Calcutta must recollect that in regard to the Navy they are neither the Law nor the Gospel, and it will ever be found by them that the Squadron under my Command is steered by Compass alone.
> I lament exceedingly to hear of murmurings and Complaints against officers, particularly when upon investigating the statements, they are found void: and I cannot possibly meet requisitions coming through the Supreme Government without a dereliction of duty.
> It has been imagined that I could forego upon grounds which I knew to be trivial, the orders of His Majesty in Council, as well those from the

Right Honourable the Lords Commissioners of the Admiralty, tending to enforce the Blockade of Java and the Moluccas.

In a second instance I am solicited by the Merchants of Calcutta not to afford protection to Neutrals, particularly Americans, who ask for it, and to prohibit their sailing for fourteen days after the departure of our Fleets! to such entreaties I have been obliged to return a Negative. The Blockade I shall modify, but the Orders I receive must be obeyed. . . .

Drury seems to have written to the Supreme Government in much the same tone, adding, for the merchants' benefit, an announcement of his intention of cautioning his officers against going out of their way to protect the Bengal trade. As he was simultaneously, and openly, planning to transfer the whole naval establishment to Trincomalee, making Coringa and Negapatam the refitting ports, the builders and contractors of Bombay and Madras were making those settlements equally hostile to him. Fresh complaints were made, in which connection the following dispatch may be quoted, chronologically a little out of place.

His Majesty's Ship Russel
Madras Roads: 15th February 1810.

Sir,

An extrordinary Letter from the Merchants of Calcutta to the Supreme Government of India, a copy of which has been transmitted to me by the Honble the Vice President in Council who declined forwarding it to the Honble the Court of Directors to lay before the Lords Commissioners of the Admiralty as a Complaint against me. My Letter which these Gentlemen make the motive for complaint, was one written to repel the unfounded complaint made by the same body against Captain Bremer of the *Rattlesnake*, which was also to have been laid before their Lordships.

Having the honour of filling the highest official Situation in India, binds me to a rigid discharge of my duty, without looking to the right, or left, for either approbation or censure, and standing perfectly indifferent as to the opinion of Men collectively or individually, endeavouring at the same time to maintain the most unreserved and cordial intercourse with the Government of India, which never has been broken.

Striking at peculation, and wasteful expense as well as various adoptions which certainly interfere both with Calcutta and Bombay, in placing the Squadron for certain refits more independent of both, has given more than offence to Speculation and Peculation, but my endeavours to settle the great Harbour of Trincomalee with Chinese Cultivators and Native Artificers (and which from the ready co-operation of General Maitland, who upon this, as other occasions where the Public Welfare is the object, exceeds expectation, but never falls short of it) has opened wide the mouths of India upon me, but whose unwholesome noise their Lordships will I am sure treat as it merits. I have little doubt that in a very short time the foundation will be completely laid to render Trincomalee the finest Port in India, without any expence worthy of consideration, so little, that sooner than not give Trincomalee the trial, I would pay it.

Their Lordships perspicuity needs no further comment from me on the supposed grievances of Merchants and complaints against the Commander in Chief, and their Lordships will approve the conduct of an Officer whose object is the Public Welfare, and whose measures are not to be given up to Cabal. . . .

I have the honour to be

Sir,

Your most obedient
humble Servant
Wm O'B. Drury.

It may be noted in this connection that the Calcutta merchants were always willing to pillory the Admiral, not only because their trade was always more exposed to losses than that of Bombay, but also because they did not know their victim personally. The naval commander-in-chief was hardly ever seen at Fort William. Sir Edward Pellew paid a hasty visit to the fort just before he left India, and that was probably the only time he visited it. Wellesley had urged him to come, shortly before he himself left for England; but the meeting never took place. Drury had, in all probability, never been there in his life. Madras was where Admirals lived. It was there and at Bombay that an Admiral would live ashore and meet all the shipowners at dinner. Pellew's friendship was with Lord William Bentinck, and it was Sir George Barlow's daughter—when Barlow was governor of Madras—that one of his sons married. He had friends, again, at Bombay, notably the great shipowner, Mr. Forbes, who would make caustic comments on the Calcutta merchants' grievances, saying that their opium did more harm than their rice did good. If Drury had any friends, they would be at Madras or Penang. The merchants of Bengal could tear his character to pieces in the certainty they would never meet him at a dinner party. Those of Bombay did their grumbling in private or in the newspapers. They did not compose offensive petitions and sign their names at the foot. The Admiral, whoever he might be, was a man they had to live with afterwards.

Drury quitted Madras in October and proceeded straight to Bombay, where he received reports of Captain Wainwright's operations in the Persian Gulf, where the frigates *Chiffonne* and *Caroline* were smoking out the pirate stronghold of Rusal-Khyma with the assistance of seven of the Company's cruisers. He did not remain there for long, coming south again to Colombo in December, remaining there for part of January 1810, and so back to Madras in February. This was an unusually early time of year for an Admiral to appear on the coast. But the occasion, too, was unusual. A scheme was afoot for ending these French depredations at a blow. The French islands were, at last, to be attacked.

CHAPTER XX
Lord Minto and Admiral Drury

THE mystery which surrounds the capture of Mauritius is simply the mystery of why it was never attacked before. Napoleon, as we have seen, had been surprised to find it still in French hands in 1808 and rightly incredulous of René Decaen's courtly explanation. Napoleon's threat to India had certainly saved the French islands in 1798–1801. Thereafter they were successively saved by the Company's orders—Wellesley was to defend India with the 'smallest possible extension of expenditure'[1]—and by the division of the East Indies station in 1805–7. This was the period, incidentally, of Barlow's rigid economy rule which left Pellew little scope even in his raids on Java. In 1808–9 there was the scare about Persia followed by the scare about the Portuguese colonies. Thenceforward the remaining obstacle was 'the determined spirit of penury' prevalent in India. This spirit, inculcated by Lord Castlereagh, was the ruling and sole principle of government under Sir George Barlow 'displayed in every public advertisement and introduced into every secret despatch.'[2] Lord Minto only gradually freed himself from it, assisted a little by the lamentation of the merchants at Calcutta.[3]

But Minto's dawning conviction that the capture of the French islands would be, in fact, an economy, would have carried little weight at India House had Hamelin's squadron been less successful. There were five frigates based on Mauritius in 1809, with two corvettes and several privateers, and they were doing considerable damage. More important still, they were inflicting losses on the East India Company itself. Until this time it had been a rare occurrence for an East Indiaman to be taken, whatever the havoc wrought among privately owned shipping. Only seven Indiamen had been captured during the years 1793–1801 and of these one was retaken. Several of the smallest class were taken in the period 1803–5,

---

[1] *Despatches of Wellesley.* Ed. S. J. Owen. P. 581.

[2] *Despatches of the Marquess Wellesley.* Ed. S. J. Owen. P. 804.

[3] In 1803 a London merchant could still write, in a letter to a friend in Calcutta 'I hope there will be no idea of an expedition . . . against Batavia and the isles Mauritius. But the rage for extending our dominions is the proper character of Lord W——y's government.' *The Intercepted Letters*, 1804.

two more serious losses being the H.C.S. *Brunswick* (1,200 tons) in 1804, and the H.C.S. *Warren Hastings* (1,200 tons) in 1805. The average was little more, nevertheless, than one a year, and most of the victims were of 500 to 600 tons.[1] Now, in 1809, no less than five Indiamen were taken, the *Europe*, *Streatham*, *Windham*, *United Kingdom* and *Charlton*; all of them of the 800-ton class, and several very richly laden. This entirely unprecedented loss, almost equal to the entire damage sustained during the last war, fell in a year when, as it happened, five more Indiamen foundered at sea. With three ships wrecked, there was a total loss that year of thirteen sail. Although the French were responsible for less than half of the damage, the general impression was alarming. The atmosphere in Leadenhall Street, as well as in Fort William, was perceptibly more warlike.

The Admiralty, advised by Sir Roger Curtis in 1800,[2] had previously suspected that Mauritius, if captured, would prove costly and useless. From 1806, when the Cape was taken afresh, the Navy had used Capetown and Simon's Bay as bases for a blockading squadron. Towards the end of 1808 came orders from the Admiralty to tighten the blockade. Admiral Bertie loyally did his best, wearing out his ships[3] in an effort to cut off the island's food supply. The occupation of Rodriguez did not represent, however, a change of policy but merely an attempt to make the blockade more effective. The events, nevertheless, of 1809 proved the turning point in naval policy. For while it was apparent, on the one hand, that the French frigates could come and go despite the blockade, it was equally apparent on the other hand, that St. Paul's had offered only a feeble resistance to the landing of September 21st. At the moment, in fact, when the French squadron was proving most mischievous, the suspicion dawned that its base was more vulnerable than had been supposed. If St. Paul's could be captured overnight, with the local militia too spiritless to retake it, might not the Ile de France prove as easy a conquest? Could it survive, in any case, if Bourbon were already captured? Naval opinion was fairly summarized, perhaps, by the author who pointed out that Mauritius would always, in French hands, be a 'focus of intrigue with the Native Powers' and 'Not the present, nor any future, nor any possible superiority of the British Navy can wholly prevent a clandestine intercourse on the part of the enemy with Asia, whilst he holds his footing on the Mauritius.'[4]

[1] *A Register of Ships*. Revised by H. C. Hardy, 1813.
[2] *Spencer Papers*. N.R.S. Vol. LIX Curtis to Spencer, 28th November, 1800, p. 238.
[3] Ad. 1/63 Bertie to Admiralty 1st July, 1810.
[4] M.S. *Proposal for the Total Expulsion of the French from Maritime India*. Anon. 1809. BM. MSS. Stowe 865.

When, in March 1810, the Governor-General invited Admiral Drury to confer with him on urgent business at Madras, he was still cautious enough to be thinking of Bourbon rather than of Mauritius. The news of Rowley's raid had convinced him that the conquest of Bourbon would be relatively easy, and he had accordingly decided to postpone an alternative scheme for attacking Java.[1] Admiral Drury, with whom he had had some previous correspondence, maintained that a small addition to the proposed military force (six thousand men instead of four thousand) would justify an attack, not on Bourbon, but directly on Mauritius. Although Lord Minto had refused to take that risk without further information, it would seem that Drury came to Madras in some expectation of the Governor-General changing his mind. Much to the Admiral's annoyance, Lord Minto was immovable and refused, on March 12th, and subsequently, all naval co-operation save for an escort to go with the transports. He explained, however, that he was preparing a second expedition, to follow on the heels of the first, supposing it successful and supposing favourable conditions were reported for attacking Mauritius. Lord Minto's strategy was apparently sound, for failure against Mauritius would be far less serious if there were a neighbouring base to which the defeated expedition could withdraw. But Drury no doubt argued that the attack on the one island would reduce—would in fact eliminate—all chance of surprising the other.

Drury evidently intended to lead the expedition in person and had concentrated his squadron with that end in view, so that 'in April, nearly every ship was collected and ready to proceed.' To have taken his squadron outside his station, as Drury was apparently prepared to do, would have been extremely irregular. But Minto discouraged this idea and preferred to rely for his naval co-operation on Commodore Rowley and the ships already there. His convoy comprised a 50-gun ship, two frigates and fourteen transports, in which he embarked 3,650 troops. Minto wrote on this occasion as follows:

> March 26, 1810.
>
> I am just sending an expedition to make the conquest of the Isle of Bourbon. There is the fairest prospect of success. I propose to follow up the blow by attacking the Mauritius, generally called the Isle of France. . . .
>
> A second expedition must be sent against the Isle of France, and a much larger force: including those going now about 10,000 men. The first will sail from Madras about May 1; the second will probably depart from India in August.[2]

[1] A. G. Field. *The Expedition to Mauritius in 1810.* Unpublished MS. thesis in the library of the University of London.
[2] *Lord Minto in India, 1807–1814.* Ed. by the Countess of Minto, 1880, p. 243.

The first expedition duly sailed in April and arrived at Rodriguez in June 1810. Meanwhile, Lord Minto was hard at work collecting the troops, stores and ships needed for attacking the Mauritius itself. There were difficulties, especially over doing the work in time, and the convoy actually sailed not in August but September. It seemed to many experts that the expedition would have to be postponed until April 1811. But Lord Minto would not agree to that plan. He thought that Decaen might have been reinforced by then. In this, his instinct was perfectly sound. Napoleon had not forgotten the French islands and would soon, in any case, learn of their predicament. On 17th April, 1809, he wrote to Decrès from the Schönbrünn

> ... il est egalement necessaire à penser à envoyer 3 frégates à l'Ile de France. Je n'ai plus dans cette colonie que 5 frégates, parmi lesquelles il y'en aura probablement 1 ou 2 qui seront prises. . . .[1]

This was after the 'Division Hamelin' had sailed and it does not appear that any more frigates were sent until the *Astrée* and *Mouche* sailed early in 1810.[2] Before then, on January 5th, Decaen made a last desperate appeal for ships, men, money and supplies. Napoleon, on receiving this, issued orders (as Minto thought he would) for immediate aid on a large scale—five ships of the line, eight frigates, corvettes and transports with 1,200 or 1,500 men. These orders, perhaps slightly unrealistic, finally produced three 40-gun frigates, each with 200 troops, which sailed for Mauritius on 2nd February, 1811; two months after the island had fallen. Minto foresaw Napoleon's reaction and resolved to persevere with his preparations for the second expedition. He did not at first find Drury very co-operative. Following their disagreement in April the Admiral had dismissed his squadron to different stations between Canton and the Persian Gulf; one detachment, for example, being sent to occupy Amboyna and Banda afresh and land there 'part of the Madras European Regt. who were three months ago in a state of outrageous Mutiny and Rebellion.' Drury was therefore furious when told in July that the Mauritius was to be attacked that autumn. This had been Minto's intention all along, but to Drury it seemed merely the result of vacillation. He replied rather sulkily that he had collected his squadron for just such a purpose not three months ago, and that now the ships were all dispersed. He might get some of them together by September or October. But the *Belliqueux* had been sent

---

[1] *Correspondance de Napoleon avec le Ministre de la Marine 1804–15.* Two vols. Paris, 1838. Vol. II, p. 49.

[2] M. E. Fabre. *La Guerre Maritime dans l'Inde sous le Consulat et l'Empire.* Paris, 1883, p. 65.

home, and the *Russel* was much in need of repair. Then there was the China fleet and the country trade returning to India to be protected—and the Indiamen to go through the Straits of Sunda, too. He consented, however, to do what he could, sending the whole correspondence to the Admiralty with a gesture of derision.

His Majesty's Ship *Cornelia*
Madras Roads 29th July 1810

Sir

I am induced to lay before the Right Honorable the Lords Commissioners of the Admiralty the accompanying letter, as it relates to the attack of the Isle of France, that their Lordships may be satisfied the Squadron under my Command is always ready, in spite of the indecision of Indian Governments and the rejection last April of my entire Squadron for that Service, assembled in consequence of the most exigent Letters of the Governor General for me to meet him at Madras, which I did against the Monsoon and for nothing.

I have the honour to be
Sir
Your most obedient
humble Servant

(P.R.O. Adm. 1/182)   Wm O'B Drury

The final decision of the Supreme Government did not reach Drury until August 18th, soon after which date he reported to the Admiralty that he was collecting all the ships he could to serve with the expedition. He added that 'In acting for the public good it behoves me to set aside the Consideration of serving under a superior officer, and with that idea I shall accompany my Squadron to the Mauritius.' The 'superior officer' referred to was the commander-in-chief at the Cape, Admiral Bertie. It was a detachment from his squadron, under Commodore Rowley, that was blockading the island; and he was, of course, sure to be present when it was attacked. The plan involved a converging of forces from India and the Cape, and Bertie was naturally informed of Lord Minto's plans. What Drury had forgotten was that, in proceeding to the Mauritius, he was quitting his station without orders; a serious offence in itself. Also, in magnanimously offering to serve under a superior officer, he had lost sight of the possibility of that officer not requiring his assistance.

Lord Minto remained serenely determined that the expedition should sail that year, and arrive before the hurricane season, that is, by mid-November.

I have been pretty nearly alone at times [he wrote on September 19th] in thinking it practicable to make the attempt before next April, a delay which might probably have been fatal to the ultimate success. . . . The French . . . employ the hurricane months, when the blockading squadron is obliged to quit the ground, to throw in supplies, and we are informed that, in consequence of the apprehensions excited by our late measures, the most positive assurances have been given to the Governor of the Isle of France that troops, military stores, and all other means of defence shall be dispatched from Europe this very season. It is of great consequence, therefore, that *we* should be at Port Louis to receive such supplies from France, rather than Monsieur De Caen. This is one of several reasons and certainly the strongest, which has made me *damnatus obstinatus mulier* (vide Cowslip's translation) and determined me to push off the expedition now, whether it was possible or not. The weight of opinion was strong against me in all quarters, but when once the point was decided, all hands concurred lustily in the execution, and lo and behold! everything is actually afloat. Three divisions of troops from three Presidencies are now on their passage, with a very perfect equipment, having six weeks to perform a voyage which *may* be done in one month; five weeks is a fair allowance, so as to arrive at Rodriguez before November 1. And this reminds me of a Piedmontese gentleman, who said that he had watched the quarrels of mules with men for several years, but had never in any instance found the mules in the wrong. . . .[1]

The division of transports from Madras sailed on September 22nd, with the *Cornwallis* and *Psyche*. The ships from Bengal were left to the protection of the *Illustrious* (74), those from Bombay to that of the *Doris* (36). Drury sailed independently on the 23rd in the *Russel* (74), accompanied by the *Clorinde* (38), *Cornelia* (32), *Bucephalus* (36), *Phaeton* (38) and *Hesper*. The *Diomede* and *Ceylon* were already off the French islands, having gone on ahead, the latter carrying Major-General Abercromby. The *Hecate* and one or two other vessels were to follow. It was Drury's purpose to arrive before the slower-sailing transports so as to make all arrangements before they arrived. Following this plan, he reached Rodriguez on October 21st, and was on his way to the Mauritius when on October 24th he fell in with Vice-Admiral Bertie in the *Africaine*, with whom, and under whose orders, he returned to Rodriguez. What then occurred is best told in Drury's words.

His Majesty's Ship *Russel*
Mathurion Bay
Island of Rodriguez
8th Nov. 1810.

Sir

My various Letters by this conveyance will inform their

[1] *Lord Minto in India 1807–1814.* Ed. by the Countess of Minto, 1880. Pp. 244–56.

Illustrious
Cornwallis
Clorinde
Cornelia
Doris
Psyche
Ceylon
Hesper
Hecate
Eclipse

Lordships of my arrival with a Squadron of fast sailing ships off the Mauritius and of my meeting Vice Admiral Bertie, who at the moment before an attack was made on the Isle of France, ordered me back to India. Although I have now left ten Ships of my Squadron with Vice Admiral Bertie, there can be no doubt but the assistance of the *Russel*, *Phaeton* and *Bucephalus*, Vice Admiral Bertie is sending me back to India with, might be of the most essential service in the landing of the Troops.

I beg here to represent to their Lordships, I cannot but feel myself insulted and injured by Vice Admiral Bertie who has from his Seniority, wrested from me my legitimate right of acting with, and seeing concluded, the enterprise of an Expedition from India under my immediate auspices, supported by my utmost efforts of co-operation, at the requisition of the Government of India.

As Admiral Bertie told me he had their Lordships *orders* to take me and my Squadron under his Command; and that he would send me back to India before the attack on the Isle of France: I beg leave to enclose my correspondence with him, for their Lordships information and

> I have the honor to be
> Sir
> Your most obedient
> humble Servant
> Wm O'B. Drury.

(Adm. 1/182.)

The reason Bertie gave for sending Drury back to India was that he could not sanction his continued absence from his station. That he was technically in the right is beyond question. That he was generous may be doubted. Drury returned rather sadly to Madras and died there on 6th March, 1811. Before that date he heard of the fall of Mauritius. His consolation then was that he was on the point of sailing with another expedition to Java.

Obituary

On the evening of March 6, Vice-Admiral William O'Bryen Drury, Commander-in-Chief in the East Indies.—He had not been in good health since he arrived in that country; but the severe illness immediately preceding his death was only of 24 hours duration. He was waiting the arrival of some ships from Bencoolen to proceed with the expedition against Java; and had, two days previously, fixed that the expedition should sail on the 13th; and it is a singular circumstance, that the *Minden*, 74, which had been fitted out, at Bombay, for his flag, and the arrival of which, at Madras, he had, for several days, been so anxiously expecting, appeared in the offing just as he expired. His remains were interred in St. Mary's church, Madras, on the following evening. . . .

On February 25th, before sailing from Calcutta to join Drury at Madras, Lord Minto gave, among his reasons for accompanying the fleet in person, the final one that 'as Admiral Drury acts under a distinct authority and is fond of acting for himself' he, Minto, could not otherwise be certain that his plan would be carried out. Before the Governor-General arrived, Drury was acting under a still more distinct authority. And it was with Commodore Broughton that Lord Minto sailed for Java.

CHAPTER XXI

The Battle of Grand Port

AFTER the hurricane season in 1810, Captain Lambert resumed the blockade of Mauritius at the end of March. He had with him the *Iphigenia* (36), *Leopard* (50), *Magicienne* (36) and some smaller vessels. In Port Louis were the *Vénus* (40), *Manche* (40) and *Entreprenant* corvette. The *Bellone*, *Minerve* and *Victor* were at sea but expected to return. At Madras, Lord Minto was assembling his force for the capture of Bourbon, and at the Cape Captain Josias Rowley, with the *Boadicea* (38) and *Sirius* (38), was preparing to join Lambert and supersede him. The latter's squadron, too weak for its purpose, was reinforced in the meanwhile, in April, by the *Nereide* (36) commanded by Nesbit Willoughby. It was known that the attack on Bourbon was to be made and suspected that one on Mauritius would follow. The immediate task was one of reconnaissance preliminary to the latter operation, and Willoughby began his patrol to the south-east by revisiting the Riviere-Noire which he had raided before. There he located the French frigate *Astrée*, latest reinforcement from Cherbourg, which had been unable to enter the blockaded Port Louis. Then he went on (on April 30th) to reconnoitre the small harbour of Jacolet, where he found a merchantman protected by two shore batteries and decided to cut her out, together with a schooner, by a night attack. As a first step it would be necessary to silence the batteries, which was done by marines and sailors numbering a hundred. One battery was taken that night and the other the following day. After some fighting on shore, and after destroying the batteries, works, magazine, stores and signal house, Willoughby re-embarked his force with little loss, bringing with him some captured officers. The merchantman was found to be American and was left, but the schooner was brought away. Jacolet was evidently judged unsuitable for the landing of a larger force, but the raid served to show that the local militia was unlikely to offer any serious resistance. It also enabled Willoughby to demonstrate British respect for private property and courtesy towards prisoners (who were exchanged soon afterwards). Shortly afterwards, Commodore Rowley left Pym of the *Sirius* to continue the blockade while he himself went to Rodriguez to meet the expected transports from Madras. The *Nereide* went with him but Willoughby, the expert in combined operations, had been nearly killed on June 15th by the accidental bursting of a musket and recovered barely in time to be of use.

During the attack on Bourbon, which began on July 7th, the blockade of the neighbouring island was abandoned. All the men-of-war were needed to cover the landing, which was successful and indeed but ineffectively opposed. By the 9th Mr. Farquhar had landed and assumed office as governor, and the *Sirius*, *Iphigenia*, *Nereide* and *Staunch*, gun-brig, then returned hastily to resume the blockade. In the light of subsequent events, it seems not improbable that the four thousand men who had conquered Bourbon could have gone on to attack Mauritius without much risk of losing the first island or of failing against the second. The information that Decaen's militia numbered over ten thousand had not, however, in India, been qualified by Willoughby's report that they would not fight. The captors, therefore, of Bourbon had no orders to attack Mauritius, but were rather to await the arrival of the second expedition towards the end of the year. In the meanwhile, it was decided to undermine the opposition by propaganda. Mr. Farquhar had printed for this purpose a proclamation addressed to the inhabitants of Mauritius. It described their present state in the gloomiest terms and contrasted it with the happiness which would follow an (unresisted) British conquest. The only views of Britain, it seemed, were 'justice, commerce, and plenty.' Then Farquhar added, more recklessly, that 'Our Government is generous . . . the French pay in paper . . . and we pay in Spanish coin.' The distribution of this literature was entrusted to a squadron under the orders of Captain Pym of the *Sirius*, the other ships being the *Iphigenia*, *Nereide* and *Staunch*. As an opening move, the *Nereide*, Willoughby's ship, carrying a special 'commando' unit of a hundred soldiers and three officers, was to capture the Ile de la Passe at the entrance to Grand Port, which town and neighbourhood could then be inundated with propaganda. It was not, apparently, intended to retain the island indefinitely (for which purpose the troops would hardly suffice), but Grand Port was one place, clearly, at which the final landing in force might be planned and this possibility was borne, no doubt, in mind.

In comment on this plan of campaign, it is clear that the initial error was that made by Lord Minto in April. It is probable that a slightly larger force, as Drury urged, might have captured both islands in one operation. But, apart from that, Minto had rejected the Admiral's help and sent off his first expedition without allowing Drury to strengthen the squadron with which the troops were to act. This squadron had been weakened (unknown to Minto) in March, by the departure of the *Raisonable* (64) and soon afterwards by the departure of the *Leopard* (50), both ordered home by the Admiralty, probably for the docking they must have needed. This meant that Rowley had with him some five frigates, opposed, in theory, by four French frigates (either at Port Louis or likely to return there), but actually, since the arrival of the *Astrée*, by five. Minto was thus relying, in his plans, on a naval superiority which did not exist. The next error was in Rowley's decision to remain with the *Boadicea* (38) at St. Paul's, and direct the blockade from there. He was capable and distinguished and he had several reasons, no doubt, for doing what he did. Bourbon had to be defended, French ships might call there, not knowing that it had fallen, and the governor would be much happier with the Commodore and his frigate at hand. The result was, however, to deprive the blockading force of its most experienced senior officer and reduce it to an actual inferiority as compared with the force it was to contain.

To call this inferiority 'actual' is not quite accurate, for two of the French frigates were on a cruise. But they had sailed on March 14th and five months was quite a long time for a frigate to be at sea. On the other hand, a blockade would imply a certain dispersion of the squadron, if only to watch the two main ports. And, whereas the *Vénus* and *Manche* were 40-gun ships, the *Iphigenia*, *Magicienne*, *Sirius* and *Nereide* were of 36 guns and with a far lighter broadside. These considerations were not, presumably, forgotten, but recent events—the raid on Jacolet, the fall of Bourbon—had given everyone unbounded confidence. Any English frigate could capture any French frigate irrespective of size—in fact, could probably capture two. Willoughby, the ablest of the captains, was a hothead and possibly overshadowed Pym, his senior officer. At any rate, the operations against the Ile de France went gaily forward and were planned, indeed, with great skill. Leaving the *Iphigenia* and *Magicienne* off Port Louis, Captain Pym brought the *Sirius*, *Nereide* and *Staunch*, brig, to Grand Port. A first attempt on the Ile de la Passe failed on the night of August 10th to 11th because of adverse weather conditions. The second attempt, on the 13th to 14th, succeeded so well that the officer defending the fort surrendered without destroying his signal book. According to James, the fort mounted four 24-pounders, nine 18-pounders, three 13-inch mortars and two howitzers, and was held by two officers and eighty regular soldiers. His expressed inability to describe the fortifications is no great loss as they are still there; as are two of the 13-inch mortars.[1] The capture

---

[1] H. C. M. Austen. *Sea Fights and Corsairs of the Indian Ocean.* Mauritius. See text and illustration, p. 140.

was made by the boats of the *Sirius* and *Iphigenia*, the island being then garrisoned by fifty of the special troops. Captain Pym now sailed to join the *Iphigenia* off Port Louis, leaving Willoughby with the *Nereide* and *Staunch* to continue the propaganda war. Between Pym and Willoughby there was no love lost at this time, Willoughby being furious that Pym had captured the Ile de la Passe before he (the real expert) had arrived.

Willoughby was now, nevertheless, in his element and began an exhilarating series of operations in what we should call 'commando' style. He began on the 17th by the capture—after a six-mile approach march— of the fort on Pointe du Diable. From there he marched along the coast, supported by the ship's boats, to 'Vieux Grand Port,' the village which Mahébourg had superseded. After distributing leaflets and after a skirmish with a company of militia, Willoughby's one hundred and seventy men were all re-embarked. This was on August 17th, and Willoughby landed again on the following day. Meeting now with no military opposition, he sent the *Staunch* to join Captain Pym and landed afresh with his men on the 19th and 20th. The inhabitants proved friendly and were further won over by the model behaviour of the landing party. All, in fact, was going splendidly until, on the 20th at 10.0 a.m., five ships were seen heading for the south entrance. The *Nereide* was anchored just behind the Ile de la Passe and Willoughby managed to reach her by midday, after a pull of nearly five miles to windward in his gig. His other boats followed more slowly.

There could be little doubt, of course, as to the strange ships' identity. It was Duperré's squadron—two frigates and a corvette, with prizes. Willoughby had now a difficult decision to make. The French had five frigates to the British four, but three were still presumably in port. If Duperré knew of the capture of the Ile de la Passe, he would probably go round to Port Louis, where he would encounter Pym's three frigates, a force barely equal to his own. But his appearance would presumably be the signal for the other three frigates to come out of harbour, creating impossible odds for Pym. Now, the trade wind blowing normally from the south-east, Grand Port was easy to enter (with a pilot) but difficult to leave; Port Louis easy to leave but difficult to approach. To prevent the French squadron uniting, therefore—and to save Pym's squadron from annihilation—the best policy seemed to be to lure Duperré's ships into Grand Port, cripple them as they entered and trust to the trade wind, the damage and the battery on the Ile de la Passe to keep them there. Willoughby therefore hoisted French colours on the island and the *Nereide* and made the signal to indicate that the British were off the Gunner's Quoin on the north side of the island. The French ships then made the private signal and were answered, thereupon giving their numbers and so revealing themselves (not very surprisingly) as the *Bellone*, *Minerve*, *Victor* and two prizes; these last being, in fact, the *Windham* and *Ceylon*, Indiamen.

In an extremely critical situation Willoughby chose the lesser of two evils. But the weakness of his plan lay in the absence of about 160 of the 281 men by whom the *Nereide* should have been manned. The Ile de la Passe, furthermore, had nine guns, at most, facing seawards and these without artillerymen. The need for gunners had not originally been overlooked, for the troops employed included an officer (Lieutenant Aldwinkle), a sergeant and a dozen gunners of the Madras artillery. These had not, however, been included in the garrison of the Ile de la Passe. Willoughby had taken these with him to attack the fort or battery at Pointe du Diable. They were still with him on the 18th, when the sergeant deserted and one of the gunners was wounded. The remainder were with him on the 20th, and now, as the French squadron approached, they and their officer were in the heavier boats still laboriously rowing off the from the shore. The modern reader is apt to assume that the loading and firing of a muzzle-loading cannon was relatively simple; and so, in a sense, it was. But the problem, as with the even simpler modern rifle, is not merely how to fire but how to hit the target. And whereas the essentially 'commando' type infantrymen on the Ile de la Passe could undoubtedly fire the guns, provided they were loaded, it was a question whether they would hit anything and more of a question whether they could reload quickly and fire again with effect or indeed without hurting themselves. The drill for fighting a battery was exact and complex and implied months of hard training. All this occurred to Willoughby, no doubt as the French ships entered the channel. Looking up the harbour towards Vieux Grand Port, he could see, in the distance, the boats which contained more than half his seamen, gunners and all his artillerymen. In the *Nereide* he could fight one battery, no doubt, with the men on board— who were probably, for the most part, sailmakers, cooks, carpenters, caulkers, stewards and sick bay attendants. Had he remembered to see that the 'idlers' had learnt their gun drill? If he had not, it was too late now (the leading French vessel, a corvette, the *Victor*, was almost within range. . . .)

It is easier to criticize a battle than fight one. But critics who have studied this action have been at a loss to reconcile Willoughby's ability and courage with his lack of success. There is, however, no great mystery about it. He was, first and foremost, the expert in combined operations. He was happiest in organizing an opposed landing on a moonless night, with boats to touch down at 3.30 a.m. and the flotilla to be divided between beaches A, B and C. He was an inspiring leader ashore in the Cochrane manner and fancied himself as a tactician; not without reason. The result of his semi-military bent was that his crew spent half their time on shore training with small arms. When accidentally wounded in June, he had been obviously instructing them himself in musketry. And in these operations round Grand Port (as formerly at Jacolet) he not only had all his best men on shore but was with them himself and always in the lead. Most other captains would have put a lieutenant in command, not from lack of enterprise but from a belief that their ship was their main responsibility. Willoughby's specialization would have mattered less had the *Nereide's* crew been trained in gunnery by someone else. But, as luck would have it, Willoughby's predecessor was Robert Corbet, whose cruelty had driven the seamen to mutiny in 1809. Corbet was a specialist in seamanship (see page 367) who nearly killed his men at sail drill but failed to train them in target practice. Without disparagement of Willoughby, it would be fair to say that he fell between two stools. Had he been more of a sailor, he would not have been caught with so many of his best men on shore. Had he been more of a soldier, he would have had his artillerymen on the Ile de la Passe, with seamen to help them rather than picked grenadiers.

Some such thoughts as these may have passed through Willoughby's mind during the time between noon, when he came aboard, and 1.30, when the *Victor* was approaching the *Nereide*. Astern of the corvette came the *Minerve* and following her the *Ceylon*, prize. Willoughby, at 1.40, struck his French ensign, hoisted British colours and opened fire. Had he realized the ineffectiveness of his shore battery, he would probably have allowed the *Victor* to pass. He preferred, however, to engage the *Victor* and leave the *Minerve* to the guns on the Ile de la Passe. The surprise was complete, so much so that the *Victor* surrendered at once—escaping, however, before she could be secured. For an instant, the Frenchmen felt themselves in a trap, with perhaps the whole of the island in enemy hands. But the *Minerve's* crew were reassured on finding themselves unharmed. For the amateur gunners on the Ile de la Passe had begun the battle by accidentally exploding a hundred cartridges, killing three and injuring twelve among themselves. Five of the guns facing seawards were dismounted and the marksmanship of the remainder is probably fairly represented by the shot fired at the *Minerve* which killed a man in the boat returning from an attempt to secure the *Victor*. It does not seem that the *Nereide* fired with much greater effect. Mrs. Welland, an English prisoner in the *Ceylon*, saw the shot fall in the sea and pointed out to her husband that there must be some mistake—shot should *never* be used in saluting a Commodore! She was hustled below in haste but ran little risk where she was—only one man on board was killed and none wounded. The *Minerve*, too, with twenty casualties, suffered lightly for a ship that was too surprised to return the fire. The *Ceylon* passed in turn, followed by the *Bellone*, the *Windham* heading westwards and being ultimately (and rather oddly) recaptured by two unarmed boats' crews from the *Sirius*. By a miracle, the *Nereide's* boats were allowed to pass the *Minerve*, *Ceylon* and *Victor* and were alongside, apparently, before the *Bellone* (Duperré's flagship) arrived. The French ships anchored well up the harbour, out of mortar range, removing as they went the buoys which marked the channel. The position now was that the French were in their harbour, almost unharmed, with Willoughby still holding the entrance. He decided to stay where he was, sending a boat to inform Pym of what had happened.

Captain Pym learnt something of the position on August 21st from the prisoners in the *Windham*, which ship he sent to warn Commodore Rowley. Then he picked up Willoughby's boat and knew the worst. He instantly decided that his best chance was to collect his squadron and attack Duperré's ships in harbour. The French, although so greatly superior, were in two fragments and his hope lay in destroying one, the only one he could reach, before the other arrived. It was just possible if he acted swiftly and if Hamelin acted slowly, and there was nothing else he could do. He arrived with the *Sirius* off the Ile de la Passe, late on the morning of the 22nd, and saw the *Nereide* signal 'Ready for action' and 'Enemy of inferior force.' This latter signal (which a subsequent court martial properly called 'injudicious'), nearly led to an immediate attack with the two frigates only, an action only averted through the *Sirius* running aground and not being refloated until the morning of the 23rd. By then the two frigates were joined by the *Iphigenia* and *Magicienne*, and at 4.0 p.m., with the *Nereide* leading, the whole squadron stood in to the attack. So far Pym's plan had worked well, and, in fact, the other three French frigates did not appear until the 27th, leaving Pym with ample time to destroy Duperré's squadron. He had four frigates with which to attack two (heavier) frigates, a corvette and a captured Indiaman. His superiority, however, was slight if account be taken of the reinforcements which the French ships might (and did) receive from the shore.

Although the *Vénus*, *Astrée* and *Manche* did not arrive until after the action, their presence imposed on Pym a haste which he would, no doubt, in other circumstances, have avoided. A day spent in reconnaissance of the channel would not have been wasted, and even an attack on the following morning would have been preferable. At the same time, it is absurd to represent this as an attack through unknown navigational hazards. For Willoughby, at any rate, had been all over the harbour from the 17th onwards, and if no soundings were taken or rough chart made, the fault was his. The French had taken up a position among the shoals between Mahébourg and Vieux Grand Port, and all would depend on the English ships' ability to keep off the coral reefs. The inexplicable feature of the events which followed was Pym's failure to keep in the track of the *Nereide*. Willoughby had the only pilot (a negro) and had been over the ground in his ship's boats. His was the only ship that reached her allotted position. But the *Sirius*, conned by Mr. Lesly, master of the *Nereide*, followed a course of her own and came to grief over a quarter of a mile from the French ships. The *Magicienne* and *Iphigenia* kept clear of the *Sirius* but equally ignored the track of the *Nereide*. The *Magicienne* grounded accordingly on another shoal, whereupon the *Iphigenia* dropped anchor where she was, in six fathoms. The result was that the *Sirius* and *Magicienne* were immobile, with few or no guns bearing on the enemy, while the *Iphigenia* engaged the *Minerve* at a range of about 450 yards. The *Nereide* was abreast of the *Bellone* and distant from her less than 200 yards.

It thus came about that the action was initially between two English frigates and two French, the latter assisted by a corvette and an Indiaman and with occasional help from a few guns on shore; one of them directed by Decaen himself. The battle would have been more equal if the opposing frigates had been of something like the same size. But the *Bellone* (44) had 18-pounders as against the 12-pounders of the *Nereide*, and the *Iphigenia* (an 18-pounder frigate) was only about equal to the *Minerve*. The vital phase of the action began at about 5.15 p.m. and ended at 8.30 p.m. when the *Nereide* ceased fire. The French had in that time reduced the *Nereide* to a mere wreck with Willoughby seriously wounded and most of his men casualties. The other English frigates had suffered little and one of them was still afloat. As against this, the *Bellone*, *Minerve* and *Ceylon*, their cables cut, had drifted aground 'in a heap,' with the smaller *Victor* beyond them and farther on the same shoal. Duperré himself was a casualty and Bouvet had taken command, shifting to the *Bellone* from the *Minerve*. Willoughby now sent a boat to the *Sirius* to report on the situation. The *Nereide* had drifted down towards her opponents, anchoring again near them, and still under fire from the *Bellone*. Willoughby could do nothing more and suggested either an effort to tow the *Nereide* out by boats, or else the removal of her crew and setting her on fire in the hope of destroying the *Bellone* and her neighbours. Perhaps the boats were lacking for either plan for Captain

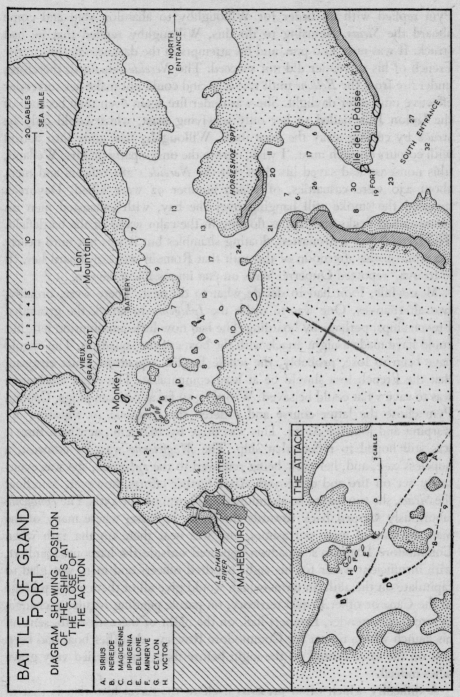

BATTLE OF GRAND PORT

DIAGRAM SHOWING POSITION OF THE SHIPS AT THE CLOSE OF THE ACTION

A. SIRIUS
B. NEREIDE
C. MAGICIENNE
D. IPHIGENIA
E. BELLONE
F. MINERVE
G. CEYLON
H. VICTOR

THE ATTACK

Pym replied with an order for Willoughby to abandon ship and come aboard the *Sirius*. Refusing to do this, Willoughby replied that he had struck. It was now 11.0 p.m. and his attempts in the darkness to inform the French of his surrender did not succeed. The *Nereide* remained, therefore, under fire from the *Bellone* until 1.50 a.m. and could not make her surrender effective until after daylight. She was under fire again even then because of the Union Jack nailed to her only surviving mast, which could only be struck by cutting away the mast itself. Willoughby had gone into action with colours on each mast. 'I wish,' wrote the unsympathetic Mrs. Welland, 'this nonsense had saved his ship.' Of the *Nereide's* 281 officers and men, about 230 were casualties, of which number 92 were killed. Daybreak revealed the smoke still hanging over the bay, with exhausted men on bloodstained decks and bodies floating in the calm water of the battlefield. The *Nereide* was a dismasted, floating shambles but it was not until nearly 3.0 p.m. on the afternoon of the 24th that Roussin went on board her. 'Il le trouva,' reported Duperré, 'dans un état impossible a décrire. . . .'

Meanwhile, Pym had to decide what to do next. There were, broadly, two alternatives. One was to order the *Iphigenia* to attack the grounded French ships, perhaps by boarding. She had now little ammunition left, but could have made a night attack with the boats of the squadron. This would have been to lose, probably, the whole English squadron while ensuring that the French loss should be at least comparable. The other alternative was to save what could be saved. Wrongly, so far as one can judge, Captain Pym chose the latter course and ordered the *Iphigenia* to withdraw by warping and join the *Sirius*. This was done by 10.0 a.m., at which time it was still hoped to refloat that ship. The *Magicienne* was, by contrast, a hopeless case, and, her crew being removed to the *Iphigenia*, she was eventually set on fire and destroyed. After further efforts, however, to refloat the *Sirius*, she too had to be abandoned and burnt on the 25th. The *Iphigenia* laboriously warped back towards the Ile de la Passe, where many of the men she carried were put ashore, and was near there on the 27th when Commodore Hamelin's squadron appeared outside the harbour. Lambert, with insufficient water for his eight hundred officers and men, was glad to capitulate on the 28th on terms which would give all of them a free passage to the Cape or other British territory, on parole pending regular exchange. Before this surrender, Lambert had, on the night of the 27th–28th, sent off his launch with a report for Commodore Rowley. Another boat had been sent on the same errand on the night before that. They carried very grave news indeed.

A difficulty which often presents itself to the naval historian is that of accurately representing a naval action by a diagram. He realizes that the diagram must be inexact and can, at best, show roughly the situation at a given time. Ships are less static than bodies of troops and, apart from that, theirs is a battlefield almost without features and one which it is rarely helpful to explore. One of the exceptions to the rule is the Battle of Grand Port, this British defeat of 1810. For the diagram made of this action by Mr. H. C. M. Austen has two fixed points of reference, to which the positions of the other ships can be related.[1] Where much might be doubtful, the position in the action of two frigates is known; and known for the sufficient reason that they are still there. It was in 1933 that Mr. Austen, then Harbour Engineer, located the wrecks of the *Sirius* and *Magicienne* and recovered from the latter eight of her 12-pounder guns and five of her 24-pounder carronades. So the diagram on page 391, based on that made by Mr. Austen, is less fanciful than some diagrams that are better known.

The problem of what to do next now devolved on Commodore Rowley. From the *Windham*, on August 22nd, Rowley learnt of the impending attack on Grand Port and sailed that evening with the *Boadicea* (38) and the *Bombay* transport, both ships carrying troops. They were delayed by the same wind that delayed Hamelin and did not sight the Ile de la Passe until the 29th, after all was over. He was chased off by the *Vénus* and *Manche* and returned to St. Paul's, quickly sending off the transport *Emma* to cruise off Rodriguez and warn all friendly shipping of what the position was. Besides the *Boadicea* his only force now comprised the sloops *Otter* and *Staunch*. The immediate question was whether Decaen would now try to recapture Bourbon. The naval force at his disposal, counting the *Iphigenia*, now included five frigates and two corvettes, which would be ample to cover such an operation, had all been ready for sea. On the other hand, Decaen knew of the coming British expedition and probably thought that the defence of the one island was problem enough in itself. Be that as it may, he exploited success only to the extent of ordering the *Iphigenie* (late *Iphigenia*) and *Astrée*, with the *Entreprenant* corvette, to cruise off Bourbon. They sailed for this purpose from Port Louis on September 9th and, on the 12th, saw what they took to be the *Boadicea* at St. Denis. The frigate they there located was, in fact, a new arrival, the *Africaine* (38), commanded by Robert Corbet, chosen for his experience on the station. The *Boadicea*, with the *Otter* (16) and *Staunch*, was at St. Paul's, where Rowley had heard, by message overland, of Corbet's arrival. All these English vessels put to sea and Bouvet, finding himself outnumbered, withdrew towards

[1] See *Sea Fights and Corsairs of the Indian Ocean*. H. C. M. Austen, Mauritius, 1935, p. 148.

Mauritius, pursued by his opponents. The *Africaine*, much faster than her consorts, drew ahead of them during the night and overtook the French frigates when they were about two or three hours from Port Louis. Corbet engaged them both in a fierce night action, suffered 163 casualties out of a crew of 295, and struck his flag at 5.0 a.m. on the 13th, he himself being mortally wounded. The *Boadicea* was then four or five miles away and becalmed, the two sloops out of sight. Rowley retook the shattered and dismasted *Africaine* that evening.

The time was now near for the coming of the expedition against Mauritius, and a first symptom of its approach was the arrival of the frigate *Ceylon* (32), sent from Madras to inform Rowley of what was happening and when. She also carried Maior-General Abercromby and his staff sent to make a preliminary reconnaissance of the landing-places. Captain Gordon of the *Ceylon* expected to find Rowley's squadron off Port Louis, which he sighted on September 17th. Commodore Hamelin promptly put to sea with the *Vénus*, *Manche* and *Victor* and captured the *Ceylon* in a night action on the 17th–18th. Commodore Rowley appeared in the morning with the *Boadicea* and his two sloops, recovered the *Ceylon*, captured the *Vénus* (with Abercromby aboard) after ten minutes' fighting[1] and reached something like equality with Hamelin. For, of the five frigates in Port Louis, only two (*Manche* and *Astrée*) were ready for sea. By October 19th, Rowley was off Port Louis with the *Boadicea* and *Vénus* (renamed *Nereide*) and could fairly claim to have regained control of the situation even before Admiral Bertie arrived in the *Nisus*. More than that, Rowley had sufficiently reconnoitred the island to be able to point out a suitable landing-place for troops. Much of the credit for the ultimate conquest is properly his. His also, however, is part of the blame for the defeat which preceded it, which his presence would almost certainly have prevented.

While admitting that Rowley had initially made a tactical error, it is only fair to point out now how magnificently he recovered the initiative. The capture of the *Vénus* (Hamelin's flagship) was the turning-point but it was followed by the astonishing achievement of refitting his own squadron in a matter almost of days. The *Vénus*, luckily, carried most of the stores taken from a captured storeship. But to remove the *Africaine*'s lower masts and replace them with those of the *Windham* was something of a feat and performed at that very largely by soldiers.

In the course of a few weeks [wrote Captain Basil Hall], as if by magic (and the influence of such a mind as Rowley's falls little short of the magician's

[1] In this action the *Vénus* lost only nine killed and seventeen wounded. The *Boadicea* had only two wounded.

touch), all four frigates were fitted for sea, and again ready for action, re-masted, re-equipped, and re-manned. . . .

But it remained for Admiral Bertie to outline the services which gained Rowley his baronetcy.

A momentary superiority had been obtained by the enemy, but it was promptly and decisively crushed by the united zeal, judgment, perseverance, skill and intrepidity of Captain Josias Rowley, the value and importance of whose services, long, conspicuous, and distinguished as they have been, fully justified his being selected as the senior officer conducting the blockade of the Isle of France. In the present instance, Captain Rowley, almost alone and unsupported but by the never-failing energies and resources of his active and intelligent mind, under circumstances, as may easily be imagined, of extreme anxiety, mortification and disappointment, in a few hours not only retook two of His Majesty's Ships, but captured, also, the largest frigate possessed by the enemy in those seas, and thus restored the British naval pre-eminence in that quarter, which his talents had so long successfully contributed to maintain.

On this subject, Captain Hall points out that:

. . . if the incidents above related had not taken place at so great a distance from home, the renown of Sir Josias Rowley would assuredly have proved no less general in the country at large than it is, and ever must remain, in the Navy.

The Battle of Grand Port cannot, however, be said to have had momentous strategic consequences. The immediate danger was of units attached to the combined expedition coming severally into an area believed to be under British control. The *Africaine* was such a ship, although fortunate in learning the position at Bourbon before she actually met the enemy. The *Ceylon's* capture was a more unfortunate example of the risks being run and might easily have involved the permanent loss of the military commander-in-chief. With the General and his staff captured, Willoughby taken and Corbet dead, and a few more such specialists lost, the success of the expedition would have been problematical. Especially serious would it have been if the *Boadicea* had been taken and the *Africaine* left in French hands. Without Rowley, without Lieutenant Street and the engineer, Lieutenant Blakiston, without the masters of the *Boadicea* and *Africaine*, Major-General Warde would have succeeded to a difficult, perhaps impossible, task. That the worst did not happen was due to the hard fighting which preceded disaster, leaving temporarily crippled the frigates which might have made French naval superiority complete. The Battle of Grand

Port left the *Bellone*, *Minerve*, and *Nereide* out of action for months to come, and the recapture of the *Africaine* and *Ceylon* was made possible by the damage each had suffered before surrender. French exploitation, moreover, of success, was hampered, no doubt, by the heavy casualties sustained which must have made it difficult to man even the ships that were still fit for sea. Due to these and other causes, the worst did not happen and Admiral Bertie arrived to find Captain Rowley still at his post, the French ships blockaded, the work of reconnaissance done and the experts (or some of them) still available. As against this, the defeat at Grand Port and the capture of the *Africaine* had revealed the weaknesses in the Navy which the Americans rediscovered in 1812; the neglect of gunnery and the over-confidence in innate national superiority. Of these weaknesses a new generation of French officers, Duperré, Bouvet and the rest, had taken advantage before the Americans appeared on the scene. It is a fact which figures more prominently in French histories than in British. But the French success at Grand Port did not, as it happened, even delay the fall of Mauritius. Overwhelming forces were on their way, and when Duperré, on October 24th, sighted seventeen sail off Port Louis, he knew that the war at sea was, as far as he was concerned, finished. His frigates could do no more and he moored them as floating batteries to protect Port Louis, sending many of their men to man the shore batteries. He was no longer thinking of any offensive operations. His problem was how to save his only naval base.

CHAPTER XXII

The Capture of Mauritius

THE assembly of the forces from India and the Cape with the forces already in the vicinity of the French islands was no easy matter. And the time-table was further complicated by the fact that yet other forces were coming from England; including, it would seem, the tonnage in which some troops from the Cape were to embark. There also came from England, and more rapidly, the frigate *Nisus* (38) commanded by Captain Philip Beaver. This officer was another expert in combined operations and especially chosen for this service. The *Nisus*, being newly-built, made a fast passage out, leaving Plymouth on 22nd June, 1810, reaching Madeira in eight days and sighting Table Bay on August 22nd. At Capetown was Rear-Admiral Bertie, and what followed is best told in Beaver's own words:[1]

> I arrived at the Cape, on the 23rd of August, and the morning I went to pay my respects to Admiral Bertie, two officers came in with news of our having taken the Isle of Bourbon. This is good—and I have no doubt but its companion will quickly follow its fate. There is no man-of-war here besides ourselves and the *Olympia* cutter; so that I have hoisted the Admiral's flag, and am to carry him to Mauritius, which is closely blockaded by his squadron. Troops will there meet us from India, and ere long another jewel will stud the crown of England. It is difficult to assign a reason why this measure has not been resorted to before, for the island has, for many years, nourished a vile nest of buccaneers against our Oriental commerce.

Bertie was hoping for the ships to arrive in which the Cape contingent could embark, but he lost patience, sent a hundred men of the 87th Regiment on board the *Nisus*, and sailed in her on September 4th. His first desire was to make contact with his blockading ships off Mauritius and he arrived off that island, after meeting contrary winds, on October 2nd.

> We made the Isle of France on the 2nd instant, and hove to before the town, where our appearance seemed to produce considerable bustle along

[1] Capt. W. H. Smyth, R.N. *The Life and Services of Captain Philip Beaver*, London, 1829.

the shores, and on board two frigates and a corvette in Port Louis. But to our utter astonishment, we saw nothing of our own vessels, though we continued cruizing off and on for a couple of days, without any attempt of the enemy to attack us. Lost in conjecture, we ran down to Bourbon to procure intelligence, and being baffled by light winds off St. Paul's Bay, Commodore Rowley, with Colonel Keating, the governor of the island, came on board. Judge, if you can, what a damper we experienced, on hearing the bitter tidings of the loss of all our ships in an unsuccessful attack upon the anchorage of Port Sud Est. What a feather for France!

It was as well that the *Nisus* did not arrive much sooner. As things were, Rowley's squadron was feverishly re-equipping and the French frigates still mostly crippled. By October 15th Rowley's frigates were ready for sea and Bertie shifted his flag to the *Africaine* and sailed with her, the *Nisus*, *Boadicea* (38), *Nereide* (late French *Vénus*, 44), *Ceylon* (36) and *Staunch*, brig. The *Otter*, sloop, was sent back to England but the remaining ships appeared off Port Louis, somewhat to the French surprise. The squadron approached near enough to ascertain that six frigates and two sloops were in harbour—near enough, indeed, to draw the fire of the batteries and see the smoke ascending from the furnaces on Tonnelier Island where the French shot was being heated. The Admiral and General Abercromby then went on to Rodriguez in the *Africaine*, leaving Rowley to draw up plans for the landing, the actual conduct of which was to be entrusted to Beaver. With the *Boadicea*, *Nisus* and *Nereide*, Rowley went through the motions of blockading Port Louis by day, mainly as cover for an intensive reconnaissance at night. There can be no doubt that Rowley had long since chosen the area for the landing and now needed only to choose the actual beaches and anchorage. 'The whole of the north coast,' writes Mr. H. C. M. Austen,[1] 'had been carefully sounded by Commodore Rowley and Lieutenant Street (of the *Staunch*) with Lieutenant Blakiston of the Madras Engineers and the masters of the *Africaine* and *Boadicea*.' To this one might add that Captain Willoughby had also explored this coastline, including Flat Island, and that credit must go to Willoughby and others for eliminating other possibilities and so contributing to the final plan.

The difficulty of landing on the Isle of France was due, primarily, to the inhospitable rocks by which its coast is fringed. Careful survey had revealed a breach in this natural defence at a point just opposite Coin de Mire—the island which the English called the Gunner's Quoin. Within the passage was Mapou Bay, which had a good beach and which—unlike the neighbouring Grand Bay—was undefended. This was carefully recon-

[1] H. C. M. Austen. *Sea Fights and Corsairs of the Indian Ocean*, Mauritius, 1935.

noitred by parties of experts, the passage itself being buoyed on the eve
of the landing. Soundings revealed a good anchorage within a mile of the
shore and the anchorage off Flat Island was already known. Busy nights
were spent with lead-line and compass, a cutter from the *Nisus*, with
Lieutenant Bowler, being captured in the process. Those officers, meanwhile, who were less actively occupied, went in daylight to the islands
and tried to shoot hares and curlews for the ward-room table. Days passed
and patience dwindled, and it was not until November 24th that Rear-
Admiral Bertie's flag was seen.

The delay was caused by the non-arrival of the Bengal and Cape
divisions of transports. Rear-Admiral Drury had appeared with part of
the East Indies squadron (see page 381) and had been sent away again,[1]
but the *Illustrious* (74) was overdue and with her the troops from Bengal.
Bertie waited at Rodriguez, hoping to concentrate his forces, but finally
concluded that the season was too advanced to wait any longer. Abercromby
agreed to make the attempt with the Madras and Bombay contingents alone
and the fleet sailed from Roderiguez on November 22nd. The Bengal
division came in sight at this juncture and brought the total number to
sail to nearly seventy. The force now comprised the *Illustrious* (74),
Cornwallis (44), *Africaine* (38), *Boadicea* (38), *Nisus* (38), *Clorinde* (38),
Menelaus (38), *Nereide* (38), *Phoebe* (36), *Doris* (36), *Cornelia* (32), *Psyche*
(32), *Ceylon* (32), and the sloops *Hesper, Eclipse, Hecate, Actaeon* and
Staunch, together with numerous transports and auxiliaries. An Order of
Battle in the Mauritius Archives gives the total number of troops, probably
accurately, as 6,848, including marines serving ashore but excluding sailors.
The plan had been, no doubt, for a force of ten thousand men and this is the
strength which has sometimes been given. Bertie did not wait for his
slow-moving armada but went on ahead in the *Africaine* and, joining
Rowley, withdrew his squadron farther out to sea in order to lull the
enemy's suspicions. That Decaen was deceived is more than doubtful.
What he really needed at this juncture was radar; and that, by some accounts,
was what, for all practical purposes, he had. For several inhabitants of
Mauritius claimed, at different times, the gift of second sight by which
they could detect ships at the distance of 90 or even 400 miles. Be that
as it may, the fleet kept away from the island for a few days, waiting for
the right weather conditions, and it was not until the 29th that it moved
in to the attack.

[1] One justification for Bertie's action in this matter was to be found in the dangerous state
of the *Russel* (74). Built in 1764, she was as old as the *Blenheim* had been when she foundered.
She needed docking and was in no state to encounter a hurricane, as Drury himself recognized.

This interval was used by Captain Beaver in perfecting his plans for the landing. The landing tables and diagram for the 1st Division have survived and are given by Prior,[1] who was present as an officer of the *Nisus*, from which Beaver and Abercromby directed operations. The boats for this leading division, or first wave, numbered 47 and carried 1,555 infantry. In addition, 10 more boats were armed with 6-pounder and other guns, manned by seamen and artillerymen, and 2 boats with 4½-inch howitzers. The gunners and seamen numbered 160, bringing the total force to 1,715. These boats were to assemble alongside 5 named frigates, on board which the troops were to assemble. The landing craft were divided into a right

Plan of the Landing of the British Army in

MAPOU BAY, ISLE OF FRANCE

Novr. 29th 1810

Distribution of Boats for debarking the 1st Division

Ships' Boats	No. of men to be Carried	From what Ship	No. of men in each Ship	What Regiment	Total
Nisus's Flat, barge and two Cutters	154				
Boadicea's Flat, barge and two Cutters	110				
Africaine's Flat, barge and Yawl	110	Nisus	407		
Castlereagh's Launch	33			Flank Battn.	547
Ceylon's Flat, Barge, Pinnace and Large Cutter	140	Ceylon	140		
Clorinde's Flats, Barge, and Two Cutters	154				
Cornelia's Flat and three Cutters	90	Clorinde	479		
Cornwallis's Flats, Pinnace and two Cutters	145				
Pitt's Flat Boats	90			84th Regt.	898
Doris's Flat, Barge and two Cutters	106				
Lushington's Flats and Yawl	120				
Alexander's Flats	100	Doris	369		
Upton Castle's Flats	43				
Psyche's Flat	50				
Phoenix's Flat and Psyche's Cutter	110	Ceylon	160	59 Regt.	110
					1,555
Artillery and Seamen					
Pitt's Launch one 6 Pdr. Arty. Men 8 } 20					
Hesper's Cutter with Lascar Gunners 12 } 20	40				
Pitt's Yawl Seamen from Nisus 20					
Alexander's Launch one 6 Pdr. Arty. Men 8 } 20					
Africaine's Cutter with Lascar Gunners 12 } 20	40				
Alexander's Yawl Seamen from Clorinde 20					160
Phoenix's Launch one Howitzer Arty. Men 7 } 20					
Hecate's Cutter with Lascar Gunners 13 } 20	40				
Phoenix's Yawl Seamen from Doris 20					
Preston's Launch 1 Howitzer Arty. Men 7 } 20					
Eclipse's Cutter with Lascar Gunners 13 } 20	40				
Preston's Largest Cutter, Ceylon's Seamen 20					
					1,715

[1] James Prior. *Voyage in the Indian Seas*, London, 1820.

wing under Captain Briggs, R.N., and a left wing under Captain Lye, R.N., each wing carrying approximately 1 battalion of infantry. The gunboats were distributed as follows: 2 in advance of each flank, 1 on each flank, 2 ahead, and the remainder (including the 2 howitzers) in rear.

Arrangement of the Boats for Landing the 1st Division

Cornwallis
G. ◁ B.
G. ◁ B.
Clorinde

Africaine
G. ◁ B.

◁ } Nisus's Flats Grenadrs. 12th

◁ } Doris's Barge and 2 Cutters L.I. 33rd Nisus's Seamen ◁ Pitt's Yawl
◁ Boadicea's Flat L.I. 33rd 6 Pdr. ◁ Pitt's Launch
Lascar Gunners ◁ Hesper's Cutter

◁ } Ceylon's Flat and Boats Dett. 56th

Nisus
G. ◁ B.

◁ } Boadicea's barge & 2 Cutters C. Hewett's Comy.

◁ Africaine's Flat Grenadrs. 33rd

◁ } Do. Barge and Yawl L.I. 12th Doris's Seamen ◁ Phoenix's Yawl
◁ Castlereagh's Launch Do. 4½ Howitzer ◁ Doris's Launch
◁ } Clorinde's Flats Grenadrs. 84th Lascar Gunners ◁ Hecate's Cutter

Right Wing — Flank Battalion Captain Thos. Briggs, R.N.

Nisus
◁
Gig

◁ } Doris's barge and 2 Cutters

◁ } Alexander's Flats

◁ } Cornelias's Flat and 3 Cutters

◁ } Cornwallis's Flats and Boats

Battalion

Ceylon's Seamen ◁ Preston's Cutter
4½ Howitzer ◁ Do. Launch
Lascar Gunners ◁ Eclipse's Cutter

Cornelia
G. ◁ B.

◁ } Pitt's Flats

◁ } Doris's Flat and Boats

◁ } Lushington's Flats and Yawl

Companies

Clorinde's Seamen ◁ Alexander's Yawl
6 Pdr. ◁ Launch
Lascar Gunners ◁ Africaine's Cutter

Left Wing — 84th Regiment Captain W. T. Lye, R.N.

◁ Upton Castle's Flat
◁ Psyche's Flat } L.I. 84th

◁ Do. Cutter
◁ } Phoenix's Flats Grenadrs. 59th

Pyche's
G. ◁ B.
G. ◁ B.
Doris

G. ◁ B.
Boadicea

Both Prior and Beaver himself wrote accounts of this landing and both deserve at least partial quotation.

On the morning of the 29th . . . [Prior writes] . . . the breeze being particularly favourable, and the day one of the finest that could be chosen, the fleet stood toward the shore; in front appeared the rugged reef and sun-burnt hills and vallies of the prize for which we were to contend; behind followed more than sixty sail of large vessels, filled with armed men anticipating victory, and steering steadily and rapidly to the point of debarkation. This spot was Mapou Bay, formed by a small curve in the land, and discovered in the night excursions of our boats. It is situated in the straits dividing Mauritius from the islet called the Quoin, and which had been hitherto scarcely known to the English as a practicable channel for shipping. The bay was undefended, as far as could be ascertained, by works; and an opening in the reef promised to admit as many boats abreast as would suffice to land the first division of the army.

In the mean time signals to 'prepare for battle'—'Have troops in readiness for landing'—'Supply three days provisions,' occupied the attention of those who had not more active duties to perform. We anchored a little after twelve o'clock, something less than a mile from the shore; on the beach all was quiet; not a gun or a soldier was to be seen. Two brigs-of-war took their stations close to the opening in the reef, to sweep the woods with grape, in case of opposition, while the flag ship (*Africaine*) and *Nisus*, remaining a little without, covered them; several other frigates, with the *Illustrious*, seventy-four, and transports, kept still further out, but as near as the crowded state of the anchorage permitted. This, however, is very extensive, the water being likewise deep, and so clear that, though several fathoms below the surface, the beds of coral under the bottom of the ship were so distinct to the eye as the paper on which I write.

I have already said, that Captain Beaver, who had again joined us, was charged with the very important duty of disembarking the army. The arrangements made by him were such, that in little more than an hour, two thousand men had been embarked, the boats placed in their proper stations, and preceded and flanked by gun-boats: the whole of the division now moved toward the shore, presenting a most magnificent and interesting spectacle. . . . While pulling to the beach, we on board could not but feel the most lively anxiety for the event, and continued gazing intently till we saw the troops land, form, and advance, without a musket being fired. The explosion of a magazine in Grand Bay, two or three miles to the westward, seemed as if the enemy intended to retreat and make a stand nearer to Port Louis. . . .

According to Captain Beaver and his biographer, the operation was not as smoothly carried out as Prior, being an onlooker, supposed. To begin

402

with, Beaver's own gig was swamped while towing behind the *Nisus* with the loss of his copy of the signals. It was probably too late in the day to make much difference, but worse was to follow, as Beaver explains:

> Having anchored (soon after 11.0 a.m.) we hoisted out all the boats; but owing to some of the troops, who were to be on the right flank, having been put on board the *Nereide*, which was anchored the furthest to the left, it was near two o'clock before we pulled towards the shore. We then, however, gave way, and landed in a quarter of an hour without experiencing any obstacle, the enemy blowing up the magazine at Grand Bay, and retreating. It was well to be able to disembark and advance without a struggle, for circumstances did not combine as I could have wished. A strong tide was made to the westward, which prevented the flat and heavy boats from preserving the necessary order; but still better might have been obtained. . . . It was on the whole, very short of what I intended. Our troops formed, and started off for the capital at about five o'clock, except one brigade; and by half-past eight, I had landed most of the troops, European and Native, and all the ammunition, food and spirits which the General had requested of me. . . .
>
> On the morning of the 30th considerable trouble and some confusion arose from disembarking sepoys, pioneers, and artillery at one spot, when I had expressly directed another. . . .

It seems possible that Captain Beaver was a little too absorbed (as staff officers incline to be) in the perfecting of organization as an end in itself as apart from victory. However, he landed the army and it is proper now to note the sequel.

The first brigade landed, that of Lieutenant-Colonel Keating, was termed the 'Reserve.' This meant that Keating's was supposed to hold the bridgehead while the 1st Brigade passed through it. The landing, however, being unopposed, Keating's brigade was allowed to push on, its defensive role being taken over by the 4th Brigade. Keating led his men along the beach for about a mile and then turned inland through the woods. That night there was a slight skirmish with the French troops which had withdrawn from Fort Malartic. The advance was resumed at daybreak but the leading formation halted in a position short of the Tombeau River while the other troops, some only landed that morning, came up into line. They were still forming at 2.0 p.m. on November 30th when General Decaen rode forward to reconnoitre them.

Decaen, it is clear, was in no mood to sell his life dearly at the head of his army. For one thing, he had no army. He had originally brought out

403

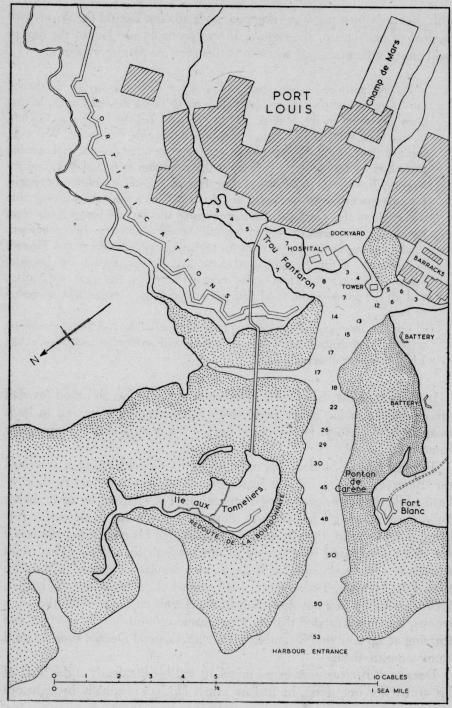

with him between 1,200 and 1,300 regular infantry. He had not been reinforced and his regulars had dwindled to about 800. To these he could add
some 400 men from what had been the garrison of Bourbon, 50 artillerymen,
400 marines and 75 marine artillerymen. With his staff and 60–80 cavalry,
Decaen had perhaps 2,000 regular soldiers and marines.[1] But of these a
fairly high proportion were needed for the seaward defences of Port Louis.
To counter-attack an enemy landing he would need to rely very largely
on the militia, which seems to have numbered about 3,000 men. As the
total European and Eurasian population numbered only 9,000 and free
coloured folk another 5,000, the militia can certainly never have mustered
10,000, a figure which has sometimes been given. There were, it is true,
some 80,000 slaves, of whom Decaen had once proposed to arm 4,000. But
this plan had been strongly opposed—with good reason—and nothing had
come of it. Much depended, therefore, on these 3,000 militia or those of
them within easy reach of where the landing took place. About this militia
force Keating had an opinion based partly on observation of the equivalent
body which had helped to defend Bourbon, partly on intelligence work
conducted from that island.

> The great mass of the inhabitants are Creoles, certainly allied to their
> mother country, but having existed so long without her protection under
> an intercourse carried on with great difficulty for many years, and now
> suffering from severe and cruel imposts, ruled with a military tyranny and
> their commerce annihilated, it cannot be expected they will be hearty in
> staking the remains of their property and their persons in the defence of a
> Government they are dissatisfied with, especially when by experience they
> know their persons and their property, their religion, and their customs will
> be respected, and protected by their enemy (as in Bourbon), with the
> additional and great inducements of a present market for their immense
> quantities of colonial products now lying in their warehouses. . . .[2]

(Keating to Castlereagh.)

Keating's opinion was one which Decaen, with even better information,
probably shared. He had evidently planned, therefore, to defend Port
Louis against a frontal attack (which he could have done). Supposing there
were a landing elsewhere in considerable strength, he knew that a defence
of Port Louis would be impossible. For one thing, it was incompletely
fortified. For another there was no relieving force within thousands of

[1] The two battalions (107th and 108th) which Sercey had brought out were mutinous
and had been sent back to France in 1798. See, however, Appendix K.

[2] "Bengal Secret and Separate Consultations." Quoted in *The Expedition to Mauritius in
1810. A MS. thesis in the Library of the University of London. By A. G. Field.

miles. All he could do, in that event, would be to give battle outside the town and attempt to gain reasonable terms of capitulation by a defensive victory. And even this plan depended on the willingness of the militia to stand their ground under fire. Beyond all this reasoning, Decaen had his own motives for welcoming a chance to capitulate. He had been marooned on the Ile de France since 1803 and was heartily tired of the place. His chances of making it the base for an invasion of India had dwindled and vanished and the governorship in itself, to an ambitious soldier, meant nothing. While he had been doing garrison duty, his contemporaries were being promoted. His rivals were Marshals of the Empire, Counts and Barons. If he could gain terms which would leave him free to return to France, he could even now gain rank and fame in Europe. He had only to ensure that his capitulation should be honourable. He must return, but not in disgrace.[1]

Thinking on these lines—and he would have been scarcely human to have thought very differently—Decaen made a rather dashing reconnaissance at the head of his cavalry, withdrawing again with a slight wound and some idea of his opponent's strength. He decided to give battle on the hill feature between the Tombeau River and Port Louis, and drew up his troops astride the road which was the axis of the British advance. The French numbered about three thousand five hundred men with four guns and a howitzer, the force being commanded by Decaen's second-in-command, General Vandermaesen. Decaen himself had returned to Port Louis, presumably to ensure that it remained in his hands to bargain with. It might possibly have been attacked from the sea while its defenders were deployed elsewhere.

From the foregoing account it will be seen that General Abercromby did not push on with any reckless speed. His main difficulty was probably one of supply. Early on the 30th he asked for naval co-operation and—the Admiral being now off Port Louis—Captain Beaver sailed along the coast. Seeing English colours flying over the battery at Cannonière Point, he stood on for Baie aux Tortues.

> At half-past one [he wrote], I anchored to the eastward of bay Tortuse, and observing French colours flying, sent the first lieutenant, with a strong party, to take possession of the batteries; a service accomplished without any loss, as the enemy retreated with such precipitation, as to throw down the lighted matches without discharging the guns.

[1] See *A Voyage to Terra Australis* by Matthew Flinders, p. 490. In fact, Decaen was acquitted by court martial and appointed commander-in-chief in Catalonia, with 30,000 troops. He had a success at Villafranca in 1813 and was appointed commander-in-chief in Holland. He survived the restoration, rallied to Napoleon in 1815, and died of cholera in 1832.

The *Nisus* was thus covering the army's right flank on the eve of the action which took place on December 1st. The troops were still in position short of the Tombeau River and did not advance until the following day-break. With a superiority, now obvious, in numbers, Abercromby out-flanked his opponent in orthodox fashion, sending a battalion of sepoys to occupy Long Mountain and another column to seize the coastal batteries covering Tombeau Bay and Baie aux Tortues. He then ordered a frontal attack, before which the French militia broke and fled.

December 1st—At dawn of day [wrote Captain Beaver] I perceived a column of our troops near the works: they had been despatched to cover the right flank, by occupying them, but finding us already there, were enabled to rejoin the main body; and the communication being thus secured, I immediately sent a day's provision for twelve thousand men. A cannonade soon after commenced from the enemy's lines, on a hill a-breast the ship, as our soldiers advanced, which though pretty brisk for a time, totally ceased by half-past nine. I found that the advanced guard had had a sharp brush with the enemy, who were strongly posted, but were forced to retire, leaving two guns, some tumbrils, and a few wounded men behind them. The weather was uncommonly fine, but the troops complained of a grievous want of water.

December 2nd—All our boats were employed in landing and transporting provisions for the army; and the seamen on shore were eminently useful in dragging the cannon over apparently unsurmountable obstacles [i.e. the Tombeau River, the bridge being demolished]. The General came on board and breakfasted with me, after having enjoyed a shave and a clean shirt: he was well satisfied with affairs on the whole, for the enemy had receded with each of our advances and the only stand they made scarcely merited the name of a skirmish. Between nine and ten o'clock, a flag of truce came out of Port Louis; and after much extravagant bravado and insolence on the part of Governor de Caen, the Isle of France was surrendered by capitulation, on the 3rd. I wish I had been of greater consequence at this moment; the terms were rather demanded than supplicated, and are far too advantageous for such an undeserving and inferior garrison . . . they are actually allowed to march with their arms, their eagles, and fixed bayonets. Is not this too much? What can justify such concessions? 'Oh' cry out some people, 'these honours are of no real importance; they are only trifles founded on opinion.' But is it not to the influence of opinion that the French owe more of their conquests, than to physical strength? Will any one be found hardy enough to rise in the House of Commons, and move a vote of thanks on this occasion?

Decaen might actually have haggled still more on December 2nd had not the long-expected Cape Division arrived on that day with another two thousand troops on board. These, with sailors ashore, would bring the English total to nearly ten thousand, representing an overwhelming superiority. If Major-General Warde and Commodore Rowley were insufficiently brutal in negotiation, as Beaver considered, it was not from lack of strength but lack of time. Granted that the hurricane season at Mauritius is from January to March, it is also noteworthy that hurricanes also happen there in December. This fact would not be overlooked in 1810, as a hurricane in 1808 had begun as early as November 21st, causing the loss of three Indiamen off Rodriguez. Those to be stationed at Mauritius for any length of time wanted to enter the harbour. Others were anxious to leave the area before worse befell, or else were due back at Madras to take part in the expedition to Java. The result was that, Bertie keeping no very strict control, all the ships entered Port Louis. Beaver was contemptuous, thinking that they would be safer at sea.

> Early on the 6th [he wrote], I ran down off the Port, where we anchored in eleven fathoms, and made the signal for a pilot to take us in. Every ship, whether man of war, or transport, without order or regularity, seems determined to force inside, and the mouth of the harbour is completely blocked up by shipping of all sorts and sizes; some of which, as might be expected, are on shore. Every kind of mooring is snapped up, whether good or bad, adequate or inadequate for the seizer. The four French frigates, which were moored for defence across the entrance, are still suffered to remain in the same station: such confusion, such gross neglect I never before witnessed.

The *Nisus* was warped into harbour on the 7th and found herself moored among 10 other men-of-war, 4 of the East India Company's cruisers, numerous transports, 6 captured frigates, 2 captured corvettes and 30 prizes. 'If one ship should catch fire,' Captain Beaver commented gloomily, 'it is most probable that the whole fleet would be destroyed, and [he added more cheerfully] the town also.' He was left at Port Louis as Commodore when Admiral Bertie sailed on the 8th.

The first significant event of Beaver's command at Mauritius was the appearance on 5th January, 1811, of a strange sail. She was decoyed almost into Port Louis by French colours and boarded smartly enough to secure the dispatches she carried for Decaen. Besides signifying to Decaen his recall, now unnecessary, these dispatches informed him that three French frigates were following a fortnight later with troops and supplies. Beaver accordingly sent to sea some of the ships that were with him—the *Phoebe*

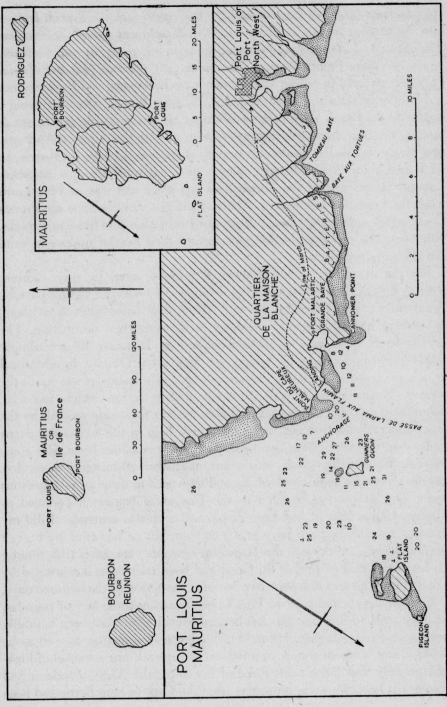

PORT LOUIS
MAURITIUS

MAURITIUS
OR
Ile de France

PORT LOUIS   PORT BOURBON

BOURBON
OR
REUNION

MAURITIUS

RODRIGUEZ

PORT BOURBON

PORT LOUIS

FLAT ISLAND

Port Louis or
Port North West

TOMBEAU BAYE

BAYE AUX TORTUES

BATTERIES

CANNONIER POINT

QUARTIER
DE LA MAISON
BLANCHE

Line of March

FORT MALARTIC

GRANDE BAYE

CAPE MALHEUREUX

POINT DU DIABLE

LANDING

PASSE DE L'ARMA AUX FLAMIN

ANCHORAGE

GUNNERS QUOIN

FLAT ISLAND

PIGEON ISLAND

409

(36), *Galatea* (36) and *Racehorse* (18)—hoping to lure the French frigates into the harbour mouth and then have this detachment cut off their retreat. The *Nisus* and *Astrea* (36) remained in port but ready to sail. Unfortunately, the three French frigates, *Renommée* (40), *Clorinde* (40) and *Nereide* (40) were delayed in sailing and did not leave Brest until 2nd February nor arrive off the Mauritius until May 6th. By then Beaver, after surviving a hurricane on March 18th–19th—faithful to his principles he put to sea to meet it, with the *Astrea* in company—had gone with the *Nisus* on April 4th, first to the Seychelles Islands to occupy them and, second, to Madras, to fetch specie for the bankrupt colony which England had now acquired. Captain Schomberg of the *Astrea* took his place and was in Port Louis when the French at last arrived. The trap did not work because the French Commodore approached Grand Port, not Port Louis, and did that at night. Nor could the two frigates do much against their heavier opponents until the *Astrea* joined them.

But the troop-laden French ships, if initially saved by their caution, were in urgent need of water. They attempted to land for the purpose on Bourbon but were foiled by the surf. When they sailed again from there, Schomberg had no difficulty therefore in guessing their destination. The nearest fresh water was in Madagascar and to Tamatave he accordingly followed them, locating his quarry on May 20th. Despite an additional vessel, as compared with the French, Schomberg's squadron was much the weaker. Nevertheless, in the extremely gallant action which followed, Schomberg captured the *Nereide* and *Renommée*; a feat made possible by the misconduct of the *Clorinde*, which gave little help in the action and eventually fled, watering at the Seychelles and finally reaching Brest. Her commander, Captain St. Cricq, was court martialled, dismissed the service, expelled from the Legion of Honour and sentenced to three years' imprisonment. On his passage to Elba in the *Undaunted* Napoleon confided to Captain Ussher that he had been dissatisfied with this sentence. 'I did my utmost,' he explained, 'to have St. Cricq shot, but he was tried by French naval officers. . . .' So well did Napoleon remember the affair that, finding on his return to France that St. Cricq had been released and reinstated by Louis XVIII, he sent him back to prison for the period of the hundred days.

Captain Beaver returned to Port Louis, bringing three lacs of pagodas, on June 27th, to find that this last belated French effort had been faithfully dealt with in his absence. He refitted his battered squadron as well as he could, being 'without a stick or a fathom of rope . . . nor a morsel of junk' and on July 2nd sailed with three of his ships, the *Nisus*, *President* and *Phoebe* for Java. This was on orders from the Cape (where Bertie had been

succeeded by Admiral Stopford). He sighted Australia on August 6th—
'without a vestige of tree or shrub of any kind, being all of a quaker-like
drab colour, except when broken by dingy cliffs'—and noted that 'a more
barren, uninviting land I never beheld.' He ran on the 13th through the
Straits of Bali 'all my charts of which resemble [it] just as much as they do
the Sea of Marmora, and no more,' and reached Batavia on the 20th. The
city had fallen on the 9th but Admiral Stopford was able to make good use
of his services in attacking Cheribon and Samarang. His comments were
fairly acid to the end and he died at the Cape in 1812 of enteritis; in other
words, of inflammatory constipation.

CHAPTER XXIII

The Conquest of Java

WHEN Lord Minto heard of the fall of Mauritius at Madras on 25th January, 1811, he described it in a letter as a service 'the most important as it is universally considered here, and as in truth I believe it to be, that could be rendered to the East India Company and the nation in the East.' This event should properly have deprived the French of their only naval base east of the Cape. It did not do that, unfortunately, because it had been preceded by events in Europe which placed the Netherlands and the Dutch overseas possessions in the power of France. Under stricter French control, the colony of Java had been forced to accept a French governor, who could make it a fresh naval base, even more strategically placed than Port Louis had been and protected by diseases as well as by navigational hazards. Whereas the Ile de France surrendered on 3rd December, 1810, two French frigates sailed from Nantes on the 28th, carrying General Jansen, destined to succeed Daendels as Governor-General of Java. These were the *Meduse* and *Nymphe*, and the *Sappho* corvette sailed from Bordeaux at much the same time with the object of bringing Daendels back to France. These vessels were dispatched in ignorance of what had happened at Mauritius—and indeed three frigates were, as we have seen, sent to carry aid there. They show, however, that Napoleon was well aware of Batavia's importance, whether as subsidiary or alternative to Mauritius, and that use would soon be made of it. We know, moreover, that Bouvet, after Decaen's capitulation, and after returning to France, petitioned Napoleon for leave to return to the Indian Ocean with an 80-gun ship. This plan, reminiscent of Linois, was rejected. He was offered instead two frigates and a corvette with which to operate from Batavia, and he would undoubtedly have gone there had not news arrived of that city's fall.[1] We know, furthermore, that the *Renommée*, *Clorinde* and *Nereide* (see page 410) which sailed for Mauritius in February 1811 had Batavia as what James calls their 'succedaneous destination.'

While Napoleon could thus make plans for an effective use of Batavia,

[1] M. E. Fabre. *La Guerre Maritime dans l'Inde sous le Consulat et l'Empire*, Paris, 1883, p. 104.

he could not as easily prevent Lord Minto from guessing what his plans were likely to be. And to see Java in French hands was to the Governor-General of India an unpleasing spectacle, even with no French men-of-war actually based there. Pellew's raids had shown that Java was vulnerable and Minto now intended nothing short of conquest. 'I have still,' he wrote, 'one object more . . . which will fill up the whole scheme of my warlike purposes, and which will purge the Eastern side of the globe of every hostile or rival European establishment.' To this purpose he had turned even before the good news had come from the Ile de France.

As at Mauritius, however, the eventual conquest was preceded by operations which began the year before. Amboyna, captured in the previous war and afterwards restored, was taken again in 1810 by Captain Edward Tucker with the *Dover* (38), the *Cornwallis* (44) and *Samarang* (18), and Banda fell to Captain Christopher Cole with the *Caroline* (36), *Piémontaise* (38) and *Barracouta* (18). Cole's exploit was the more remarkable of the two and it was he, by Drury's orders, who organized the leading division of the fleet destined to capture Java in 1811. That division was at Penang on May 18th. A second division from Madras, sailing with the *Phaeton* shortly after the first, foregathered with it at Penang and then went on in company with Cole to Malacca, where another division appeared from Bengal. As Drury had since died, the latter's contingent was led by Commodore W. R. Broughton of the *Illustrious* (74). The military commander-in-chief was Lieutenant-General Sir Samuel Auchmuty, and his force comprised nearly twelve thousand men. Vessels of the East India Company's marine were present under Commodore John Hayes, and Captain Sayer, with the *Leda* (36), *Minden* (74) and *Procris* (18), was already off Java, making feint attacks and preventing any Dutch reconnaissance.

About this expedition the most remarkable feature was the presence of the Governor-General of India in the *Modeste* frigate, commanded by his son. This cannot be deemed, unfortunately, an early example of a supreme commander being placed over naval and military forces. He might, had he chosen, have assumed command of the army, but actually did no more than advise and finally arrange for the civil government of Java. He gave various good reasons for going but admitted what was probably the real one in a letter to his wife which reads 'you will easily conceive what a gratifying break this kind of adventure must make in the monotony of my not less laborious life at Fort William.' Apart from this, however, Minto performed a great service by quietly insisting that the expedition should proceed despite Drury's dictum that a fleet which left Madras after March 1st could never reach Java at all.

As regards the date of sailing from Madras, it had nevertheless been left to a dangerous period of the year. How narrowly the second convoy from Madras was to escape disaster may be gathered from Beaver's account of his visit there shortly afterwards. He came to fetch specie for Mauritius (see page 410) and arrived in a mood of self-congratulation at having taken the degree-and-a-half channel (then little known) and so shortened his voyage by nearly a thousand miles. In the event, however, he was glad not to have made a still shorter passage.

> On the 14th of May the *Nisus* anchored in Madras roads, where the whole shore exhibited evidence of recent devastation, and the beach was literally strewed with the wrecks of every description of vessel . . . it was stated that a storm of the severest description had commenced in the eastern quarter on the 2nd instant . . . angry blasts of wind, torrents of rain, and a peculiar rolling sea. . . . Large trees were torn up by the roots. . . . But in the road-stead, the effect of this visitation exceeded all description: a hundred and twenty ships and vessels either bilged or foundered, and were all lost! It was providential that the expedition against Java had sailed two days before, or the whole armament, comprising the squadron of India, twelve Company's cruisers and sixty transports with twelve thousand soldiers on board . . . [had been lost].

Besides country craft, the vessels lost included the *Dover*, frigate, and *Chichester*, store-ship. Prior, also there in the *Nisus*, writes:

> The horrors of the night are said to have been indescribable. Many of the native vessels . . . foundered at their anchors. . . . On shore, large trees were torn up by the roots, doors and window-shutters dashed with violence from their hinges, palings, sentry-boxes, every thing in short capable of being seized by the wind, overturned and carried away.[1]

Regret, however, at the damage sustained was as nothing to the relief felt that it was no worse. And the loss of life was less, it was found, than might have been expected, considering that this was the worst storm experienced at Madras since 1782.

The fleet left Malacca in small, escorted divisions, round about June 17th.

> . . . it was despatched [wrote Lord Minto] towards its destination in a number of small divisions, which sailed successively, each under charge of a frigate, and attended also by sloops of war or Company's cruizers. The *Modeste* was not attached to any division, and, being sure of overtaking the earliest and swiftest, we remained at anchor till the whole had departed. The fleet consisted of 81 sail of all description. . . .

[1] J. Prior. *A Visit to Madras . . . in the year 1811*, London, 1821.

... The *Modeste* sailed from Malacca on June 18. We soon passed a great part of the fleet, and left them in the Straits of Singapore. ... On the 29th anchored close to the island of Panambangan, which was the first rendezvous from Malacca. ...

At Penang, Malacca[1] and again at Panambangan the troops were landed in the interests of health. From the latter place the *Minto*, schooner (Captain Greig) was sent to reconnoitre uncharted seas towards the west coast of Borneo and reported back to Panambangan before the bulk of the fleet arrived there.

> Commodore Broughton [wrote Lord Minto] who is the most cautious navigator that ever wore a blue coat, was not satisfied to abide by Greig's report, but ordered the *Modeste* to go ahead and reconnoitre the whole passage to the Rendezvous, thinking very properly that I had better be drowned than he. As I was entirely of the same opinion I accepted the service very thankfully. In reality I knew that George [i.e. Captain the Hon. G. Eliot] was much fitter to perform the duty than any other officer in the fleet and I thought it would be amusing to myself.

The *Modeste* was in sight of Java on July 25th, the day on which news came of Rear-Admiral Stopford's approach. Stopford was commander-in-chief at the Cape in succession to Bertie. Hearing of Drury's death and of the Java expedition, he took the unusual step of quitting his station in order to assume temporary command of another. Circumstances justified him and Lord Minto wrote thankfully:

> The little Commodore's brief hour of authority came to an end to the great relief of all in the fleet and army. There could not be a man less fit for the important situation into which chance had brought him. ...

In fact, however, it was under Broughton's command that the landing took place on August 4th. Chillingehing, the place chosen, is about twelve miles east of Batavia, and was undefended. The credit for the swiftness of the landing went to Captain Cole of the *Caroline*, who pushed the leading troops on shore before the Dutch patrols could arrive on the scene. In point of fact, the new Governor-General, Jansens, had collected his forces at Meester-Cornelis, an inland camp, where they were in no position to counter-attack the coast. The whole army was ashore by the evening of the 4th, and Batavia surrendered on the 8th. It was not until the following day

[1] Minto's reception at Malacca was described by a Malay eye-witness, Abdullah, as follows: 'And all the great men who were there to welcome him stood a long way off; and not one of them dared to offer his hand, they only raised their hats and perspired.' F. Swettenham. *British Malaya.*

that Rear-Admiral Stopford arrived in the *Scipion* (74) and superseded Broughton, to the latter's speechless indignation. The fleet now comprised 4 ships of the line, 14 frigates and 7 sloops, with 8 of the Company's cruisers under Commodore John Hayes. The only naval opposition might have come from the 2 French frigates *Nymphe* (40) and *Meduse* (40), which brought General Jansens to Java. These fled, however (not unreasonably) from Sourabaya, and reached France safely. Jansens was defeated on August 25th but did not finally surrender until September 18th. Before then, on the 15th, Stopford sailed for Sourabaya, leaving Broughton in the *Illustrious* (74) off Samarang, to co-operate with the General, Sir Samuel Auchmuty. Marines and seamen were serving ashore, some of the latter as (of all things) horse artillery and known as the Marine Light Dragoons.[1]

The surrender of Java was reported to the Admiralty by Commodore Broughton on the 19th, in words which were probably very characteristic. He enclosed a copy of the terms of capitulation, explaining that they had been agreed

> without reference to me the Senior Naval Officer on the spot, or the Honble Rear-Admiral Stopford. . . . In a great conjunct expedition of this nature I though it my duty to represent the same to Lieut. General Sir Samuel Auchmuty. . . .
>
> (Adm. 1/184.)

Broughton was restored to his command by the departure of Stopford and reported, on October 4th, on the state of the Dutch defences.

> In my visit to the Port of Gressie and Sourabaya I remarked that since the destruction of the Enemys Ships by Sir Edward Pellew, they had erected the strong fortress of Fort Louis to prevent ships entering the Port, and had sunk fourteen vessels to obstruct the passage, but they appear to have all drifted away, and except one large ship, do not impede the passage.
>
> The Entrance to the river of Sourabaya is strongly protected by two heavy Batteries of twenty-seven and seven guns. . . .
>
> The establishment of Grissie has no force, not even a battery, neither is there at Sourabaya except at the Pier Heads.
>
> As to Batavia there are no works of any kind for its protection or the canal, except an old ruinous fort without a gun, and the island of Onrust with the Arsenal etc. was destroyed by Captn. Tucker in the *Dover* near two years since, nor is there the remains of defence existing in any part of the Bay. . . .

[1] For a detailed account of this expedition see *English Expeditions to the Dutch East Indies during the Revolutionary and Napoleonic Wars*. S. G. Rainbow. Unpublished thesis, University of London, 1933.

PLATE XI. Admiral Sir Nesbit Josiah Willoughby (1777–1849), called 'The Immortal,' from the oil painting by Thomas Barber at Birdsall House, Malton

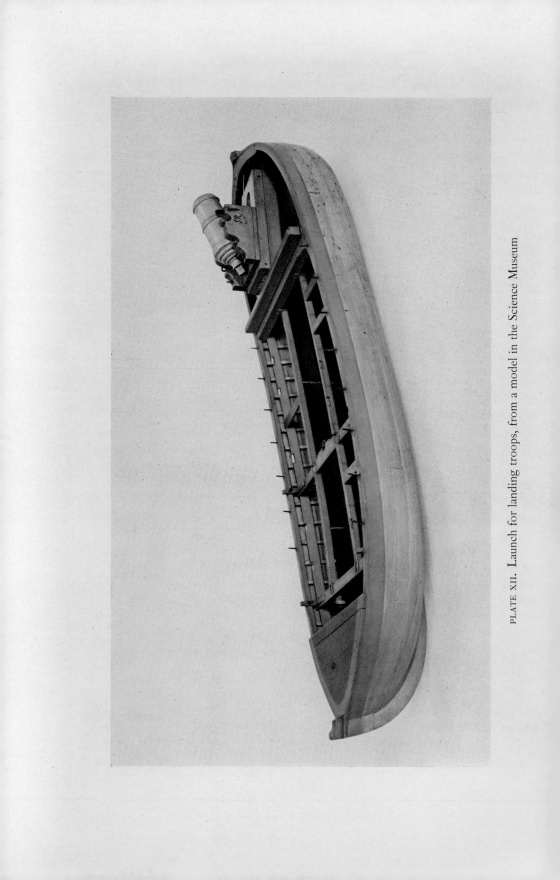

PLATE XII. Launch for landing troops, from a model in the Science Museum

Batavia was indeed little fortified but one defence it still retained, as Broughton ended by admitting.

> I am sorry to inform their Lordships that the Squadron is sickly, from the nature of the climate and its pernicious effects, which I always dreaded, has been severely felt by the seamen and marines that have landed, particularly the latter. We have in the *Illustrious* buried 31 men, and have now 120 in the Sick Report. I hope a change of station will benefit her crew.

In fact, the *Illustrious* lost 71 men before she left Java, and the squadron as a whole lost 221, including 9 officers. Nor did these losses end when Broughton was back at Madras, for he left 7 frigates and 2 sloops to guard Java and the Straits of Sunda 'to intercept any force the enemy may send out from Europe,' and these were still there in March 1812. By then the squadron had dwindled to a total of 1 74-gun ship, 10 frigates, 5 sloops, 1 hospital ship at Penang and the sheer hulk at Bombay. Broughton was not to remain commander-in-chief for long but the last word on the Java campaign may properly be his, and extracted from his letter of 4th October, 1811. (Adm. 1/184.)

> I am extremely happy to congratulate their Lordships upon the conquest of the valuable Island of Java and its Dependencies, wherein the evils adverted to are done away by the total fall of all the Enemy's settlements in the East, and on taking possession of Macassar and Coupang on the Island of Timor the French Flag will no longer fly in the Eastern Seas.

CHAPTER XXIV

The End of the War

ITH the capture of Java, the naval war in the East was at an
end. Having no base anywhere near India, Napoleon gave up
all idea of naval operations there. From 1812, therefore, to
1815, the East Indies squadron, much reduced in strength, merely stood
guard against the French and the Americans, without actual conflict with
either. The first event was the arrival of the new commander-in-chief,
Vice-Admiral Sir Samuel Hood, K.B., who came within the limits of the
station in February and arrived at Madras on 5th April, 1812. Hood, the
younger brother of Viscount Hood and also of Lord Bridport, was an
extremely distinguished officer and far more senior than his predecessors
in this command had been on their arrival. Aged just fifty, he had been a
flag-officer since 1807 and a Vice-Admiral since 1811. His immediate
problem was what to do with Captain Broughton, whose broad pendant he
at first ordered to be struck. Later, Hood changed his mind and decided to
send Broughton to England, with pendant still flying:

> . . . under consideration of the very able services of Commodore Broughton,
> in the command of His Majesty's Ships in India, since the death of the late
> Commander-in-Chief and judicious conduct therein.
>
> (Ad. 1/184.)

But Hood then discovered that Broughton's main object in going home
was to demand a court martial on Rear-Admiral Stopford for trespassing
on what was temporarily Broughton's station. This made the Admiral alter
his plans afresh, thereby bringing upon himself the wrath of Broughton,
whose ship, the *Illustrious*, he took as his flagship. Hood resented
Broughton's 'mode of application, dictating and even threatening' and took
steps, after the commodore went, to guard himself against the expected
slander.

> I must entreat their Lordships' support [he wrote on 1st July, 1812]
> at this distance when unable to reply to any representation he may chuse
> to make to their Lordships, and which from the tenor of his letters I have
> every reason to expect.

It seems from other correspondence that Broughton was guilty of having 'publicly made improper observation on my [i.e. Hood's] conduct.' Broughton, on the other hand, described himself as going home 'a much injured officer.' His complaints did him no good, however, for he was given no reward for his recent services and not employed again until 1815. He never reached flag-rank and retired soon afterwards with a colonelcy of marines by way of consolation.

Once rid of Broughton, Hood reported to the Admiralty that much of his squadron had still to be deployed off Java and that few ships were available for service elsewhere.

> . . . But to keep up this force [off Java] with a distribution of the Ships to watch the extensive coast of this Country, I fear we shall not have a Squadron equal thereto, and it will be necessary always to keep a centrical Force prepared in case of an Enemy's Squadron making its appearance in India, and thereby prevent that hazard to the Trade which might otherwise be occasioned.
>
> (Ad. 1/184.)

The Admiralty were unimpressed, however, by this remote possibility and wanted frigates and sloops to guard against American cruisers. They presently ordered home the frigates *Doris*, *Modeste*, *Bucephalus* and *Cornelia*, the sloops *Procris*, *Barracouta* and *Samarang*. It was indeed high time that some of these ships went home. They returned, many of them, from Java in August 1812, with crews 'much debilitated from the effects of Java Fever and Dysentery.' But, apart from that, the question had already been raised as to whether ships should be allowed to remain indefinitely on a foreign station. It was Lord Cochrane who, some years previously, produced in Parliament a list of ships in the East Indies and pointed out that

> . . . The *Centurion* had been there eleven years, the *Rattlesnake* fourteen years, came home the other day, with only one man of the first crew—the *Fox* frigate, under the command of his brother, had been there fifteen years —the *Sceptre* eight years—the *Albatross* twelve, etc. Not one farthing of pay had been given all that period to all those men. He had made a calculation on the *Fox* frigate, and supposing only one hundred of the men returned, there would be due to the crew £25,000, not including the officers. What became of these sums all the while?[1]

What, indeed? By 1812 most of these ships had returned home but others, like the *Sir Francis Drake* (32), *Piémontaise* (38) and *Phaeton* (38) had been there a considerable time. As for the seamen, who could be paid only at a home port, their lot was admittedly hard.

[1] Thomas, Earl of Dundonald. *The Autobiography of a Seaman*, London, 1861, p. 384.

Sir Samuel Hood's immediate interest, however, was in the development of the port of Trincomalee, which he (like Drury) wanted to make the principal naval base and dockyard; one argument for which being that it lay in a Crown Colony, not in the territory of the East India Company. Hood went there in the autumn of 1812, ordered the harbour, the town, Nicholson's Cove and the surrounding country to be charted and mapped, and began to make plans for the arsenal he hoped to establish. A principal motive was economy, Hood having already, it is said, effected a 30 per cent saving on victualling and other expenses. He hoped, no doubt, for still greater efficiency in a naval establishment in Ceylon. Matters were, however, to be held up in April 1813, by an epidemic which carried off a quarter of the four thousand native inhabitants and nearly a hundred of the garrison. But his stay there is memorable also for the fact that the *Illustrious* was there joined by Lieutenant Basil Hall. This event was not important in itself, but Hall was afterwards to write those *Fragments of Voyages and Travels*, from which we gain a good idea of life in the East Indies Squadron in those last and uneventful years of the war. From them also we learn a great deal about Hood, as also about Hall himself.

Hall came out as a junior lieutenant in the *Volage*, which sailed from Spithead on 25th March, 1812, and carried as passenger Sir Evan Nepean, the former Secretary of the Admiralty, then recently appointed governor of Bombay. With the *Volage* went the *Princess Caroline* (74), and the *Theban* frigate, with six East Indiamen bound for China. Having parted with the Indiamen, the *Volage* came into Bombay on August 12th, refitted there and then sailed for Trincomalee. There Hall was transferred to the flagship as fifth lieutenant, and in line, he hoped, for (eventual) promotion. The Admiral himself was living ashore and there broke it to Hall that his name was not on the Admiralty List for promotion.

> Had the Admiral fired one of the flagship's thirty-two pounders, double shotted, down my throat, he could not have demolished more completely my bodily frame work than this fatal announcement shattered to pieces the gilded crockery-ware of my fondest hopes. . . . As I recovered my scattered senses, however, I recollect gazing at the anchorage from the open window of the Admiralty House, near which we stood. The flag-ship then lay just off Osnaburg Point, with her ensign . . . dropped, in the calm, so perpendicularly from the gaff-end, that it looked like a rope more than a flag, while its reflection, as well as that of the ship herself, with every mast, yard, and line of the rigging, seemed, as it were, engraved on the surface of the tranquil pool, as distinctly as if another vessel had actually been inverted and placed beneath. I have seldom witnessed so complete a calm. The

sea-breeze . . . had not as yet found its way into the recesses of the inner harbour, which, take it all in all, is one of the snuggest and most beautiful coves in the world. And such is the commodious nature of this admirable port, that even the *Illustrious*, though a large 74-gun ship, rode at anchor in perfect security, within a few yards of the beach, which at that spot is quite steep to, and is wooded down to the very edge of the water. . . .

The pity is that Hall's descriptive powers were not earlier applied to the East Indies. For little was now happening there, and little likely to happen. It is true that the news came on 4th January, 1813, of the war with the United States—news which reached Muscat from Frankfort. It is true, also, that this war soon led to the appearance of the Boston privateers *Hyder Ali* (12) and *Jacob Jones* (20). The former was captured off the Nicobars in May 1814. The *Syren* (18) never arrived, having been taken off the Cape. But these were small fry and created less excitement than the launch of the teak-built *Cornwallis* (74) at Bombay, first of a series to be built of that excellent wood; the *Cornwallis* herself being rather delayed in completion because of the capture of the *Java* in which her copper sheathing was being brought from England.[1] Sir Samuel Hood was at Bombay by the end of 1813, and then spent the summer of 1814 in a cruise to the eastward. With the *Minden* (74) he visited Acheen, Penang and Pontiana, and was back at Madras that autumn. Unfortunately, Hood paid little attention to the dangers of the climate and a visit he now paid to what had been Tippoo Sultan's palace at Seringapatam brought on an attack of malaria. He returned to Madras and died there on 24th December, 1814. During that last three days' illness he sent for his flag-lieutenant and secretary, and said:

> It will be too hard, Walcott, to die in this cursed place; but should I go off, let nothing deter you from going home and accounting to the Admiralty for my command of the East India Station.

These were almost his last words and in January 1815, Basil Hall was writing his obituary for the *Bombay Courier*:

> Sir Samuel Hood possessed in a peculiar degree the qualifications which form a great commander: to the calmest and most accurate judgment, he added a presence of mind and rapidity of perception, under all changes of situation, that enabled him to turn every event, which arose even out of unforeseen difficulties and dangers, to the purpose he had in view. In common

---

[1] The *Java* also carried General Hislop, governor of Bombay, together with his staff and some naval officers and men on their way to join the East Indies Squadron. (See *Naval Chronicle*, Vol. 29, p. 242; Vol. 31, p. 59.)

with Nelson he was anxious and impatient where there remained a doubt that the foe could be grappled with; but when the battle once began, his matchless intrepidity, his coolness, and the precision with which all his orders were given, diffused a confidence that was almost uniformly attended by victory.

He was intimately versed in astronomy, as far, at least, as it is connected with navigation. In geography, ship-building, and fortification, and in many branches of mechanical philosophy, he was also well skilled. He studied, without exception, the languages, and, as far as possible, the laws and customs, of every country he visited. . . .

Although Hood had opportunity for exploration and for learning Malay, his last command gave little scope for his intrepidity and coolness in battle. The appearance of these few American privateers, however, gave fresh grounds for relief that Mauritius was now in British hands for there were many American seamen familiar with the Eastern Seas who would gladly have made it their base of operations. As things stood, the Indian Ocean, tempting as it might be as a cruising ground, represented almost the extreme limit of a privateer's radius of action. The United States frigate *President* was under orders to sail for the East Indies when she was captured off Sandy Hook on 15th January, 1815. War came nearer, however, to India when two American sloops, the *Peacock* and *Hornet* (20), sailed for the East in January. They were chased off the Cape by the *Cornwallis* (74), first ship of the line to be built in India, and the *Hornet* escaped only by jettisoning her guns, and so could do no more than return home. The *Peacock* sailed on alone and, on June 30th, in the Straits of Sunda, encountered the East India Company's sloop *Nautilus* (14). Peace had already been made but the commander of the *Peacock* affected ignorance and attacked the *Nautilus*, continuing to fire until she struck. It was a singularly pointless aggression, the result perhaps of the cruise threatening otherwise to end so tamely, and gained nothing but needless bloodshed. With these last shots, fired actually in time of peace, the war in the Eastern Seas can be said to have finished.[1]

[1] In 1814 the East Indies Squadron comprised:—

Minden	74	Africaine	40	Clorinde	32
Stirling Castle	74	Manilla	38	Owen Glendower	32
Medway	74*	Revolutionnaire	38*	Volage	24
Cornwallis	74	Doris	38	Acorn	24
		Phoenix	38	Baracouta	18
*Going out with		Leda	38	Hecate	18
convoys.		Hussar	38	Hesper	18
		Theban	38	Procris	18
		Trincomalee	38	Samarang	18

Just as the war in the Indian Ocean had begun gradually without dramatic overture—a rumour, a whispered possibility, a strong expectation—so it died away slowly and without finale. All real fighting ended in 1811 but some routine duties remained, some ships to build, some pirates to watch, some privateers to pursue. The sound of cannon became less frequent, the complaints of the merchants less pitiable and the war in Europe more remote. Little was happening in 1812 and 1813, and then, in 1815, came a final flicker of naval activity, a last booming of guns heard in these eastern waters. Then these guns, too, ceased to fire, the echoes died away, and the Eastern Seas were left at last in peace.

Appendices

APPENDIX A

Duclos-Legris

Some facts relating to Linois and the *Marengo* are taken from a MS. volume in the National Maritime Museum entitled *Journal of a Voyage to the Indies* by Duclos-Legris. This MS. comprises sixty-seven double-sided pages of text and seventy-seven full-page illustrations, some in colour but mostly in Indian ink. Duclos-Legris is a bourgeois name of the St. Malo region. The author of this MS. actually came from Landerneau and appears in the Archives Nationales BB 3/252 as a 'Matelot a 30 fr.' who was wounded when the *Marengo* was taken. Otherwise, we know from the journal itself that he first went to sea in 1792, first as mousse, then as pilotin. He was taken prisoner in 1795 but exchanged, served in a privateer in 1797, was captured again and remained a prisoner until the war ended in 1801. He joined the *Marengo* in 1803 as coxwain of the 'petit canot' and remained in her until taken in 1806. He was a prisoner from then until 1814 and spent the last part of his enforced leisure in copying out and illustrating a journal he had kept while the *Marengo* was at sea. Beginning this work after 1811—the date of the watermark in the paper he used—and perhaps in 1813–14, he was probably still engaged on it when finally released at Dieppe on 30th May, 1814.

APPENDIX B

Ship's Company of the 'Marengo'

The establishment of the *Marengo* is given in a return made by Linois before sailing (Archives de Marine, BB[4] 185) and is as follows:

Capt. de Vaisseau	1		Premier Maitres	1
Capt. de Fregate	1	Charpentiers	Second Maitres	1
Lieuts. de Vaisseau	5		Aides Maitres	3
Enseignes de Vaisseau	6			
Officiers d'artillerie	2		Premier Maitres	1
Officiers de Santé	1	Calfats	Second Maitres	1
Officiers civils	1		Aides Maitres	2
Aspirants	14		Premier Maitres	1
		Voiliers	Second Maitres	1
			Aides Maitres	1
Manœuvre	Premier Maitres	1	Matelots	Premier Classe	49
	Second Maitres	2		2e Classe	43
	Contre Maitres	4		3e Classe	59
	Quartier Maitres	15		4e Classe	80
Canonniers Militaires	Premier Maitres	1	Novices		134
	Second Maitres	1	Mousses		72
	Aides Maitres	11	Capitaines d'Armes		1
Canonniers des Classes	Premier Maitres	1	Soldats de Garnison		75
	Second Maitres	3	Armuriers		1
	Aides Maitres	16	Proposés de vivres		6
Timonnerie	Chefs	2	Surnumeraires		7
	Second Chefs	3	Garçons de Confiance		13
	Aides	13			
Pilotes Cotiers		1			

The actual, as opposed to the established strength, was rather different and excessive, especially in fourth-class seamen and boys. The 'supernumeraries' evidently included the Admiral's staff—two aides-de-camp, secretary, clerk and assistant clerk. Before sailing, there were apparently 626 men on board the ship and 11 in hospital. Duclos makes the total 593. The *Belle Poule* had 274; *L'Atalante*, 248; and *Semillante*, 215.

STATEMENT OF PRIZES TAKEN BY OUR SQUADRON IN THE INDIES:

Cruise	Description	Name	Nature of Cargo	Tonnage	Where captured	Value Piastres	Total*
First	Indiaman	Countess of Sutherland	Rice and Cotton	1,500	At Sea	150,000	
„	Merchantman	Eliza Ann	Cloth	450	Bencoolen	60,000	
„	Merchantman	Menatchy	Cinnamon and Pepper	40	„		
„	Merchantman	Admiral Rainier	Nankeen and Tea	200	Pulo Aor	4,000	5,271,000
„	Indiaman from Bombay	Henriette	Calico and Opium	400	At Sea	27,000	
„	Merchantman	Althea	Indigo	800	At Sea	110,000	
„	Merchantman	Burnt with warehouses	„	„	Bencoolen	920,000	
„	Merchantman	Malay brig	Pepper	120	At Sea	6,000	
Second	Merchantman	Upton Castle	Grain	500	Canal de Mozambique	99,000	
„	Merchantman	Charlotte	Rice	700		100,000	
„	Indiaman from Bombay	Pearl	Sugar-candy Cordage	400	Sadras	180,000	1,300,000
„	Indiaman	Princess Charlotte	Sugar, Canvas and Saltpetre	800	Vizigapatam	152,000	
„	Merchantman	Hope	Dry Goods and Indigo	750	At Sea	430,000	
„	Merchantman	Barnaby	„ „	400	On shore at Vizigapatam	330,000	
Third	Merchantman	Heroine	Rice	300	At Sea	120,000	
„	Merchantman	Pigeon	Rice	500	At Sea	130,000	150,000
„	Merchantman	Fortune	Rice	160	Sunk	30,000	

* [This last column represents estimated British loss, not the totals from the previous column.—C. N. P.]

STATEMENT OF PRIZES TAKEN BY OUR SQUADRON IN THE INDIES—contd.

Cruise	Description	Name	Nature of Cargo	Tonnage	Where captured	Value Piastres	TOTAL
Fourth	Indiaman	*Brunswick*	Cotton and Sandalwood	1,100	Off Ceylon	30,000	
Fourth	Merchantman	*Resource*	Slave-trade goods	400	African Coast	24,000	240,000
Fourth	Merchantman	*Rolla*	Slave-trade goods	200	African Coast	16,000	
Fourth	Indiaman	*Sarah*	Cotton and Sandalwood	1,100	Off Ceylon	180,000	

STATEMENT OF PRIZE-MONEY RECOVERED BY US

					Amount Paid
1st Cruise	..	..	..	1,271,000	
¼ deducted	..	..	..	312,000=	959,000 Piastres
2nd Cruise	..	..	..	1,000,000	
¼ deducted	..	..	..	250,000=	750,000 Piastres
3rd and 4th Cruises	..	..	..	150,000	
¼ deducted	..	..	..	37,500=	112,500 Piastres

Recapitulation of English Loss

1st Cruise	..	..	..	..	5,271,000
2nd Cruise	..	..	..	..	1,300,000
3rd Cruise	..	..	..	..	150,000
4th Cruise	..	..	..	..	240,000
			Total	..	6,961,000 Piastres

APPENDIX D

Officers of the China Fleet

It would seem that the China fleet of 1804 contained rather more tactical skill and operational experience than might be expected. James Farquharson, who commanded the *Alfred*, had been with the other China ships which deceived Sercey in 1797. *He* would have thought of using the blue ensign even if it had occurred to no one else. The idea originally came, according to Biden, from Sir Richard Strachan. Dance himself had had no more exhilarating experience than being captured in 1780 but Timmins, his adviser at Pulo-Aur and his former third officer, had seen service. To quote Biden:

> Captain Timins had served in the navy; he was a midshipman in the *Experiment*, Captain Sir James Wallace, when she captured the famed *Belle Poule* after a most desperate night action. . . . Mr. Timins was also present at the arduous and well contested battle of the Dogger Bank, in the *Preston*, of 50 guns; he served, during this severe engagement, as aide-de-camp to Captain Graeme. . . .

Timmins had several brothers, his eldest being present as a marine officer at Trafalgar and retiring as colonel. Two others were in the Navy, one being a lieutenant at the Battle of Copenhagen. John Timmins himself had been a lieutenant in the *Indefatigable*, and it was perhaps because of this family background that the *Royal George* became so smart a ship. Nisbet, the chief mate, had been acting-lieutenant in the *Monarca* (64), serving under Hughes against Suffren. Hay, the second mate, had seen active service in the H.C.S. *Pigot* in 1794. Biden himself, whom Timmins had taken as an orphan from Greenwich Hospital School, had been acting-midshipman under his patron in the *Indefatigable*. As for the *Royal George* herself, if not equipped for war in 1804, she was certainly capable of being so armed. She had carried a Letter of Marque in 1798 (when a mate who assaulted the captain was sentenced by court martial to two years' imprisonment in the Marshalsea and was lucky to escape the death penalty). She was actually armed with sixty-three guns in 1808 and manned by 500 men. Biden is emphatic that Linois could not have been deceived—'Surely he could tell, at noon-day, whether the Indiamen fired from two decks or one. . . ?'—but one of his own stories tells against him. He narrates how Sir Edward Pellew once sent the *Royal George* the message 'tell the captain if he had not his main topmast staysail in the brails, I should have taken his ship for a frigate.' Making every allowance for Biden's partiality, we may take it that the *Royal George* looked formidable, and where Pellew was so nearly deceived, Linois may have been even more so.

But other ships also had their quota of talent. Captain W. S. Clarke had been a lieutenant in the Navy. Captain Henry Meriton was the man who bluffed the French frigate *Medée* (36) into surrendering to him, and Captain Hamilton had been present at the same affair. Captain Torin had been chief officer of the *Pigot* in the action of 1794 and his chief mate, Mr. Boyce, had seen service under Sir C. Mitchell. The list could, no doubt, be extended but it is evident, without any detailed analysis, that the China fleet had no great need of the advice of Lieutenant Fowler. (See *Naval Discipline*, by Christopher Biden, 1830, page 215, *et seq.*).

APPENDIX E

Note on the Rainier Family

From information kindly supplied by Captain J. W. Rainier, R.N. (Retired)

The relationships of the Rainier family are best shown in diagrammatic form, as follows:

Daniel Regnier
(Huguenot refugee from Poitou)

Peter Rainier (second son)

Daniel Rainier   *Peter Rainier*   John Rainier   Other children
b. 1741?   b. 1742
Admiral
d. 1808

John Spratt Rainier   *Peter Rainier*   Daniel Rainier
b. 1778   b. 1784
educated at   Captain, R.N.
Tonbridge School.   d. 1836
Rear-Admiral, R.N.
d. 1822

Elizabeth Rainier   descendants   descendants
m. McQueen

Peter Rainier, the Admiral who figures largely in this book, entered the Navy in early life after some previous experience in the Merchant Service, and rose to command the *Ostrich* sloop in 1775. He went out to India in the *Burford* (64) in 1779 but was home in 1782. After peace was made, he was in France between 1785 and 1786 and then at sea again, on the Jamaica station, in 1790. He served in India from 1794 to 1805 and then struck his flag, being elected afterwards as Member of Parliament for Sandwich. He died, still unmarried, in 1808, leaving his two nephews as Captains, R.N., several of whose descendants have also served in the Navy. Mount Rainier National Park in Washington serves to commemorate the family name in the United States. Peter Rainier was one of the members of the Royal Naval Club in 1792. There is mention of him in *Her Majesty's Navy* by

431

C. Rathbone Low, *c.* 1890, Vol. II, pp. 161–163. In a contribution to the *United Service Journal* of 1839, entitled 'Leaves from my Log Book' (p. 507) he is described as:

> ... an immense, corpulent man, seated in a commodious arm-chair that ran upon gun-trucks; it strongly reminded me of Neptune's car, and certainly the old gentleman who sat in it was no bad personification of the sea god himself. . . .

The oil painting by Devis, reproduced as frontispiece to this book, was probably painted after his return from India in 1805. More revealing than any painting, however, is the letter he wrote to his nephew, Peter Rainier, on his promotion to command the *Caroline* in 1805. As one of the few of his private letters known to exist, it is here reproduced in full. The reference in the first sentence is to the wife of Lord William Bentinck and the reference in the last sentence to Hoseason, the Admiral's former secretary, later the friend and adviser of Sir Edward Pellew.

TRIDENT at Sea,

2nd April 1805.

My dear Nephew,

I hope you will have had the good sense to avail your self of every advantage from Lady William's kind partiality towards you, in the improvement of your manners and address, and in engaging and recommending your self to the notice and attention of the ladies as the only means of softening the austerity of a clownish awkwardness on first being introduced into their company, which Young Gentlemen of our profession are so particularly liable to than any others owing to their being so often and so long kept from their enlivening society. I don't ever recollect having seen you dance, if you have not as yet learnt that necessary accomplishment, I would recomment you to apply your leisure moments to acquire it and endeavour to excel in it, never mind from whom unless you have an option left you. You may both learn and improve in it by dancing with the young officers on the Quarterdeck. How many that have nevertheless been thought good dancers never had any other school!

To your instructions from Lady William add the perusal of Chesterfield's letters, the Spectator and other popular authors of good fame, for 'tis only by such kind of reading and keeping good company that you can acquire a competent knowledge of the English Language and a facility of expressing yourself with propriety in writing and in conversation. This is real education, which, like repentance, is the work of our life's time. What we learn at Schools in our younger years hardly deserves the name. But above every other consideration, except what regards Religion and Virtue, let the attainment of the knowledge of your duty in the distinguished situation you hold most occupy your time and attention: a situation which, as I have often told you, the First Nobleman in the land may envy for his son. Begin with the one idea that your professional attainments have hitherto been very trifling thro' want of that experience which can only be acquired by length of servitude and opportunity and may even then be wanting. The proper preparation of mind in the first stage of progress in any Art or Science consists in being duly sensible of our ignorance in it, that we know nothing yet as we ought to know. Presumption is the reverse of this in pretending to a knowledge we have no claim to from experience, and it is therefore a certain barrier to improvement. This remark is no more applicable to you than any other young man in your situation but certainly is not less so, you may be assured.

Eagerly embrace every opportunity of adding to your fund of knowledge which, reduced to practice at every opportunity, becomes experience. A very prominent and important object of your station and dignity is the command of men which affords a large scope for the display of your abilities of mind as well as the duties of humanity and justice, and moreover opens to you a great insight into human nature, tho' but too often into its most debased state. To speak practically, I advise you frequently to muster the crew in order to become familiar to their tempers, their manners and dispositions from your own knowledge and not the information of your Officers, many of whom are not very liberal in their ideas, or are but too often influenced in their description of them to you by prejudices and private animosities and resentments. Consider your self at all times their advocate when any complaint is brought against them, and never proceed to punishment but on the fullest conviction by proper evidence and never by simple hearsay unless on very extraordinary atrocities, and then the evidence should at least amount to strong presumption of the crime being committed. A like conduct should be your rule when a member of a Court-Martial, only, being then under a most solemn oath, you should be proportionally more cautious in forming your opinion for a sentence.

Be attentive to all their complaints and relieve their little wants when it is in your power. Few are their rights but never suffer them to be infringed by yourself or those under you. Abstain most religiously from ever reviling them with foul or abusive language, or suffer your officers to do so; 'tis highly unbecoming to your character and theirs, as Officers, as Gentlemen, and as Christians. Discourage by every means allowed you and by your own virtuous example all those vices they are principally addicted to, and when obliged to punish them let them see the object is the Vice and not the Man, for the reformation of the whole, and to establish that state of discipline your duty calls upon you for. Never punish with too much severity. When an offender becomes incorrigible by the allowed measure of punishment, have recourse to a Court-Martial were it even for drunkeness only. I believe an example now and then of that kind would be found to be highly useful, and tend to reform a whole Squadron. It is not legal to stop any man's allowance of Provisions, whole or in part by way of punishment, tho' it is to put more water to the allowance of Spirits of very drunken characters.

One obvious means of gaining in your profession is by associating with your brother Officers, particularly with those senior to you, to gain information not only on general points of service but also of the particular forms generally used, as on all occasions so with respect to the method of keeping the Ship's Books, inspecting and auditing the Warrant Officer's accounts, weekly and monthly, the Purser's at every time of re-victualling, and examining strictly into the particulars stated in his Quarterly account with the Victualling Office; informing yourself thoroughly of the tenour of the several Acts of Parliament passed for the encouragement of Seamen with regard to advances of every kind, nature of their discharges from the Ship's Books to Hospitals, or being invalided or turned over to other ships, as omission of your duty in some instances is punished with pecuniary fines on Yourself, and frequently attended with stoppages in the payment of your wages which may expose you to various embarrassments. In short you should understand thoroughly the business of a Captain's Clerk for whose conduct the Service holds you responsible, and it requires but a very small portion of your leisure time to become perfect in it. If you have not got the book of Printed Instructions you should endeavour to get one or buy Riddel's publications where they are all abstracted but this book is useful also in many respects, particularly in understanding the above duty.

You should not by any means neglect to comply with the Admiralty and Naval Instructions of every kind, reading regularly to the Ship's Company as therein appointed the Articles of War, and Abstract the several Acts of Parliament above mentioned, avoiding the error young men are apt to fall into, often affectedly, of being above learning your duty in these points. Whenever you receive orders from a Commanding Officer don't be content with a simple perusal of them, but look them over every now and then that you may not mistake their meaning. In cases of doubt whether as to rules of Service or professional practice always ask the opinion of your brother officers who are most competent to give you information. I recommend Captain M. Osborn, Captain Bingham and Captain Cockburn, but no matter whom rather than expose yourself to a hazard of doing wrong. But follow no one's faults or absurdities, however praiseworthy their examples may be in other respects!—so also with respect to myself, endeavour to imitate and excel me in all commendable points; in those that are not so, do otherwise.

Be sure to show every respectful attention to Sir Edward Pellew, address him always by the title of His Excellency, I am persuaded you will meet with a friend and counsellor in him if you conduct yourself toward him with propriety. His character you know stands very high in the Service and that deservedly. Never take any man's character on hearsay particularly if to his disadvantage, not fetch or carry tales, but always speak the truth without the least prevarication, tho' tis not necessary or prudent always to speak the whole truth. Be as little absent from your Ship as possible and keep a very economical table, giving your Officers good white wine, only having a little choice Madeira or Claret for extraordinary visitants. Follow the example of your most economical brother officers in these matters, without becoming sordid, or niggardly.

Exercise your Crew frequently, at great guns and small arms, reefing and furling sails, and (what is too much neglected) heaving up the anchor, catting, fishing them. The more actively they are employed the less time they have to employ on evil and undutiful and immoral subjects, but never do any work on Sundays, if it can be avoided.

Avoid all profane cursing and swearing and all obscene expressions, particularly conversation at table, for a man is certainly the worse for having listened to or read any thing of that nature, and will one time or other have reason to repent for his indiscretion in that way. Alas: 'tis too much we are obliged to hear!—I leave it to Lady William Bentinck's good counsel to dissuade you from marrying too early—some deference is certainly due to your good Father's advice. As I am persuaded Her Ladyship has said every thing to you on the subject that good sense can suggest, I forbear saying any thing more to you on the subject. But continue to be of the opinion that marriage is a religious moral obligation, and ought to be entered into early in life. The precise time must be left to every one's discretion and the laws and customs of his native country. With reference to the disposal of my estate, I have already given you a hint of what I may do, but remember the great uncertainty of all riches, and the weakness of the Human Mind.

Few of our profession have passed through it under more unpleasant circumstances that I have done, but the goodness of God here pre-eminently distinguished me through life, and particularly during the last ten years of it, which I have ever cheerfully acknowledged but have not made the return I ought to have done. This I speak from melancholy conviction and not from any affectation.

> When all thy Mercies, O my God
>   My rising soul surveys
> Transported with the view I am lost
>   In wonder, love and praise.

Yet how shall words, etc., etc., *vide: Spectator*, Volume VII.

I hope Lady William was perfectly satisfied with your kind treatment on board the *Caroline*. I thought you parted too soon and was concerned the next day I had not stopped you. We passed Trincomaly 30 leagues to the East of it withal making a single trip. If I don't forget shall send you a few books for your instruction in Religion and the knowledge of your profession. You should be very attentive in the improving yourself in the Arithmetical Knowledge of it, such as the Curves of Chase to come up with enemy with the least possible loss of time. And buy Clark on Naval Tactics. This being the 3rd April, our last ten days have not been very favourable to our progress.

I pray God to bless you and make you a wise Captain and an able Commander and give you good success. I rec'd your letter of the 10th ultimo— Hoseason will tell you my sentiments upon it.

I remain, my dear nephew,
Your affectionate uncle and very humble
servant,
PETER RAINIER.

This letter of advice is typical of the period as well as typical of the writer. In one respect at least the nephew was evidently to follow the precept rather than the example of his uncle. For, despite his remarks on early marriage, the Admiral was (and died) a bachelor.

APPENDIX F

Sir Edward Pellew's General Orders

His Majesty's Ship *Culloden*,

Bombay Harbour,

19th March, 1805.

MEMO.

The Ships Comprising the Squadron under Rear Admiral Sir Edward Pellew are as far as circumstances will permit to be kept in a State of constant readiness for Sea and Action and every opportunity is to be embraced by their Commanders for completing their Water, Provisions and necessaries up to four months at least without waiting for any particular directions on that Head, whenever they go into Port.

The Lords Commissioners of the Admiralty having thought proper to increase the allowance of Necessary Money to the Pursers of the Fleet, the respective Captains are called upon to be particularly careful to keep their Ships well supplied with Coals, Wood and Candles, at least equal to the time for which their Bills are drawn and they are on no account to sign Necessary Bills until it has been ascertained upon full enquiry that the whole amount was actually laid out, and the articles absolutely received on board. The Commander in Chief recommends particular attention to the expenditure of necessaries and suggests the propriety of the respective Captains establishing the daily expense of each article upon the most frugal plan, a return always to be made on the back of the Weekly Accounts as under:

Weekly expence of necessaries

Coals in Bush.	Candles, Pounds	Oil in Gallons	Wood pr Cwt.

The Commander in Chief is instructed by the Lords Commissioners of the Admiralty to cause the strictest frugality to be observed in the Expenditure of the Public Stores, not only on account of the very high price Naval Stores bear in this Country but also on account of the great difficulty of procuring them in sufficient Quantity for the Fleet on home Service. Under

437

these particulars it is that the Commander in Chief calls upon the respective Commanders to second their Lordships' views by paying the strictest attention possible to the expenditure of Stores and the conduct of their respective Warrant Officers, whose Monthly accounts are to be scrutinized and will be frequently called for by the Admiral.

The first Lieutenant and Master are called upon to attend the daily expences as they arise, whereby they may greatly assist their Captains in correcting an abuse which is become very alarming and of considerable extent.

No Ropes, Sails or Stores whatever are to be condemned without a regular Survey nor are any Sails to be repaired, or any running Ropes unrove or replaced without the necessity being scrutinized before the first Lieutenant and Master, should the Captain not be in the way; and Stores which may be hereafter condemned are not to be converted without Orders from the Commander in Chief.

The first Lieutenant and Master are also to attend the stowage of the Warrant Officers' Store Rooms to see that no injury may ensue from carelessness or inattention on that Head.

All demands for Stores are to be accompanied with the Books of the remains on Charge, signed by the Captain, and a Copy of the last Supply is to attend it, signed by the proper signing officers.

No Iron bound Casks for Bread or any other article are to be Demanded of the Contractor but under absolute necessity, which must be expressed in the Body thereof; nor are any Water or other Iron bound Casks to be shaken; but returned to the Contractor when necessary.

No Buffalo Beef is to be received by any of the Squadron, the Contractor having engaged to supply the Squadron with Ox Beef.

No Stay sails are to be kept in the brails at Sea but always hauled down when required for wearing, and Jibbs and stay sails, when down, to be immediately stowed in a cloth. It is recommended whenever the Ships are lying too with their Main Top sail aback, that all Stay Sails whatever should be hauled down.

No Sick are to be sent to the Hospital until examined by the Surgeon of the Flag Ship.

No Flags or Colours are to be made use of to cover Officers' Cotts or Hammocks, or for any other private purposes, and the respective Signal Officers are charged with observance of this order, for a neglect of which they will be made accountable.

The Ships Company are to be put in three Watches; and when in Port a division of the Watch always to be on Deck by night.

Ship visiting among the People is absolutely forbid except by relations of known good Character, and then but on particular occasions.

Boats are never to be sent on Shore without a Petty Officer in them; who is not to leave the Crew; but should the duty require a Petty Officer to leave the Boat, a second one is always to be sent in her for the occasion.

All Boats are to leave the Shore the moment the Evening Gun fires, unless waiting for a Commissioned Officer who is expressly on duty.

The Commander in Chief is extremely particular, that the Meal times of the people are not broken in upon, and that Boats are not sent away at such periods: He will hoist a red Pendant at the Main when he makes it Noon, that all the Crews may dine at the same time, and one hour and a half will be usually allowed; the Crews are to Breakfast at 8 Bells, and sup at ½ past 5 P.M.

If not compelled by urgent circumstances the Ships Company's are not to work between the hours of Eleven and Two.

Loosing Sails etc. will be performed always at day break and whenever it may be thought proper to wash the lower Deck they are to be finished before breakfast.

The Admiral directs that the Ships of the Squadron wash cloaths on the same days of the Week, viz. Tuesdays and Fridays; should Rain prevent their drying the following day must be adopted. Cloaths are to be hung between the main and fore Masts only in Harbour.

The Commander in Chief having considered the difficulty and expence that young men labour under in this Country to furnish themselves with European Cloathing as also the inconvenience of wearing them on Service in this Climate, gives his permission to Commissioned Officers appearing on Deck in round Hatts either Black or Coloured, with cockades and Uniform half Coats with side arms. Petty Officers are permitted to wear round Jackets made as Uniform with Pantaloons and waistcoats either nankeen or White, with round Hatts as above, but on Public Parade days officers of every description are expected to wear their proper Uniforms and Cocked Hatts.

Marine Officers are permitted the same indulgence on Duty and may mount Guard without the Sash.

The Commander in Chief most strictly forbids any officer whatever from appearing in Coloured Cloaths, either on shore or on board, and takes this opportunity to call to their remembrance the Orders of the Lords Commissioners of the Admiralty on that Subject during the year 1796, which Order will be most strictly enforced.

Every Boat in the Fleet is to have the Signal Flags No. 226 painted on her Stern, for all Boats and Persons immediately to repair on board and it is to be explained to the Crews.

All working parties sent on Shore are to be attended by a Lieutenant and a proportion of Petty Officers, nor are Launches ever to be sent Watering or attend Ships without a Lieutenant in them.

The particulars of all desertions (if any) are to be Communicated to the Commander in Chief in writing as soon as possible signed by the Officer commanding the party and Countersigned by the Captain of the Ship.

Whenever any Ship arrives in Port where the Flag is flying an officer is immediately to be sent on board to copy Orders, without waiting for a Signal for that.

No Stores are to be purchased without an Order from the Commander in Chief, but under circumstances of peculiar necessity, particulars of which are to be directly communicated in writing, and should by accident any Ship be so much damaged as to render her incapable to join the Commander in Chief without repair, a report is to be forwarded to him with an Estimate of three respective Ship Builders (the Carpenter of the Ship to be one) before any expence is incurred, unless upon such Estimate the Ship can be repaired under the sum of 200£.

No fresh Beef is to be purchased if the price thereof should exceed 8d per Pound and whenever any purchases are made, report thereof in writing is to be delivered by the first opportunity

APPENDIX G

H.C. Ship 'Fame'

When the H.C. Ship *Fame* was captured by the French frigate *Piémontaise* in September 1806, she was sent to the Ile de France with a prize crew under the command of Charles Baudin, then an 'enseigne' in the French Navy. Baudin found in the cabin of the *Fame* a book, the property of her commander, James Jameson, and inscribed by him during his previous command of the *Arniston*. Jameson was not on board, being a prisoner, and Baudin kept the book. He rose to flag rank and in 1836 was employed in convoying transports between Toulon and Algiers. It was then, apparently, that he met Jameson for the first time, and returned his book to him, recording in the fly leaf the circumstances of this thirty years loan. The book is now in the possession of Professor C. R. Boxer, to whom I am indebted for the photograph of the inscription, which is here reproduced to the exact size of the original. See *L'Amiral Baudin*, Jurien de la Gravière, Paris, 1888, pp. 39, 106.

James Jameson

Ship Ariston

Le Cap.ne Jameson, à qui ce livre a appartenu, lorsqu'il commandait le vaisseau l'Ariston, de la Compagnie anglaise des Indes orientales, passa du commandement de l'Ariston à celui de la Fame, autre vaisseau de la Comp.ie percé à 40 canons.

La Fame fut prise sur la côte Malabare, au mois de Sept.bre 1806, par la frégate la Piémontaise, sur laquelle je servais alors comme enseigne. Je fus chargé du commandement de cette prise, que je conduisis à l'Isle de France. Le Cap.ne Jameson ayant été obligé de quitter son vaisseau après sa capture, ce livre est resté dans sa chambre et a passé en ma possession, où il est depuis plus de trente ans.

Suffren, en mer, 15 octobre 1838
Charles Baudin

442

APPENDIX H

Remarks on Nangasakie Harbour, Japan, by Fleetwood Broughton Reynolds Pellew Esq., Captain of His Majesty's Ship "Phaeton."

Nangasakie, Oct. 6th 1808.

Nangasackie Harbour . . . is perhaps one of the finest and safest harbours in the World considered in all points of view, and one which has been probably the least described. This arises not only from the Policy of the Japanese themselves which is constantly directed to the exclusion of strangers and the prohibition of all kinds of Foreign Manufactures or innovations of any kind, but also from the great silence always maintained by the Dutch, who for nearly 150 years have been the only nation since the expulsion of the Portuguese who have been permitted by the Japanese to trade in any way with them. The Dutch who find this traffic a profitable one, are of course interested not only to conceal its publicity but are anxious that the idea of great danger should be annexed to the voyage to these parts, on this account they have never published any Charts of their routes, or communicated for the benefit of other Nations any of their discoveries, which I believe however to be very limited, and it is certainly notorious to all Navigators that the Dutch of all maritime Nations have least conduced to the benefit of that Science, in general from a narrow and mean policy of keeping to themselves what discoveries they may have made, their charts are less to be depended on than any in the World, the Longitude being invariably determined by the Dead Reckoning, and the modern and important improvements rendered to Navigation appear by them either to be unknown or unregarded. Two Russian Ships on Discovery remained some months at Nangasackie during the year 1804, I believe, and I understand that from them a very good Account may be expected. I have reason to believe the *Phaeton* the first English ship that ever entered the harbour, and the account which I give may be depended on for its accuracy. . . . [He remarks on the difficulty of finding the harbour, which is invisible from the sea, hidden by an island which looks like a part of the coast. He describes how he found the entrance and brought the *Phaeton* to anchor off Papenburgh Island.]

. . . As it was dark I manned and armed three Boats and went up to the town, where nothing was laying but three large Junks and innumerable small craft of different sizes. Guard Boats of a large size and many small ones continually watched us, but gave us no annoyance, the sound of Gongs their signals of alarm were frequently heard. The harbour runs up from the town a little way due north, but the water is there shallow and forming nothing more than a River. The Island of Dezema on which all the Houses of the Dutch Factors are situated, near the Southern extreme of the town, is connected with it by a bridge of Stone, the Dutch colours were flying on a staff there. We went with the Boats within Pistol shot, and had it been an object would have landed; it is impossible to conceive a greater state of misery than that which these unfortunate Dutch Factors are doomed to live in, a strict Guard is kept on the Island from which they are never suffered to depart, not a Book of any description is allowed them, and any attempt to smuggle them or any other goods which are all prohibited would certainly be attended with Death: on the appearance of a Ship, two of the Eight of which the Establishment consists are permitted to go down to the Ship with an Officer of the Japanese who has them in custody; two came out to Papenburgh to meet the *Phaeton*, then under Dutch Colours, and as they appeared not to suspect what we really were, I sent a Boat and took possession of them. At first they shewed a reluctance to enter the Boat, but the Crew drawing their Swords, the Japanese jumped overboard, and they entered the Boat. On coming on board they faithfully assured us that no Ships had been there for the present season, or since the *Mount Vernon* an American Ship employed on this service has left it. Their appearance corroborated their statement of the extreme strictness of the Japanese in preventing the importation of any European Manufactured goods, hardly allowing them common wearing apparel. These they obtain from the Ships when they arrive, and more by connivance than consent, and by the absence of the Ships of the present Season they appeared much in want of a supply of this kind, as they were meanly dressed: such is the extreme caution of the Japanese that on their leaving the Shore they are searched at three different places on their way to the beach and an accurate inventory taken of every article about their persons, even to their keys, pencil case etc etc etc. and the whole of these they are obliged to account for at their landing or run the Peril of losing their lives. We prevailed on them to accept a Pair of shoes and a Hat each, leaving their old ones on board as they supposed the Japanese would not remark the difference between these articles and the ones they brought on board, but though we offered them wine and every thing we supposed acceptable they constantly refused expressing the greatest terror at the Idea. About 10 at night a Boat from the Governor came to demand what we wanted and from whence we came but would not come alongside, keeping off, we were obliged to send a Boat to take her message: I felt inclined to mention the real purport of our visit; but at the pressing solicitation of the two Prisoners consented to say that we were a ship from Bengal in want of Provisions. They endeavoured to convince us that if we said an English Ship our wants would not have been supplied, but the real reason was, the fear that the Japanese would retort on the unfortunate Factory, for the disquiet which our appearance had occasioned them as well as the neglect with which we were obliged to treat their accustomed Port Regulations. This they might have been induced to do when they found from our message that we were not come for Trade but only to annoy the Dutch with whom they know we are at war. This boat was directed to bring a European Sailor as an hostage for the safe return of the Dutchmen, they faithfully promised to treat him well, and return him next morning when they would send us Wood, Water and Vegetables, but though I have no doubt that they would have kept their promise, I would on no account consent, which must in some degree have astonished a people who have been accustomed to think so meanly and to carry so high a hand with the Dutch. I also insisted before I released the Prisoners to their sending some Bullocks, this it seems militated much against their Regulations, as they never yet have given any Ships Bullocks, but offering abundance of Pigs and Goats. The Boat returned with this Answer, and we were prepared to expect a visit from some of the Principal Men who always remain on board with a Guard in the Dutch Ships whilst they are loading and unloading, but our appearance with the number of Guns and Europeans on board to which they had been so unaccustomed, together with the Boats having been up the Harbour, the Launch with the Carronade in her bow, had inspired so much dread that not one would venture on board. The next morning they sent us Water & Vegetables, the water is brought off in large tubbs, very clean, which stand in the middle of their Boats, and which each fill rather more than a Butt, Firewood was also sent us very good and cut in proper lengths for the purpose. A Man of some Rank attended us to oversee the whole, and though we were liberal in offers of every kind he would not accept anything in return, or be prevailed on to enter the Ship, they make an invariable rule of supplying the wants of all Ships that call there. We were also requested not to molest the Inhabitants which we promised not to do. As I still insisted on the Bullocks they made great exertions in procuring them, and in the Evening we received four good ones, 10 or 12 Goats, a quantity of Vegetables and sweet potatoes and more Wood and Water—we were certainly the first vessel that ever procured Bullocks at Nangasackie, they are valuable to them as we were told by the Dutch from their using them wholly as beasts of burden, and all conveyances of utility and pleasure are drawn by them. . . . the People much resemble the natives of China in their appearance, dress, and manner of life, nor do I perceive them to be at all more courageous or energetic . . . during all the time they seemed to hold us in great dread—The night I went up in the Boats, I landed at a Village opposite Nangasackie at a pretty good substantial looking house, when the Inhabitants all fled in dismay. . . . The *Phaeton* was in Nangasackie on the 5th and 6th of October 1808.

(Signed)

(from the *Exmouth Papers*)   FLEETWOOD PELLEW

The immediate result of this affair was the suicide by *hari-kiri* of the governor of Nagasaki and the five principal military officers of the Province, the confinement under house-arrest of the Prince of Hizen for several months 'during which his fate was in suspense,' the suicide by drowning of three of the men who had acted as interpreters, and the orders by which the inhabitants of the Prince's district were forbidden for months to open the front of their houses. A less immediate result was a Japanese 'thirst for vengeance' which made Dr. Ainslie carry out his mission under Dutch colours in 1813.[1] The eventual result is said to have been the founding of the Japanese Navy.

[1] *Report on Japan to the Secret Committee of the English East India Company*. By Sir Stamford Raffles, 1812–16. Kobe, 1929. See Ainslie's report, p. 153.

APPENDIX K

The Blockade of Mauritius

A book could be written on the problems of maintaining a blockade with sailing ships, and a long chapter at least on the blockading of Mauritius. From the following documents some idea may be gained of what the problems were. The first is an extract of a dispatch from Pellew to the Bengal Government dated 4th January, 1806:

> From an attentive examination of the subject, assisted by the opinion of Commodore Osborn and other officers whose experience confirms their judgment, it would be requisite to employ a force of not less than twelve Ships of War to attain the full advantage proposed to be derived from such a Blockade, namely two ships of the line, six Frigates and four Sloops, which (divided into two Squadrons) by an alternate relief, might preserve an invariable Blockade, and allow sufficient opportunity for their passage to and from India, to victual and refit.
>
> The longest period which the Ships employed on this Service have hitherto been able to maintain their station has been ten weeks for, altho always victualled for six months, the length of the passage occupies the whole of the remaining period, exclusive of the impracticability of preserving the Health of the Crews for a greater length of time.

Osborn was undoubtedly the greatest living authority on blockading the Isle of France and the following paper, dated 1804, taken from Sir Edward Pellew's manuscript book of 'Nautical Remarks' (*Exmouth Papers*, N.M.M.), is most probably written by him:

> If ordered to cruize off the Mauritius during the existence of a French War, I conceive the thing of most consequence to be attended to is securing the weather approach to the Island, as owing to its situation in the South East Trade wind, almost all vessels bound to it get to the Eastward before they shape their course for it, more especially those belonging to France and her allies, who on drawing in with the Weather land, are immediately informed by Signals if any Enemy is off the Port, in which case they find shelter in Port Bourbon or at the anchorage in the mouth of the Grand Riviere, therefore to cut them off from this resource it is absolutely necessary for a ship to keep constantly to windward, which is neither so difficult or dangerous, or even unpleasant as is generally supposed. . . . [He goes on to recommend] a Cordon round it of six Ships stationed in the following manner:

Between Gunner's Quoin and Flat Island .. .. .. a frigate
Ten miles north of Point Diable .. .. ditto
Ten miles south of „ „ .. .. ditto
Between Port de Savenne & Point Brabant, a mile Frig. or Sloop
Off Black River .. .. ditto
Close in with Port Louis .. .. a frigate

But as long as the Enemy have a Line of Battle Ship in this Country
there should of course be one in the Blockading Squadron whose station
should depend on the French ship being in Port or at Sea; if the first, she
should take the station of the Frigate north of Point Diable; a small Brig
or Tender attached to the Senior Officer would prove serviceable in keeping
up a communication between the whole and prevent the necessity of any
ship quitting the station allotted her. . . .

The third document, printed in the *Naval Chronicle*, Vol. 29 (1813),
p. 127, is signed I. S. S., but not dated:

The best disposition for the annoyance of an enemy is to have two of
the fastest sailing frigates to windward, as all French ships make that part
of the island; one frigate between Port South-East (or Bourbon), and the
Gunner's-quoin (Coin de Mire); and another between Port Bourbon and
Brabant; the former ship should always be sufficiently to windward to
weather Diable, as otherwise a ship might enter the port, which was the case
in our last cruise; when the *Belle-poule* got in unmolested, owing to the
Phaeton not being able to weather that point. The two ships should, if
possible, be always in sight from each other's mast-heads; a sloop of war be
off the Black river; with a frigate (or line-of-battle ship, according to the
state of the port) off Port Louis; and another frigate close off Flat
island and the Gunner's quoin; which, I think, would be sufficient to block
the whole island. But as the nights frequently are extremely dark, and the
ships off Port Louis may not be quite close to the harbour, it is to be recommended that boats armed, with rockets etc. to make signals, should be sent
close in, with orders to return before daylight; which was practised in my
first cruise. . . . A frigate should always be stationed off St. Denys because,
from the height of the hills at the Mauritius, and the signals established,
French ships approaching that island frequently get away, and run down to
Bourbon. . . . It would be a good expedient to have a small schooner or
lugger, as a tender, to communicate between the several ships and the
commodore, to convey prisoners, necessaries etc. without being exposed
to the chance of any thing slipping through the blockade; for frigates which
have come down to leeward for the purpose of such communication, have
been known to consume several days in regaining their respective stations. . . .

APPENDIX L

The Garrison of Mauritius in 1810

There is much conflicting evidence as to the strength of Decaen's land forces. The figures given include the following:

(a) *Duperré's dispatch*, which enumerates 1,725 regular soldiers and marines, including 300 foreigners (evidently Irish) but not including any militia.

(b) *English dispatches*, which mention 1,300 regular troops, including 500 Irish, and over 10,000 militia.

(c) *Charles Grant's History of Mauritius*, which gives the National Guard as 2,000 in 1799, with 3,000 black and mulatto slaves armed or trained as gunners.

(d) *Prior's Narrative*, which estimates the French as 1,400 soldiers and sailors other than those manning the batteries, with from 2,000 to 3,000 militia.

(e) *The report of the court martial which tried Decaen*, and which should be authoritative. This gives the French 2,300 men and about 800 National Guards of whom only a third could carry arms. The accuracy of this report is lessened by the guess it includes of the English strength: 23,590, including 14,850 Europeans.

As regards the irregular forces, the estimate of 10,000, if ever correct, must have included Decaen's African battalions. These may have reached a strength of 4,000, but the news of what the slaves did in the Island of Bourbon at the time of its fall led, apparently, to these units being disbanded again (see *A Voyage to Terra Australis*, Flinders, p. 471). The units which remained may well have had a paper strength of between 2,000 and 3,000, with 800 actually available (armed or not) on the day of battle. For the regular forces the varying figures given between 1,300 and 2,300 differ perhaps mainly in excluding or comprising the sailors and marines. It is odd to have the defeated side admitting to more troops than the victors noticed, but much here depends on definition.

LIST OF DOCUMENTARY AND PRINTED SOURCES

1. *Archives.*
   (*a*) Public Record Office. Adm. 1/50, Adm. 1/55 to 1/63, Adm. 1/167 to 188. The volumes consulted are the Admiralty in-letters from Commanders-in-Chief on the East Indies and Cape of Good Hope Station, covering the period 1793–1814. This series is roughly in chronological order, according to the dates at which the dispatches were received; by no means necessarily in the order in which they were sent. Included with the dispatches are copies of all official correspondence between the Commanders-in-Chief and the Indian Governments. This correspondence is also to be found in the India Office Record Department, the series there including the enclosures which the Admiralty records lack but lacking the Admiralty comments written in the margin or on the back.
   (*b*) Archives Nationales, Paris. BB3 Series, 196 and 210, BB4 Series, 44, 86, 117, 129, 139, 185, 208, 239 and 252. BB5 Series, 6 Batiments de l'État, Matricule 1791 á 1807. Inventaire de BB4 1–1052 (Inv. 969). Supplement de l'inventaire 693 de BB4, 1752–1830 (Inv. 935).

2. *Other Documentary Material.*
   British Museum. Add MSS. 37, 283 f. 323; correspondence between the Marquess Wellesley and Admirals Rainier and Pellew, 1804–1805. Add MSS. 29, 210 f. 75; anonymous paper describing the western side of India including the Portuguese possessions. Stowe 865, p. 10; anonymous proposal 'for the total expulsion of the French from Maritime India,' dated 1809.
   National Maritime Museum. The Exmouth Papers, correspondence both private and official of Sir Edward Pellew, Lord Exmouth. Journal of Duclos-Legris, seaman in the *Marengo.*
   Private Sources. Papers lent by Sir Herbert Richmond, M. P. J. Charliat and Captain J. W. Rainier, R.N. (Ret.).

3. *Bibliographies.*
   A Bibliography of British Naval History. G. E. Manwaring, 1930.
   Bibliography of Naval History. Hist. Association Leaflet 61, Part II.
   Maritime and Naval History, an annotated bibliography. R. G. Albion, Harvard, 1951.

4. *Printed Books.*
ANON.
   The Asiatic Journal and monthly Register for British and Foreign India etc. Vol. XVIII, 1835. London. Article entitled 'Outward Bound.'
ANON.
   Journal du voyage de *la Mouche* No. 6 . . . expediée pour l'ile de France et Manille en 1808. Paris, 1857.
ANON.
   Account of the Conquest of Mauritius with some notices on the history, soil, products, defences, and the political importance of this island. By an officer who served in the expedition. London, 1811.
ANON.
   A short account of the Prince of Wales's Island or Pulo Penang in the East Indies. London, 1788.

ANON.
Papers respecting the trade between India and Europe. Printed by order of the Court of Directors. London, 1802.

ANON.
The intercepted letters taken on-board the Admiral Aplin East Indiaman, translated from the Moniteur of the 16th of September: to which is prefixed the French Official Account of the engagement of Linois' Squadron with the East-India Fleet. 2nd ed. London, 1804.

ASIATIC ANNUAL REGISTER.
Vol. XII. 1810–11.

AUBER, PETER.
An Analysis of the Constitution of the East India Company. London, 1826.

AUSTEN, H. C. M.
Sea Fights and Corsairs of the Indian Ocean, being the Naval History of Mauritius from 1715 to 1810. Mauritius, 1934.

BARLOW, G.
The story of Madras.

BARROW, JOHN.
A Voyage to Cochin China in the years 1792 and 1793. London, 1806.

BLANC DE VOLX, J.
Du Commerce de l'Inde. Paris, 1802.

BLANC DE VOLX, J.
État commerciale de la France au commencement du XIXe siècle. Paris, 1893.

BONNEFOUX, LE BARON DE.
Dictionnaire de marine à voiles et à vapeur, par MM. le Baron de Bonnefoux et Paris, Capitaines de Vaisseau. Vol. I. Paris, n.d.

BORY DE ST. VINCENT.
Voyage dans les Mers d'Afrique. 1804.

BORY DE ST. VINCENT, J. B. G. M.
Voyage to, and travels through the four principal Islands of the African Seas, performed by order of the French Government during the years 1801 and 1802 (translated). London, 1805.

BOSANQUET, AUGUSTUS.
India seventy years ago. London, 1881.

BRADSHAW, JOHN.
Rulers of India. Sir Thomas Munro and the British settlement of the Madras Presidency. Oxford, 1894.

BROWNE, DOUGLAS G.
A forgotten battle: a study in obscure Naval History. *Blackwood's Magazine*, 1912.

BURKE, EDMUND.
The Works of the Right Honourable Edmund Burke. Vol. II. London, 1855.

CAMPBELL, ARCHIBALD.
A Voyage round the World, from 1806 to 1812. Edinburgh, 1816.

CAREY, W. H.
The good old days of Honorable John Company. Three vols. Simla, 1882.

CAYLA, J. M.
Histoire des vaisseaux le Vengeur et la Belle-Poule. Paris, 1855.

CHARLIAT, P. J.
La Marine de l'Empereur. Article in *La Mer et l'Empire*, 2e Serie, Ligue Maritime et Coloniale Française.

CHATTERTON, E. KEBLE.
  Ships and ways of other days. London, 1913.
CHATTERTON, E. KEBLE.
  The Ship under Sail. London, 1926.
CHATTERTON, E. KEBLE.
  The old East Indiaman. 2nd ed. London, 1933.
CHEVALIER, E.
  Histoire de la Marine Française sous la première république. Two vols. Paris, 1886.
CHEVALIER, HENRI.
  Vie et aventures du capitaine de corsaire T. Souville (1777–1839).
CLEVELAND, RICHARD J.
  A narrative of voyages and commercial enterprises. (Reprinted.) London, 1842.
COMPTON, H.
  (See Eastwick, R. W.)
COOK, CAPTAIN JAMES.
  A Collection of Voyages round the World; performed by Royal Authority, containing a complete Historical Account of Captain Cook's 1st, 2nd, 3rd and Last Voyages. Four vols. Vol. II. London, 1790.
COTTON, SIR EVAN.
  East Indiamen, the East India Company's Maritime Service. London, 1949.
CUNAT, CHARLES.
  Histoire de Surcouff.
CUNNINGHAM, W.
  The Growth of English Industry and Commerce in modern times. Vol. III (Modern times, Part II). Cambridge, 1912.
CUPPLES, GEORGE.
  The Green Hand. Adventures of a naval Lieutenant. First published in 1849. London, 1900.

DARTON, F. J. H.
  The Life and Times of Mrs. Sherwood (1775–1851). London, 1910.
DECOURT.
  Document quoted in Revue d'Histoire des Colonies. Tome XXVI. 1933.
DE GUIGNES.
  Voyages à Peking, Manille et l'ile de France faits dans l'intervalle des années 1784 à 1801. Three vols. Vol. III. Paris, 1808.
D'EPINAY, A.
  Renseignements pour servir à l'histoire de l'Ile de France jusqu'à 1810. Dupuy, 1890.
DESJARDINS.
  Campagnes de la frègate la Manche dans les mers de l'Inde. Le Havre, 1843.
DOUGLAS, JAMES.
  Glimpses of old Bombay and Western India. London, 1900.
DUNDONALD, EARL OF
  The autobiography of a seaman. London, 1861.
DUNN, SAMUEL.
  A new Directory for the East-Indies. A Work originally begun upon the plan of the Oriental Neptune, augmented and improved by W. Herbert, W. Nichelson, now . . . further enlarged . . . Fifth edition. London, 1780.

EAMES, J. B.
  The English in China, 1600–1843. London, 1909.

EASTWICK, R. W.
A Master Mariner. Being the life and adventures of Captain Robert William Eastwick. Edited by H. Compton. London, 1891.

EDGELL, T. C. P.
English Trade and Policy in Borneo and the adjacent islands, 1667–1786. Unpublished thesis, University of London, 1935.

EDWARDES, S. M.
The Rise of Bombay, a retrospect. Bombay, 1902.

EGERTON, HUGH EDWARD.
Sir Stamford Raffles: England in the Far East. London, 1900.

ELMORE, H. M.
The British Mariner's directory and guide to the trade and navigation of the Indian and China Seas. London, 1802.

FABRE, E.
La Guerre Maritime dans l'Inde sous le Consulat et l'Empire. *Revue Maritime et Coloniale*, Vol. 78. Paris, 1883.

FIELD, A. G.
The expedition to Mauritius in 1810 and the establishment of British Control. MS. Unpublished thesis in the Library of the University of London. 1931.

FIELD, COLONEL C.
Old times afloat: a naval anthology. London, 1932.

FLETCHER, R. A.
In the days of the tall ships. London, 1928.

FLINDERS, MATTHEW.
A Voyage to Terra Australis: undertaken for the purpose of completing the discovery of that vast country. Two vols. Vols. I and II. London, 1814.

FORBES, JAMES.
Oriental Memoirs: a narrative of seventeen years residence in India. Two vols. London, 1834.

FORBES, R. B.
Remarks on China and the China Trade. Boston, 1844.

FORREST, CAPT.
A treatise on the Monsoons in the East Indies. Calcutta, 1782.

FRASER, EDWARD (ed.)
The Mariner's Mirror, Vol. 13. 1927. Journal of Commander Thomas Colby, R.N., 1797–1815.

FROBERVILLE, LÉON HUET DE.
Souvenirs de l'Ile de France.

FROBERVILLE, LÉON HUET DE.
Ile de France. Le Combat du Grand Port et la fin de l'occupation Française. Mauritius, 1910.

GALLOIS, M. NAPOLEON.
Les Corsaires Français sous la République et l'empire. Two vols. Vol. II. Le Mans, 1847.

GARNERAY, L.
Voyages, aventures et combats.

GAUTIER, M. L. E.
Biographie du Général Decaen. Caen, 1850.

GILIBERT DE MERLHIOIRE.
De la liberté des Mers et du Commerce. Paris, 1818.

GIRARD, FULGENCE.
(See Lecomte, Jules).
GRAHAM, MARIA.
A Journal of a residence in India. Edinburgh, 1812.
GRANDPRÉ, L. DE.
A Voyage in the Indian Ocean and to Bengal, undertaken in the years 1789 and 1790. Translated from the French. Two vols. London, 1803.
GRANT, CHARLES, VISCOUNT DE VAUX.
The History of Mauritius or the Isle of France, and the neighbouring islands; from their first discovery to the present time. London, 1801.
GRANT, ROBERT.
The expediency maintained of continuing the system by which the trade and government of India are now regulated. London, 1813.
GRAVIÈRE, LE CONTRE-AMIRAL E. JURIEN DE LA.
Guerres maritimes sous la République et l'Empire. Two vols. Paris, 1869.
GRAVIÈRE, VICE-AMIRAL JURIEN DE LA.
Les Gloires Maritimes de la France. Paris, 1888.
GRAVIÈRE, VICE-AMIRAL JURIEN DE LA.
L'Amiral Roussin. Paris, 1888.
GRAVIÈRE, VICE-AMIRAL JURIEN DE LA.
L'Amiral Baudin. Paris, 1888.
GROSE, MR.
A Voyage to the East Indies. New ed. Two vols. London, 1772.
GUIGNES, DE.
(See De Guignes).

HALL, CAPTAIN BASIL, R.N.
Narrative of a voyage to Java, China, and the great Loo-Choo Island. London, 1840.
HALL, CAPTAIN BASIL, R.N.
Fragments of voyages and travels. Second Series. London, 1840.
HALL, CAPTAIN BASIL, R.N.
Fragments of voyages and travels. Third Series. London, 1840.
HALL, COMMANDER W. H.
Narrative of the Voyages and Services of the *Nemesis*, 1840–1844. London, 1844.
HAMILTON, WALTER.
East India Gazetteer. London, 1815.
HANNAY, DAVID.
The Sea Trader, his friends and enemies. London, 1912.
HARDY, CHARLES.
Register of Ships employed in the service of the Hon. the United East India Company, from the union of the two companies, in 1707, to the year 1760 . . . to which is added from the latter period to the present time. London, 1799.
HARDY, H. C.
A Register of Ships employed in the Service of the Honorable the United East India Co. from the year 1760 to 1812. Revised by H. C. Hardy. London, 1813.
HENCHMAN, THOMAS.
Observations on the reports of the Directors of the East India Company, respecting the trade between India and Europe. 2nd edition. London, 1802.
HERPIN, E.
Mahé de la Bourdonnais et la Compagnie des Indes. Saint-Brieuc, 1905.
HICKEY, WILLIAM.
Memoirs, edited by Alfred Spencer. Vol. IV (1790–1809). London, 1925.

HODGSON, G. H.
Thomas Parry, Free Merchant (1768–1824). Madras, 1938.
HORSBURGH, JAMES.
Directions for Sailing to and from the East Indies, China, New Holland, Cape of Good Hope, etc. Two vols. London, 1809–11.
HOSKINS, H. L.
British routes to India. New York, 1928.
HUET DE LA FROBERVILLE.
(See Froberville, Léon Huet de).

JOHNSON, J.
The Oriental Voyager; or descriptive sketches and cursory remarks on a voyage to India and China, in his Majesty's Ship Caroline, performed in the years 1803–6. London, 1807.
JOHNSON, JAMES.
The influence of tropical climates on European Constitutions. London, 1813.
JOHNSON, W. BRANCH.
Wolves of the Channel (1681–1856). London, 1931.
JONQUIÈRE, C. DE LA
L'Expédition d'Égypte, 1798–1801. État-Major de l'armée, Section Historique, 6 vols. Vols. III–V. Paris, c. 1920–21.
JURIEN DE LA GRAVIÈRE.
(See Gravière, J. de la.)

KAYE, JOHN WILLIAM.
The administration of the East India Company. London, 1853.

LARREY.
Expédition en Égypt et en Syrie. 1803.
LAUGHTON, J. K. (ed.)
The Naval Miscellany, Vol. I. Navy Records Society, Vol. XX. London, 1902. Journals of Thomas Addison. 1801–1830.
LECOMTE, JULES, ET FULGENCE GIRARD.
Chroniques de la Marine Française, 1789 à 1830. Two vols. Paris, 1836–37.
LEE, IDA.
Commodore Sir John Hayes, his voyage and life (1767–1831). London, 1912.
LINDSAY, LORD (ed.).
Lives of the Lindsays, Vol. IV. An adventure in China, Hon. Hugh Lindsay. Wigan, 1840.
LINDSAY, W. S.
History of Merchant Shipping and ancient Commerce. Four vols. Vol. II. London, 1874.
LLOYD, C. C.
The Keith Papers, Vol. II. Navy Records Society, Vol. XC.
LOCKHART, J. G.
Blenden Hall. London, 1930.
LONG, W. H.
(See Parsons, G. S.)
LORD, WALTER FREWEN.
Sir Thomas Maitland, the mastery of the Mediterranean. London, 1897.

Low, C. R.
History of the Indian Navy (1613–1863). Two vols. Vol. I. London, 1877.

Lubbock, Basil.
The Blackwall Frigates. Second edition. Glasgow, 1924.

Mackintosh, Robert James (ed.).
Memoirs of the life of the Right Honorable Sir James Mackintosh. Two vols. London, 1835.

Macpherson, David.
Annals of Commerce. Four vols. Vol. IV. London, 1805.

Macpherson, David.
The History of the European Commerce with India, to which is subjoined a review of the arguments for and against the trade with India and the management of it by a chartered Company. London, 1812.

Malleson, Colonel C. B.
Final French Struggles in India and on the Indian Seas. First Published, 1878.

Marryat, Captain.
Newton Forster; or, the Merchant Service. London, 1838.

Masefield, John.
Sea life in Nelson's time. London, 1905.

Masefield, John.
The travels of Marco Polo the Venetian, with an introduction by John Masefield. London, 1907.

McCulloch, J. R.
A Dictionary, practical, theoretical, and historical, of Commerce and Commercial navigation. New edition, London, 1854. First published, 1832.

Meares, John.
Voyages made in the years 1788 and 1789, from China to the North West Coast of America. London, 1790.

Milbert, M. J.
Voyage pittoresque à l'Ile de France, au Cap de Bonne-Espérance et à l'ile de Teneriffe. Two vols. Vol. I. Paris, 1812.

Milburn, William.
Oriental Commerce; containing a geographical description of the principal places in the East Indies ... with their Produce, Manufactures and Trade.... Two vols. London, 1813.

Mill, James.
The History of British India. (Continued by H. H. Wilson.) Vols. VI and VII. London, 1840–45.

Minto, Countess of (ed.).
Life and Letters of Gilbert Elliot, First Earl of Minto, from 1807 to 1814, while Governor-General of India. London, 1880.

M'Leod, John, M.D.
Voyage of his Majesty's Ship Alceste, to China, Gorea, and the Island of Lewchew, with an account of her ship-wreck. Third edition. London, 1819.

Money, William Taylor.
Observations on the expediency of Shipbuilding at Bombay for the service of His Majesty and of the East India Company. London, 1811.

Montefiore, J.
A Commercial Dictionary: containing the present state of Mercantile Law, practice and custom. London, 1803.

MOREAU DE JONNES.
Aventures de Guerre au temps de la République et du Consulat. Paris, 1893.
MORRIS, HENRY.
The life of Charles Grant. London, 1904.
MORSE, H. B.
The Chronicles of the East India Company trading to China, 1635–1834. Four vols.
Oxford, 1926.
MORTIMER, THOMAS.
A General Dictionary of Commerce. London, 1810.
MOULIN, H.
Les Marins de la République. Paris, 1883.

NAVAL CHRONICLE.
Vols. 1–39.
NEALE, WILLIAM JOHNSON.
The Port Admiral: a tale of the War. London, 1833.
NEWBY, T. C.
The Court Martial, a tale of military life. Two vols. London, 1844.
NORMAN, C. B.
The Corsairs of France. London, 1887.

OWEN, S. J. (ed.).
A Selection from the Despatches, Memoranda, and Other papers relating to India, of
the Marquess Wellesley, K.G., during his government of India. Oxford, 1877.

PARKINSON, C. NORTHCOTE.
Trade in the Eastern Seas, 1793–1813. Cambridge, 1937.
PARKINSON, C. NORTHCOTE (ed.).
The Trade Winds. London, 1948.
PARKINSON, C. NORTHCOTE.
Samuel Walters, Lieutenant R.N. Liverpool, 1949.
PARLIAMENTARY PAPERS.
Vols. 1808–13.
PARSHAD, I. DURGA.
Some aspects of Indian foreign trade. London, 1932.
PARSONS, G. S.
Nelsonian Reminiscences: leaves from Memory's log. Edited by W. H. Long. London,
1905.
PERCIVAL, ROBERT.
An account of the Cape of Good Hope. London, 1804.
PHILIPS, C. H.
The East India Company, 1784–1834. Manchester, 1940.
PICARD, ERNEST.
Memoires et journaux du Général Decaen, publie avec Introduction, Notes et Cartes
par Ernest Picard. Vol. II. Second edition. Paris, 1910.
PITOT, ALBERT.
L'Ile de France. Esquisses Historiques (1715–1810). Mauritius, 1899.
POPHAM, SIR HOME.
A description of Prince of Wales Island, in the Streights of Malacca: with its real and
probable advantages and sources to recommend it as a marine establishment. London,
1805.

P*

PRENTOUT, HENRI.
L'Ile de France sous Decaen (1803–1810). Essai sur la politique coloniale du premier empire et la rivalité de la France et de l'Angleterre dans les Indes Orientales. Paris, 1901.

PRIOR, JAMES.
Voyage along the Eastern Coast of Africa to Mosambique, Johanna, and Quiloa; to St. Helena etc., in the Nisus Frigate. London, 1819.

PRIOR, JAMES.
Voyage in the Indian Seas in the Nisus Frigate, 1810 and 1811. London, 1820.

PRIOR, JAMES.
A visit to Madras; being a sketch of the local and characteristic peculiarities of that Presidency in the year 1811. London, 1821.

RAINBOW, S. C.
English Expeditions to the Dutch East Indies during the Revolutionary and Napoleonic Wars. Unpublished MS. thesis in the Library of the University of London. 1933.

RENOUARD DE SAINTE-CROIX, F.
Voyage commercial et politique aux Indes Orientales, 1803–1807. Two vols. Paris, 1810.

RICHMOND, SIR H. W. (ed.).
Private Papers of George, second Earl Spencer, First Lord of the Admiralty, 1794–1801. Vol. IV. 1924.

RICHMOND, SIR H. W.
The Navy in India, 1763–1783. London, 1931.

ROBERTS, P. E.
India under Wellesley. London, 1929.

ROUIRE, DR.
La Question du Golfe Persique. Revue des Deux Mondes. Vol. 16. Paris, 1903.

ROUVIER, CHARLES.
Histoire des Marins Français sous la République (1789–1803). Paris, 1868.

SAINTOYARD, J.
La colonisation Française pendant la periode Napoleonienne (1799–1815). Paris, 1931.

SAMUELSON, JAMES.
India, past and present, historical, social and political. London, 1890.

SCHOMBERG.
Naval Chronology. Vol. 4.

SCOTT-WARING, MAJOR.
Observations on the Present State of the East India Company. Fourth edition. London, 1808.

SETON-KARR, W. S.
Selections from Calcutta Gazettes, 1798–1805. Three vols. Calcutta, 1868.

SMYTH, H. WARRINGTON.
Mast and Sail in Europe and Asia. London, 1906.

SMYTH, CAPTAIN W. H.
The life and services of Captain Philip Beaver, late of His Majesty's Ship Nisus. London, 1829.

SPEARS, J. R.
The story of the American Merchant Marine. New York, 1910.

SPENCER, ALFRED.
(See Hickey, William.)

STAPLETON, COMMANDER G.
The Blue Peter. Vol. 14. No. 151. October, 1934. Article on Minicoy.
STEEL, DAVID.
Elements and Practice of Naval Architecture. Two vols. London, 1805.
STEEL, DAVID.
List of the Royal Navy. London, 1810.
STEPHEN, J.
War in disguise; or the frauds of the neutral Flags. London, 1805.
SURCOUF, ROBERT.
Un corsaire Malouin. Paris, 1890.
SURCOUF, ROBERT.
Un capitaine corsaire, Robert Surcouf. Paris, 1925.
SWETTENHAM, F.
British Malaya. London, 1920.

TILBY, A. WYATT.
The English People Overseas. Vol. II. British India, 1600–1828. 1911.
TOMBE, CHARLES.
Voyage aux Indes Orientales pendant les Années 1802–1806. Revu et augmente ...
par M. Sonnini. Two vols. Vol. I. Paris, 1810.
TWINING, W. II. G.
Travels in India a hundred years ago. London, 1893.

VALENTIA, GEORGE, VISCOUNT.
Voyages and Travels to India, Ceylon, the Red Sea etc., in the years 1802–1806.
Four vols. Vol. I. London, 1811.

WALLACE, JAMES.
A Voyage to India. London, 1824.
WATHEN, JAMES.
Journal of a Voyage in 1811 and 1812, to Madras and China. London, 1814.
WELLESLEY, MARQUESS OF.
(See Owen, S. J.)
WELLINGTON, DUKE OF.
Supplementary despatches and memoranda of Field-Marshal Arthur Duke of
Wellington, K.G. India, 1797–1805. Edited by his son the Duke of Wellington.
Two vols. Vol. I. London, 1858.
WHALL, W. B.
The Romance of Navigation. London, n.d.
WILSON, H. H.
(See Mill, James.)
WYATT TILBY.
(See Tilby, A. Wyatt.)

INDEX

(*Note*. For Names of Vessels, see under 'Ships').

Abercromby, Sir John (1772–1817), Commander-in-Chief, Bombay, 1809–11
  arrival off Mauritius, capture and rescue of, 394
  at Roderiguez, 398
  directing the landing at Mapon Bay, 400
Abercromby, Major-General, Sir Ralph (1734–1801), military command given to, 173
  his death, 179
Abercromby, Sir Robert (1740–1827), 63
Acapulco, trade of, 42
Acheen, 76
  value of, 12
  Admiral Sercey in roads of, 101
Achin, 73, 370
  cruisers to patrol off, 319
Acre, 151
Adams, Capt. Charles, of the *Carysfort*, 112
Adamson, Alexander, 77
Aden, Sultan's offer to surrender, 152
  British refusal to accept, 153
Affleck, P., 68
d'Aguilar, Raphael, Governor of Philippines, 40
Agulhas Bank, The, 274
Alaba, Don Martin, 138
Alava, Don Ignacio de, 157
Aldwinkle, Lieutenant, officer in charge of gunners, 387
Alexander, Captain, of the *Carysfort* frigate, 101
Alexandria, 173
  capture of, by Bonaparte, 147
Allas, Straits of, 105
Amboyna, 22, 91, 378
  Admiral Rainier off, 94
  possession of, 94, 95
  rebellion in, 136
  taken in 1810 by Captain E. Tucker, 413
Amoy, silks from, 40
Andamans, 319
  possibilities as a naval base at the, 59
Anderson, Dr., his discovery of the uses of Nopal, 361
Anjouan, slaves from, 16
Anson, Admiral Lord, interception of register ship by, 43
Anson's Bay, 156
Antwerp, 187
Arabs, in Batavia, 26
Arden, Lord, 65, 68
Armenians, in Batavia, 26
d'Arsonval, 196
Auchmuty, Lieutenant-General Sir Samuel, 413, 416
Austen, H. C. M., 129
  his diagram of Battle of Grand Port, 393

Baco, M., republican, 97
  hustled away from Mauritius, 99
Baie Aux Tortues, Mauritius, 406

Baird, General, 149, 170
  his march, 178, 179
Balasore, 14, 181
Baldwin, Mr., 60
Balfour, Baker and Hart, Firm of, 350
Bali, Straits of, map of, 296
  Captain Beaver in the, 411
Ball, Captain A. J., 141, 170, 358
Banca, Straits of, 224
Banda Islands, 22, 378
  Admiral Rainier occupies the, 94
Banks, Sir Joseph, 362
Bantam, Kingdom of, pepper from, 22
Barbados, 292
Barlow, Sir George, 373
  Governor-General, 288
  Pellew's memorandum addressed to, 300
  his rigid economy, 375
Barrow, Sir John, reference to his Voyage to Cochin China, 26
Batavia, 18, 22, 29, 30, 31, 48, 173, 250, 412
  strategic position of, 23
  plan of, 24
  description of, 26
  effort to reproduce Holland at, 27
  diseases prevalent in, 28
  American ships in, 46
  requests to Admiral Rainier for protection of, 74
  Admiral Rainier's orders for blockade of, 163
  disease in, 171
  danger of French control of, 300
  surrender of, 415
Bathurst, Captain, 212, 221
  in command of detachment, 206
Baudin, Charles, 368
Beaulieu Le Loup, commander of *La Forte*, 125
  mistaken for Sercey, 126
  incompetence of, 129
Beaver, Captain Philip, 398
  in Cape, 33
  in Mozambique, 38
  his remarks on Mozambique, 49, 50
  of the *Nisus*, 397
  perfecting his plans for landing at Mapou Bay, 400
  his account of the landing, 403
  capitulation of Isle of France to, 407
  his death at the Cape, 411
Bencoolen, 73, 240
  position of, 13
  Linois's ruse at, 210
  raid on, 219
Bengal, 30, 73, 304
  strategic position of, 11
  trade with Pondicherry, 14
  rate of mortality in, 29
  trade with Goa, 36
  trade with Danes, 45
  English territory in, 47

Bengal—*continued*
  ships sent out for protection of trade by Government of, 63
Bengal, Bay of, 14, 59, 259
  value of, 12, 13
  lack of naval protection in, 84
  hunting ground of privateers, 287
Bentham, Jeremy, his description of Captain John Blankett, 142
Bentinck, Lord William, Governor of Madras, 214
  Rainier's dispatch to, 217
  his orders, 219
Bergeret, French Naval Captain, of the *Psyche*, 259
Bertie, Rear-Admiral Albemarle, 364
  his orders to Drury, 380
  of the *Nisus*, 394
  his regard for Rowley, 395
  at Capetown, 397
  Africaine now flagship of, 398
  in Roderigue, 398
  entering harbour at Port Louis, 408
Billard, Captain, 365
Bingham, Captain A.B., of the *St. Fiorenzo*, 207
Binot, 196, 205
  in Pondicherry, 201
Blair, Captain, 141
Blakiston, Lieutenant, 398
  Engineer, 395
Blankett, Rear-Admiral John, 56, 170
  at the Cape, 84, 86
  the Red Sea project, 140
  character of, 141
  delays during voyage of, 143
  at Mocha, 149
  he tries to impress Arabs, 152
  his reluctance to sail for Red Sea, 153
  Wellesley's suggestions to, 173
  occupation of Suez by, 175
  death of, 178
Blauenberg, 272
Bombay, 263
  as centre of Government, 11
  strategic position of, 12, 13
  lethargy in, 49
  Admiral Cornwallis at, 62
  English ships for, 212
  Pellew in, 286
  Dundas in, 339
  naval hospital at, 356
'Bombay Jack,' saying of, 50
Bon, General, 145
Bonaparte, Jerome, 294
Bonaparte, General, or the Emperor Napoleon, 167, 188
  his expedition to Egypt, 139
  visit to Suez of, 145
  capture of Alexandria by, 147
  his success, 182
  his anger with Linois and Captain Larue, 234
  dispatches from, 248
  his treatment of Decaen, 309
  Decaen's appeals to, 365
  abandons plans for naval war in the East, 418
Borneo, 22
Boston, 45

Bourbon, Island of, 14, 200
  French settlers in, 15
  geographical location of, 19
  products of, 19
  population of, 20
  arrest of Governor of, 71
  Surcouf sights, 311
  attack on, 383
Bourdonnais, M. Mahé de la, First Governor of Mauritius, 15
  character of, 15
  introduction of manioc by, 16, 19
  choice of position for capital by, 17
Bouvet, Pierre, his early voyage, 210
  of the *Minerve*, 368
  taking command of *Bellone*, 390
  his withdrawal, 393
Bowers, 351
Bowler, Lieutenant, capture in a cutter of, 399
Braithwaite, Colonel, 62
Bremer, Captain, 372
Brest, 66, 284
  expedition from, 286
Bridport, Lord, 418
Briggs, Captain, R.N., in landing at Mauritius, 401
Britain, Great, war declared against, 66
Broughton, Captain W. R., 382
  of the *Illustrious*, 413
  cautious navigator, 415
  his command of landing east of Batavia, 415
  superseded and then restored to command, 416
  return to England of, 418
Brown, Major, military commander at Malacca, 93
Bruce, Fawcett and Co., ship owners, 77, 260
Bruilhac, Captain of the *Belle Poule*, 202, 229
Bruix, French Admiral, 188
Budach, Governor, 136
Buque, M. de, 122
Burnel, M., authority on affairs of Mauritius, 97
  at Mauritius, 99
Burnyeat, Captain, 110
Bussora (Bushire), information received from, 148
Butcher's Island, 356
Byng, Captain George, of the *Belliqueux*, 363

Caffarelli, 195
Caille, Abbé de la, 15
Caillean, Louise Victorine, wealthy creole and wife of Sercey, 122
Calcutta, 13, 26, 340
  as base, 11
  vulnerability of, 12, 13
  Portuguese in, 39
  Commodore Cornwallis at, 56, 60
  Sir George Barlow at, 301
Calder, Vice-Admiral Sir Robert, 286
Callamand, Captain, 58
Camperdown, Battle of, 135
Campo-Formio, Treaty of, 181
Cannonière Point, Mauritius, 406
Canterbury, Archbishop of, 56
Canton, 37, 221
  interest of, 13
  Dutch factory at, 29, 30

Canton—*continued*
    Danish ships in, 44
    American ships in, 45
    Select Committee of Super Cargoes at, 105
    map of, 322
    Rear-Admiral Drury at, 326
Cape, The, or Cape of Good Hope, 18, 22, 33
    Dutch possession of, 32
    American route round, 46
    Admiral Cornwallis passed, 63
    British acquisition of, 81
    Linois sailing for, 271
Cape Delgado, 37
Cape Frio, 368
Cape Lopez, 368
Capetown, importance of, 34
    architecture of, 48
Cape Verde Islands, 67
Caraud, *Coureur* captained by, 75
Cavaignac, Father of General, 210
Cavendish, interception of register ship by, 43
Cavité (or Cavita), Philippines, 43, 138
    naval port and arsenal of, 39
    garrison in, 40
    shipbuilding in, 42
    Spanish squadron laid up at, 119
Celebes, 22
Ceram, 22, 46
Ceylon, 76, 78, 279
    importance of, 34, 35
    Linois's squadron in, 200
Chandernagore, 13, 181
Chatham, Earl of, 65
    orders of, 68
Chatigam, 14
Cheduba, 319
Cherbourg, 187
Cheribon, 31, 411
Chillingehing, place chosen for landing, 415
China, 13, 29, 30
    trade with Goa, 36
    trade with Denmark, 44
Chinese, in Batavia, 26, 28
    in Manila, 40
Choiseul, Duc de, Naval administration of, 11
Clark, Captain William, of the *Victorious*, 112, 113
    recalled to India, 119
Clarke, General, arrival of, 81
Clive, Lord, 163
    Governor of Madras, 201
Cochrane, Hon. B., the Victualling Contractor at
    Madras, 339
    return to England of, 350
Cole, Captain Christopher, 413
    credit for swiftness of landing due to, 415
Collot, 145
Colombo, 80, 83, 86, 91, 92
    importance of, 35
    Portuguese found in, 39
    Rainier's seamen mutinied at, 132
Comoro Islands, 142
    King of the, 50
    Linois called at the, 241
Constantia, vineyard of, 34
Conway, M., 55

Cook, Captain James, visit to Batavia of, 28
    his care of sailors, 358
Cooke, Captain, of the *Mornington*, his capture,
    125, 127
Cooke, Captain Edward, 135, 137, 138
    of the *Sybille*, 112, 113
    ordered to proceed to Macao, 120
    protecting the Bay of Bengal, 124
    fatally wounded, 1799, 129
Cooper's Island, 25
    description of, 26
Copong, conquest of Dutch settlement of, 136
Corbet, Captain Robert, 367, 388
    contemporary of Willoughby, 366
    Africaine commanded by, 393
    in action and mortally wounded, 394
Corfu, French army at, 133
Coringa, 244, 340
Cornish Admiral, Manila taken by, 43
Cornwallis, Commodore the Hon. William, 58,
    63, 69
    his appointment, 56
    character of, 57
    promotion of, 59
    extract from his *Life and Letters*, 60
    letter to Admiralty, 62
    proceeding home, 63
    as Rear-Admiral, 66, 67, 68
Cornwallis, Lord, 59
    order of, 45
    securing brother's naval appointment, 56
    sailing for England, 62
    news of his death, 286
Coromandel Coast, 35, 85, 133
    strategic position of the, 11
    Rainier on the, 112
    Linois making for, 241
Corps-du-Garde, 15
Craig, Major-General Sir James, 88, 100, 116
    troops under, 81
Cranssen, Dutch Governor, 172
Cranstown, Rt. Hon. Captain the Lord, *Raison-able* commanded by, 65
Crawang, 23
Cuddalore Roads, Admiral Rainier's squadron at,
    204
Cullen, Colonel, in Pondicherry, 201
Culver Cliff, 252
Curtis, Sir Roger, 32, 164, 376
    his concern about troops, 168

Dacca, 14
Daendels, Governor-General of Java, 412
Damietta, 173
Dance, Captain Nathaniel, in command of China
    fleet, 223
    perplexed, 227
Danish East India Company, The, 44
Dawson, Captain, of the *Dedaigneuse*, 328
Decaen, René, General Decaen's younger
    brother, 309, 375
Decaen, General, 50, 237, 266, 294, 384, 399, 405
    his career, 189
    orders received by, 192
    Linois's dislike of, 193

Decaen, General—*continued*
escape from Pondicherry, 206
his dispatches, 233
Linois's feud with, 247, 271
Napoleon's treatment of, 309
in command of naval forces at Mauritius, 364
directing shore gun on English ships in Grand
Port, 390
decides to give battle, 406
he surrenders Isle of France, 407
Decrès, Admiral Denis, 275, 285, 368, 378
French Minister of Marine and Colonies, 187
dispatch from Decaen to, 233
appeals to, 248
Napoleon's letter to, 309
Deguilas, Raphael Maria, Governor of Manila, 259
Dekker, Dutch Rear-Admiral, 211, 237, 272
Delagoa Bay, 37
Preneuse enters, 130
Delarue, Captain, French Navy, 248
of the *Marengo*, 229
carrying Admiral's letter, 233
Demaun, 36
Demeuron, Colonel, 201
Denmark, ships from, 18
possessions in the East of, 44
Desaix, General, 151
Dessolles, 190
Diamond Harbour, Commodore Cornwallis's
arrival at, 56
Dickson, Captain Sir Archibald, 245
Diego Rais, or Diego Royes, 77 (*see also*
Roderigue)
Diu, 36
Dondra Head, 214
the *Marengo* off, 241
Draper, Colonel, Manila taken by, 43
Drieu, privateersman, 101
Drury, Vice-Admiral O'Brien, 365, 369, 373
protection of slave trade by, 66
his arrival at Madras, 312
in command of expedition to occupy Macao, 317
his expedition assembled at Prince of Wales
Island, 320
his character, 320
arrival at Macao of, 321
his occupation of Macao, 325
his visit to Canton, 326
he leaves Macao, 333
Pellew hands over his command to, 334
in Penang, 370
Lord Minto's discussions with, 377
instructed to attack Mauritius, 378
sailing in the *Russel*, 380
his orders from Bertie, 380
death of and obituary, 381
Dryon, Straits of, 166
Duckworth, Admiral Sir John, 292, 309
Duclos-Legris, French sailor and diarist, 29, 228,
277
wounded, 274
Dundas, Rt. Hon. Henry, Lord Melville, 81, 120,
139, 261
one of H.M. Principal Secretaries of State, 66
his suggestions, 173. *See also* 265, 293

Dundas, the Hon. Philip, his request for funds, 288
Governor of Penang, 290
at Bombay, 339
Dundonald, Earl of, Lord Cochrane, 346
representations made by, 419
Dunkirk, 47
Duperré, Captain, 365, 368, 396
his squadron nearing Ile de la Passe, 386
lured into Grand Port, 389
a casualty, 390
Dupleix, policy of, 11
Duplessis, arrest of, 71
Dutch, 13
settlement in Mauritius of, 17
commercial importance of, 22
trade with Japan, 30
possession of Colombo by, 35
lack of interest in Holland shown by, 50
Dutch East India Company, garrisoning outposts
by, 22
policy of, 29
Dutch East Indies, The, 22, 29

East Africa, slaves from, 18
trade of, 36
Portuguese settlements in, 37
East India Company, 338
interest in China of the, 13
monopoly of the, 44
policy of to prevent colonization, 48
allowances to naval officers and men, paid by
the, 344
Eastwick, Robert William, Captain and part-
owner of *Endeavour*, 125
his account of engagement between *Forte* and
Sybille, 126, 127
Edam, 25, 171
description of, 26
Edmund, Mr. Charles, Surgeon in the *Russel*, 362
Egypt, Bonaparte bound for, 139
French in, 173
Elgin, Lord, 167
Eliot, Captain the Hon. George, 415
Elphinstone, Admiral Sir George Keith, 60, 83,
88, 154
acquisition of Cape by, 81
preparations of, 86
surrender of Dutch squadron to, 87
departure for England of, 90
a Scotsman, 92
plans for conquering Mauritius prepared by, 100
Elphinstone, Mr., one of the Select Committee in
Macao, 333

Fairlie, Gilmore and Co., 318
Fallofield, E. H., Member of Council, 92
False Bay, 32, 34
Admiral Linois's squadron at, 200
Faria, St. Bernado Alexe de Lemos e, Governor
of Macao, 323
Farquhar, Mr., Governor of Bourbon, 384
Fernando Po, Island of, 272
Ferrier, Captain, 218
orders to, 219
senior officer at Bombay, 308

Ferrol, 173, 285
Flinders, Captain, explorer, 362
Flushing, 187
Forbes, Mr., the Shipowner, 373
Forbes, Smith and Co., 77
Forfait, French Minister, 187
Fort Belgica, 22
Fort Cornwallis, Penang, foundation of, 12
Fort Dauphin, Madagascar, 31
  harbour of, 21
  Linois arrives at, 271
Fort Lodowic, 31
Fort Malartic, 403
Fort Marlborough, 49. See also Bencoolen
Fort Nassau, 22
Fort Ostenburg, Ceylon, protection of Trinco-
  malee by, 35
  capitulation of, 80
Fort St. George, see Madras
Fort William, see Calcutta
Foul Point, 21
Fowler, Captain, killed, 162
Fowler, Lieutenant, 224, 226
France, Isle of, see Mauritius
French, 57, 67
  policy of the, 11
  as settlers in Bourbon, 15
  annexation of Colombo by, 35
  Revolution, 55
  in Egypt, 173
  their designs on Portugal, 315
French East India Company, The, 15
Fresne, Chevalier de, his role in fortification of
  Pondicherry, 14
Friars Hood, Ceylon, 73
Frigate's Island, 22
Fulgueras, Don Mariano Fernandez de, Spanish
  Governor General in Manila, 258

Galega, or Agalega Islands, 22, 200
Ganges, River, value of the, 11
Ganteaume, Rear-Admiral, 146, 178
Gardanne, General, his mission, 309
Gardner, Sir Alan, 65
  Rear-Admiral, 66, 67
Gardner, Captain Alan Hyde, son of Admiral, 91
  of the Heroine, 112
  invalided home, 113
Garneray, Louis, 129
Gaspar, Straits of, 231
Genoa, French Army at, 133
George II, H.M. King, 65
George III, H.M. King, 65
Gibraltar, 173
Goa, 57, 86, 177, 204, 315
  Portuguese capital at, 35
  trade by, 36
  architecture of, 48
Goate, Lieutenant William, 166
Golconda, 14
Governor-General of the Indies, power of the, 29
Graham, Maria, 50
Grand Bay, 398
Grand Port, Mauritius, 15, 247, 395
  harbour of, 18

Grand Port, Mauritius—continued
  force guarding, 365
  possible landing at, 384
  luring Duperré's ships into, 386, 389
  plan of ships' positions in Battle of, 391
Grandpré, his opinion of Pondicherry, 13
Grant, Captain, of the H.C.S. Brunswick, 266
  his report on the encounter with Admiral
    Linois, 271
Grant, Charles, Viscount de Vaux, extract from
  History of Mauritius by, 18
Greig, Captain, his report on uncharted seas, 415
Grenville, 182
Grey, Lieutenant, of the Adamant, 131
Griessie, or Gressec, 31, 296, 302, 303, 304
  scheme to destroy two ships at, 301
Guadeloupe, 191
Guadeloupe, Governor of, Linois's appointment as,
  275
Guernsey, 64
Guinea, Gulf of, 272
Gunner's Quoin, Rock named the, 386, 398
Guy, Captain Dornal de, 365
Guzerat, 214

Halgan, Captain, 229
  of the Berceau, 225
Hall, Lieutenant Basil, 33
  joins the Illustrious, 420
  works written by, 420
  obituary written by, 421
Hall, Mr., 339
Hallowell, Captain Benjamin, 313
Halstead, John, 113
Hamburgers, trade competition in East from the,
  44
Hamelin, Commodore, 365, 394
  appearance outside Grand Port of squadron of,
    392
Hargood, Captain W., convoy protected by, 158
Harris, General, 117
Hartsinck, Admiral, 218, 237, 255, 294
  in Batavia harbour, 231
Hayes, Commodore John, 413
  cruisers under command of, 416
Hayward, Captain Thomas, on the Swift, 112
l'Hermitte, Captain, 124
  commander of frigate, 121
  of the Preneuse, 129
  taken prisoner, 131
Hickey, William, 294
  extract from memoirs of, 56
  his memoirs, 287
Hills, Captain Will, in Bombay in the Hobart, 112
Hindoos, in Batavia, 26
Hislop, General, Governor of Bombay, capture of,
  421
Hobart, Lord, 77, 118
  Admiral Rainier's discussions with, 91
Hogue, Davidson and Co., 318
Holkar, the Mahratta chief, 252
Holland, war declared against, 66
  on English side, 74
Hood, Vice-Admiral Sir Samuel, 418
  report rendered by, 419

Hood, Vice-Admiral Sir Samuel—*continued*
  plans made by, 420
  death of and obituary, 421
Hood, Lord, 65, 418
  promotion as Vice-Admiral, 66
  occupation of Toulon by, 67
Hooghly, River, 62, 340, 370
  strategic value of, 11
Horsburgh, Captain, 158
Hoseason, Admiral Rainier's secretary, 338
Houdoul, Captain, French privateer, 132
Howe, Rt. Hon. Richard, Earl, commands
  Channel Fleet, 65, 69
Hughes, Sir Edward, the coastal strip at Ceylon
  taken by, 35
  in Madras, 339
Hunter, Dr. surgeon, 357
Hutchinson, General, 176, 178

Ile de Passe, or Ile de la Passe, 247
  attempt on, 385
  men put ashore from *Iphigenia* at, 392
Ile-du-Roi, Admiral Sercey at, 105
India, 18
  Dutch trade with, 29
  native armies organized by English in, 36
  trade with America, 45
Indians, in Manila, 40
Inman, Commissioner, 339

Jacatra, Java, 23
Jacatra River, Java, 26
Jacolet, The harbour of, 383
Jamaica, 65, 66
James, Silas, extract from his narrative, 36
James, William, naval historian, 86
Jansen, General, 412, 415
  surrender by, 416
Japan, 29
  Dutch trade with, 30
Java, 23, 304
  as centre of Dutch East Indies, 22
  exports of, 30
  map of, 296
  French Governor of, 412
  surrender of, 416
Javanese, in Batavia, 26
Jeffreys, surgeon of the *Dover*, 362
Jena, Battle of, 309
Jervis, Vice-Admiral Sir John, K.B., on expedition
  to W. Indies, 67
Jidda, merchants of, 145
  Blankett's visit to, 152, 174
Johnson, J., author of *Oriental Voyager*, quoted,
  32, 360
Junkceylon, 370

Kandy, Ceylon, native King of, 35
Karikal, 14
Keating, Lieutenant-Colonel, 366
  his brigade landed at Mapou Bay, 403
Kedah, Sultan of, 13
King, Captain, instructions to, 63
Kosseir, 151, 173
  Blankett sails for, 176

Kutch, Gulf of, 214
Kuyper, 170

Laccadives, the, 266
Ladrones, the, 332
Laing, David, member of English crew, 96
Lambert, Captain Peter, 112
  his handling of the mutiny in the *Suffolk*, 134
  of the *St. Fiorenzo*, 260
  of the *Iphigenia*, 368
  blockade of Mauritius by, 383
  surrenders, 392
Lascars, 33, 343, 346
Latouche-Treville, 188
Leclerc, General, 190
Leeward Islands, The, 66
Lefebure, 248
  aide-de-camp, 233
Leger, 205
  Decaen's colleague, 196
  in Pondicherry, 201
Lemême, Captain, commands privateer, 132
Lennox, Captain Charles, his bluff, 106
Lesly, Mr., Master of the *Nereide*, 390
Light, Captain Francis, 12, 101
Lind, Captain James, 244
Linois, Rear-Admiral, C. A. L. Durand de, 221,
  229, 237, 238, 253, 368
  his career, 192
  Decaen's dislike of, 193
  escape from Pondicherry of, 206
  map of his two voyages, 209
  his ruse at Bencoolen, 210
  his attempt on the China fleet, 214
  his position on trade route, 224
  he reaches Isle of France, 232
  his plan to intercept trade, 241
  Decaen's feud with, 247
  news of his operations, 264
  plan of voyages of, 270
  Linois sails for Cape, 271
  he receives news of English capture of Cape, 272
  surrender to British squadron by, 274
  a prisoner and his later retirement, 275, 278
Linois, Enseigne de Vaisseau Durand, 274
Lloyd, Lieutenant-Colonel, 175
Locker, Mr. Hawke, Pellew's secretary, 339
Losack, Captain, detachment under, 90
Louis XVI, 71
  policy of, 11
Louis XVIII, 368
Lucas, Dutch Rear-Admiral, his voyage to the
  Cape, 85, 86
Lucas, Captain Richard of the *Arrogant*, 112
  in Penang, 103
  his death, 113
Luconia or Luzon, island of, 39, 48
Lushington, Stephen, Chairman of the East India
  Co., 120
Lye, Captain, in landing at Mauritius, 401

Macao, 13, 35, 48, 95, 156
  trade of, 36
  population of, 37
  naval force at, 239

Macao—*continued*
  the *Blenheim* in, 291
  a danger to England, 315
  Drury arrives at, 321
  map of, 322
Macassar, Straits of, 291
Mackerel, Mr., passenger in the *Mornington*, 125
Macnemara Comte de, lynching of, 55
Madagascar, 14, 16, 271
  slaves from, 16, 18
  exports of, 19
  ports of, 21
  provisions from, 77
Madeira, 33
  Dutch squadron sighted off, 85
Madras, 13, 43, 49, 61, 67, 84, 91, 292, 304, 410
  strategic position of, 11
  Commodore Cornwallis in, 56
  Admiral's residence in, 57
  Rainier at, 70
  Bentinck made Governor of, 214
  during mutiny of Vellore, marines landed to occupy, 293
  Pellew arrives at, 317
  map of, 344
  diagram of Admiral's house in, 345
  naval hospital at, 355
  plan of naval hospital, 356
Madura, or Manara, 31
Magallon, General, 97
  in charge of troops, 98
  as Governor-General of Mauritius, 208
  transferred to Bourbon, 208
Magon, René, former Governor of Mauritius, 122
Mahé, 13, 57, 58
  settlement of, 21
Mahebourg, 390
  Captain Willoughby marches to, 386
Mahrattas, the, position of, 11
  resistance of, 36
Malabar Coast, 13, 35, 286
  pepper from, 22
  Commodore Cornwallis on the, 57
  protection of, 251
Malacca, 78, 86, 181
  strategic importance of, 22
  occupation by Captain Newcome of, 80, 93
  fleet leaves, 414
Malacca, Straits of, 12, 59, 63, 73, 263
  Admiral Linois near mouth of, 224
  Admiral Pellew in the, 253
Malartic, Comte de Anne Joseph Hippolyte Maurès, 121, 123, 124
  Governor of Mauritius, 71
  non-committal conduct of, 99
  his death, 208
Malaya, 12
Malays, 28
  junks taken from, 72
  in ships, 343
Malcolm, Captain Pulteney, of the *Fox*, 112, 137
Malcolm, Brigadier-General, 370
Malroux, Captain, 132, 162
Mangalore, 121
  ships cruising off, 148

Manila, Philippines, 48, 263
  description of, 39
  population of, 40
  subsidy from Mexico for, 41
  American ships in, 46
  events in Europe, saved by, 119
  strategic possibilities of, 258
  Semillante blockaded at, 274
Manning, Mr., in command of *Concorde*, 61
Mapou Bay, a good beach and undefended, 398
  landing of the British Army in, 400
Markham, Admiral, 284, 295
Maroondah River, 171
Marryat, Captain F., 262
Masulipatam, French port of, 14
  French squadron off, 244
Mauritius, 14, 50, 96, 159, 167, 173, 182, 375, 384
  as naval base, 12
  geographical description of, 15
  colonization by Dutch of, 15
  population of, 16
  supplies of foodstuffs to, 19
  trade with Portuguese, 39
  American ships visiting, 46
  news of French Revolution came to, 55
  epidemic of smallpox, 56
  Governor of, 71
  blockade of, 74
  letter from Elphinstone to Admiralty about, 88
  Sercey reaches Port Louis, 99
  rebellion in 1798 at, 130
  Admiral Linois's squadron refitted in, 266
  Admiral Pellew's detachment off, 292
  Decaen in command of naval force at, 364
  Drury told to attack, 378
  difficulty of landing at, 398
  General Decaen surrenders, by capitulation, 407
Meares, John, 30
Mecca, 145
Mediterranean, warning received by fleet in, 66
Meester-Cornelis, an inland camp, 415
Melun, 149
Melville, Lord, Rt. Hon. Henry Dundas, 265, 293. *See also* under Dundas
Mendoca, Don Antonio Manoel de Mello Castro e, Portuguese Governor of Mozambique, 49
Mexicans, presence in Manila of, 40
Milburn, extracts from his *Oriental Commerce*, 25, 46
Minto, Lord, 382, 412
  Barlow's successor, 304
  his decision to occupy Macao, 317
  his discussions with Admiral Drury, 377
  in Madras, 383
  his visit to Java, 413
Mitchell, Commodore, 72
M'Leod, J., extracts from his *Voyage of the Alceste*, 39
Mocha, *L'Uni* at, 132
  Blankett reaches, 143
Moluccas, 181
  possession by Rainier of Amboyna, capital of the, 94
Montagne de Faience, 15
Montagne Longue, 15

Montagu, Rear-Admiral, 70
Montandevert, Ripaud de, privateer officer, 121
Montigny, Brigadier, 196
Moreau, 189
Morne des Prêtres, 15
Mornington, Lord, Governor-General, afterwards
    the Marquess Wellesley, 124
    his decision about Aden, 153
    letters received by, 162. *See also under* Welles-
    ley
Morrow, Robert, member of English crew, 96
Motard, Captain, 364
    of the *Semillante*, 259
Mozambique, slaves from, 16
    description of, 37, 38, 39
    smallpox infected slaves from, 56
Muncherjee, Sorabjee, a Parsee ship owner, 260
Murray, Captain, 166
Murray, Lieutenant-Colonel, troops under, 149
    transfer of his troops to Aden, 152
    at Tor, 154
Murray, Hon. John, 113
Muscat, Portuguese found in, 39
Muscat, Imam of, ship belonging to the, 72

Nagasaki, Japan, 30, 307
Nantucket, 45
Napoleon, *see under* Bonaparte
Natal, 35
    coast of, 37
Navy Board, The, organization of, 338
    invalided Lists of, 353
Negapatam, Admiral Rainier cruising off, 120
    Admiral Drury's ambition for, 340
Negrais, 319, 370
Nelson, Vice-Admiral, Horatio, Viscount, 57
    Agamemnon commanded by, 65
Nepean, Sir Evan, 284
    appointed Governor of Bombay, 420
Newcome, Captain Henry, 72
    in Malacca, 80
    surrender of Malacca, 83, 93
    in Bombay on the *Orpheus*, 112
New York, 45
Nicobars, the, 319, 370
North, Governor, of Ceylon, 215
Nova Scotia, 66

Oakley, Sir Charles, 61
Oman, Seyd, Sultan of, 308
Oman, Seyd-Said of, new Ruler, 308
Onroost, 170
    dockyard of, 23
    geographical location and description of, 25
    dockyard and establishment burnt by Pellew at,
    297
Onrust, *see under* Onroost
Ontong, 23
Orange, Prince of, 78
    residence in Capetown of, 34
Osborn, Captain Edward, of the *Trident*, 112
Osborn, Captain John, 239, 250, 258, 290
    his orders, 246
    he proceeds to Bay of Bengal, 263
Osborn, Captain Oliver, 156

Osborn, Captain Samuel, of the *Centurion*, 75,
    112, 113
Ostend, 57

Page, Captain, 253
    of the *Hobart*, 94
    in command of convoy, 239
    at Pulo Aur, 254
Pakenham, Captain, 78, 138
    invention of, 65
    Rainier's instructions to, 95
    at Amboyna in the *Resistance*, 112
    plot to kill, 135
Panambangan, troops landed at, 415
Paris, war declared at, 66
Parker, interception of register ship by, 43
Parsees, in Batavia, 26
    Bombay largely owned by, 39
Patna, 14
Pellew, Admiral Sir Edward, 129, 253, 254, 289,
    290, 292, 294, 337, 339, 364, 373, 375
    captain of the *Tonnant*, 218
    to succeed Admiral Rainier, 242
    his promotion, 252
    bound for Bombay, 255
    purchase of ships by, 260, 261
    force handed over to, 262
    his protection of Bay of Bengal, 263
    his plan of operations, 264
    his dispatch to Admiralty, 268
    off the Isle of France, 274
    his quarrel with Rear-Admiral Troubridge, 278,
    279
    his memorandum to Admiralty, 281, 282
    his opinion of Troubridge, 284
    sailing from Madras, 295
    through the Straits of Sunda, 297
    in sole command of East Indies squadron, 300
    at Malacca, 306
    instructions received by, 308
    blamed for loss of ships, 312
    justifying himself, 316
    his resignation, 318
    handing over his command to Vice-Admiral
    Drury, 334
    his income, 349
Pellew, Fleetwood, younger son of Admiral
    Pellew, 297
    his visit to Japan, 307
Pellew, Captain Pownall, Admiral Pellew's elder
    son, 318
Penang, 76, 280, 304
    position of, 12, 13
    base at, 59
    Admiral Rainier sailing for, 73
    plan of, 102
    rendezvous of Admiral Rainier and Admiral
    Pellew at, 253
    Rear-Admiral Troubridge at, 290
Penmarch-Mainvielle, Brigadier, 196
Percival, Captain Robert, 32
Perim, Island of, occupation of, 140
Persia, news of French Army about to march
    through, 308
Persians, in Batavia, 26

Petrie, Mr., 257
Philadelphia, 45
Philippines, importance of, 39
  trade in, 40
  plan of, 41
  peculiarity of calendar at, 43
  British interest in, 111
Philipps, Mr. John, Master of the *Ganges*, 272
Phillips, Lieutenant, of the *Centurion*, 244
Pickett, Lieutenant, 110
Piter Bort, 15
Pitt, Rt. Hon. William, 65, 261, 293
Plymouth, a 'King's Port,' 345
Point de Galle, 84
  squadron and troops landing at, 212
Pointe du Diable, 387
Point Negrais, 251
Point Pedro, 73
Ponce, 15
Pondicherry, 20, 57, 60, 181, 187, 204, 243
  as French H.Q., 11, 13
  plan of, 14
  proximity with Tranquebar, 45
  surrender of, 62
  Admiral Linois's squadron in, 200
  Linois escapes from, 206
Pontavinda, in Spain, 233
Popham, Captain Sir Home, as Lieutenant, 13
  in the Red Sea, 176
Port au Prince, 274
Port Jackson, American ships in, 46
Port Louis, Mauritius, town and harbour of, 17
  trade of, 18
  Americans overstocking markets of, 46
  French atmosphere in, 48
  frigates in, 72
  Admiral Sercey reaches, 99
  arrival of Tippoo's emissaries at, 122
  Osborn's small squadron off, 246
  occupation of men of, 293
  Surcouf enters, 311
  refit of *Semillante* at, 364
  force guarding, 365
  Duperré's ships nearing, 386
  French ships moored as floating batteries at, 396
  plan of harbour entrance to, 404
  Decaen in, 406
  plan of, 409
Portsmouth, the *Marengo*, prize, brought into, 274
  a 'King's Port,' 345
Port Sud-Est (or Bourbon), unsuccessful attack on
  anchorage of, 398
Portugal, army destined for, 173
  a potential ally of France, 315
Portuguese, 35, 86
  slave trading by, 16
  interest in Goa by, 36
  character of, 49, 50
Praslin, Duc de, 17
Prendergast, Michael, 314
Prince of Wales Island, *see* Penang
Pringle, Rear-Admiral Thomas, 86, 89
Prior, James, extracts from his *Voyage in the
  Indian Ocean*, 27, 32
  as a surgeon, 27, 28, 361

Prior, James—*continued*
  visit to East Africa of, 37
  his account of landing of British Army at
    Mapou Bay, 402
Providence, U.S.A., 45
Prussians, trade competition in East from the, 44
Pulo-Aur, 250
  Linois arrived off, 224
  Battle of, 229
  Linois's retreat from, 233
  protection of fleet off, 286
Purmerend, 25
Pybus, Mr., 65
Pym, Captain Samuel, 368, 383
  distributing literature, 384
  capture of Ile de la Passe by, 385, 386
  his plan to attack Duperré's ships, 389
  his orders to ships, 392

Quiloa, slaves from, 16

Raffles, Sir Stamford, Pellew's acquaintance with,
  307
Rainier, Captain J. S., 113
  nephew of Admiral P. Rainier, 70
  Swift, sloop commanded by, 91
  of the *Dortrecht*, 112
  of the *Centurion* in Suez, 151
  return to India of, 252
Rainier, Admiral Peter, 69, 124, 176, 235, 238,
  245, 260, 288, 302, 337
  the *Suffolk* commanded by, 65, 67
  Commodore, 70
  movements of, 73
  in Madras, 77
  Rainier's plans, 84
  Elphinstone's departure from Cape restores
    independence to, 90
  return to Madras of, 91
  his intentions, 91
  sails for Malacca, 93
  off Amboyna, 94
  possession of Amboyna, 95
  Rear-Admiral of the Blue, 95
  on the Coromandel Coast, 112
  his expedition against Manila, 114
  on defensive, 119
  cruising, 120
  in Madras, 133
  his treatment of the mutineers in the *Suffolk*, 134
  the Red Sea Project, 141, 142, 143
  information received by, 148
  his orders to Blankett, 149, 153
  at Madras, 163
  at Penang, 165
  at Colombo, 169
  his decision to sail for Bombay, 170
  in Penang, 179
  his presence at Trincomalee, 203
  French squadron at Pondicherry escaped from,
    206
  his dispatches, 212
  his concern about the China ships, 217
  his annoyance with Lord W. Bentinck, 219
  on the Malabar Coast, 236
  his mistake, 241

Rainier, Admiral Peter—*continued*
  his plan of action, 242, 243
  situation of East Indies squadron under, 251
  chasing after Linois, 253
  handing over his command to Admiral Pellew, 254
  force handed over by, 262
  his income, 349
Rainier, Captain Peter. *See* Appendix E
Rangoon, Portuguese found in, 39
Ravenel, Commodore, mutiny suppressed by, 123
Raynal, Abbé, quotation from his account of the galleon, 42
Red Sea, 140
  map of, 144
  Blankett sailing for, 153
  troops for the, 173
Register ships, description of, 41
  interception by English of, 43
Renaud, 75
  Saint Felix's successor, 72
Richemont, Engineer-Colonel, 196
Rio de Janeiro, 33, 70
  British ships in, 218
  a neutral port, 218
Riviere Noire, 15, 366
Riviere Rampart, 15
Roberts, Mr., President of the Select Committee, Macao, 321, 325
Rochefort, 284
  French squadron at, 264
Rochon, Alexis, extract from his *Voyage to Madagascar and the East Indies*, 16
Roderigue, or Rodriguez, 24, 370
  geographical location of, 20
  occupation of, 366
  Rowley at, 384
  Bertie and Abercromby in, 398, 399
Rogers, interception of register ship by, 43
Rosetta, 173
Roussin, 368
  boarding the *Nereide*, 392
Rowley, Captain Sir Josias, 158, 377, 392, 393, 398, 408
  squadron commander, 364, 366
  at the Cape, 383
  directing blockade, 384
  capture of *Africaine* by, 394
  his achievements, 395
Rusal-Khyma, pirate stronghold, 373

St. Anne, 21
St. Augustin Bay, 21
  Admiral Linois sailed to, 241
St. Cricq, Captain, court-martialled, 410
St. Denis, 20
Sainte-Suzanne, Brigadier, 195
Saint-Felix, Rear-Admiral, M. de, 55, 58
  in Indian waters, 59
  arrest of, 71
St. Helena, 67, 273
  Admiral Cornwallis visited, 63
  Admiral Rainier reached, 257
St. Helen's, 81
St. Leger, Major-General, 117

St. Paul, Bourbon, 20
  force guarding, 365
St. Vincent, Admiral the Earl of, 218, 292
Saldanha Bay, 33
  Lucas in, 87
Salem, 45
Samarang, 31, 411
  rebellions of natives of, 301
Sambelangan, 31
San Bernadino, Straits of, 259
Sapi, Straits of, 105
Saumarez, Admiral Sir James, 192
Saunders, Edward, member of Council, 92
Savane, 15
Sayer, Captain, 413
Schomberg, Captain, 410
Serampore, Danish factory at, 44
Sercey, Rear-Admiral, Marquis P. C. C. Guillaume de, 97, 120, 146, 368
  minor troubles on his voyage to Mauritius, 98
  in Mauritius, 99
  his attention to commerce destruction, 100
  in action with British ships, 104, 105
  in Batavia, 105
  his wasted opportunities, 106
  his wife, 122
  at Sourabaya, 124
  Beaulieu le Loup mistaken for, 126
  retirement of, 131
Seringapatam, 59
  storming of, 149
  visited by Sir S. Hood, 421
Seychelles, the, 14
  description of, 21
  Sybille to proceed to, 178
  French ships sailing for, 266
  Beaver occupies, 410
Shaw, Mr., valuable assistance for Rainier from, 94
Shereef of Mecca, character of the, 151
Ships:
  Note. H.M.S. indicates a ship of the Royal Navy. H.C.S. (Honorable Company's ship) indicates an East Indiaman. Warships of other nations, privateers and merchantmen are included in the same alphabetical list.
  Abercrombie, troopship, 115
  Acorn, H.M.S. (24), 422
  Actaeon, H.M. sloop, 399
  Adamant, H.M.S. (50), blockading French Islands, 130
  Adèle, French privateer, 159
  Admiral Aplin, country ship taken by Surcouf, 311
  Admiral Gardner, merchantman, 289
  Admiral Rainier, merchant brig, 231
  Africaine (40), 380, 395, 399, 400, 422
    frigate commanded by Robert Corbet, 393
    shattered and dismasted and refitted by Rowley, 394
    flagship of Admiral Bertie, 398
  Agamemnon (64), commanded by Captain Horatio Nelson, 65
  Aigle, H.M. sloop, 218
  Albatross, H.M.S. (18), 151, 152, 153, 165, 203, 212, 255, 262, 268, 280, 300, 419

Ships—*continued*

Albatross, H.M.S.—*continued*
  in Red Sea, 143
  approaching Suez, 146
  condemned, 303
Albion, H.M.S. (74), 218, 219, 240, 250, 253,
    260, 262, 268, 285, 293, 300, 303, 308
  protecting convoy to England, 318
Alerte, French privateer schooner, requisitioned
    by Sercey, 100
  capture of, 101
Alfred, H.C.S., 226
Alnwick Castle, H.C.S., 318
Althea, H.C., extra ship, 277
Amboyna, H.M. sloop (brig), 112, 136, 152, 153,
    165, 195
  in Spice Islands, 148
Amelia, H.M.S. (38), 368
Amelie, French privateer, 287
America, H.M.S. (64), 84, 86
Antelope, H.C. sloop, 174
Apollon (16), French privateer, 121, 132
  captured by Blankett, 142
Ardaseer, country ship renamed as H.M.S.
    Arrogant, 356
Arethusa, H.M.S. (38), Sir Edward Pellew on
    board, 64
Arethuse, French frigate (40), 368
Argo, H.M.S. (44), 67
Ariel, H.M. sloop, 56
Arniston, H.C.S., 82
Arrogant, H.M.S., floating hospital, 356
Arrogant, H.M.S. (74), 84, 104, 112, 120, 144,
    148, 156, 164, 165, 177, 212, 262
  visit to Madras, 95
  off Acheen, 101
  in action, 104
  in Madras, 133
Asia, country ship. *See Sir Francis Drake*
Asia, H.C.S., 244, 341
Astrea, H.M.S. (36), 410
Astrée, French frigate, 378, 383, 393
Atalanta, H.M. sloop, 56, 57
Atalante, French frigate, 55, 198, 241, 266
  on a mission to Muscat, 209
  cruising in Bay of Bengal, 258, 260
  loss of, 272
Athenienne, H.M.S. (64), 252, 254, 255
Aurore, slaver in which Surcouf served, 107
Aventurier, Dutch sloop (18), 211, 225, 296
  destroyed by Pellew, 297
Bader-Bux, country ship, Houdoul's capture of
    the, 132
Baker, merchantman, 149
Barnaby, country ship, 244
Barracouta, H.M. sloop (18), 370, 413, 419, 422
Bato, Dutch ship (74), 237, 272
Belier, French corvette, 198
Belle-Poule, French frigate (44), 204, 210, 241,
    246, 266
  at Brest, 198
  sent to reconnoitre, 230
  cruising in Bay of Bengal, 258, 260
  an encounter with Blenheim, 269
  at the Cape, 272

Ships—*continued*

Belliqueux, H.M.S. (64), 181, 292, 295, 300, 303,
    314, 352
  cruising off Point de Galle, 306
  fitness of crew, 363
  escort, 370
  sent home, 378
Bellona, Dutch frigate (28), 87
Bellone, French privateer, 293, 347, 364
Bellone, French frigate (44), 383, 396
  Duperré sent to sea in the, 368
  lured into Grand Port, 387
  Duperré's flagship, 389
  aground, 390
Bellone, H.M.S. (28), British frigate, 300, 303
Belvidere, H.C.S., 148
Bengal, H.C.S., 244
Berceau, French corvette, 208
  sent to reconnoitre, 224
Bien Aimé, French vessel taken into H.E.I.C.
    service, 62
  cruising of, 63
Blenheim, H.M.S. (74), 285, 298, 342, 351
  flagship of Troubridge, 265
  in encounter with Linois's ships, 269
  disaster of the, 291
  sank off Madagascar, 299
Boadicea, H.M.S. (38), 393, 398, 399, 400
  Rowley directing operations from the, 385
Bombay, H.C. frigate (32), 83, 93, 95, 300, 303
  with Pakenham in Moluccas, 113
  of the Bombay Marine, 261
  transport, 393
Bombay Anna, country ship, 158, 174
Bombay Castle, H.C.S., 226
Bonne-Citoyenne, French corvette, 98
Braave, H.M.S. (38), capture of *La Surprise* by,
    122
  at Mocha, 152
  in blockade of Batavia, 163
  in Rainier's squadron, 165
Braave, Dutch ship (40), 87, 90
Britannia, H.C.S., 63
Brule-Gueule, French frigate (32), 100, 120, 124,
    129, 146, 156
  wrecked, 130
Brunswick, H.C.S., 277, 376
  a leaky ship, 257
  captured by Linois, 266
  a total loss, 272
Bucephalus, H.M.S. (36), 380, 419
Calcutta, H.C.S., 222
Camel, H.M., storeship (24), formerly (44), 130
Cannonière, French frigate (40), 364
  formerly the English *Minerve*, 293
  in the China Seas, 315
Caroline, H.M.S. (36), 212, 239, 254, 260, 262,
    268, 300, 303, 360, 365, 373, 413
  register ship, *San Raphael*, taken by, 303
  successful cruise in Bay of Bengal of the, 366
Carron, country ship, *see Duncan*, H.M.S.
Cartier, brig, 108
Carysfort, H.M.S. (28), 101, 112, 114, 120, 146,
    148, 156
  sent back to England, 166

Ships—*continued*
Casthor, Dutch ship (44), 87
Castle Eden, H.C.S., 314, 341
Centurion, H.M.S. (50), 68, 72, 73, 78, 83, 93, 112, 114, 137, 148, 151, 152, 163, 165, 203, 211, 212, 240, 250, 253, 419
  obsolescence of, 69
  blockading by, 74
  in action, 75
  in Red Sea, 143
  approaching Suez, 146
  Rainier sailed for Bombay in, 207
  on convoy duty, 242
  in action, 244
  damaged by white ants, 251
Ceylon, H.C.S., 380, 381, 387, 395, 398, 399, 400
  aground, 390
  arrival off Port Louis, capture and recovery of, 394
Chance, country ship, 125
Charlotte, H.C.S., 277
Charlton, H.C.S., captured, 365, 368
Chichester, storeship, lost, 414
Chiffonne, French frigate (36), 178, 373
Clarisse (14), French privateer, 132, 155, 159
Cleopatre, French frigate (36), 55
Clorinde, H.M.S. (38), 380, 381, 399, 400, 422
Clorinde, French frigate (40), 410, 412
Colonel Macaulay, country ship, taken by Surcouf, 311
Comet, schooner, 162
Concorde, H.M.S. (36), 64, 203, 207, 212, 251, 262, 263, 268, 280, 300, 303
Concorde, French privateer, taken, 61
Confiance, French privateer, 159
Cormorant, H.M. sloop (20), 364
Cornelia, H.M.S. (32), 370, 380, 381, 399, 400, 419
  as flagship, 379
Cornwallis, H.C. packet, 166
Cornwallis, H.M.S., originally H.C. frigate (44), 176, 261, 263, 300, 303, 380, 381, 399, 400, 413
  operating in China Seas, 291
  in Malacca, 307
Cornwallis, H.M.S. (74), launch of, at Bombay, 421
  chases privateer, 422
Côte D'or, French ship, 198
  detained, 206
Countess of Sutherland, country ship, 210, 277
Coureur, French brig, 75, 82, 100
Courier, French privateer, 160
Creole, French corvette, 365
Creole, slaver, 107
Crescent, H.M.S. (36), 86
Crown, H.M.S. (64), 56
Culloden, H.M.S. (74), 255, 262, 268, 285, 295, 300, 303, 313, 334
  Pellew's flagship, 252
Cybèle, French frigate (40), 62, 63, 72, 100, 120, 187
  flagship of Rear-Admiral de Saint Felix, 55
  chase of, 61
  in action, 75
  in Port Louis, 99

Ships—*continued*
Daedalus, H.M.S. (32), 141, 151, 152, 163, 165, 177
  sent to Cape, 143
Daphne H.M. sloop (20), Elphinstone sailing for England with the, 90
Dasher, H.M. sloop (18), 212, 239, 253, 262, 300, 303
David Scott, H.C.S., 318
Dedaigneuse, H.M.S. (36), 212, 239, 254, 255, 262, 268, 280, 300, 303, 308, 320, 364
  under Rainier's command, 203
Deux Soeurs, French privateer, 287
Diana, country ship, capture of, 108, 109
Diana, H.M. cutter (12), 303, 317
Diomede, H.M.S. (44), 67, 72, 73, 76, 78
  blockading by, 74
  in action, 75
  loss of the, 80
Diomede (44), 380
Dispatch, H.M.S., in bad state of repair, 59
Doris, H.M.S. (36), 380, 381, 399, 400, 419, 422
Dortrecht, Dutch ship (66), 87, 112
Dover, H.M.S. (38), 362, 413
  under Drury's command, 317
  lost in Madras Roads, 414
Drake, H.C.S., 361
Drake, H.C. sloop, 83, 174
Duncan, H.M.S. (38), 261, 263, 268, 290, 300, 303
Earl Camden, H.C.S., 226 et seq.
Earl Mornington, country ship, 125
Echo, H.M. sloop (18), 84, 86
  visit to Madras, 95
Eclipse, H.M. sloop, 381, 399
Eliza Ann, country ship, 277
Elizabeth, Dutch East Indiaman, 348
Emilie, French privateer, 107
Emma, merchantman, 393
Endeavour, country ship, 125
Entreprenant, French corvette, 383, 393
Europa (74), Spanish ship, 139, 157
Europe, H.C.S., 365, 371
Fama, Spanish frigate, 157
Favourite, country ship, 101
Fidèle, French frigate, 71
Flora, H.M.S. (36), 64
Fly, H.M. sloop (14), 113, 174
Foudroyant, H.M.S. (80), 187
Forte, H.M.S., previously French frigate (44), 100, 120, 124, 153, 155, 165, 368
  flagship of Admiral Sercey, 98
  mutiny suppressed in, 123
  her last cruise, 124, 125, 126
  a wreck, 128
  sunk in Red Sea, 174
Fortune, French privateer, 287
Fortune, country ship, 77
  taken by Surcouf, 311
Fox, H.M.S. (32), 90, 112, 114, 119, 137, 146, 149, 152, 153, 156, 165, 174, 203, 251, 258, 262, 300, 303, 419
  disguised, 138
Galatea, H.M.S. (36), 410
Ganges, country brig, 224, 226
  at Pulo Aur, 272

Ships—*continued*
General Goddard, troopship, 115
Gloire, French privateer, 160
Goonong Assi, H.M. fireship, 114
Grampus, H.M.S. (50), 218, 239, 254, 255, 262, 263, 300, 364
Grand Hirondelle, French privateer, 159
Gran Para, Portuguese ship, 241
Greyhound, H.M.S. (32), 265, 280, 299, 303, 317
  lost on coast of Luconia, 320
Harrier, H.M. sloop (18), 259, 263, 298, 364
  operating in China Seas, 291
  damaged in gale, 299
Harriet, H.C.S., 70
Havick, Dutch sloop, 87
Hecate, H.M. sloop (18), 380, 381, 399, 422
Henrietta, country ship, 231, 277, 278
Henriette, French privateer, 287, 364
Heroine, H.M.S. (32), 76, 78, 83, 90, 93, 112, 120, 166
  in Madras, 71
Hesper, H.M. sloop (18), 380, 381, 399, 422
Hobart, H.M. sloop (18), 83, 103, 112, 136, 165, 172
  commissioned, 93
  in Spice Islands, 148
  condemned by survey, 166
Hope, H.C.S., 226
Hope, M.H. sloop, 86
Hornet, U.S. sloop, pursuit of the, 422
Houghton, H.C.S., 63, 67
Howe, H.M.S. frigate, 261, 263
Hussar, H.M. ship (38), 422
Hyder Ali, U.S. privateer, 421
Illustrious, H.M.S. (74), 380, 381, 399, 418
  overdue at Roderiguez, 399
  Broughton of Samarang in, 416
  men lost from sickness on board, 417
Imperieuse, H.M.S. (38), 158, 164, 165
Intrepid, H.M.S. (64), 156, 164, 165
Iphigenia, H.M.S. (36), 368, 383, 385
  dropped anchor and engaged in action, 390
  surrendered, 392
  See Iphigenie
Iphigenie, French frigate, late H.M.S. Iphigenia, 393
Iphigenie, French privateer, 132, 159, 162
  sinking of the, 163
Jacob Jones, U.S. privateer, 421
Jane, country ship, 160
Jaseur, H.M. sloop, 317, 347
  French brig bought by Pellew, 305
Java, H.M.S. (32), 298
  sank off Madagascar, 299
Java, H.M.S. (38), capture of, 421
Jean-Bart, privateer, 75
Jean Labdam, country ship, 311
Jehangeer, country ship, 149
Jena, French corvette (18), taken by the Modeste, 364
Jeune Adèle, (32), privateer, 289
Jupiter, H.M.S. (50), 86, 90, 130, 307
Kent, H.C.S., captured by Surcouf, 162
Kortenaar, Dutch ship (64), 237, 296
  burnt, 306

Ships—*continued*
Lady Castlereagh, H.C.S., 222
Lady Shore, H.C.S., pillage of, 100
Lancaster, H.M.S. (64), 203, 212, 240, 258, 262, 263, 285
  stationed off Port Louis, 247
  sent to protect fleet off Pulo-Aur, 286
  escorting China fleet to St. Helena, 291
Lansdowne, H.C.S., 160
Laurel, H.M. sloop (22), 364
Leda, H.M.S. (36), 413, 422
Leopard, H.M.S. (50), 56, 67, 152, 153, 165, 174, 364, 383
  Blankett's ship, 141
  ordered home, 385
Lion, H.M.S. (64), 187, 333
Lord Camden, H.C.S., 115
Lord Hawkesbury, 115
  whaler, 95
  captured by Sercey, 99
Lord Macartney, H.C.S., 115
Lucia, Spanish frigate (36), 139, 157
Macassar, H.M.S. (32), 300, 303
Magicienne, H.M.S. (36), 368, 383, 385
  grounded, 390
  set on fire and destroyed, 392
Malabar, French storeship, 198
Malartic, French privateer, 159
Manche, French frigate (40), 365, 368, 383, 385, 393
Mangles, country ship taken by Surcouf, 311
Manilla, H.M.S. (38), 422
Manship, H.C.S., 160
Marengo, French ship (74), 204, 237, 258, 266, 343, 364
  how armed, 196
  in action, 227
  off Dondra Head, 241
  in action, 244
  grounded on the Ile de Passe, 247
  in encounter with Blenheim, 269
  at the Cape, 272
  plan of last voyage of, 273
  reduced to shattered hulk, 274
Maria, Dutch storeship, 87
Maria de la Cabeya, Spanish ship (36), 139
Maria Riggersbergen, Dutch ship (36), 296, 347
Maria Wilhelmina, Dutch ship (14), 296
  captured by Pellew, 297
Marie-Francaise, French transport, 198
  detained, 206
Marquesetta, Spanish ship, 138
Mars, H.M.S. (74), 218
Meduse, French frigate (40), 412, 416
Medway, H.M.S. (74), 422
Melampus, H.M.S. (36), frigate, 64
Menelaus, H.M.S. (38), 399
Minden, H.M.S. (74), 413, 421, 422
  fitted out as flagship of Vice-Admiral Drury, 381
Minerva, H.M.S. (38), 56, 60, 61, 62, 64, 368, 371
  cruising on Malabar Coast, 57
  Commodore Cornwallis in, 58
  heaved over, 59

Ships—*continued*

Minerva, H.M.S.—*continued*
  repair of, 63
  captured by the Bellone, 365
Minerve, French frigate. *See Minerva*
Minerva, captured by *Bellone* and renamed, 383
  with other French ships being lured into
    Grand Port, 387
  in engagement with *Iphigenia*, 390
  aground, 390
  out of action, 396
Minto, schooner, 415
Modeste. See L'Emilie, 107
Modeste, H.M.S. (36), 303, 364, 370, 413, 414, 419
Moineau, French corvette, carrying Baco and
  Burnel, 100
Monarch, H.M.S. (74), 84
  Elphinstone sailing for England with the, 90
  visit to Madras of the, 95
Mongoose, H.M. armed vessel, 164, 165
Monmouth, H.M.S. (64), 313
  flagship of Rear-Admiral Drury, 312
Montanes, Spanish ship (74), 139, 157
Montrose, country ship, captured by Admiral
  Sercey, 99
Mornington, country ship, 261
Moselle, H.M.S. (28), 86
Mouche, No. 6, French corvette, 365, 378
Mount Vernon, American ship, 160
Mutine, French corvette, 98
  captured by British frigate, 99
Nancy, troopship, 115
Napoleon, French privateer, 287
Nautilus, H.C. sloop, surrender of, 422
Nereide, H.M.S. (36), 364, 366, 385
  commanded by Nesbit Willoughby, 383
  Willoughby hoists French colours on, 386
  in action, 390
  reduced to a mere wreck and ceased fire, 390
  boarded by Roussin, 392
Nereide (38) (late *Venus*), 396, 398, 399
  Rowley off Port Louis with, 394
Nereide, French frigate (40), 410, 412
New Endeavour, country ship, taken by
  Surcouf, 311
Niger, H.M.S. (32), 66
Nisus, H.M.S. (38), 398, 399, 400, 407, 410
  arrival off Port Louis, 394
  commanded by Beaver, 397
  operations directed from, 400
  warped into harbour of Port Louis, 408
  anchored in Madras Roads, 414
Nostra Signora de la Conception, Portuguese
  ship, capture of, 132
Nymphe, French frigate (40), 412, 416
Orestes, H.M. sloop (18), 141
  foundered, 153
Oriente, country ship, 311
Orpheus, H.M.S. (32), 68, 69, 72, 78, 83, 90,
  103, 112, 114, 120, 165, 177
  at Madras, 71
  at Malacca, 80, 93
  in Spice Islands, 148
Otter, H.M. sloop (16), 364, 366, 393
  sent to England, 398

Ships—*continued*

Pallas, Dutch frigate (36), 218, 296, 347
Peacock, U.S. sloop, action with H.C. sloop
  Nautilus, 422
Pearl, country ship, 246, 277
Pearl, H.C. packet, 162
Penelope, H.M.S. (36), 187
Penguin, country ship taken by Surcouf, 107
Perseverance, H.M.S. (frigate), 56, 57, 58
  sailing from Bombay, 60
Phaeton, H.M.S. (38), 240, 247, 259, 262, 300,
  303, 308, 320, 364, 370, 380, 419
  operating in China Seas, 291
Phoebe, H.M.S. (36), 399, 409, 410, 422
Phoenix, H.M.S. (38), 56, 58, 59, 60, 115, 422
  cruising on Malabar Coast, 57
  action with *La Resolue*, 58
Phoenix, Dutch frigate (36), 296
  destroyed by Pellew, 297
Piémontaise, French frigate (40), 364, 413, 419
  her qualities, 293
  operating in Bay of Bengal, 311
  surrendered, 314
  lascars among crew of, 343
Pitt, H.M.S. (36), a new frigate, 262, 263, 287,
  290, 292, 300, 303. *See also under Salsette*
Pluto, Dutch ship (70), 237, 296, 298
  concealment of, 306
  burnt, 306
Powerful, H.M.S. (74), 67, 292, 295, 298, 300,
  303, 314
Preneuse, French frigate (36), 100, 120, 124, 129,
  146, 156
  in Sercey's squadron, 121
  mutinous crew of, 123
  in Delagoa Bay, 130
  destruction of, 131
President, H.M.S., 410
President, U.S. frigate (44), 422
Prime, cartel ship, intercepted by Linois, 266
Prince of Wales, armed transport, 84
Princess, H.M. sloop (26), 84, 86
Princess Caroline, H.M.S. (74), 420
Princess Charlotte, H.C.S., 149, 243, 277
  captured, 244
Procris, H.M. sloop (18), 370, 413, 419, 422
Prudence, armed vessel, 164, 165
Prudente, French frigate (36), 72, 100, 120, 124,
  138
  in action, 75
  in Port Louis, 99
  capture of, 151
Psyche, French privateer (32), 241, 261, 290,
  300, 303, 380, 381, 399, 400
  in damaged condition, at Port Louis, 247
  cruising in Bay of Bengal, 259
  surrender to *St. Fiorenzo*, 260
Queen, H.C. sloop, 83
Racehorse, H.M. sloop (18), 410
Raisonable, H.M.S. (74), 364, 367 *et seq.*
  commanded by Captain Lord Cranstown, 65
  ordered home, 385
Rattlesnake, H.M. sloop (18), 84, 86, 130, 202,
  203, 207, 212, 242, 250, 254, 262, 280, 300,
  303, 372, 419

Ships—*continued*

Rattlesnake, H.M. sloop—*continued*
  visit to Madras, 95
  Troubridge's flagship, 285
Raymond, H.C. ship, captured, 121
Recovery, country ship, captured by *Forte*, 125
Régénérée, French frigate (36), in Sercey's
  squadron, 98, 100, 120
Renommée, French frigate (40), 410, 412
Resistance, H.M.S. (44), 68, 78, 83, 112, 120,
  136, 138
  a British ship of obsolete class, 69
  dispatched to China Seas, 72
  escort to Bombay, 74
  in Malacca, 80, 93
  instructions from Rainier to Captain of, 95
  cargo of nutmeg and mace, 95
  missing, 148
Resistance, Dutch ship (60), 218
Resolue, French frigate (36), 55
  at Mahé, 57
  surrender of, 58
Revenant, privateer (18), Robert Surcouf's
  ship, 287, 311
Revolutie, Dutch ship (70) or (66), 87, 296, 298
  concealment of, 306
  burnt, 306
Revolutionnaire, H.M.S. (38), 422
Rey-Carlos, Spanish ship, 138
Rolla, Botany Bay ship, 224
Romney, H.M.S. (50), 176, 180
Rose, H.C.S., 70
Royal Charlotte, H.C.S., 63
Royal George, H.C.S., 225, 226
Ruby, H.M.S. (64), 84, 86
Russel (74), 218, 240, 251, 256, 262, 268, 284,
  285, 290, 293, 295, 300, 303, 317, 370
  sent to Bay of Bengal, 305
  Drury's flag transferred to, 313
  first ship to make use of nopal, 362
  in need of repair, 379
  Drury sailing in the, 380
Russell, country ship, taken by Surcouf, 108
Rusthoff, Dutch Indiaman, burnt by Pellew's
  force, 306
St. Thomé, H.M. sloop, 165, 172
Salsette, H.M.S. (36), formerly *Pitt*, q.v.,
  frigate, 303
Samarang, H.M. sloop (18), 413, 419, 422
  bought into the service by Pellew, 305
Sambolasse, country ship, taken by Surcouf, 108
Sampson, H.M.S. (64), 67
San Fiorenzo, H.M.S. (36), 203, 207, 212, 240,
  242, 243, 250, 251, 262, 268, 300, 303, 343
  capture of *Psyche* by, 260
  surrender of *Piémontaise* to, 314
San Pedro (74), Spanish ship, 139
San Raphael, Spanish register ship, 347
  taken by the *Caroline*, 303
Sapphire, H.M. sloop, 366, 368
Sappho, French corvette, 412
Sarah, country ship, 267
Sceptre, H.M.S. (74), 86, 87, 90, 93, 218, 219,
  240, 245, 250, 253, 260, 262, 268, 280, 285,
  293, 419

Ships—*continued*

Schrikerrwekker, Dutch ship (70), 296
Scipio, Dutch sloop (18), 347
  with the Dutch squadron, 218
  taken by the *Psyche*, 305
Scipion, H.M.S. (74), Admiral Stopford arrives
  in Java with the, 416
Seaflower, H.M. cutter (14), 253, 255, 262, 295,
  300, 303
Seahorse, H.C. sloop, 113
Seine, French frigate (36), 120, 138
  in Sercey's squadron, 98, 100
Semillante, French frigate (36), 198, 210, 229,
  241, 264, 266, 274, 293
  sent to warn Governor-General at Manila,
  258
  damaged in attack, 259
  refitted in Port Louis, 364
Sensible, H.M.S. (36), a troopship, 176
Shah Kaikuseroo. See *Howe*, H.M.S.
Sheerness, H.M.S. (32), originally (44), 207,
  212, 242, 243, 245, 250, 262
  as troopship, 203
  loss of, 255
Sir Edward Hughes, H.M.S. (36), acquired
  from H.E.I.C., 263, 280, 291, 300, 303
Sireene, Dutch ship (26), 87
Sir Francis Drake, H.M.S. (32), 287, 297, 300,
  303, 419
Sirius, H.M.S. (36), 366, 368, 383, 385
  immobile, 390
  abandoned and burnt, 392
Sir Stephen Lushington, H.C.S., 115
Sphynx, H.M. sloop (20), 84, 90
  chased off False Cape by French frigate
  squadron, 96
Star, H.M. sloop (18), 84
Stately, H.M.S. (64), cruising off French
  Islands, 84
  at the Cape, 86
Staunch, H.M. brig, 384, 393, 398, 399
Stirling Castle, H.M.S. (74), 422
Streathem, H.C.S., 365, 371
Strombolo, H.M. bomb ketch, 174, 189
Success, country ship, taken by Surcouf, 311
Suffolk, H.M.S. (74), 73, 78, 83, 106, 112, 114,
  120, 146, 164, 165, 177
  commanded by Captain (later Admiral)
  P. Rainier, 65, 68
  sailing for Malacca, 93
  sick men in, 95
  mutiny in the flagship, 134
  on Malabar Coast, 148
Surprise, country ship, 122, 125
Susannah, country ship, taken by Surcouf, 311
Swallow, H.C. packet, 62
Swan, H.M. sloop, sails from Bombay, 60
Swift, H.M. sloop (16), 68, 73, 74, 83, 93, 106,
  112
  convoying by, 76
  commanded by Captain J. S. Rainier, 91
  sick men on board, 95
Sybille, H.M.S. (38), 90, 112, 119, 137, 148, 163,
  165, 177
  protecting Bay of Bengal, 124

Ships—*continued*
Sybille, H.M.S.—*continued*
  action between *Forte* and the, 126, 127
  crack ship, 129
  disguised, 138
  chasing privateer, 160
  to proceed to the Seychelles, 178
  Chiffonne captured by the, 178
Syren, U.S. privateer, 421
Terpsichore, H.M.S. (32), 203, 212, 240, 247, 258, 262, 263, 287, 290, 292, 295, 300, 303, 334
Terrible, Dutch ship (60), 218
Thames, H.M.S. (32), 56
  cruising on Malabar Coast, 57
Theban, H.M.S. (38), 420, 422
Thetis, H.M.S. (38), 67
Tigre, H.M.S. (74), 313
Tonnant, H.M.S. (74), 218
Trafalgar, country ship taken by Surcouf, 311
Tremendous, H.M.S. (74), 86, 203, 212, 240, 247, 262, 263, 287, 292
  blockading French Islands, 130
  in dock, 207
  seamen poisoned in the, 357
Trident, H.M.S. (64), 86, 90, 112, 114, 119, 137, 146, 148, 164, 177, 202, 203, 212, 238, 250, 253
  in dock, 207
  Rainier aboard the, 240
Trincomalee, H.M. sloop (16), sinking of, 163
Trincomalee, H.M.S. (38), 422
Triton, H.C.S., 63
  capture of, 110
Tromp, Dutch ship (54), 87
Two Brothers, merchantman, 362
Undaunted, H.M.S. (38), Napoleon on board the, 410
Uni, French privateer, 160
  how armed, 132
United Kingdom, H.C.S., 365, 368
Upton Castle, H.C.S., 149, 277
Venus, French frigate (40), 365, 368, 383, 385, 393
  after Battle of Grand Port renamed *Nereide*, 394
Vertu, French frigate (40), 99, 100, 120
  in Sercey's squadron, 98
Vestal, H.M.S. (28), 56
  cruising on Malabar Coast, 57
Victor, H.M. sloop (18), 176, 203, 207, 212, 240, 250, 255, 262, 300, 303, 368, 371, 383
  captured by the *Bellone*, 365
  lured into Grand Port, 387
  surrender and escape of the, 388
  drifted on to shoal, 390
Victorious, H.M.S. (74), 104, 112, 137, 146, 164, 165, 177
  cruising off French Islands, 84
  off Acheen, 101
  crippled and suffered casualties, 105
  in Madras, 114
  on Malabar Coast, 148
Virginie, H.M.S. (38), 146, 148, 156, 165, 172
Volage, H.M. sloop (22), 420, 422

Ships—*continued*
Vulcan, H.M. bomb vessel, 114, 136, 165
  in Spice Islands, 147
Walmer Castle, H.C.S., 330
Warley, H.C.S., 63
Warren Hastings, H.C.S., 293, 376
Wasp, H.M. schooner, 366
Wilhelmina, H.M.S. (32), 207, 212, 242, 244, 300, 303
  troopship, 203
  an indecisive action with *Psyche*, 246
  re-armed as frigate, 262
  as a hospital ship, 357
William, Dutch ship (14), 296
  taken by Pellew, 297
William Burroughs, country ship, taken by Surcouf, 311
William Pitt, H.C.S., 63
Windham, H.C.S., 365, 387, 393
Winterton, H.C.S., wrecked in 1792, 38
Woodcot, H.C.S., 121
Woolwich, H.M. sloop, 295
Worcester, H.C.S., 304, 306
Yarmouth, country ship captured by *Forte*, 125
Zee Ploeg, Dutch sloop (14), 296
  destroyed by Pellew, 297
Shore, Sir John, 63, 73, 113
  extract from letter written by, 74
Simon's Bay, 32, 86, 274
  navigational dangers of, 33
  landing made at, 81
Simon's Town, South Africa, settlement of, 34
Singapore, Straits of, cruisers to patrol off, 319
Smith, Captain Mathew, 67, 113
  court-martialled, 75
Smith, Admiral Sir Sidney, 151
Smyth, Captain W. H., extracts from his *Life of Captain Beaver*, 33, 39, 358, 361
Smyth, Mr., 65
Socotra, 132
Sourabaya, description of, 31
  map of, 296
South Seas, American ships in the, 46
Souza, Sir Miguel de Lima, a Portuguese resident at Bombay, 339
Spencer, Rt. Hon. Lord, 32, 177
  Rainier's letter to, 164
Spice Islands, 22, 83, 86
  American smuggling in the, 46
Spithead, 64, 252
  naval mutiny at, 133
Steward, Alexander, 314
Stewart, Captain John, 160
Stirling, Rear-Admiral Charles, 364
Stokes, Mr., 167
Stopford, Rear-Admiral Hon. Robert, 415
  successor to Bertie, 411
  supersedes Broughton, 416
  demand for court martial on, 418
Strachan, Vice-Admiral Sir Richard, 58
Street, Lieutenant, 395, 398
Suez, 173
  Bonaparte's expedition to, 141, 142, 143, 145
  shipwrights in, 146
Suffolk, Countess of, 65

Suffren, 14, 35, 80
  tactical brilliance of, 11
  position of, in 1782, 12
Sumatra, 22, 370
  use of, 12
  trade with America, 46
Sunda, Straits of, 13, 23, 73, 76, 105, 224, 295
  contrary winds in, 259
Surat, 132
  trade of, 36
Surcouf, Robert, French privateer, 107, 162
  his successes, 108, 109
  in the *Clarisse* (14), in 1798, 132
  his arrival and successes in the Indian Seas, 311
Surridge, Captain, 141
  of the *Leopard*, 177
Sweden, trade in the East of, 44

Table Bay, South Africa, 32
Tamatave, French ships at, 410
Tanabang, 23
Tappanooly, a small settlement, 365, 371
Tapson, Captain, his account of the capture of the *Diana*, 108, 109
Tellicherry, base at, 58, 62
  ships captured at, 121
Teneriffe, 173
Ternate, 22
  well fortified island of, 136
Therouart, Captain, 106
Tilsit, Napoleon came to terms with Tsar at, 309
Timmins, Captain John, 227
  his success at Pulo-Aur, 235
Timor, 22, 46
  Pakenham instructed to capture Great Timor, 95
Tippoo Sultan, 57, 120, 121, 146
  attack by, 56
  defeat of, 59
  Sercey's connection with, 119
  Bonaparte's ally, 148
  campaign against, 149
  his death, 149
Tombeau River, 403
Tonnelier Island, 398
Tor, 151
Toulon, occupation by Lord Hood of, 67
Townshend, Hon. Mr., 65
Trail, Palmer and Co., 318
Tranquebar, 73
  population and garrison of, 44
  proximity to Pondicherry, 45
  French agent at, 294
Travancore, capture of, 56
Tremenhere, Captain, Commander of the *Asia*, 342
Trincomalee, 74, 91, 92, 173, 257, 285
  position of, 12
  harbour of, 35
  citadel at, 39
  Admiral Cornwallis in, 60
  plan of, 79
  capitulation of, 80
  Rainier cruising off, 120
  Rainier anchored at, 203

Trincomalee—*continued*
  Pellew calls at, 263
  Drury's hopes for, 340
  a 'King's Port,' 345
  development of, as naval base, 420
Tromelin, M. de, 17
Troubridge, Captain E., son of Sir Thomas Troubridge, 299
Troubridge, Rear-Admiral Sir Thomas, 56, 148, 269, 278, 337, 359
  in command of squadron, 265
  his quarrel with Pellew, 278, 279
  exploring Penang, 290
  disaster to the *Blenheim*, flagship of, 291
  his fate, 299
Trou Fanfarron, Mauritius, 17
Truguet, Vice-Admiral, French Minister of Marine and Colonies, 98
Tucker, Captain, of the *Dover*, experimenting with the plant 'Nopal,' 362
  capture of Amboyna by, 413
Tuckey, extracts from his *Voyage to New South Wales*, 34
Turks, the, 173

United States of America, 30
  ships from, 18
  Dutch trade with, 29
  trade competition in East from, 44
  ubiquity of merchantmen in East, 45
  outbreak of war with, 421

Vaillant, 132
Vandermaesen, General, 195
  Decaen's Second-in-Command, 406
Van Der Sande, Captain, 230
  Commander of *L'Aventurier*, 229
Vasco da Gama, 37
Vellore, 302
  mutiny at, 293
Venice, 35, 187
  French Army at, 133
Versailles, Admiral Linois died at, 275
Vieux Grand Port, 390
  a village near Mahébourg, Mauritius, 386
Vigoureux, First Lieutenant of *La Forte*, 129
Vincent, M. Bory de St., 15
Vrignaud, Captain, 274

Wainwright, Captain, 373
Walcott, Lieutenant, 421
Waldegrave, Admiral, 141
Walters, Lieutenant Samuel, of the *Raisonable*, 367
Warde, Major-General, 395, 408
Warren, Admiral Sir John Borlase, as frigate captain, 64
  squadron commanded by, 274
Welland, Mrs., 388
Wellesley, Hon. Colonel Arthur, Duke of Wellington, 122, 149
  criticism of Penang by, 12
  commander of 33rd Regiment, 116
  his reflections, 116
  instructions to, 140
  advice of, 158
  in command of troops at Trincomalee, 167

Wellesley, Hon. Colonel Arthur—*continued*
  superseded by General Baird, 170
  his appointment as Governor at Seringapatam, 183
Wellesley, the Rt. Hon. the Marquess, Governor-General of India, 158, 163, 200
  his dispatches, 166
  his recommendations, 173
  his dispatch to Admiral Rainier, 212
Weltervreeden, 23
Wesley. *See* Wellesley, Duke of Wellington
Whampoa, 323
Whitby, Captain H., 61, 64
Whitworth, Lord, 196
Willaumez, Admiral, squadron under, 294
Williamson, Mr. T. J., 339
Willoughby, Captain Sir Nesbit, 398

Willoughby, Captain Sir Nesbit—*continued*
  Commander of the *Otter*, 366
  of the *Nereide* (36), 383
  his operations, 386
  his dilemma, 388
  seriously wounded in the *Nereide*, 390
  ordered by Pym to abandon ship, 392
Wilson, Captain Lestock, 105, 143
Wood, Captain, in H.M. Ship *Phaeton*, 263
  his objects, 264

Yambo, merchants of, 145
Yanaon, 14, 181
Ykel, M., rule of, 21

Zambesi, 37
Zanzibar, slaves from, 16
  Captain Blankett put into, 143

GEORGE ALLEN & UNWIN LTD
London: 40 Museum Street, W.C.1

Auckland: Haddon Hall, City Road
Sydney, N.S.W.: Bradbury House, 55 York Street
Cape Town: 58–60 Long Street
Bombay: 15 Graham Road, Ballard Estate, Bombay 1
Calcutta: 17 Chittaranjan Avenue, Calcutta 13
New Delhi: Munshi Niketan, Kamla Market, Ajmeri Gate, New Delhi 1
Karachi: Haroon Chambers, South Napier Road, Karachi 2
Toronto: 91 Wellington Street West
Sao Paulo: Avenida 9 de Julho 1138–Ap. 51

Edited by C. Northcote Parkinson

THE TRADE WINDS

A STUDY OF BRITISH OVERSEAS TRADE DURING THE FRENCH WARS 1793-1815

Introduction by Admiral Sir William M. James, G.C.B.

Illustrated   Demy 8vo   21s. net

It is very strange, as the editor remarks, that in an island defended, enriched and made famous by its ships and seamen the study of maritime history should be so ignored. What this volume offers is an essay in maritime history covering a period of unusual importance, and a period that has several points of contact with our own recent history, contact so close that we appear to have re-lived through 1939–45 the perils and triumphs of 1793–1815.

The authors present an authoritative statement on the main aspects of British overseas trade of their period, stressing conditions rather than the better known events. What the social historian has done in relation to political history they do for maritime history, and, in the famous words of Hakluyt, 'speak a word of that just commendation which our nation do indeed deserve.'

The contributors are C. ERNEST FAYLE (*Shipowning and Marine Insurance*, and *The Employment of British Shipping*); C. NORTHCOTE PARKINSON (*The Port of London*, and *The East India Trade*); A. C. WARDLE (*The Port of Liverpool*, *The Newfoundland Trade*, and *The Post Office Packets*); PROFESSOR C. M. MACINNES (*The Port of Bristol*, and *The Slave Trade*); BASIL LUBBOCK (*Ships of the Period and Developments in Rig*, and *Seamen*); PROFESSOR J. A. NIXON (*Health and Sickness*); LUCY FRANCES HORSFALL (*The West Indian Trade*); PROFESSOR H. HEATON (*The American Trade*).

'It is a symposium contributed by divers authors, all of them learned. It is a serious essay in history based on detailed and in some cases original research. Yet it is admirably written, admirably illustrated and admirably produced ... packed with useful, interesting and often delightful information. ... The book is an historian's treasury; full of interesting facts and of the germinating ideas that spring from facts.'   *Sunday Times*

'A book which should be read not only by those who are concerned in studying the strategic implications of the sea and ships, but by all those who wish to acquire the broader view of Imperial Defence. If the reader once picks it up, even if it be from a sense of duty, he will continue to read it for his entertainment and enlightenment.'

Journal of the Royal United Service Institution

'The story it tells, its excellent plates, diagrams, maps and statistical schedules, make the volume a work of considerable significance for the historical records of this country.'

Times Educational Supplement

by Michael Lewis

THE NAVY OF BRITAIN

Second Impression   Illustrated   Demy 8vo   30s. net

This book is a history, not of Britain's sea-power, but of that great institution which has implemented it—*the Navy of Britain*. Again, it is a history, not of the Royal Navy alone, (though that holds an important place in it) but of something much wider and of even greater national importance. It shows how dangerous it is—and, historically, how wrong—to attempt to dissociate the Royal Navy from its 'natural reserves,' since from the very earliest days of our history all have been interwoven in one common pattern, all sprung from common parents, all fostering common traditions, all seeking common ends. So this book does not follow the plan that the thoughtless might expect, and deal first with the R.N., then with the R.N.R., then with the R.N.V.R., and so on. Such vertical cuts are meaningless in the eye of History. The divisions, rather, are horizontal. 'Origins,' 'Ships,' 'Officers,' 'Men,' 'Management,' 'In Action'—these are its big headings.

It is written for those who might be expected from the nature of the case to be interested—the officers and men of the Royal Navy, and the officers and men of the Reserves who have known the sea life at first hand. But it is also meant—perhaps most of all—for the ordinary citizens who have not. These are the men and women who through the centuries have benefited by the faithful services of their Navy—that cross-section of themselves, the *whole* Navy of Britain. Here is set out for them the story of this great national heritage which, more than any one other, has changed their little island into a World Empire, and saved it, without fail or fuss, from every tyrant who has threatened it from the days of Philip of Spain to those of Hitler.

'I do not believe that anybody could have told the tale so well as the Professor of History at Greenwich whose learning is as deep as the sea and whose style is as supple and tough as a rope, as sound as a good ship, and as colourful as the speech of seamen.'

The Observer

'Here then we have a bold, outspoken, well-planned and learned book, the result of much thought and practical demonstration, let us remember, often given in the presence of officers, practised in modern naval warfare! . . . Can best be described as a Companion to the study of British naval history. Nothing like it has appeared since Commander C. N. Robinson published *The British Fleet* in 1895.'

The Mariner's Mirror

GEORGE ALLEN AND UNWIN LTD

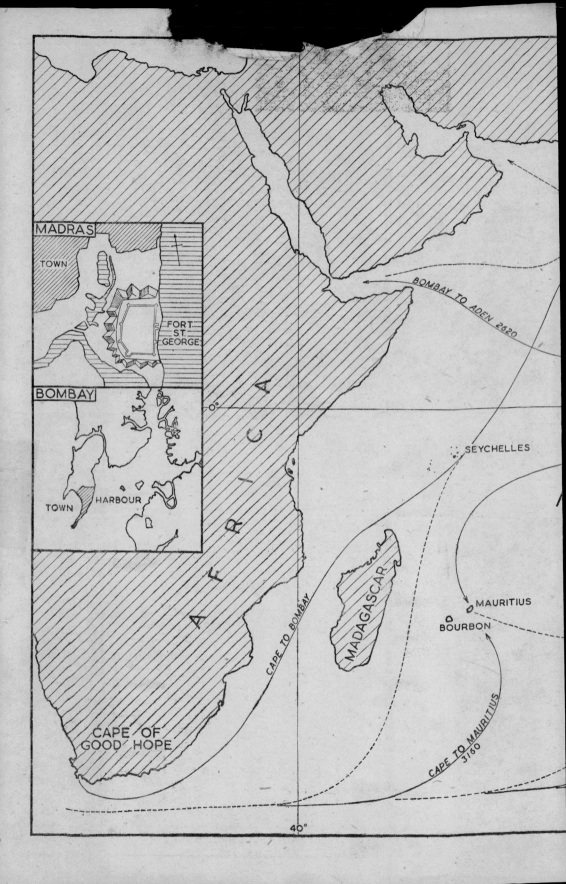

MADRAS

TOWN

FORT
ST.
GEORGE

BOMBAY

TOWN   HARBOUR

A F R I C A

BOMBAY TO ADEN 2620

SEYCHELLES

MADAGASCAR

CAPE TO BOMBAY

MAURITIUS

BOURBON

CAPE OF
GOOD HOPE

CAPE TO MAURITIUS
3160

0°

40°